BATGIRL

VOLUME 2

To the Death

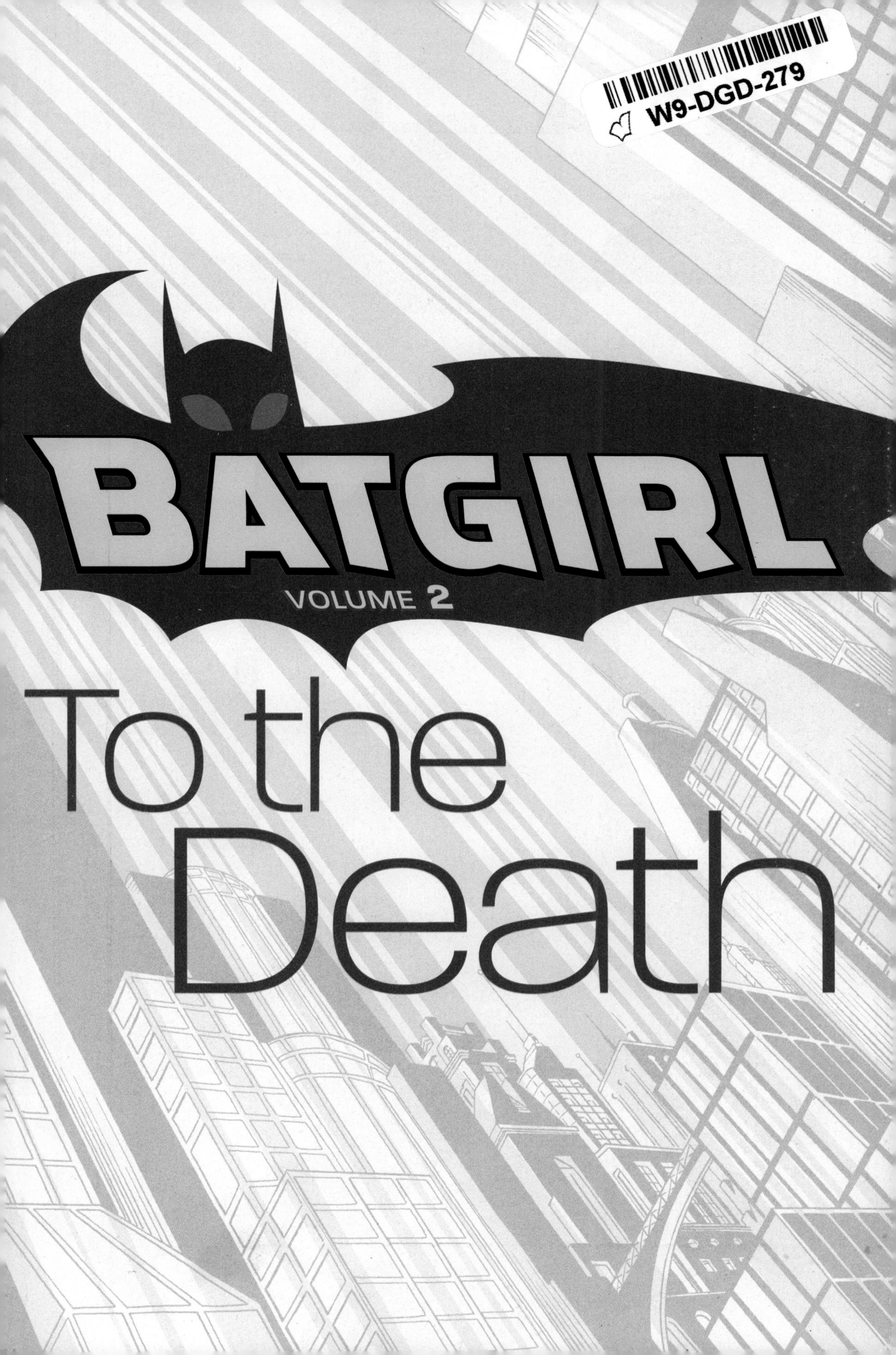

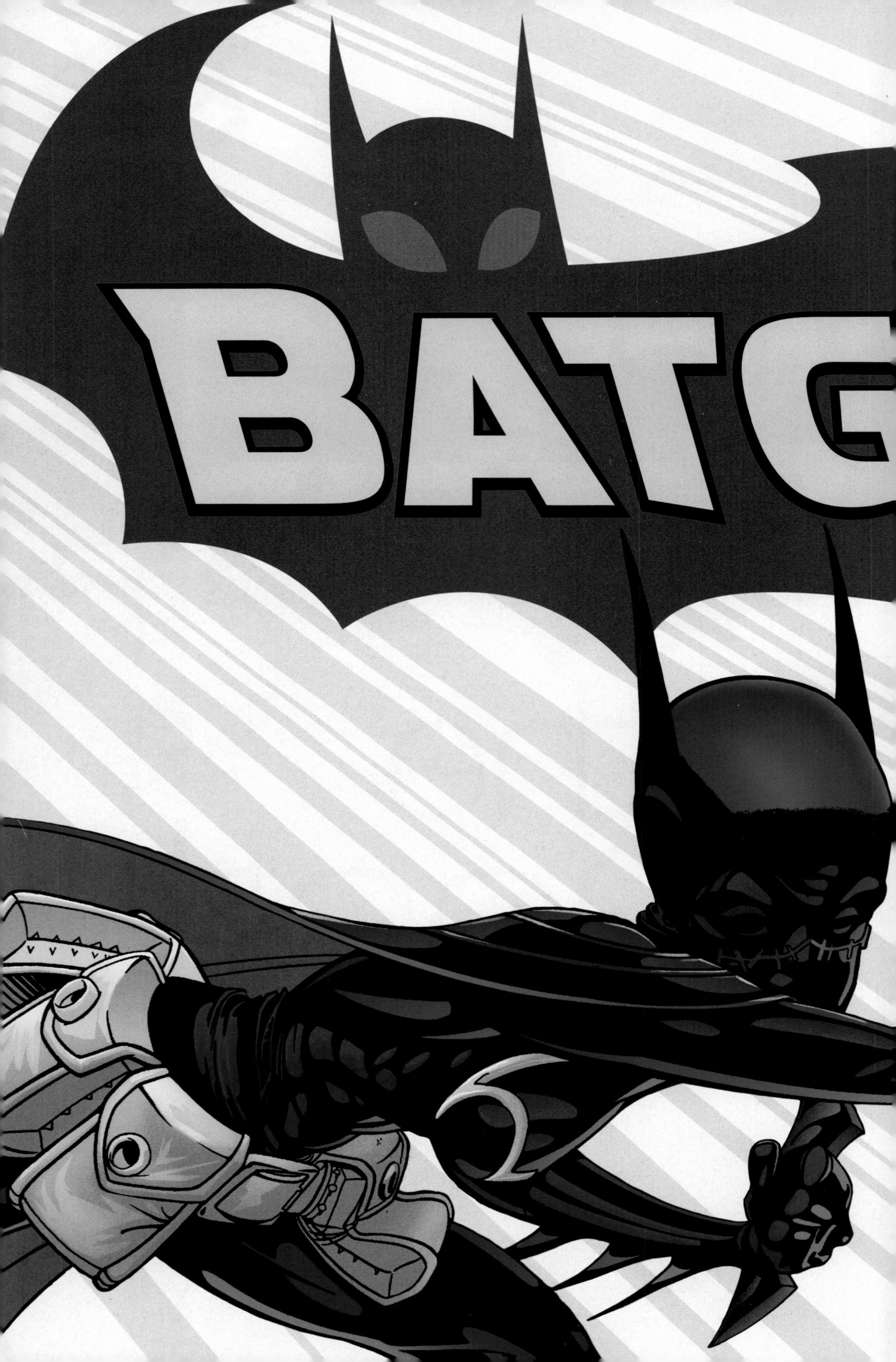
BATG

IRL

VOLUME 2

To the Death

Kelley Puckett
Chuck Dixon
Scott Peterson
Writers

Damion Scott
Alitha Martinez
Marcos Martin
Pencillers

Robert Campanella
John Lowe
Mick Gray
Alvaro Lopez
Inkers

Jason Wright
Gregory Wright
Tom McCraw
Colorists

John Costanza
Letterer

Digital Chameleon
Separations

Damion Scott,
Robert Campanella
& Patrick Martin
Collection cover artists

BATMAN
created by
Bob Kane
with Bill Finger

Dennis O'Neil
Michael Wright
Editors – Original Series

Frank Berrios
Assistant Editor – Original Series

Jeb Woodard
Group Editor – Collected Editions

Liz Erickson
Editor – Collected Edition

Steve Cook
Design Director – Books

Curtis King Jr.
Publication Design

Bob Harras
Senior VP – Editor-in-Chief, DC Comics

Diane Nelson
President

Dan DiDio and Jim Lee
Co-Publishers

Geoff Johns
Chief Creative Officer

Amit Desai
Senior VP – Marketing & Global Franchise Management

Nairi Gardiner
Senior VP – Finance

Sam Ades
VP – Digital Marketing

Bobbie Chase
VP – Talent Development

Mark Chiarello
Senior VP – Art, Design & Collected Editions

John Cunningham
VP – Content Strategy

Anne DePies
VP – Strategy Planning & Reporting

Don Falletti
VP – Manufacturing Operations

Lawrence Ganem
VP – Editorial Administration & Talent Relations

Alison Gill
Senior VP – Manufacturing & Operations

Hank Kanalz
Senior VP – Editorial Strategy & Administration

Jay Kogan
VP – Legal Affairs

Derek Maddalena
Senior VP – Sales & Business Development

Jack Mahan
VP – Business Affairs

Dan Miron
VP – Sales Planning & Trade Development

Nick Napolitano
VP – Manufacturing Administration

Carol Roeder
VP – Marketing

Eddie Scannell
VP – Mass Account & Digital Sales

Courtney Simmons
Senior VP – Publicity & Communications

Jim (Ski) Sokolowski
VP – Comic Book Specialty & Newsstand Sales

Sandy Yi
Senior VP – Global Franchise Management

Batgirl Volume 2: To the Death

DC Comics, 2900 West Alameda Avenue, Burbank, CA 91505
Printed by RR Donnelley, Owensville, MO, USA. 6/17/16.
First Printing. ISBN: 978-1-4012-6352-2

Library of Congress Cataloging-in-Publication Data is available.

PEFC Certified

Printed on paper from
sustainably managed
forests and controlled
sources

PEFC/29-31-75   www.pefc.org

BATGIRL #13 cover by Damion Scott,
Robert Campanella & Patrick Martin

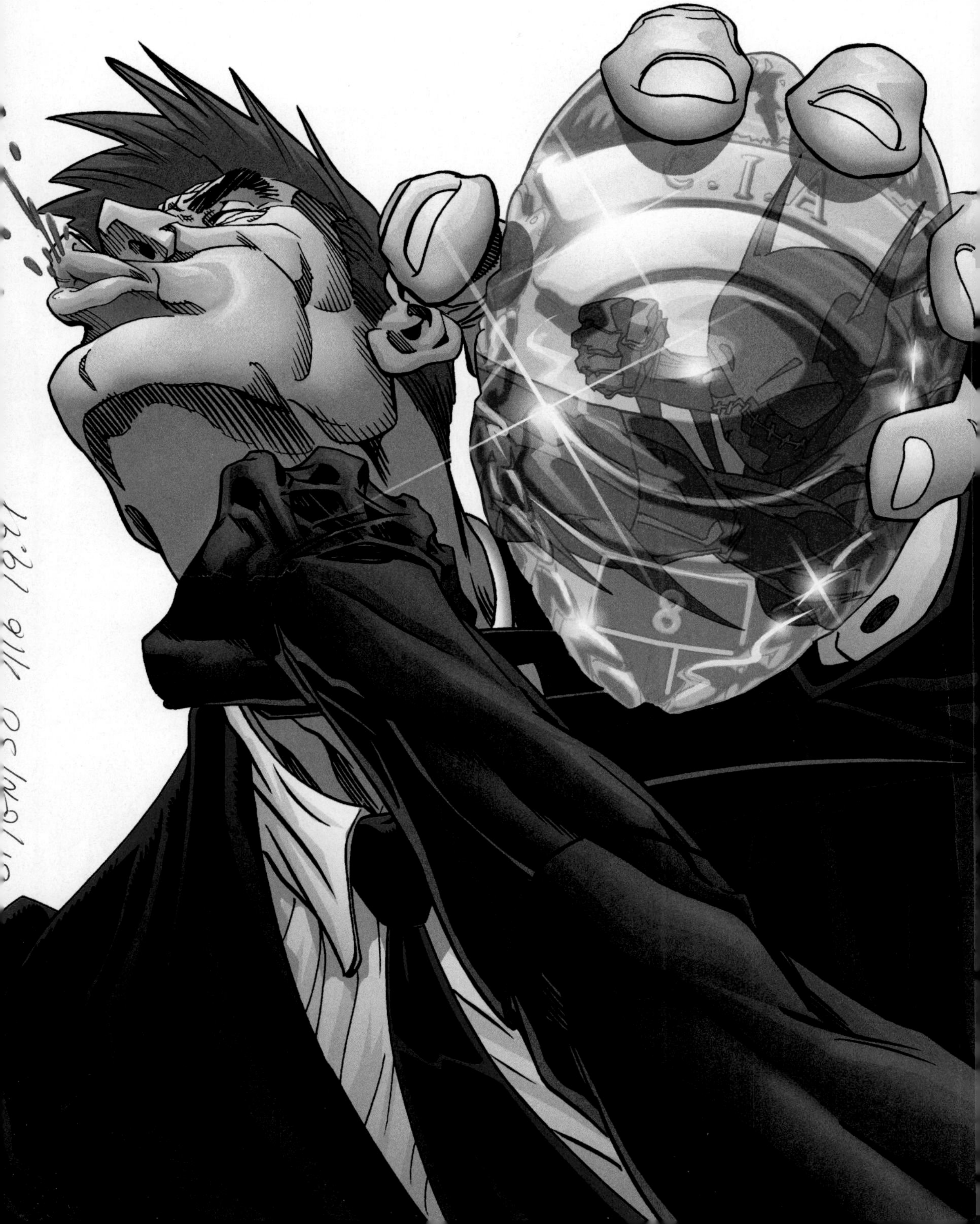
C.I.A

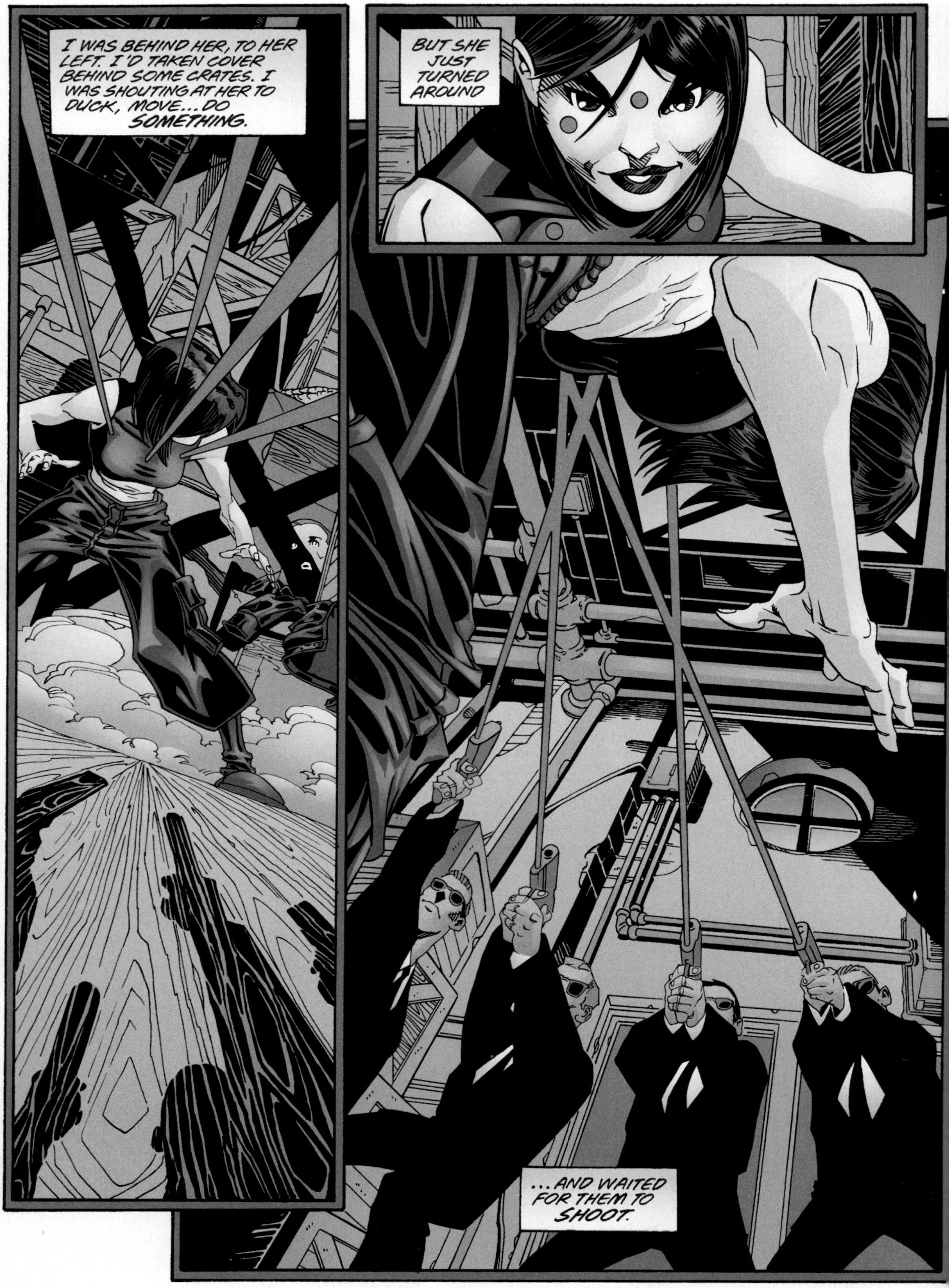
I WAS BEHIND HER, TO HER LEFT. I'D TAKEN COVER BEHIND SOME CRATES. I WAS SHOUTING AT HER TO DUCK, MOVE...DO SOMETHING.
BUT SHE JUST TURNED AROUND
...AND WAITED FOR THEM TO SHOOT.

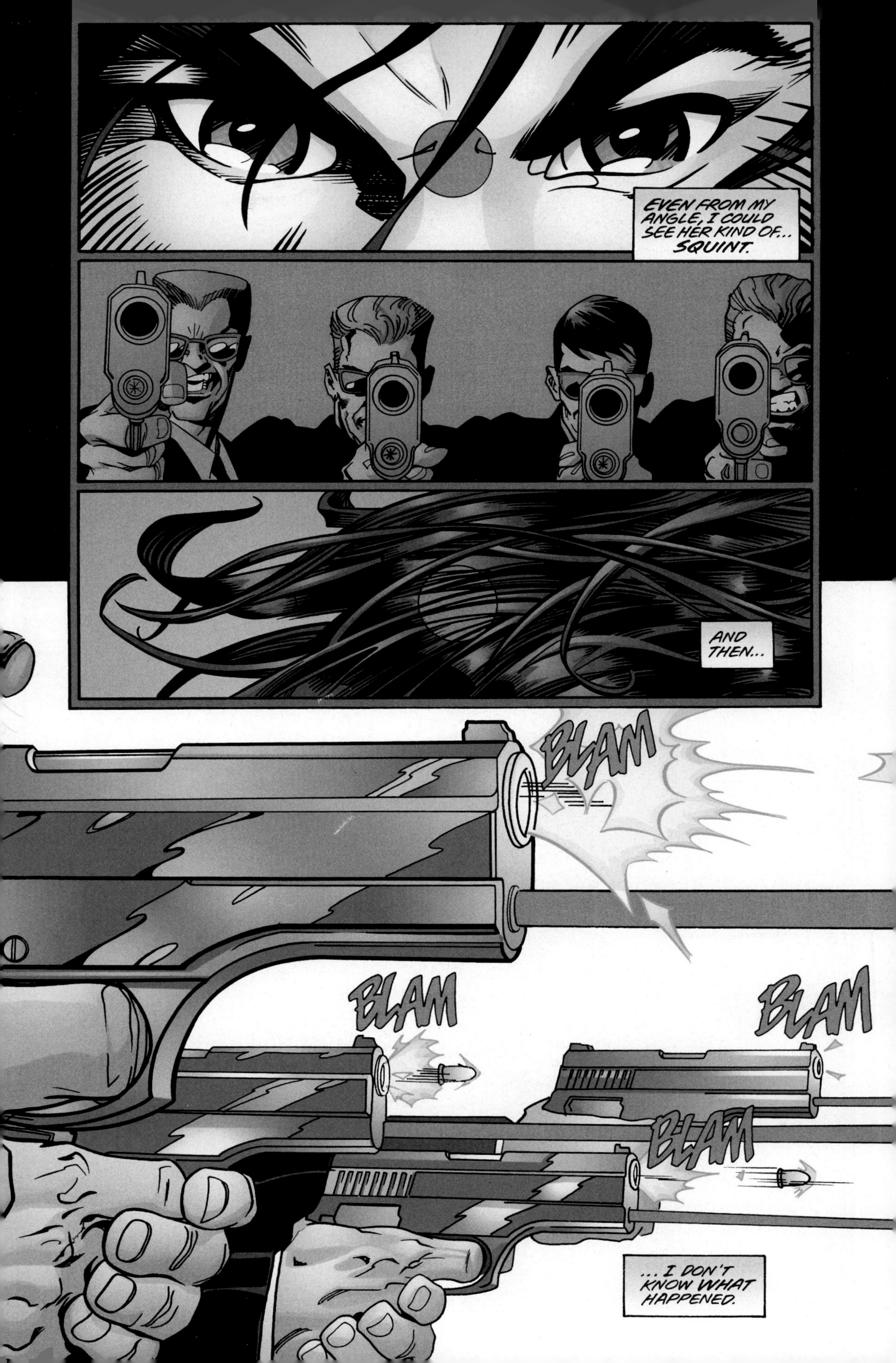
EVEN FROM MY ANGLE, I COULD SEE HER KIND OF... SQUINT.
AND THEN...
BLAM
BLAM
BLAM
BLAM
...I DON'T KNOW WHAT HAPPENED.

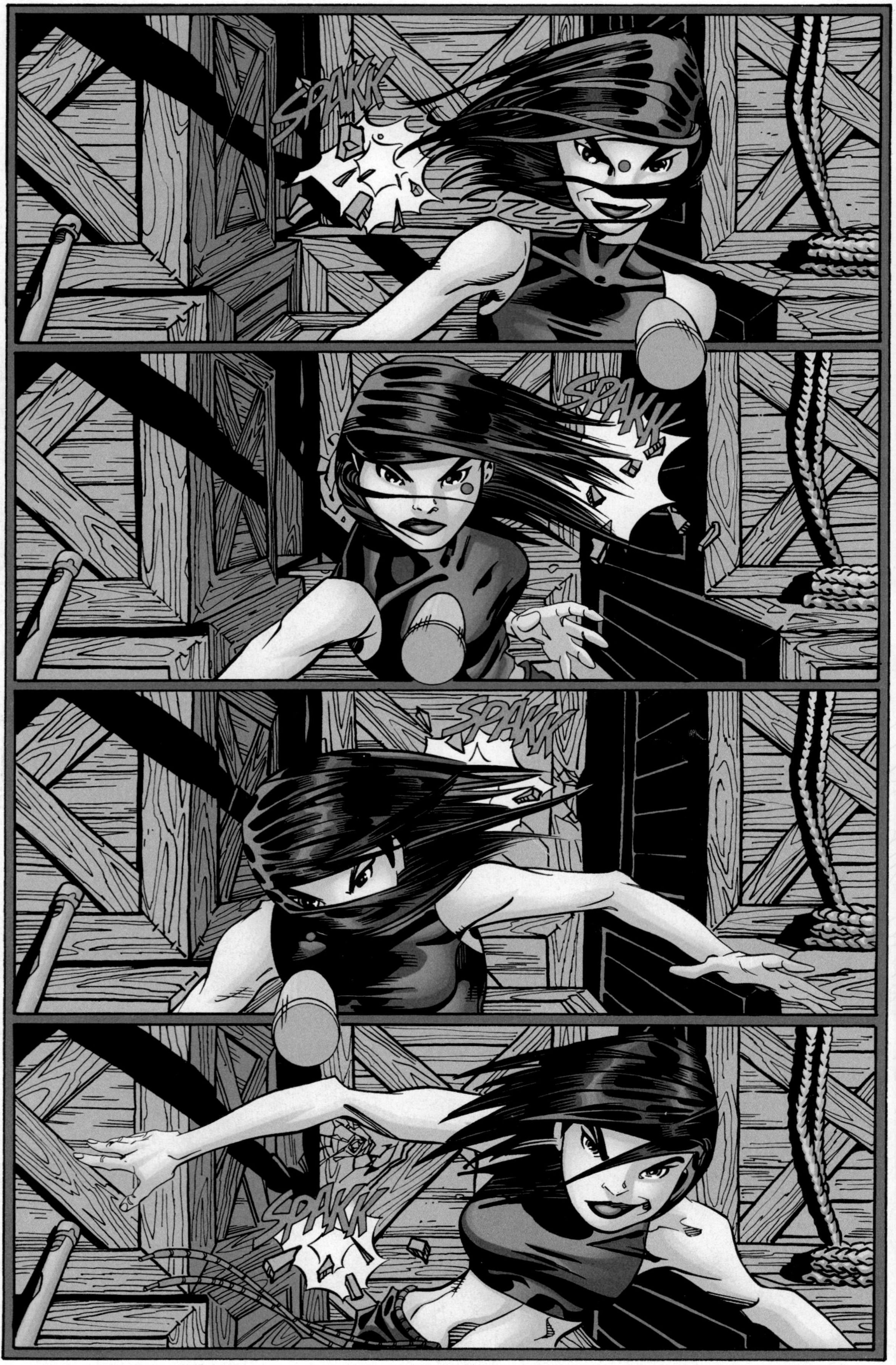
SPAKK
SPAKK
SPAKK
SPAKK

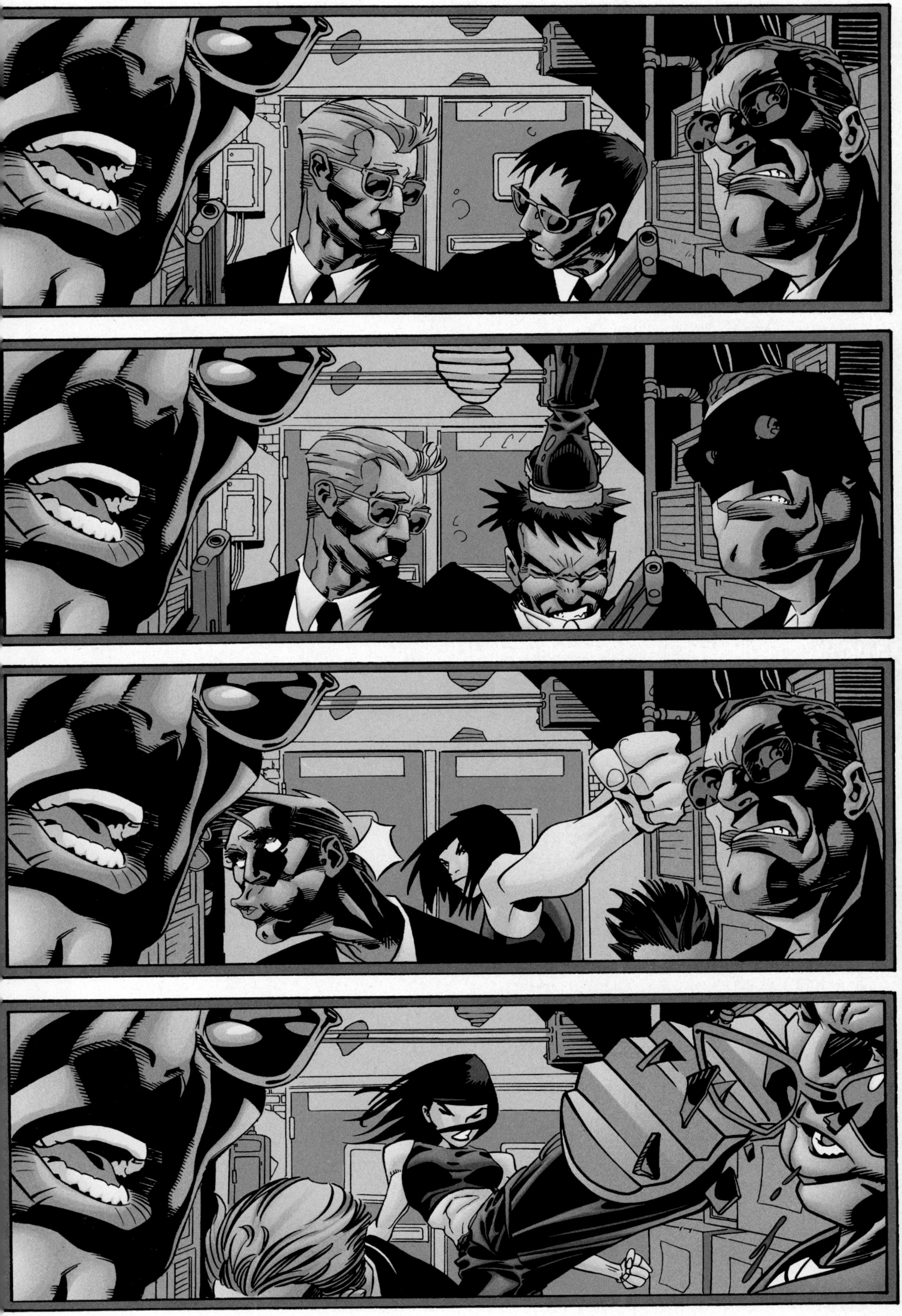

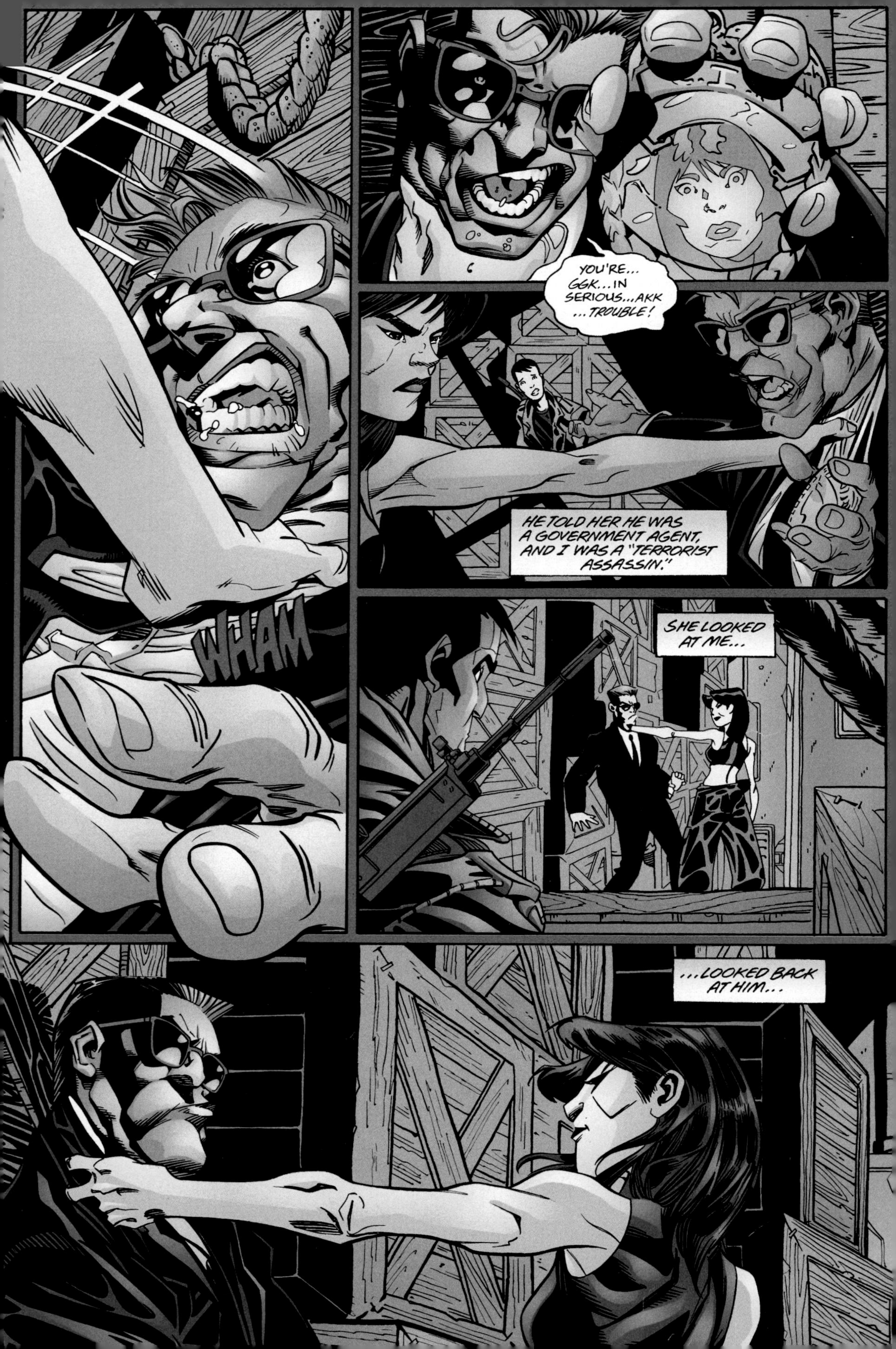
WHAM
YOU'RE... GGK... IN SERIOUS... AKK ...TROUBLE!
HE TOLD HER HE WAS A GOVERNMENT AGENT, AND I WAS A "TERRORIST ASSASSIN."
SHE LOOKED AT ME...
...LOOKED BACK AT HIM...

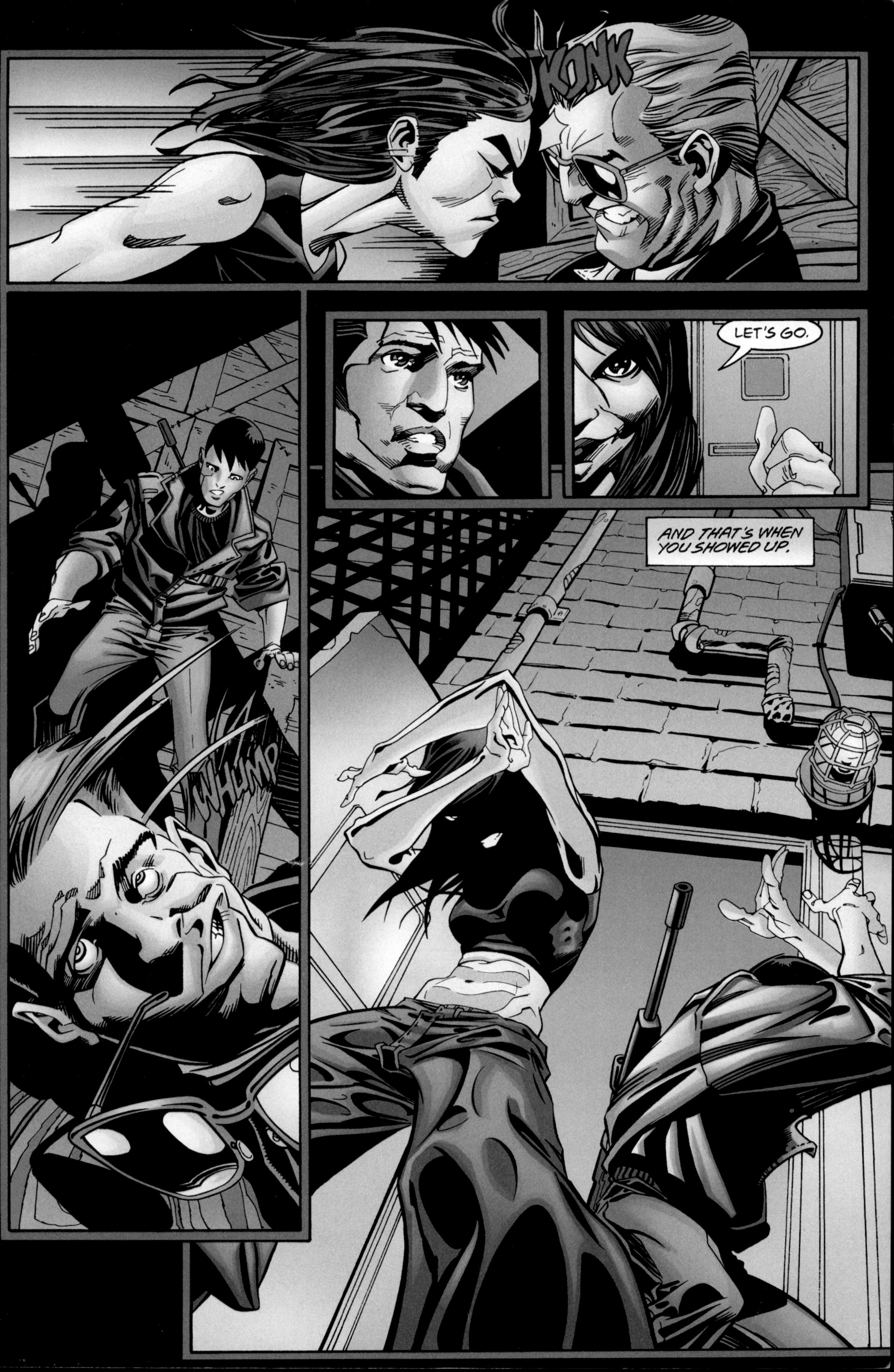
KONK
LET'S GO.
AND THAT'S WHEN YOU SHOWED UP.
WHUMP

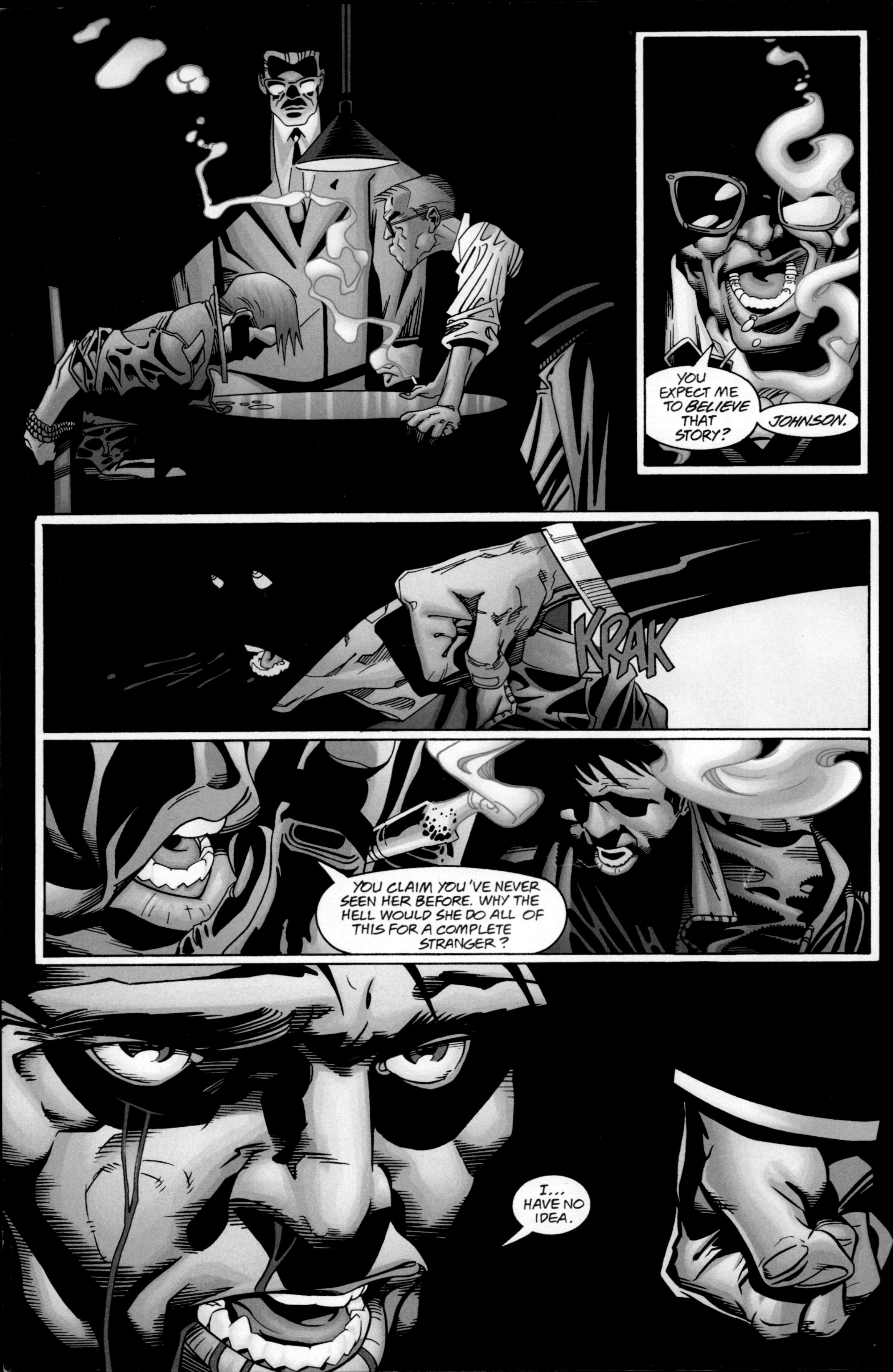
YOU EXPECT ME TO *BELIEVE* THAT STORY?
JOHNSON.
KRAK
YOU CLAIM YOU'VE NEVER SEEN HER BEFORE. WHY THE HELL WOULD SHE DO ALL OF THIS FOR A COMPLETE STRANGER?
I... HAVE NO IDEA.

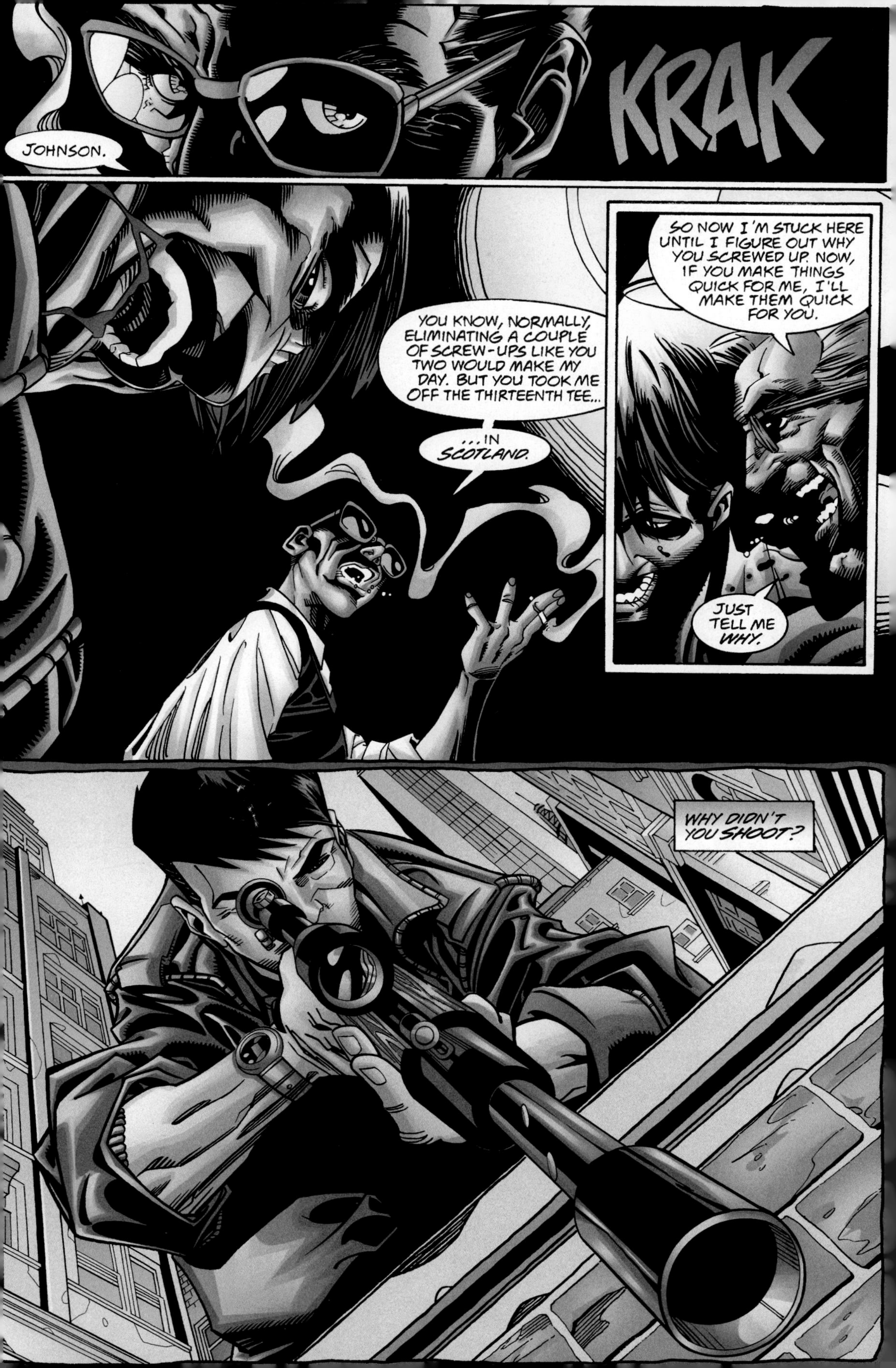
JOHNSON.
KRAK
YOU KNOW, NORMALLY, ELIMINATING A COUPLE OF SCREW-UPS LIKE YOU TWO WOULD MAKE MY DAY. BUT YOU TOOK ME OFF THE THIRTEENTH TEE...
...IN SCOTLAND.
SO NOW I'M STUCK HERE UNTIL I FIGURE OUT WHY YOU SCREWED UP. NOW, IF YOU MAKE THINGS QUICK FOR ME, I'LL MAKE THEM QUICK FOR YOU.
JUST TELL ME WHY.
WHY DIDN'T YOU SHOOT?

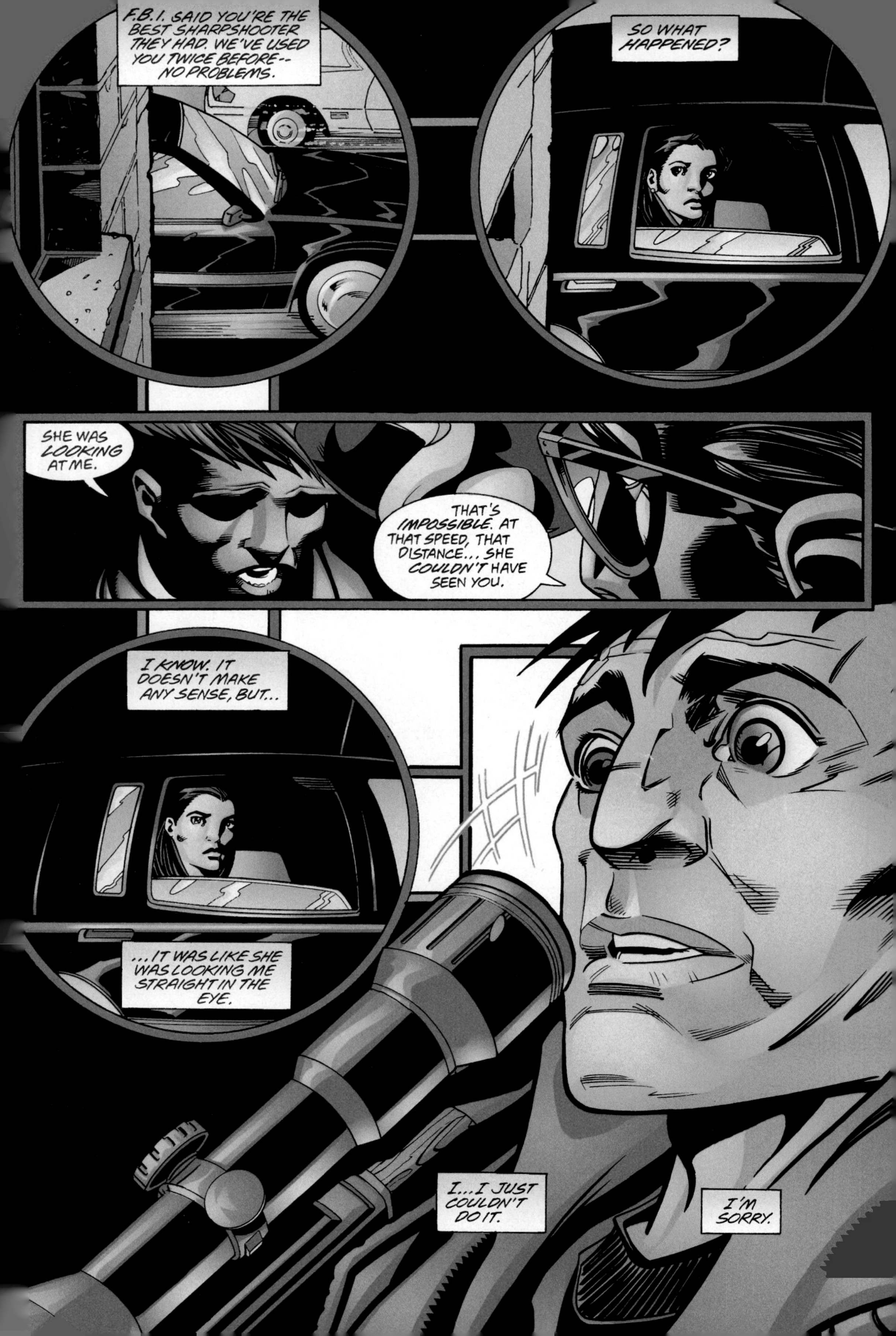
F.B.I. SAID YOU'RE THE BEST SHARPSHOOTER THEY HAD. WE'VE USED YOU TWICE BEFORE-- NO PROBLEMS.
SO WHAT HAPPENED?
SHE WAS LOOKING AT ME.
THAT'S IMPOSSIBLE. AT THAT SPEED, THAT DISTANCE... SHE COULDN'T HAVE SEEN YOU.
I KNOW. IT DOESN'T MAKE ANY SENSE, BUT...
...IT WAS LIKE SHE WAS LOOKING ME STRAIGHT IN THE EYE.
I...I JUST COULDN'T DO IT.
I'M SORRY.

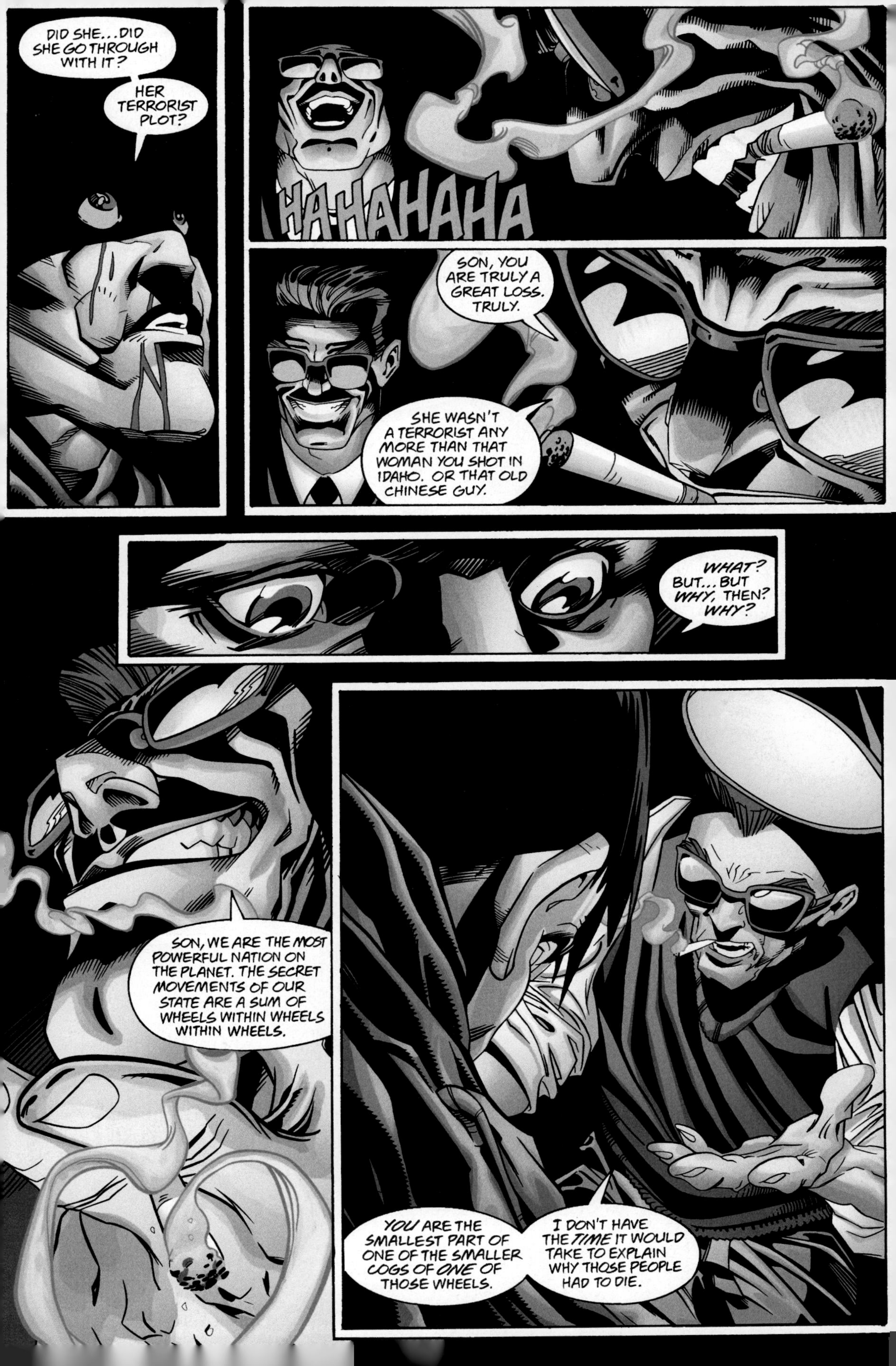
DID SHE...DID SHE GO THROUGH WITH IT?
HER TERRORIST PLOT?
HAHAHAHA
SON, YOU ARE TRULY A GREAT LOSS. TRULY.
SHE WASN'T A TERRORIST ANY MORE THAN THAT WOMAN YOU SHOT IN IDAHO. OR THAT OLD CHINESE GUY.
WHAT? BUT... BUT WHY, THEN? WHY?
SON, WE ARE THE MOST POWERFUL NATION ON THE PLANET. THE SECRET MOVEMENTS OF OUR STATE ARE A SUM OF WHEELS WITHIN WHEELS WITHIN WHEELS.
YOU ARE THE SMALLEST PART OF ONE OF THE SMALLER COGS OF ONE OF THOSE WHEELS.
I DON'T HAVE THE TIME IT WOULD TAKE TO EXPLAIN WHY THOSE PEOPLE HAD TO DIE.

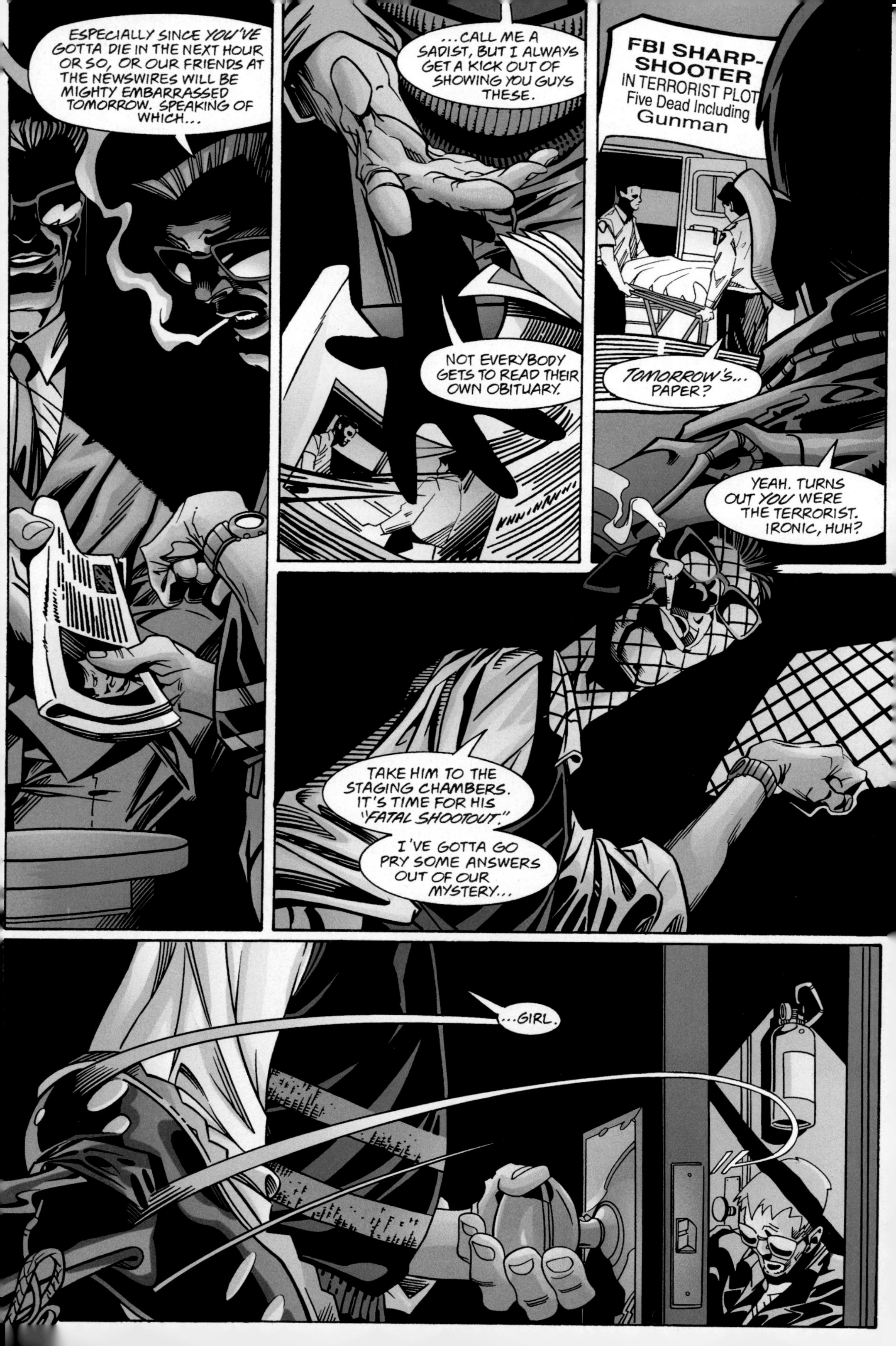

ESPECIALLY SINCE YOU'VE GOTTA DIE IN THE NEXT HOUR OR SO, OR OUR FRIENDS AT THE NEWSWIRES WILL BE MIGHTY EMBARRASSED TOMORROW. SPEAKING OF WHICH...
...CALL ME A SADIST, BUT I ALWAYS GET A KICK OUT OF SHOWING YOU GUYS THESE.
NOT EVERYBODY GETS TO READ THEIR OWN OBITUARY.
NNNNNNNN...
FBI SHARP-SHOOTER IN TERRORIST PLOT
Five Dead Including Gunman
TOMORROW'S... PAPER?
YEAH. TURNS OUT YOU WERE THE TERRORIST. IRONIC, HUH?
TAKE HIM TO THE STAGING CHAMBERS. IT'S TIME FOR HIS "FATAL SHOOTOUT."
I'VE GOTTA GO PRY SOME ANSWERS OUT OF OUR MYSTERY...
...GIRL.

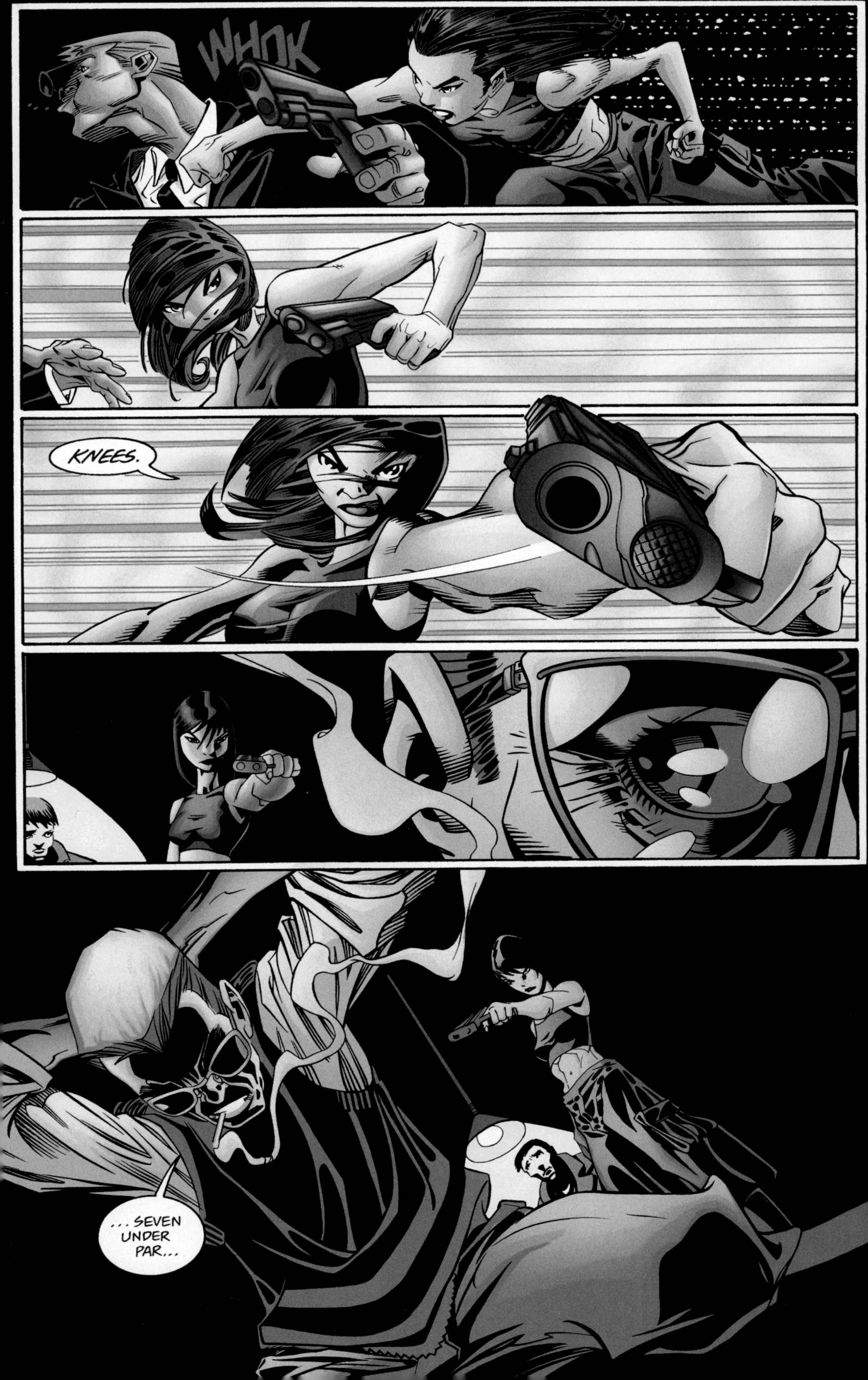
WHOK
KNEES.
...SEVEN UNDER PAR...

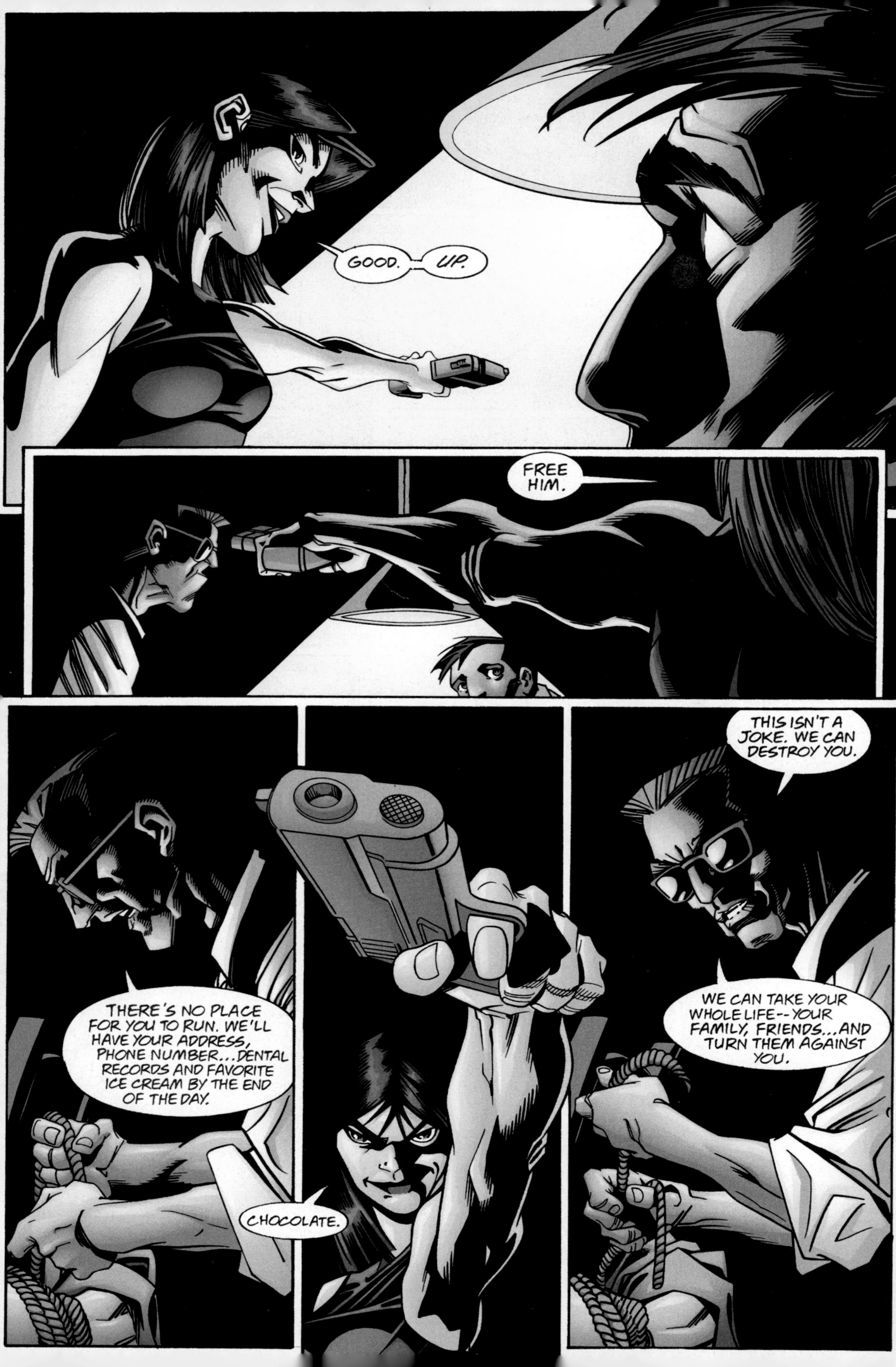
GOOD.
UP.
FREE HIM.
THERE'S NO PLACE FOR YOU TO RUN. WE'LL HAVE YOUR ADDRESS, PHONE NUMBER...DENTAL RECORDS AND FAVORITE ICE CREAM BY THE END OF THE DAY.
CHOCOLATE.
THIS ISN'T A JOKE. WE CAN DESTROY YOU.
WE CAN TAKE YOUR WHOLE LIFE--YOUR FAMILY, FRIENDS...AND TURN THEM AGAINST YOU.

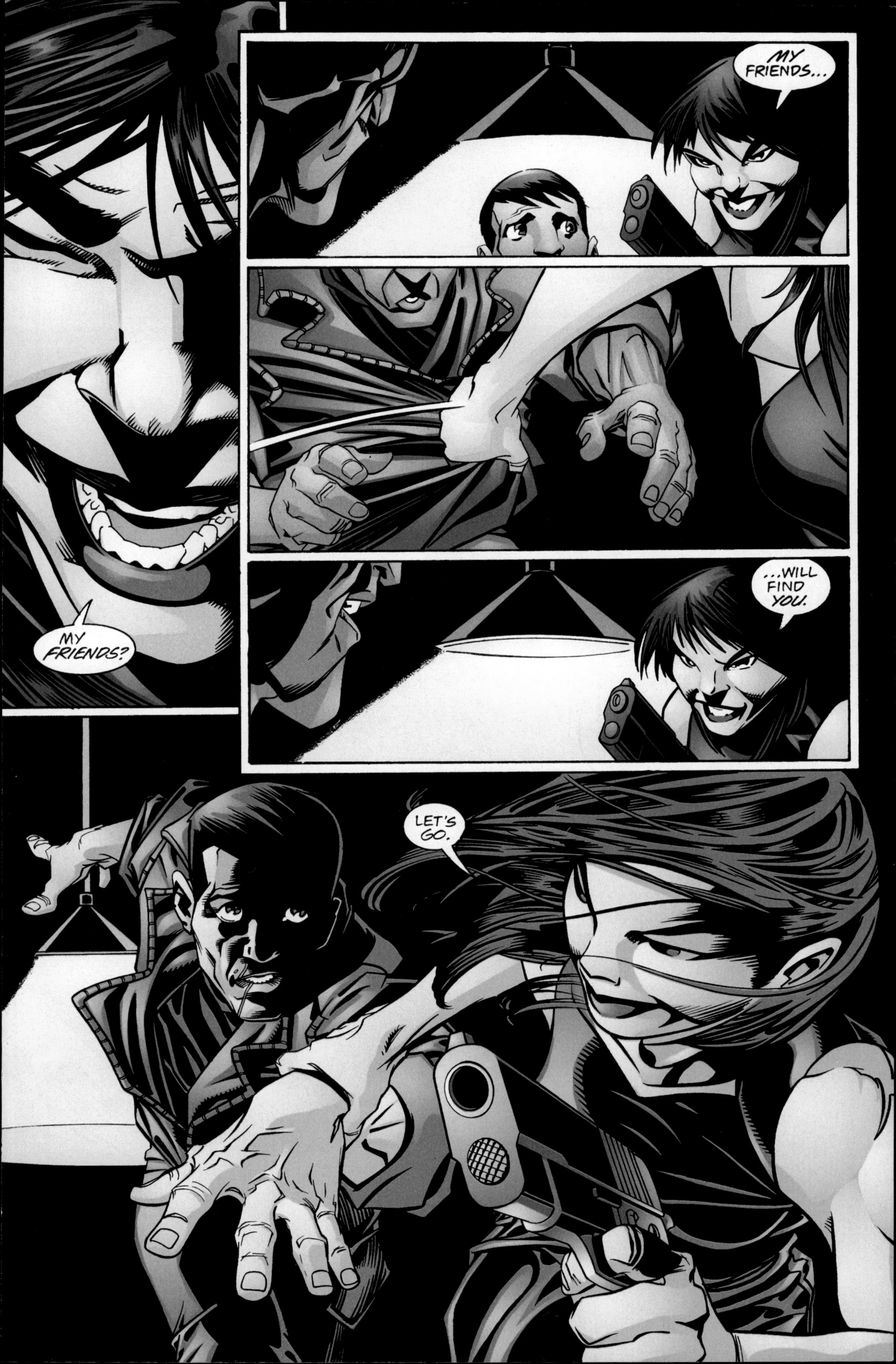
MY FRIENDS?
MY FRIENDS...
...WILL FIND YOU.
LET'S GO.

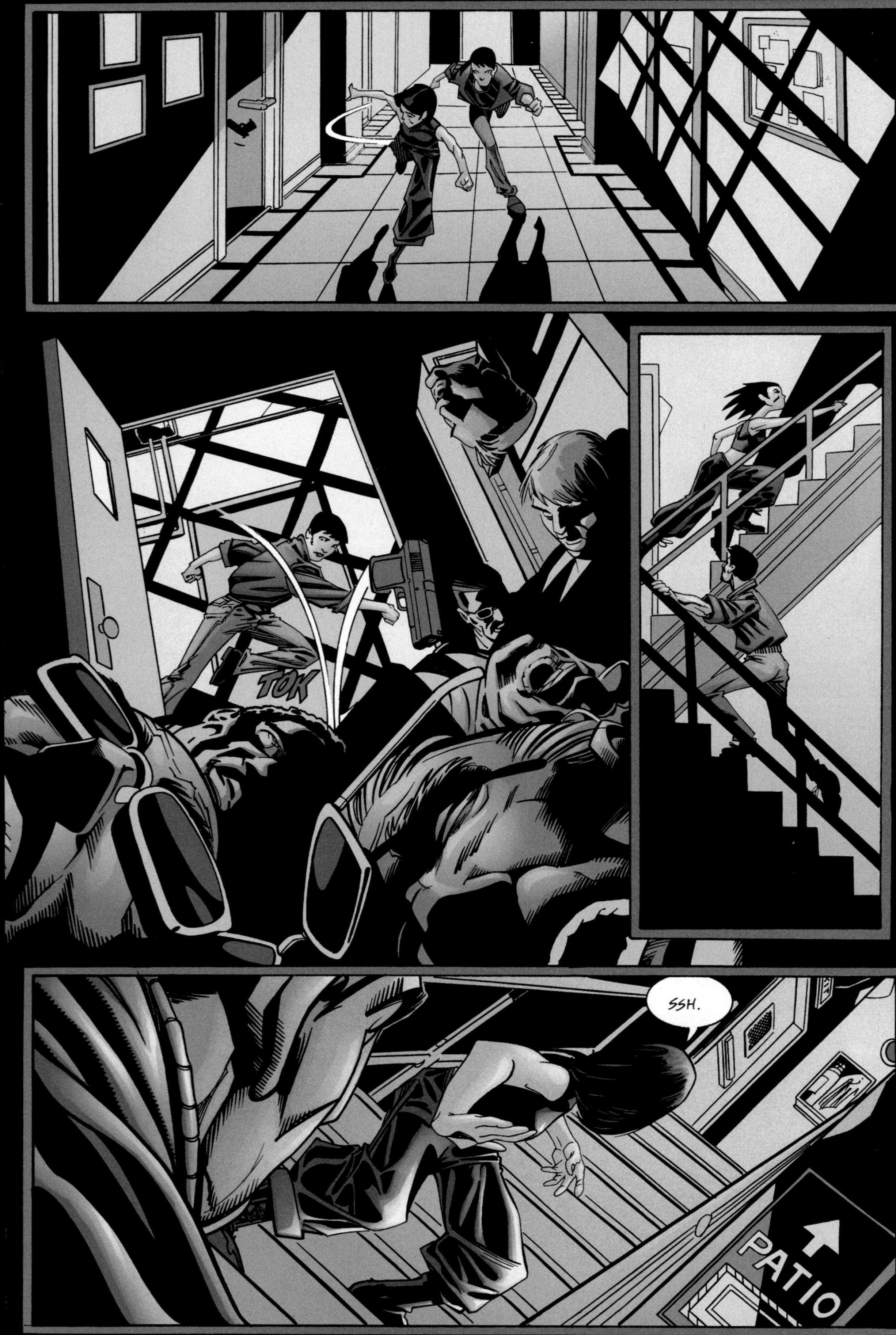
TOK
SSH.
PATIO

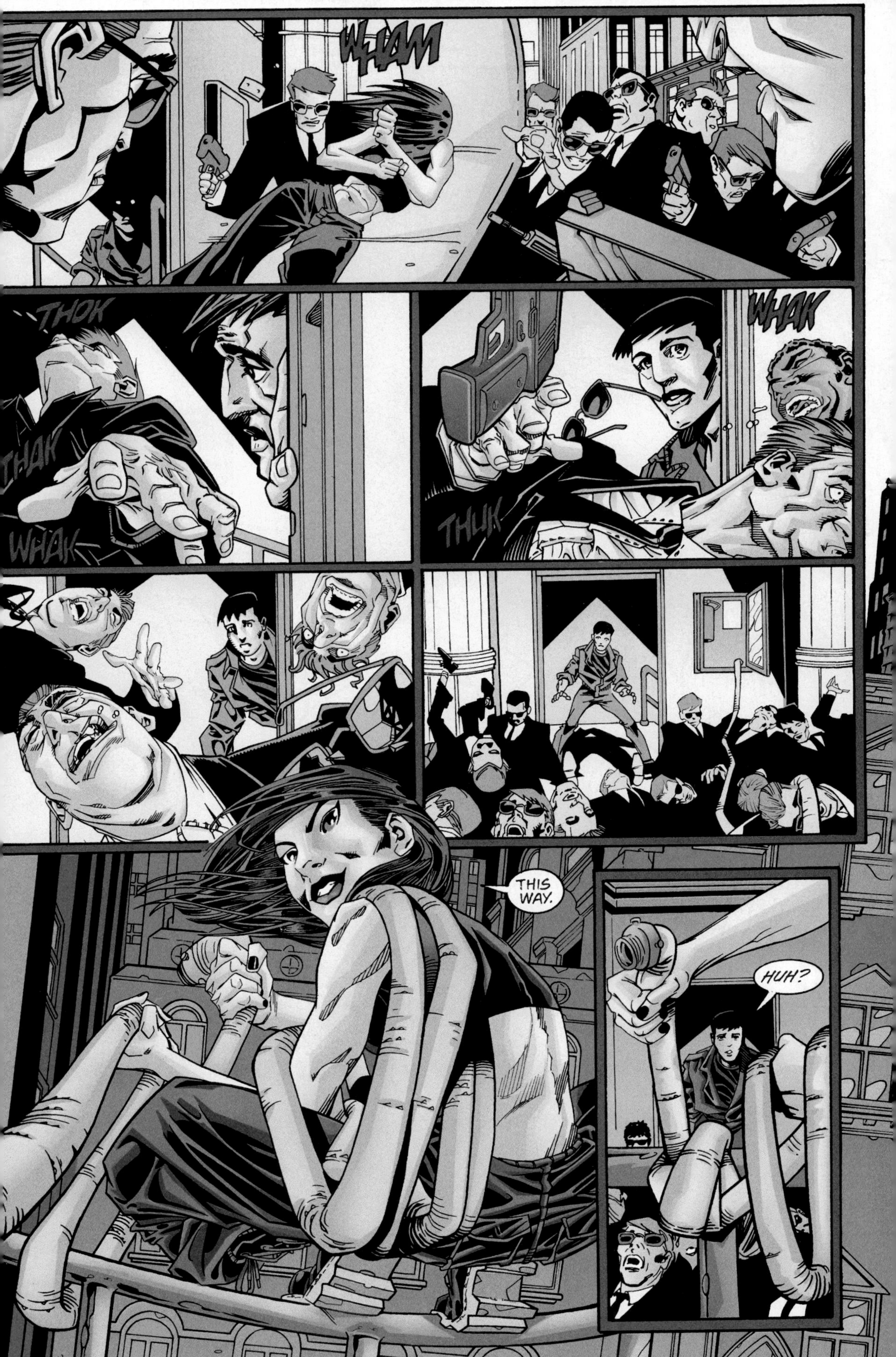
WHAM
THOK
THAK
WHAK
WHAK
THUK
THIS WAY.
HUH?

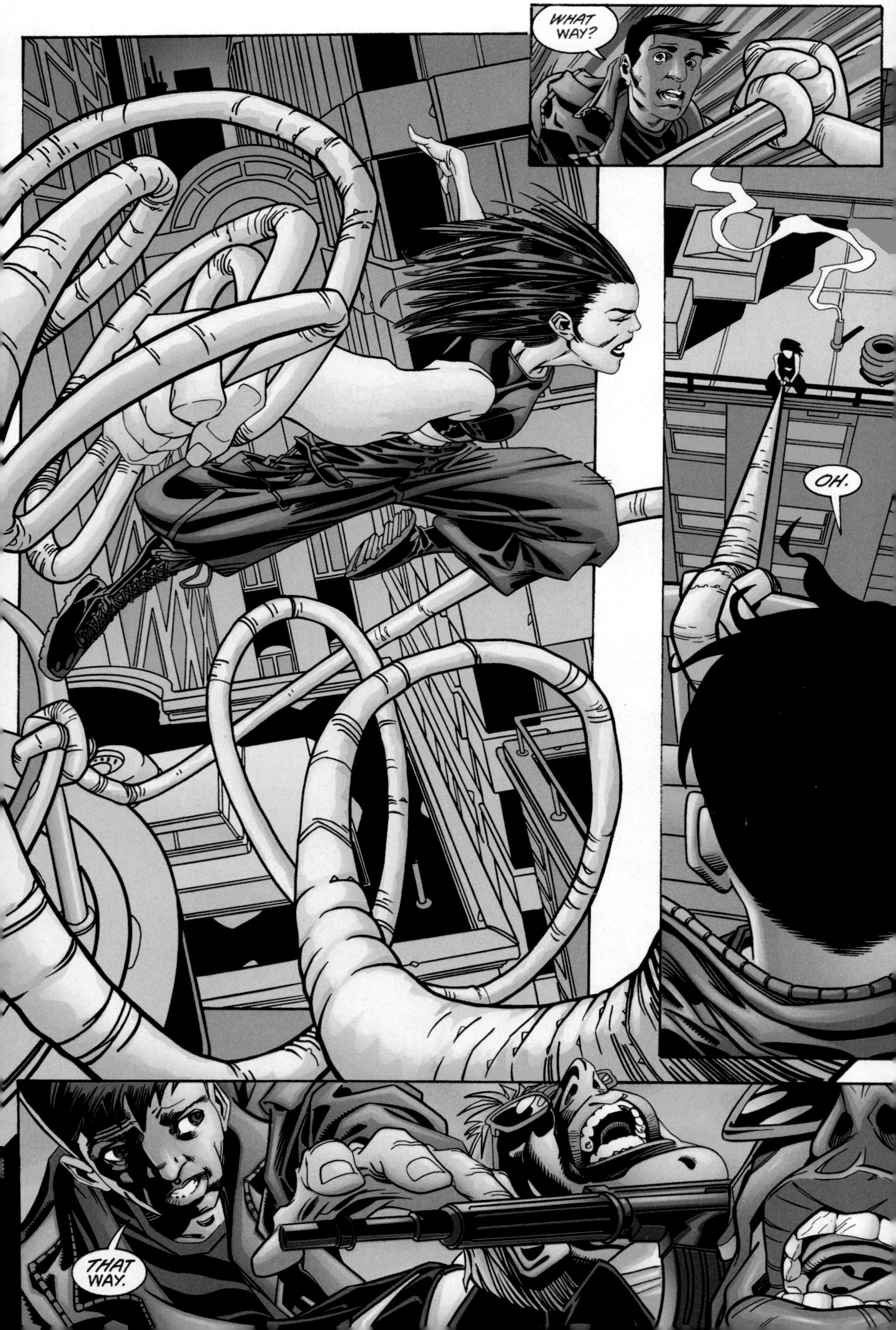
WHAT WAY?
OH.
THAT WAY.

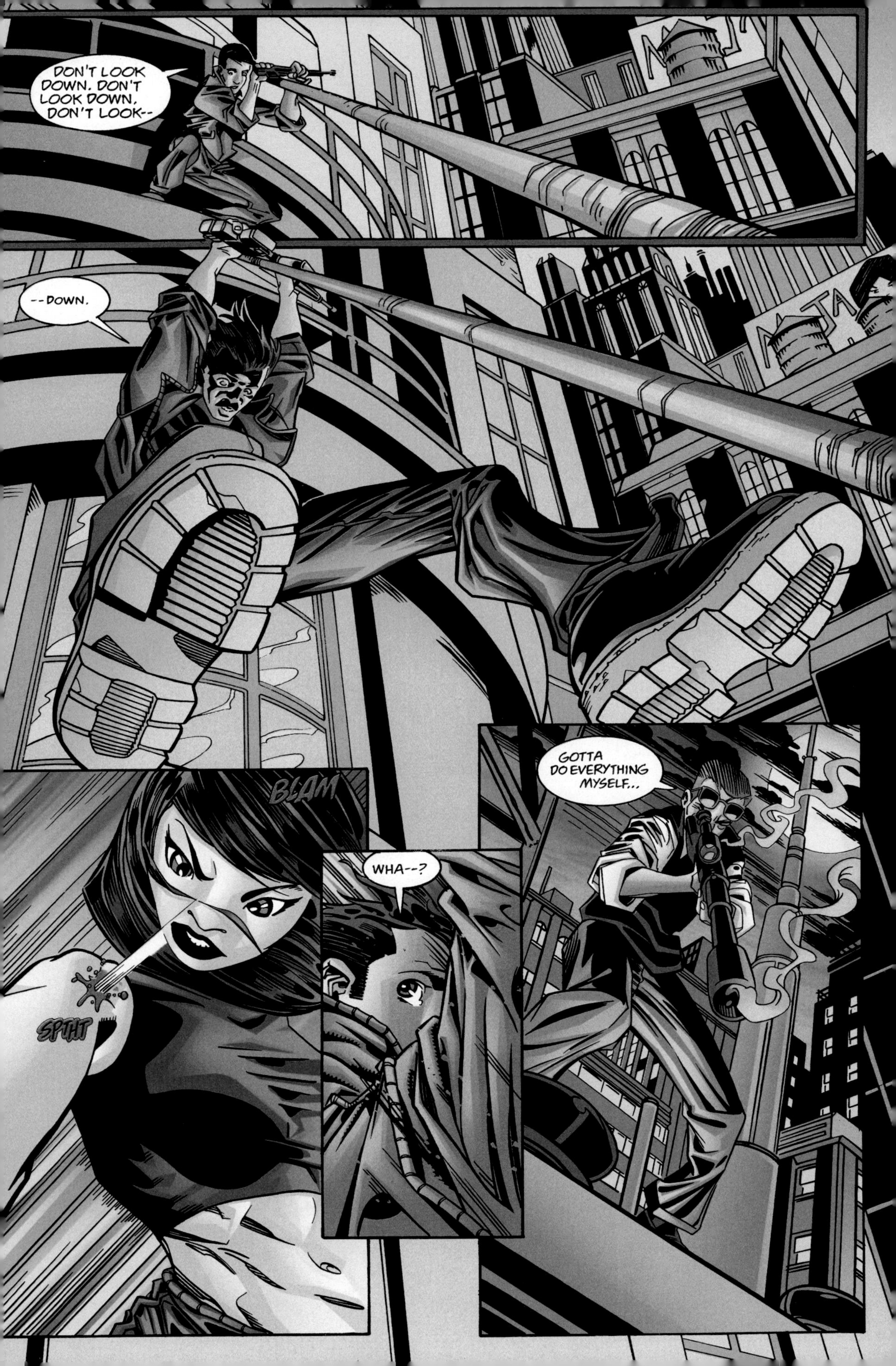
DON'T LOOK DOWN. DON'T LOOK DOWN, DON'T LOOK--
--DOWN.
BLAM
SPTHT
WHA--?
GOTTA DO EVERYTHING MYSELF...

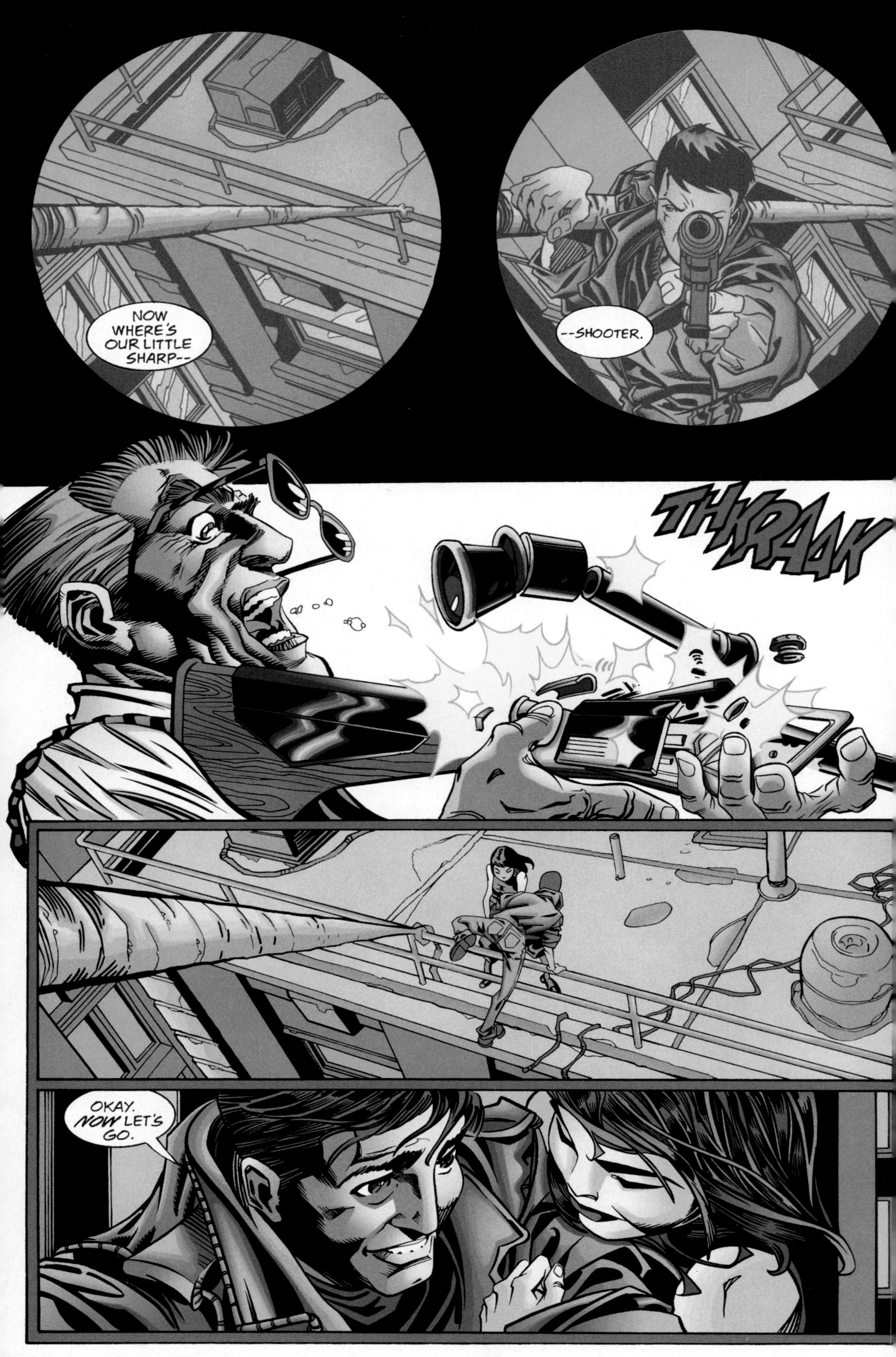
NOW WHERE'S OUR LITTLE SHARP--
--SHOOTER.
THKRAAK
OKAY. NOW LET'S GO.

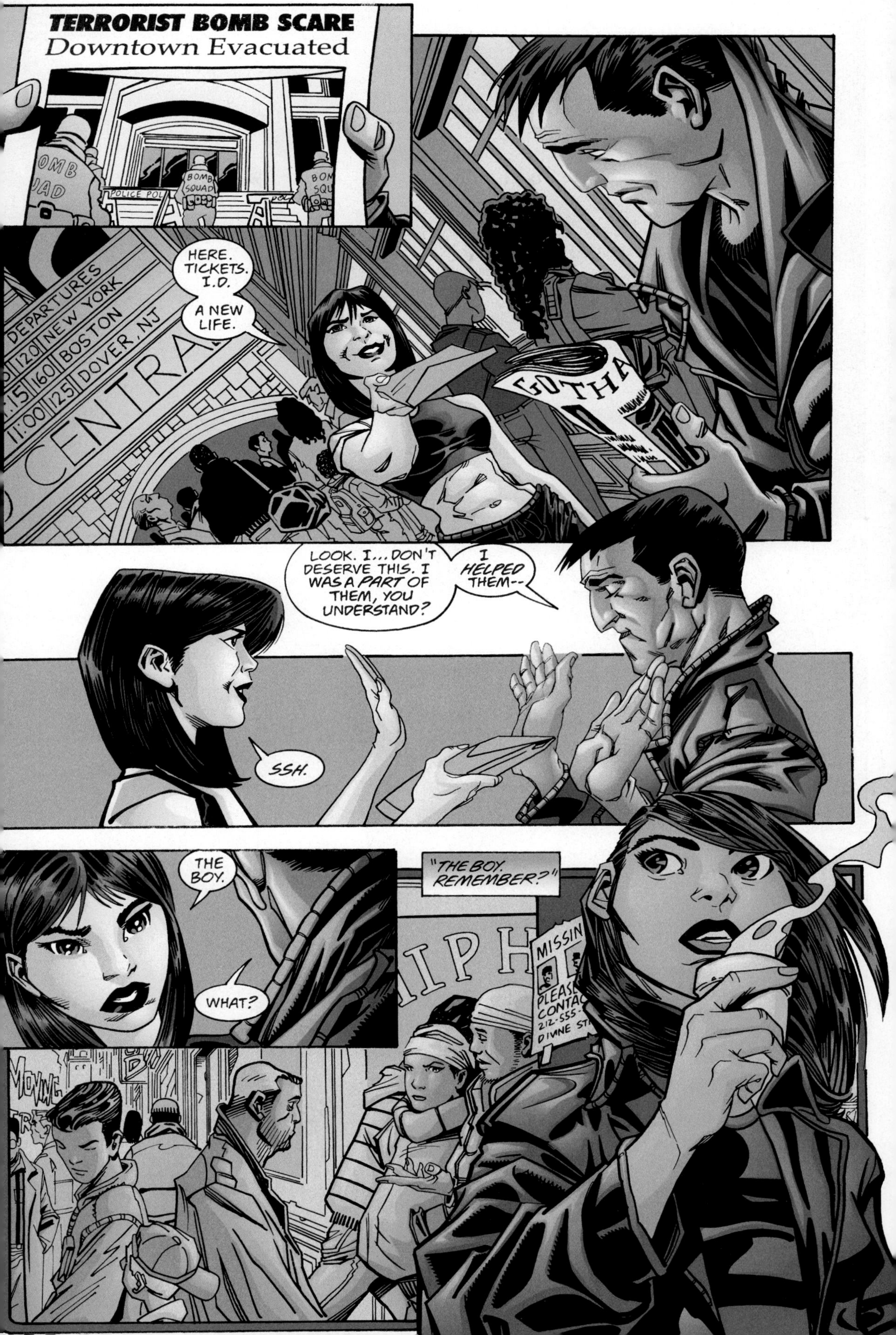
TERRORIST BOMB SCARE
Downtown Evacuated
BOMB SQUAD
POLICE
DEPARTURES
120 NEW YORK
160 BOSTON
11:00 125 DOVER, NJ
CENTRA
HERE. TICKETS. I.D.
A NEW LIFE.
GOTHA
LOOK. I... DON'T DESERVE THIS. I WAS A PART OF THEM, YOU UNDERSTAND?
I HELPED THEM--
SSH.
THE BOY.
WHAT?
"THE BOY. REMEMBER?"
MISSIN
PLEASE CONTAC
212-555-
DIVNE ST

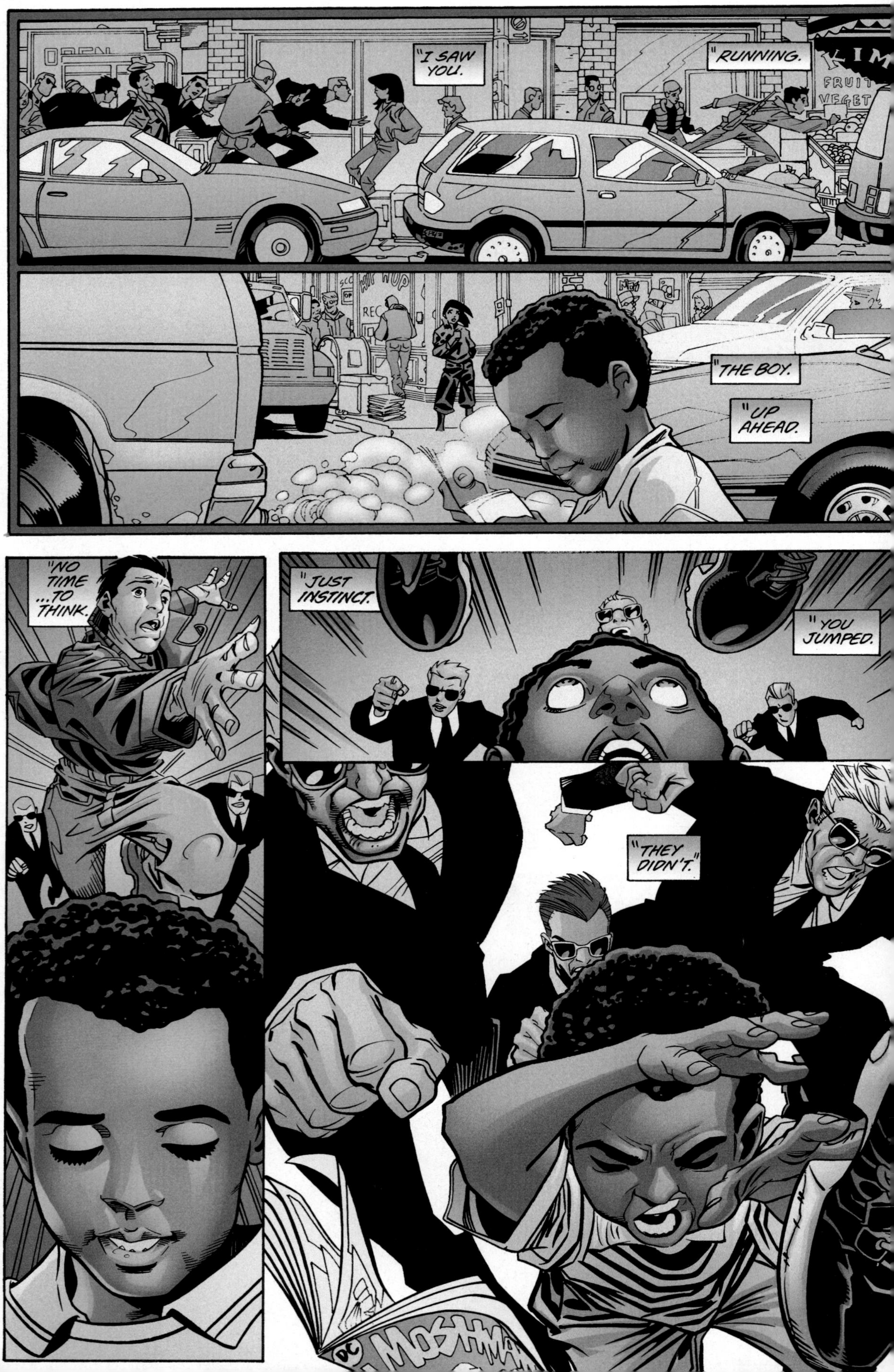
"I SAW YOU.
"RUNNING.
"THE BOY.
"UP AHEAD.
"NO TIME ...TO THINK.
"JUST INSTINCT.
"YOU JUMPED.
"THEY DIDN'T."

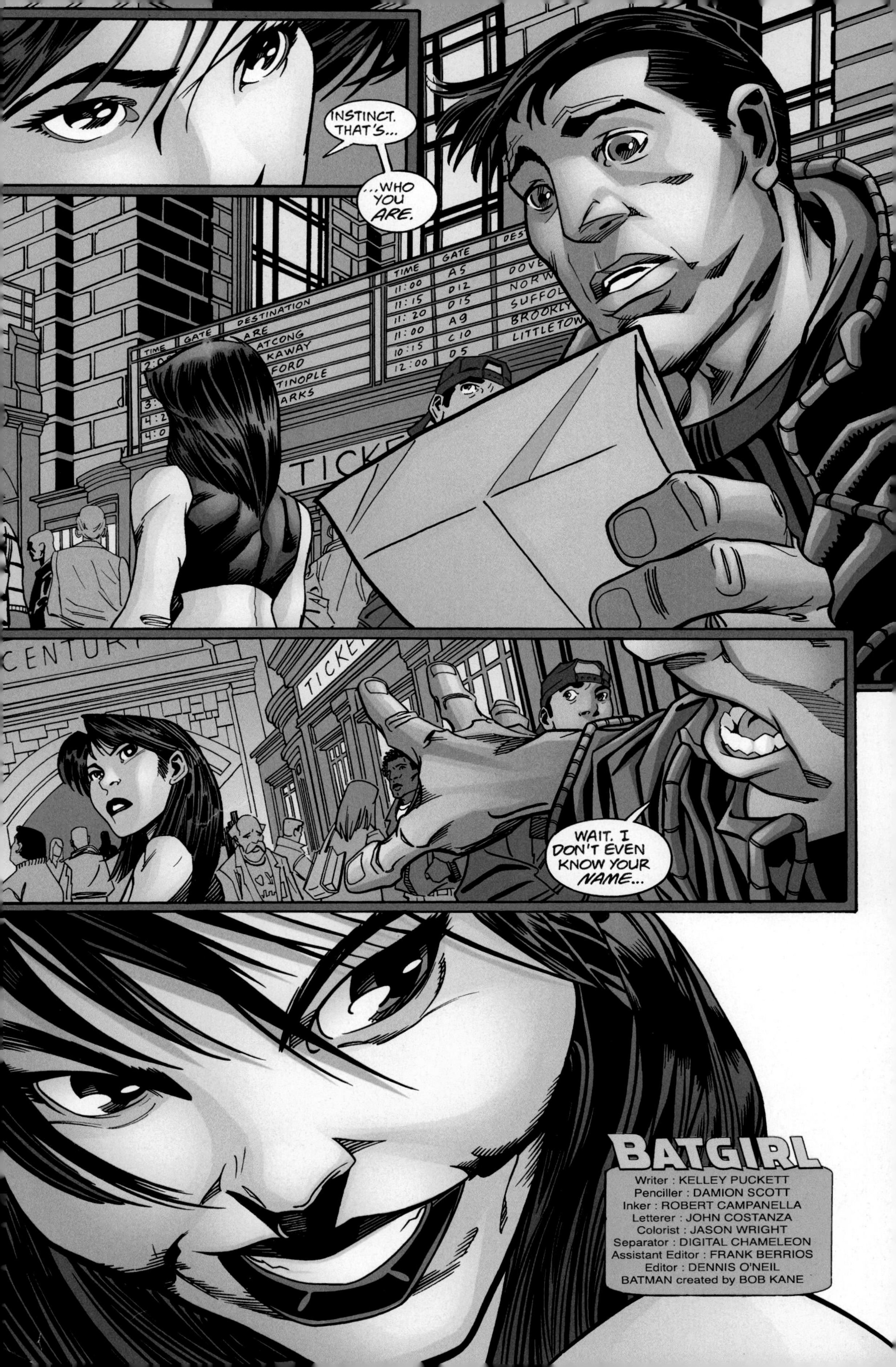
INSTINCT. THAT'S...
...WHO YOU ARE.
TIME GATE DESTINATION
11:00 A5 DOVE
11:15 D12 NORW
11:20 D15 SUFFOL
11:00 A9 BROOKLY
10:15 C10 LITTLETOW
12:00 D5
TICKE
CENTURY
TICKE
WAIT. I DON'T EVEN KNOW YOUR NAME...
BATGIRL
Writer : KELLEY PUCKETT
Penciller : DAMION SCOTT
Inker : ROBERT CAMPANELLA
Letterer : JOHN COSTANZA
Colorist : JASON WRIGHT
Separator : DIGITAL CHAMELEON
Assistant Editor : FRANK BERRIOS
Editor : DENNIS O'NEIL
BATMAN created by BOB KANE

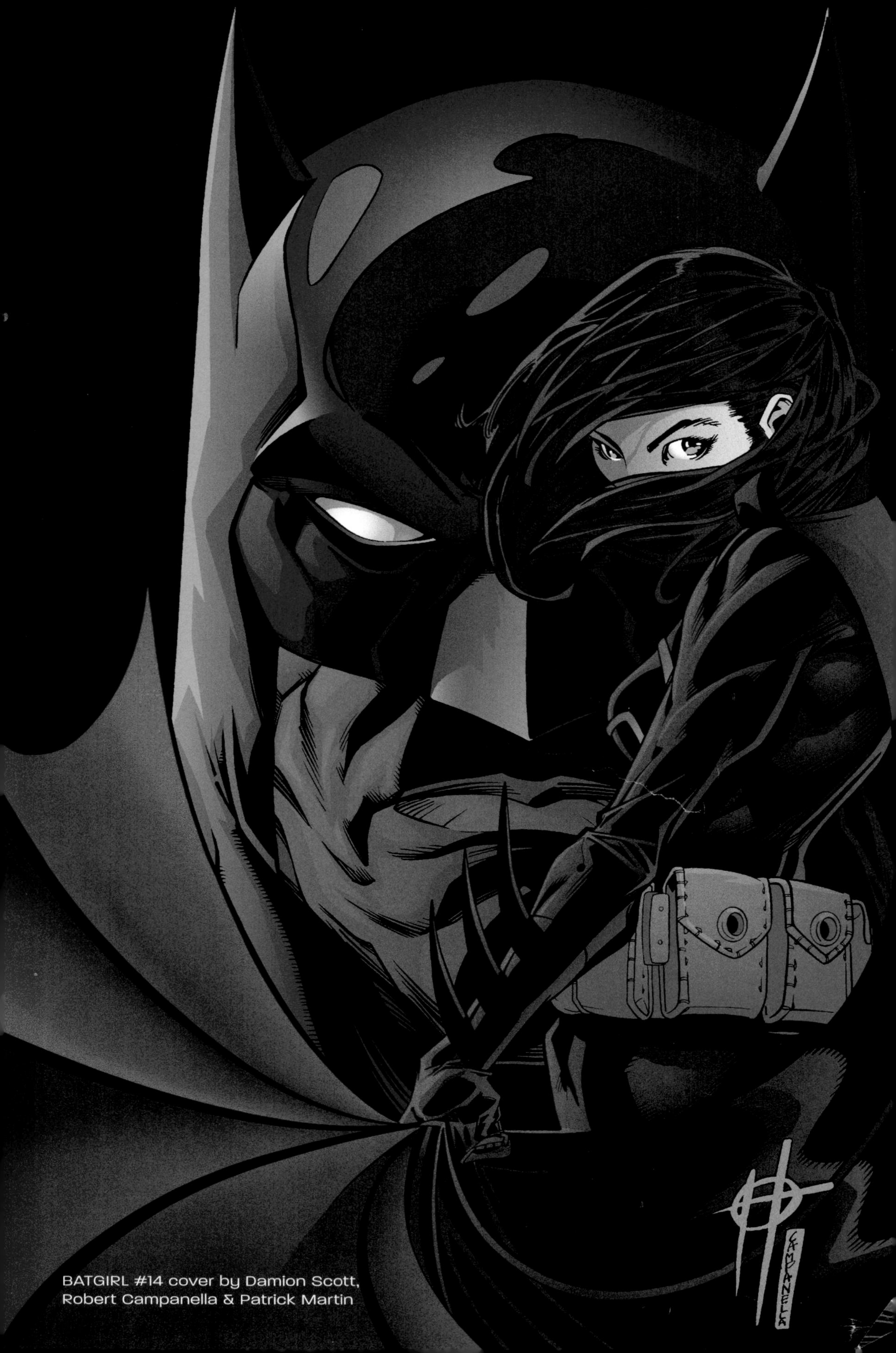
CAMPANELLA

BATGIRL #14 cover by Damion Scott,
Robert Campanella & Patrick Martin

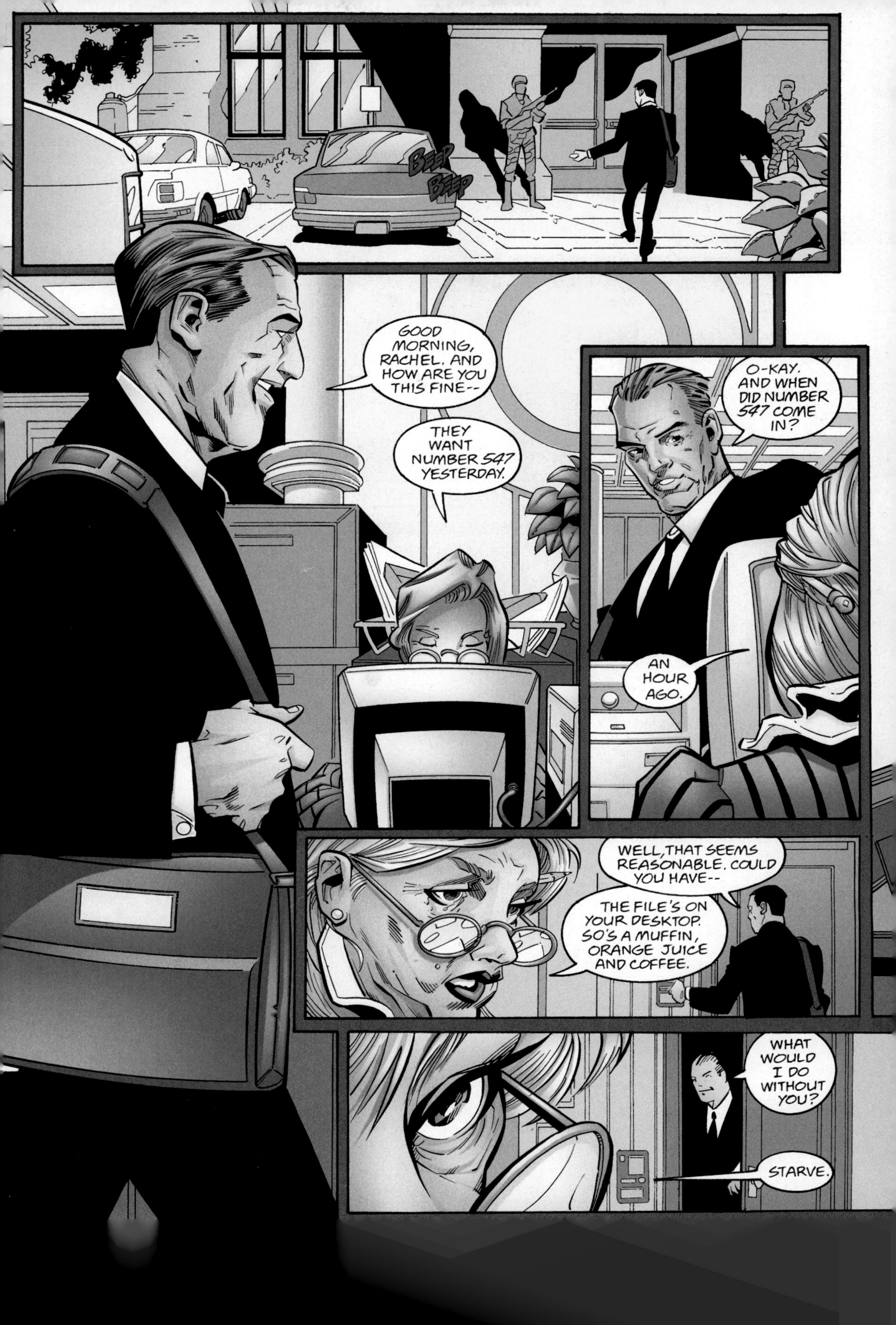
BEEP BEEP
GOOD MORNING, RACHEL. AND HOW ARE YOU THIS FINE--
THEY WANT NUMBER 547 YESTERDAY.
O-KAY. AND WHEN DID NUMBER 547 COME IN?
AN HOUR AGO.
WELL, THAT SEEMS REASONABLE. COULD YOU HAVE--
THE FILE'S ON YOUR DESKTOP. SO'S A MUFFIN, ORANGE JUICE AND COFFEE.
WHAT WOULD I DO WITHOUT YOU?
STARVE.

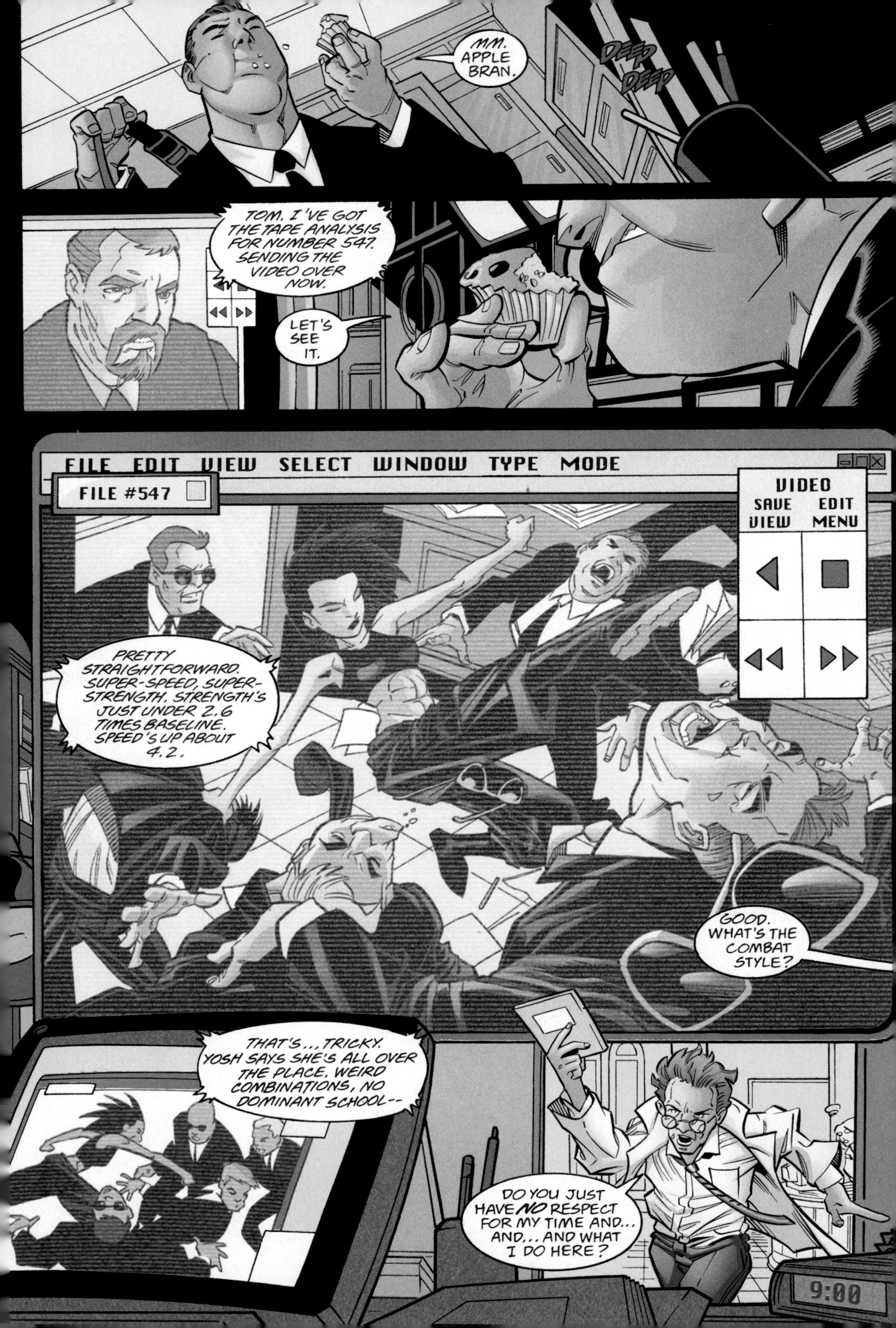
MM. APPLE BRAN.
DEEP DEEP
TOM, I'VE GOT THE TAPE ANALYSIS FOR NUMBER 547. SENDING THE VIDEO OVER NOW.
LET'S SEE IT.
FILE EDIT VIEW SELECT WINDOW TYPE MODE
FILE #547
VIDEO
SAVE VIEW
EDIT MENU
PRETTY STRAIGHTFORWARD. SUPER-SPEED, SUPER-STRENGTH. STRENGTH'S JUST UNDER 2.6 TIMES BASELINE. SPEED'S UP ABOUT 4.2.
GOOD. WHAT'S THE COMBAT STYLE?
THAT'S... TRICKY. YOSH SAYS SHE'S ALL OVER THE PLACE. WEIRD COMBINATIONS, NO DOMINANT SCHOOL--
DO YOU JUST HAVE NO RESPECT FOR MY TIME AND... AND... AND WHAT I DO HERE?
9:00

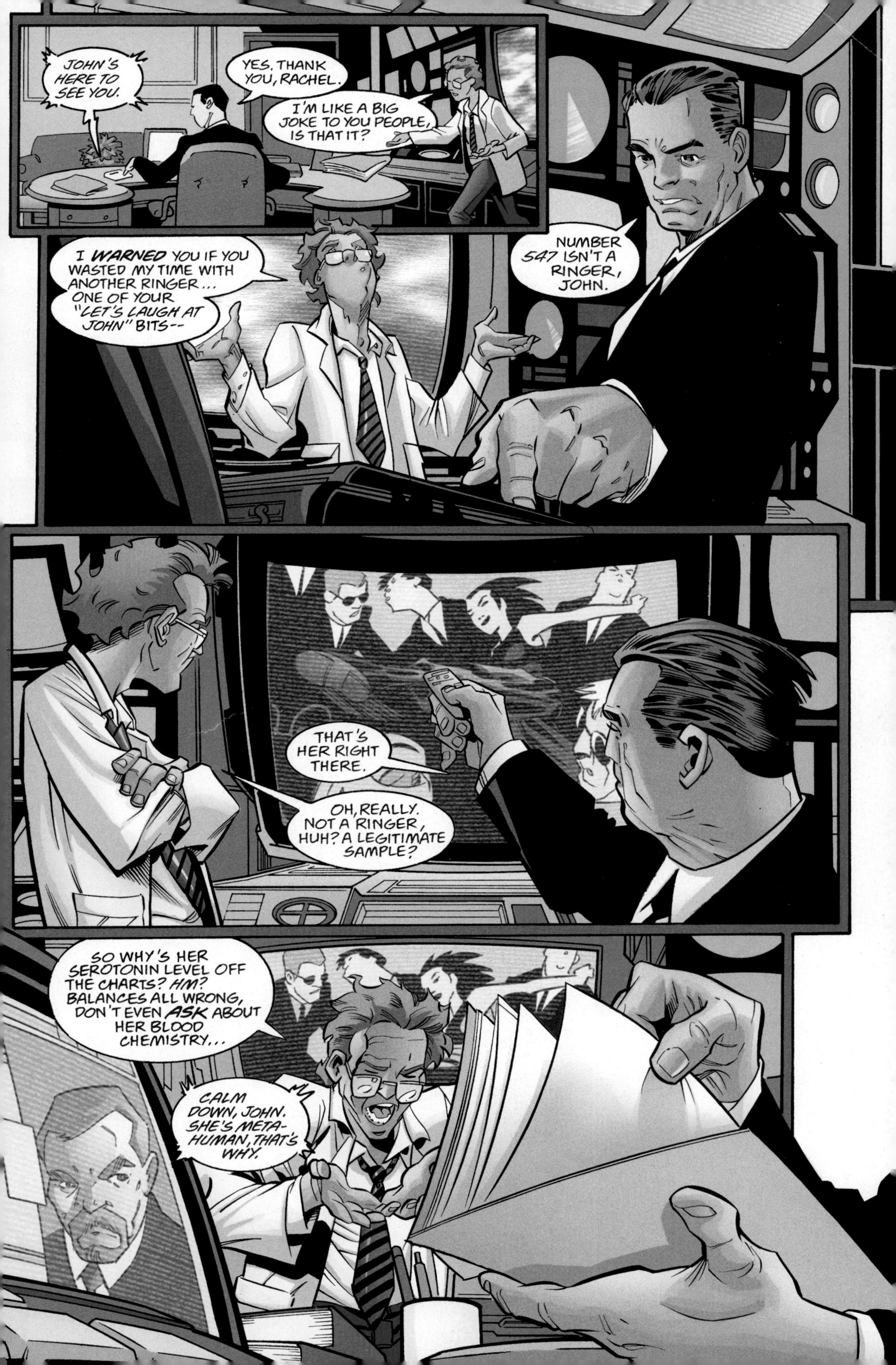

JOHN'S HERE TO SEE YOU.
YES, THANK YOU, RACHEL.
I'M LIKE A BIG JOKE TO YOU PEOPLE, IS THAT IT?
I **WARNED** YOU IF YOU WASTED MY TIME WITH ANOTHER RINGER... ONE OF YOUR "LET'S LAUGH AT JOHN" BITS--
NUMBER 547 ISN'T A RINGER, JOHN.
THAT'S HER RIGHT THERE.
OH, REALLY. NOT A RINGER, HUH? A LEGITIMATE SAMPLE?
SO WHY'S HER SEROTONIN LEVEL OFF THE CHARTS? *HM?* BALANCES ALL WRONG, DON'T EVEN **ASK** ABOUT HER BLOOD CHEMISTRY...
CALM DOWN, JOHN. SHE'S META-HUMAN, THAT'S WHY.

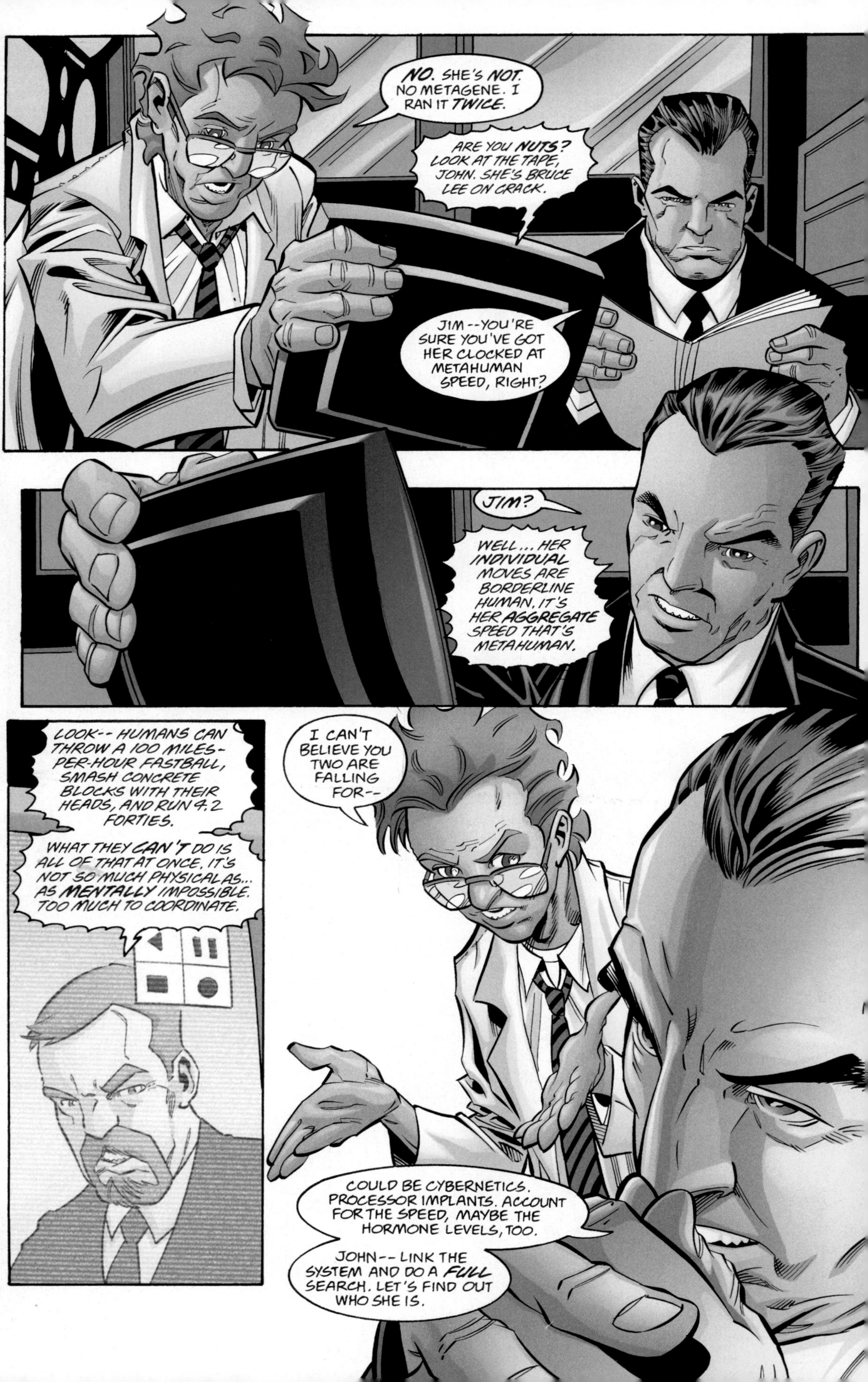
NO. SHE'S NOT. NO METAGENE. I RAN IT TWICE.
ARE YOU NUTS? LOOK AT THE TAPE, JOHN. SHE'S BRUCE LEE ON CRACK.
JIM--YOU'RE SURE YOU'VE GOT HER CLOCKED AT METAHUMAN SPEED, RIGHT?
JIM?
WELL... HER INDIVIDUAL MOVES ARE BORDERLINE HUMAN. IT'S HER AGGREGATE SPEED THAT'S METAHUMAN.
LOOK-- HUMANS CAN THROW A 100 MILES-PER-HOUR FASTBALL, SMASH CONCRETE BLOCKS WITH THEIR HEADS, AND RUN 4.2 FORTIES.
WHAT THEY CAN'T DO IS ALL OF THAT AT ONCE. IT'S NOT SO MUCH PHYSICAL AS... AS MENTALLY IMPOSSIBLE. TOO MUCH TO COORDINATE.
I CAN'T BELIEVE YOU TWO ARE FALLING FOR--
COULD BE CYBERNETICS. PROCESSOR IMPLANTS. ACCOUNT FOR THE SPEED, MAYBE THE HORMONE LEVELS, TOO.
JOHN-- LINK THE SYSTEM AND DO A FULL SEARCH. LET'S FIND OUT WHO SHE IS.

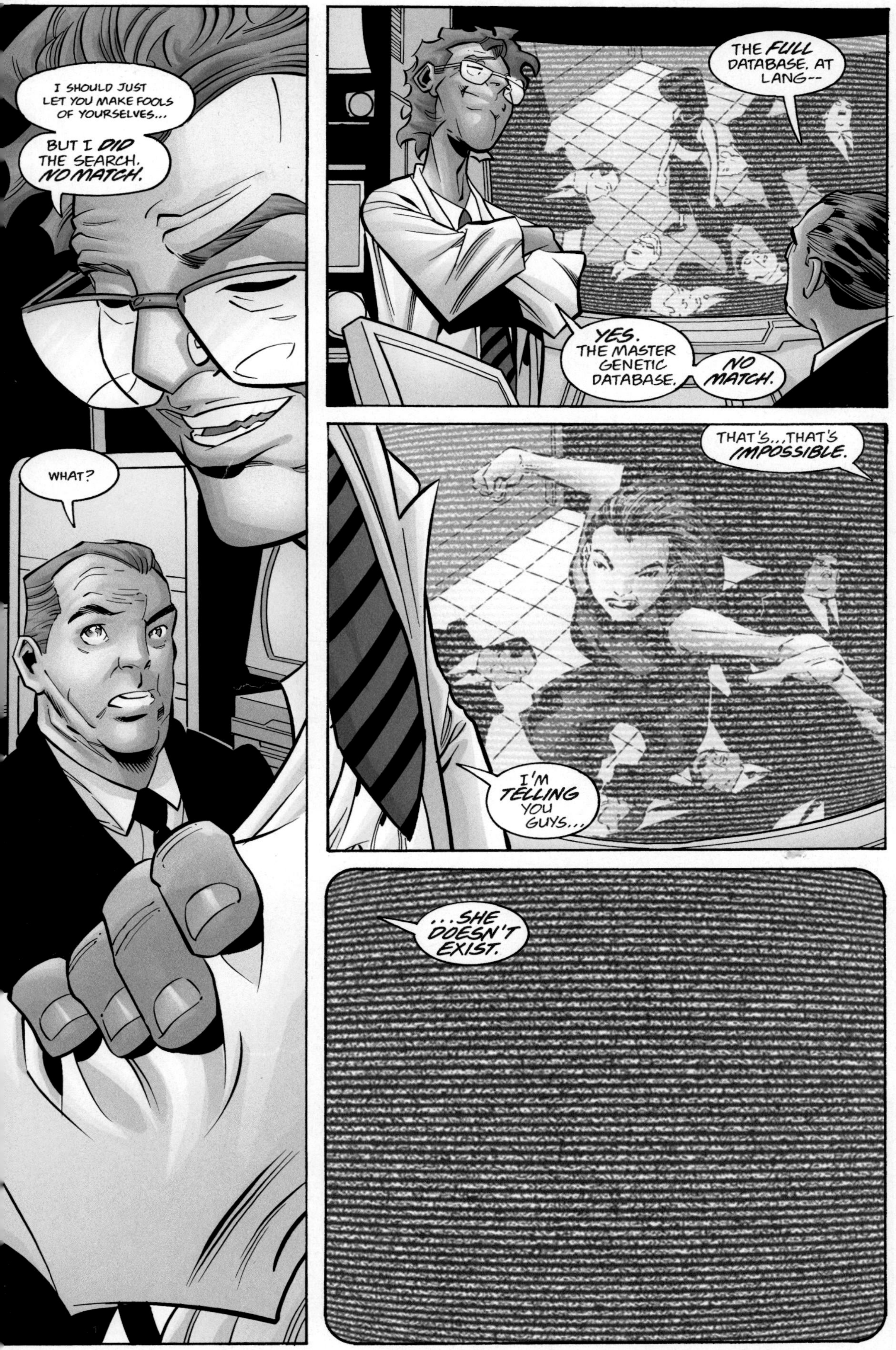
I SHOULD JUST LET YOU MAKE FOOLS OF YOURSELVES...
BUT I DID THE SEARCH. NO MATCH.
THE FULL DATABASE. AT LANG--
YES. THE MASTER GENETIC DATABASE.
NO MATCH.
WHAT?
THAT'S...THAT'S IMPOSSIBLE.
I'M TELLING YOU GUYS...
...SHE DOESN'T EXIST.

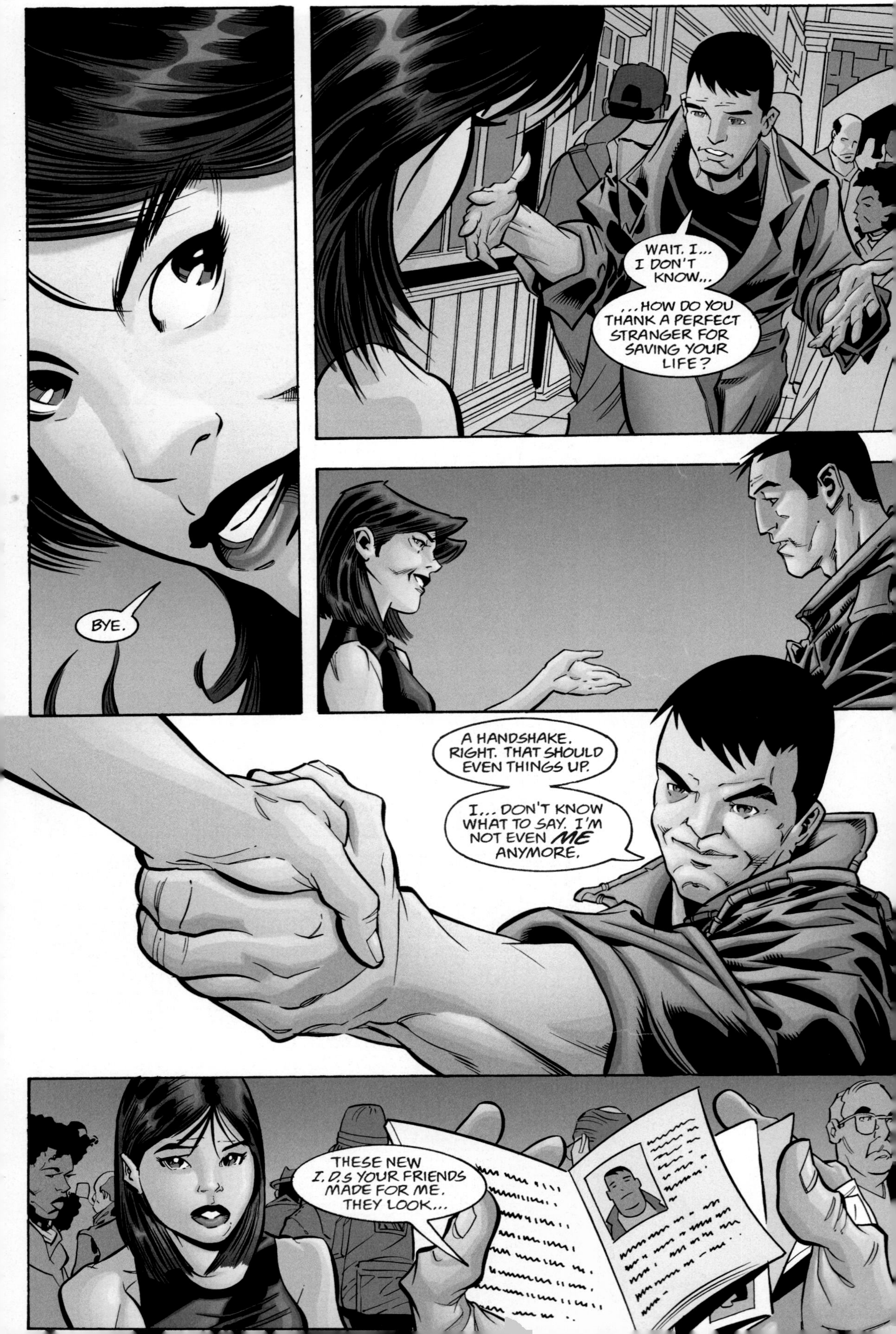
WAIT. I... I DON'T KNOW...
...HOW DO YOU THANK A PERFECT STRANGER FOR SAVING YOUR LIFE?
BYE.
A HANDSHAKE. RIGHT. THAT SHOULD EVEN THINGS UP.
I... DON'T KNOW WHAT TO SAY. I'M NOT EVEN ME ANYMORE.
THESE NEW I.D.S YOUR FRIENDS MADE FOR ME. THEY LOOK...

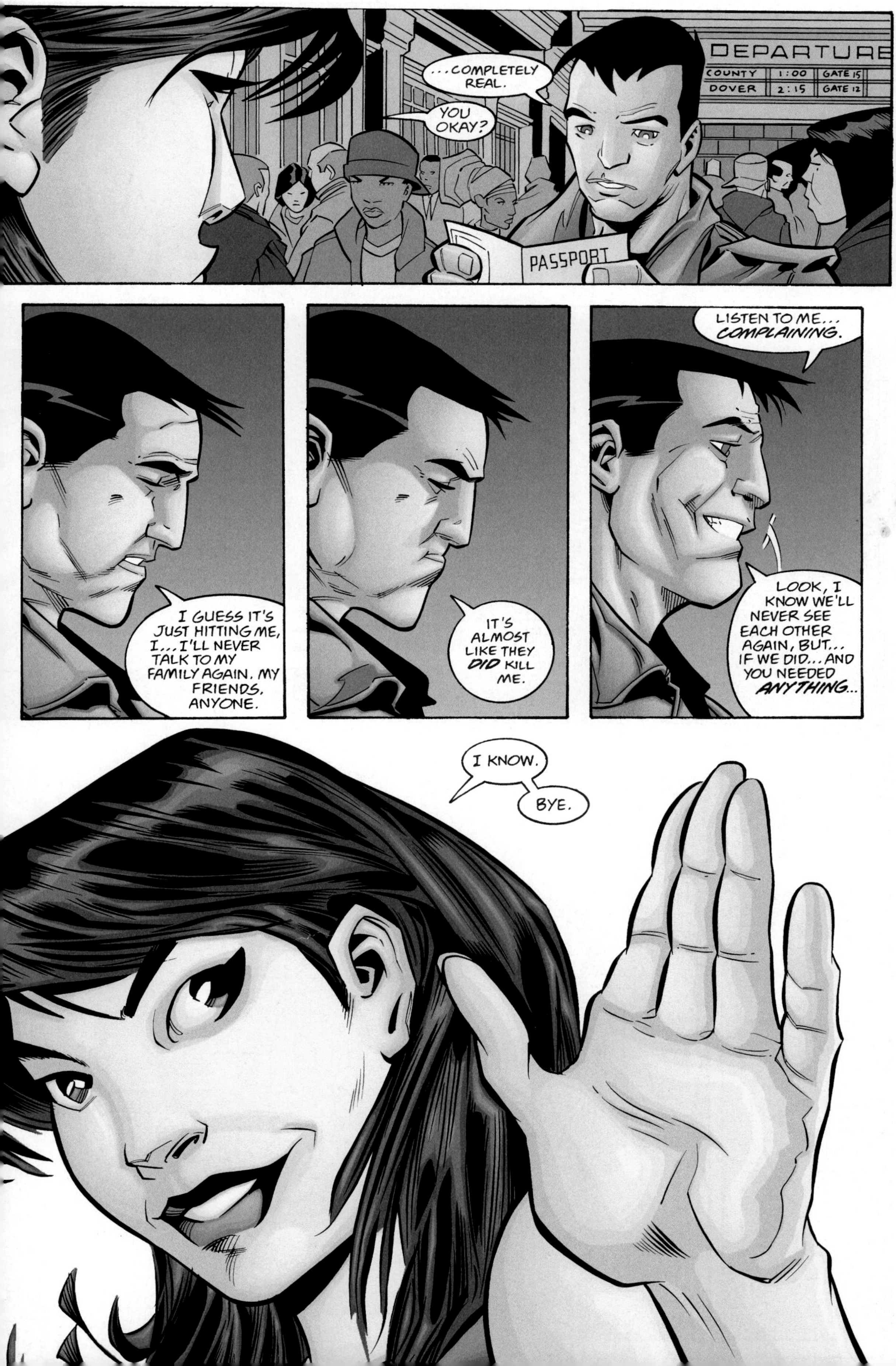
DEPARTURE
COUNTY 1:00 GATE 15
DOVER 2:15 GATE 12
...COMPLETELY REAL.
YOU OKAY?
PASSPORT
I GUESS IT'S JUST HITTING ME, I... I'LL NEVER TALK TO MY FAMILY AGAIN. MY FRIENDS. ANYONE.
IT'S ALMOST LIKE THEY DID KILL ME.
LISTEN TO ME... COMPLAINING.
LOOK, I KNOW WE'LL NEVER SEE EACH OTHER AGAIN, BUT... IF WE DID... AND YOU NEEDED ANYTHING...
I KNOW.
BYE.

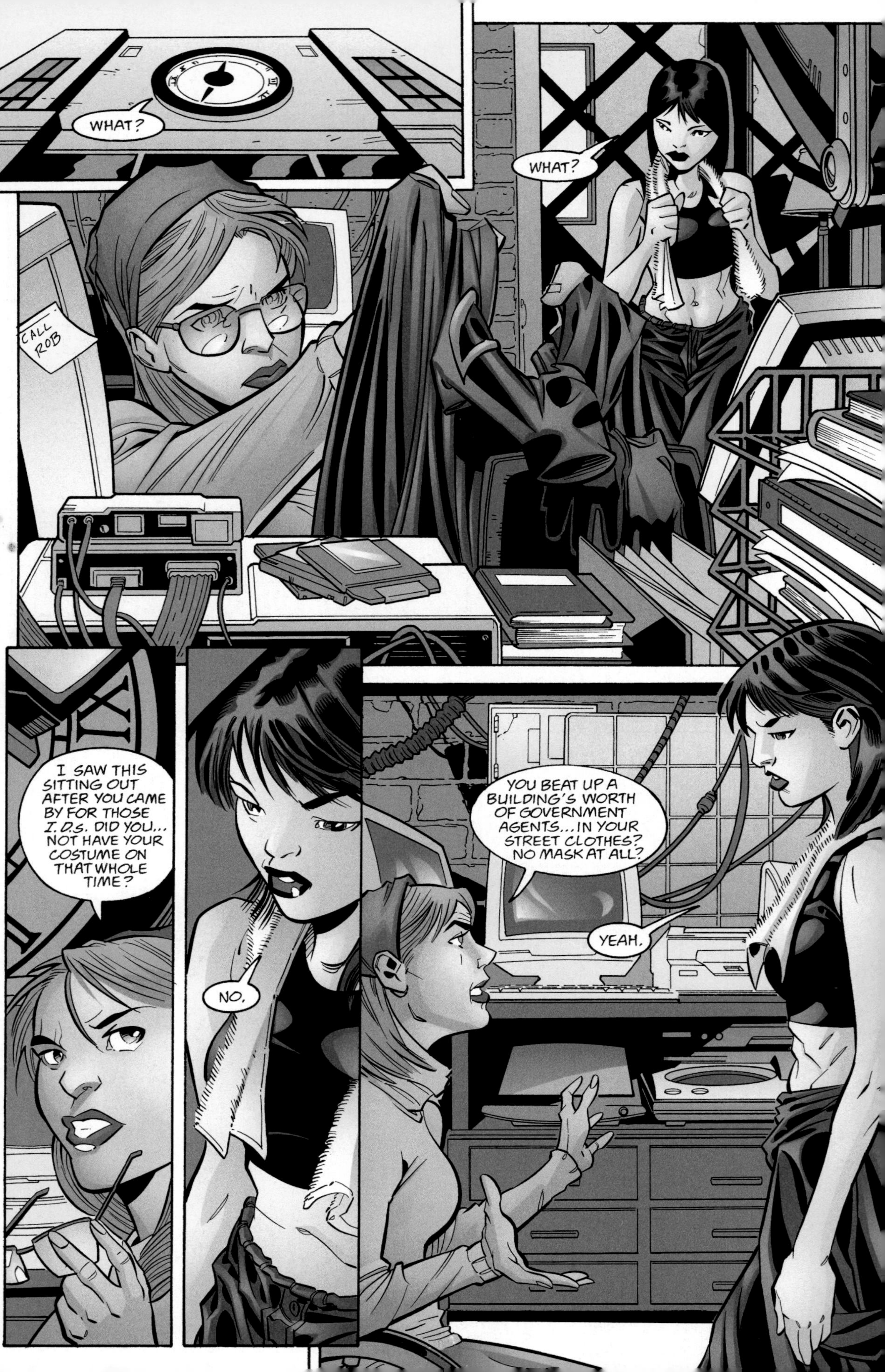
WHAT?
CALL ROB
WHAT?
I SAW THIS SITTING OUT AFTER YOU CAME BY FOR THOSE I.D.s. DID YOU... NOT HAVE YOUR COSTUME ON THAT WHOLE TIME?
NO.
YOU BEAT UP A BUILDING'S WORTH OF GOVERNMENT AGENTS... IN YOUR STREET CLOTHES? NO MASK AT ALL?
YEAH.

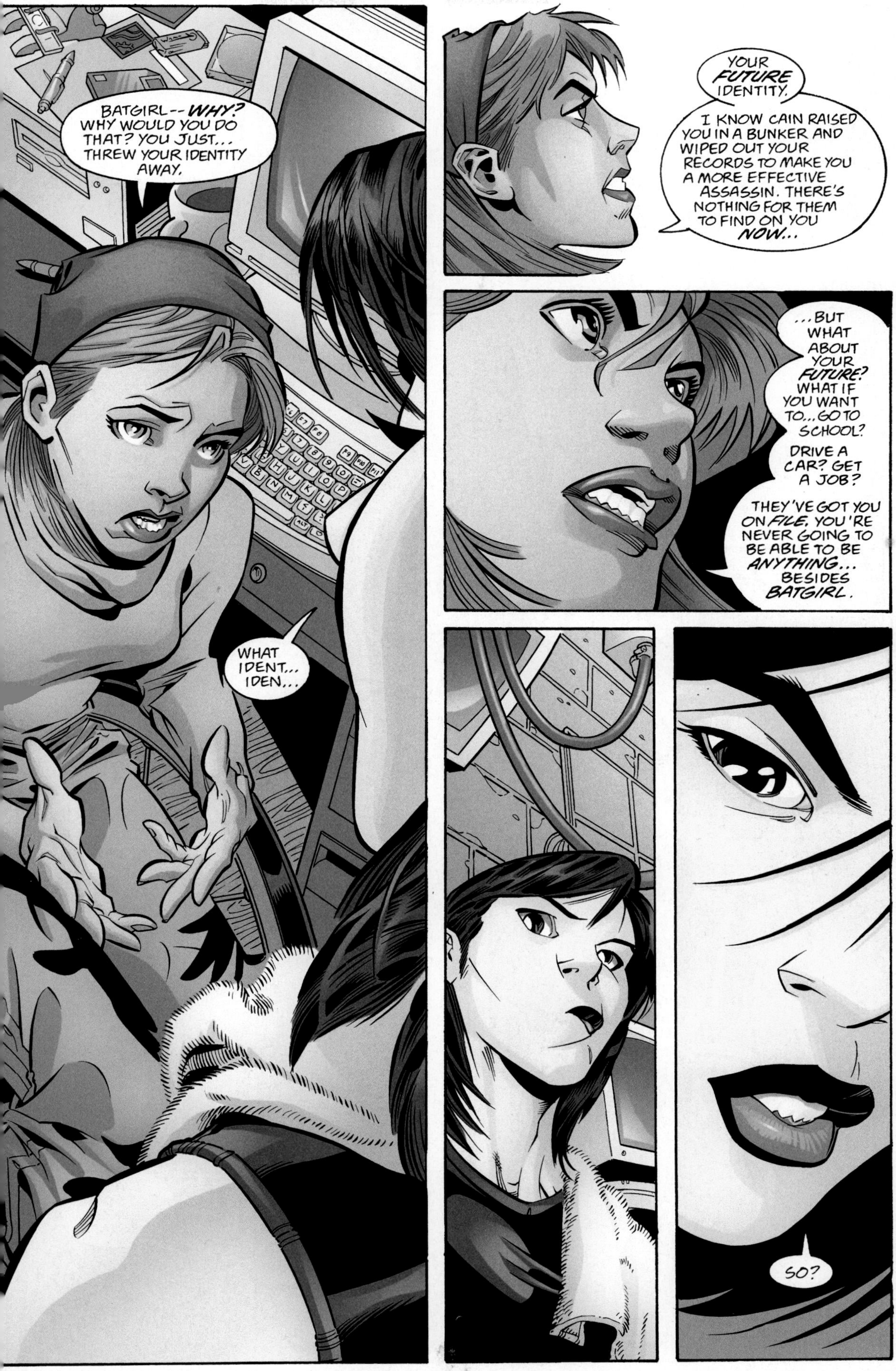
BATGIRL--WHY? WHY WOULD YOU DO THAT? YOU JUST... THREW YOUR IDENTITY AWAY.
WHAT IDENT... IDEN...
YOUR FUTURE IDENTITY.
I KNOW CAIN RAISED YOU IN A BUNKER AND WIPED OUT YOUR RECORDS TO MAKE YOU A MORE EFFECTIVE ASSASSIN. THERE'S NOTHING FOR THEM TO FIND ON YOU NOW...
...BUT WHAT ABOUT YOUR FUTURE? WHAT IF YOU WANT TO...GO TO SCHOOL?
DRIVE A CAR? GET A JOB?
THEY'VE GOT YOU ON FILE. YOU'RE NEVER GOING TO BE ABLE TO BE ANYTHING... BESIDES BATGIRL.
SO?

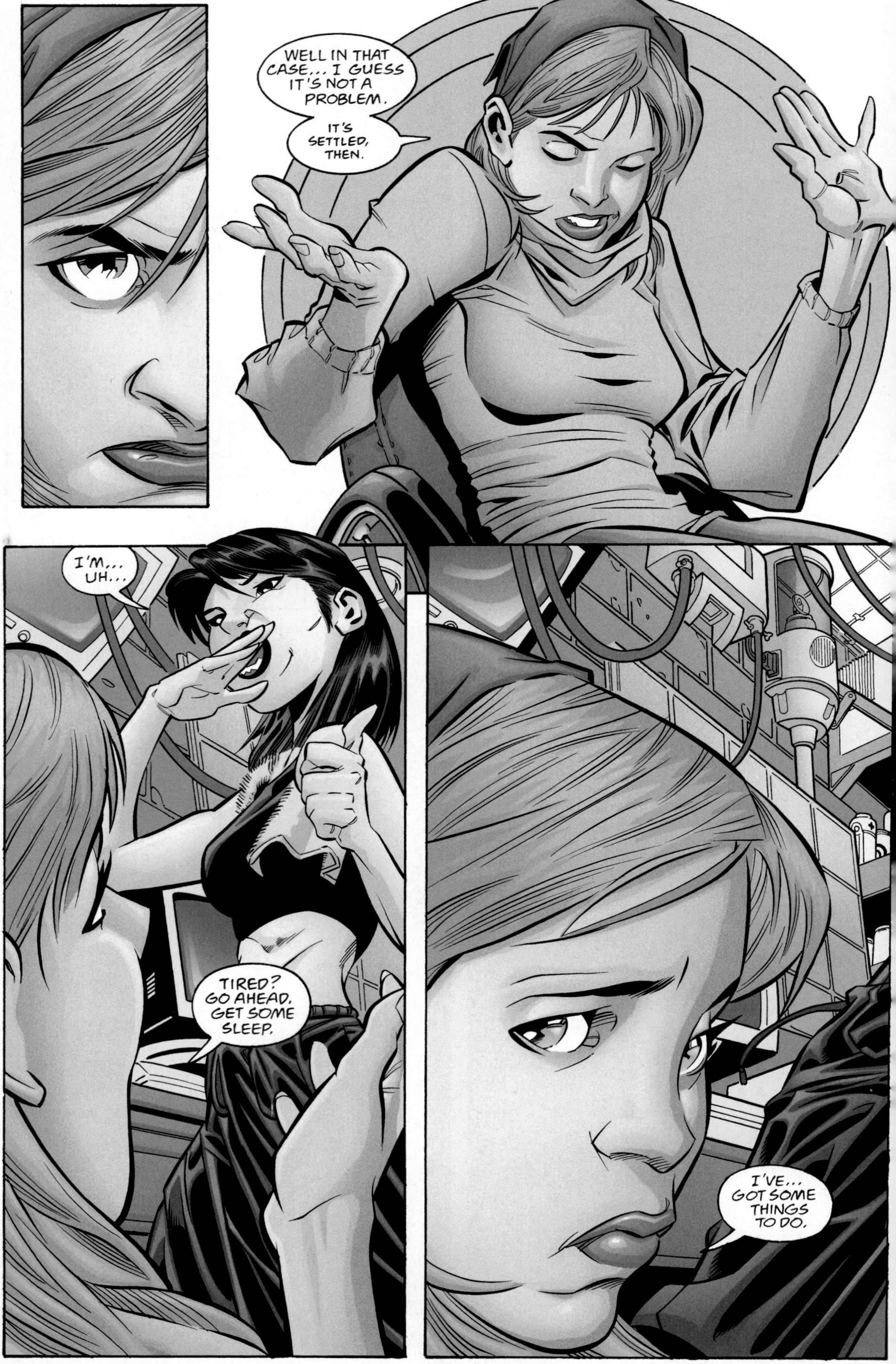
WELL IN THAT CASE... I GUESS IT'S NOT A PROBLEM.
IT'S SETTLED, THEN.
I'M... UH...
TIRED? GO AHEAD, GET SOME SLEEP.
I'VE... GOT SOME THINGS TO DO.

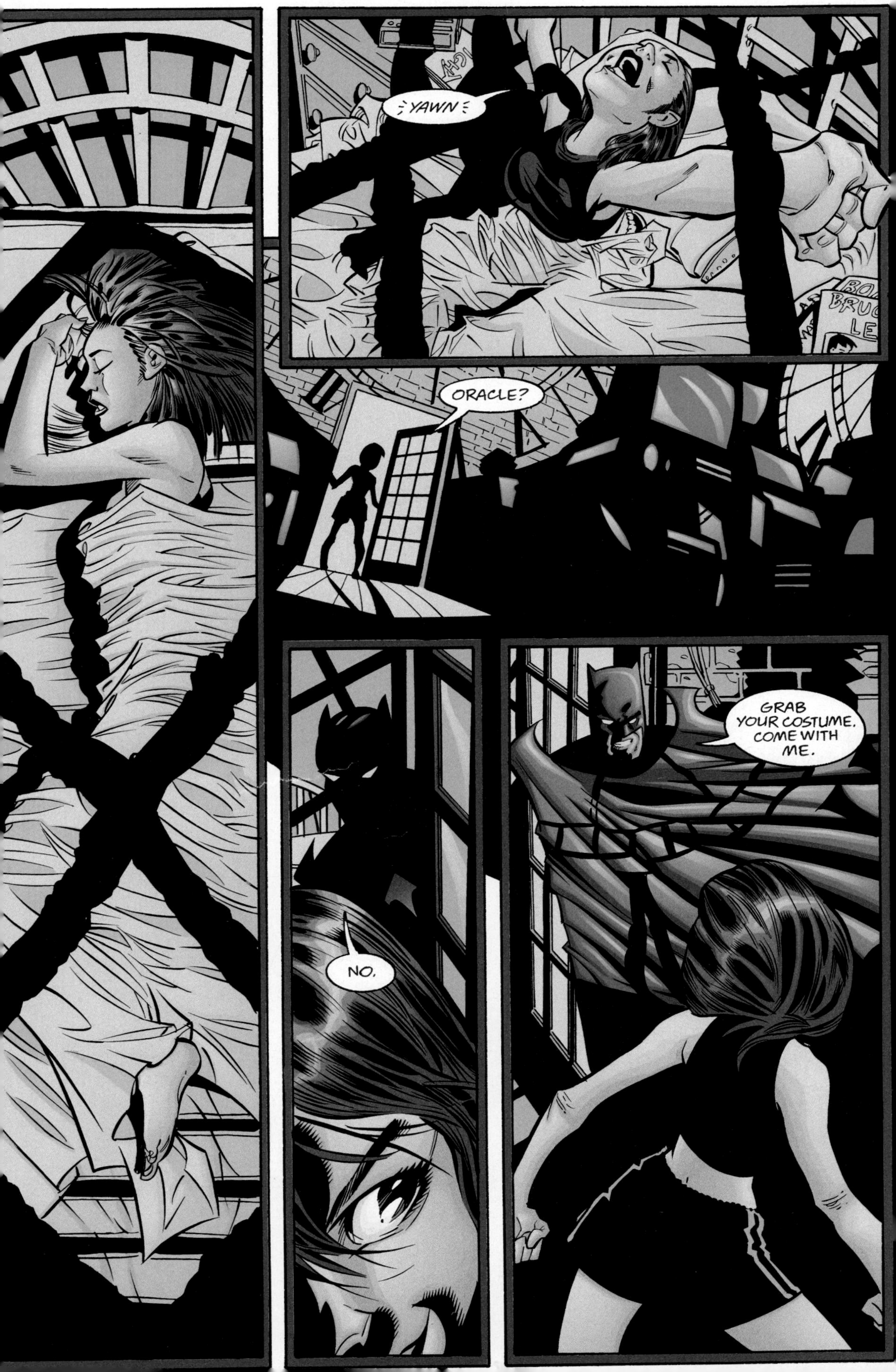
YAWN
ORACLE?
GRAB YOUR COSTUME. COME WITH ME.
NO.

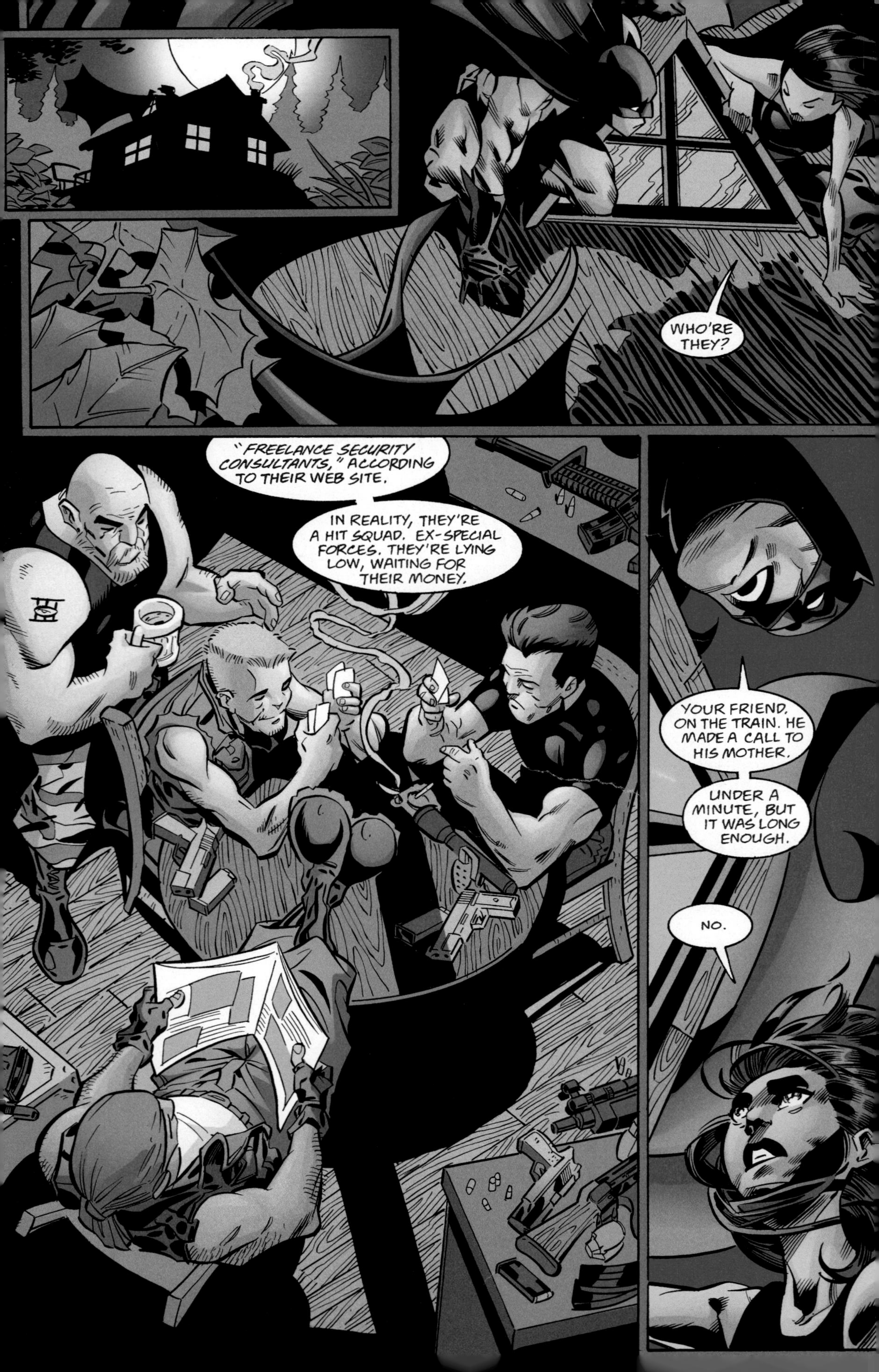
WHO'RE THEY?
"FREELANCE SECURITY CONSULTANTS," ACCORDING TO THEIR WEB SITE.
IN REALITY, THEY'RE A HIT SQUAD. EX-SPECIAL FORCES. THEY'RE LYING LOW, WAITING FOR THEIR MONEY.
YOUR FRIEND, ON THE TRAIN. HE MADE A CALL TO HIS MOTHER.
UNDER A MINUTE, BUT IT WAS LONG ENOUGH.
NO.

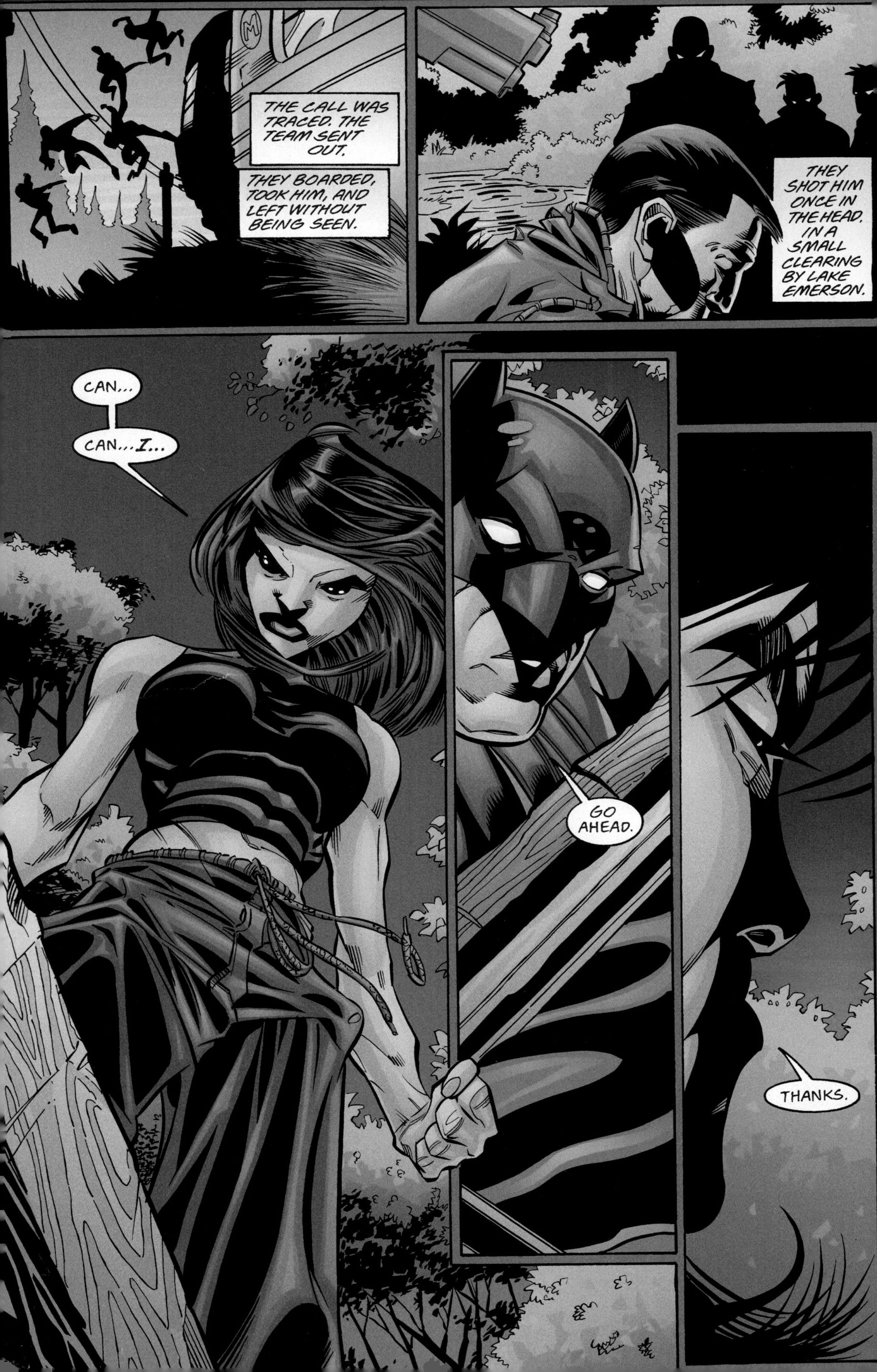
THE CALL WAS TRACED. THE TEAM SENT OUT.
THEY BOARDED, TOOK HIM, AND LEFT WITHOUT BEING SEEN.
THEY SHOT HIM ONCE IN THE HEAD. IN A SMALL CLEARING BY LAKE EMERSON.
CAN...
CAN... I...
GO AHEAD.
THANKS.

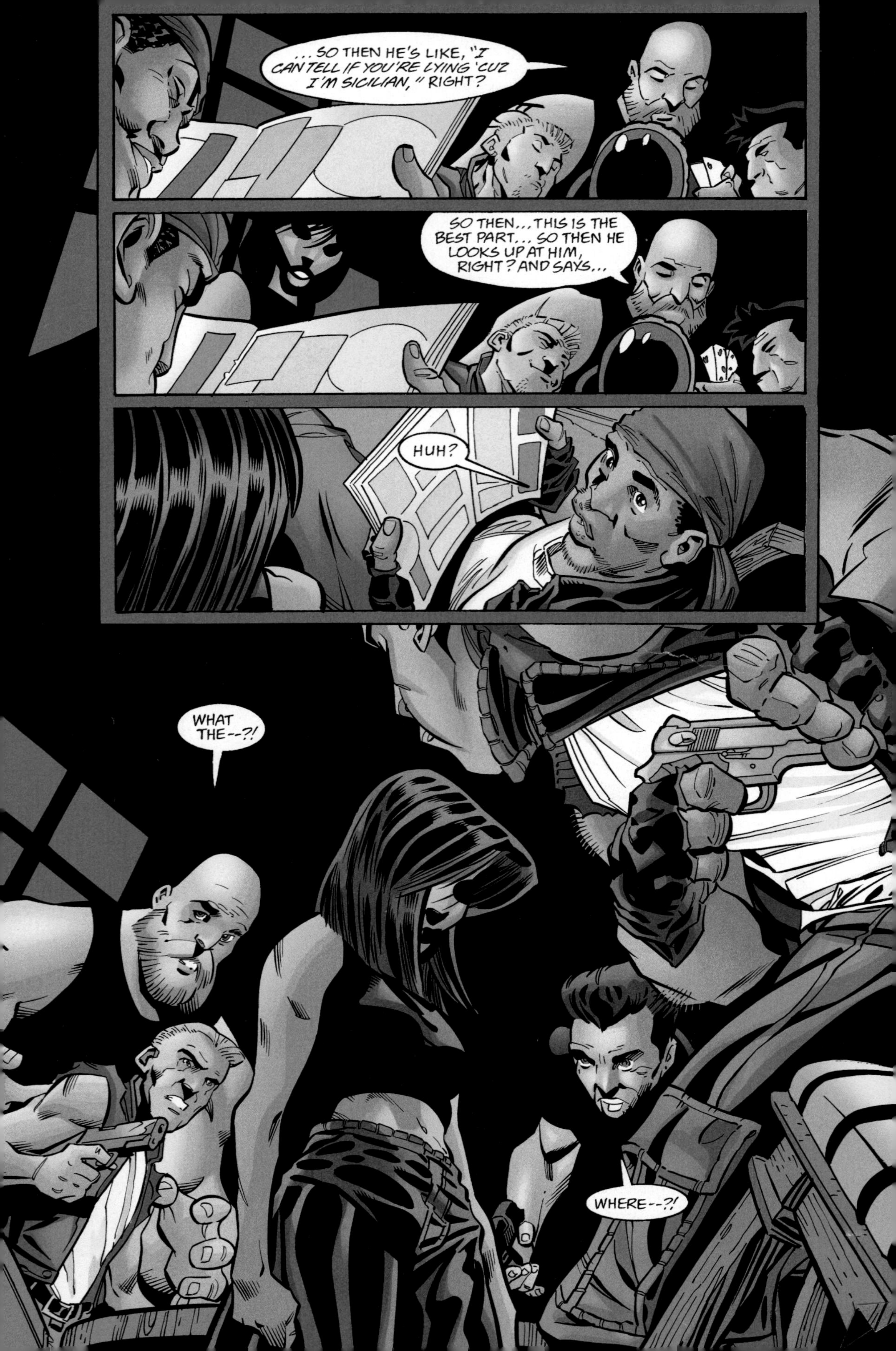
...SO THEN HE'S LIKE, "I CAN TELL IF YOU'RE LYING 'CUZ I'M SICILIAN," RIGHT?
SO THEN... THIS IS THE BEST PART... SO THEN HE LOOKS UP AT HIM, RIGHT? AND SAYS...
HUH?
WHAT THE--?!
WHERE--?!

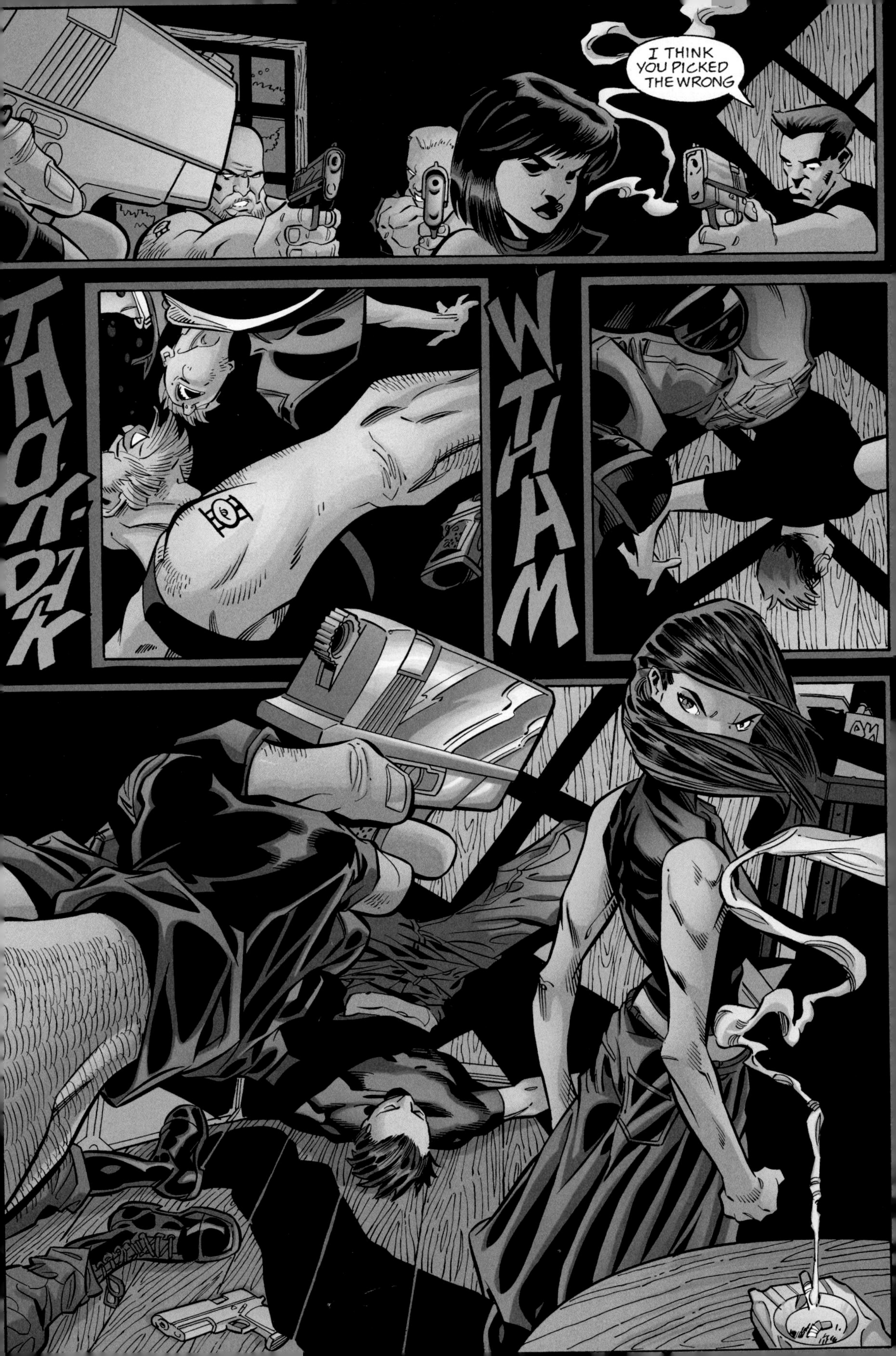
I THINK YOU PICKED THE WRONG
THOK-DAK
WHAM

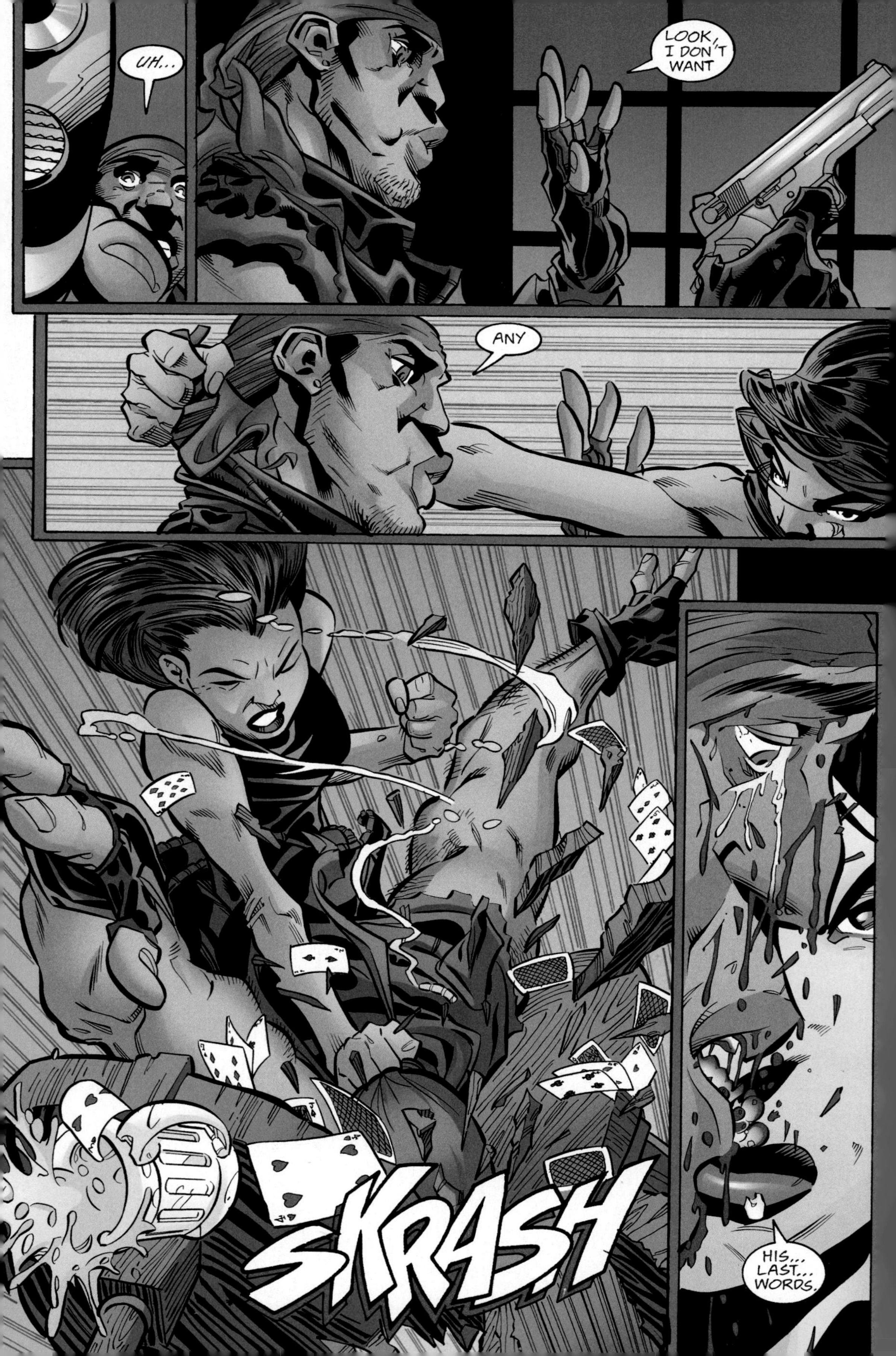
UH...
LOOK, I DON'T WANT
ANY
SKRASH
HIS... LAST... WORDS.

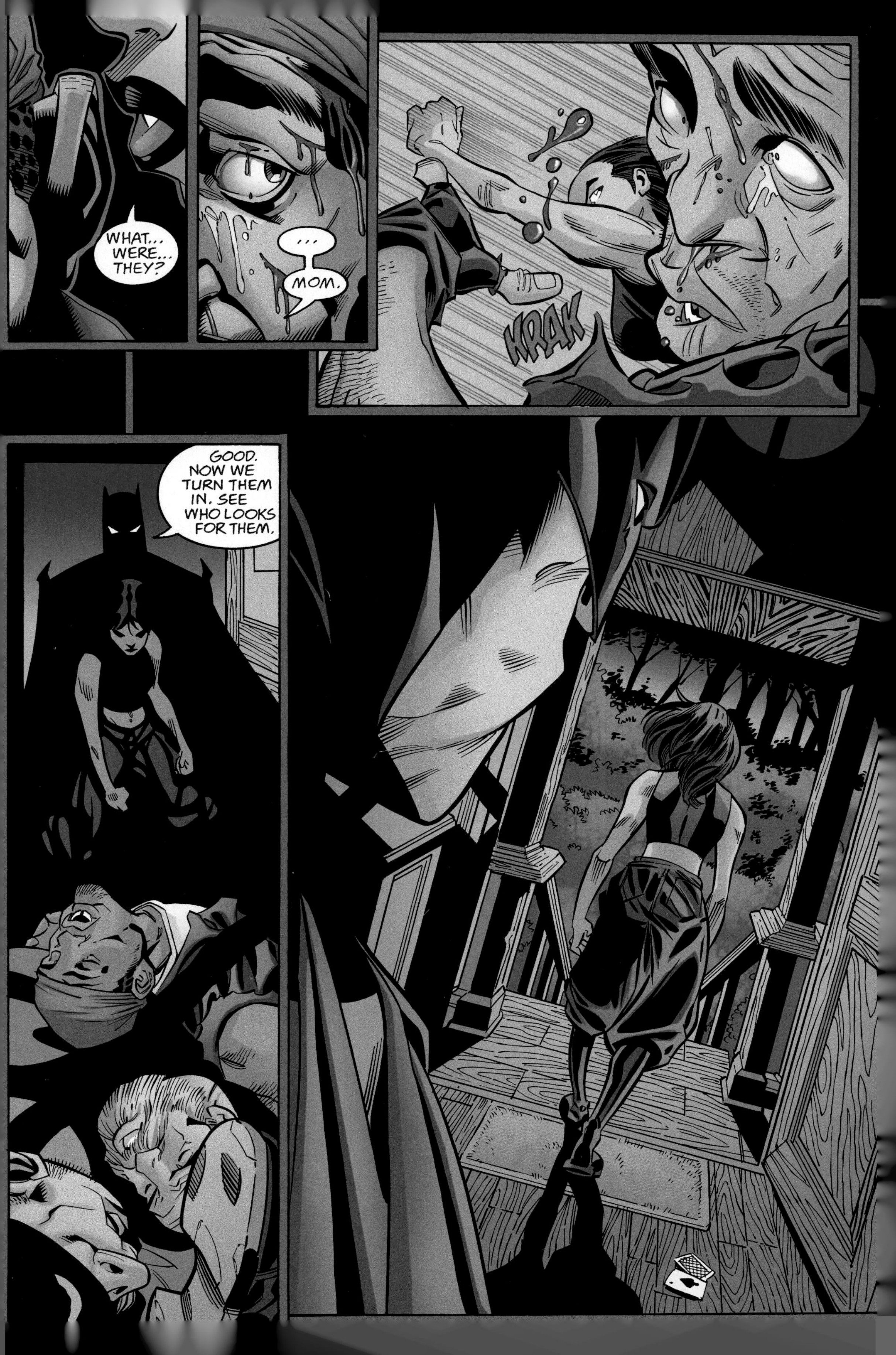
WHAT... WERE... THEY?
...
MOM.
KRAK
GOOD. NOW WE TURN THEM IN. SEE WHO LOOKS FOR THEM.

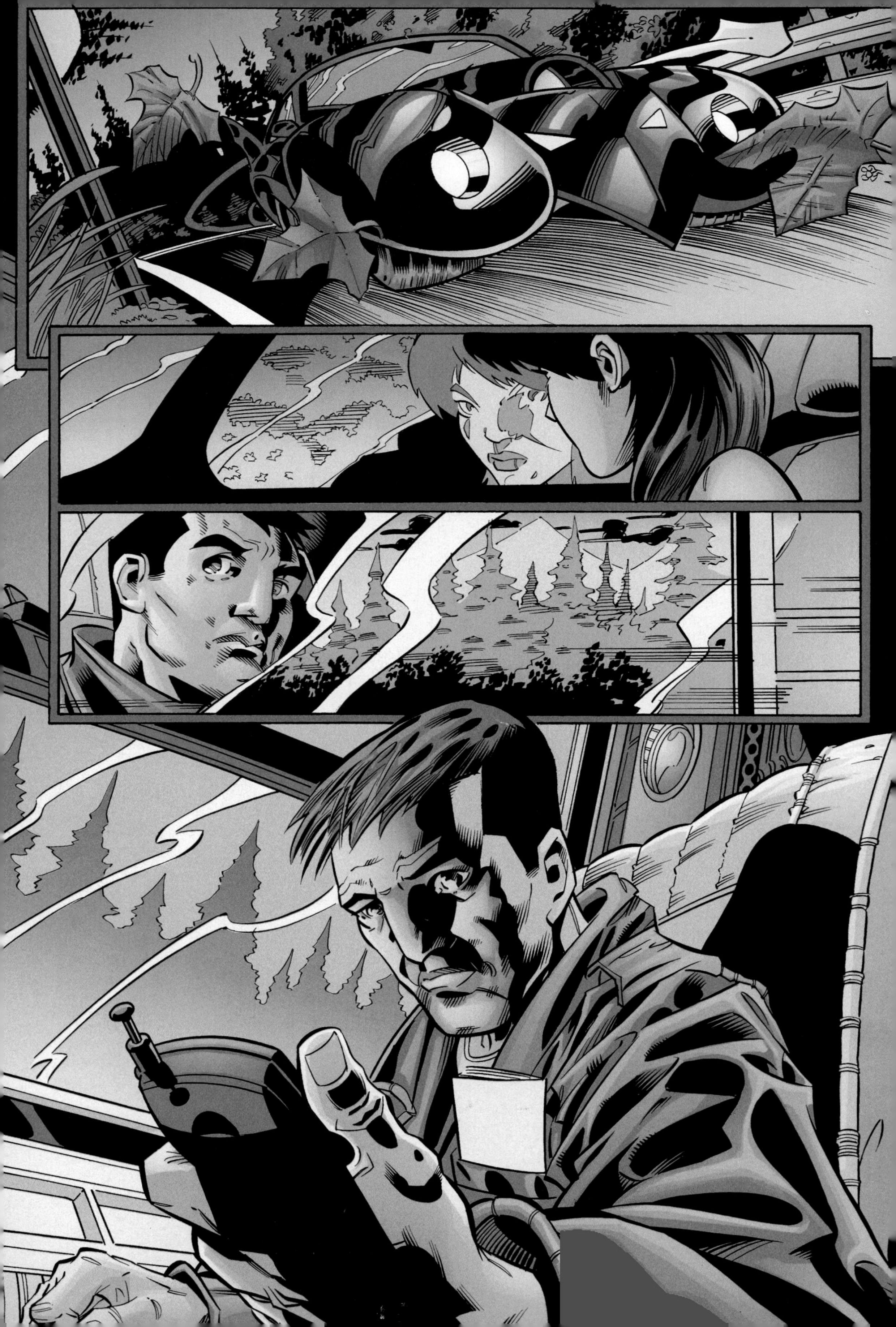

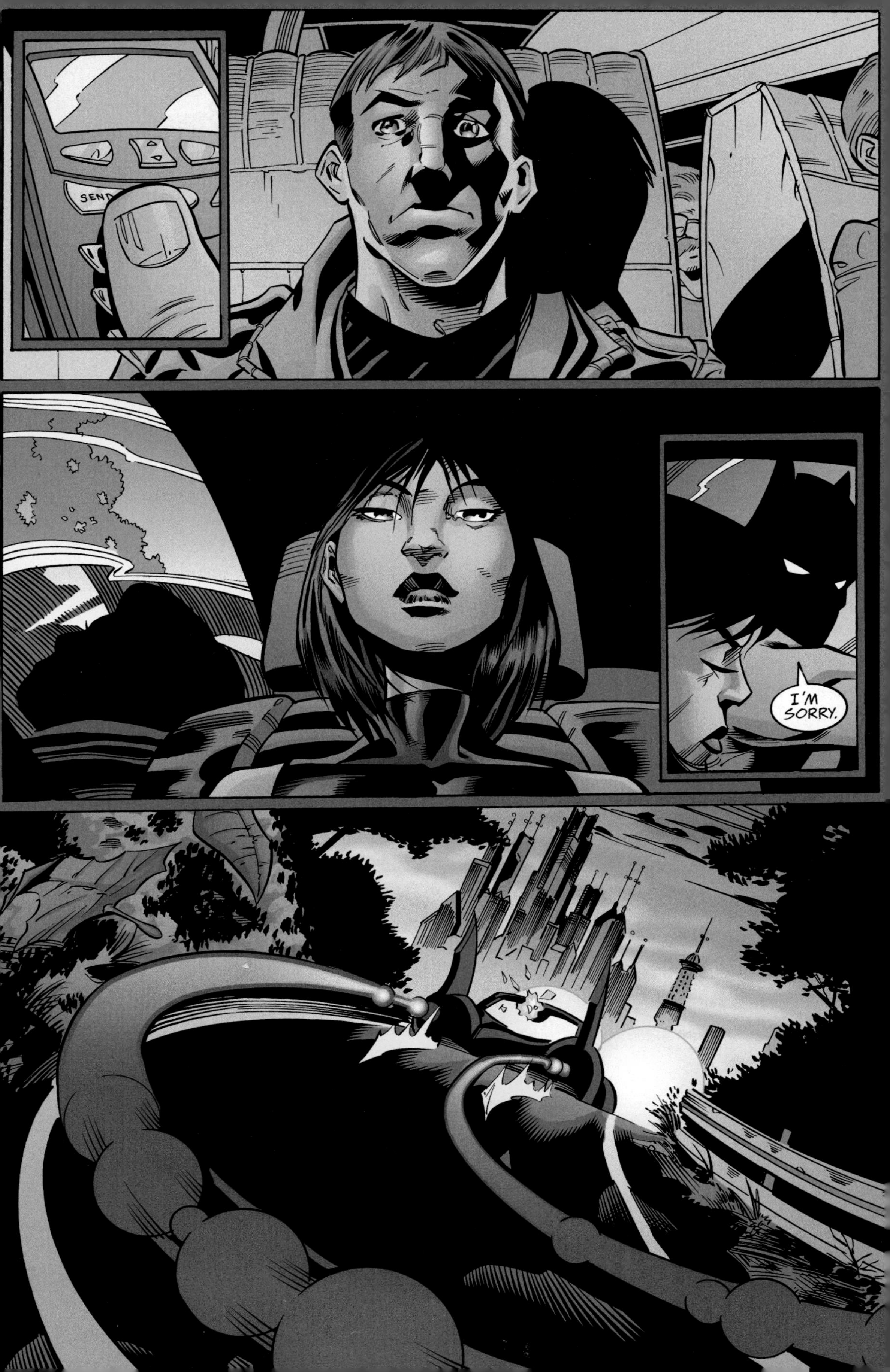
SEND
I'M SORRY.

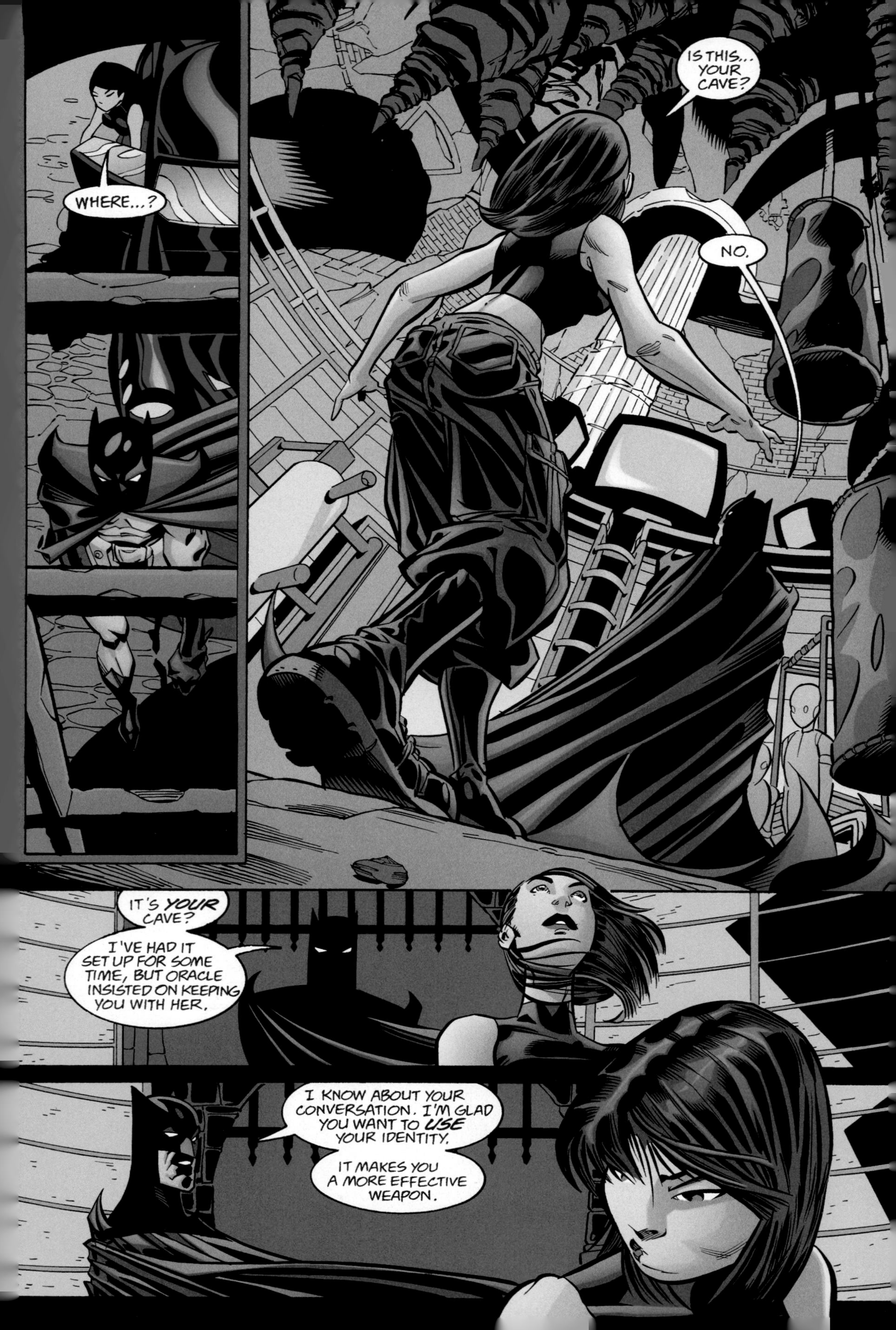
WHERE...?
IS THIS... YOUR CAVE?
NO.
IT'S YOUR CAVE?
I'VE HAD IT SET UP FOR SOME TIME, BUT ORACLE INSISTED ON KEEPING YOU WITH HER.
I KNOW ABOUT YOUR CONVERSATION. I'M GLAD YOU WANT TO USE YOUR IDENTITY.
IT MAKES YOU A MORE EFFECTIVE WEAPON.

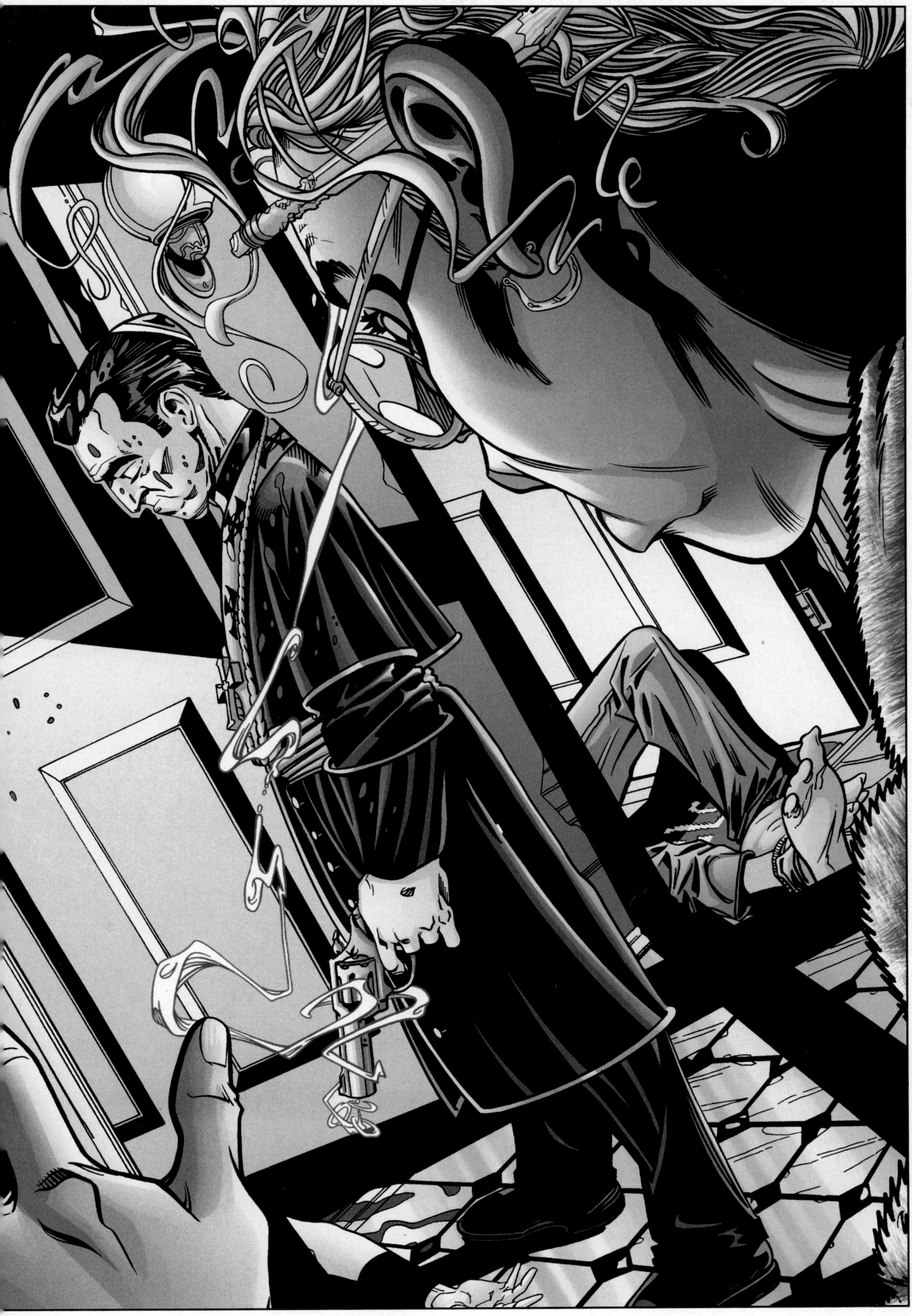

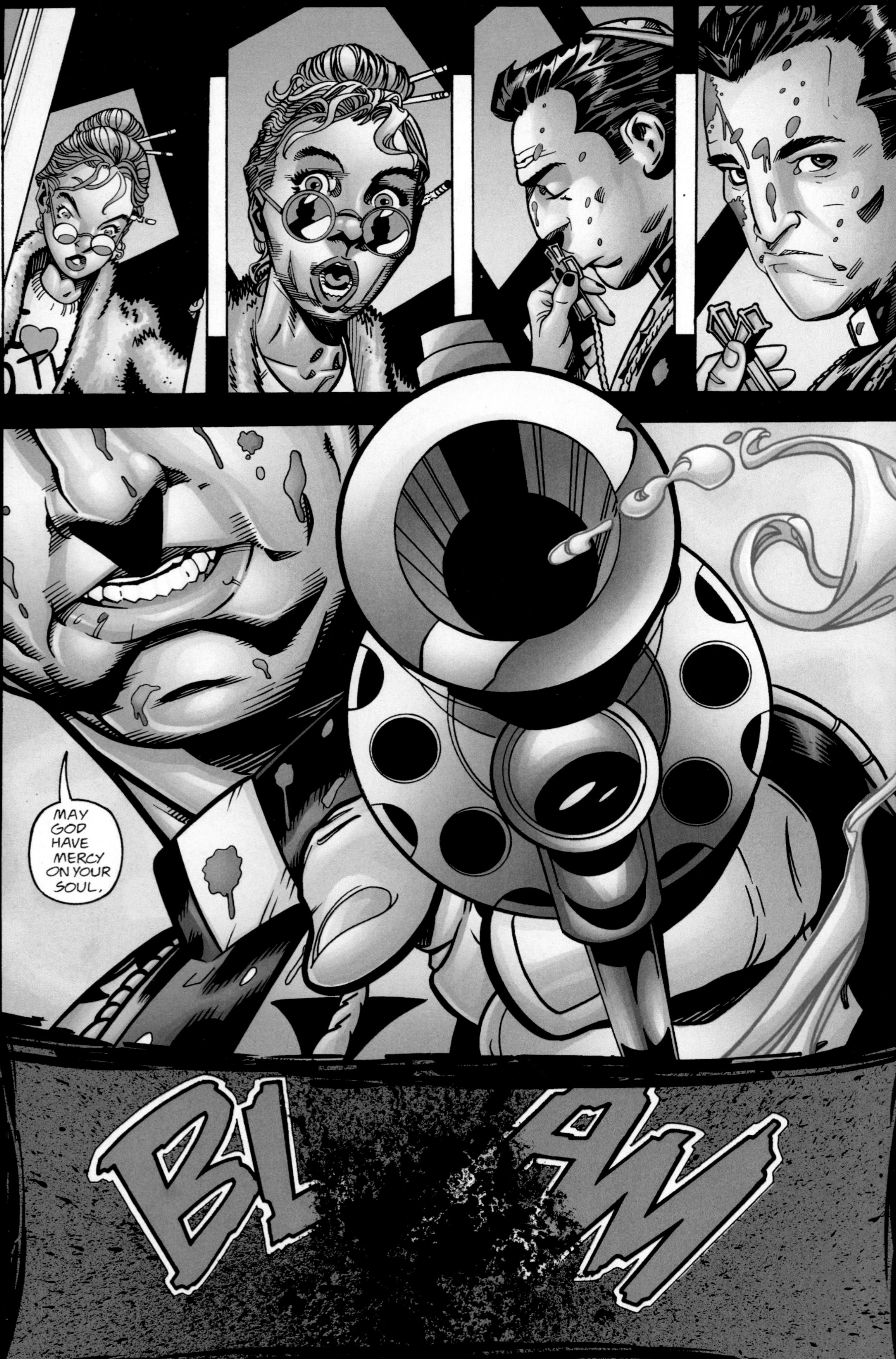
MAY GOD HAVE MERCY ON YOUR SOUL.
BLAM

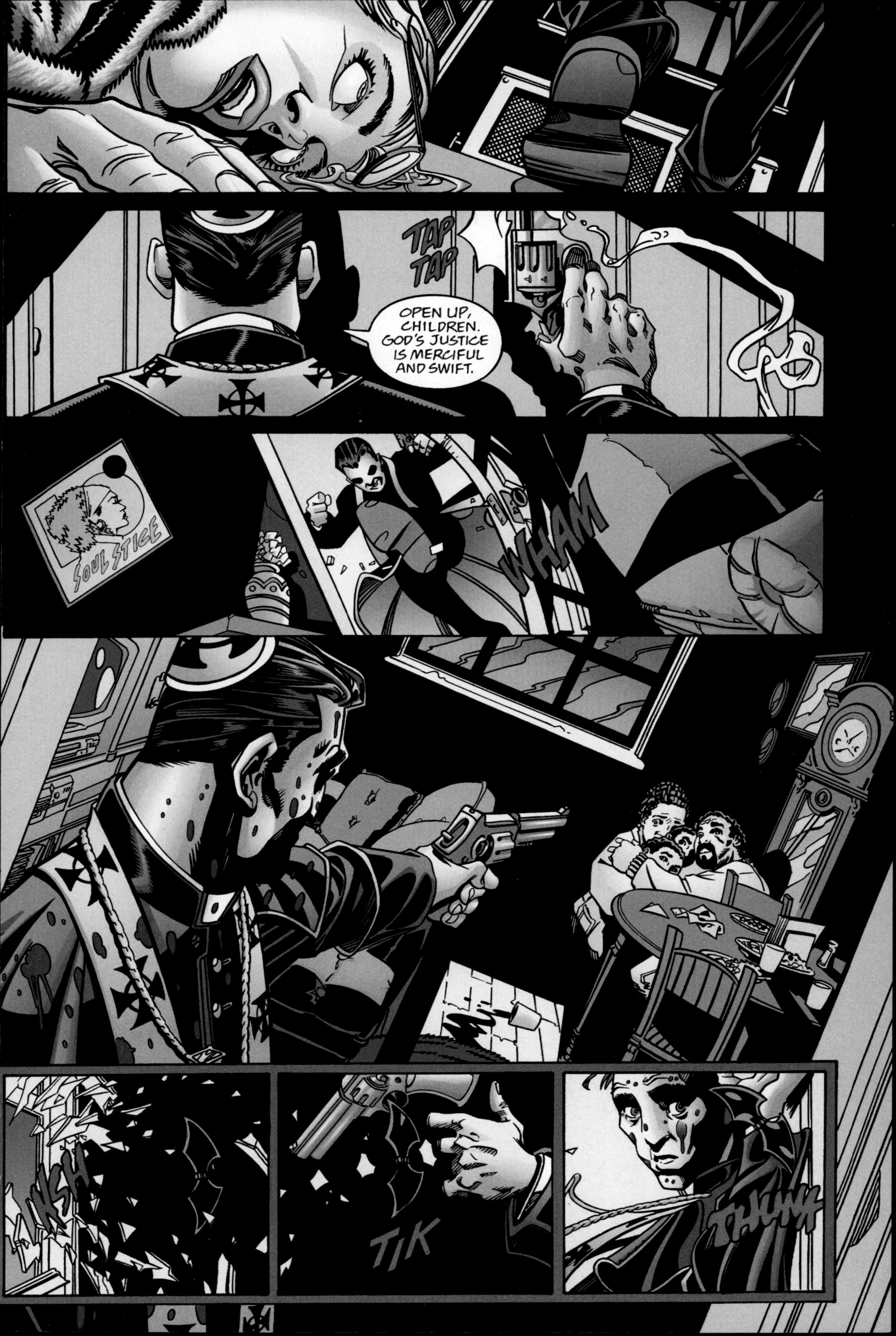
TAP TAP
OPEN UP, CHILDREN. GOD'S JUSTICE IS MERCIFUL AND SWIFT.
SOUL STICE
WHAM
TIK
THUNK

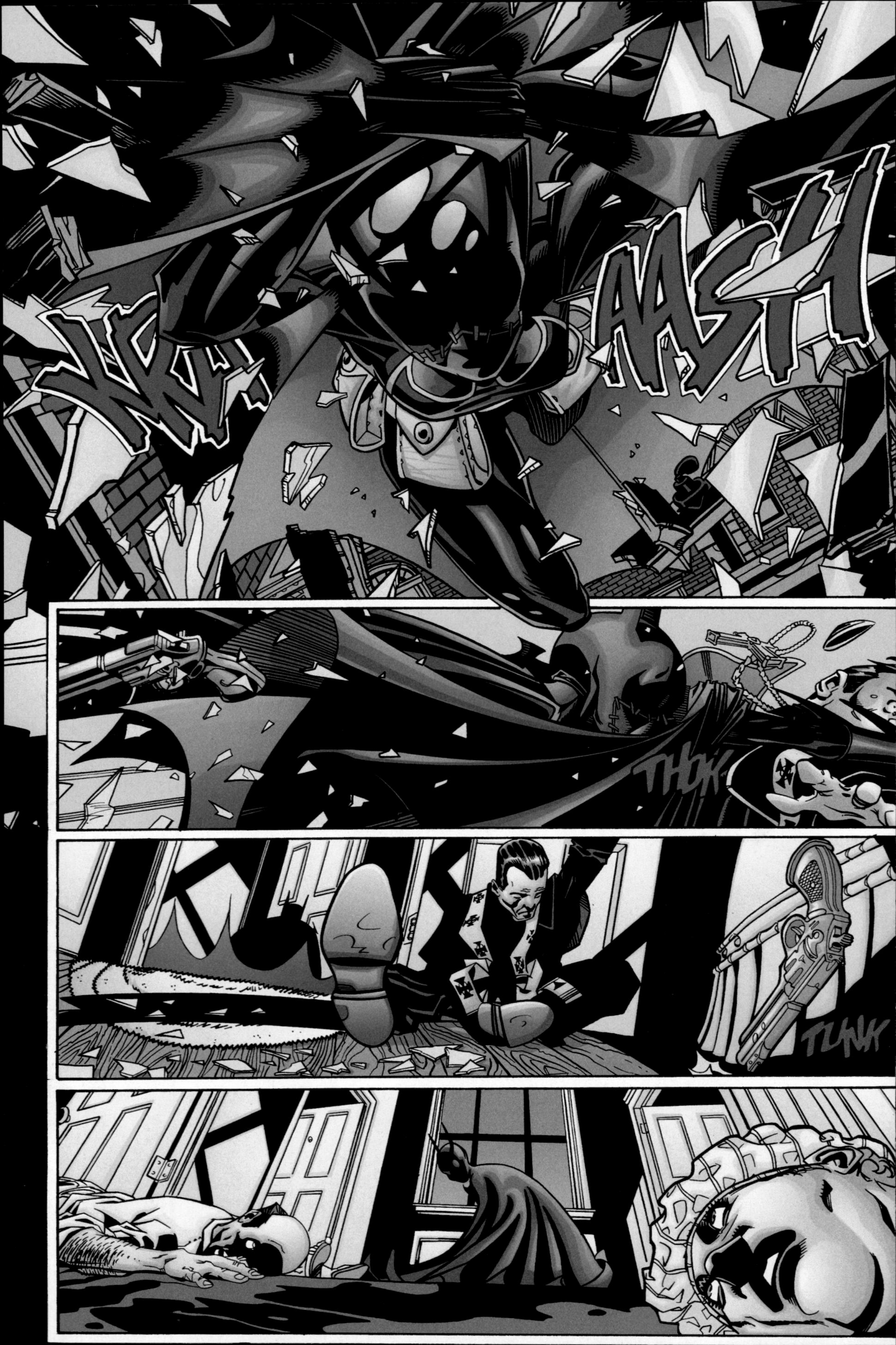
AASH
THOK
TUNK

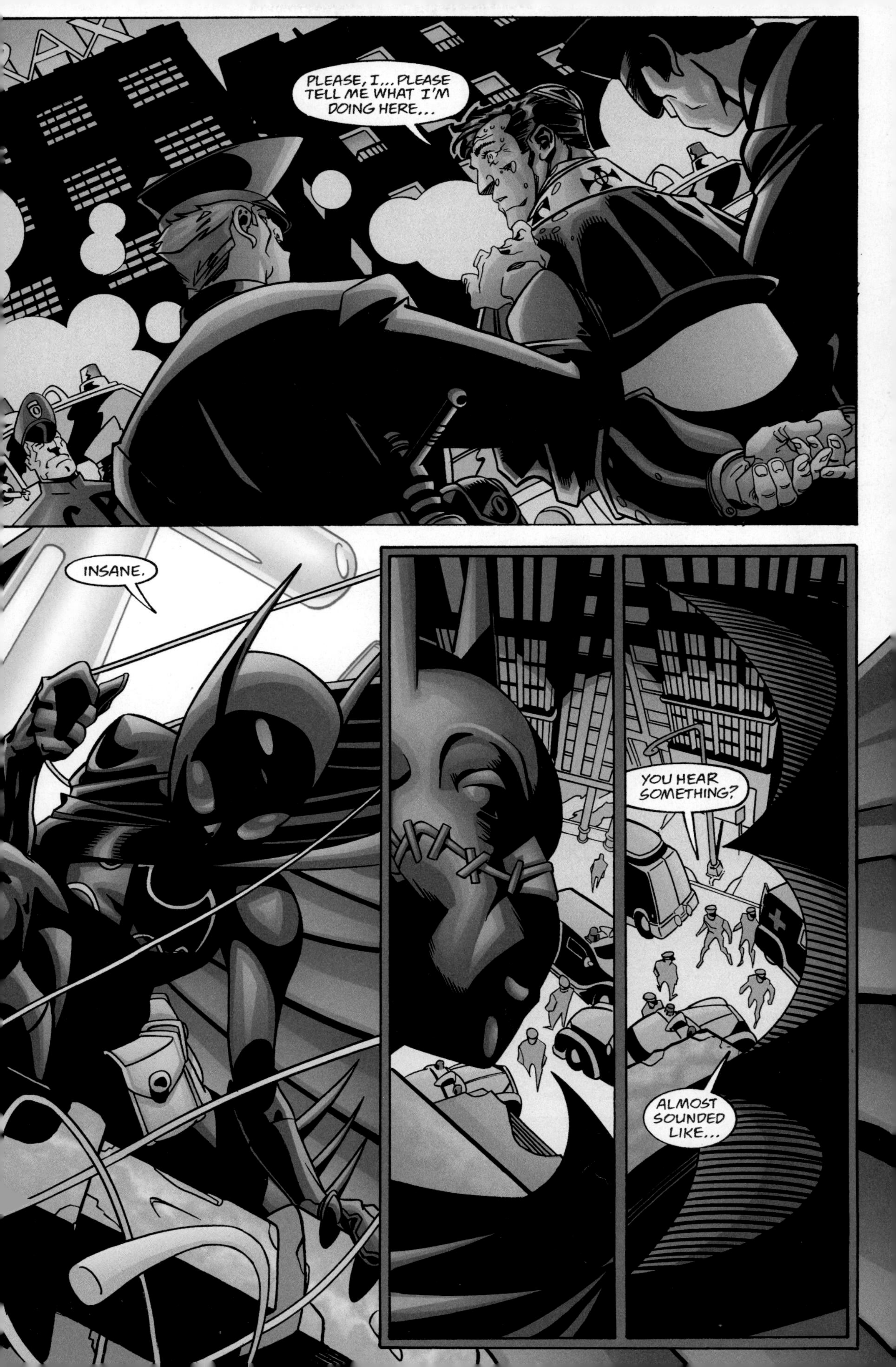
PLEASE, I... PLEASE TELL ME WHAT I'M DOING HERE...
INSANE.
YOU HEAR SOMETHING?
ALMOST SOUNDED LIKE...

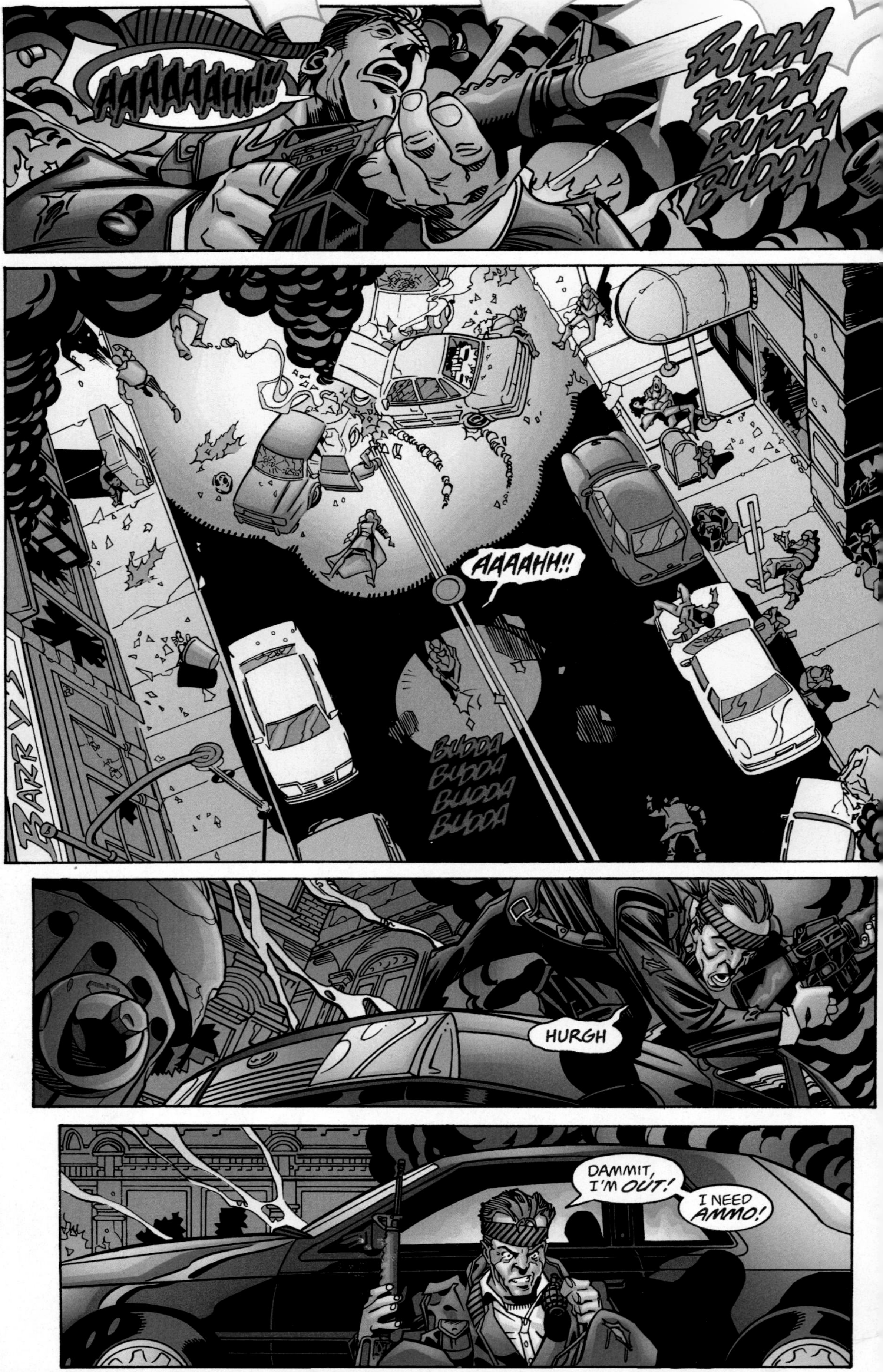
AAAAAAHH!!
BUDDA BUDDA BUDDA BUDDA
AAAAHH!!
BUDDA BUDDA BUDDA BUDDA
BARRY'S
HURGH
DAMMIT, I'M OUT!
I NEED AMMO!

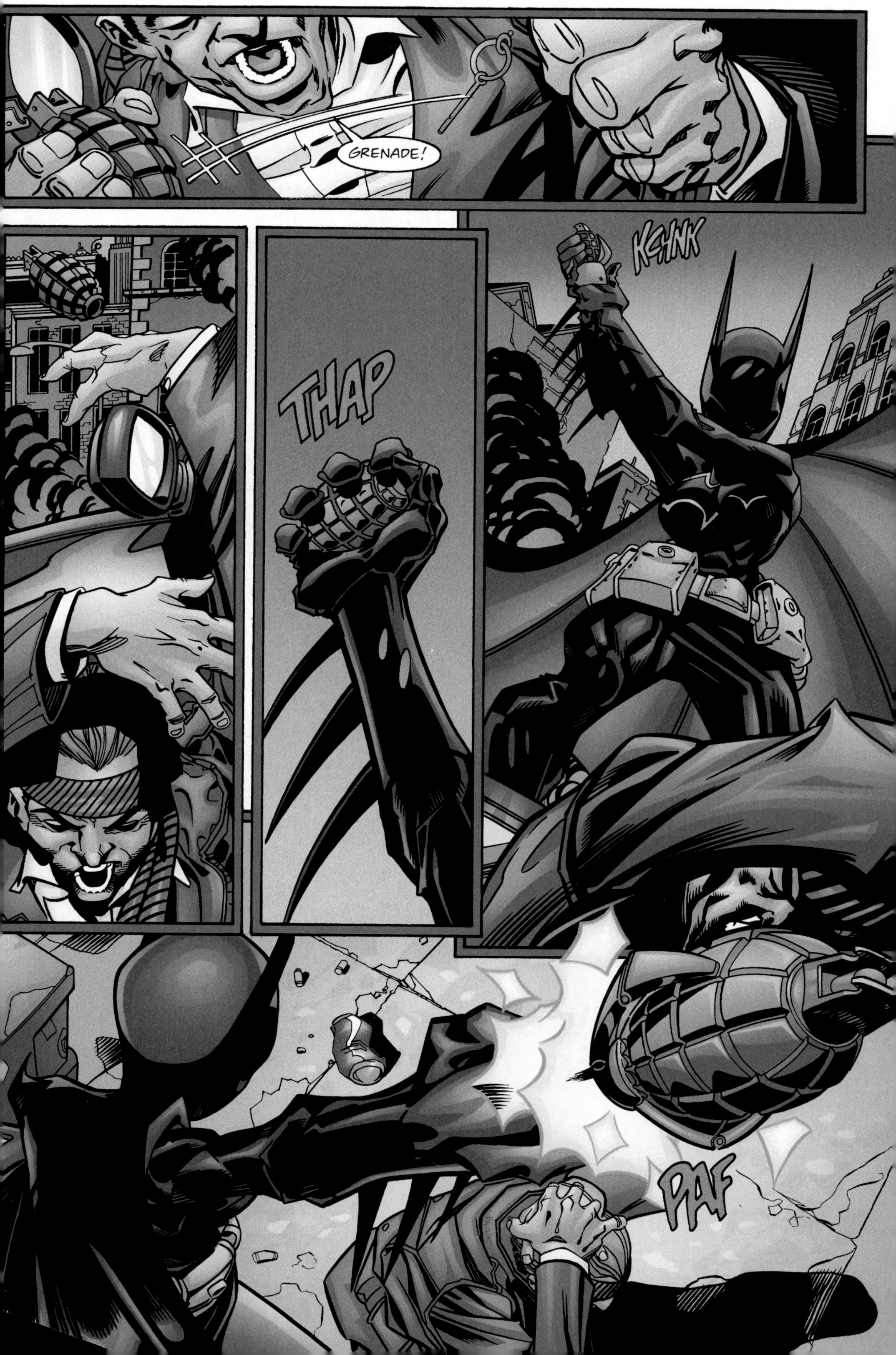
GRENADE!
THAP
KCHNK
PAF

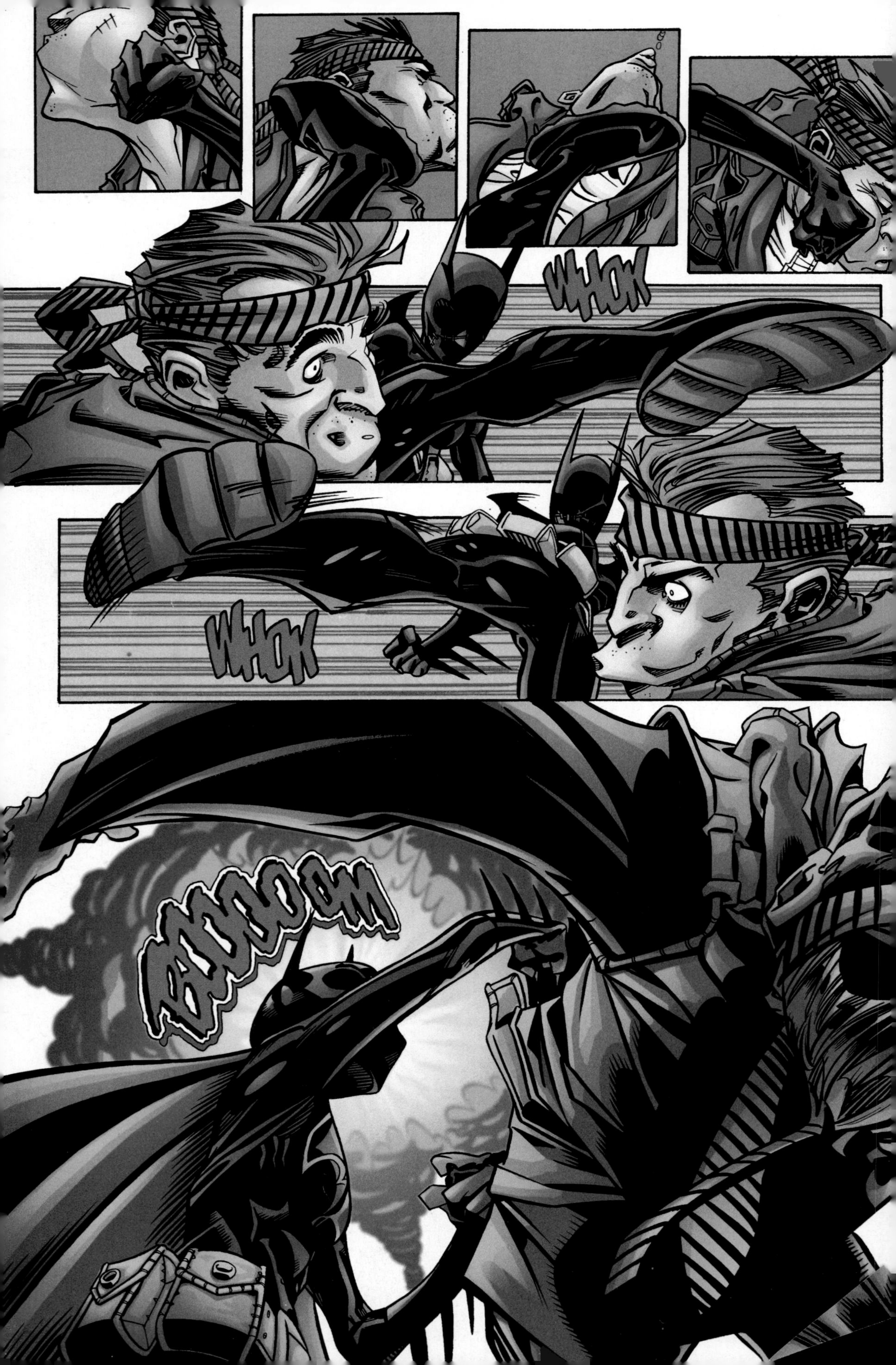
WHOK
WHOK
BOOOOM

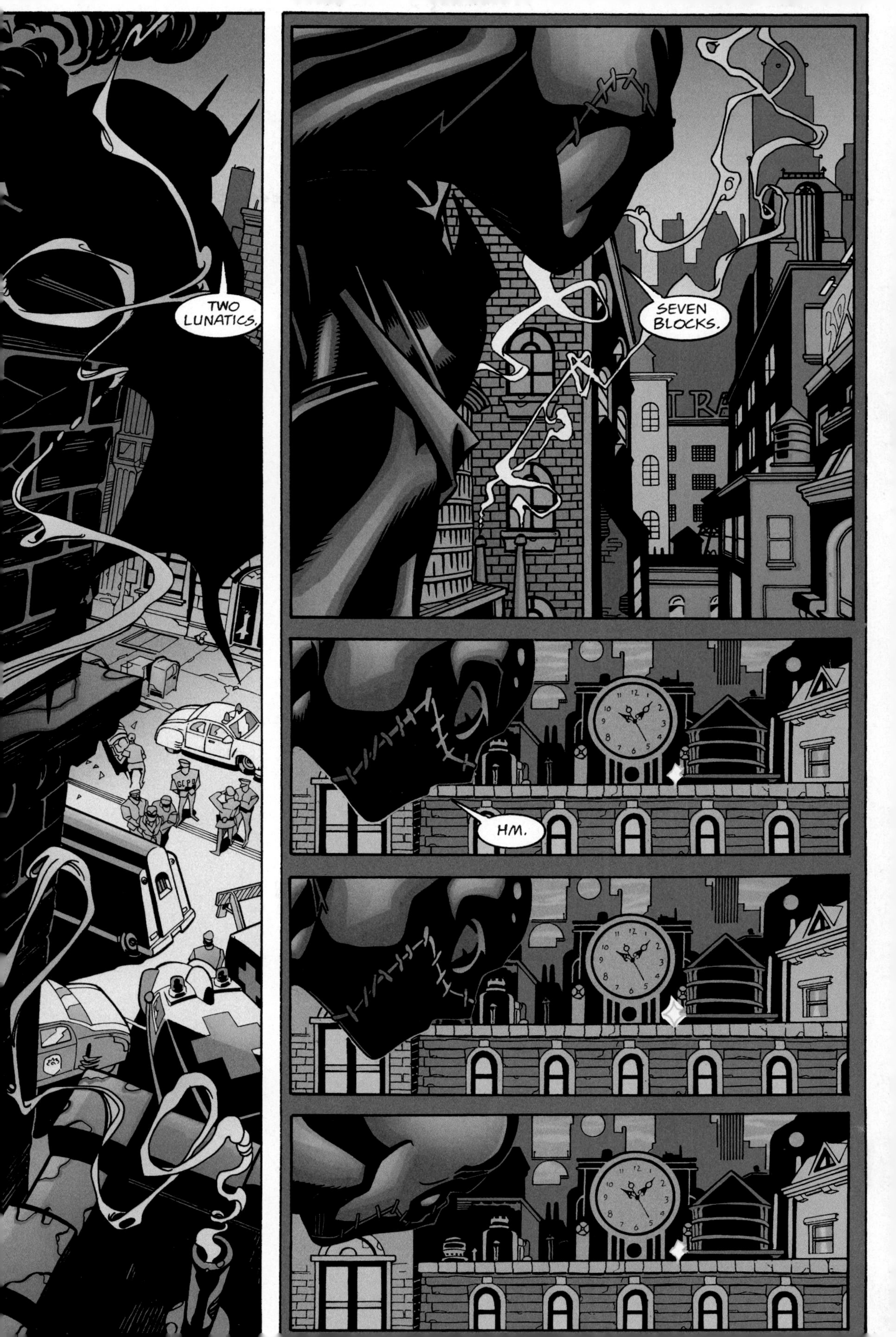
TWO LUNATICS.
SEVEN BLOCKS.
HM.

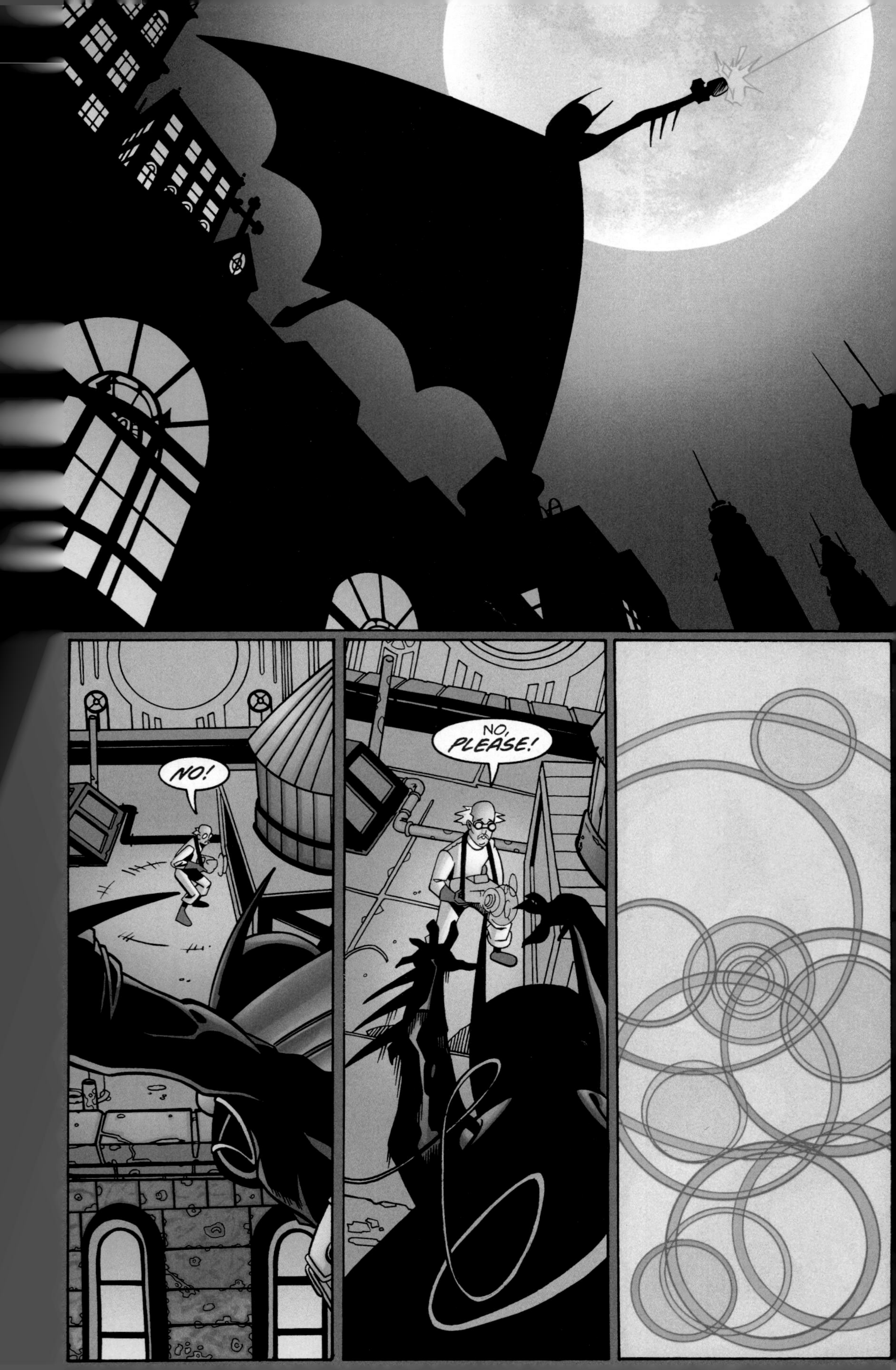
NO!
NO, PLEASE!

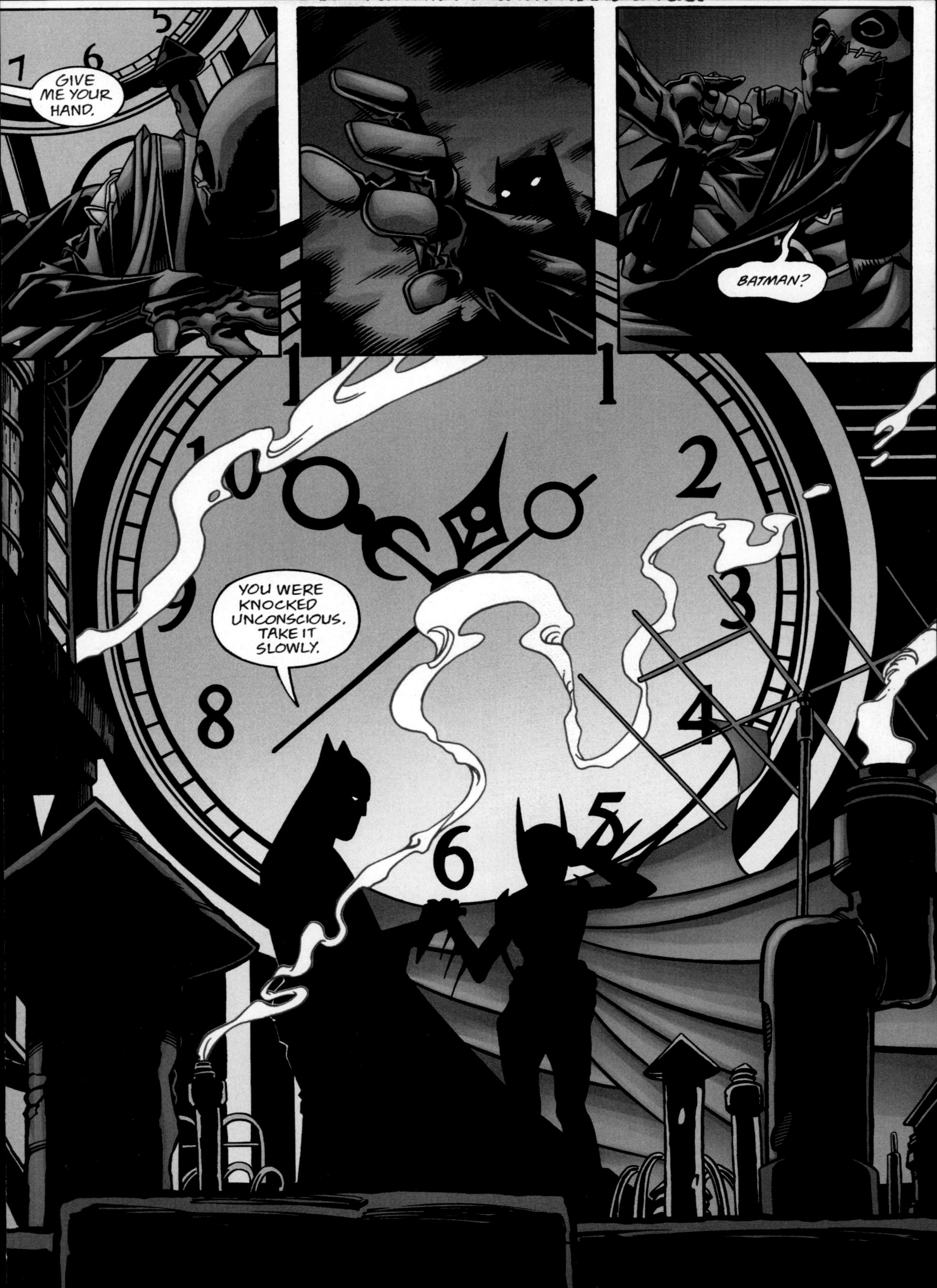
GIVE ME YOUR HAND.
BATMAN?
YOU WERE KNOCKED UNCONSCIOUS. TAKE IT SLOWLY.

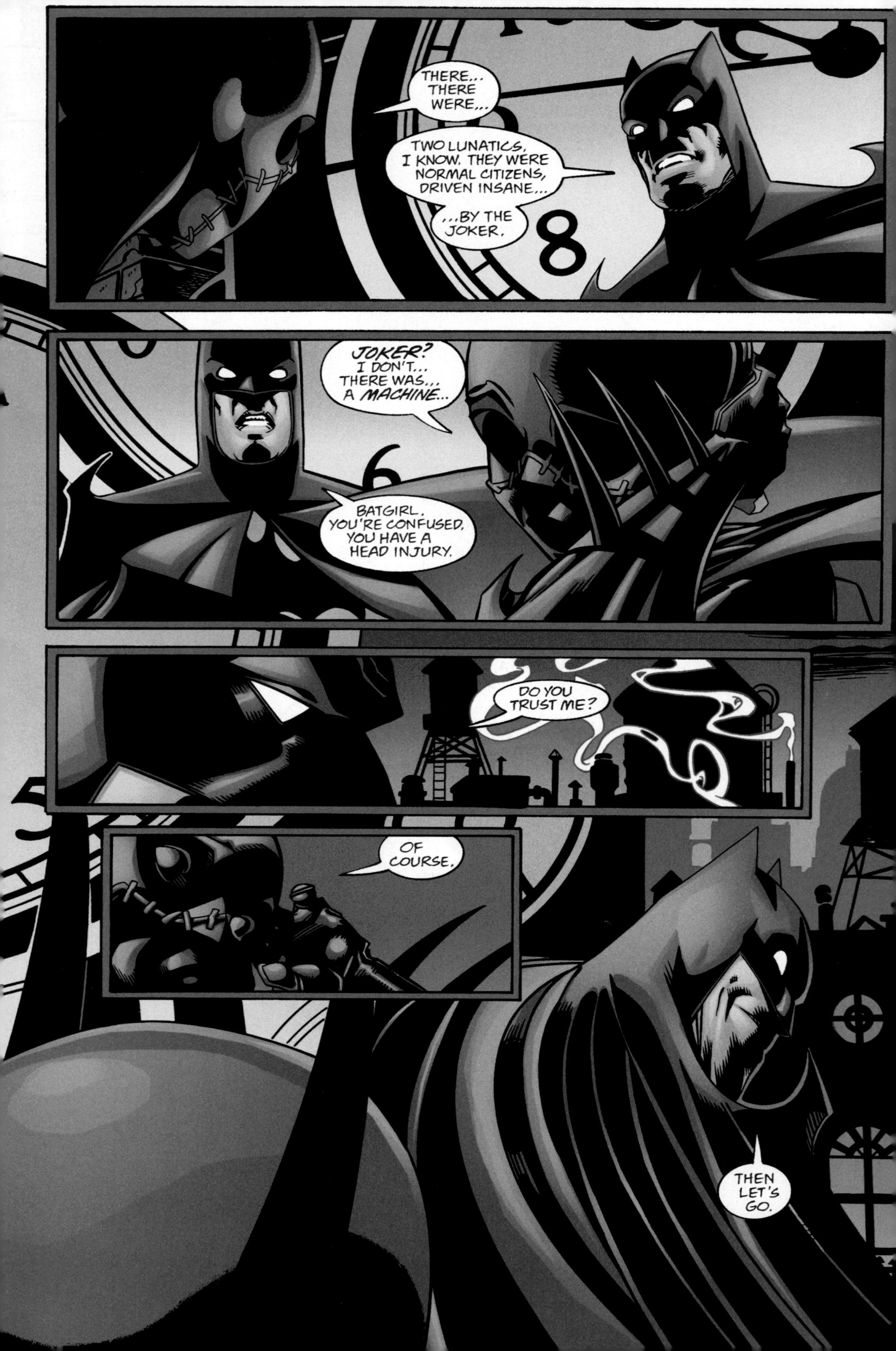
THERE... THERE WERE...
TWO LUNATICS, I KNOW. THEY WERE NORMAL CITIZENS, DRIVEN INSANE...
...BY THE JOKER.
JOKER? I DON'T... THERE WAS... A MACHINE...
BATGIRL. YOU'RE CONFUSED. YOU HAVE A HEAD INJURY.
DO YOU TRUST ME?
OF COURSE.
THEN LET'S GO.

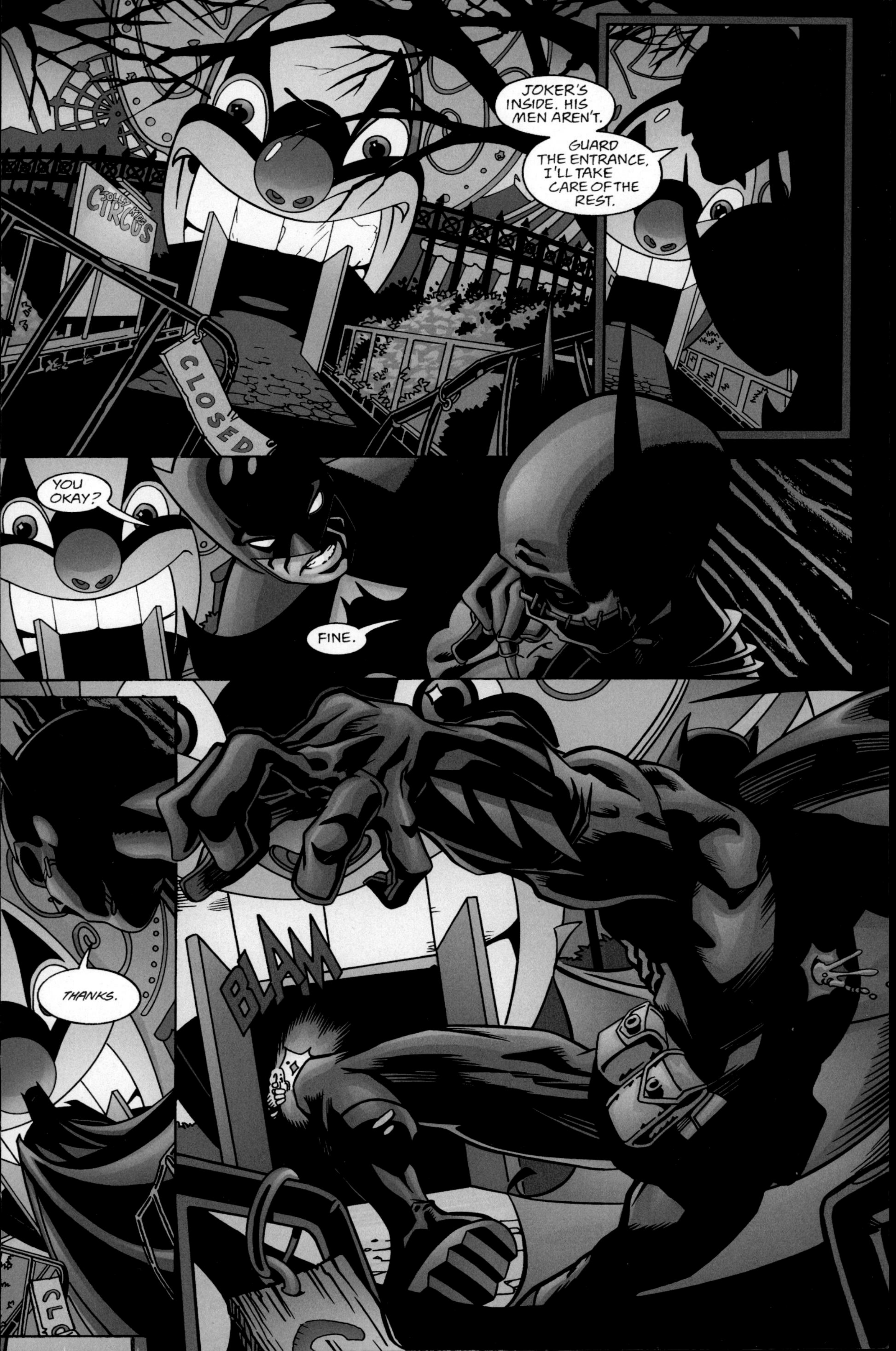

JOKER'S INSIDE. HIS MEN AREN'T.
GUARD THE ENTRANCE, I'LL TAKE CARE OF THE REST.
CIRCUS
CLOSED
YOU OKAY?
FINE.
THANKS.
BLAM

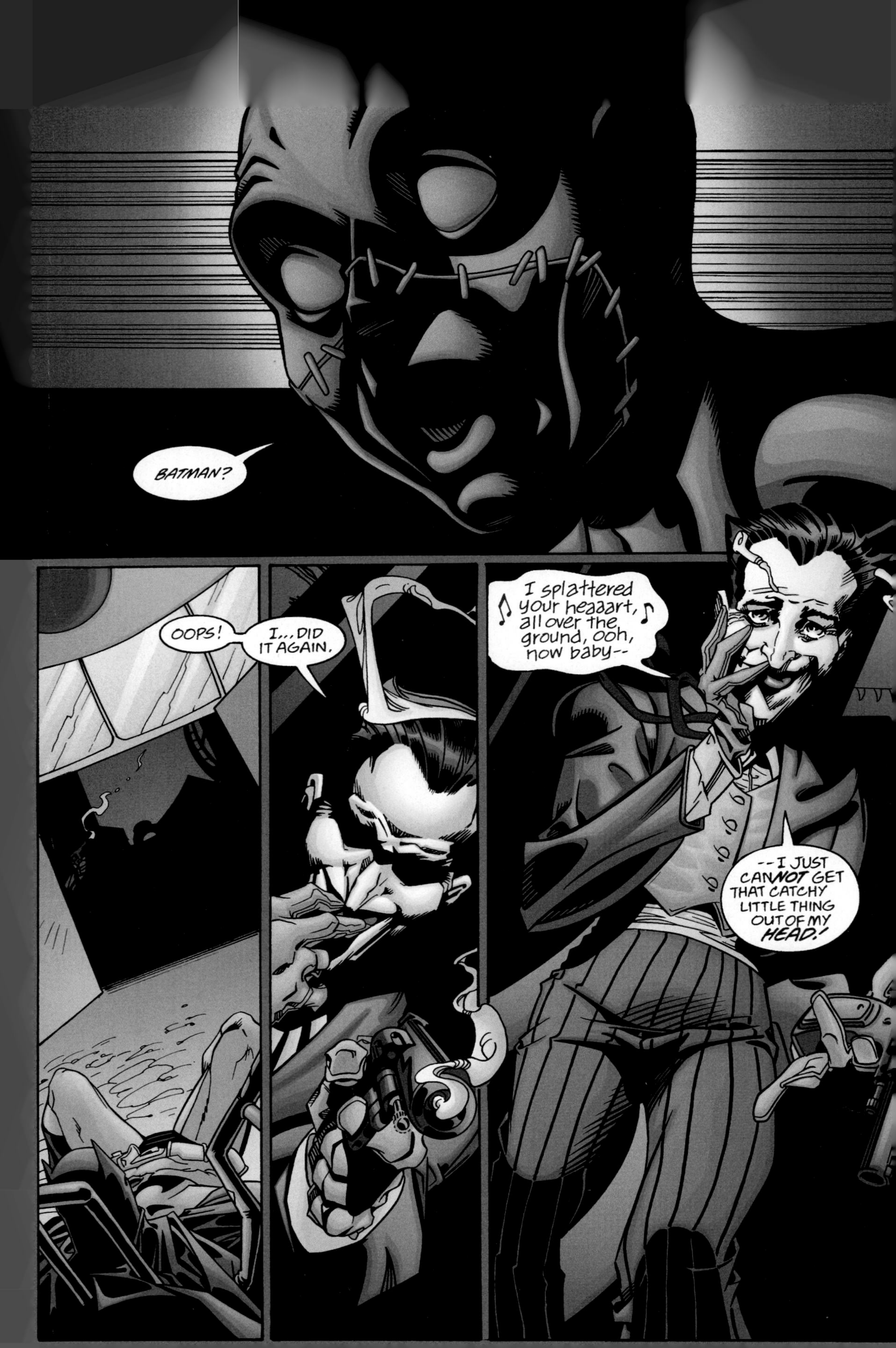
BATMAN?
OOPS!
I... DID IT AGAIN.
♪ I splattered your heaaart, all over the ground, ooh, now baby-- ♪
--I JUST CANNOT GET THAT CATCHY LITTLE THING OUT OF MY HEAD!

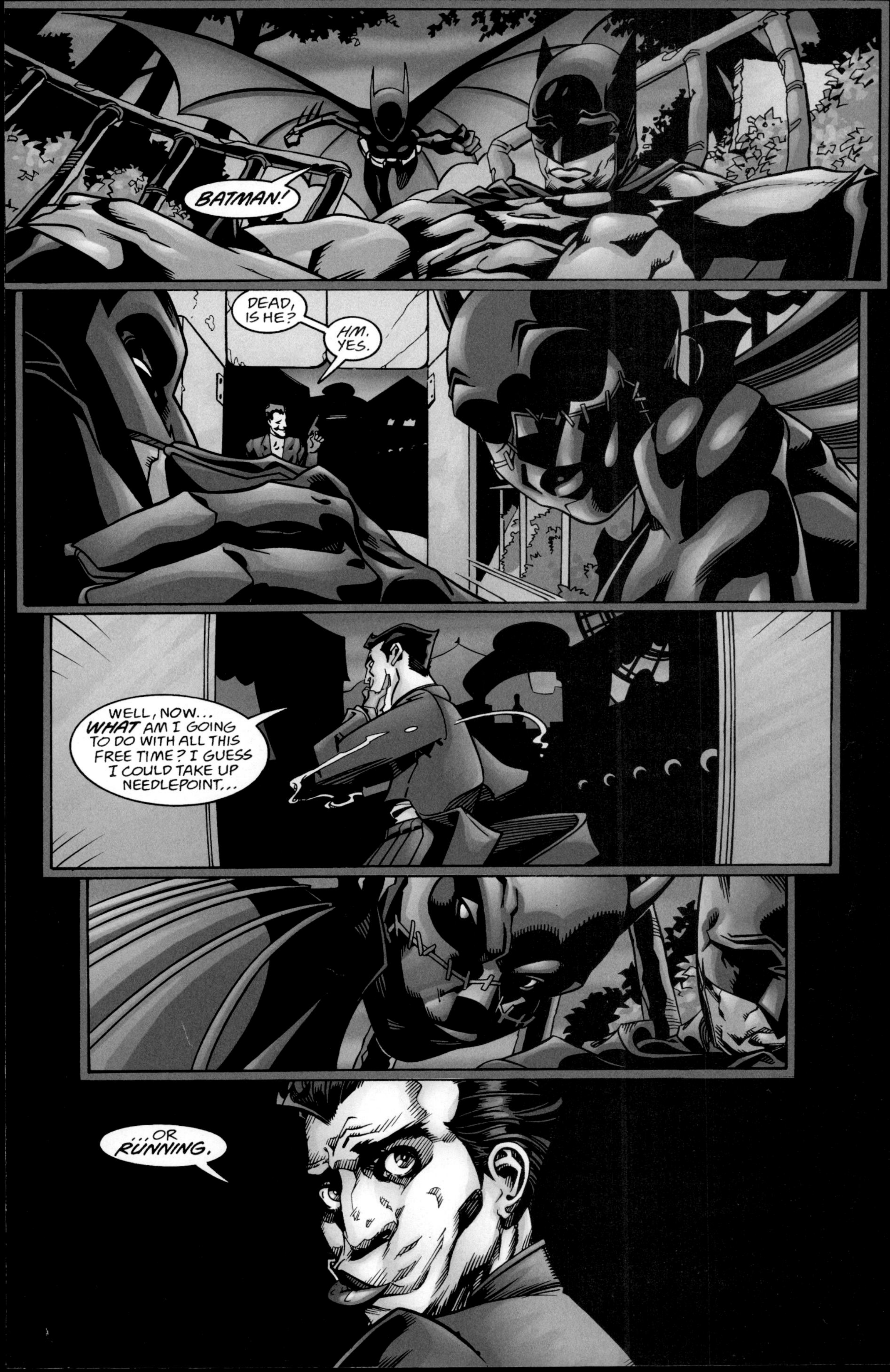
BATMAN!
DEAD, IS HE?
HM. YES.
WELL, NOW... WHAT AM I GOING TO DO WITH ALL THIS FREE TIME? I GUESS I COULD TAKE UP NEEDLEPOINT...
...OR RÜNNING.

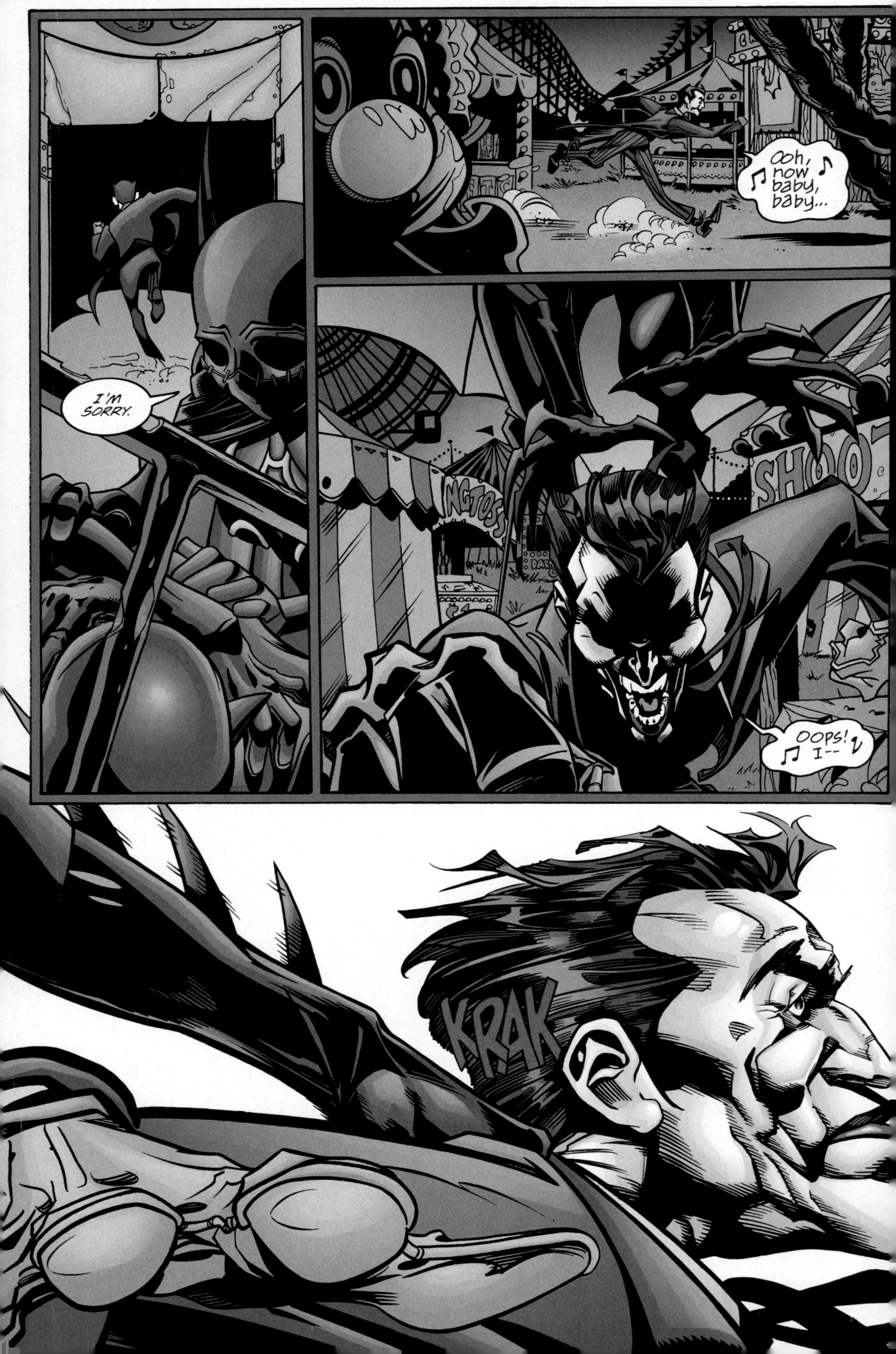
Ooh, now baby, baby...
I'M SORRY.
SHOOT
OOPS! I--
KRAK

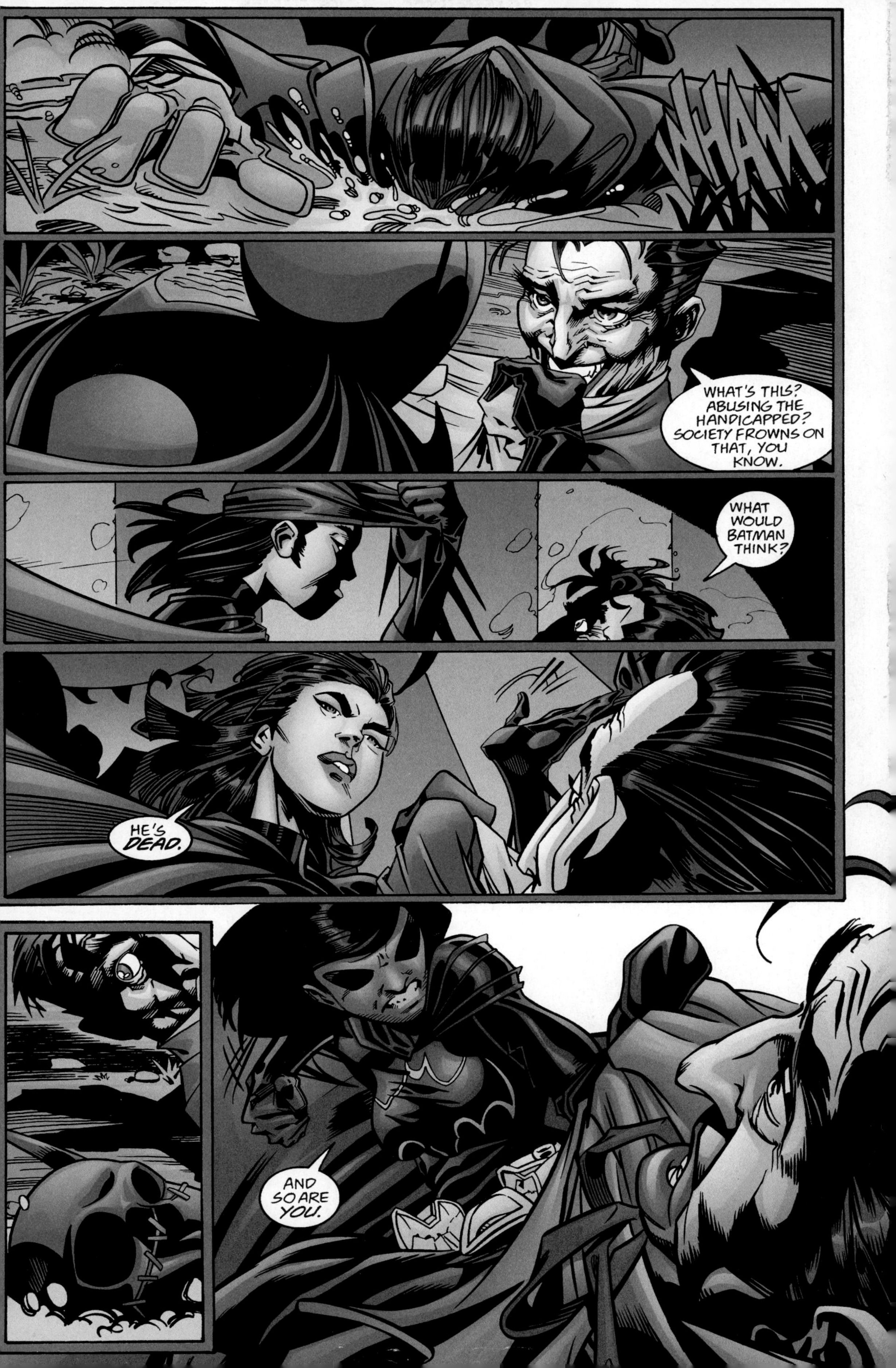
WHAM
WHAT'S THIS? ABUSING THE HANDICAPPED? SOCIETY FROWNS ON THAT, YOU KNOW.
WHAT WOULD BATMAN THINK?
HE'S DEAD.
AND SO ARE YOU.

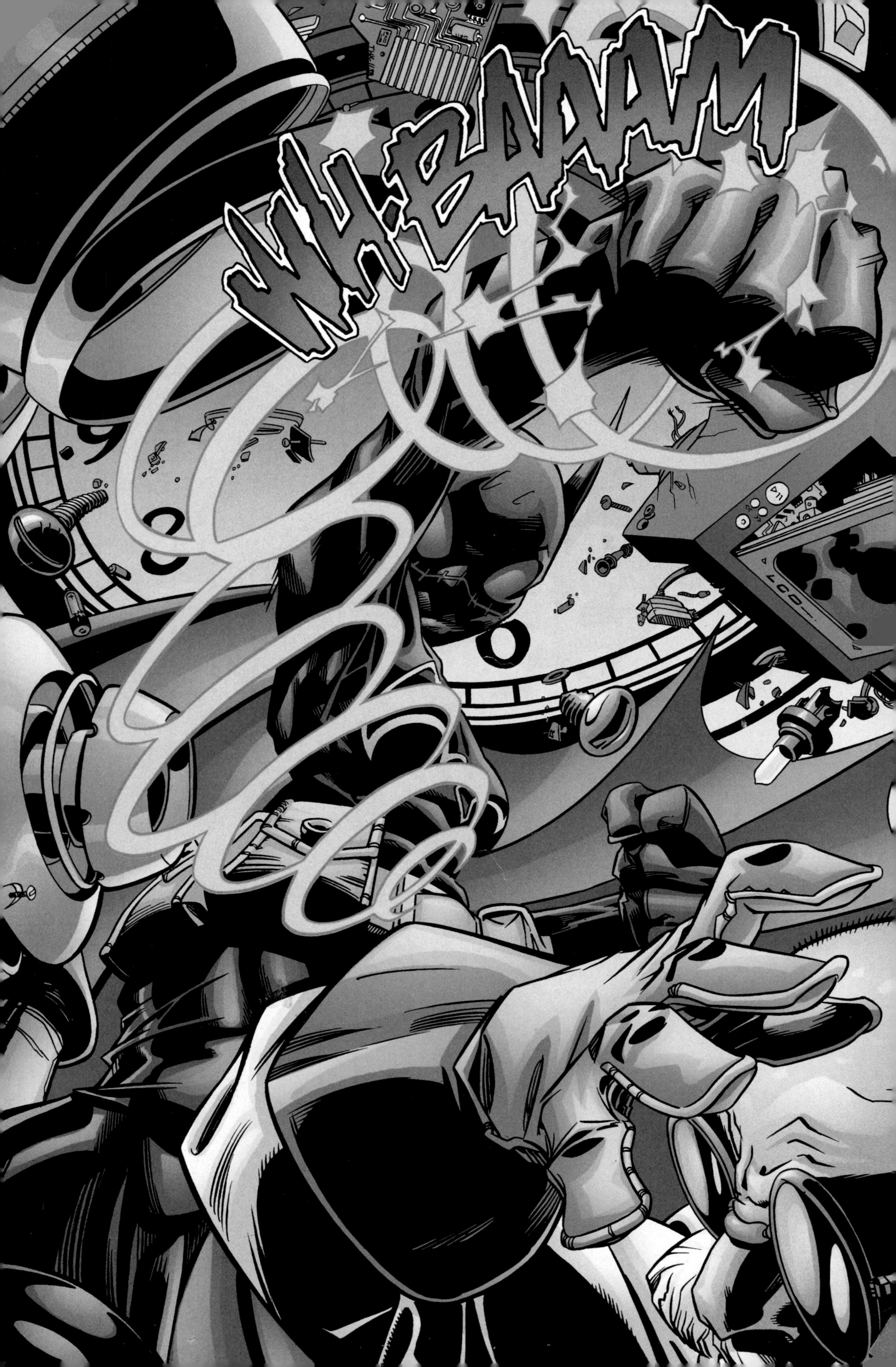
WHBAAAM

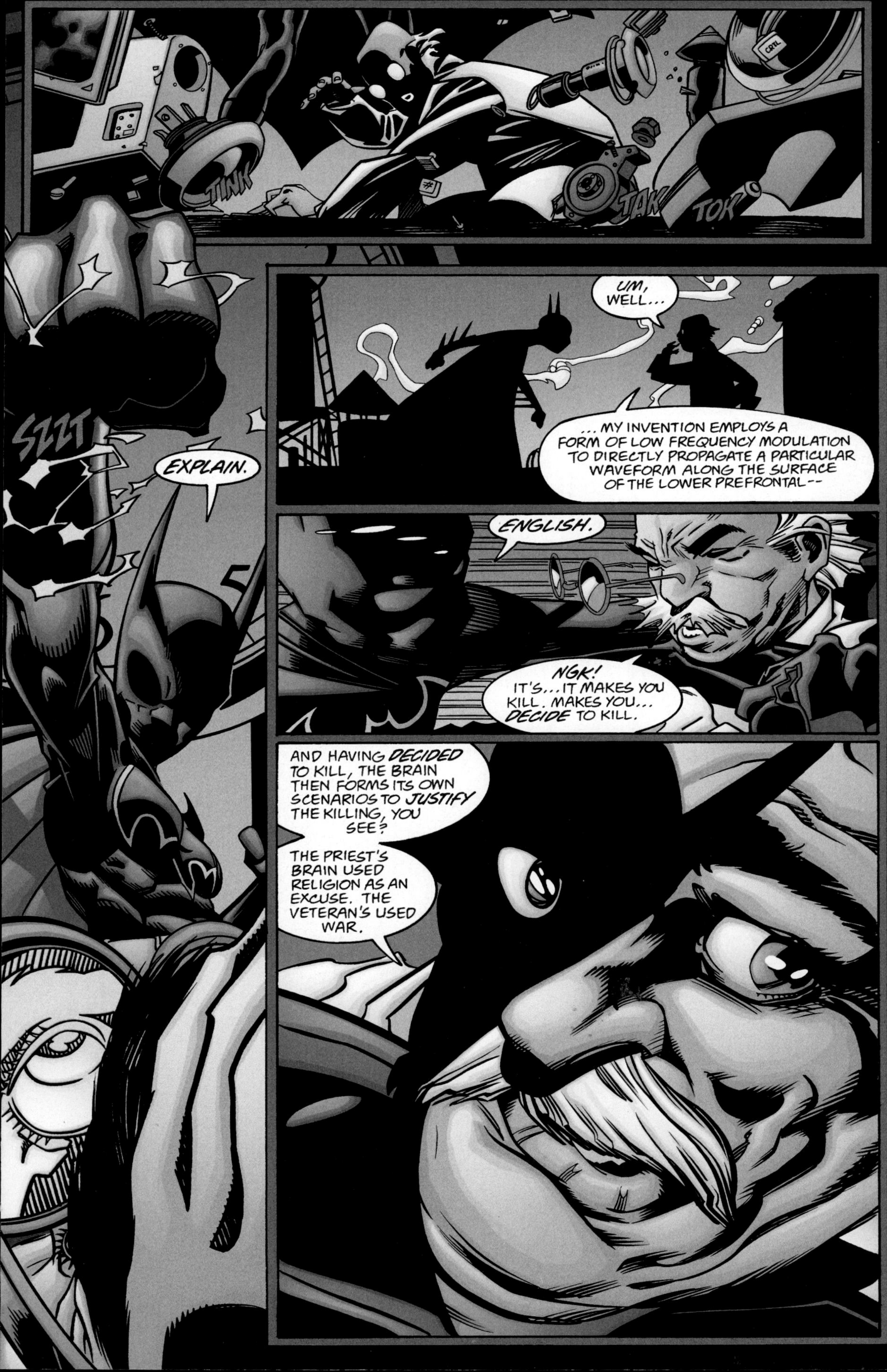
TINK
JAK
TOK
SZZT
EXPLAIN.
UM, WELL...
...MY INVENTION EMPLOYS A FORM OF LOW FREQUENCY MODULATION TO DIRECTLY PROPAGATE A PARTICULAR WAVEFORM ALONG THE SURFACE OF THE LOWER PREFRONTAL--
ENGLISH.
NGK! IT'S...IT MAKES YOU KILL. MAKES YOU... DECIDE TO KILL.
AND HAVING DECIDED TO KILL, THE BRAIN THEN FORMS ITS OWN SCENARIOS TO JUSTIFY THE KILLING, YOU SEE?
THE PRIEST'S BRAIN USED RELIGION AS AN EXCUSE. THE VETERAN'S USED WAR.

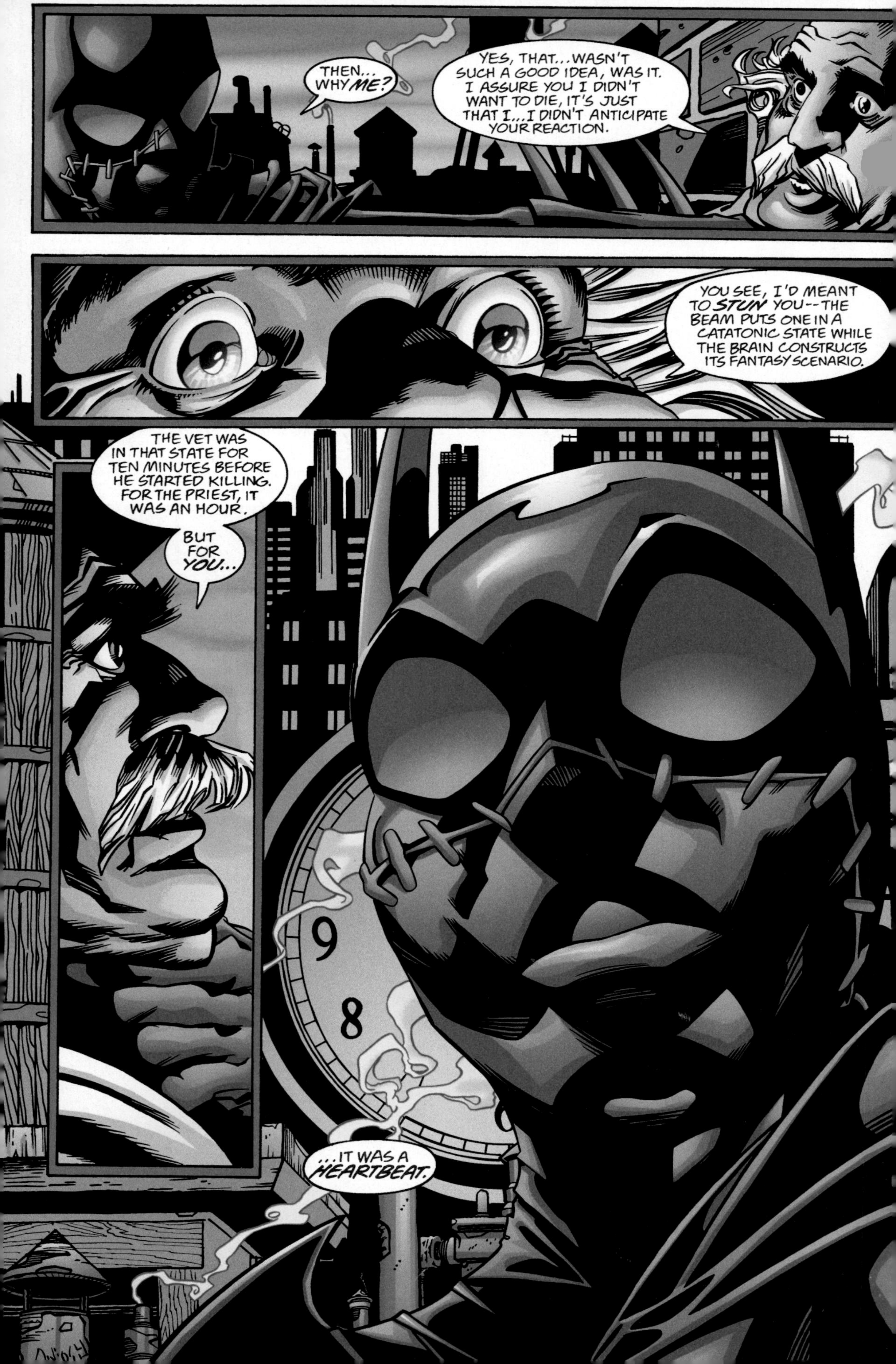

THEN... WHY *ME?*
YES, THAT...WASN'T SUCH A GOOD IDEA, WAS IT. I ASSURE YOU I DIDN'T WANT TO DIE, IT'S JUST THAT I...I DIDN'T ANTICIPATE YOUR REACTION.
YOU SEE, I'D MEANT TO *STUN* YOU--THE BEAM PUTS ONE IN A CATATONIC STATE WHILE THE BRAIN CONSTRUCTS ITS FANTASY SCENARIO.
THE VET WAS IN THAT STATE FOR TEN MINUTES BEFORE HE STARTED KILLING. FOR THE PRIEST, IT WAS AN HOUR.
BUT FOR *YOU*...
...IT WAS A *HEARTBEAT.*

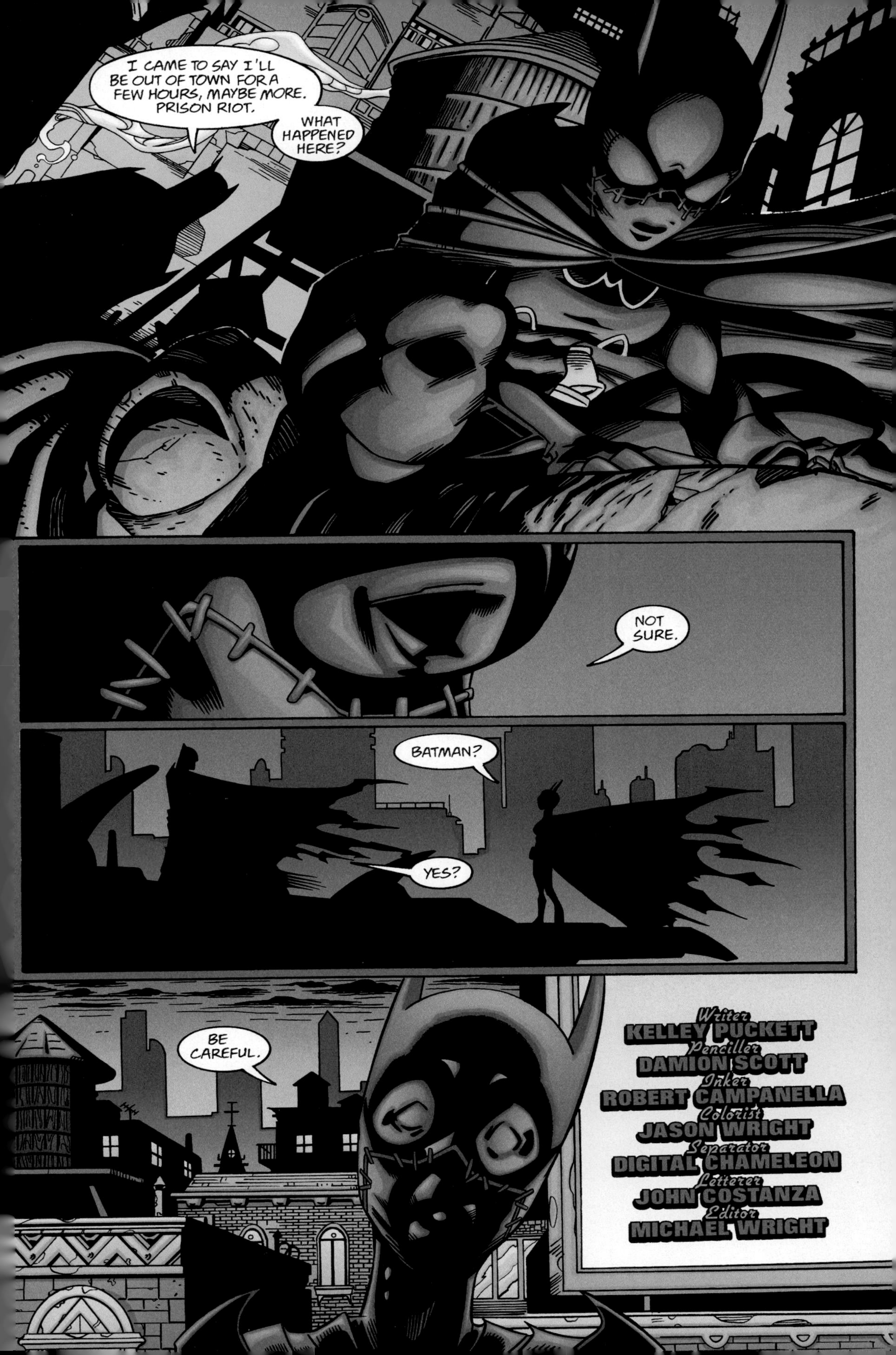
I CAME TO SAY I'LL BE OUT OF TOWN FOR A FEW HOURS, MAYBE MORE. PRISON RIOT.
WHAT HAPPENED HERE?
NOT SURE.
BATMAN?
YES?
BE CAREFUL.
Writer KELLEY PUCKETT
Penciller DAMION SCOTT
Inker ROBERT CAMPANELLA
Colorist JASON WRIGHT
Separator DIGITAL CHAMELEON
Letterer JOHN COSTANZA
Editor MICHAEL WRIGHT

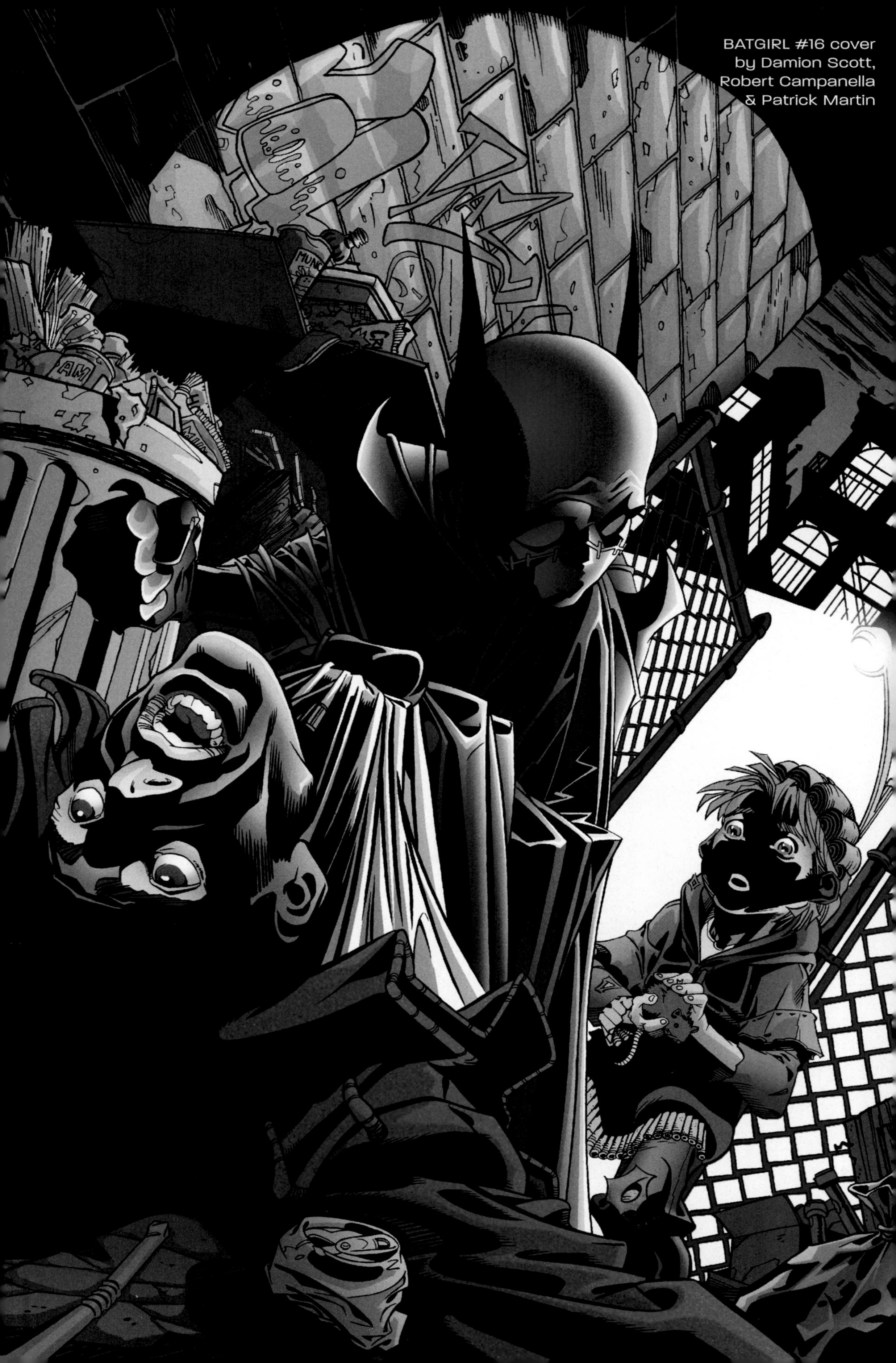

BATGIRL #16 cover
by Damion Scott,
Robert Campanella
& Patrick Martin

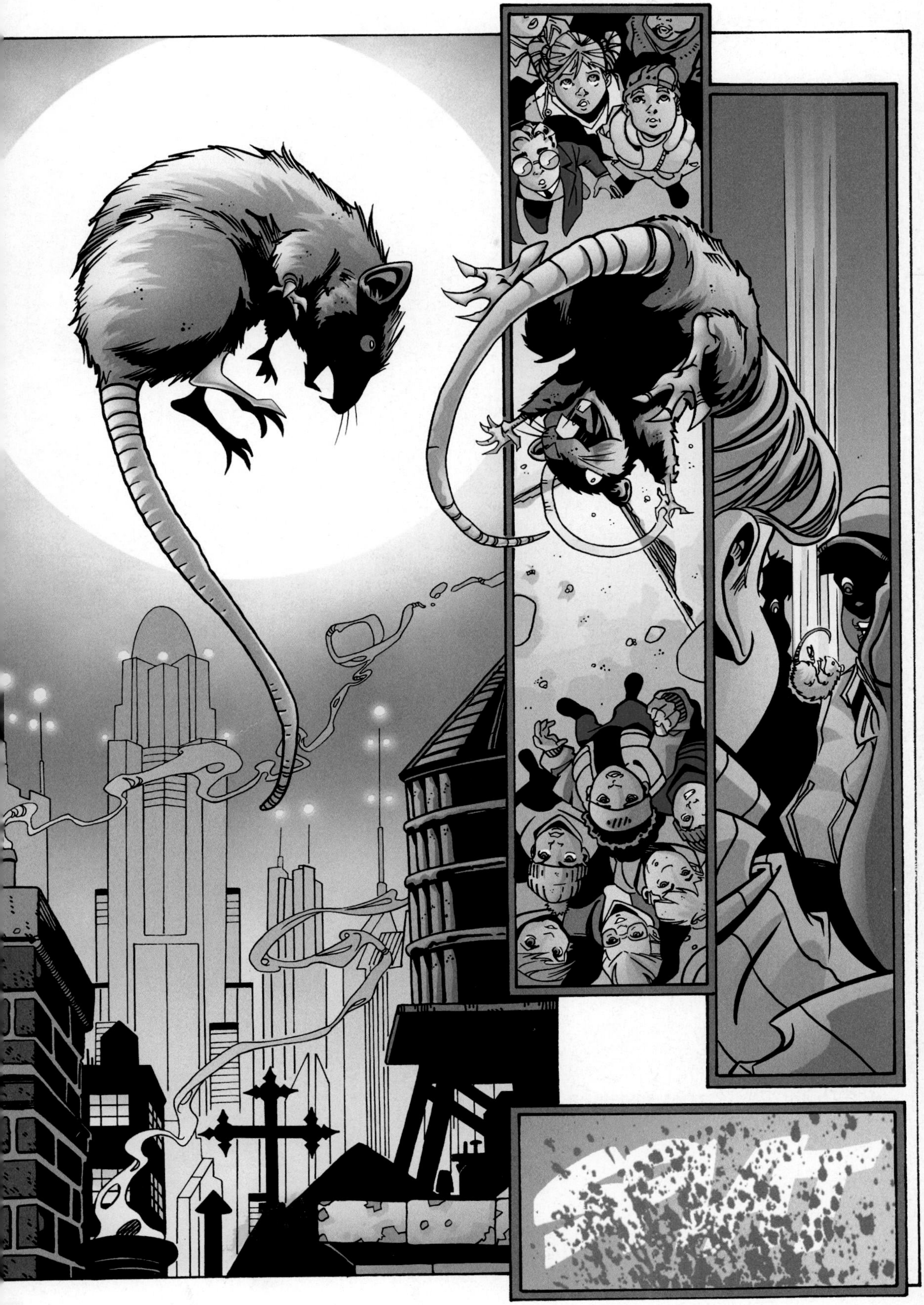

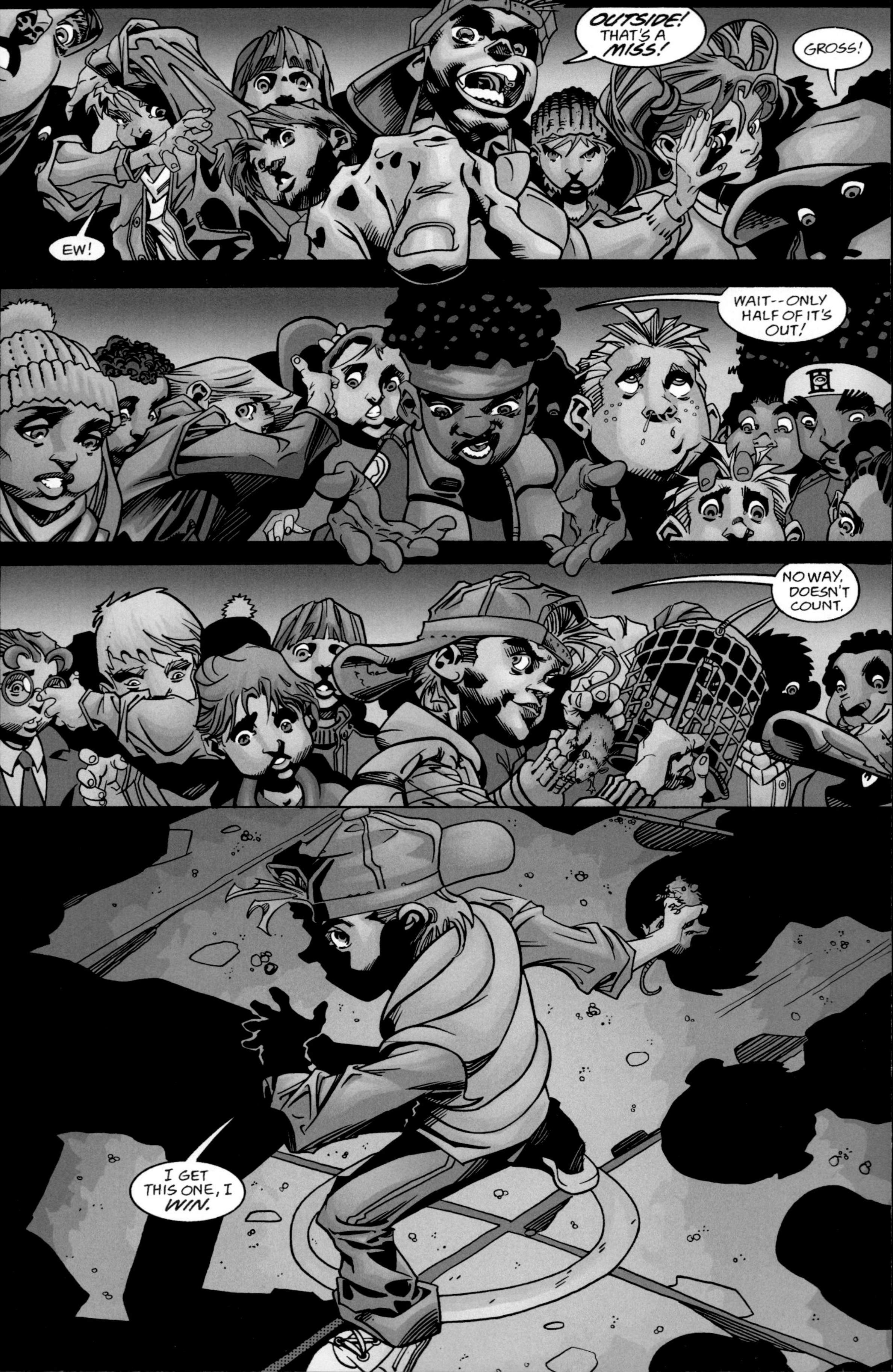
OUTSIDE! THAT'S A MISS!
GROSS!
EW!
WAIT--ONLY HALF OF IT'S OUT!
NO WAY. DOESN'T COUNT.
I GET THIS ONE, I WIN.

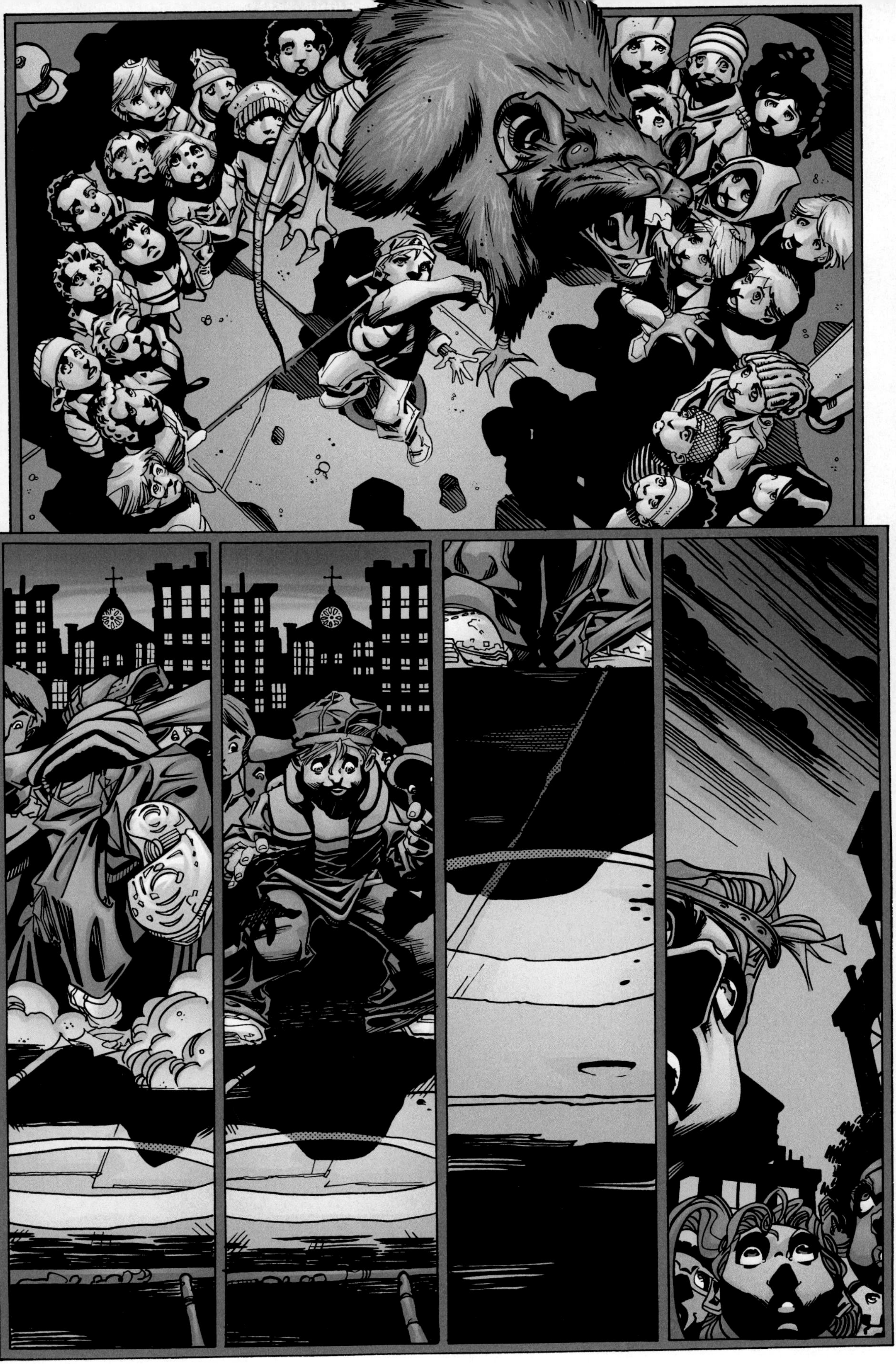

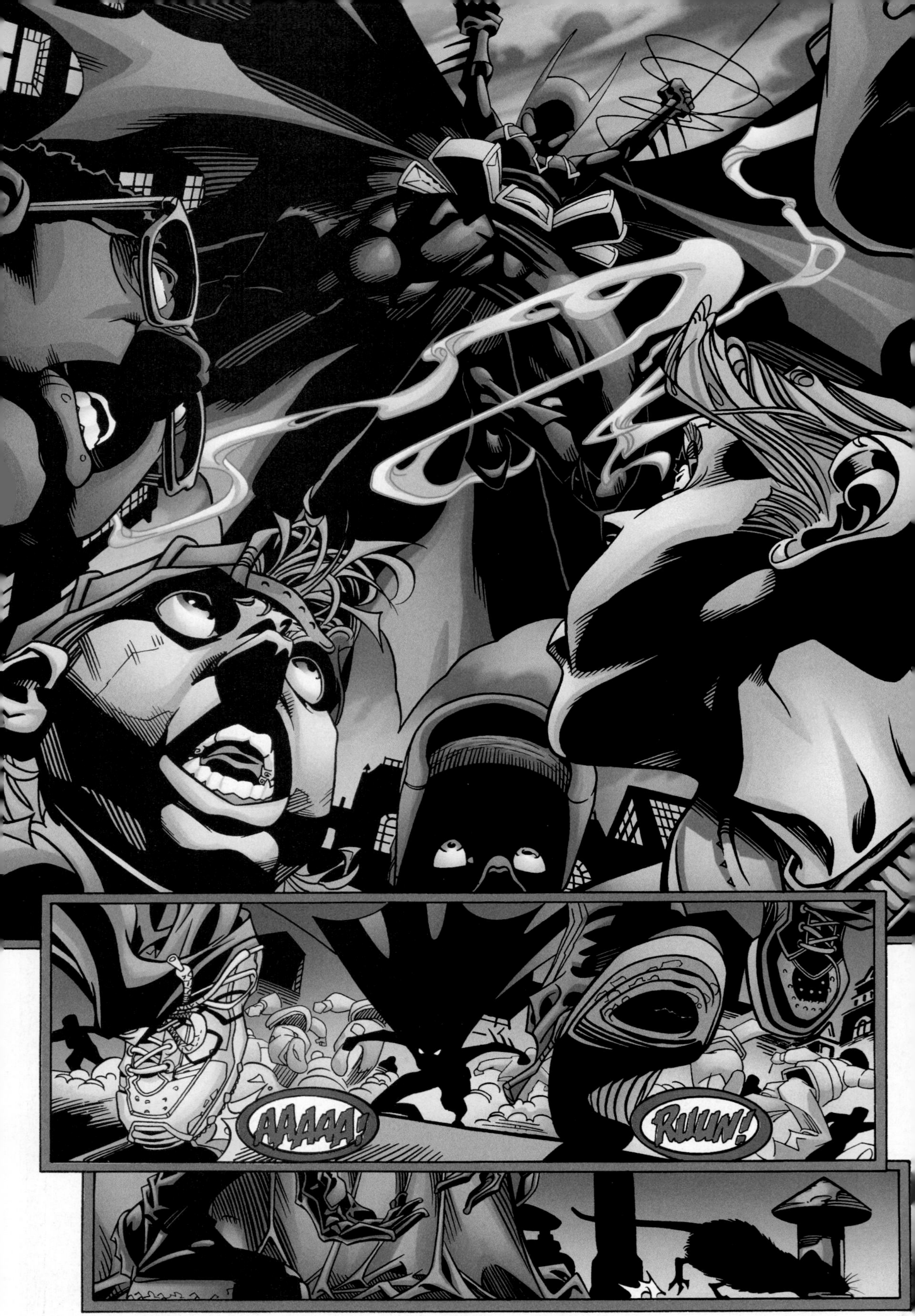
AAAAA!
RUUN!

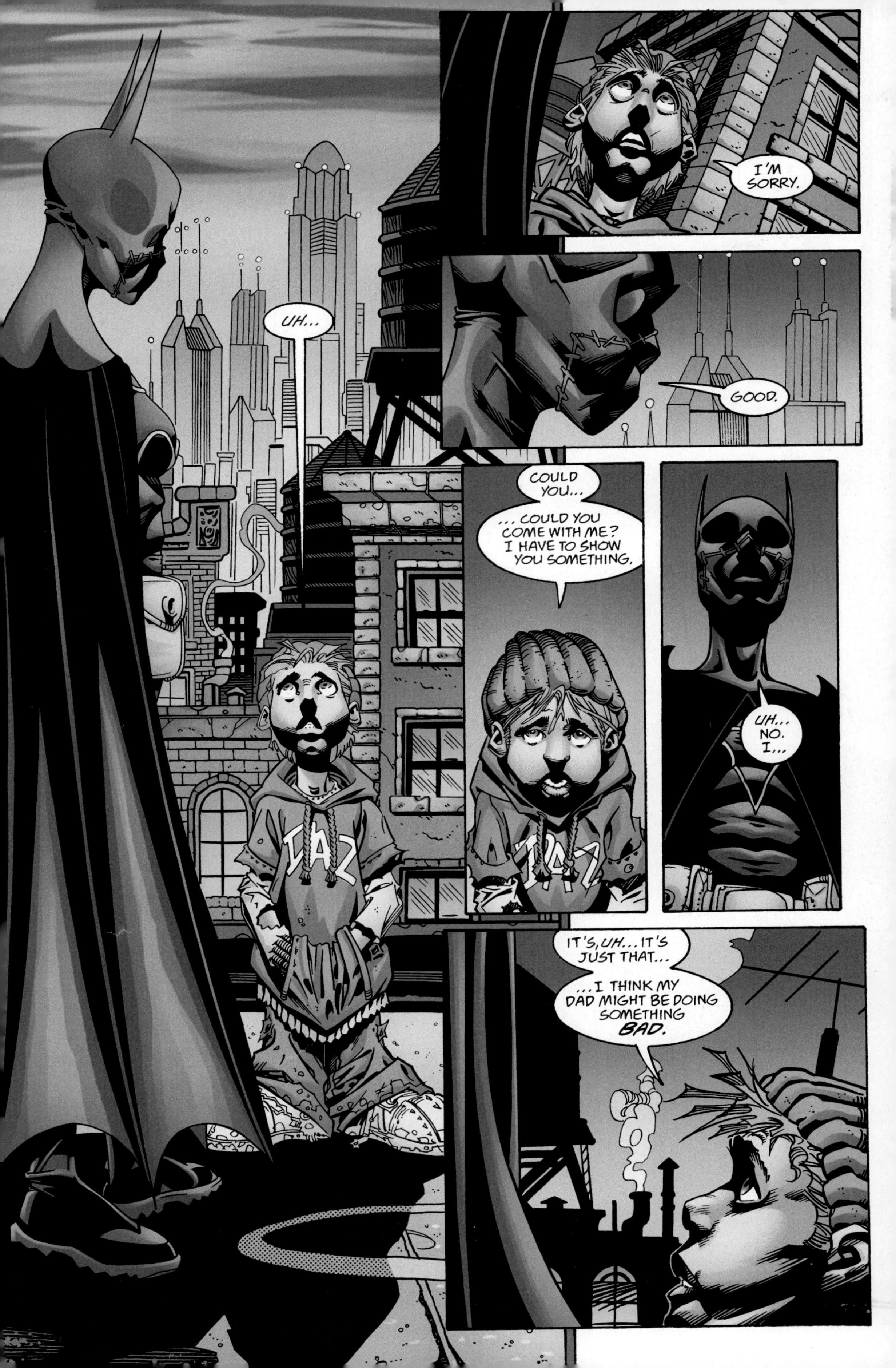
UH...
I'M SORRY.
GOOD.
COULD YOU...
...COULD YOU COME WITH ME? I HAVE TO SHOW YOU SOMETHING.
UH... NO. I...
IT'S, UH... IT'S JUST THAT...
...I THINK MY DAD MIGHT BE DOING SOMETHING BAD.

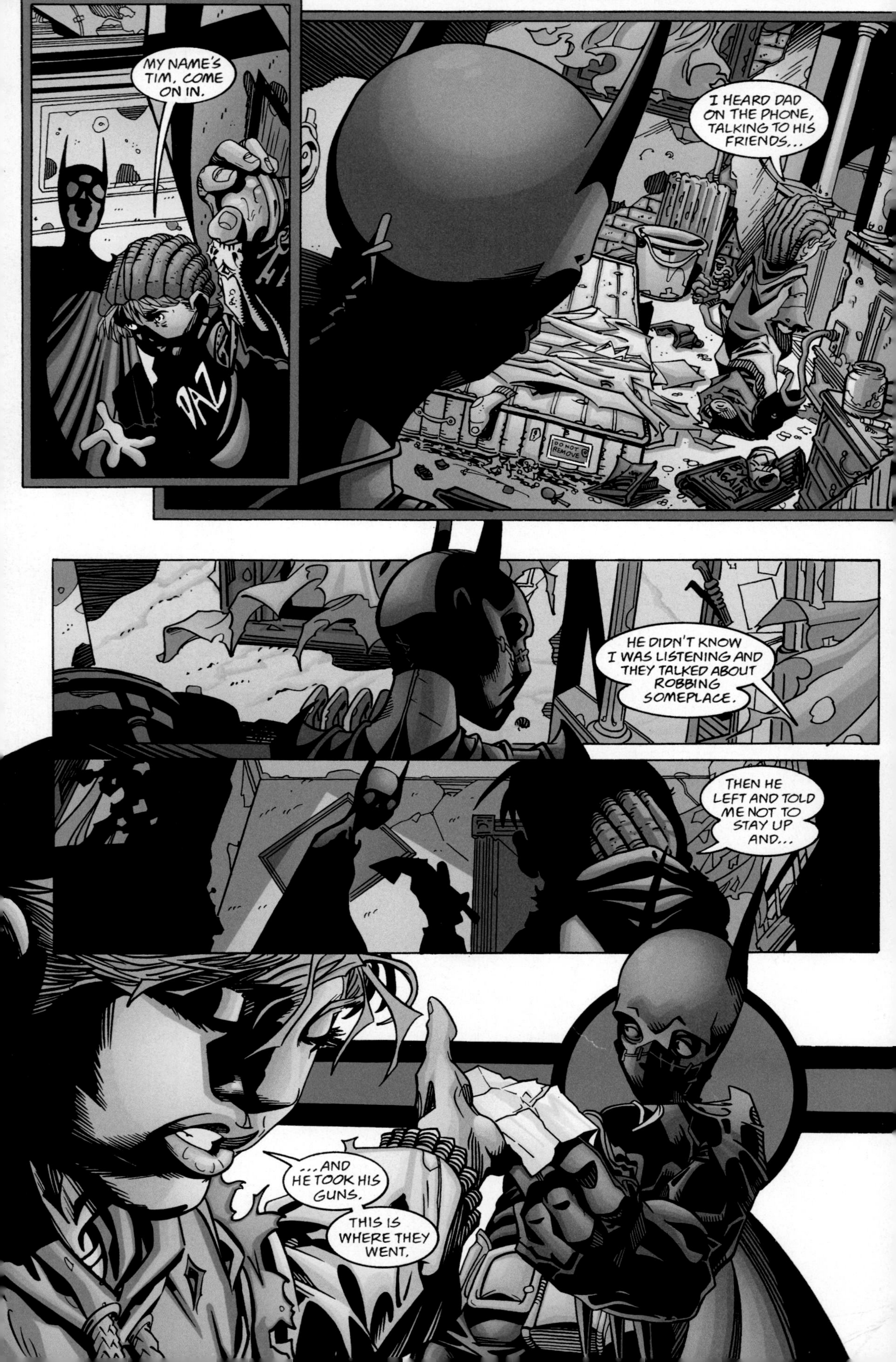
MY NAME'S TIM, COME ON IN.
I HEARD DAD ON THE PHONE, TALKING TO HIS FRIENDS...
DO NOT REMOVE
HE DIDN'T KNOW I WAS LISTENING AND THEY TALKED ABOUT ROBBING SOMEPLACE.
THEN HE LEFT AND TOLD ME NOT TO STAY UP AND...
...AND HE TOOK HIS GUNS.
THIS IS WHERE THEY WENT.

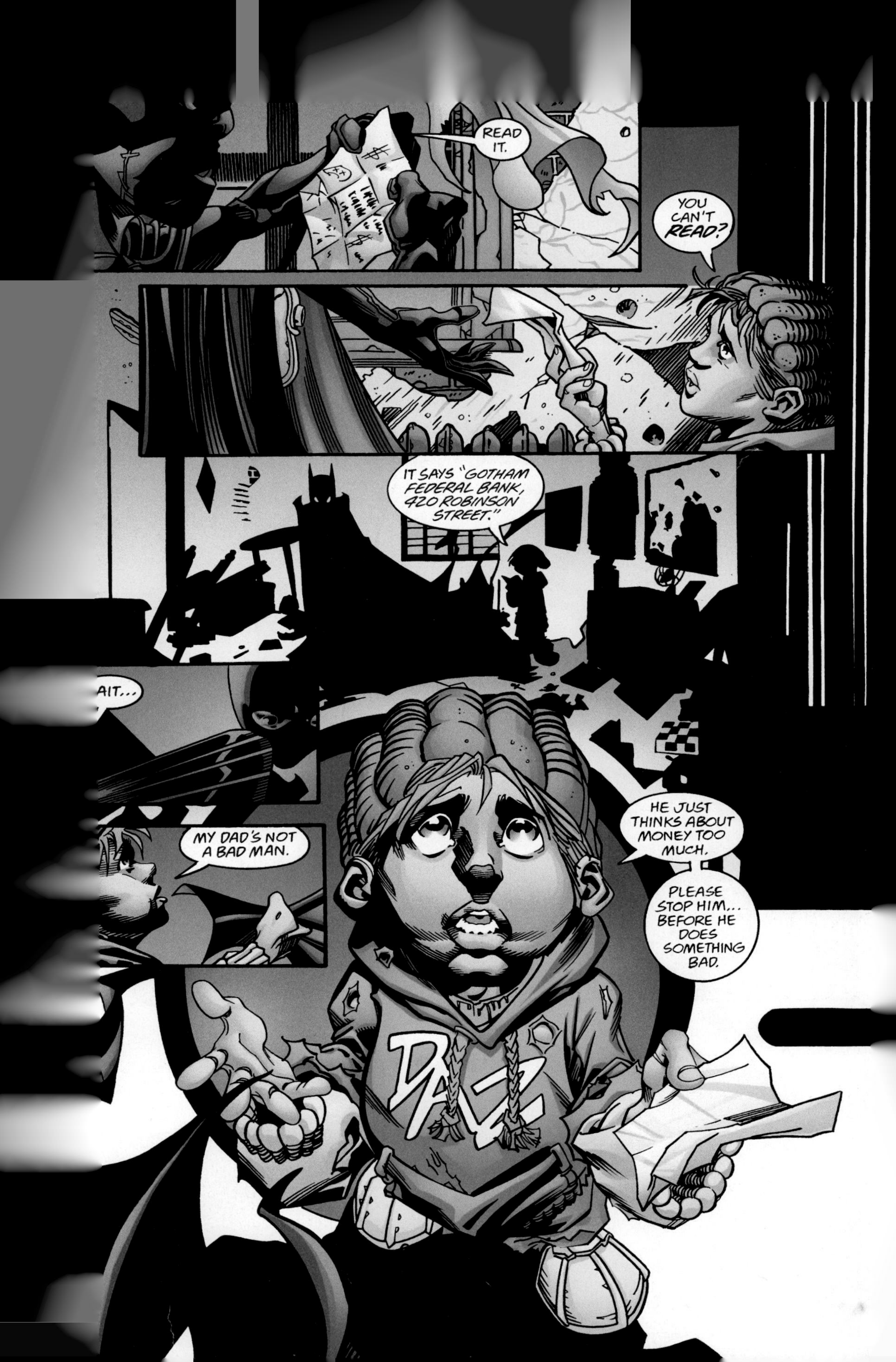
READ IT.
YOU CAN'T READ?
IT SAYS "GOTHAM FEDERAL BANK, 420 ROBINSON STREET."
MY DAD'S NOT A BAD MAN.
HE JUST THINKS ABOUT MONEY TOO MUCH.
PLEASE STOP HIM... BEFORE HE DOES SOMETHING BAD.

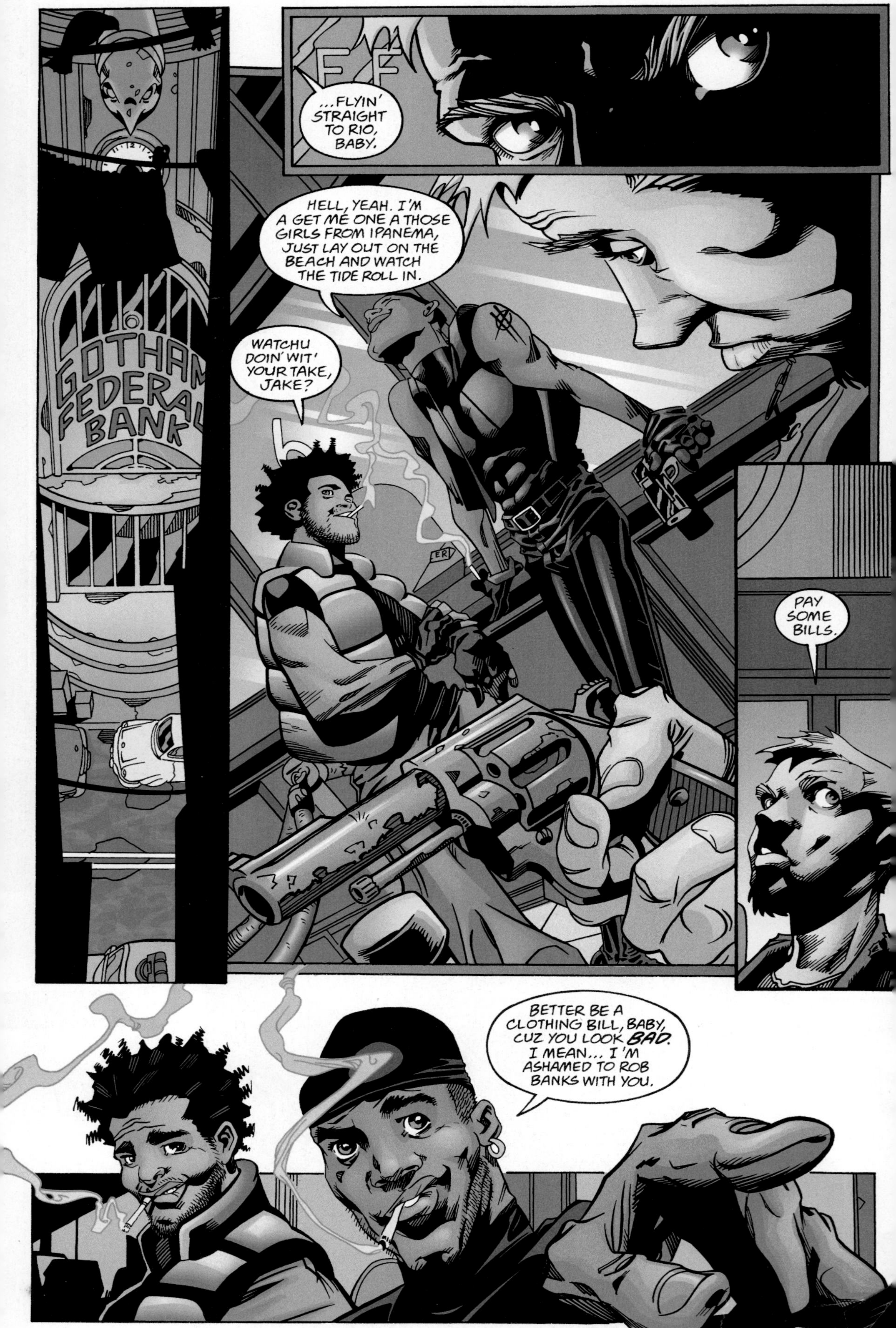
GOTHAM FEDERAL BANK
...FLYIN' STRAIGHT TO RIO, BABY.
HELL, YEAH. I'M A GET ME ONE A THOSE GIRLS FROM IPANEMA, JUST LAY OUT ON THE BEACH AND WATCH THE TIDE ROLL IN.
WATCHU DOIN' WIT' YOUR TAKE, JAKE?
PAY SOME BILLS.
BETTER BE A CLOTHING BILL, BABY, CUZ YOU LOOK BAD. I MEAN... I'M ASHAMED TO ROB BANKS WITH YOU.

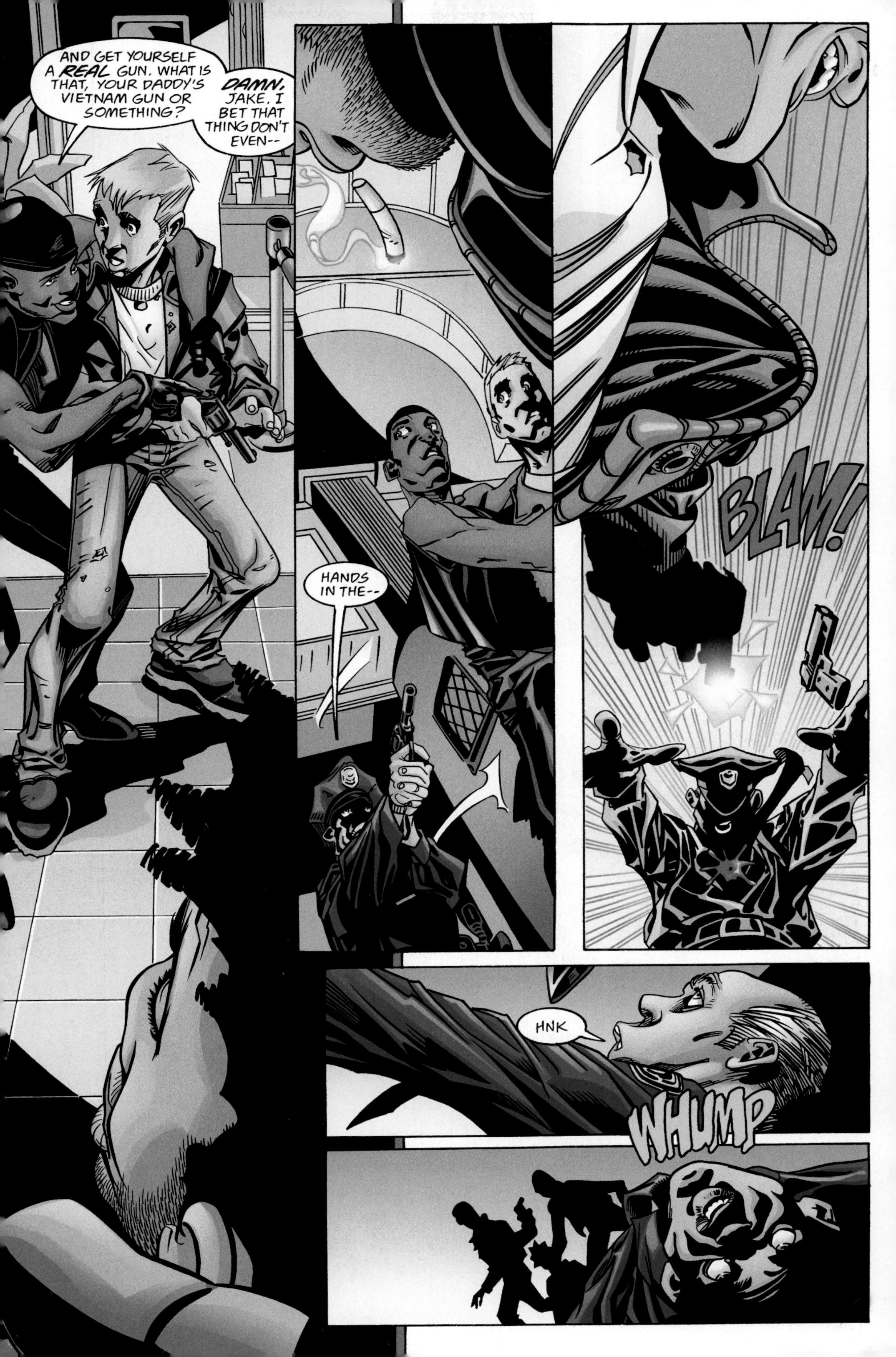
AND GET YOURSELF A REAL GUN. WHAT IS THAT, YOUR DADDY'S VIETNAM GUN OR SOMETHING?
DAMN, JAKE. I BET THAT THING DON'T EVEN--
HANDS IN THE--
BLAM!
HNK
WHUMP

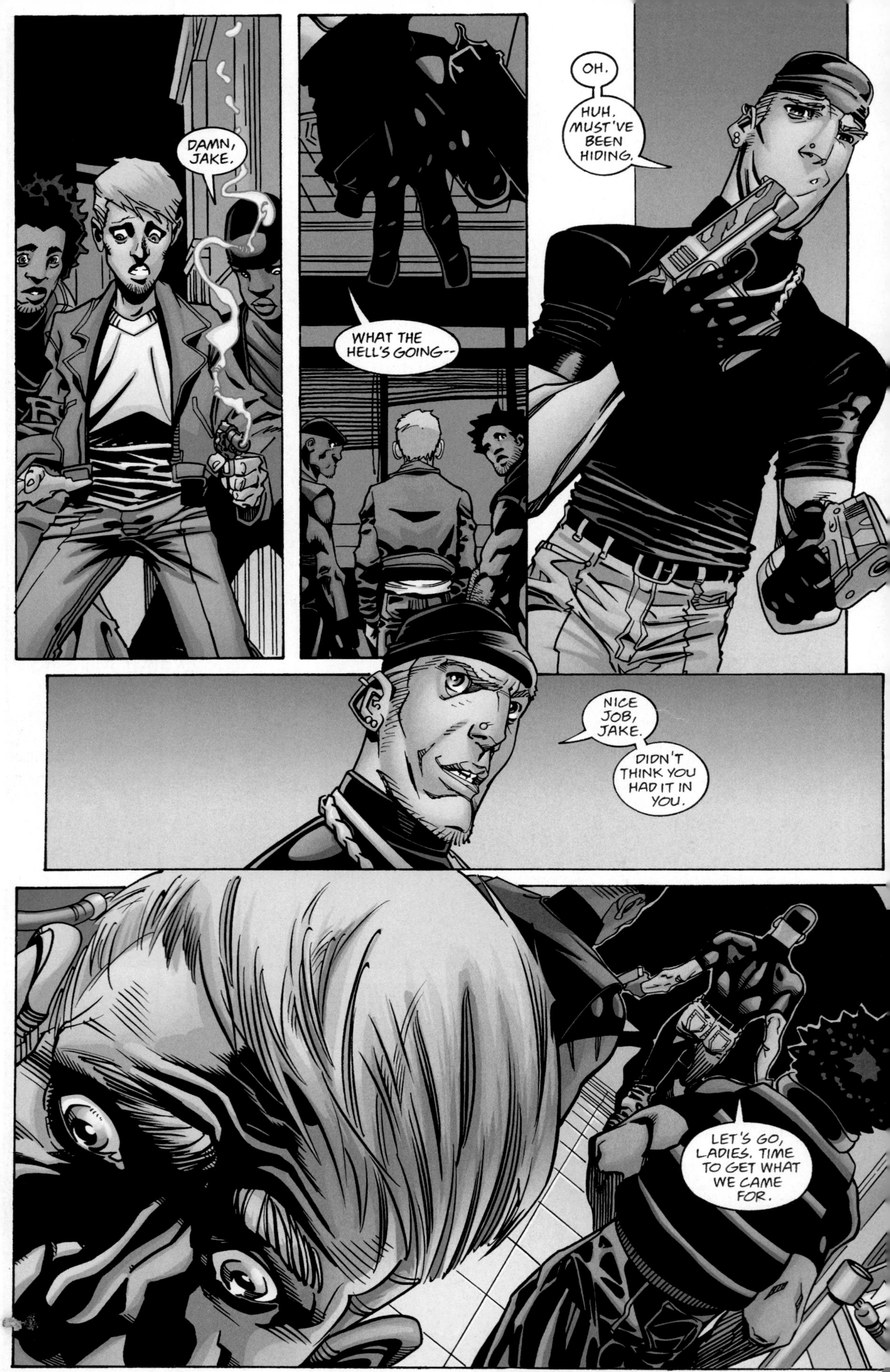
DAMN, JAKE.
WHAT THE HELL'S GOING--
OH.
HUH. MUST'VE BEEN HIDING.
NICE JOB, JAKE.
DIDN'T THINK YOU HAD IT IN YOU.
LET'S GO, LADIES. TIME TO GET WHAT WE CAME FOR.

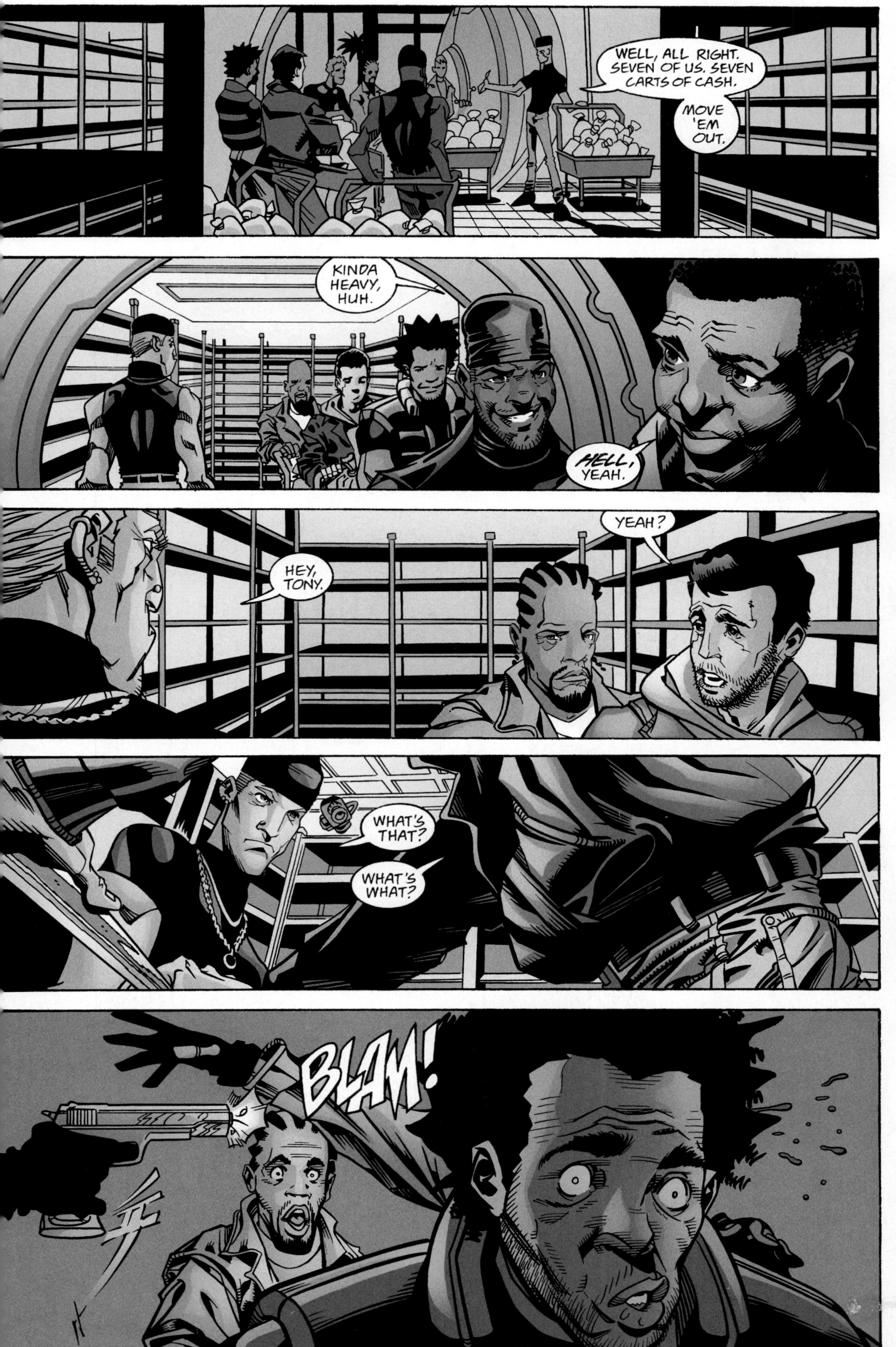
WELL, ALL RIGHT. SEVEN OF US. SEVEN CARTS OF CASH.
MOVE 'EM OUT.
KINDA HEAVY, HUH.
HELL, YEAH.
HEY, TONY.
YEAH?
WHAT'S THAT?
WHAT'S WHAT?
BLAM!

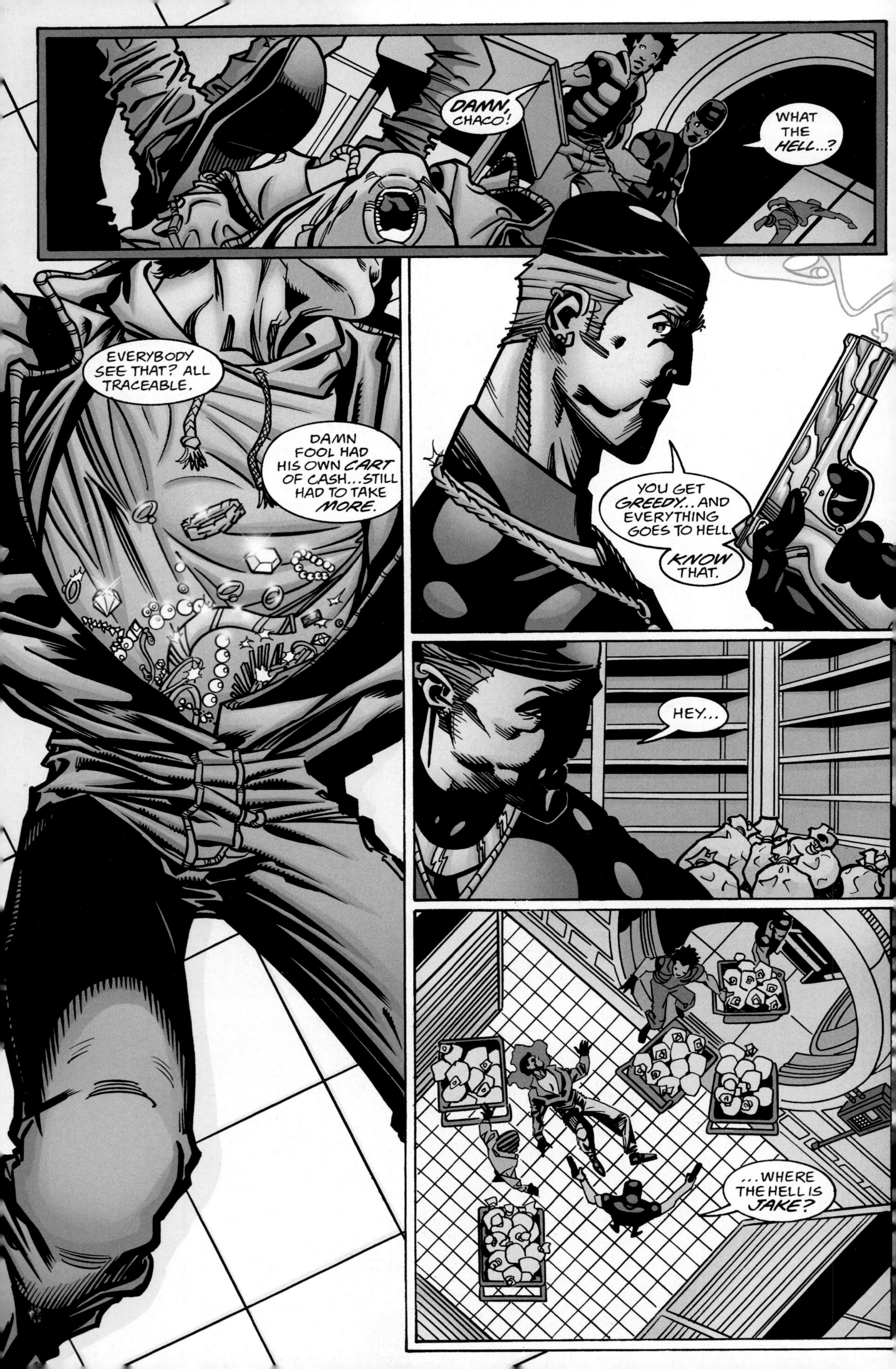
DAMN, CHACO!
WHAT THE HELL...?
EVERYBODY SEE THAT? ALL TRACEABLE.
DAMN FOOL HAD HIS OWN CART OF CASH...STILL HAD TO TAKE MORE.
YOU GET GREEDY...AND EVERYTHING GOES TO HELL.
KNOW THAT.
HEY...
...WHERE THE HELL IS JAKE?

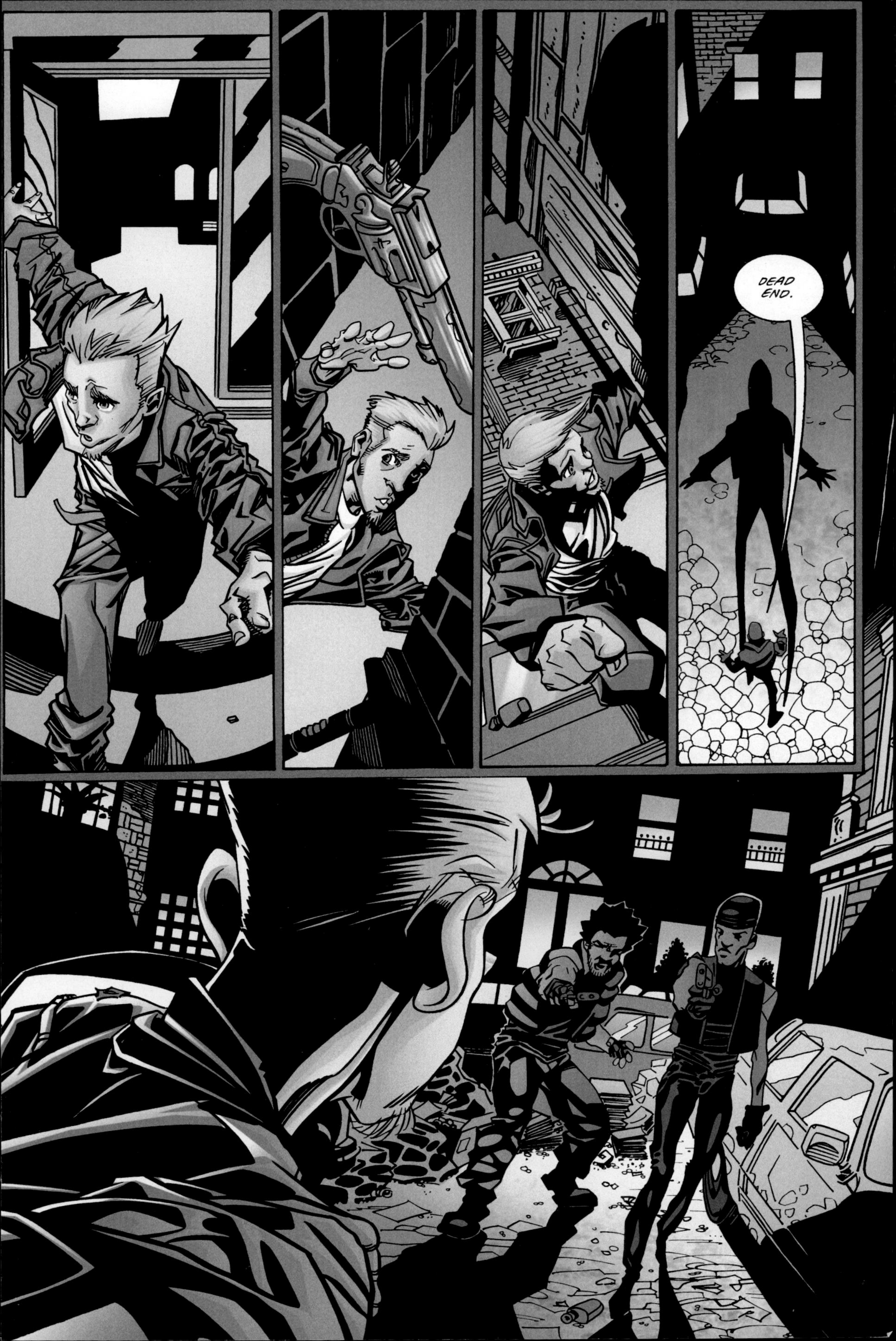
DEAD END.

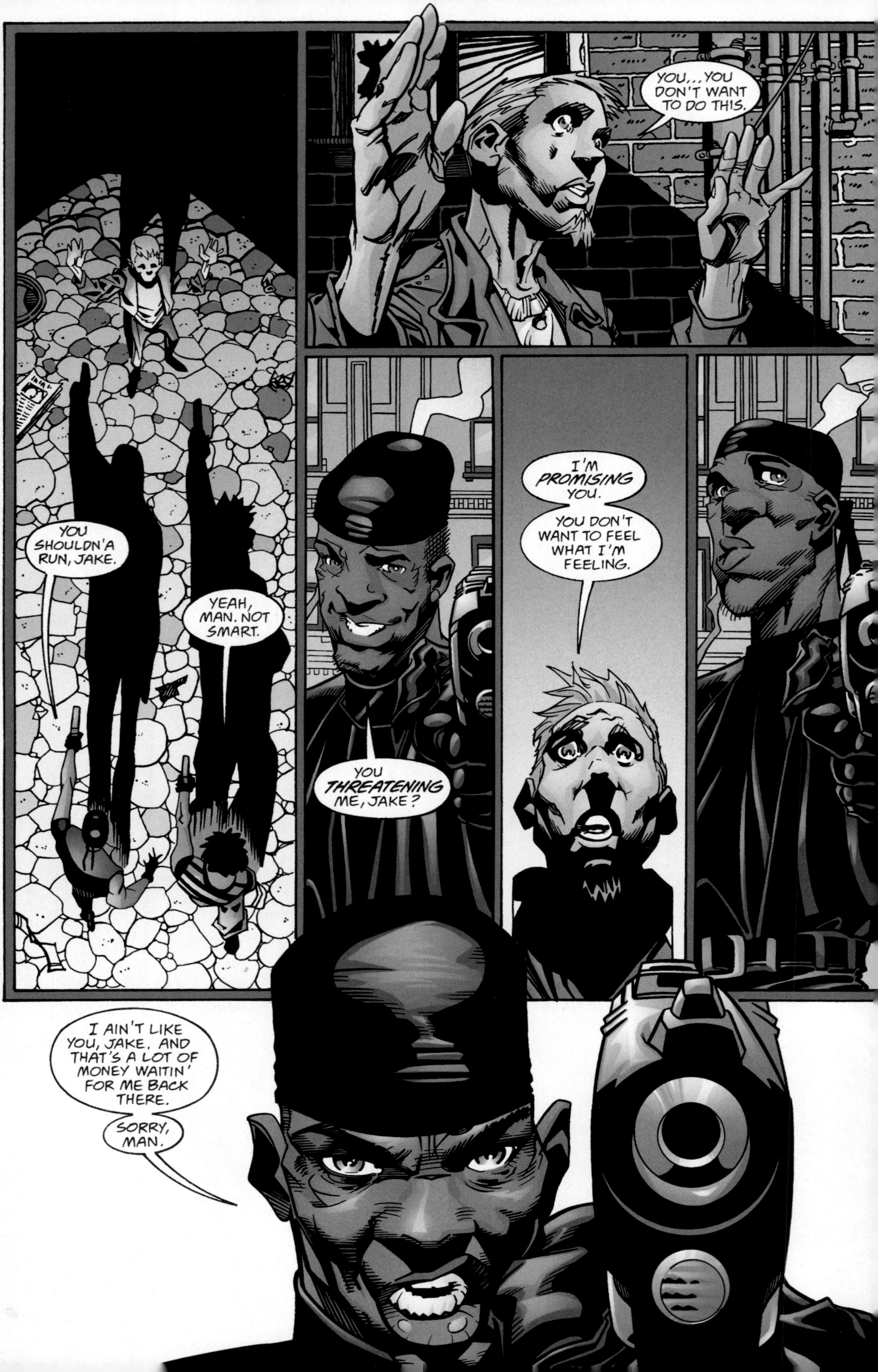
YOU,.. YOU DON'T WANT TO DO THIS.
YOU SHOULDN'A RUN, JAKE.
YEAH, MAN. NOT SMART.
YOU THREATENING ME, JAKE?
I'M PROMISING YOU.
YOU DON'T WANT TO FEEL WHAT I'M FEELING.
I AIN'T LIKE YOU, JAKE, AND THAT'S A LOT OF MONEY WAITIN' FOR ME BACK THERE.
SORRY, MAN.

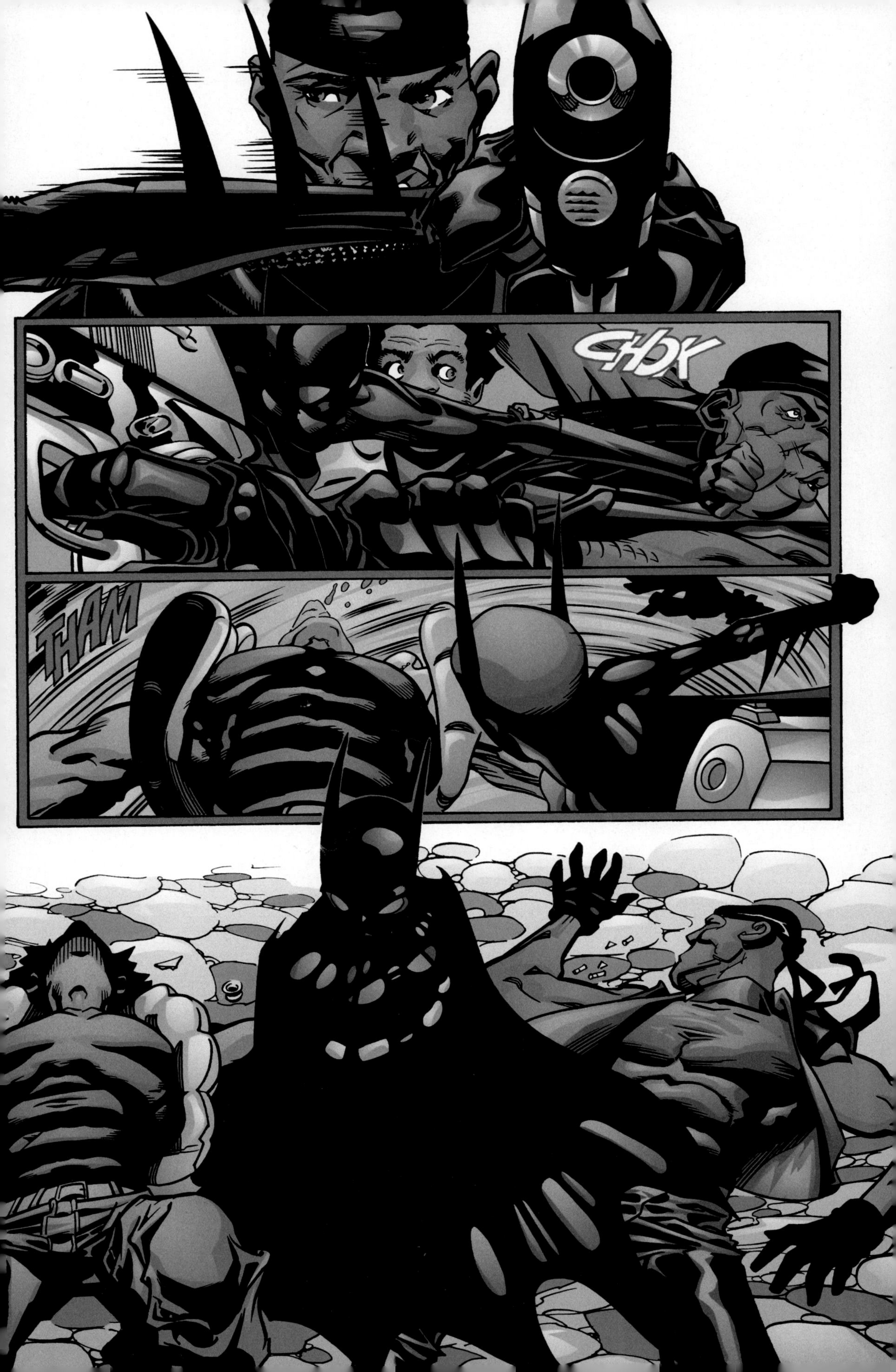
CHOK
THAM

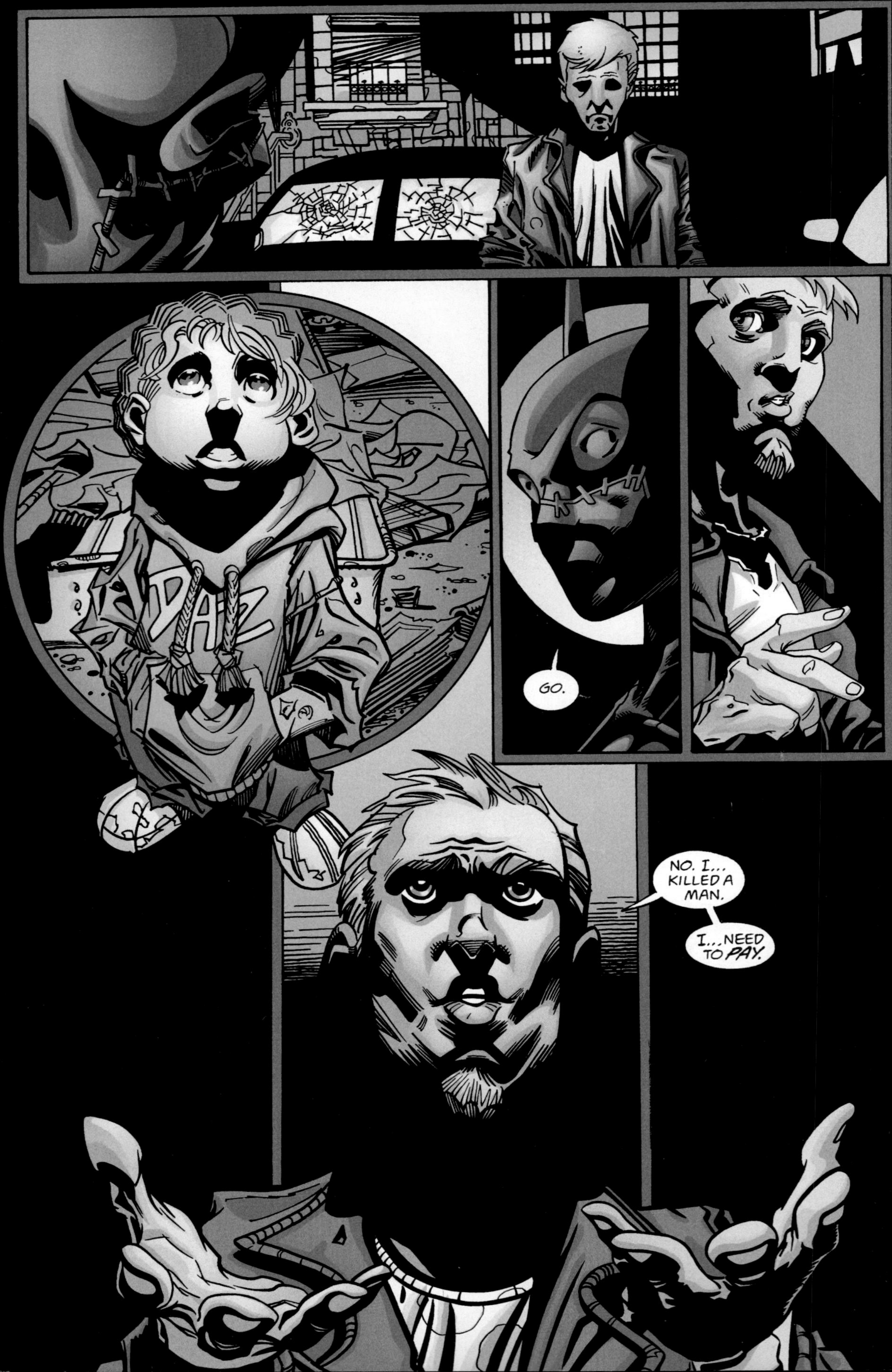
DAZ
GO.
NO. I... KILLED A MAN.
I... NEED TO PAY.

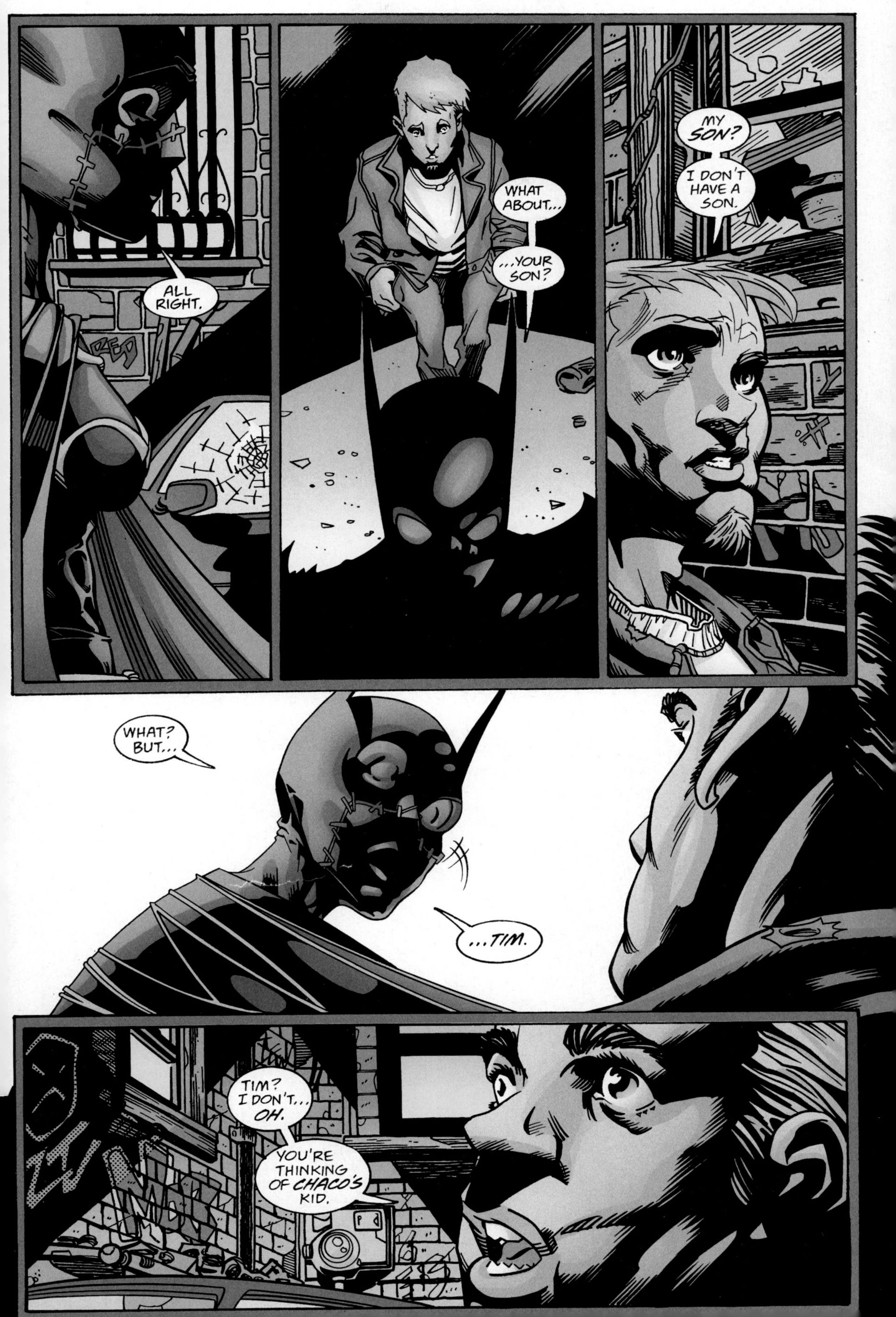
ALL RIGHT.
WHAT ABOUT...
...YOUR SON?
MY SON?
I DON'T HAVE A SON.
WHAT? BUT...
...TIM.
TIM? I DON'T... OH.
YOU'RE THINKING OF CHACO'S KID.

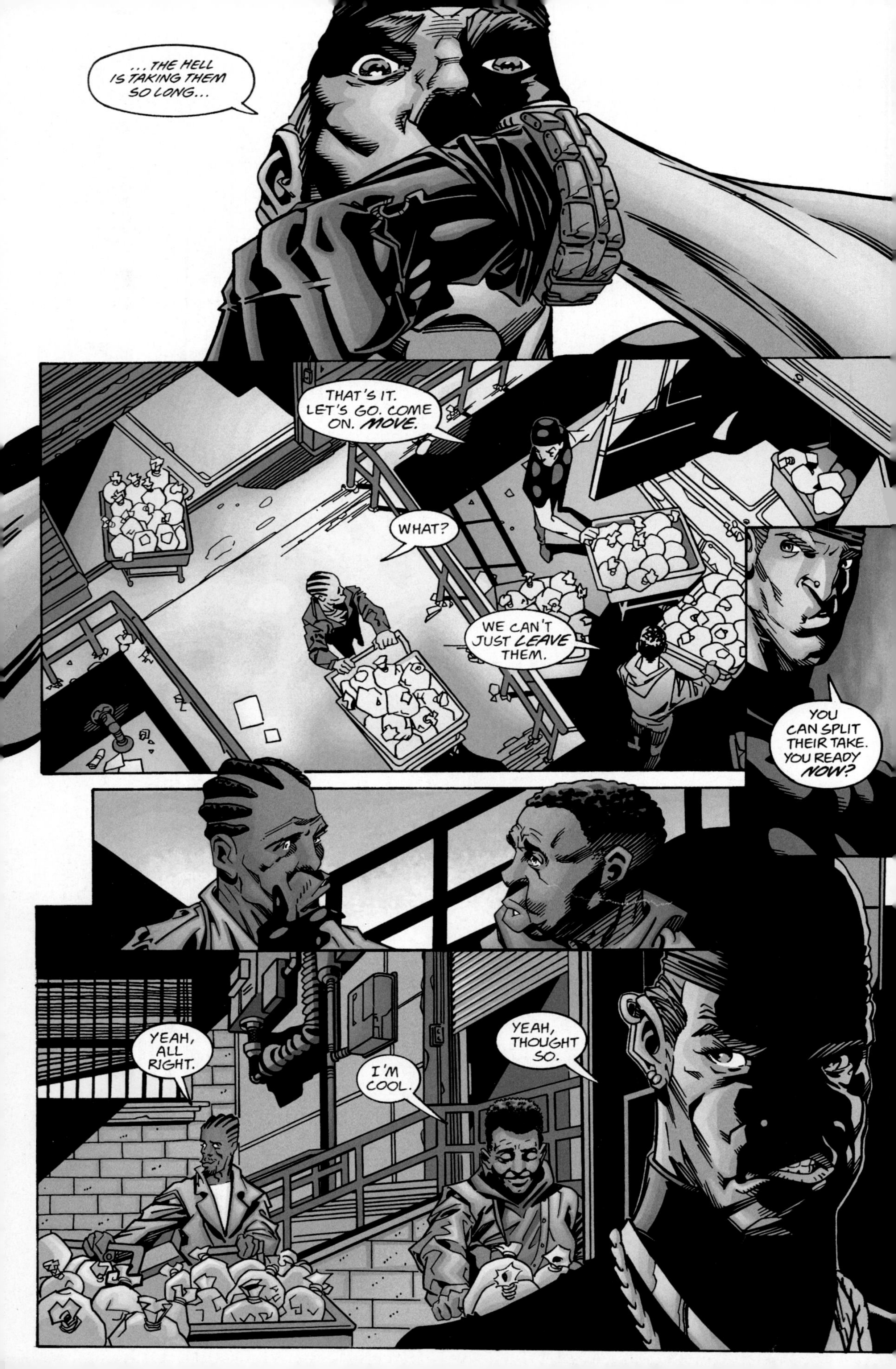
...THE HELL IS TAKING THEM SO LONG...
THAT'S IT. LET'S GO. COME ON. MOVE.
WHAT?
WE CAN'T JUST LEAVE THEM.
YOU CAN SPLIT THEIR TAKE. YOU READY NOW?
YEAH, ALL RIGHT.
I'M COOL.
YEAH, THOUGHT SO.

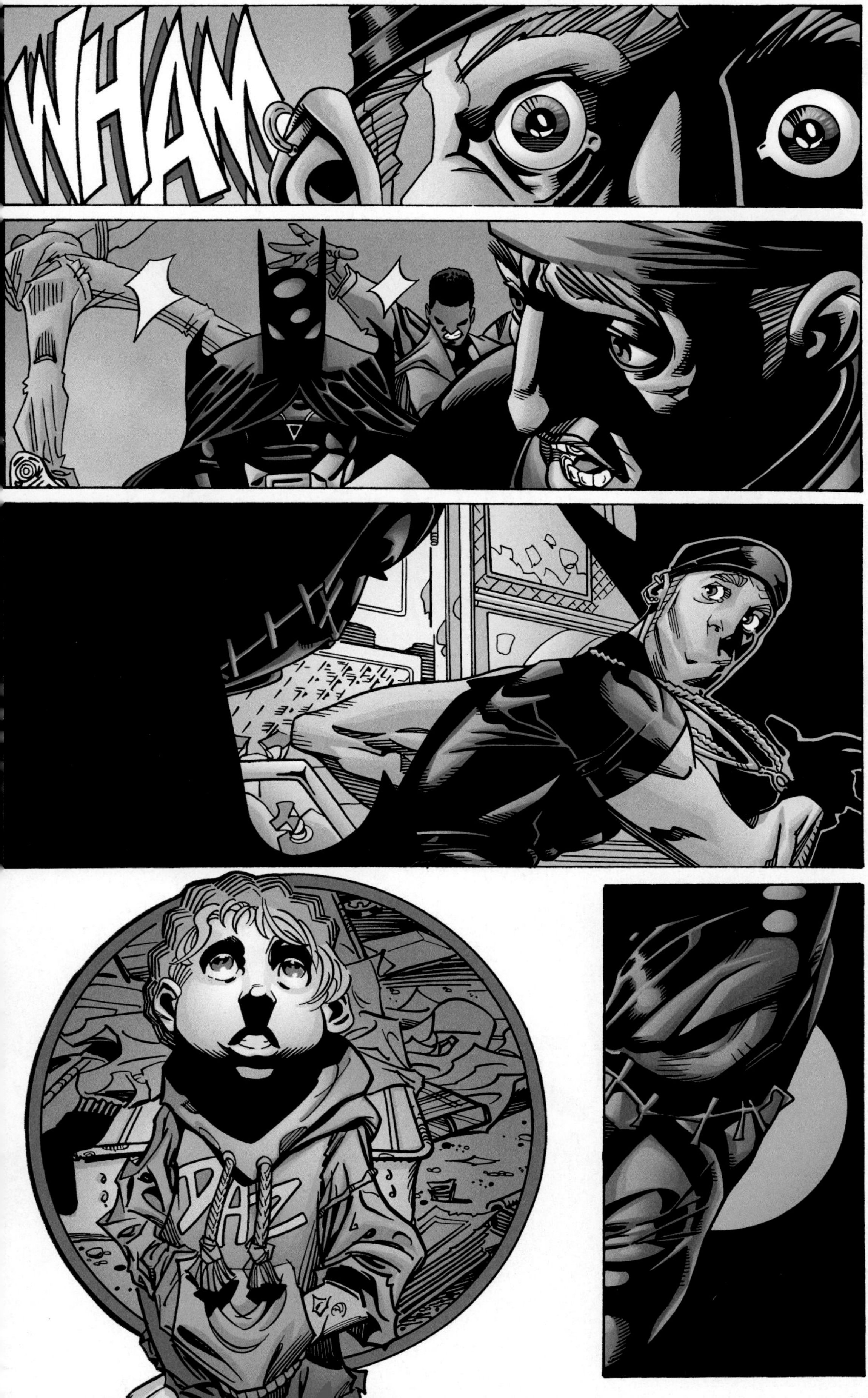
WHAM

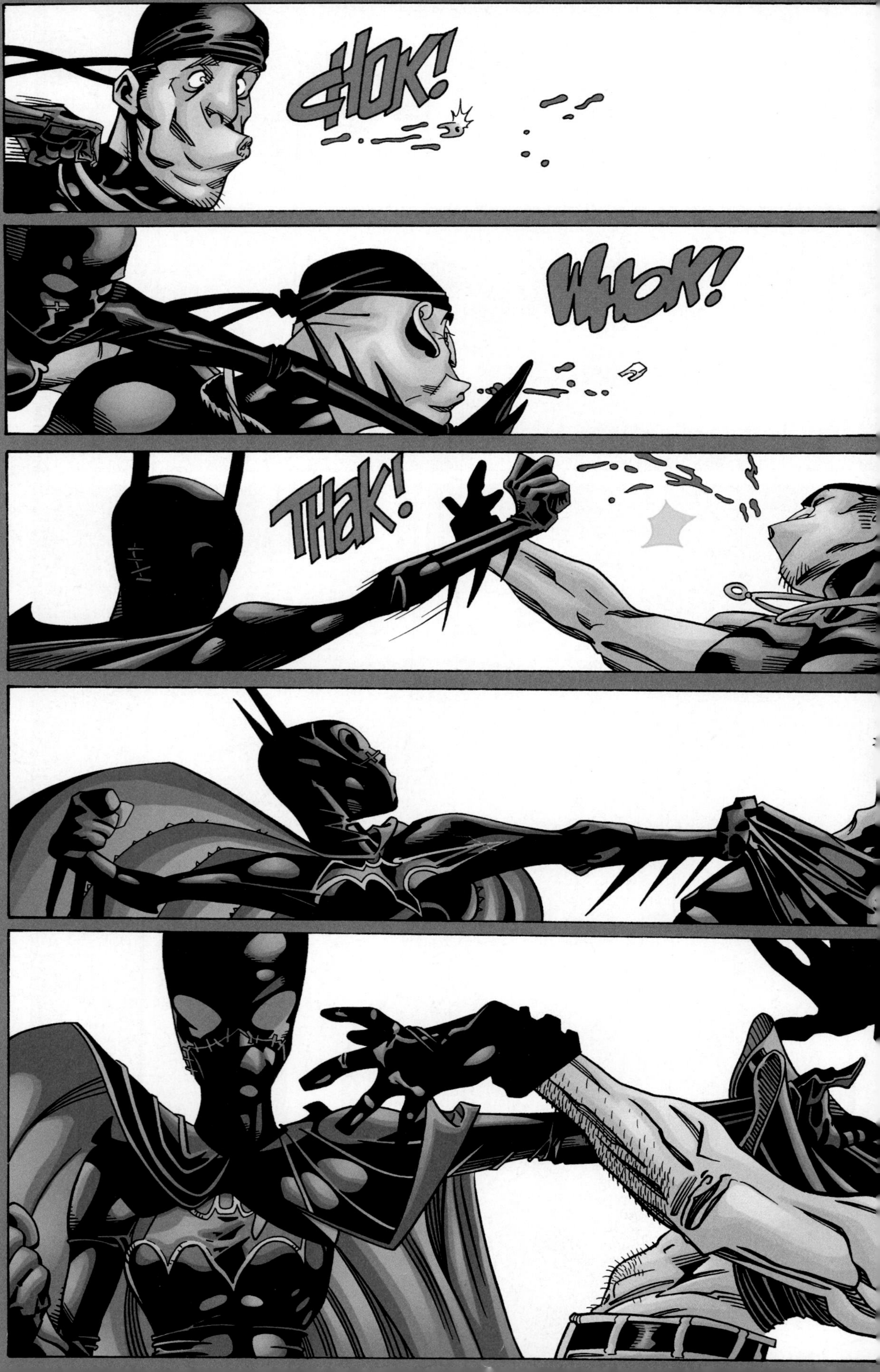
CHOK!
WHOK!
THAK!

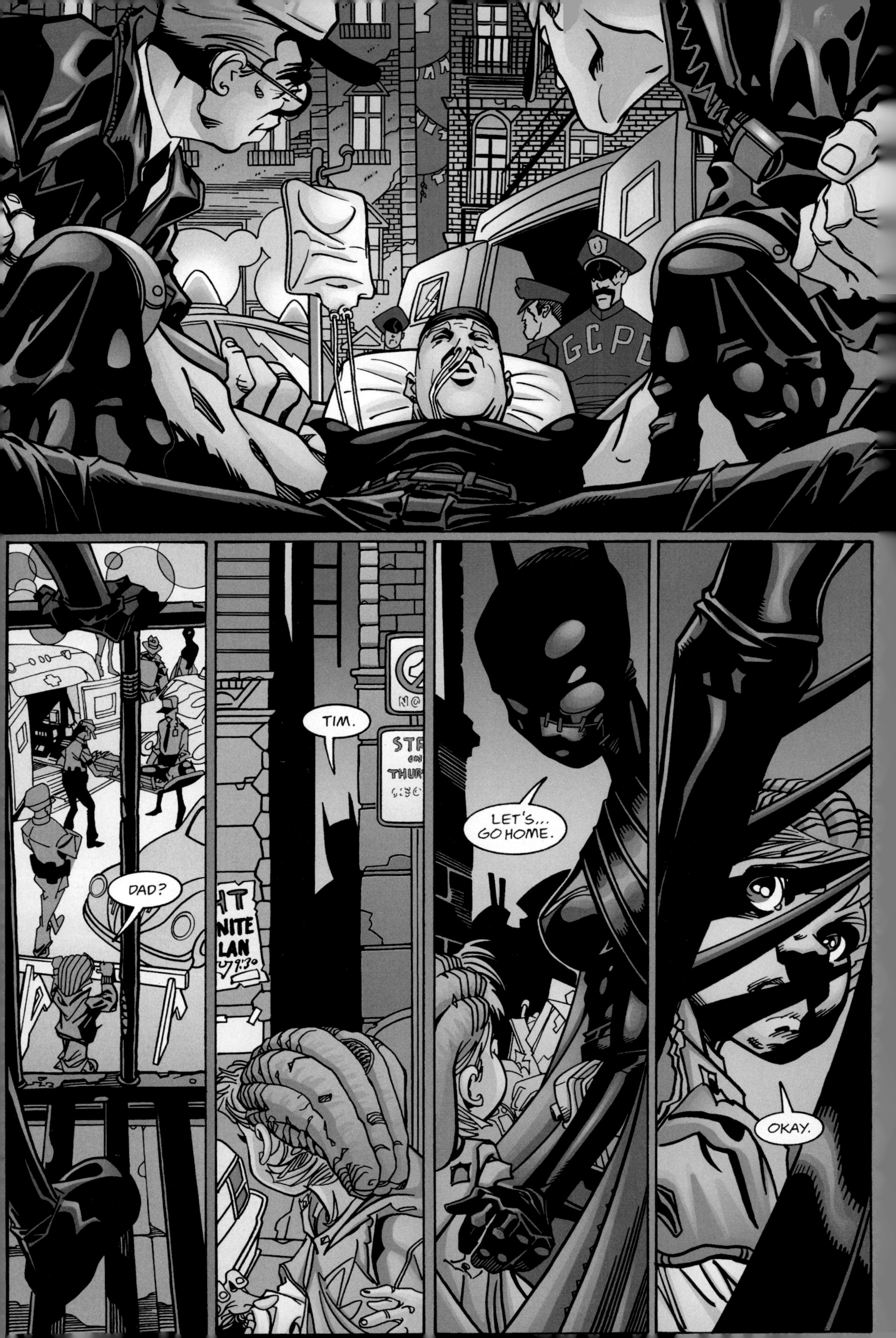
GCPD
DAD?
TIM.
LET'S... GO HOME.
OKAY.

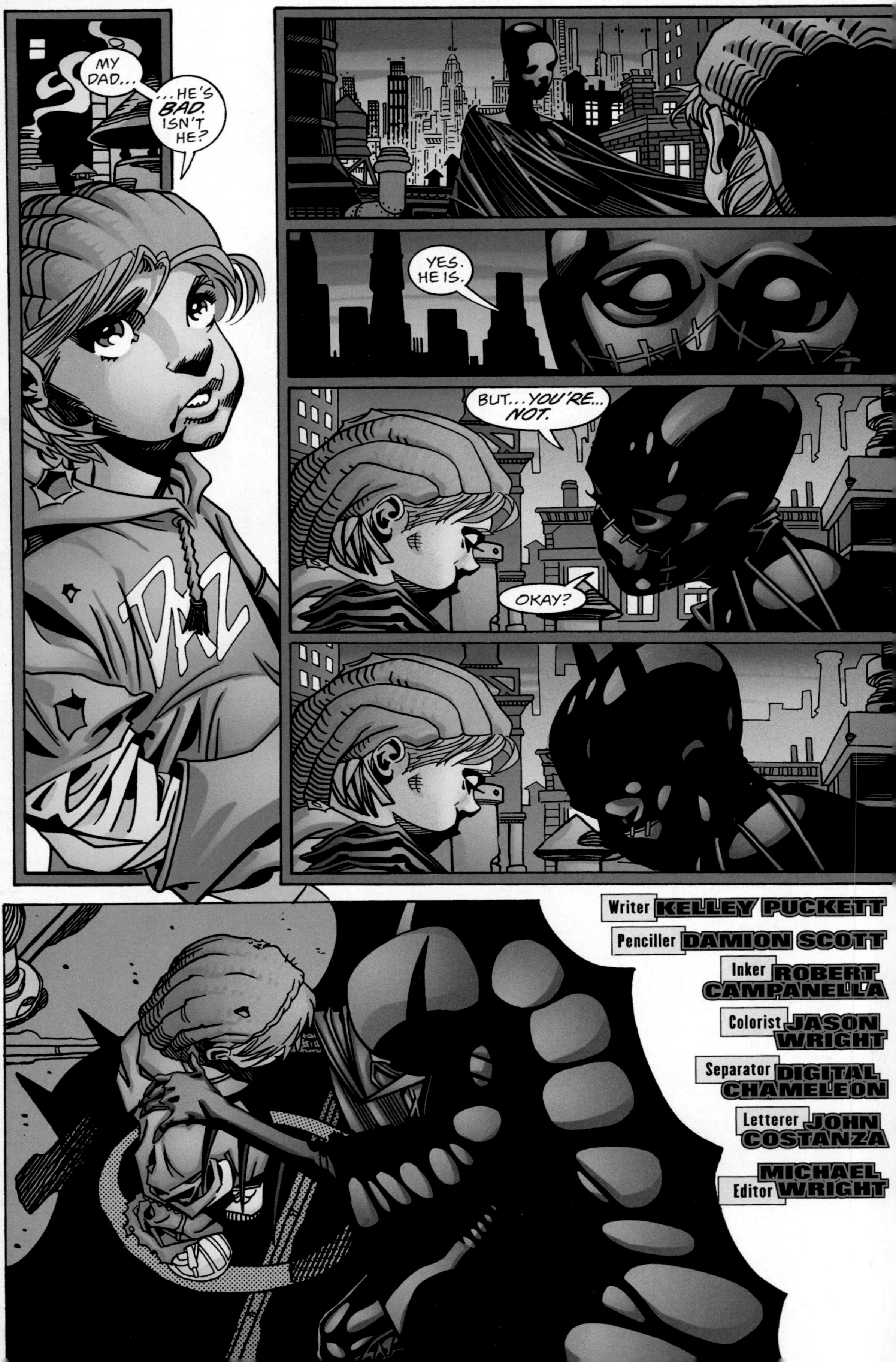
MY DAD...
...HE'S BAD. ISN'T HE?
YES. HE IS.
BUT... YOU'RE... NOT.
OKAY?
DAZ
Writer KELLEY PUCKETT
Penciller DAMION SCOTT
Inker ROBERT CAMPANELLA
Colorist JASON WRIGHT
Separator DIGITAL CHAMELEON
Letterer JOHN COSTANZA
Editor MICHAEL WRIGHT

BATGIRL #17 cover by Damion Scott, Robert Campanella & Patrick Martin

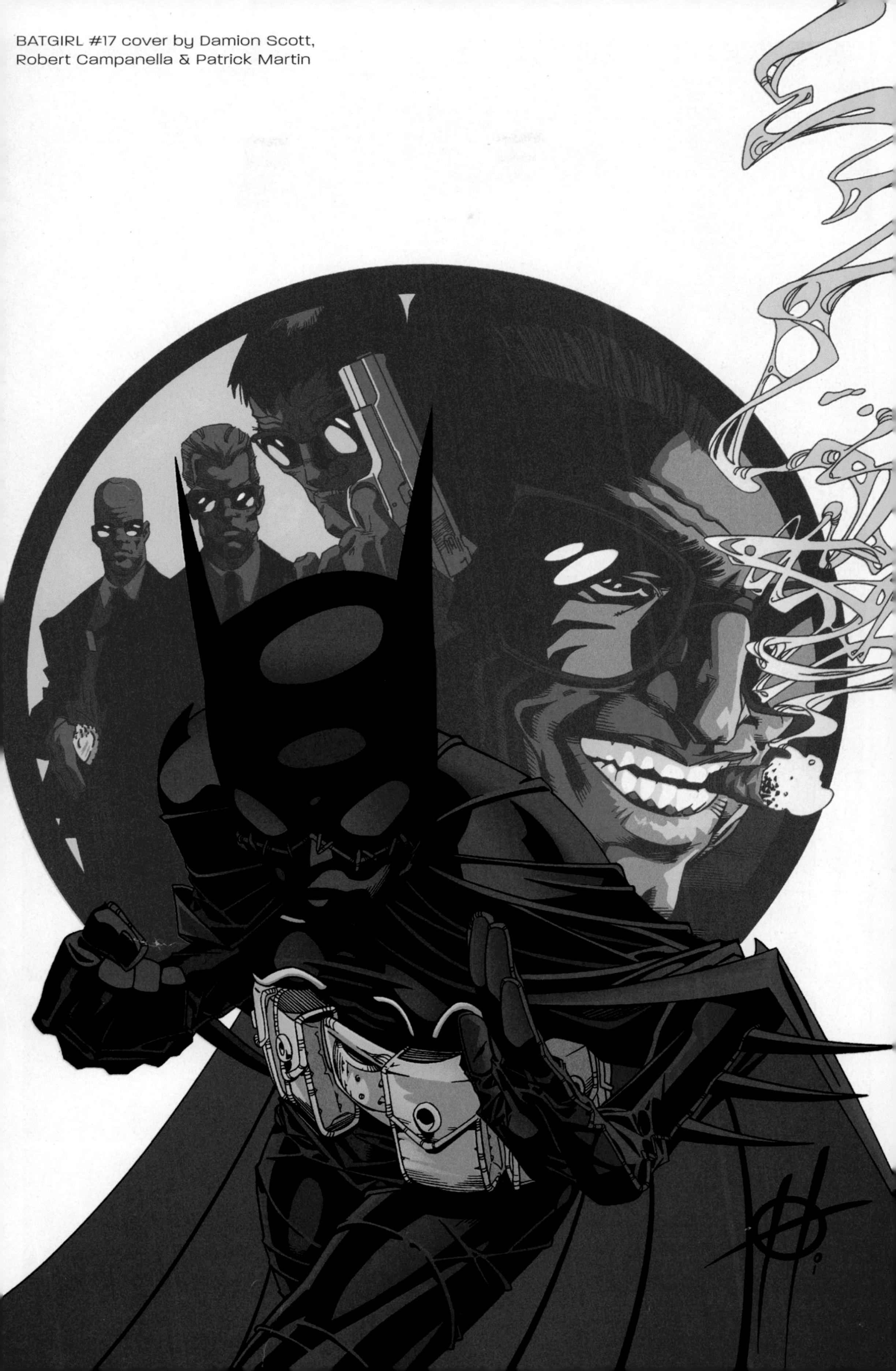

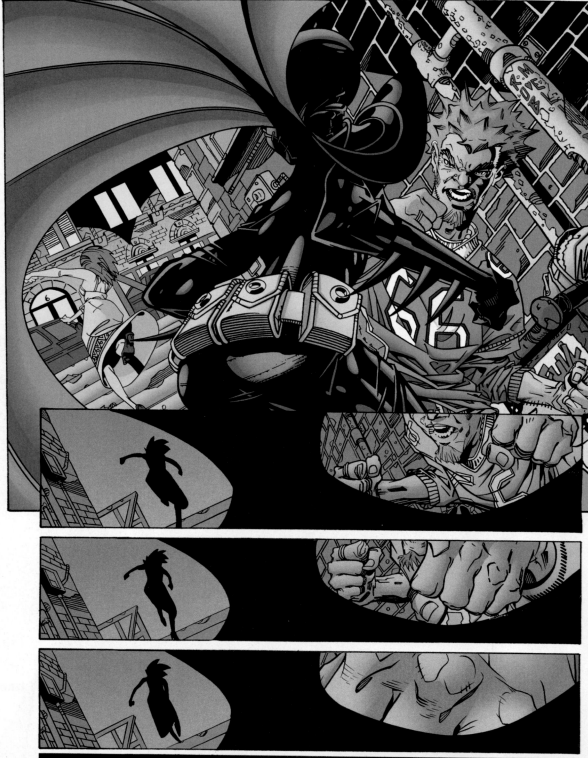

PUCKETT / SCOTT / CAMPANELLA *storytellers* / **WRIGHT** *Colors*
DIGITAL CHAMELEON *Seps* / **COSTANZA** *Letters* / **WRIGHT** *Editor*

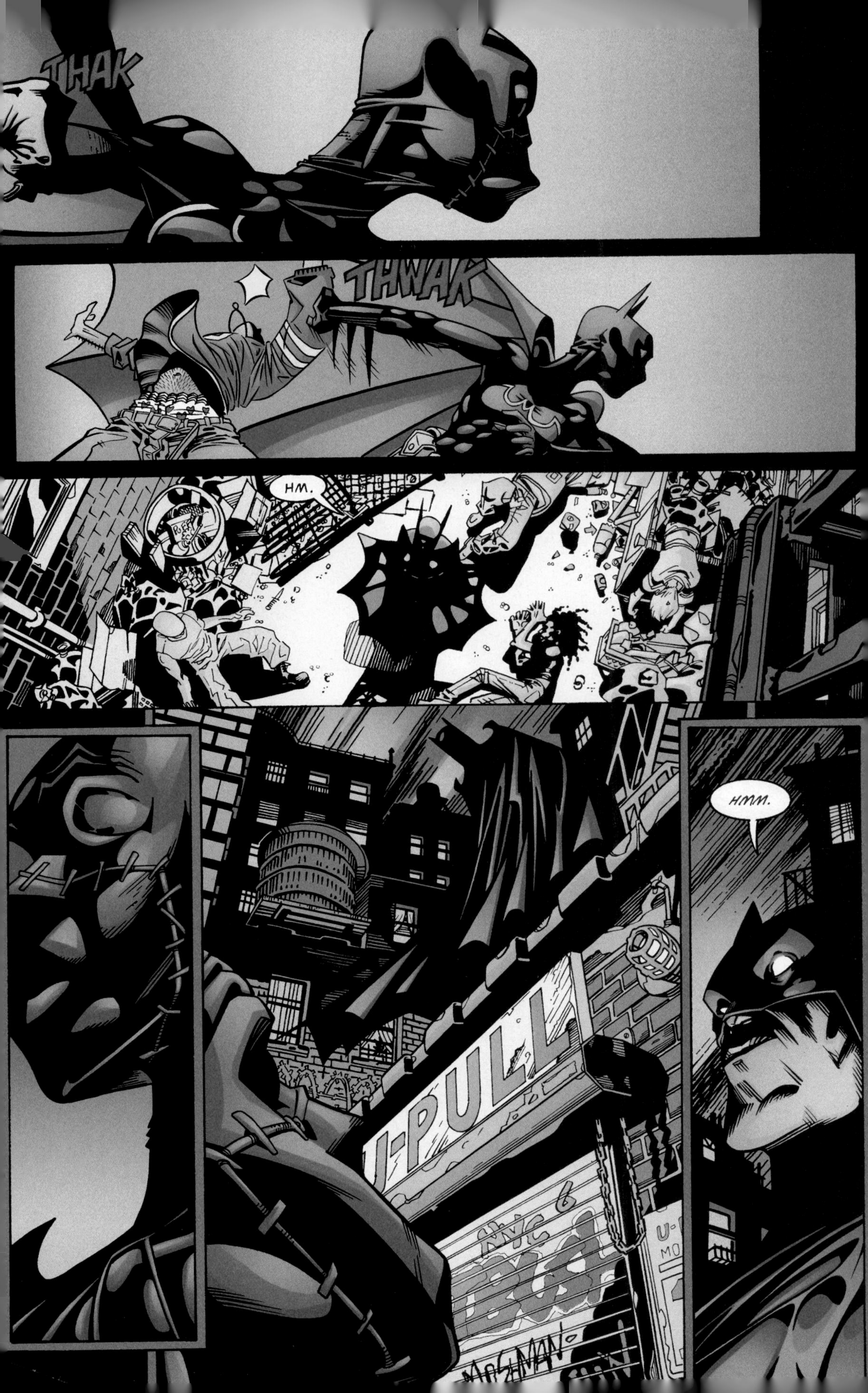
THAK
THWAK
HM.
HMM.
U-PULL

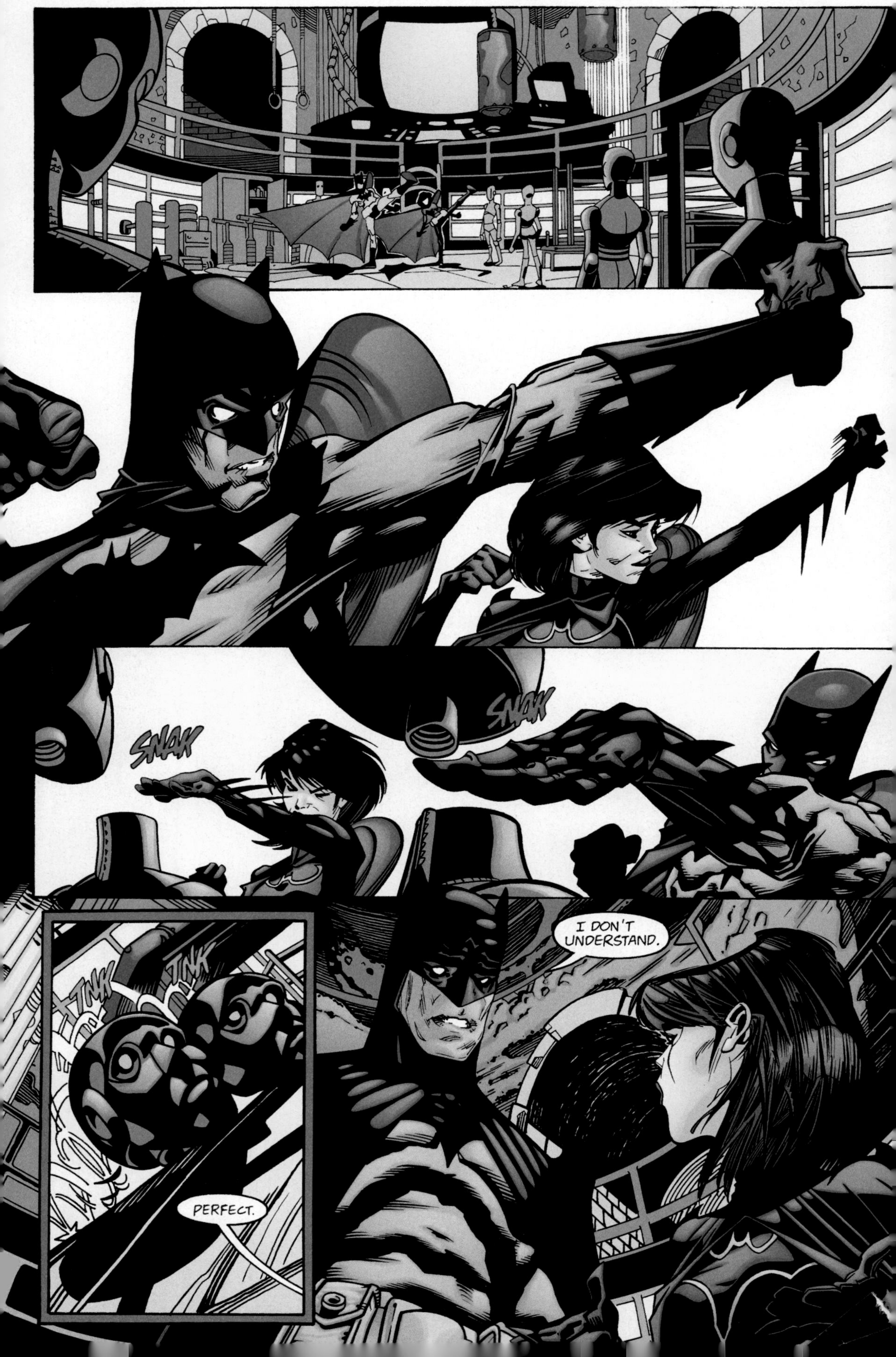
SNAK
SNAK
TINK
TINK
PERFECT.
I DON'T UNDERSTAND.

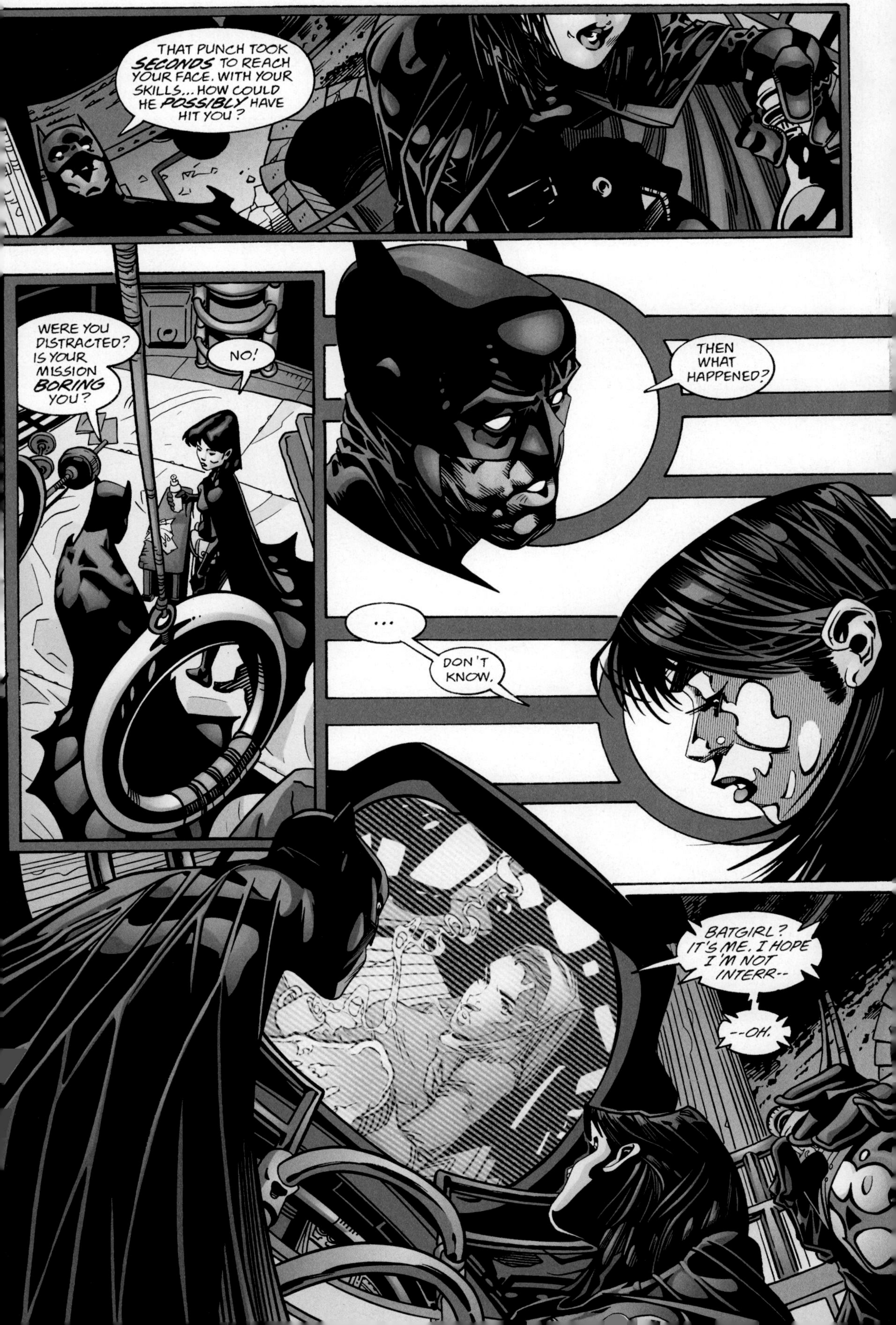
THAT PUNCH TOOK SECONDS TO REACH YOUR FACE. WITH YOUR SKILLS... HOW COULD HE POSSIBLY HAVE HIT YOU?
WERE YOU DISTRACTED? IS YOUR MISSION BORING YOU?
NO!
THEN WHAT HAPPENED?
...
DON'T KNOW.
BATGIRL? IT'S ME. I HOPE I'M NOT INTERR--
--OH.

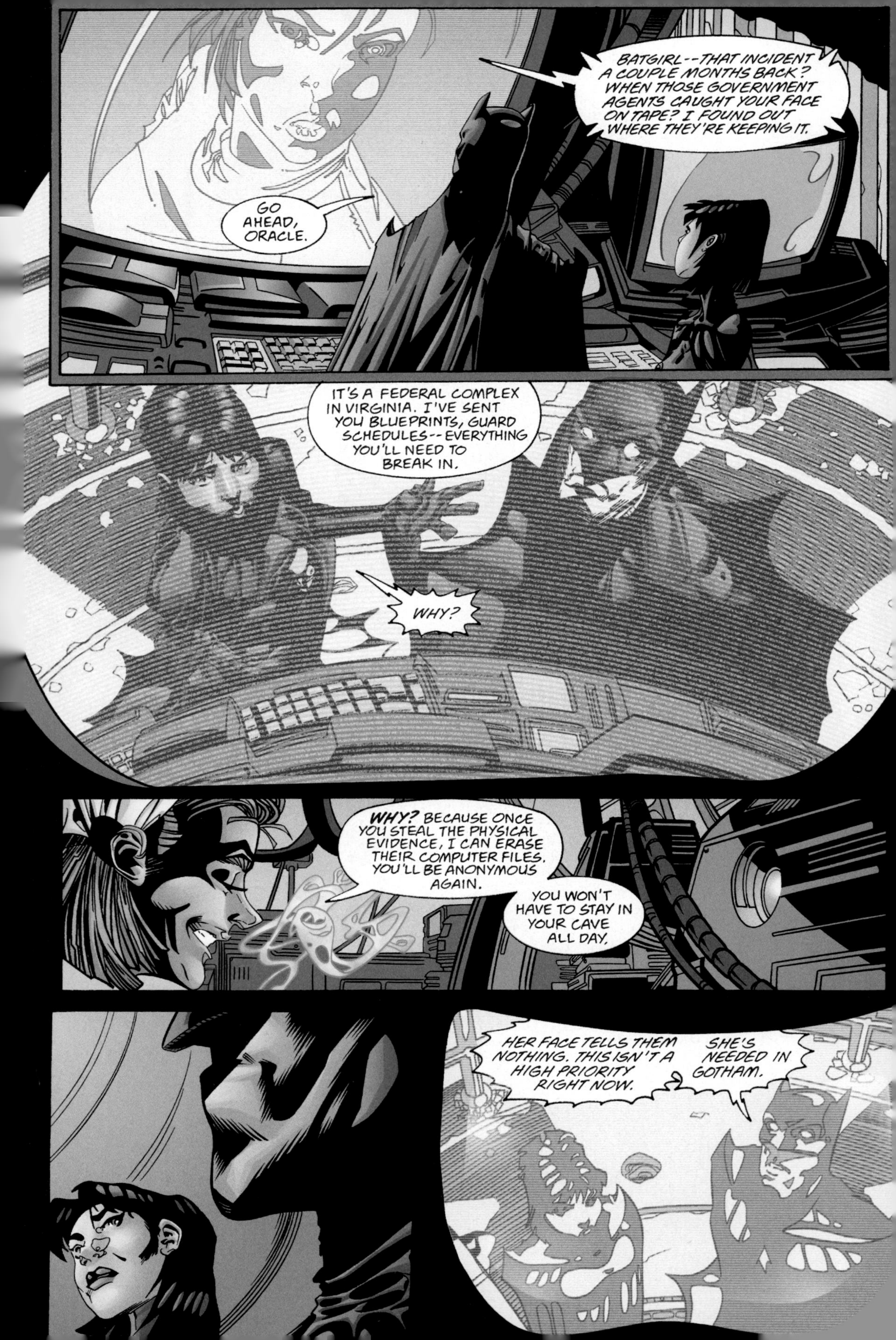
BATGIRL--THAT INCIDENT A COUPLE MONTHS BACK? WHEN THOSE GOVERNMENT AGENTS CAUGHT YOUR FACE ON TAPE? I FOUND OUT WHERE THEY'RE KEEPING IT.
GO AHEAD, ORACLE.
IT'S A FEDERAL COMPLEX IN VIRGINIA. I'VE SENT YOU BLUEPRINTS, GUARD SCHEDULES--EVERYTHING YOU'LL NEED TO BREAK IN.
WHY?
WHY? BECAUSE ONCE YOU STEAL THE PHYSICAL EVIDENCE, I CAN ERASE THEIR COMPUTER FILES. YOU'LL BE ANONYMOUS AGAIN.
YOU WON'T HAVE TO STAY IN YOUR CAVE ALL DAY.
HER FACE TELLS THEM NOTHING. THIS ISN'T A HIGH PRIORITY RIGHT NOW.
SHE'S NEEDED IN GOTHAM.

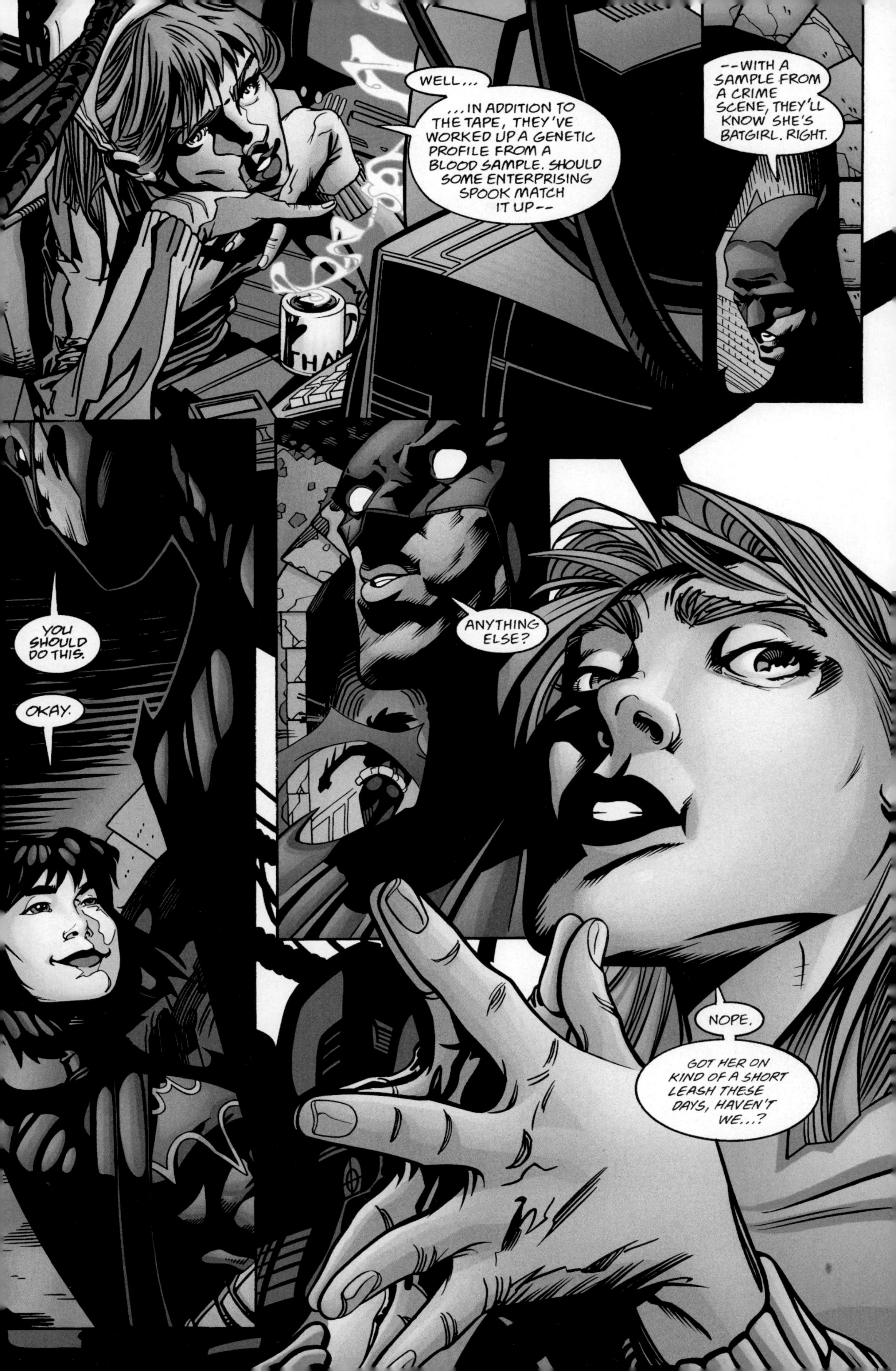
WELL...
...IN ADDITION TO THE TAPE, THEY'VE WORKED UP A GENETIC PROFILE FROM A BLOOD SAMPLE. SHOULD SOME ENTERPRISING SPOOK MATCH IT UP--
--WITH A SAMPLE FROM A CRIME SCENE, THEY'LL KNOW SHE'S BATGIRL. RIGHT.
YOU SHOULD DO THIS.
OKAY.
ANYTHING ELSE?
NOPE.
GOT HER ON KIND OF A SHORT LEASH THESE DAYS, HAVEN'T WE...?

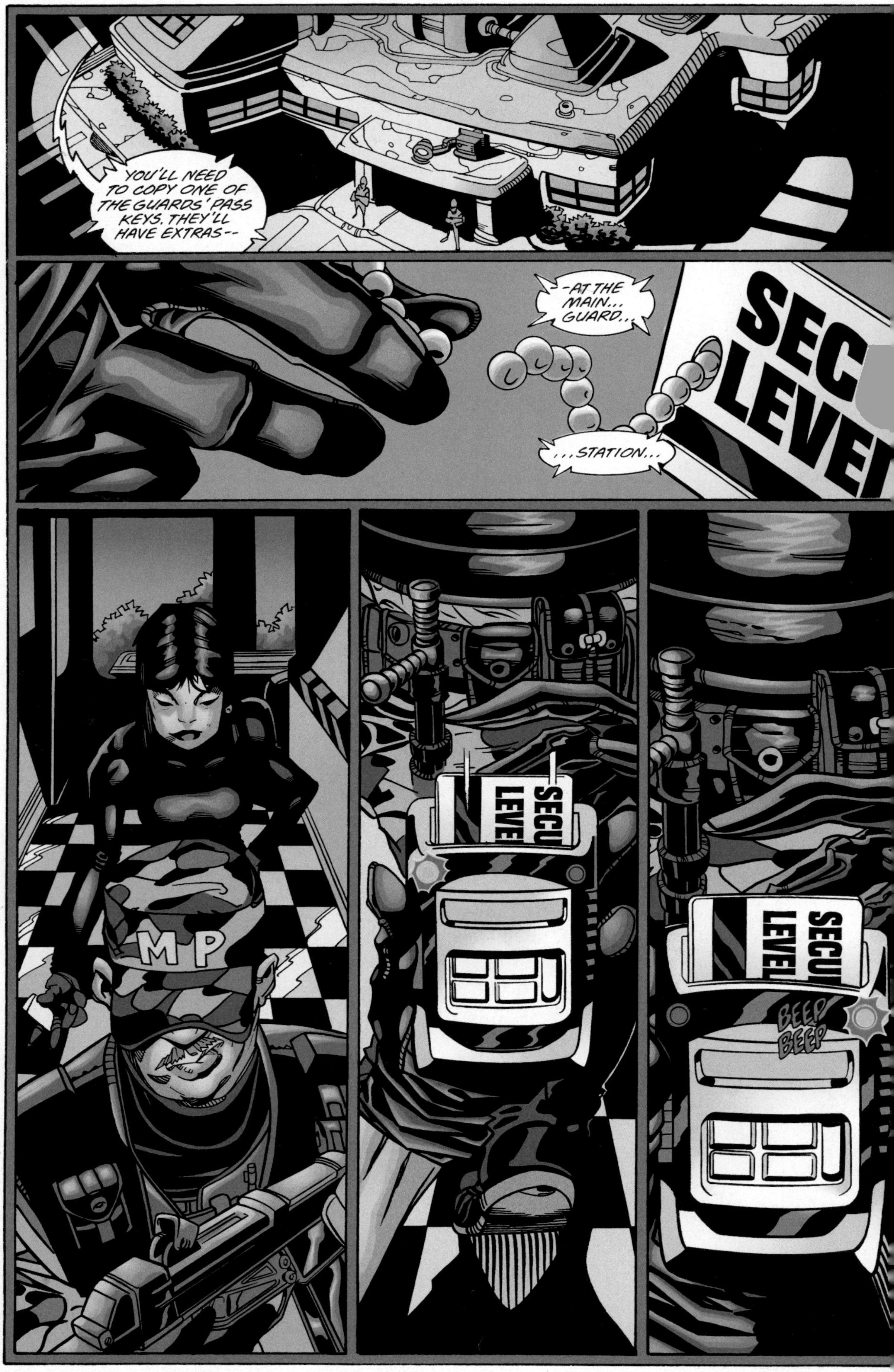
YOU'LL NEED TO COPY ONE OF THE GUARDS' PASS KEYS. THEY'LL HAVE EXTRAS--
-AT THE MAIN... GUARD...
...STATION...
SEC LEVE
MP
SECU LEVE
SECU LEVE
BEEP BEEP

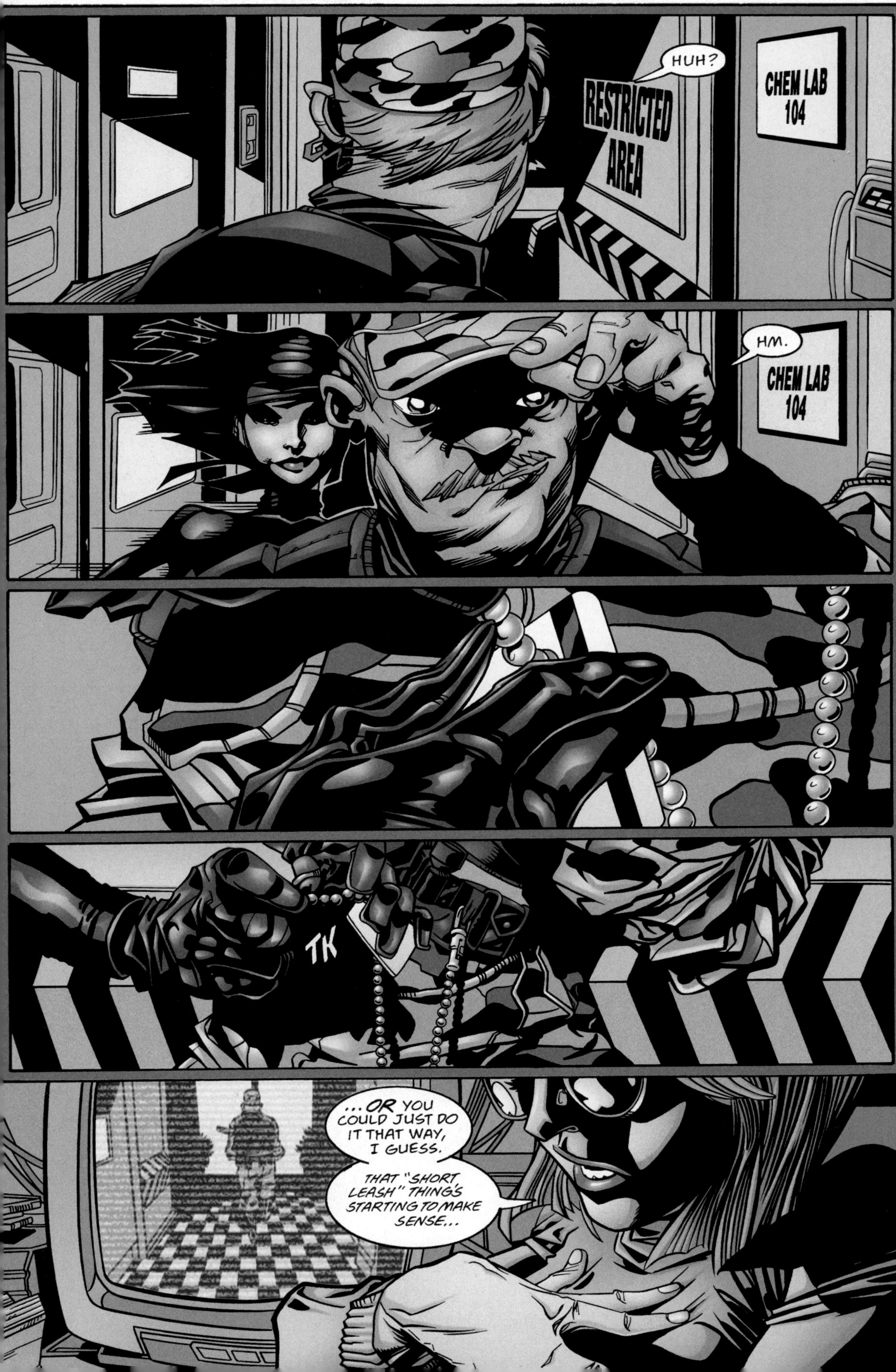
HUH?
RESTRICTED AREA
CHEM LAB 104
HM.
CHEM LAB 104
TK
...OR YOU COULD JUST DO IT THAT WAY, I GUESS.
THAT "SHORT LEASH" THING'S STARTING TO MAKE SENSE...

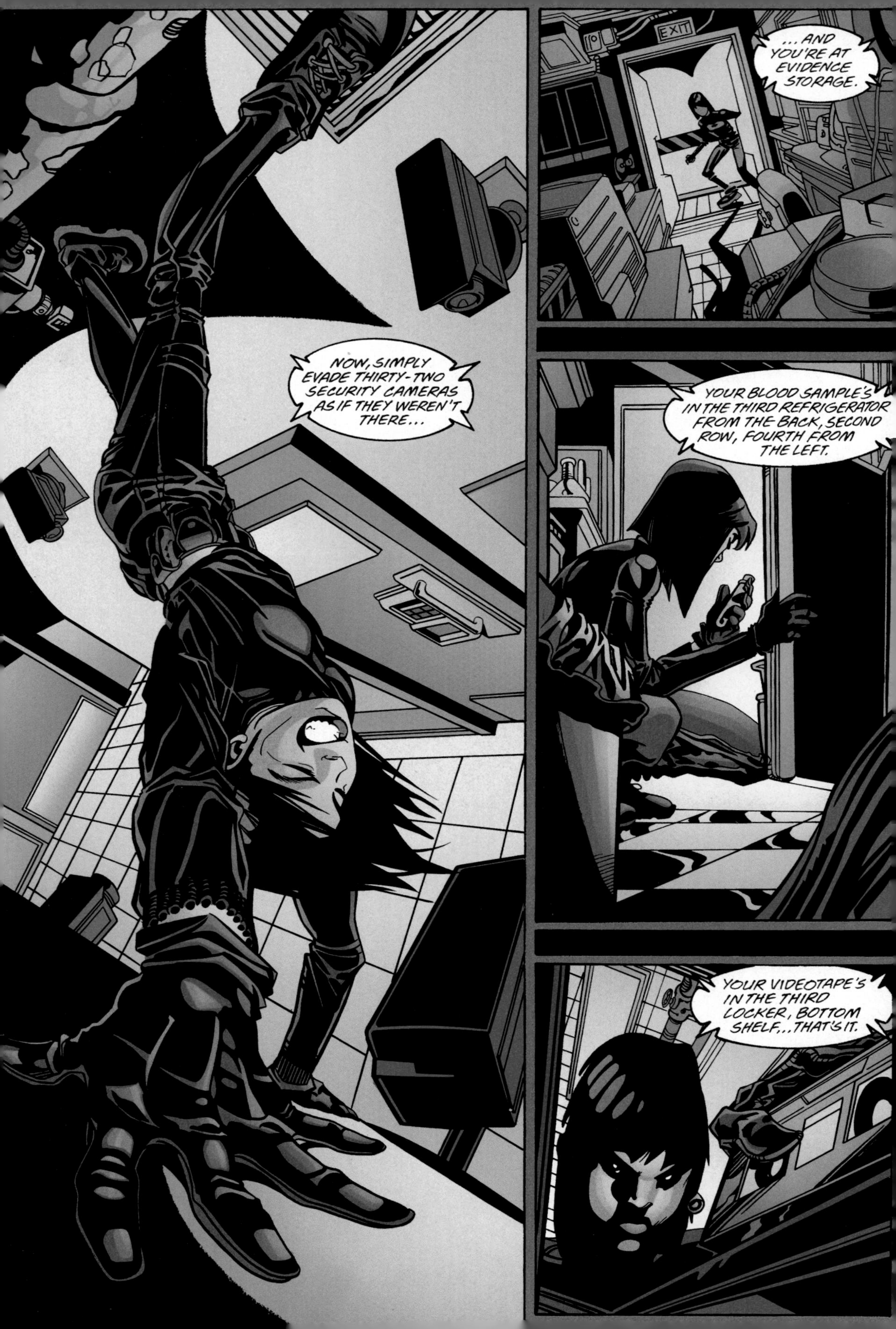
NOW, SIMPLY EVADE THIRTY-TWO SECURITY CAMERAS AS IF THEY WEREN'T THERE...
EXIT
...AND YOU'RE AT EVIDENCE STORAGE.
YOUR BLOOD SAMPLE'S IN THE THIRD REFRIGERATOR FROM THE BACK, SECOND ROW, FOURTH FROM THE LEFT.
YOUR VIDEOTAPE'S IN THE THIRD LOCKER, BOTTOM SHELF...THAT'S IT.

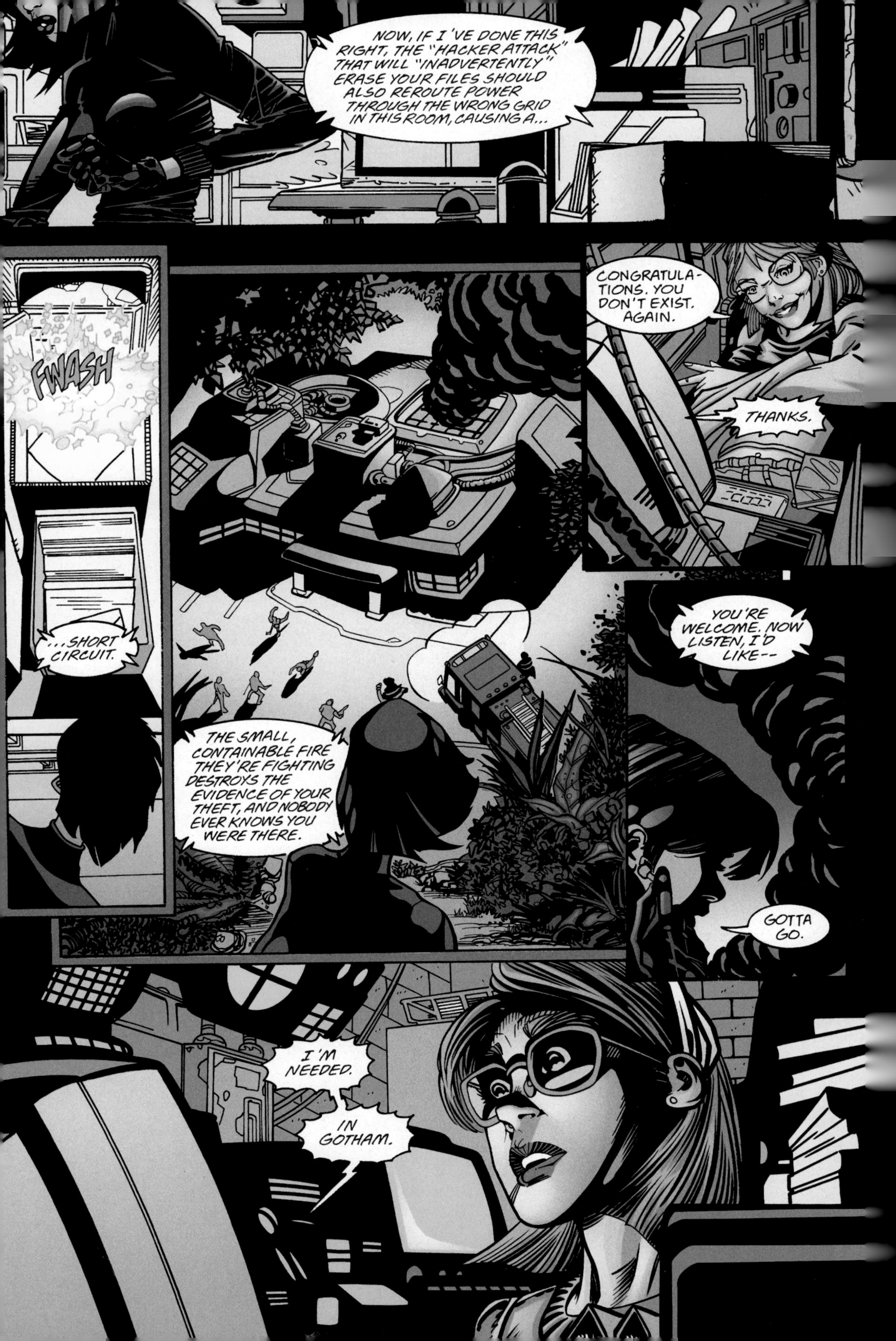
NOW, IF I'VE DONE THIS RIGHT, THE "HACKER ATTACK" THAT WILL "INADVERTENTLY" ERASE YOUR FILES SHOULD ALSO REROUTE POWER THROUGH THE WRONG GRID IN THIS ROOM, CAUSING A...
FWASH
...SHORT CIRCUIT.
THE SMALL, CONTAINABLE FIRE THEY'RE FIGHTING DESTROYS THE EVIDENCE OF YOUR THEFT, AND NOBODY EVER KNOWS YOU WERE THERE.
CONGRATULATIONS. YOU DON'T EXIST. AGAIN.
THANKS.
YOU'RE WELCOME. NOW LISTEN, I'D LIKE--
GOTTA GO.
I'M NEEDED.
IN GOTHAM.

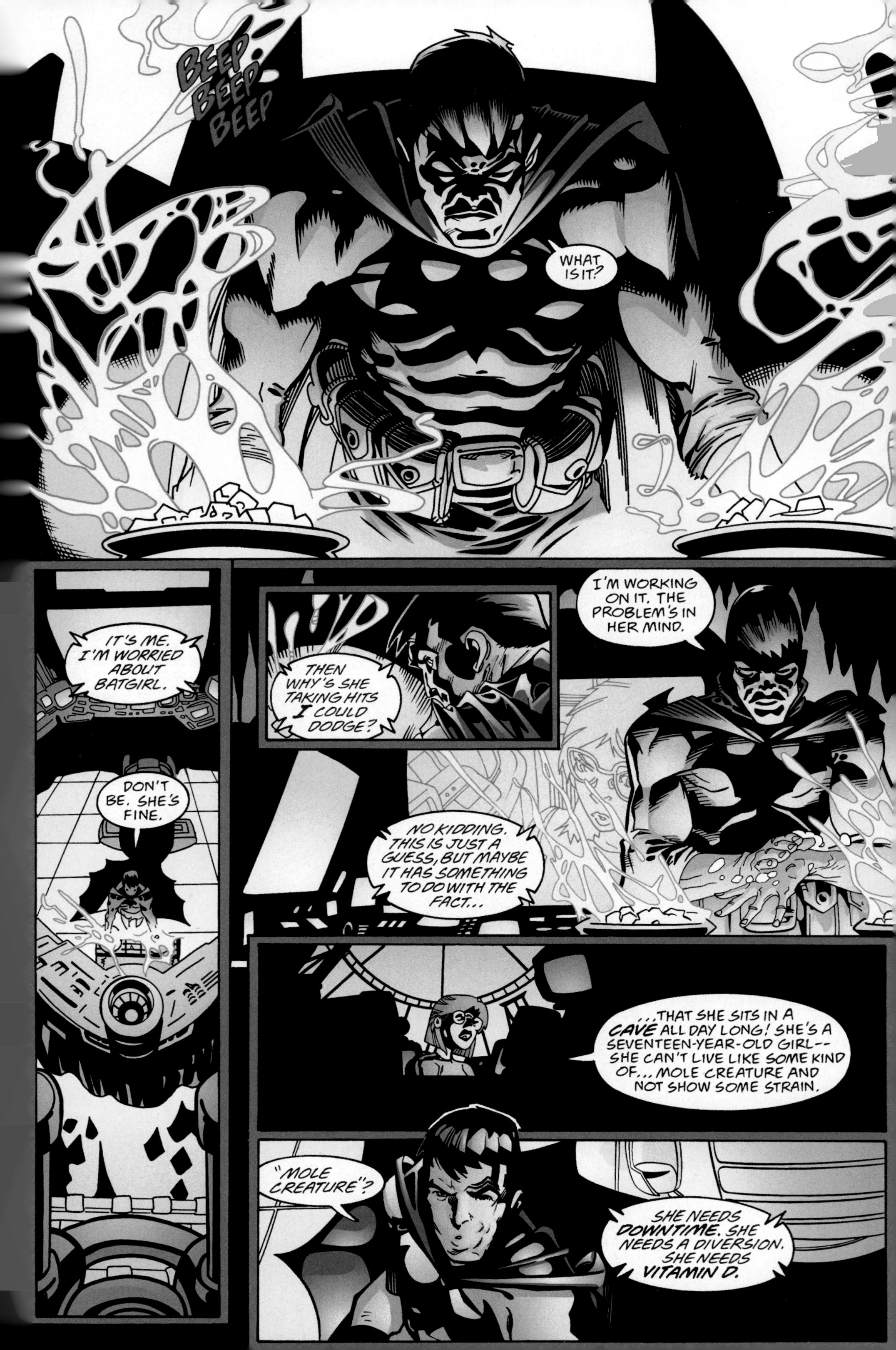
BEEP BEEP BEEP
WHAT IS IT?
IT'S ME. I'M WORRIED ABOUT BATGIRL.
DON'T BE. SHE'S FINE.
THEN WHY'S SHE TAKING HITS I COULD DODGE?
I'M WORKING ON IT. THE PROBLEM'S IN HER MIND.
NO KIDDING. THIS IS JUST A GUESS, BUT MAYBE IT HAS SOMETHING TO DO WITH THE FACT...
...THAT SHE SITS IN A CAVE ALL DAY LONG! SHE'S A SEVENTEEN-YEAR-OLD GIRL-- SHE CAN'T LIVE LIKE SOME KIND OF... MOLE CREATURE AND NOT SHOW SOME STRAIN.
"MOLE CREATURE"?
SHE NEEDS DOWNTIME. SHE NEEDS A DIVERSION. SHE NEEDS VITAMIN D.

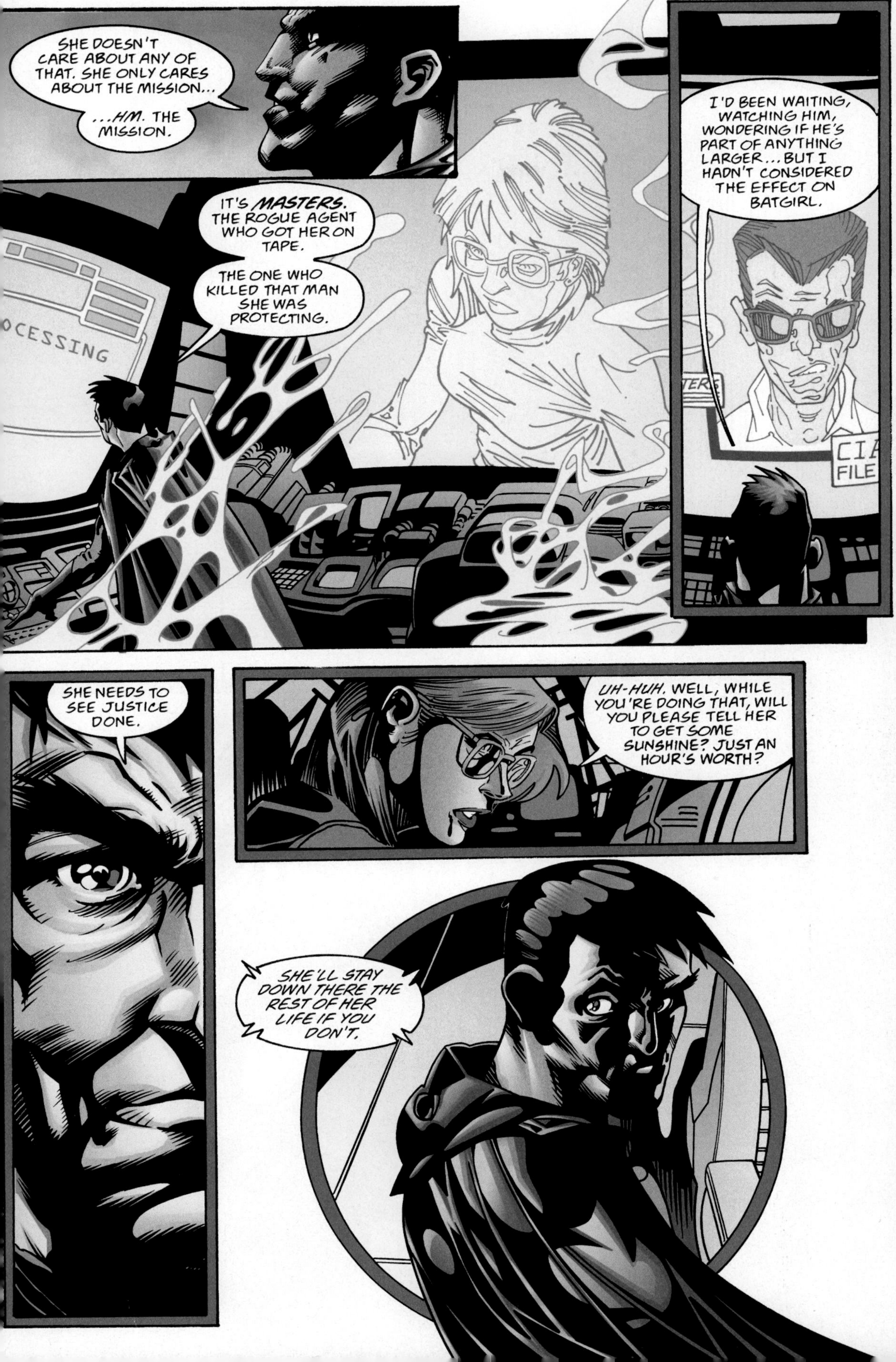
SHE DOESN'T CARE ABOUT ANY OF THAT. SHE ONLY CARES ABOUT THE MISSION...
...HM. THE MISSION.
I'D BEEN WAITING, WATCHING HIM, WONDERING IF HE'S PART OF ANYTHING LARGER... BUT I HADN'T CONSIDERED THE EFFECT ON BATGIRL.
IT'S MASTERS. THE ROGUE AGENT WHO GOT HER ON TAPE.
THE ONE WHO KILLED THAT MAN SHE WAS PROTECTING.
OCESSING
CIA FILE
SHE NEEDS TO SEE JUSTICE DONE.
UH-HUH. WELL, WHILE YOU'RE DOING THAT, WILL YOU PLEASE TELL HER TO GET SOME SUNSHINE? JUST AN HOUR'S WORTH?
SHE'LL STAY DOWN THERE THE REST OF HER LIFE IF YOU DON'T.

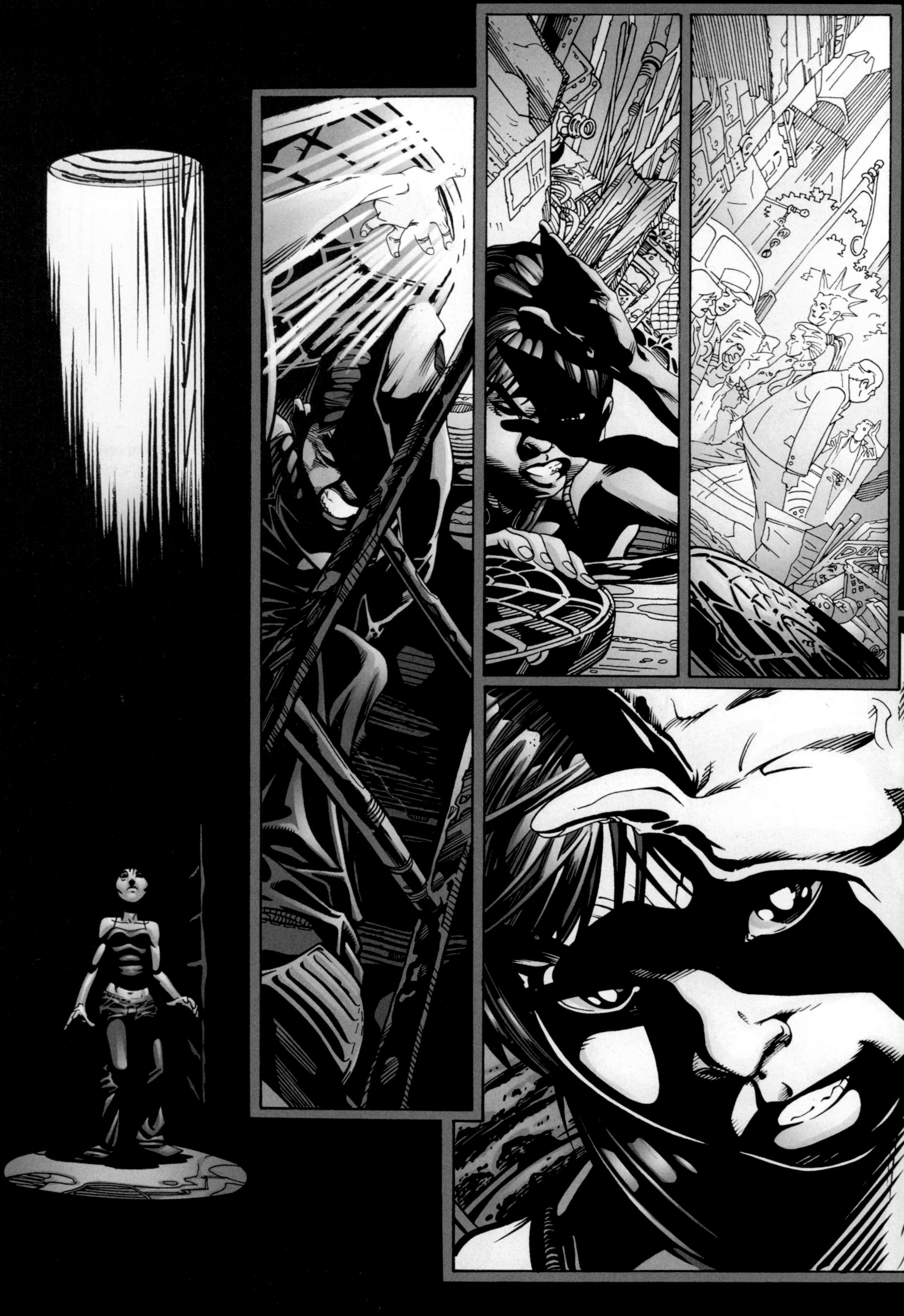

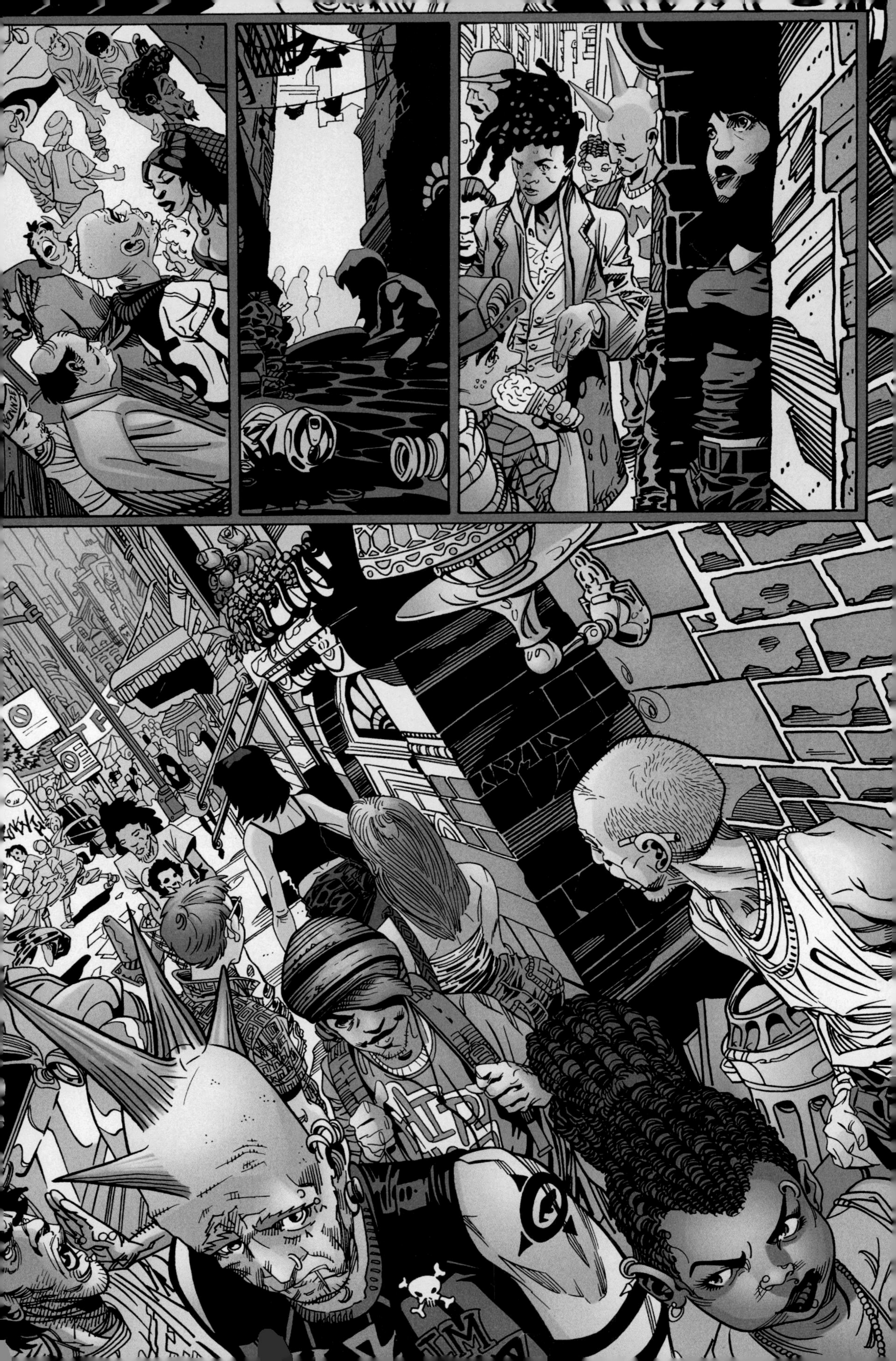

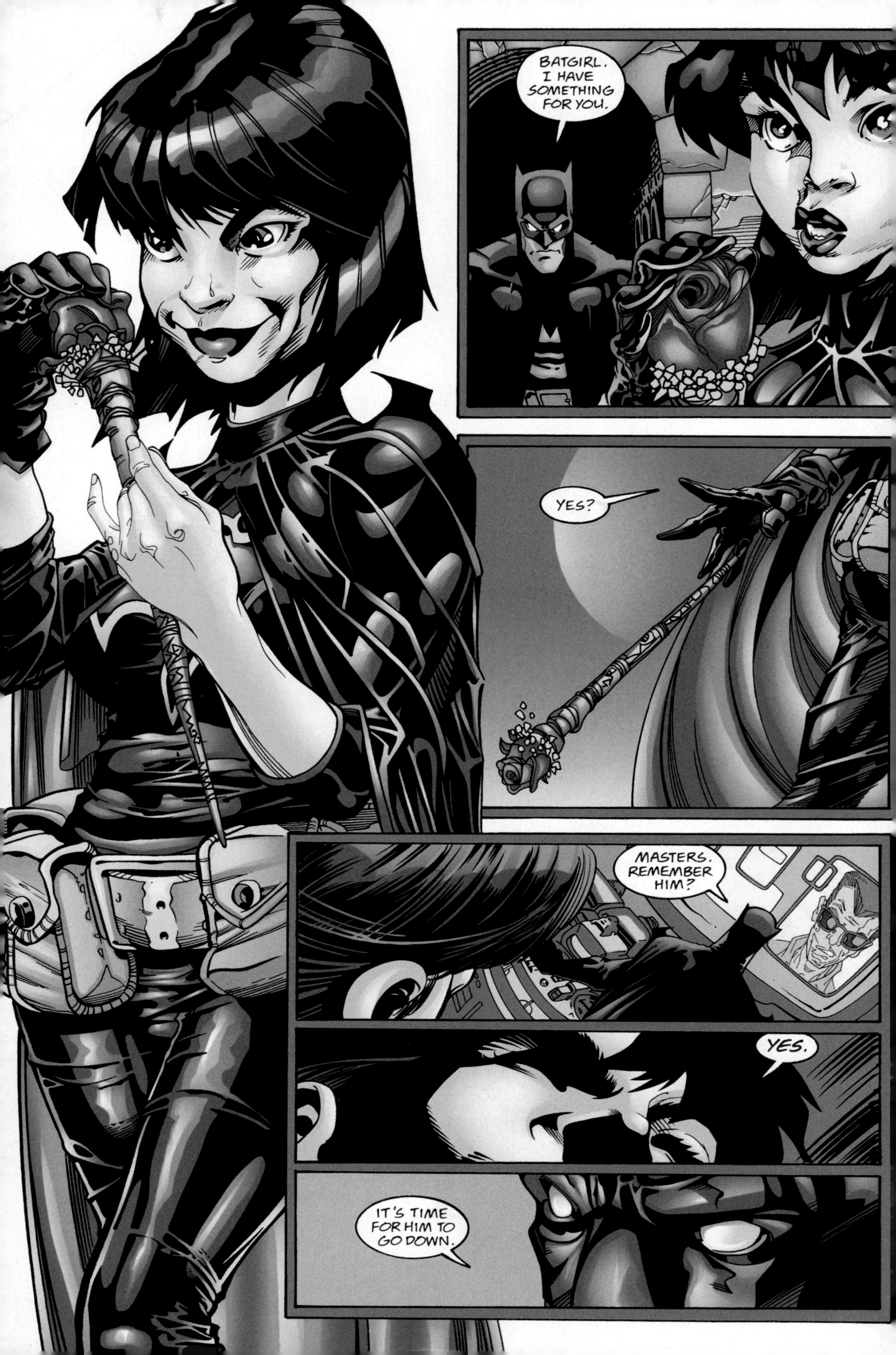
BATGIRL. I HAVE SOMETHING FOR YOU.
YES?
MASTERS. REMEMBER HIM?
YES.
IT'S TIME FOR HIM TO GO DOWN.

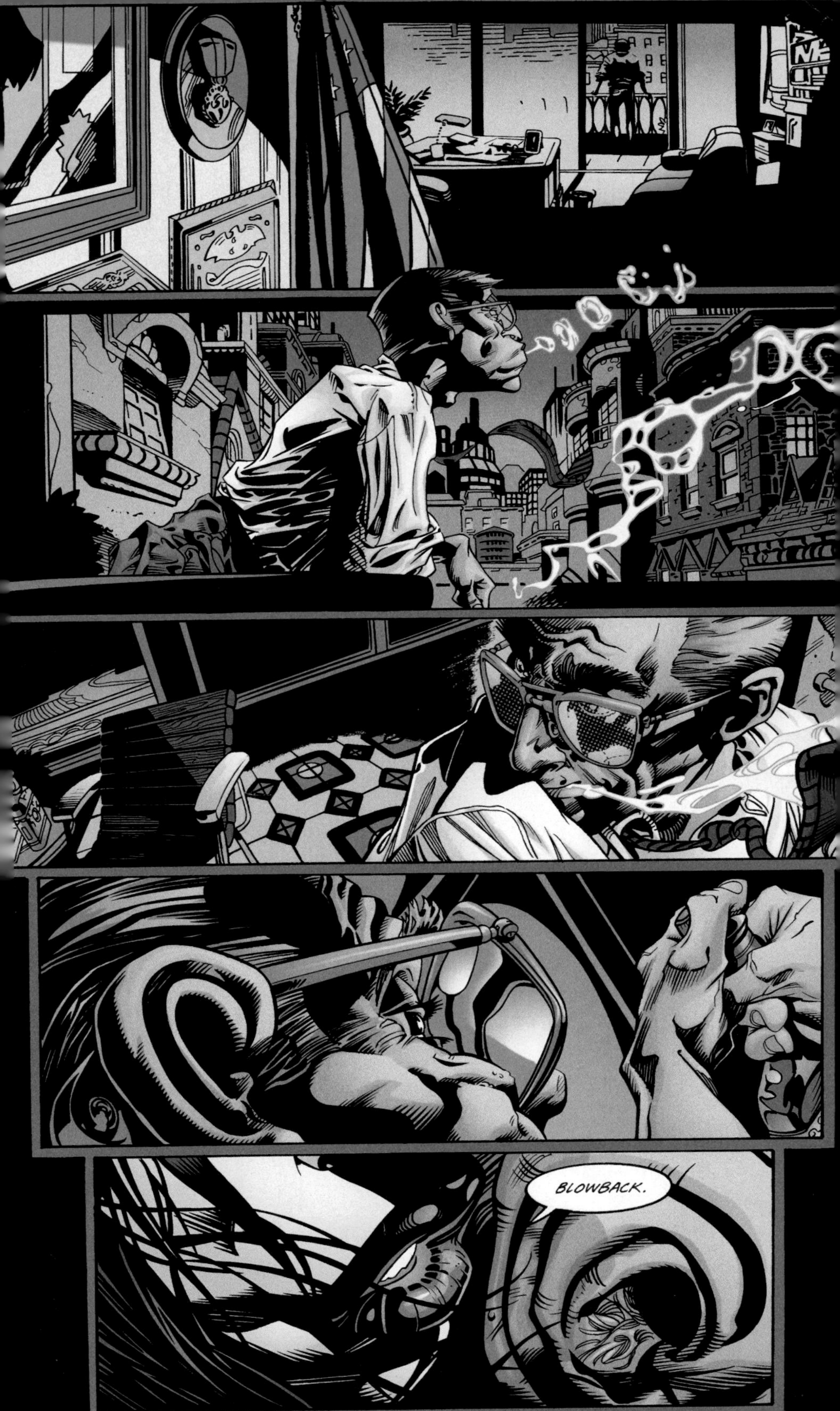
BLOWBACK.

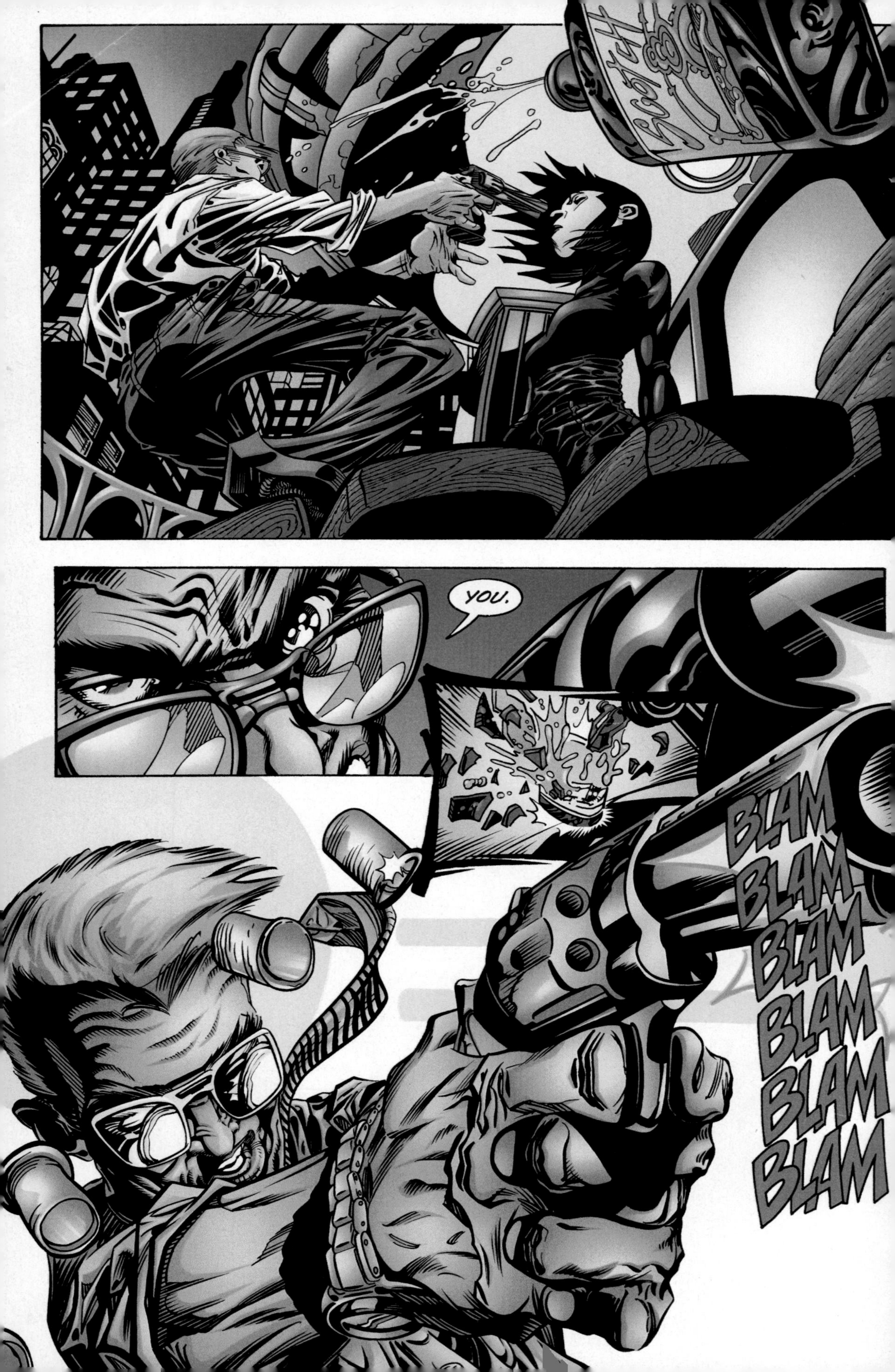
YOU.
BLAM
BLAM
BLAM
BLAM
BLAM
BLAM
BLAM

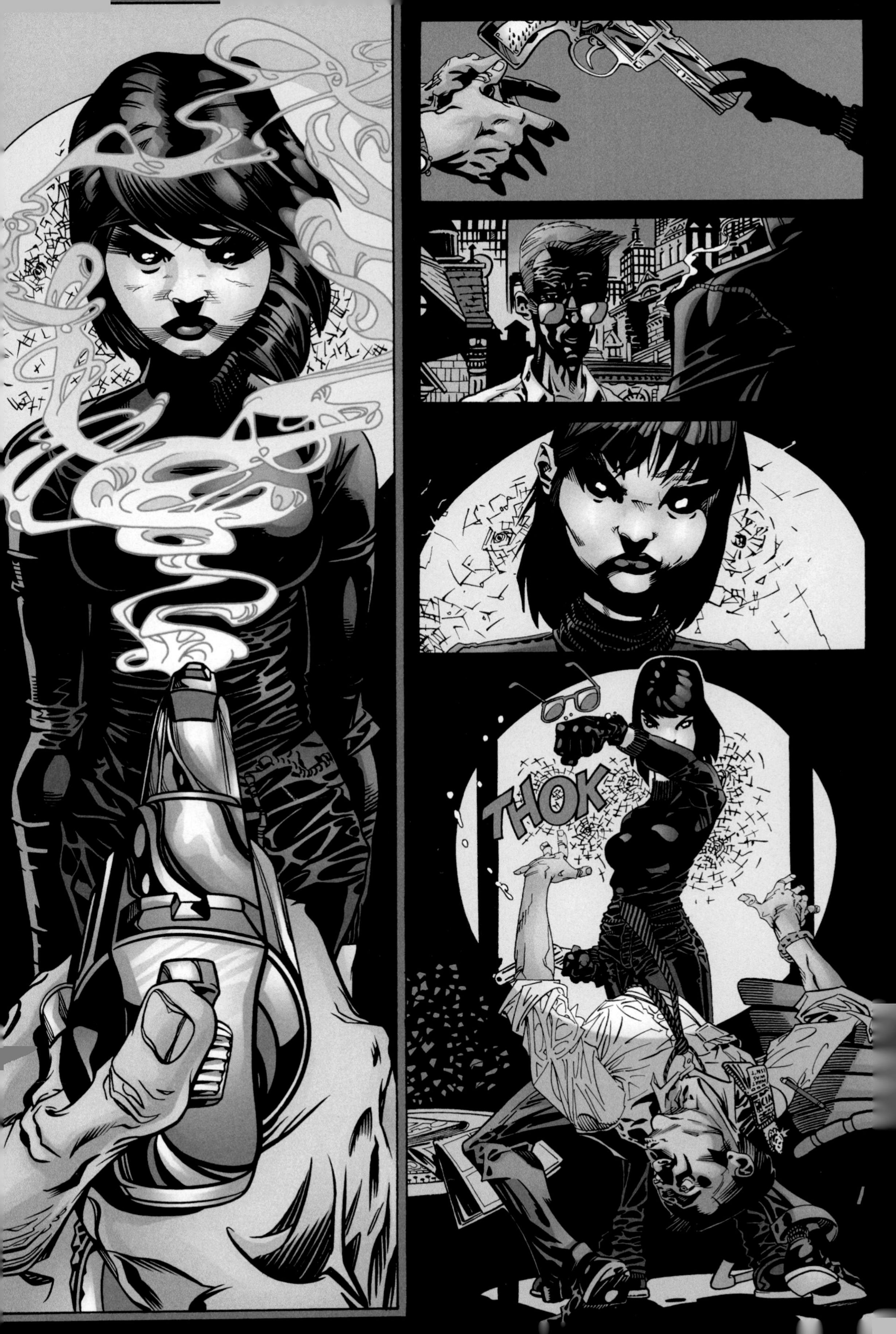
THOK

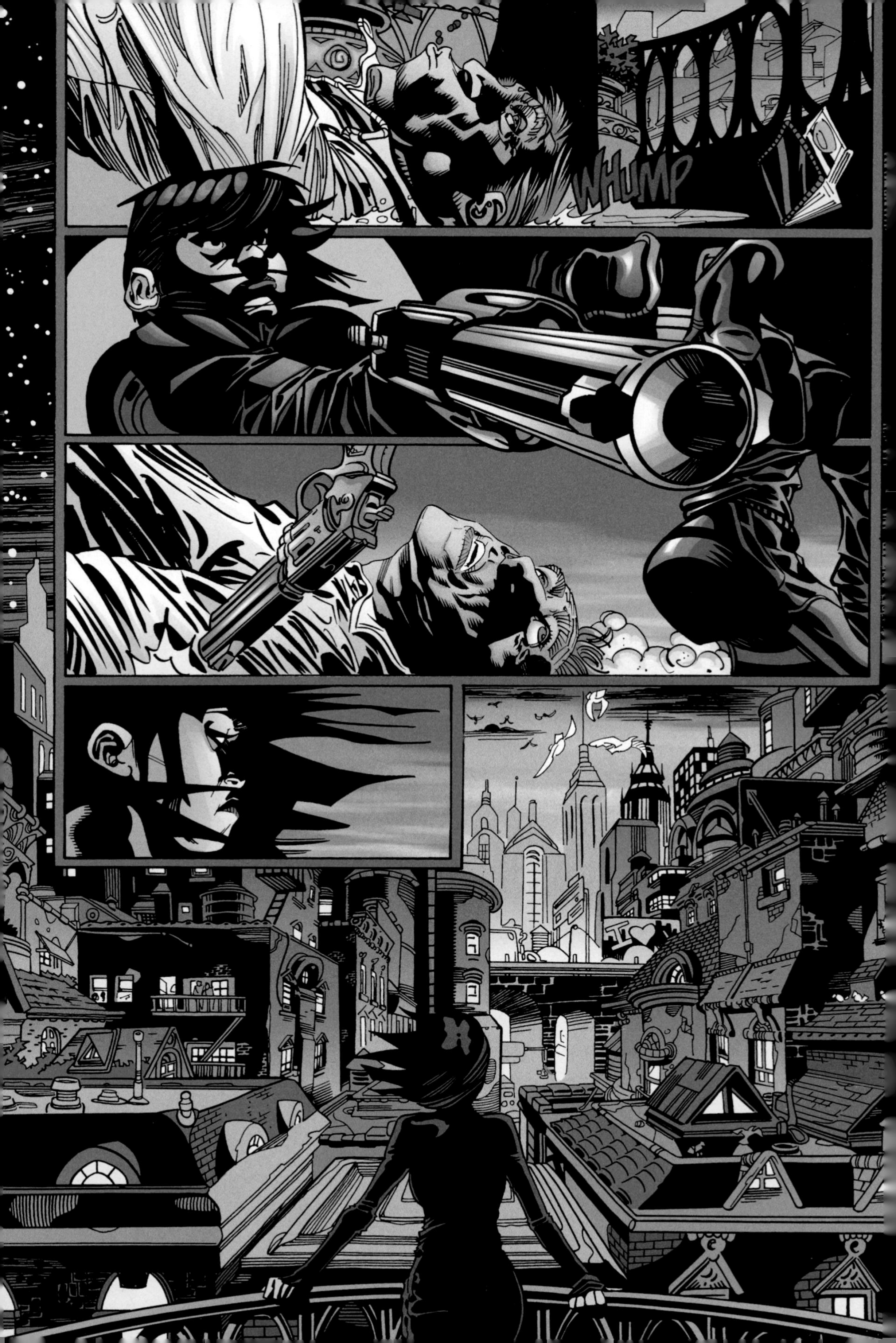
WHUMP

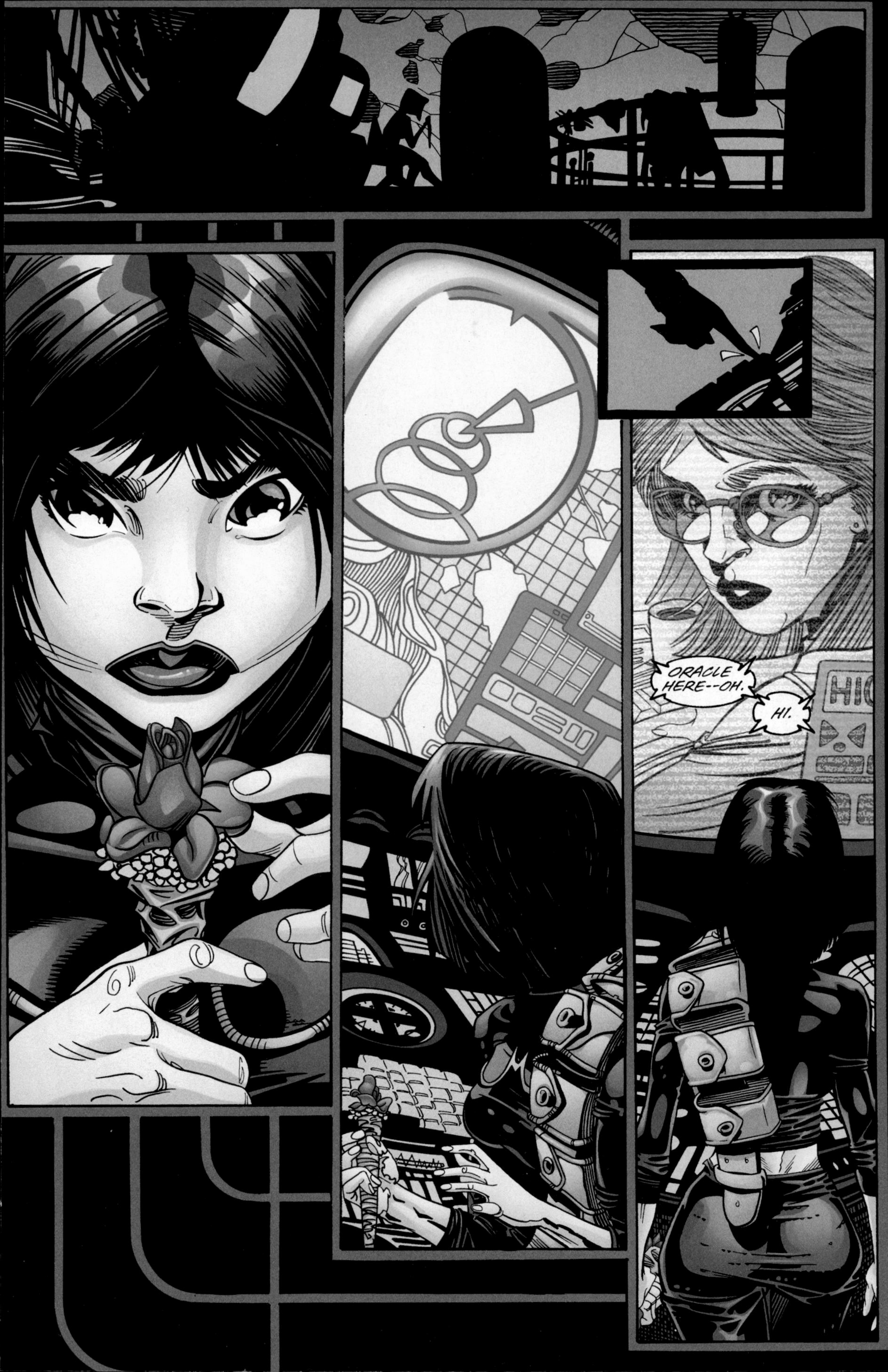
ORACLE HERE--OH.
HI.

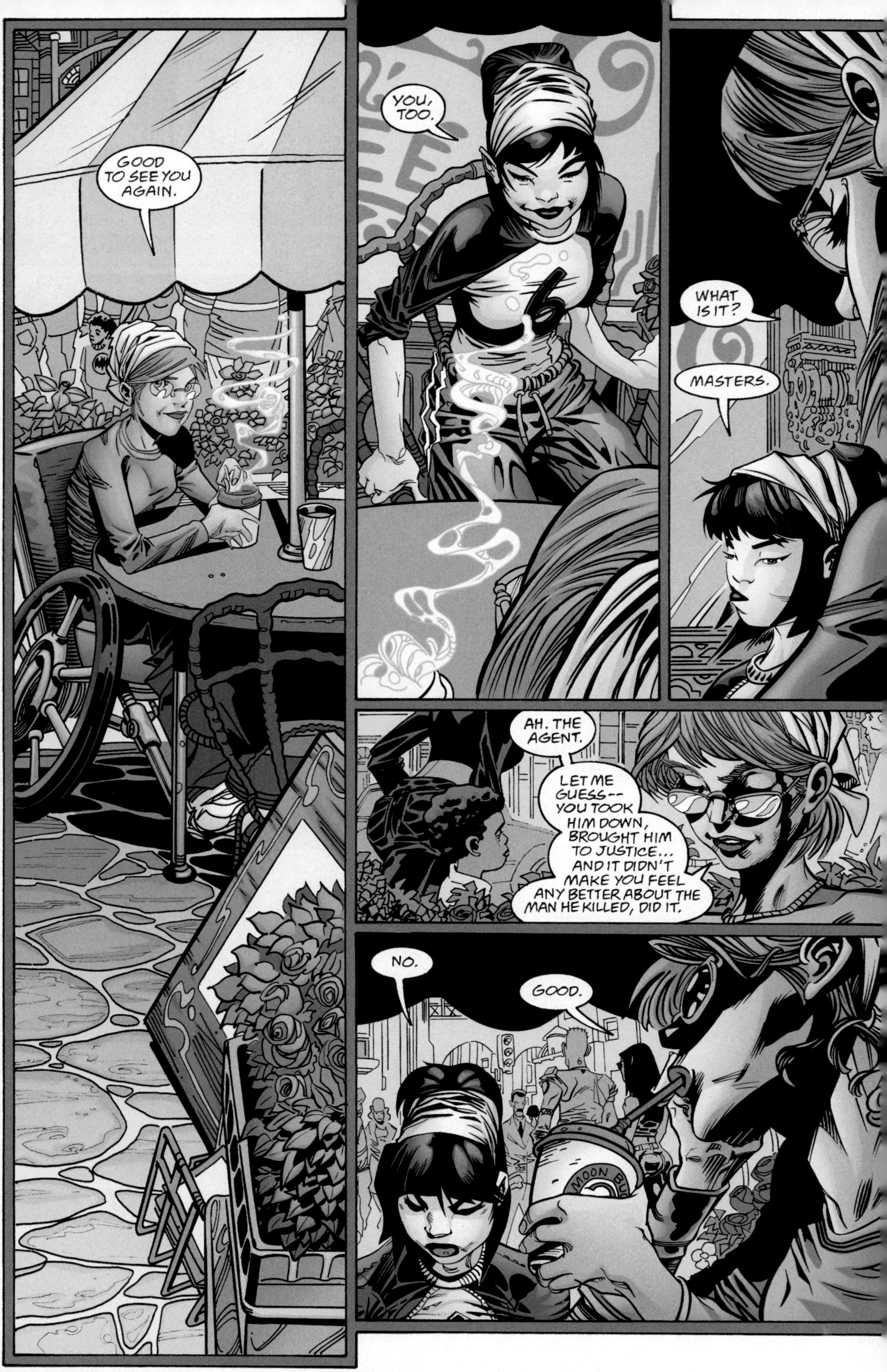
GOOD TO SEE YOU AGAIN.
YOU, TOO.
WHAT IS IT?
MASTERS.
AH. THE AGENT.
LET ME GUESS-- YOU TOOK HIM DOWN, BROUGHT HIM TO JUSTICE... AND IT DIDN'T MAKE YOU FEEL ANY BETTER ABOUT THE MAN HE KILLED, DID IT.
NO.
GOOD.

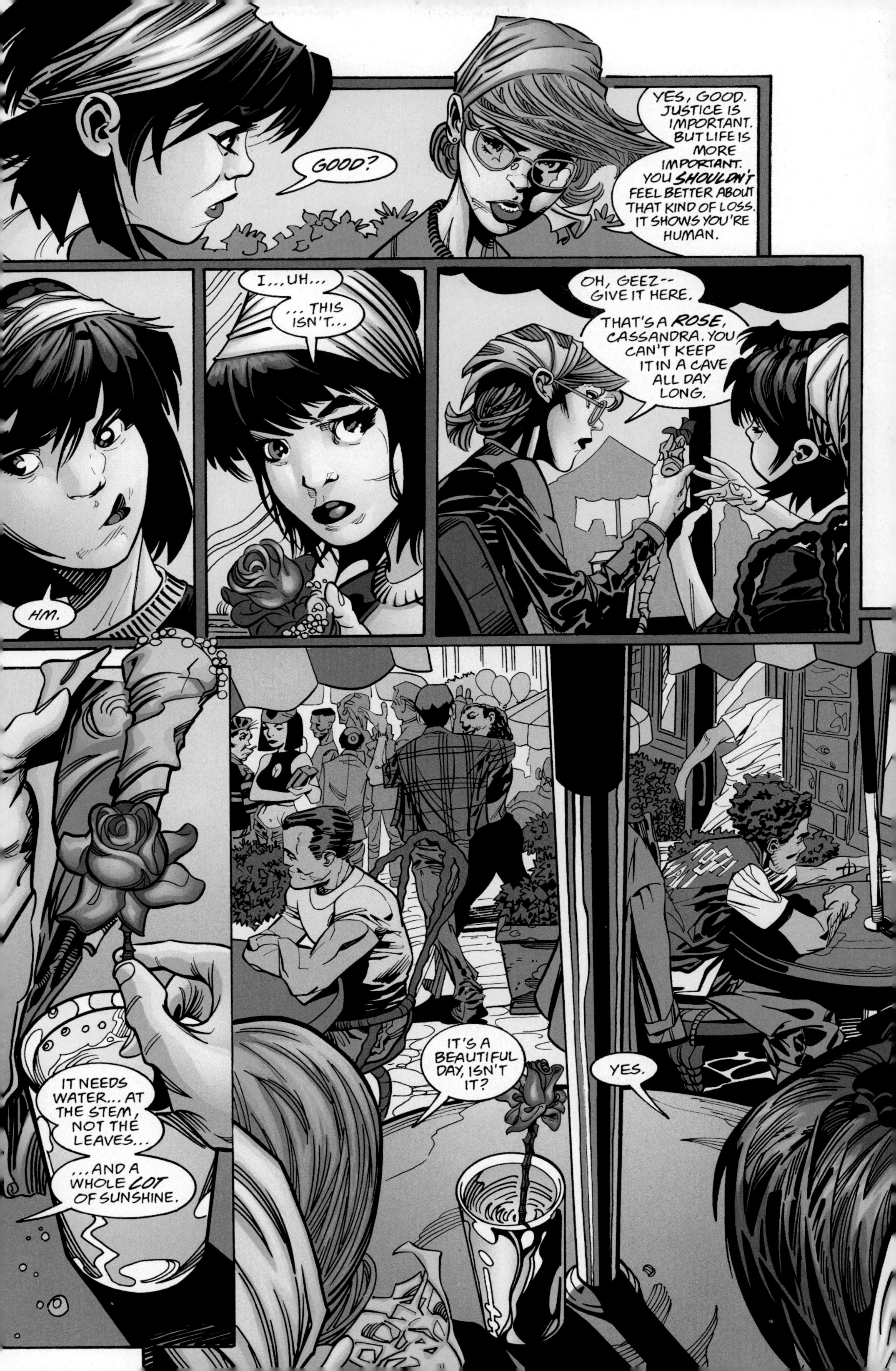
GOOD?
YES, GOOD. JUSTICE IS IMPORTANT. BUT LIFE IS MORE IMPORTANT. YOU SHOULDN'T FEEL BETTER ABOUT THAT KIND OF LOSS. IT SHOWS YOU'RE HUMAN.
HM.
I... UH...
... THIS ISN'T...
OH, GEEZ-- GIVE IT HERE.
THAT'S A ROSE, CASSANDRA. YOU CAN'T KEEP IT IN A CAVE ALL DAY LONG.
IT NEEDS WATER... AT THE STEM, NOT THE LEAVES...
...AND A WHOLE LOT OF SUNSHINE.
IT'S A BEAUTIFUL DAY, ISN'T IT?
YES.

BATGIRL #18 cover by Damion Scott, Robert Campanella & Patrick Martin

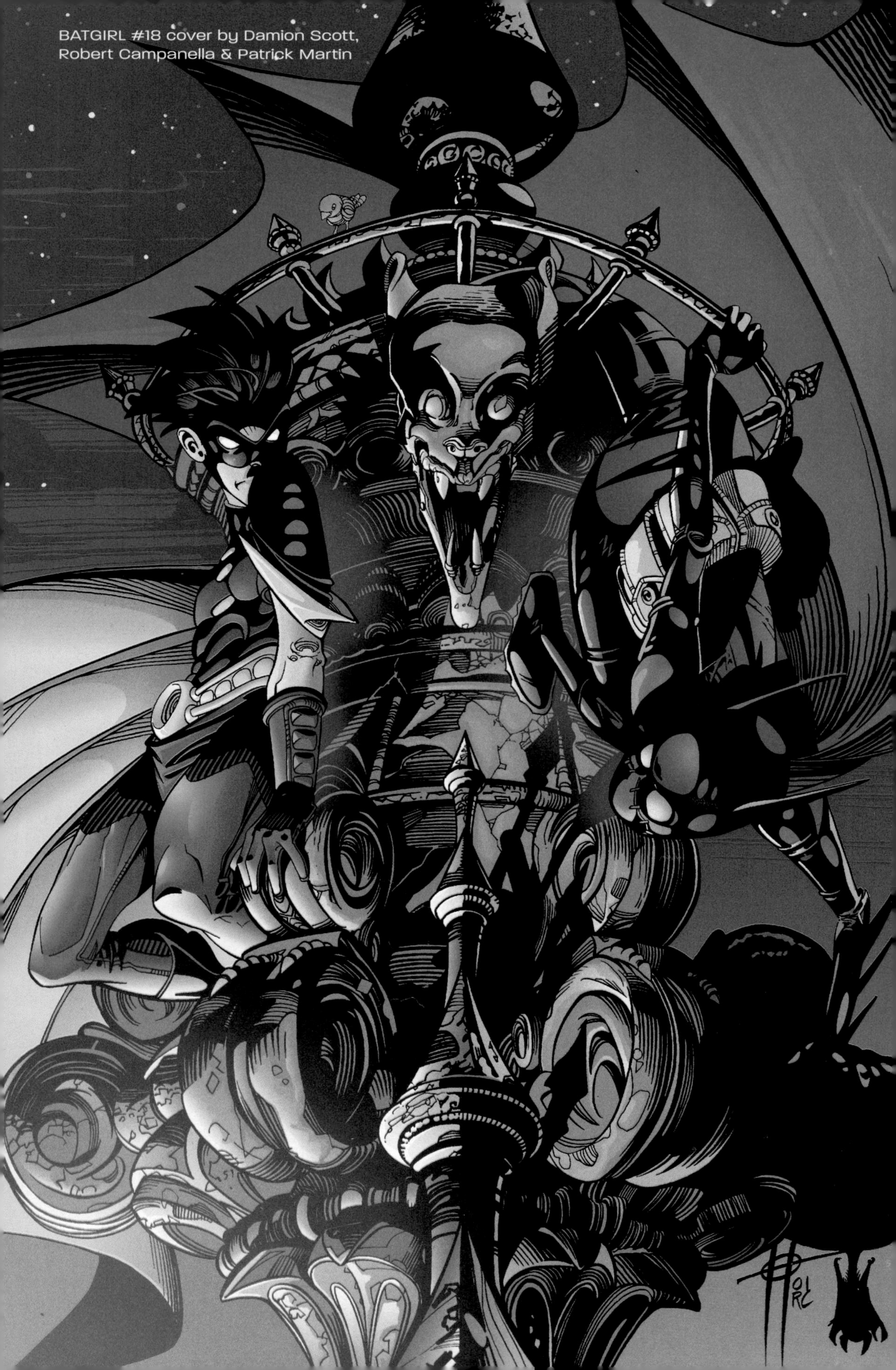

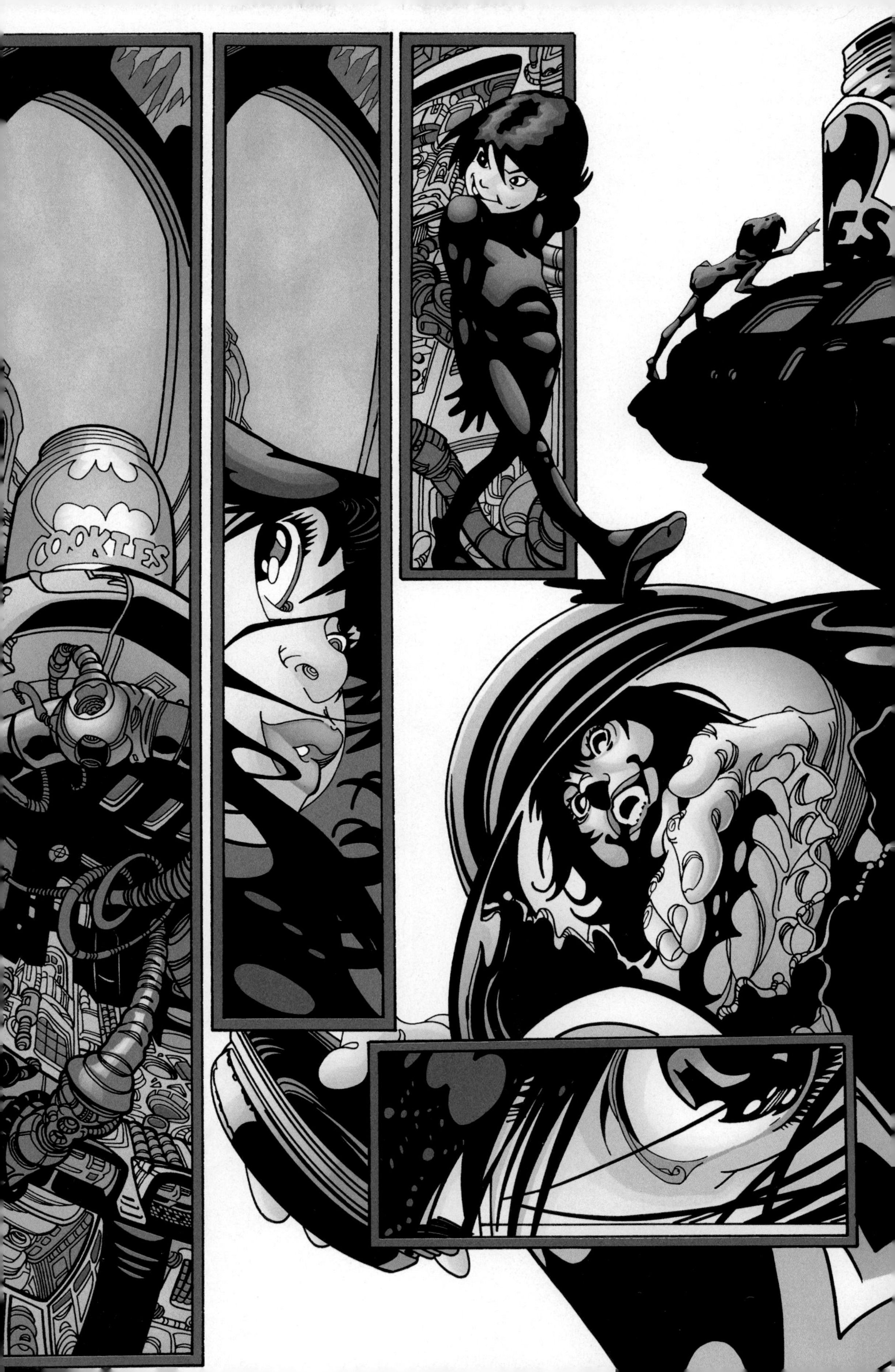
COOKIES

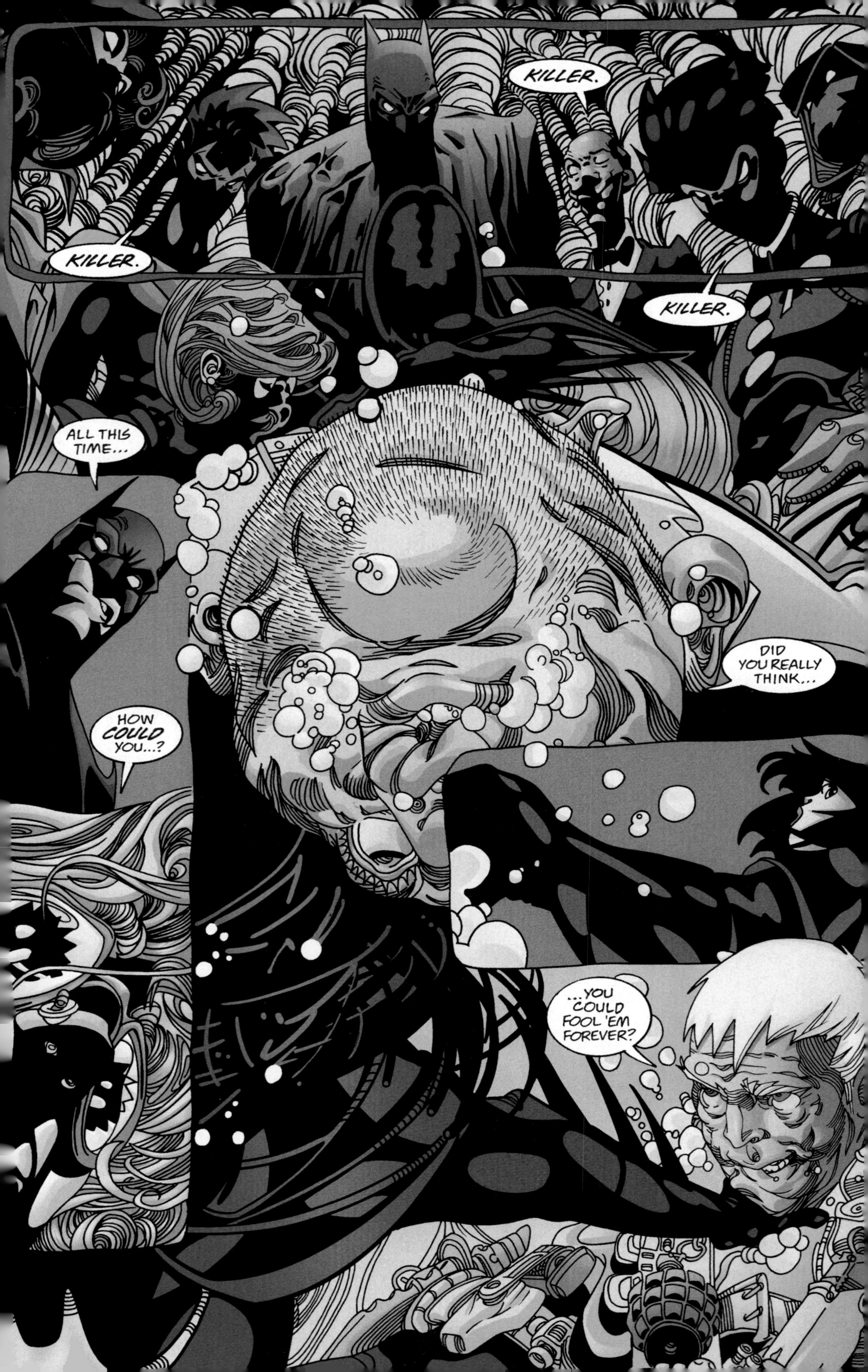
KILLER.
KILLER.
KILLER.
ALL THIS TIME...
HOW COULD YOU...?
DID YOU REALLY THINK...
...YOU COULD FOOL 'EM FOREVER?

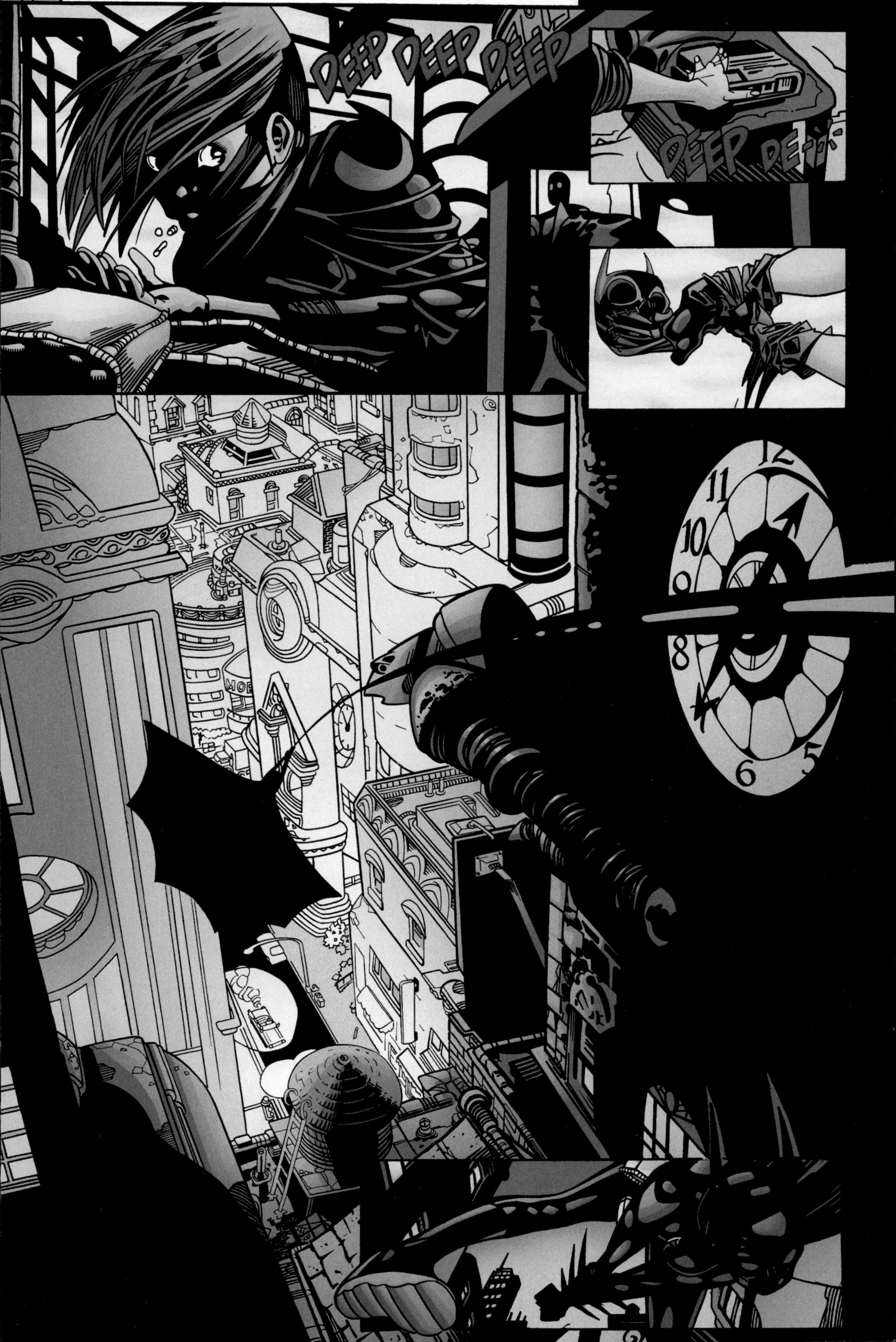
DEEP DEEP DEEP
DEEP DE-

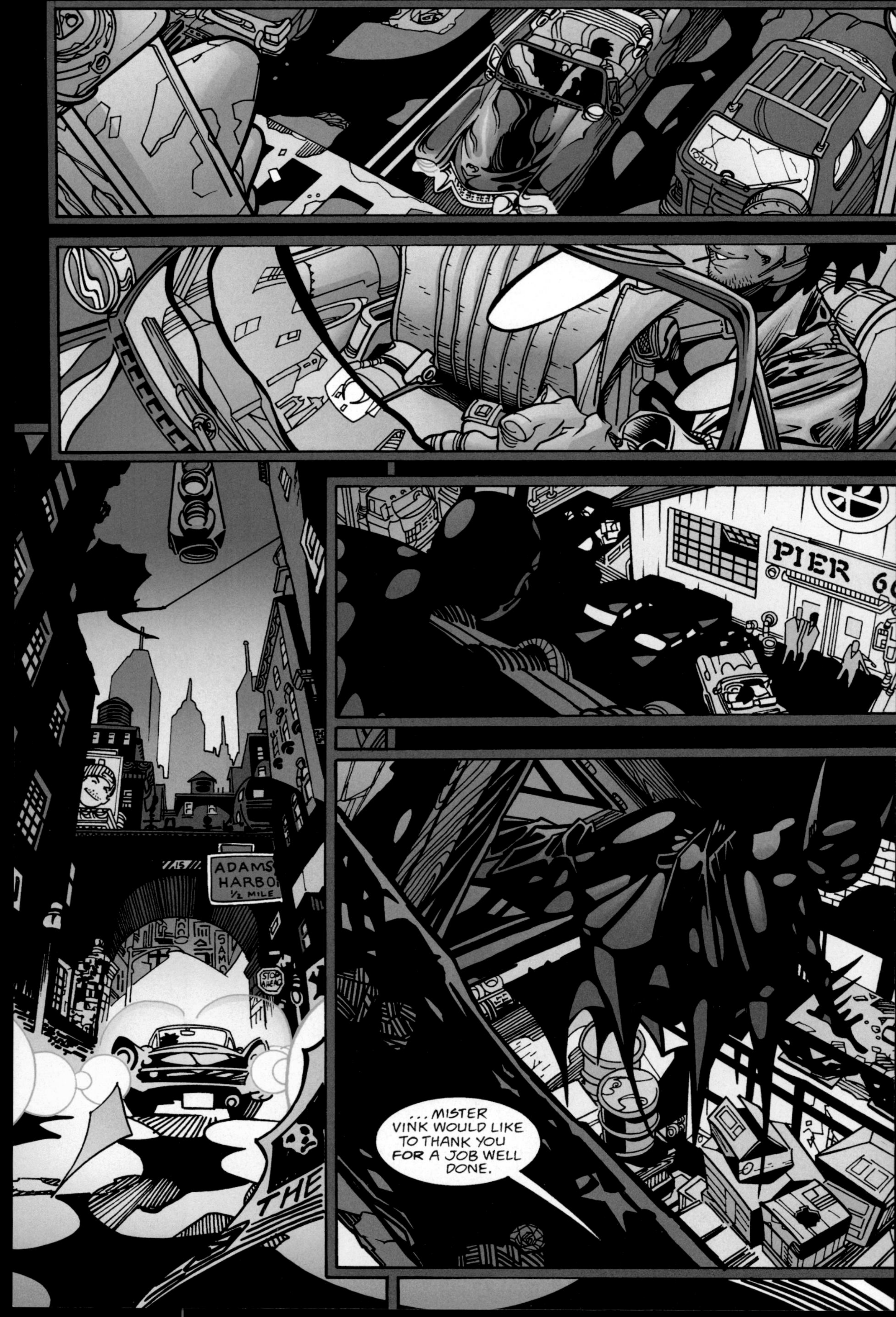

PIER 66
ADAMS HARBOR 1/2 MILE
STOP AHEAD
...MISTER VINK WOULD LIKE TO THANK YOU FOR A JOB WELL DONE.
THE

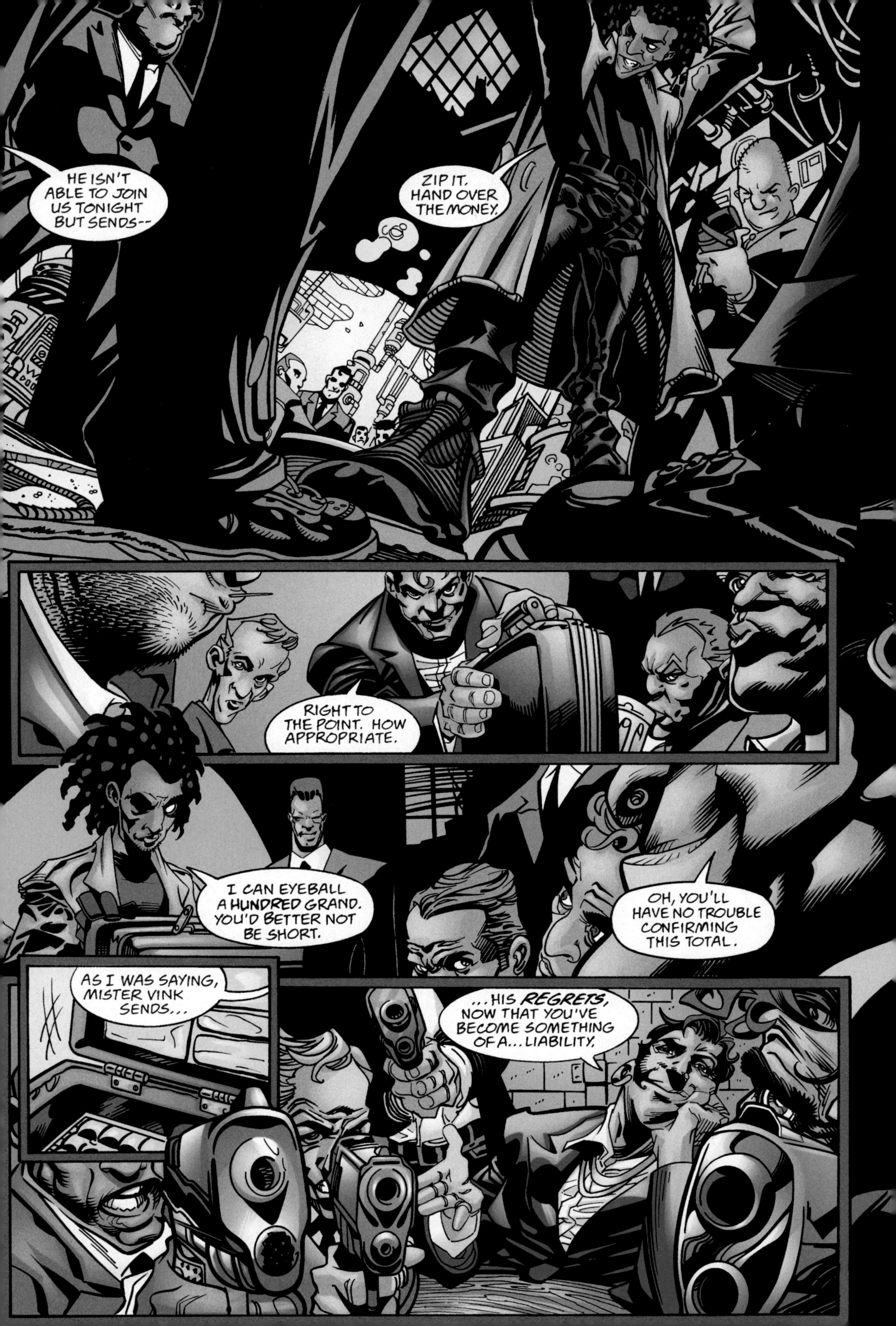
HE ISN'T ABLE TO JOIN US TONIGHT BUT SENDS--
ZIP IT. HAND OVER THE MONEY.
RIGHT TO THE POINT. HOW APPROPRIATE.
I CAN EYEBALL A HUNDRED GRAND. YOU'D BETTER NOT BE SHORT.
OH, YOU'LL HAVE NO TROUBLE CONFIRMING THIS TOTAL.
AS I WAS SAYING, MISTER VINK SENDS...
...HIS REGRETS, NOW THAT YOU'VE BECOME SOMETHING OF A... LIABILITY.

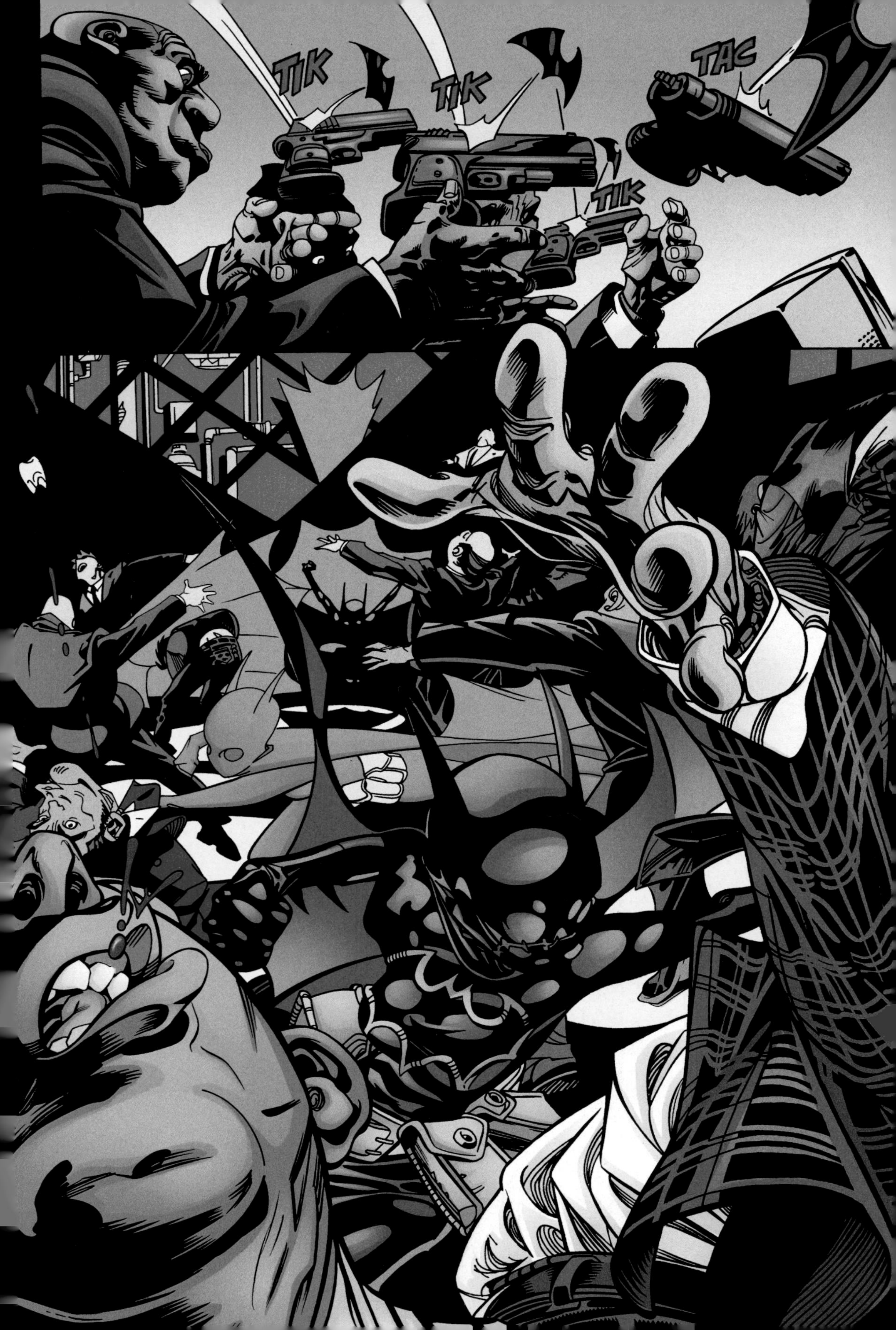
TIK
TIK
TAC
TIK

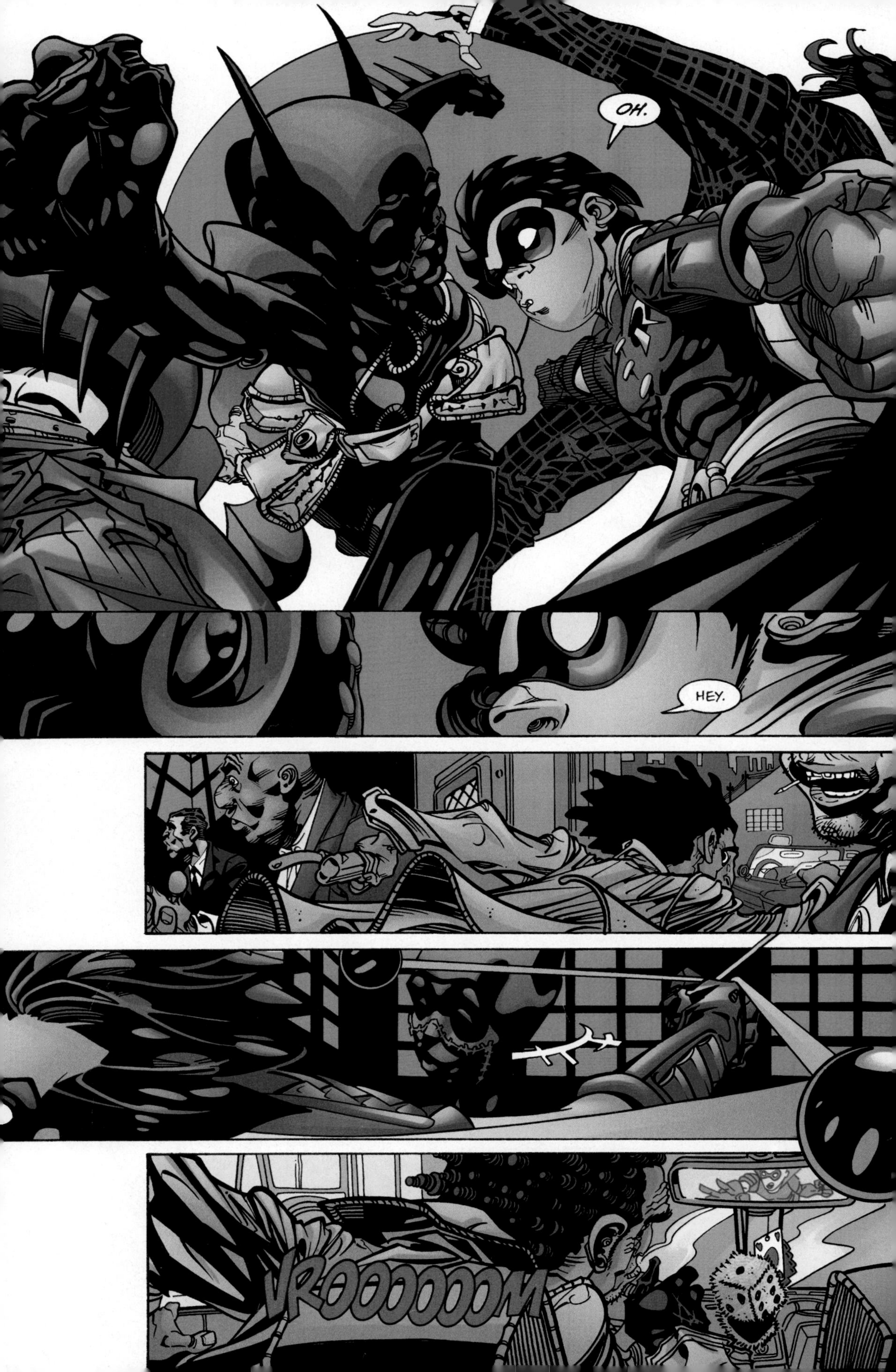
OH.
HEY.
VROOOOOOM

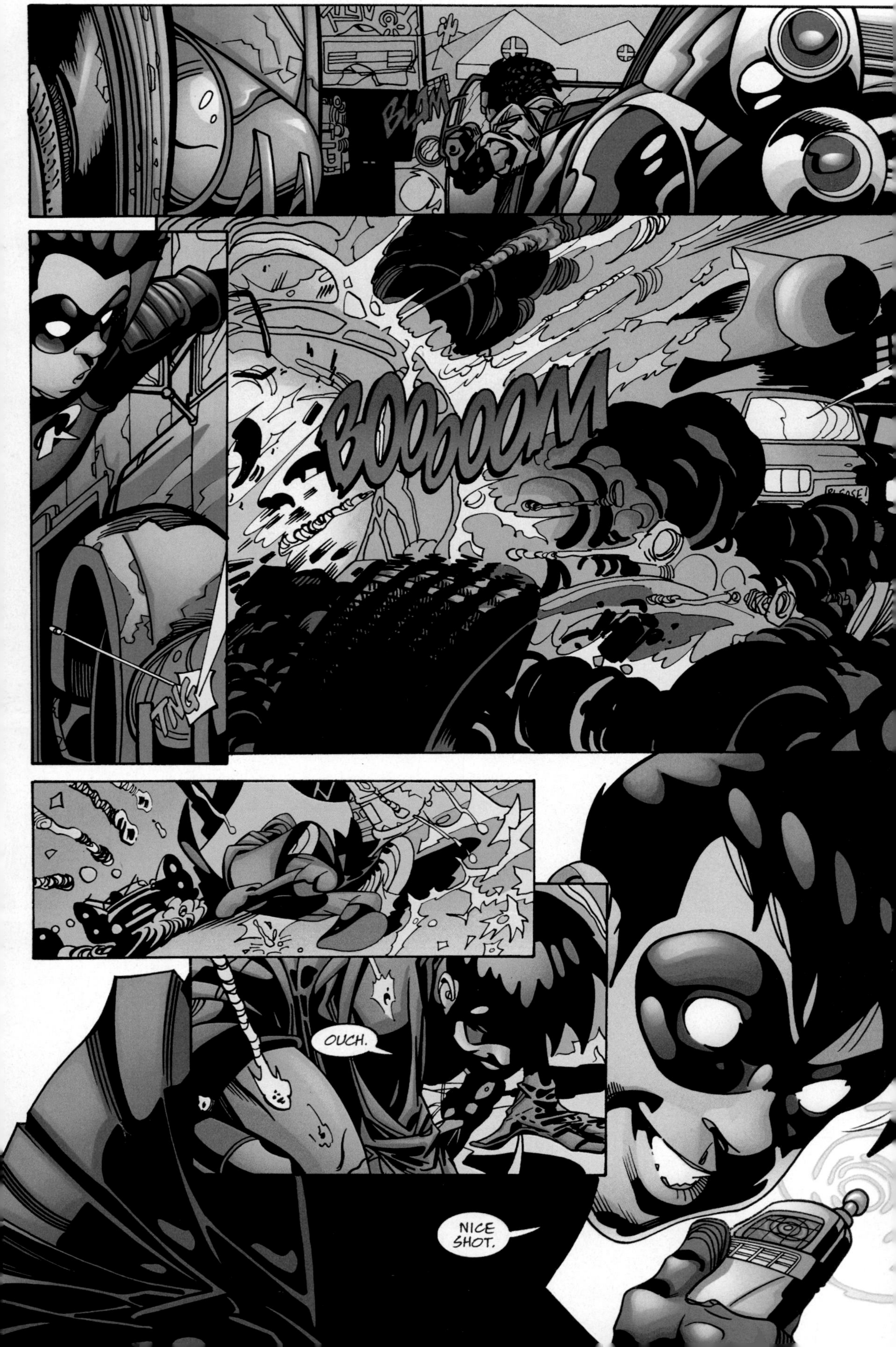
BLAM
BOOOOOM
TNG
OUCH.
NICE SHOT.

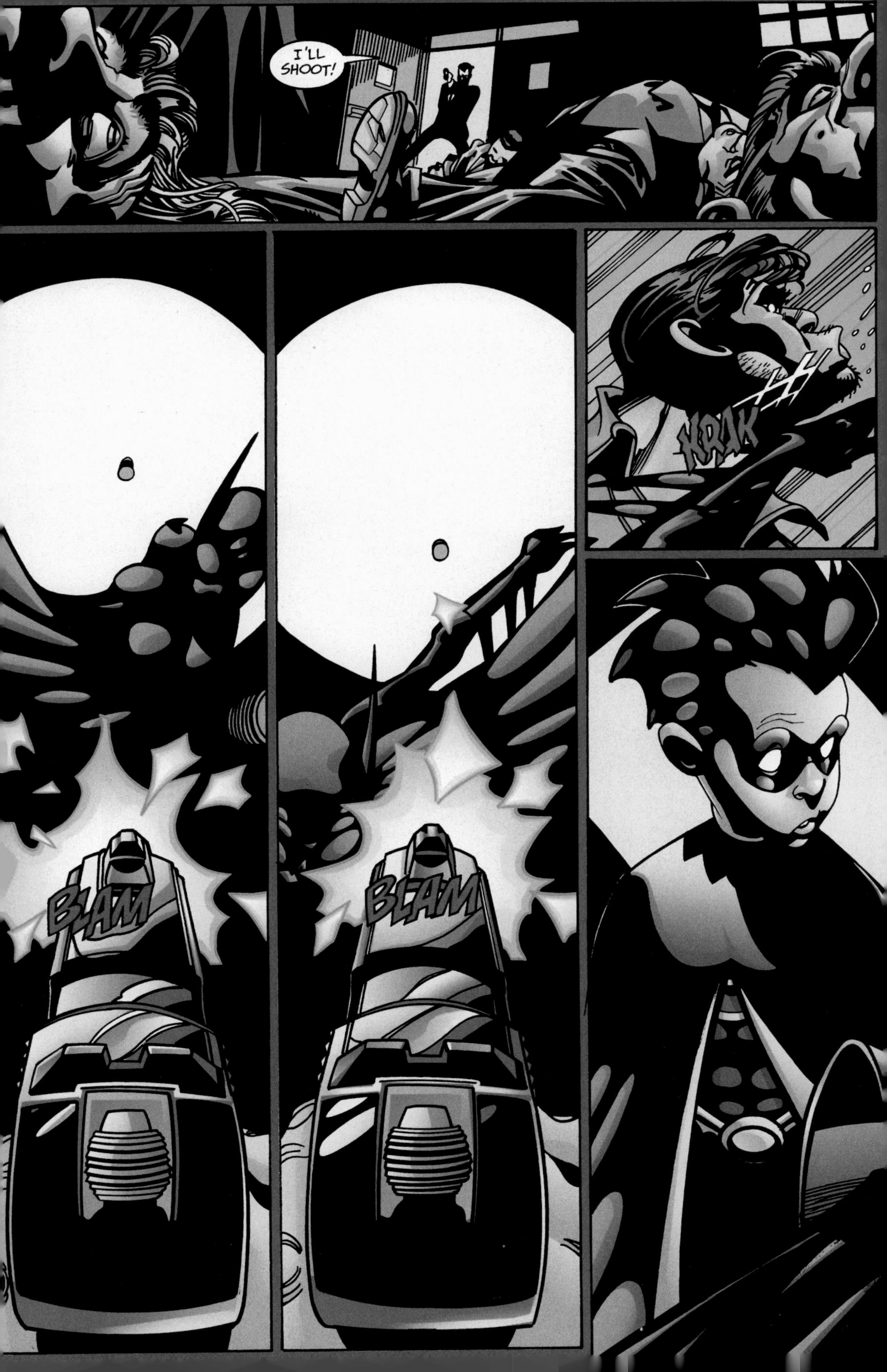
I'LL SHOOT!
KRAK
BLAM
BLAM

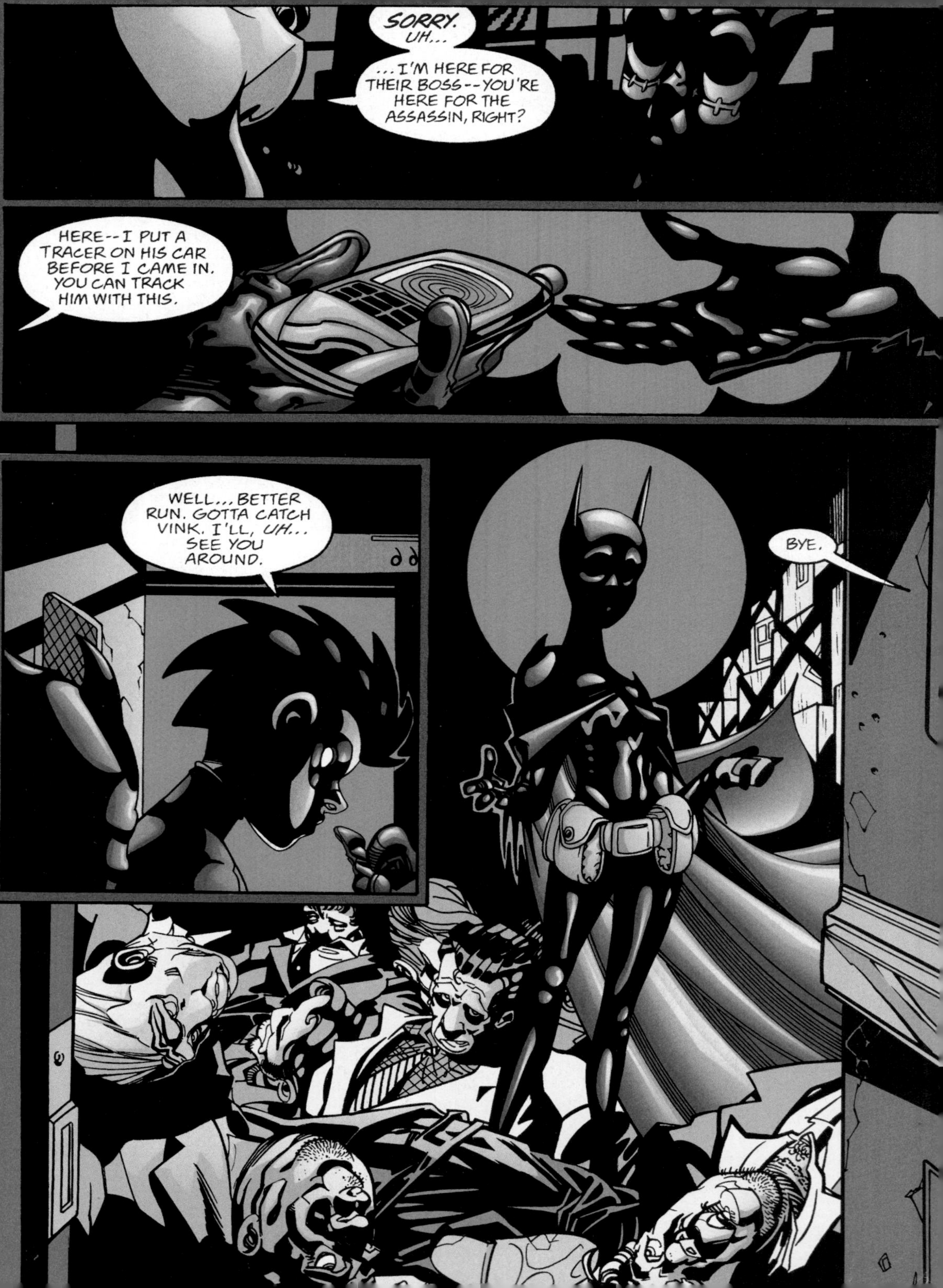
SORRY. UH...
...I'M HERE FOR THEIR BOSS--YOU'RE HERE FOR THE ASSASSIN, RIGHT?
HERE--I PUT A TRACER ON HIS CAR BEFORE I CAME IN. YOU CAN TRACK HIM WITH THIS.
WELL... BETTER RUN. GOTTA CATCH VINK. I'LL, UH... SEE YOU AROUND.
BYE.

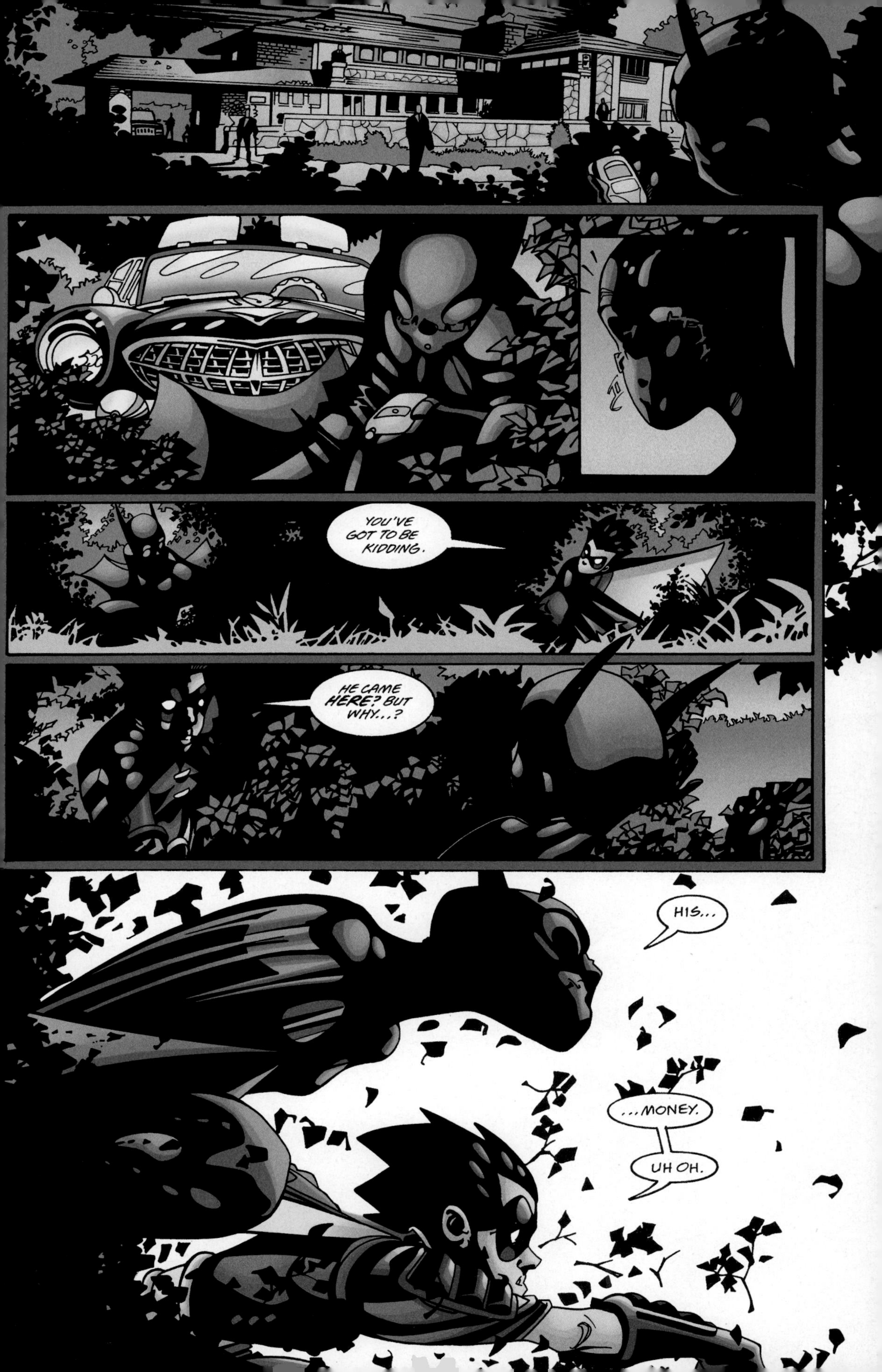
YOU'VE GOT TO BE KIDDING.
HE CAME HERE? BUT WHY...?
HIS...
...MONEY.
UH OH.

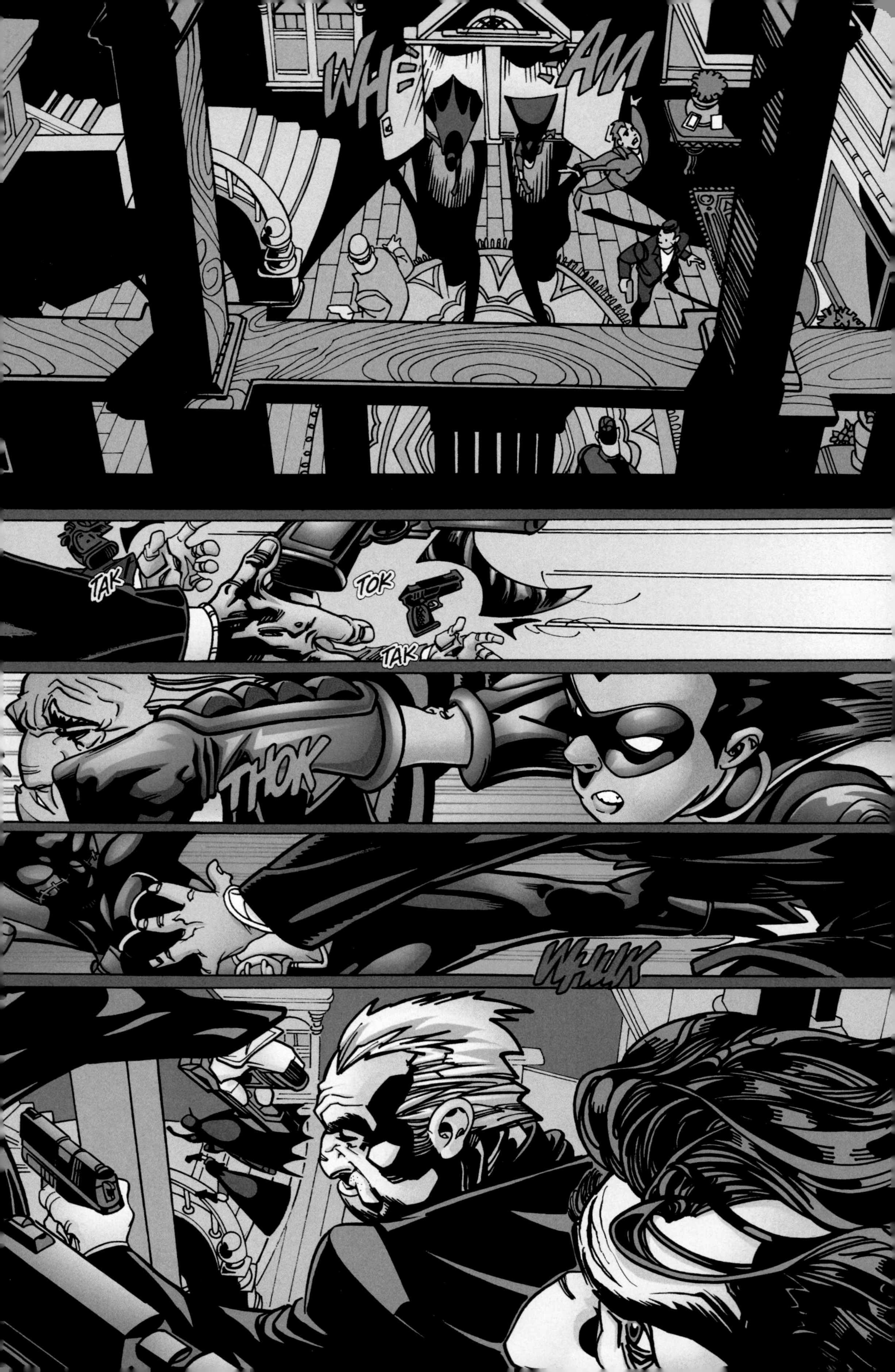
WH-
AM
TAK
TOK
TAK
THOK
WHUK

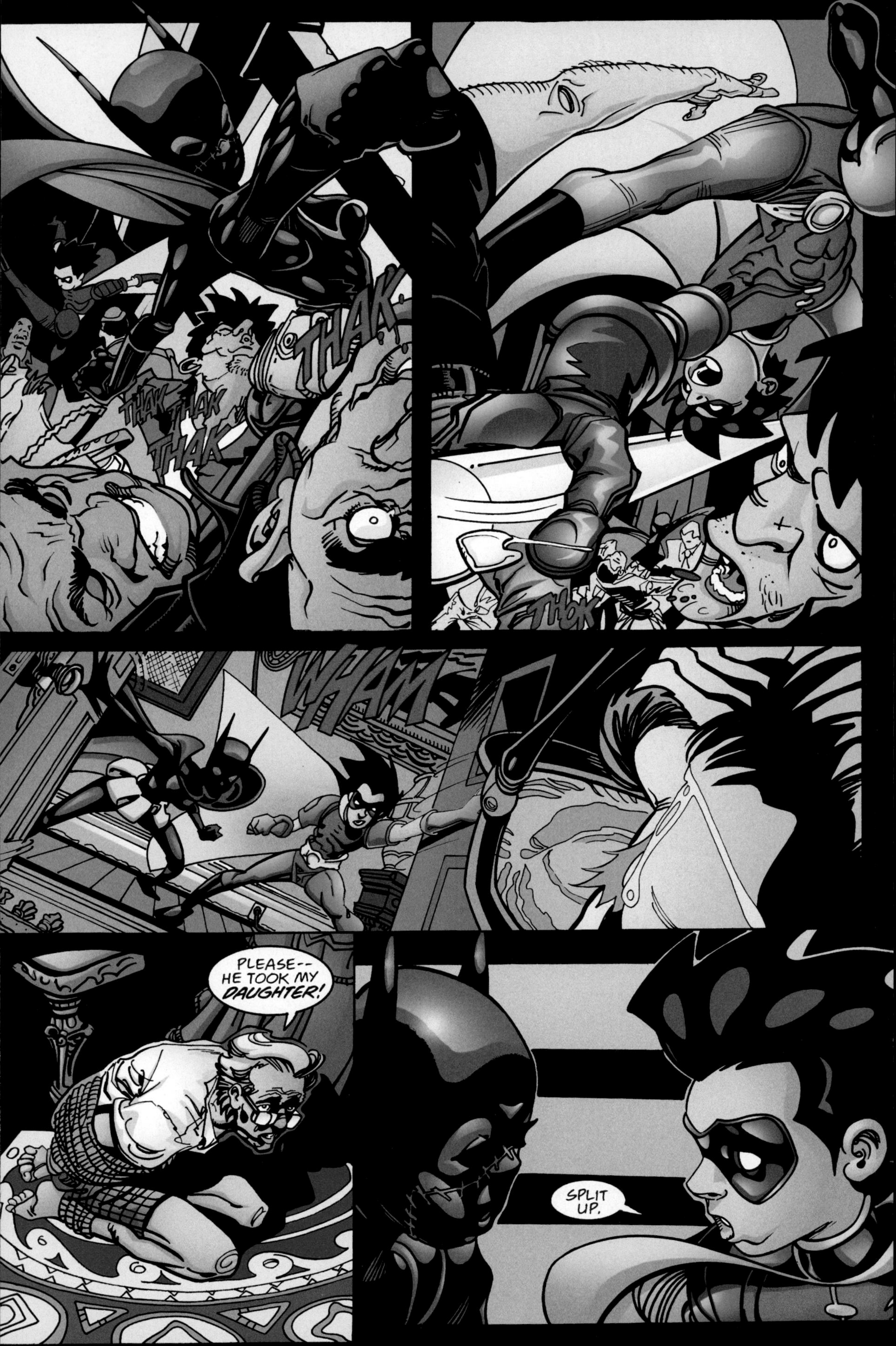
THAK
THAK THAK
THAK
THAK
THOK
WHAM
PLEASE-- HE TOOK MY DAUGHTER!
SPLIT UP.

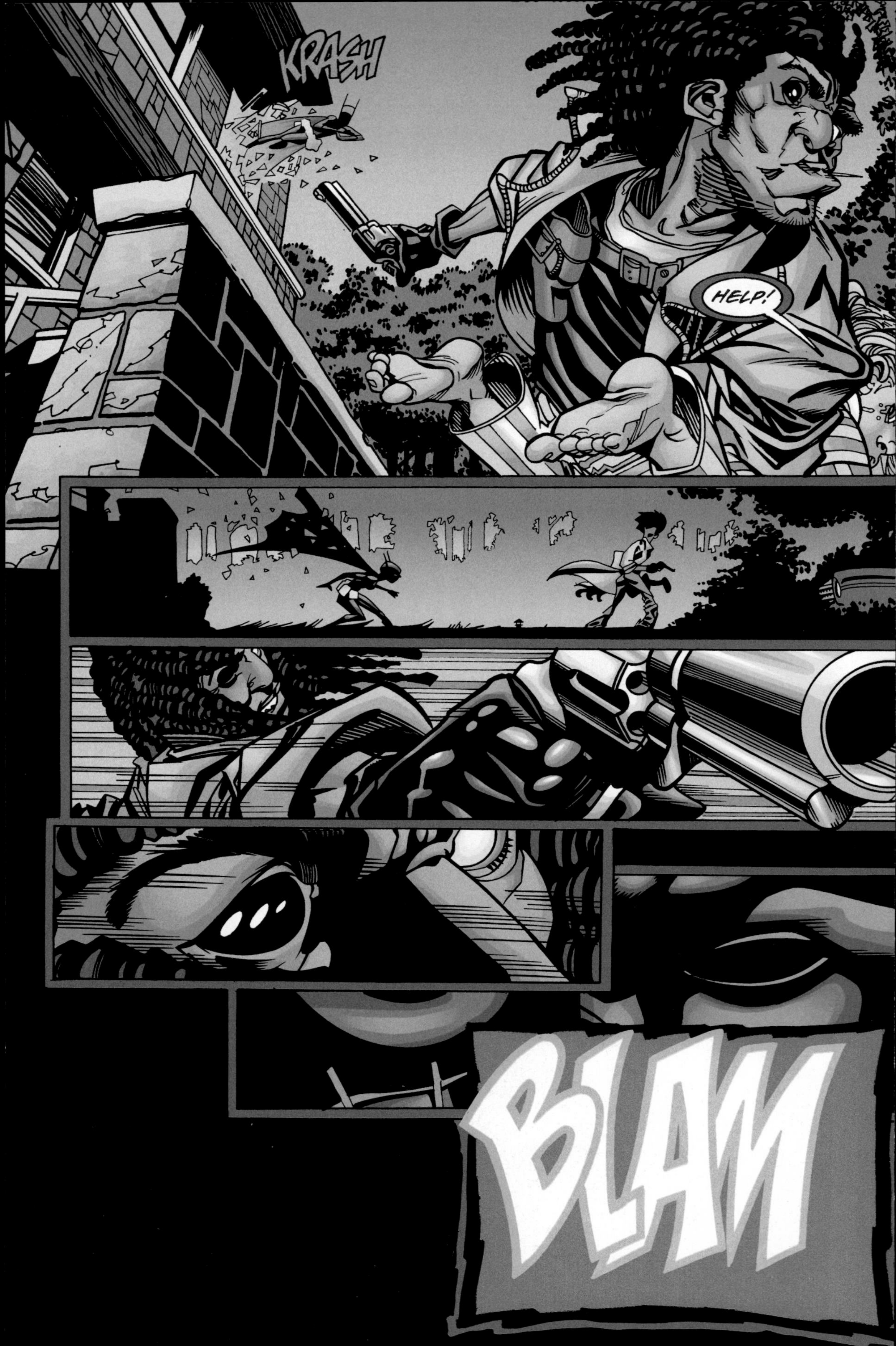
KRASH
HELP!
BLAM

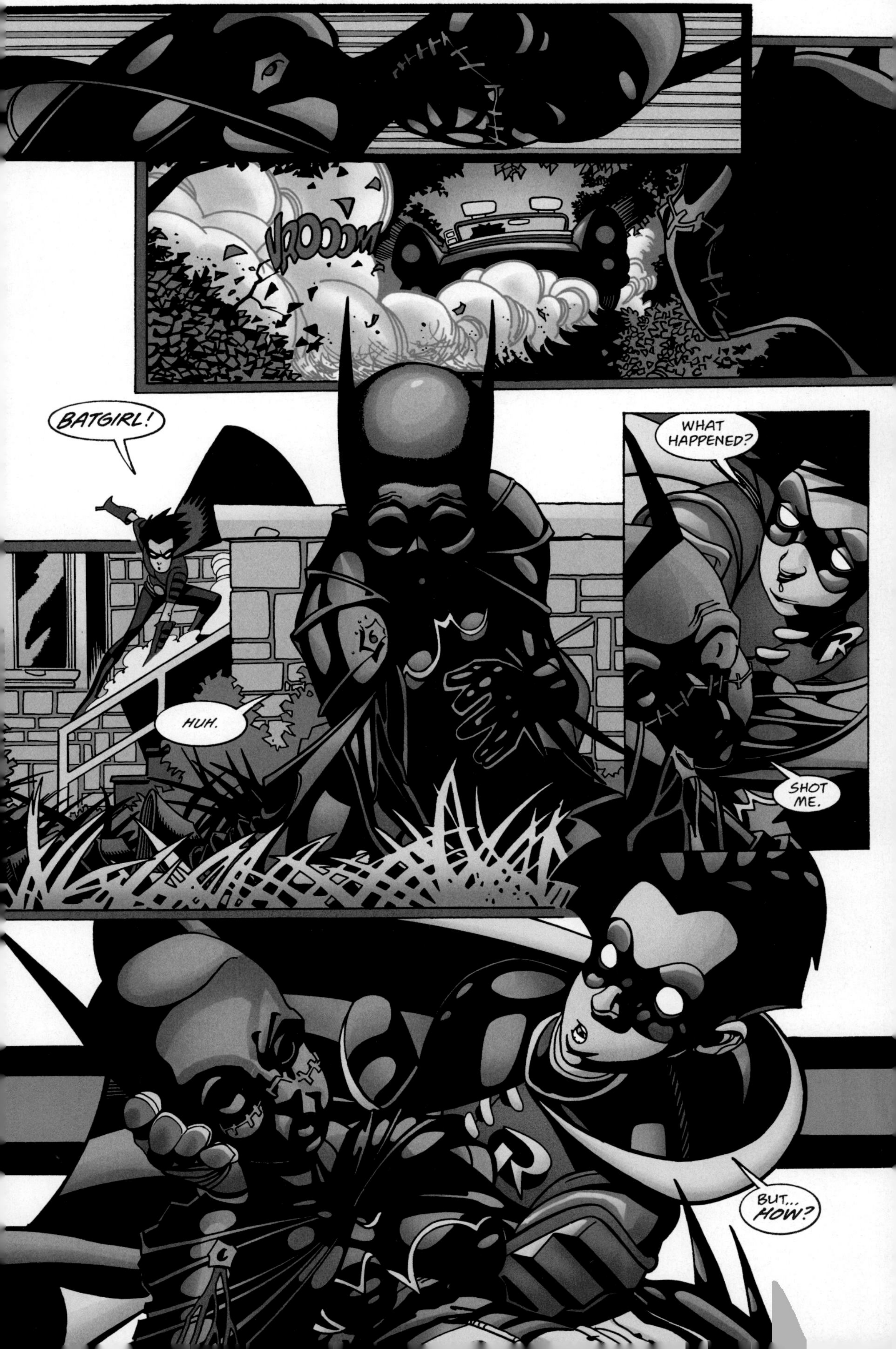
VROOOM
BATGIRL!
HUH.
WHAT HAPPENED?
SHOT ME.
BUT... HOW?

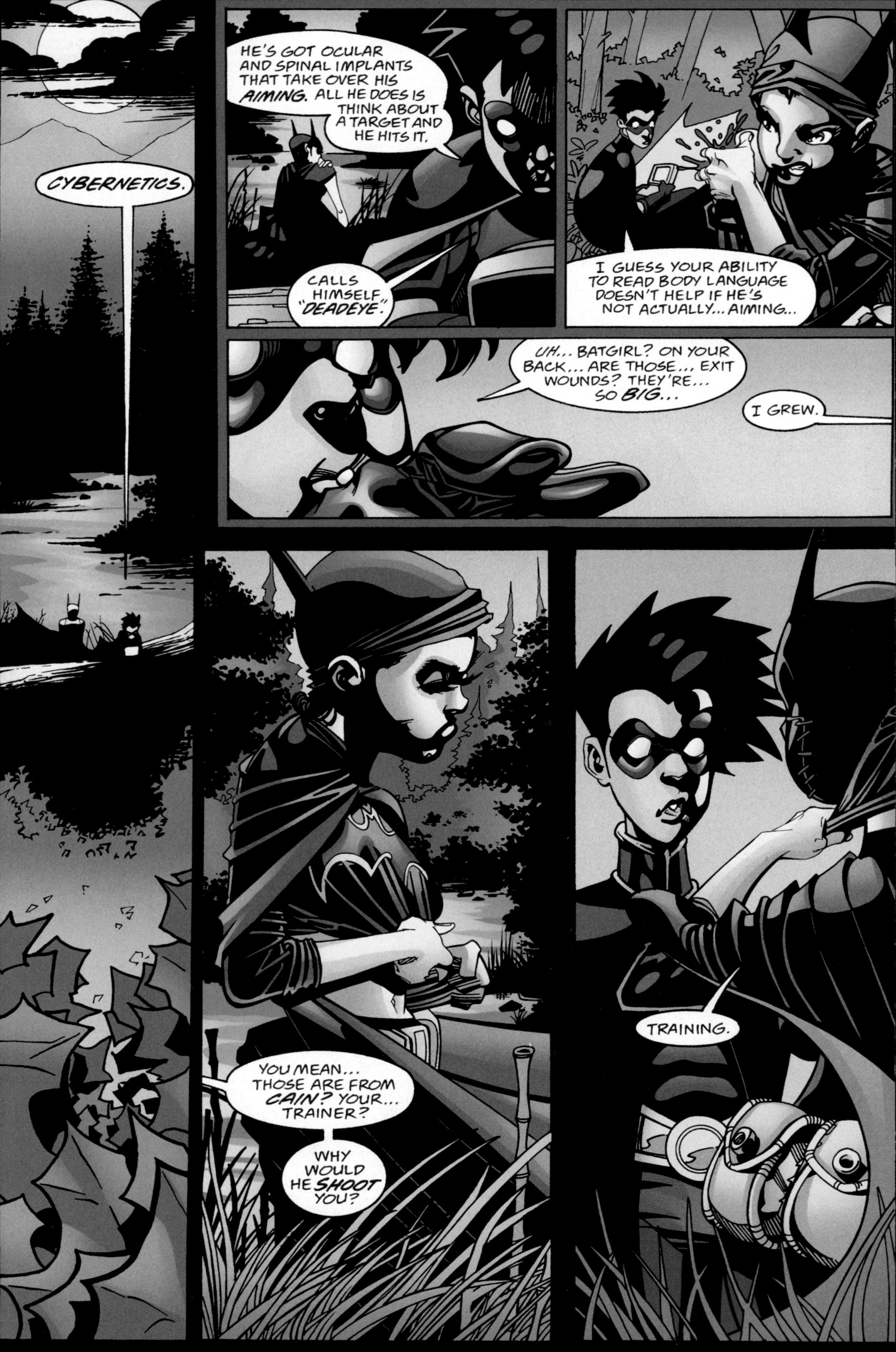
HE'S GOT OCULAR AND SPINAL IMPLANTS THAT TAKE OVER HIS AIMING. ALL HE DOES IS THINK ABOUT A TARGET AND HE HITS IT.
CYBERNETICS.
CALLS HIMSELF "DEADEYE".
I GUESS YOUR ABILITY TO READ BODY LANGUAGE DOESN'T HELP IF HE'S NOT ACTUALLY... AIMING...
UH... BATGIRL? ON YOUR BACK... ARE THOSE... EXIT WOUNDS? THEY'RE... SO BIG...
I GREW.
YOU MEAN... THOSE ARE FROM CAIN? YOUR... TRAINER?
WHY WOULD HE SHOOT YOU?
TRAINING.

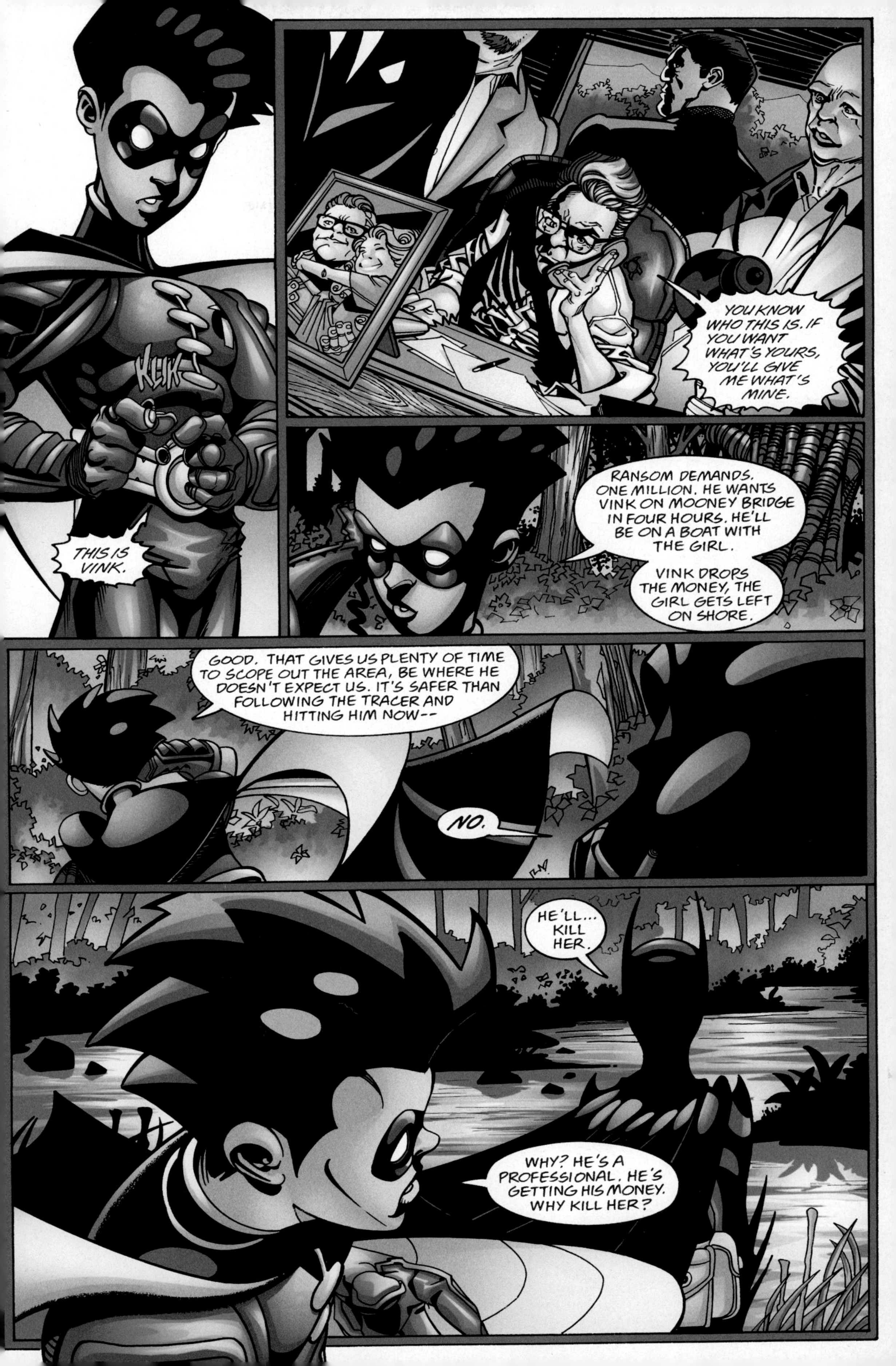
KLIK
YOU KNOW WHO THIS IS. IF YOU WANT WHAT'S YOURS, YOU'LL GIVE ME WHAT'S MINE.
THIS IS VINK.
RANSOM DEMANDS. ONE MILLION. HE WANTS VINK ON MOONEY BRIDGE IN FOUR HOURS. HE'LL BE ON A BOAT WITH THE GIRL.
VINK DROPS THE MONEY, THE GIRL GETS LEFT ON SHORE.
GOOD. THAT GIVES US PLENTY OF TIME TO SCOPE OUT THE AREA, BE WHERE HE DOESN'T EXPECT US. IT'S SAFER THAN FOLLOWING THE TRACER AND HITTING HIM NOW--
NO.
HE'LL... KILL HER.
WHY? HE'S A PROFESSIONAL. HE'S GETTING HIS MONEY. WHY KILL HER?

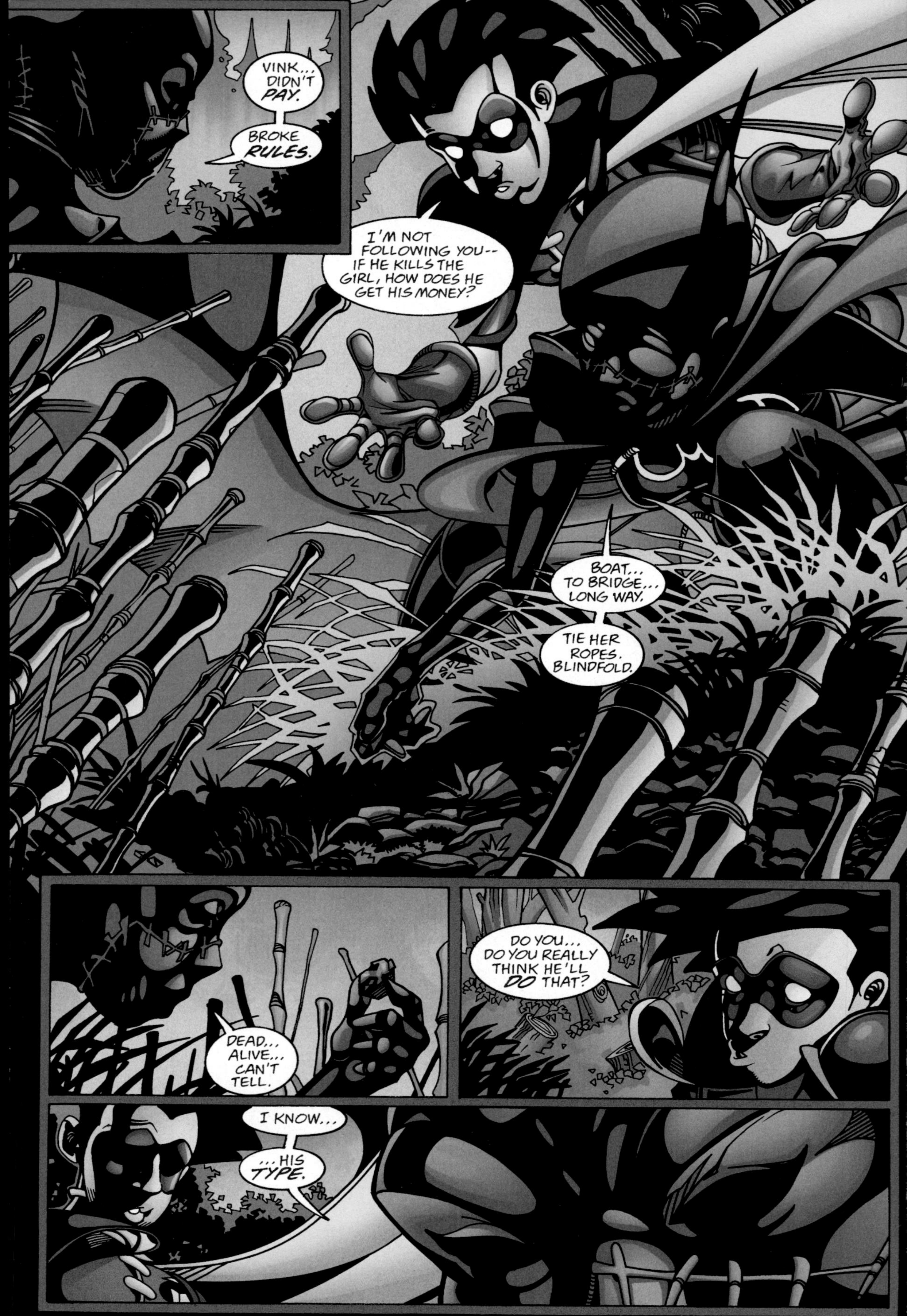

VINK... DIDN'T PAY.
BROKE RULES.
I'M NOT FOLLOWING YOU-- IF HE KILLS THE GIRL, HOW DOES HE GET HIS MONEY?
BOAT... TO BRIDGE... LONG WAY.
TIE HER ROPES. BLINDFOLD.
DEAD... ALIVE... CAN'T TELL.
DO YOU... DO YOU REALLY THINK HE'LL DO THAT?
I KNOW...
...HIS TYPE.

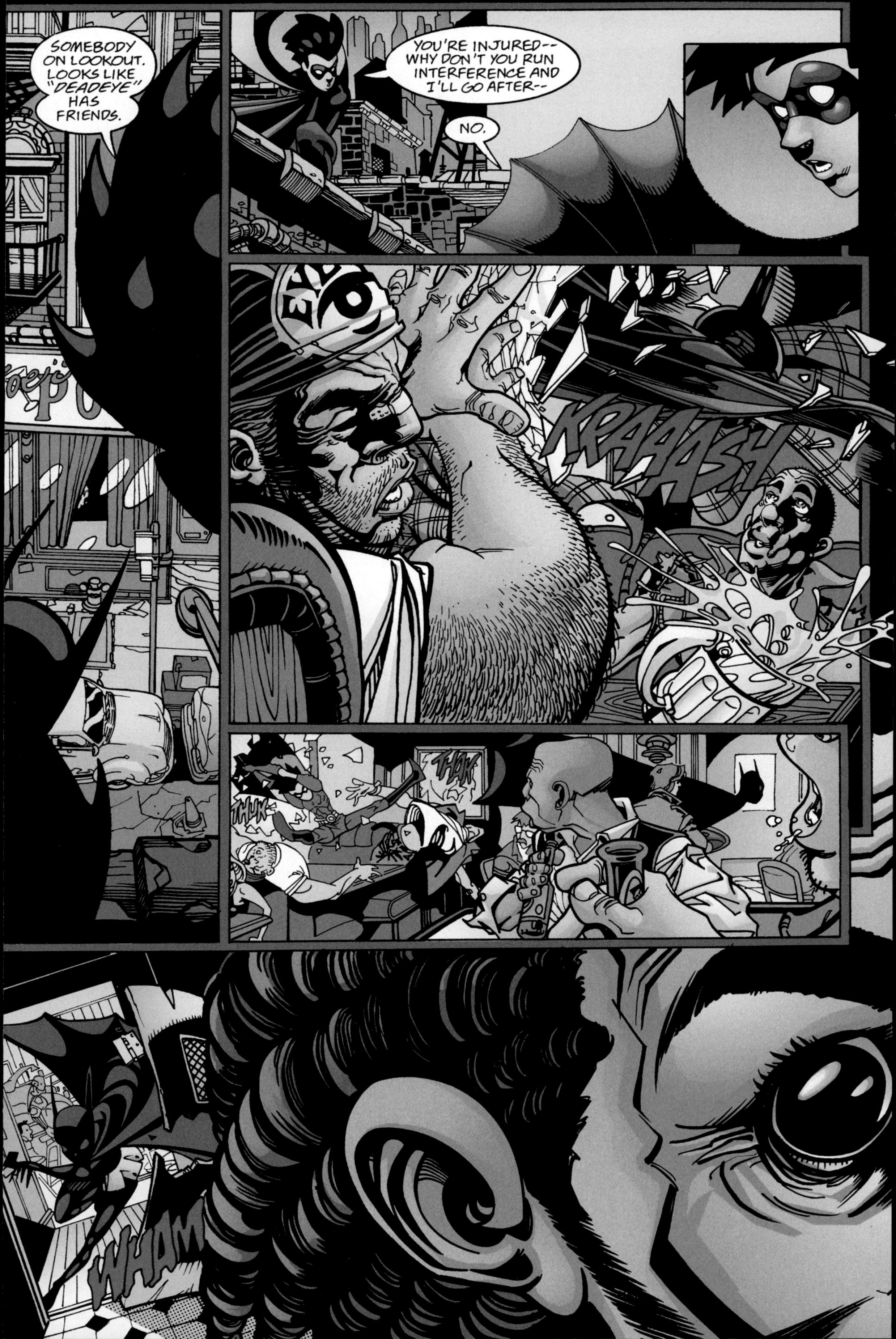
SOMEBODY ON LOOKOUT. LOOKS LIKE "DEADEYE" HAS FRIENDS.
YOU'RE INJURED--WHY DON'T YOU RUN INTERFERENCE AND I'LL GO AFTER--
NO.
KRAAAASH
THAK
THUK
WHAM

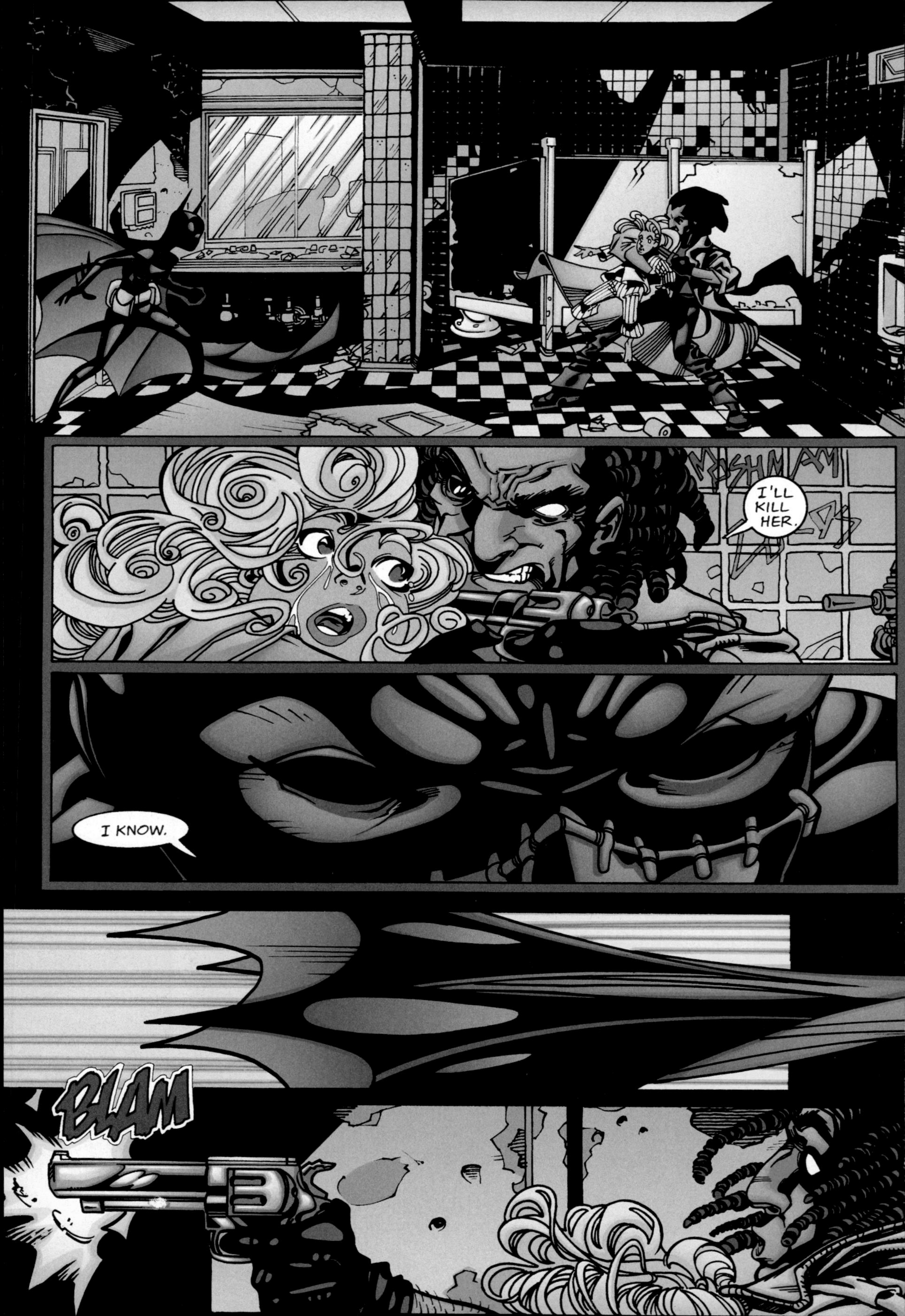
I'LL KILL HER.
I KNOW.
BLAM

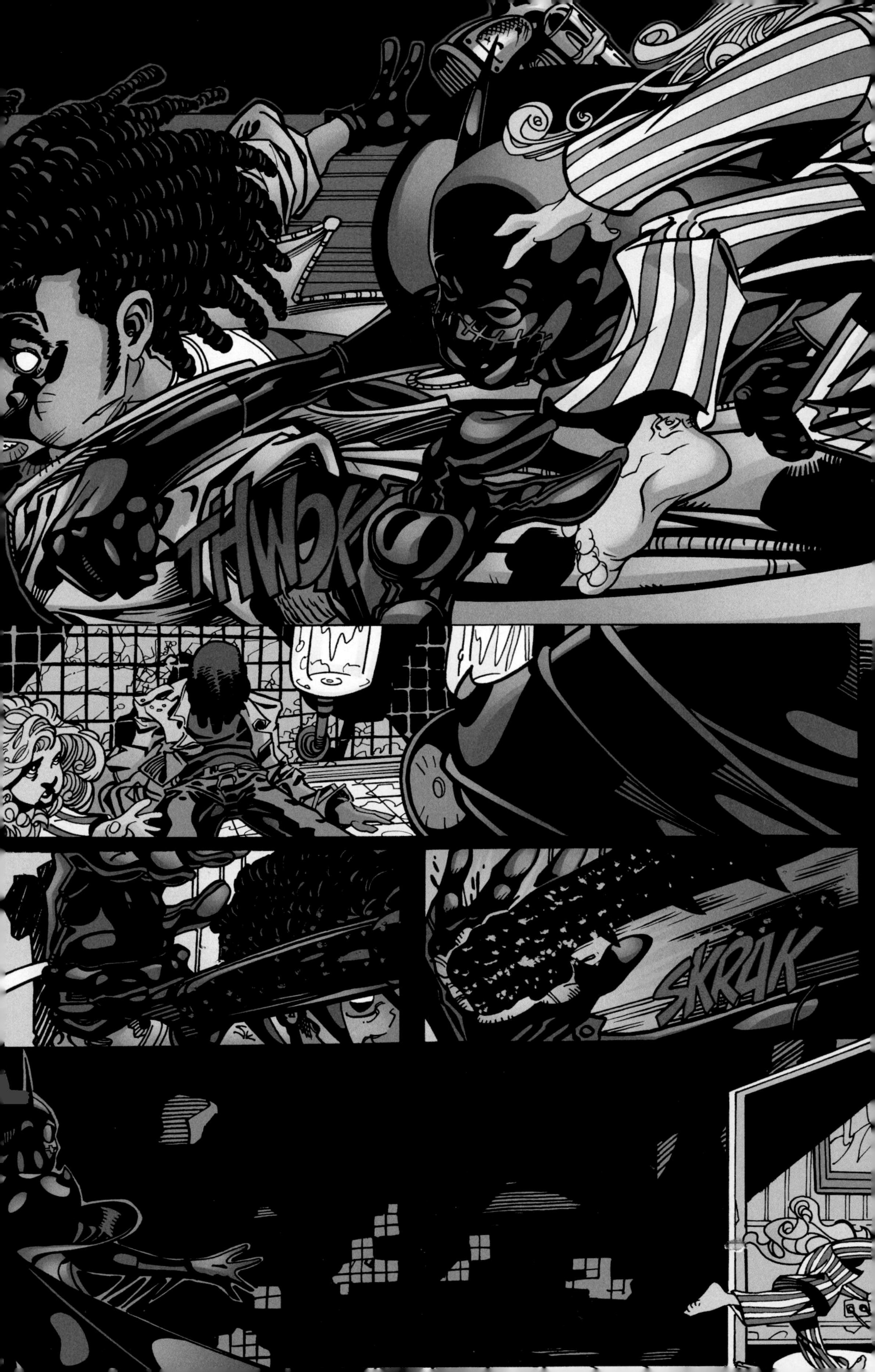
THWOK
SKRAK

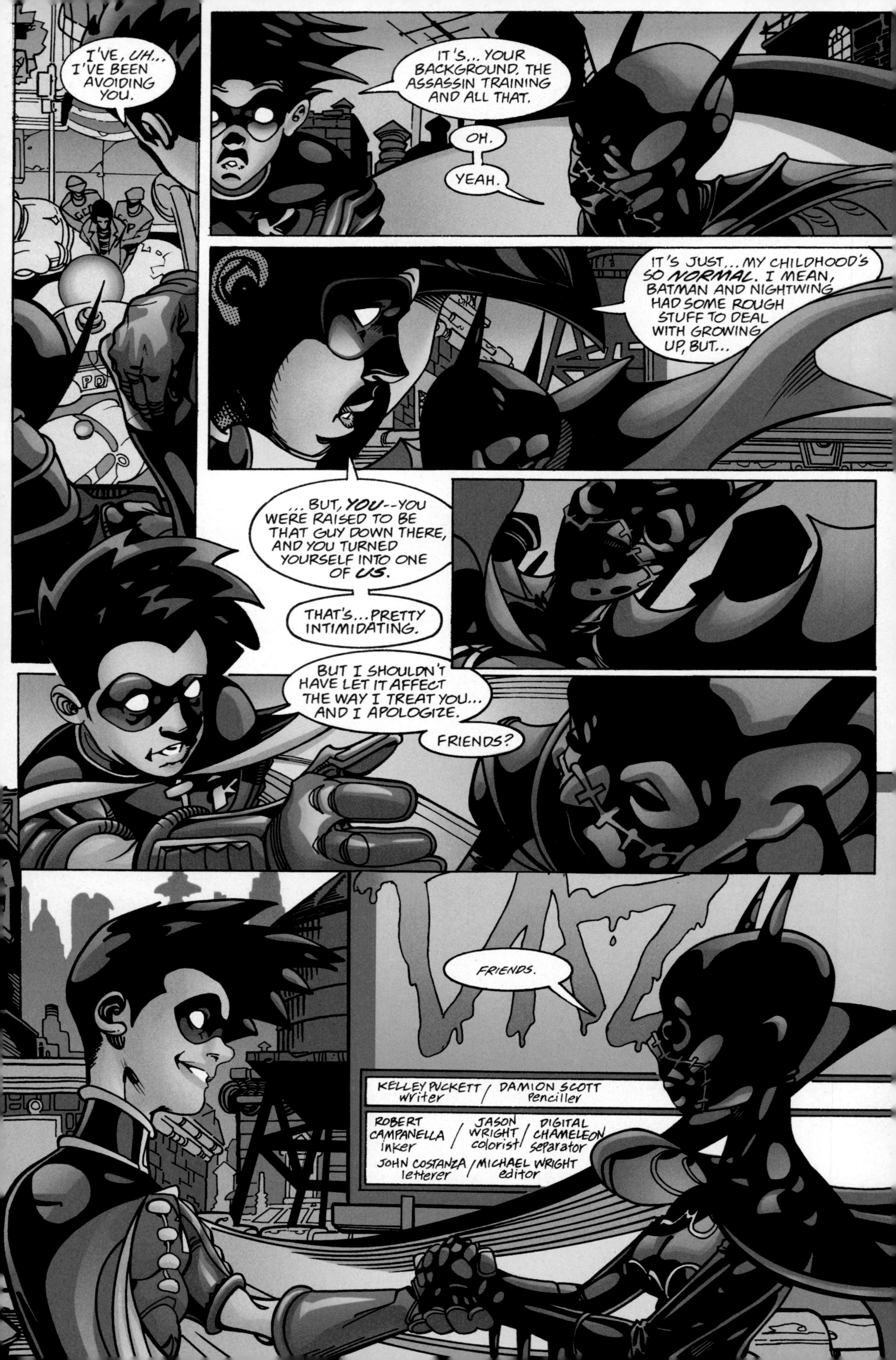
I'VE, UH... I'VE BEEN AVOIDING YOU.
IT'S... YOUR BACKGROUND. THE ASSASSIN TRAINING AND ALL THAT.
OH.
YEAH.
IT'S JUST... MY CHILDHOOD'S SO NORMAL. I MEAN, BATMAN AND NIGHTWING HAD SOME ROUGH STUFF TO DEAL WITH GROWING UP, BUT...
...BUT, YOU--YOU WERE RAISED TO BE THAT GUY DOWN THERE, AND YOU TURNED YOURSELF INTO ONE OF US.
THAT'S... PRETTY INTIMIDATING.
BUT I SHOULDN'T HAVE LET IT AFFECT THE WAY I TREAT YOU... AND I APOLOGIZE.
FRIENDS?
FRIENDS.
KELLEY PUCKETT writer / DAMION SCOTT penciller
ROBERT CAMPANELLA inker / JASON WRIGHT colorist / DIGITAL CHAMELEON separator
JOHN COSTANZA letterer / MICHAEL WRIGHT editor

BATGIRL #19 cover by Damion Scott,
Robert Campanella & Patrick Martin

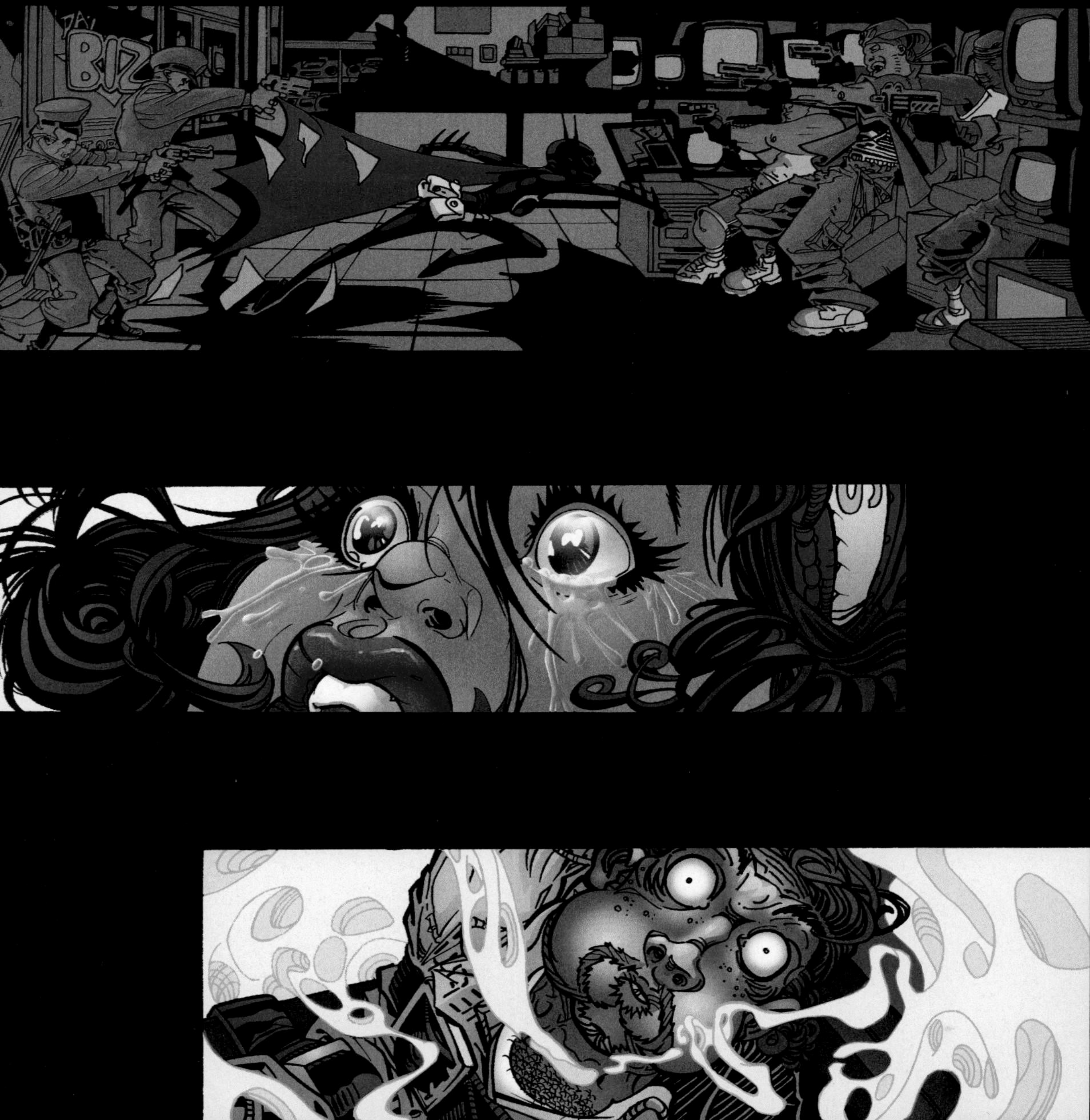

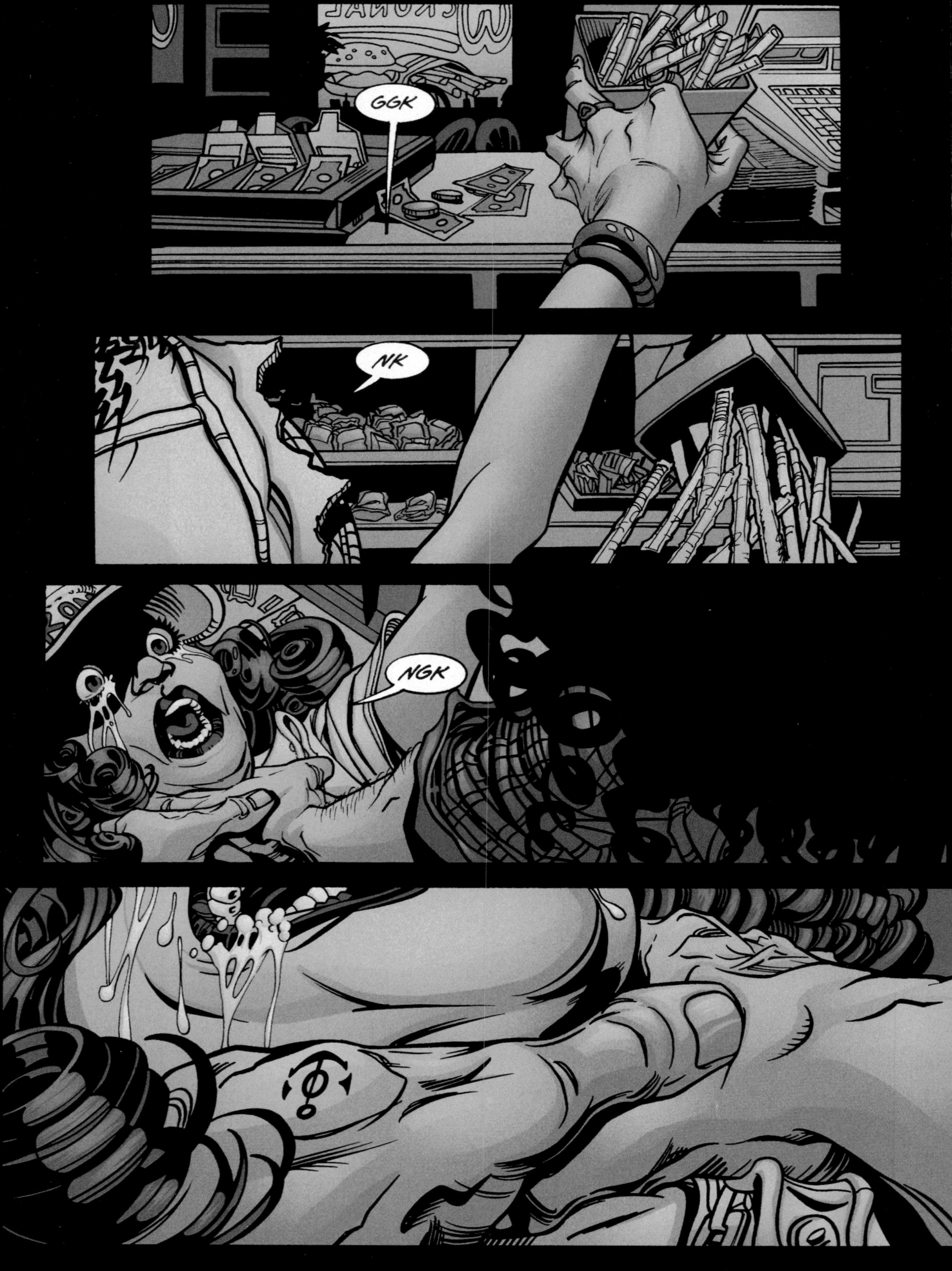
GGK
NK
NGK

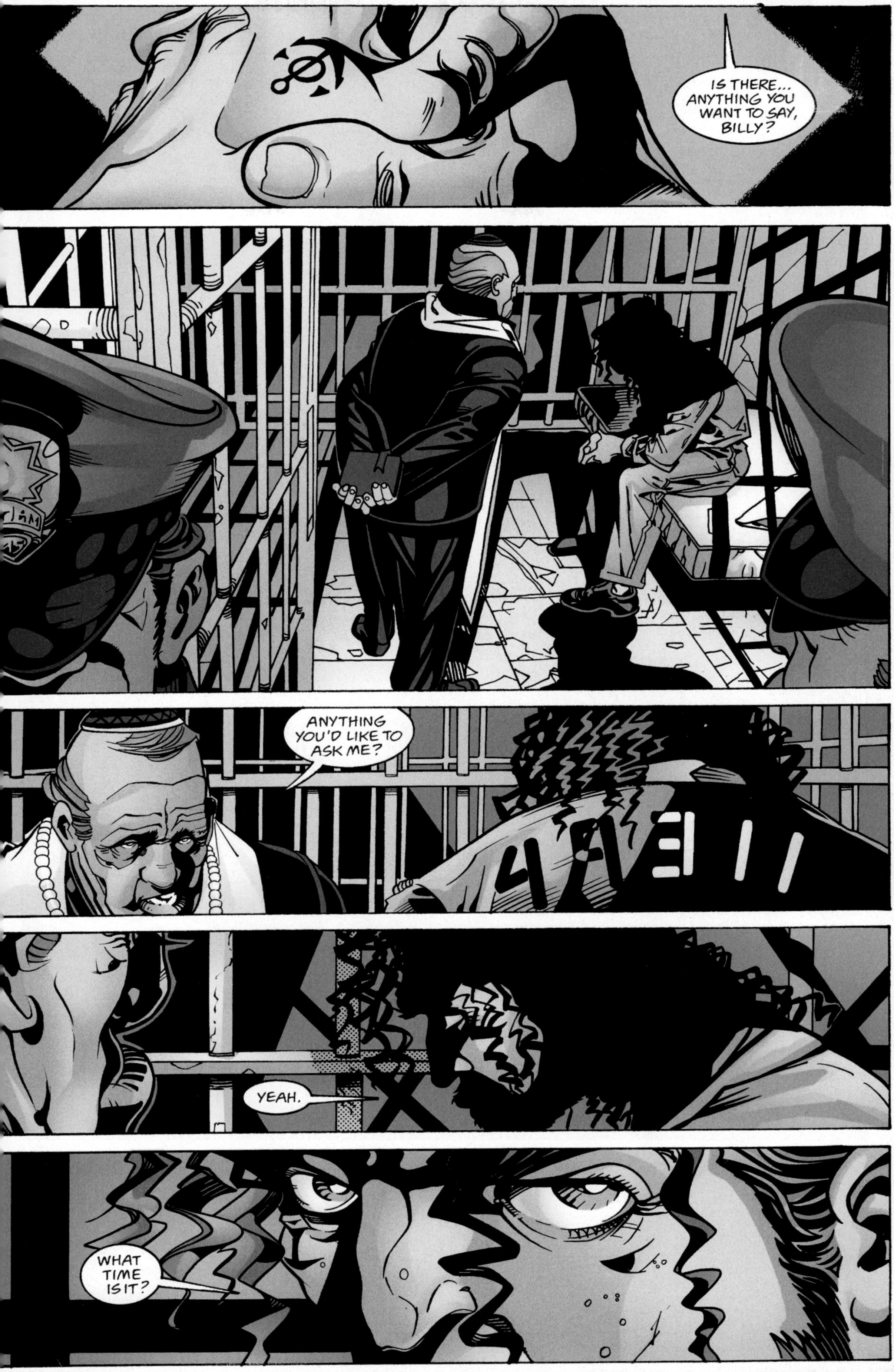
IS THERE... ANYTHING YOU WANT TO SAY, BILLY?
ANYTHING YOU'D LIKE TO ASK ME?
4 EVER
YEAH.
WHAT TIME IS IT?

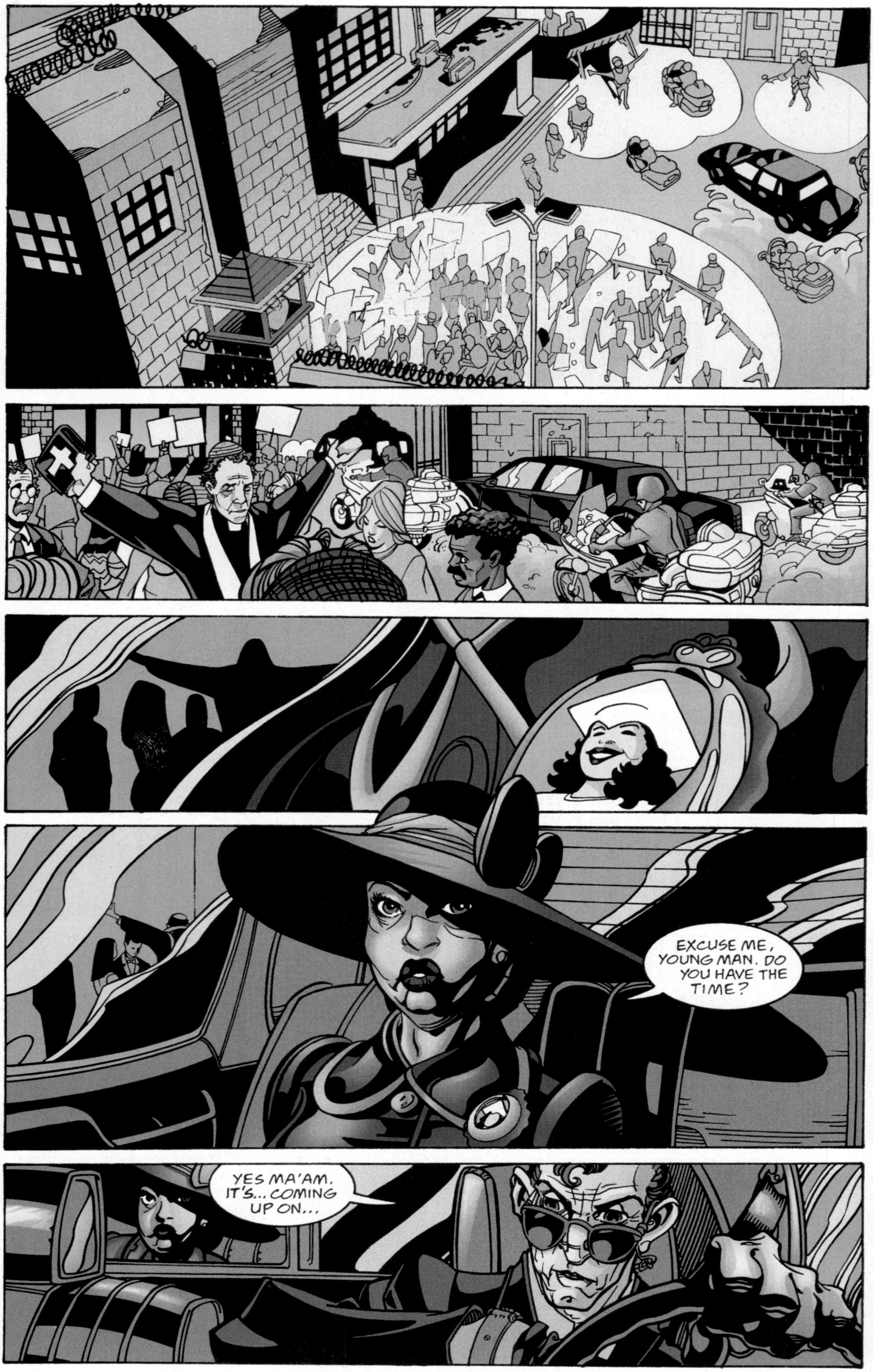
EXCUSE ME, YOUNG MAN. DO YOU HAVE THE TIME?
YES MA'AM. IT'S... COMING UP ON...

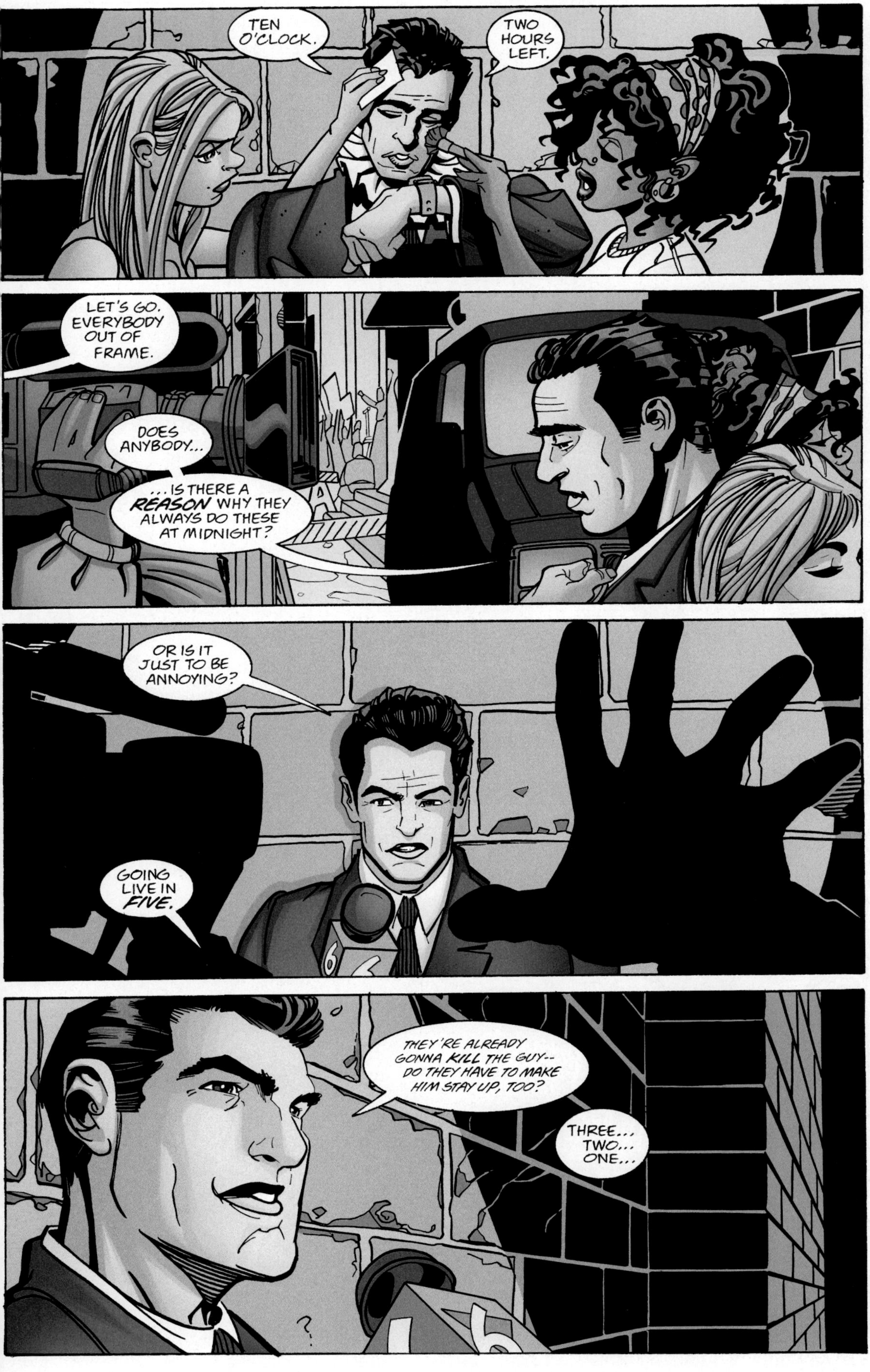
TEN O'CLOCK.
TWO HOURS LEFT.
LET'S GO. EVERYBODY OUT OF FRAME.
DOES ANYBODY...
...IS THERE A REASON WHY THEY ALWAYS DO THESE AT MIDNIGHT?
OR IS IT JUST TO BE ANNOYING?
GOING LIVE IN FIVE.
THEY'RE ALREADY GONNA KILL THE GUY-- DO THEY HAVE TO MAKE HIM STAY UP, TOO?
THREE... TWO... ONE...

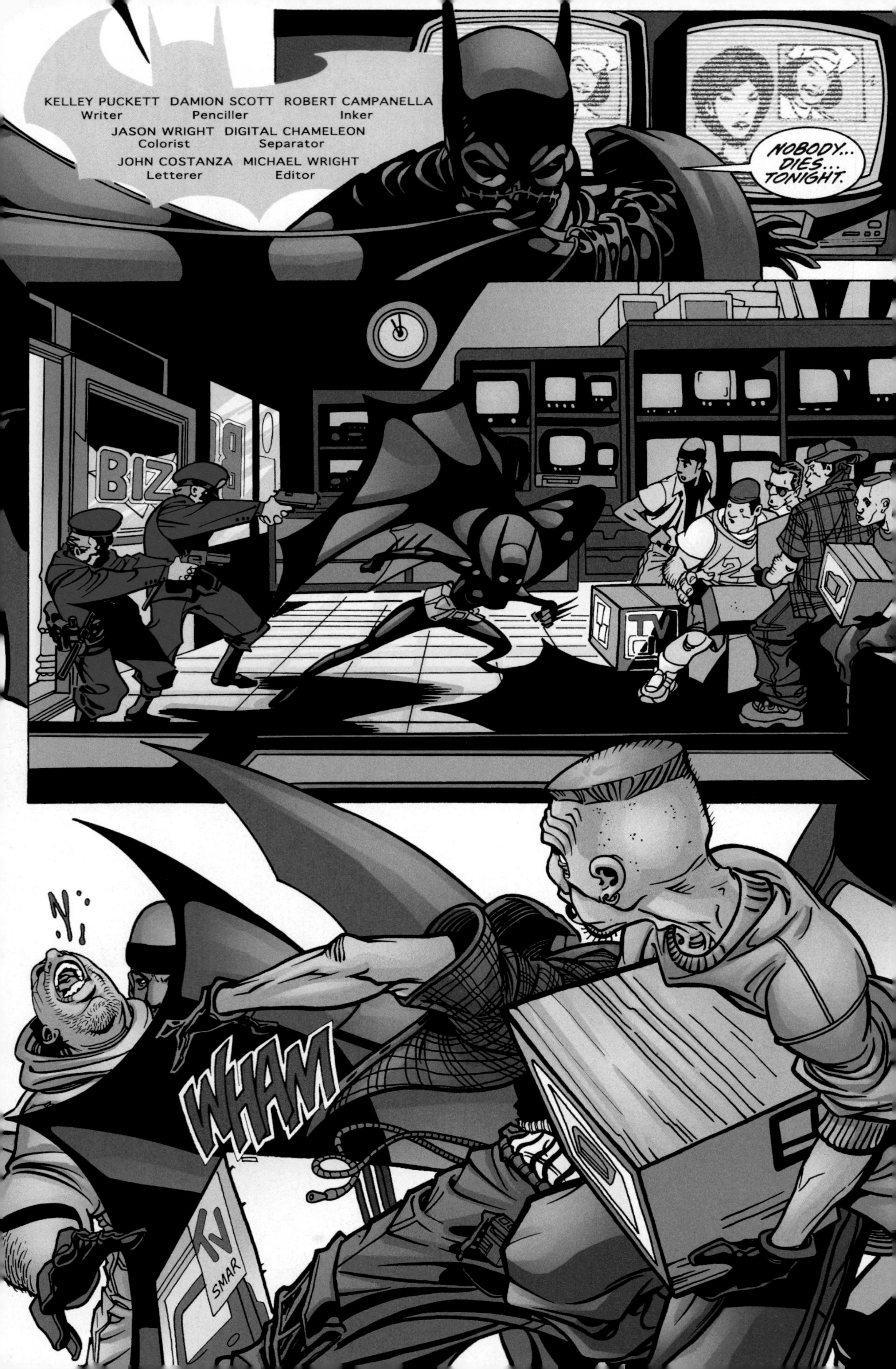
KELLEY PUCKETT Writer DAMION SCOTT Penciller ROBERT CAMPANELLA Inker
JASON WRIGHT Colorist DIGITAL CHAMELEON Separator
JOHN COSTANZA Letterer MICHAEL WRIGHT Editor
NOBODY... DIES... TONIGHT.
BIZ
TV
WHAM
TV
SMAR

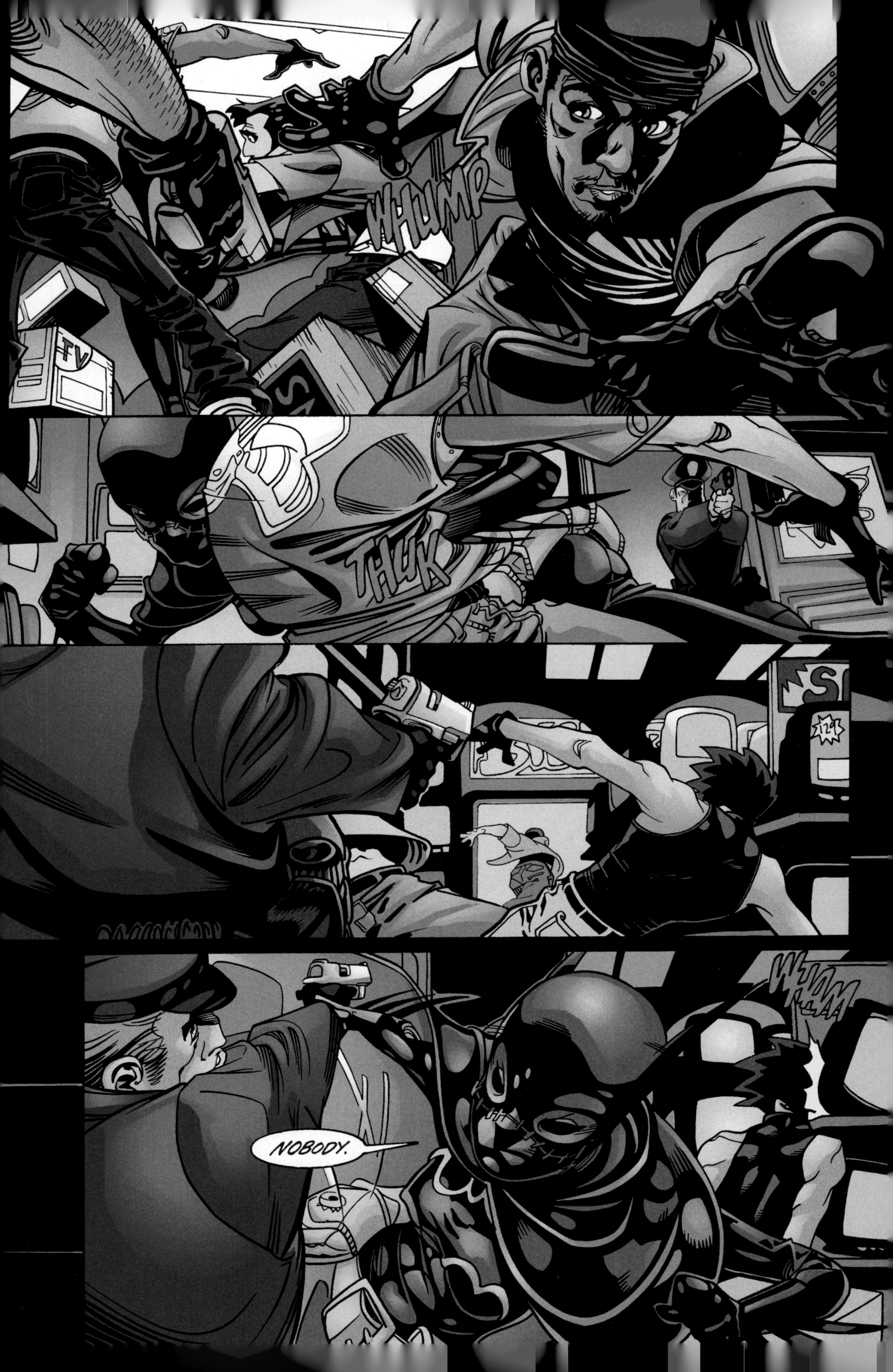
WHUMP
THUK
WHAAM
NOBODY.

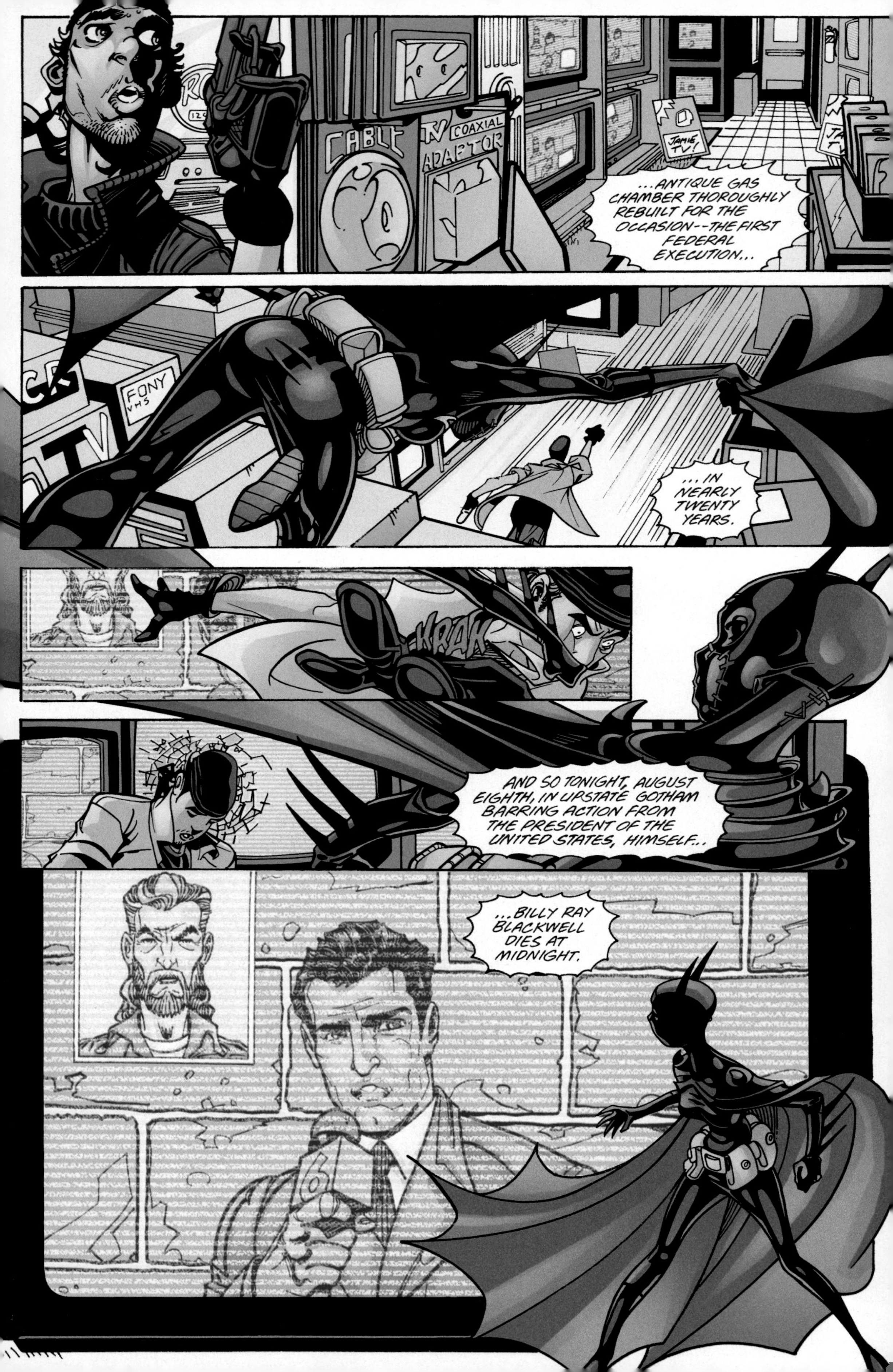
CABLE
TV COAXIAL ADAPTOR
JAMIE TV!
...ANTIQUE GAS CHAMBER THOROUGHLY REBUILT FOR THE OCCASION--THE FIRST FEDERAL EXECUTION...
FONY VHS
TV
...IN NEARLY TWENTY YEARS.
KRAK
AND SO TONIGHT, AUGUST EIGHTH, IN UPSTATE GOTHAM BARRING ACTION FROM THE PRESIDENT OF THE UNITED STATES, HIMSELF...
...BILLY RAY BLACKWELL DIES AT MIDNIGHT.

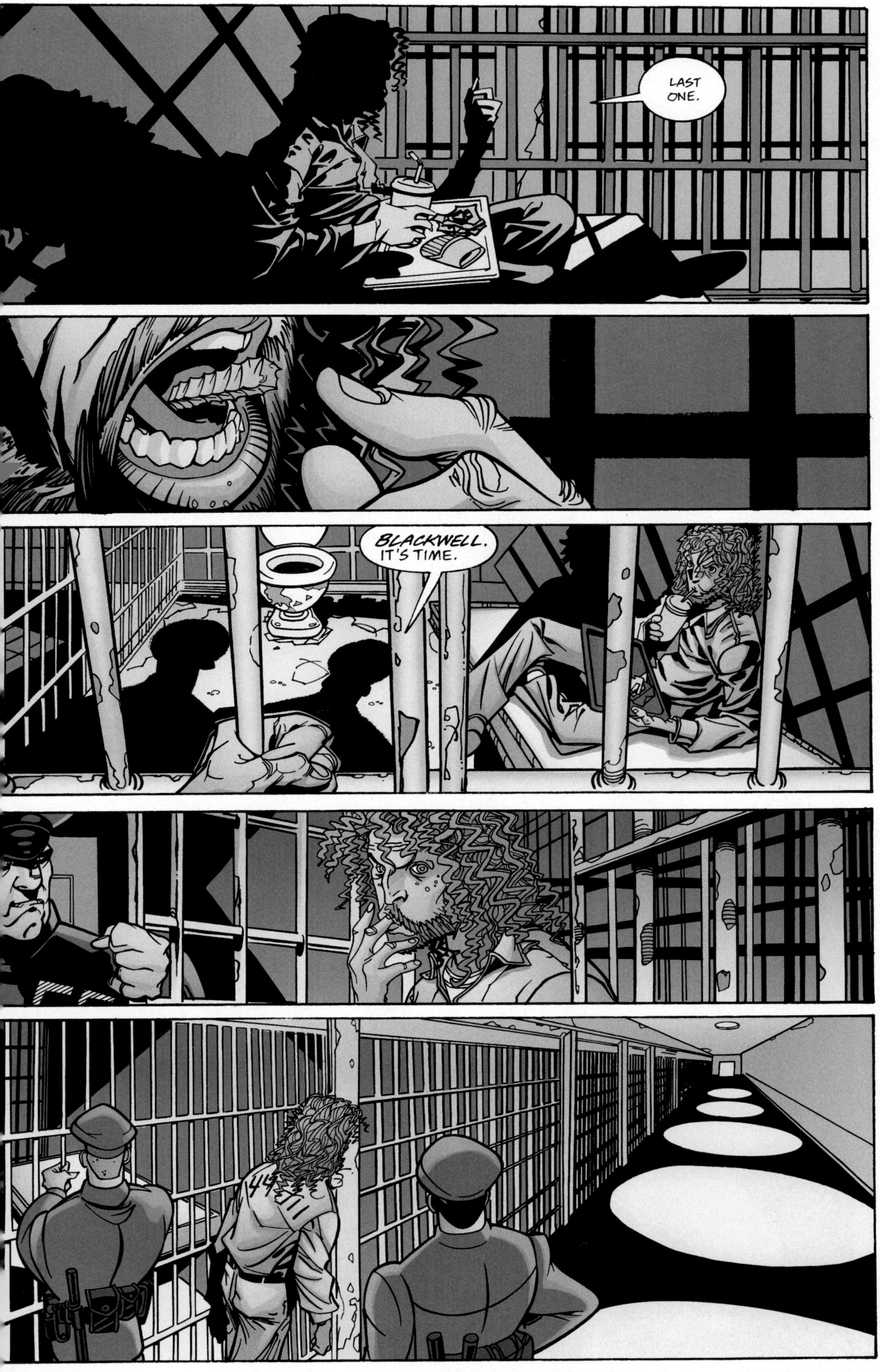
LAST ONE.
BLACKWELL. IT'S TIME.

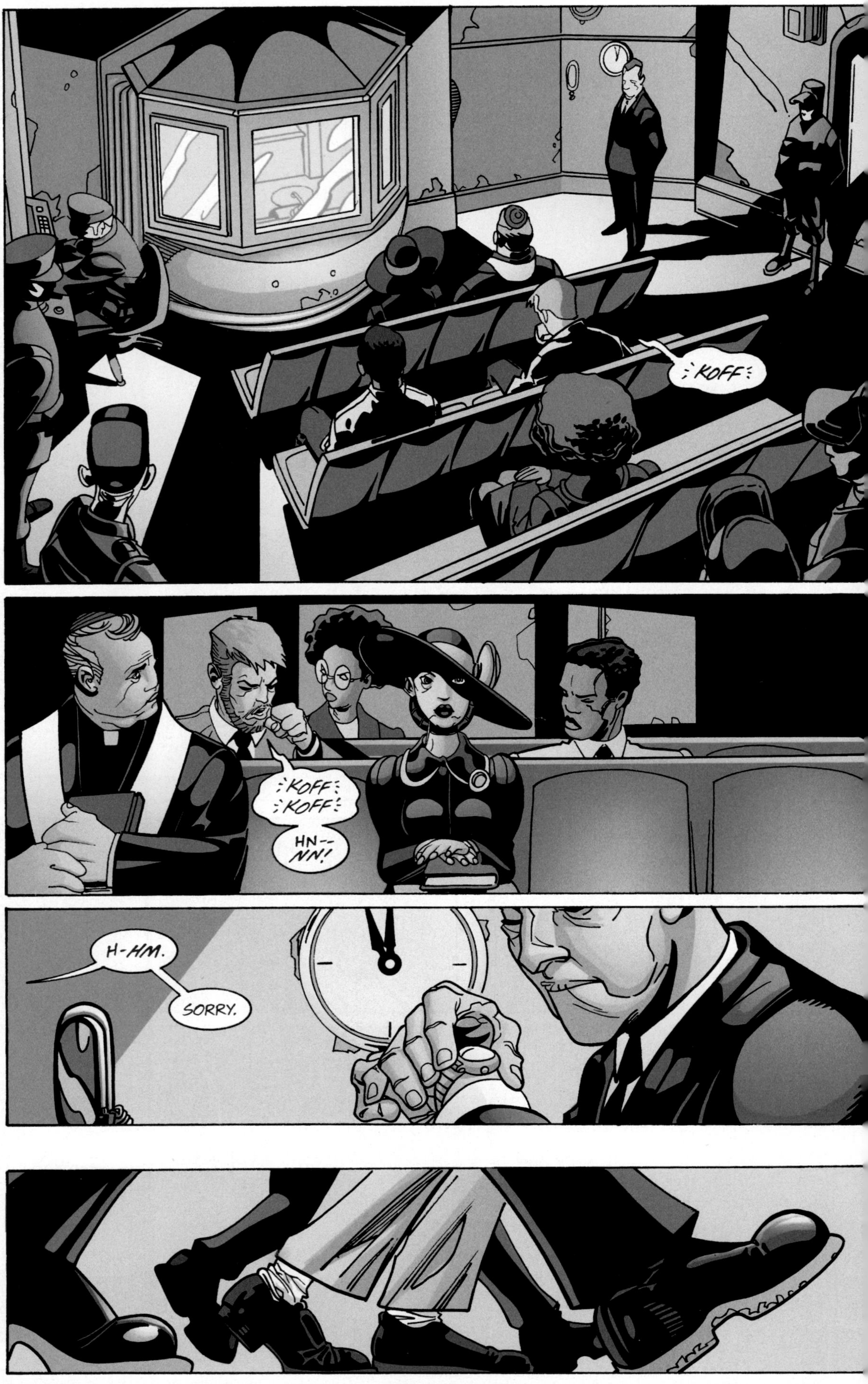
KOFF
KOFF KOFF
HN--NN!
H-HM.
SORRY.

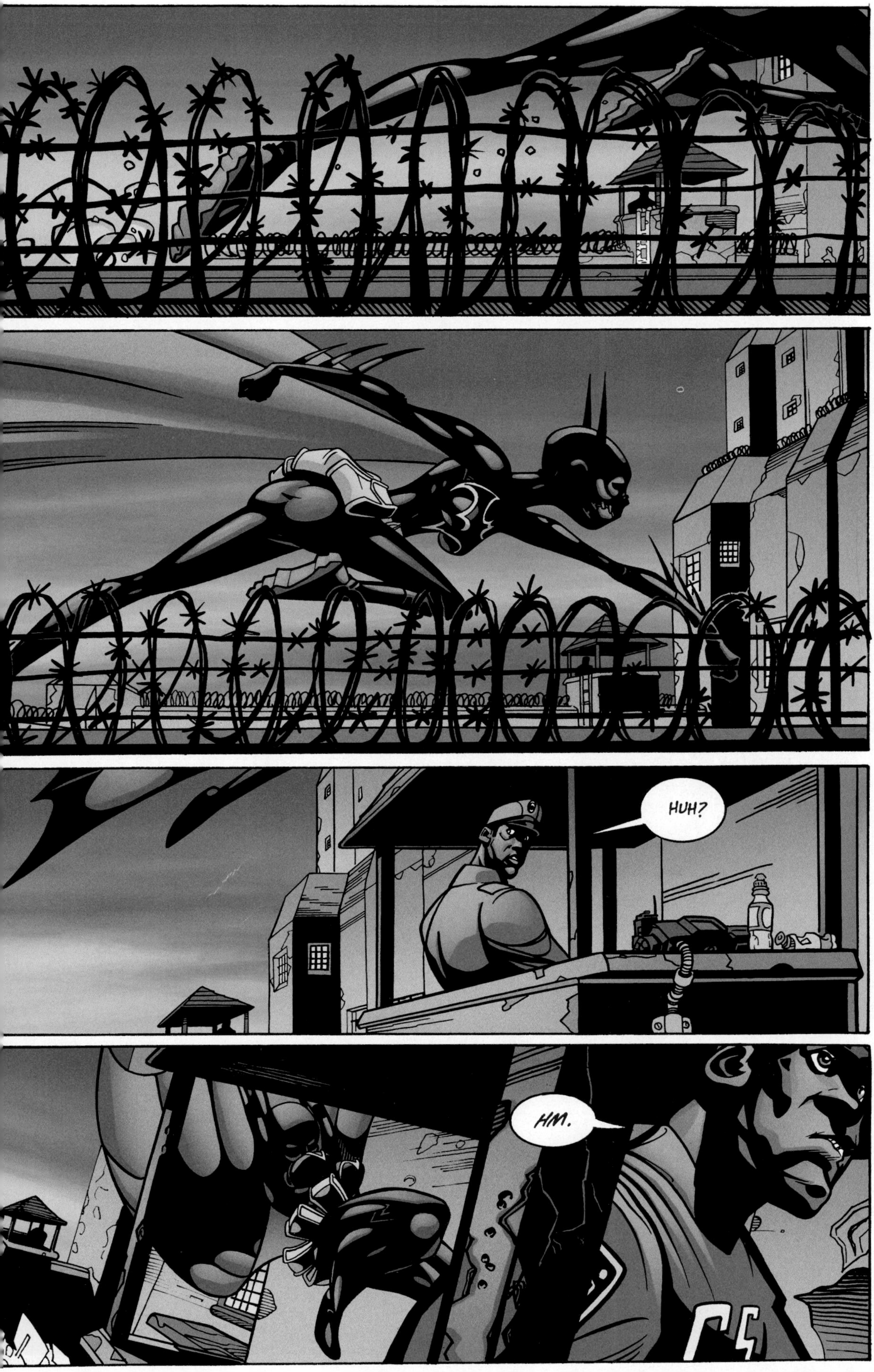
HUH?
HM.

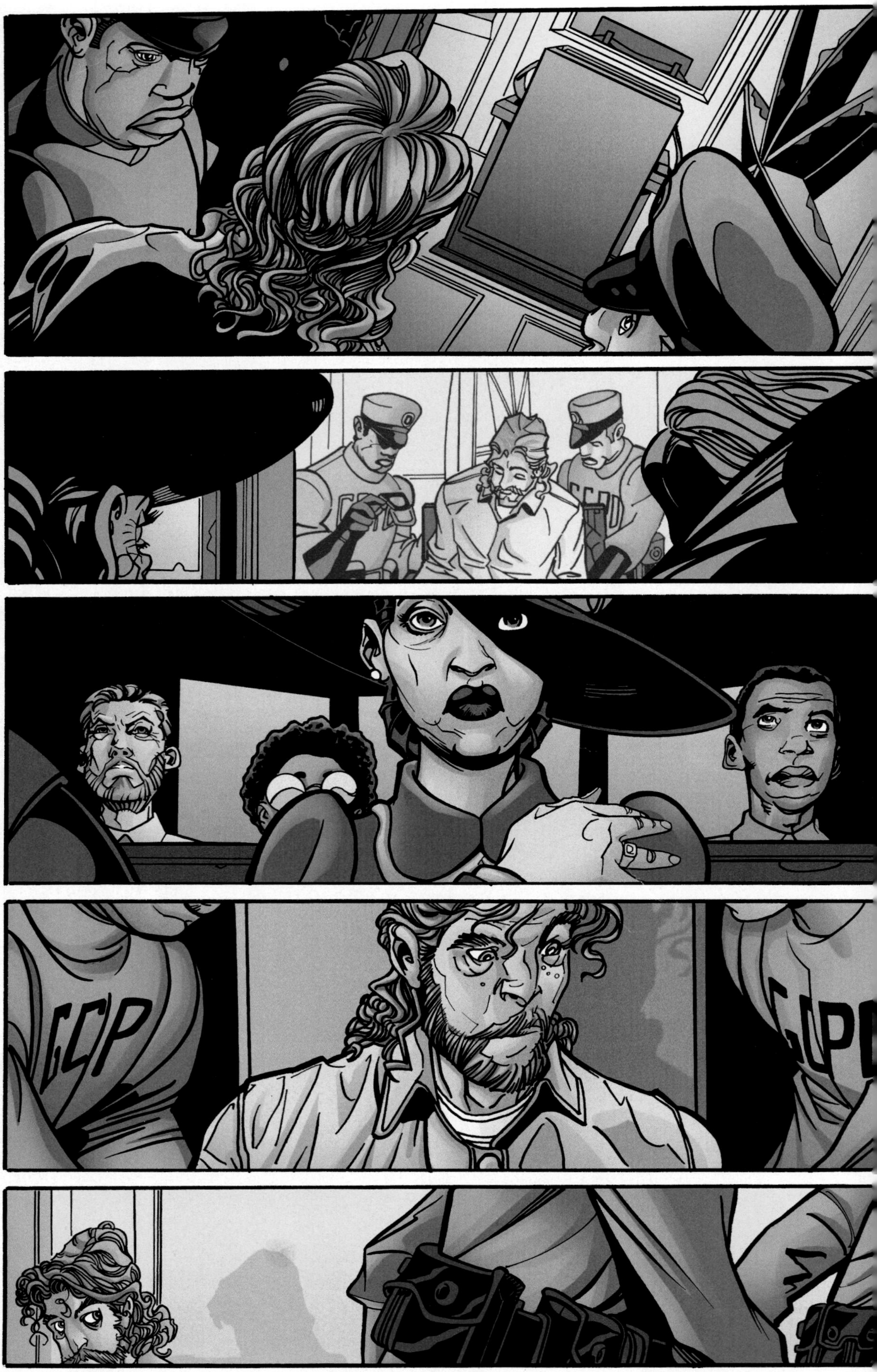
GCP

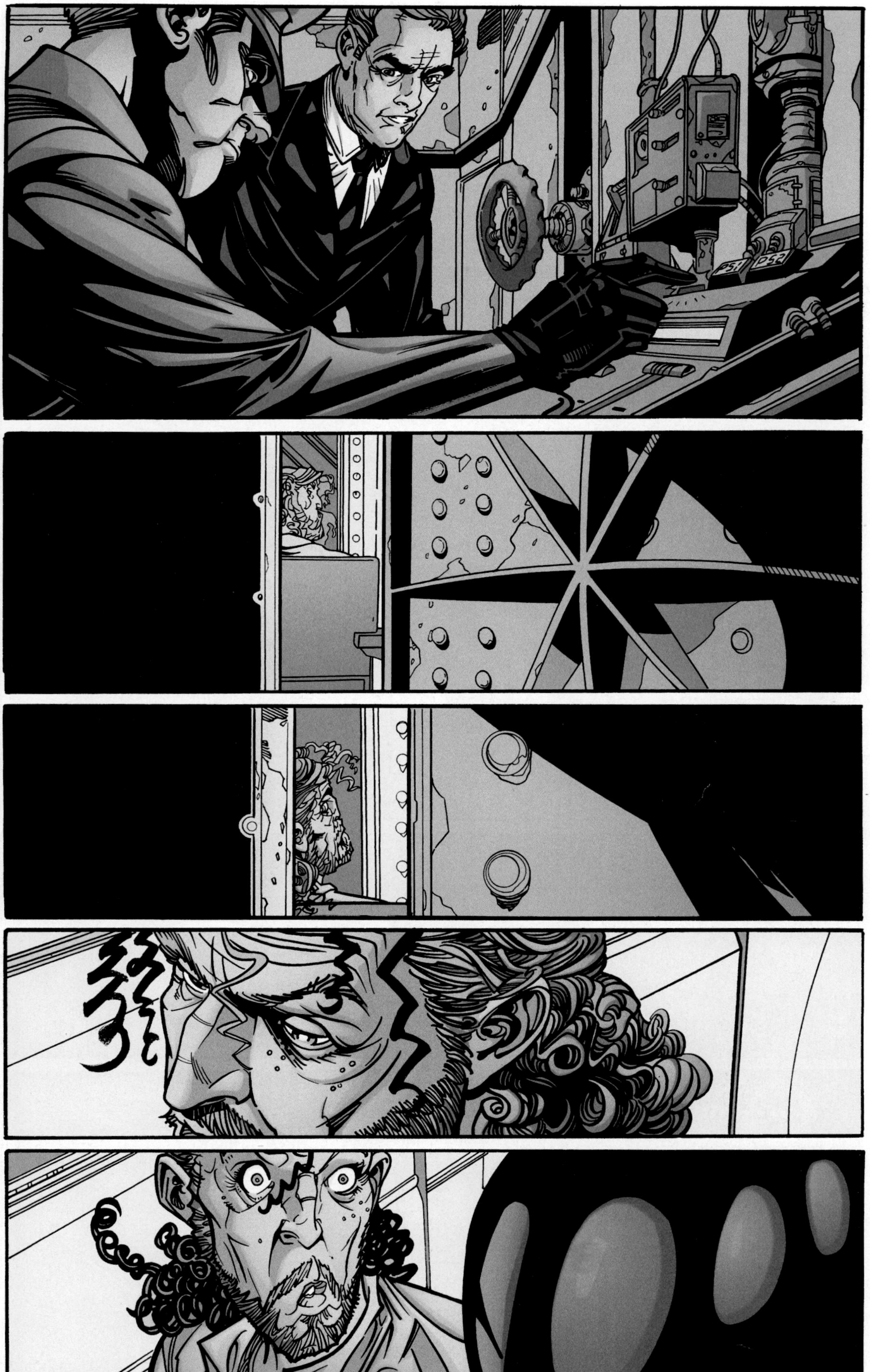
PS1
PS2

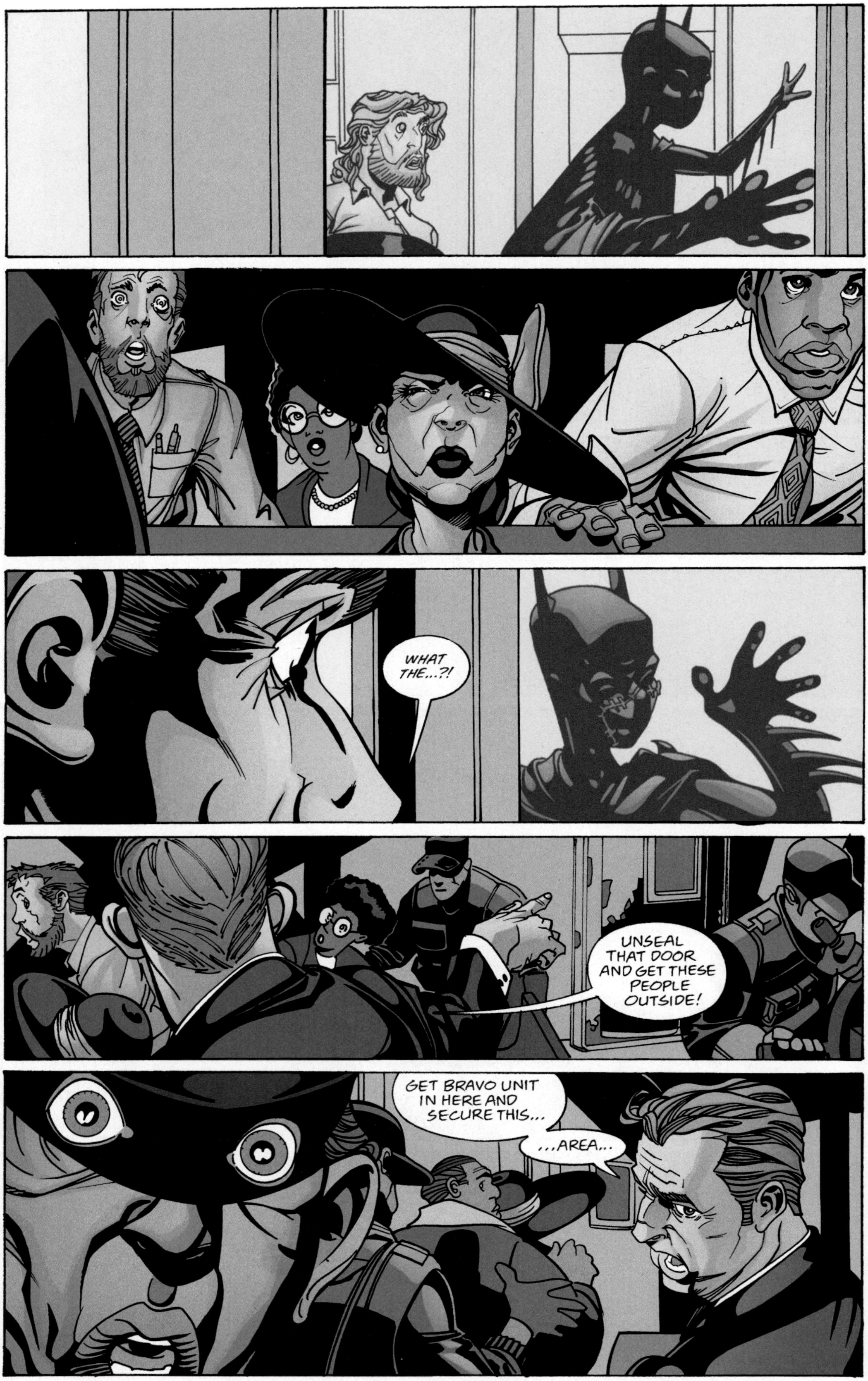
WHAT THE...?!
UNSEAL THAT DOOR AND GET THESE PEOPLE OUTSIDE!
GET BRAVO UNIT IN HERE AND SECURE THIS...
...AREA...

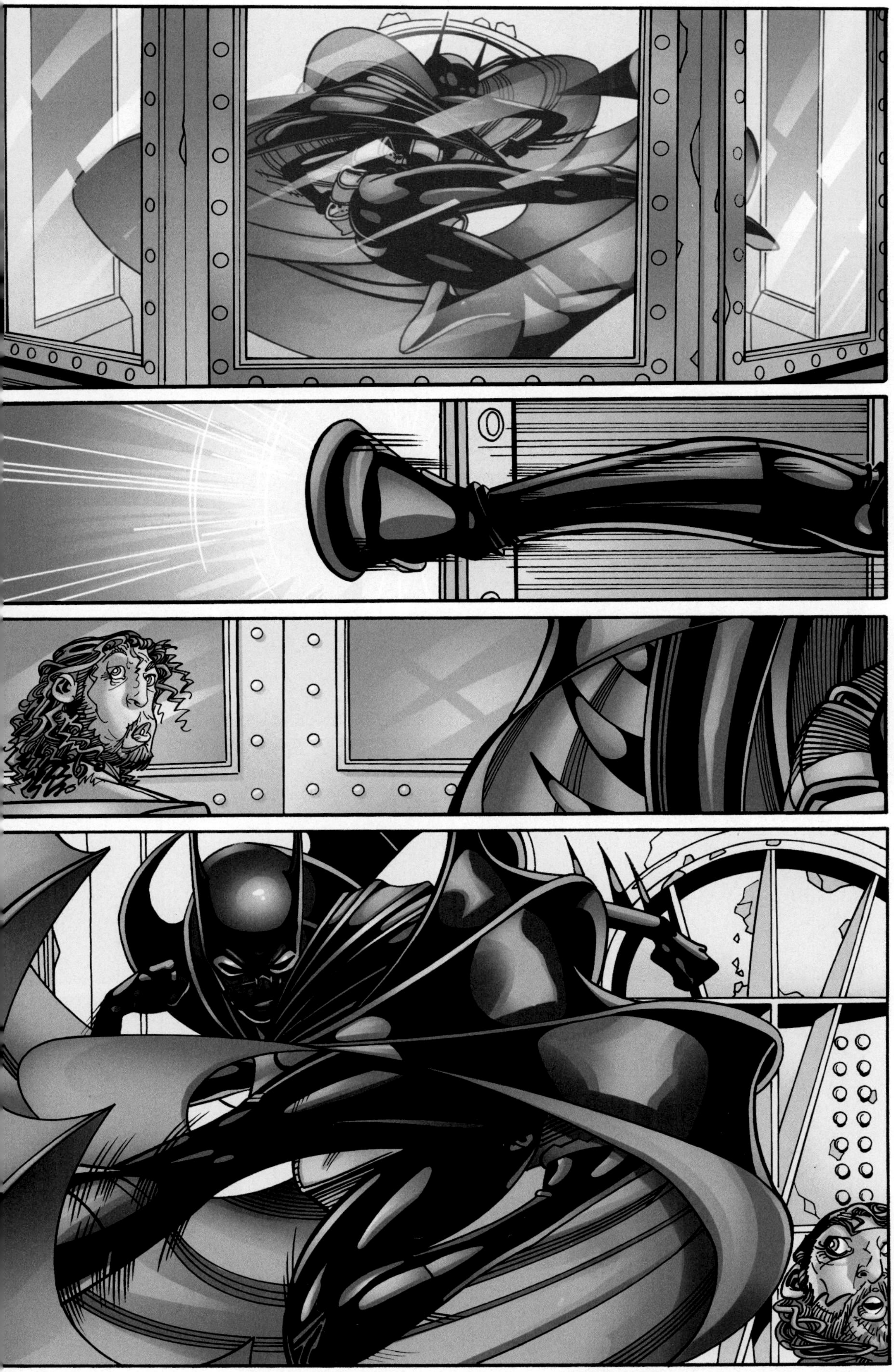

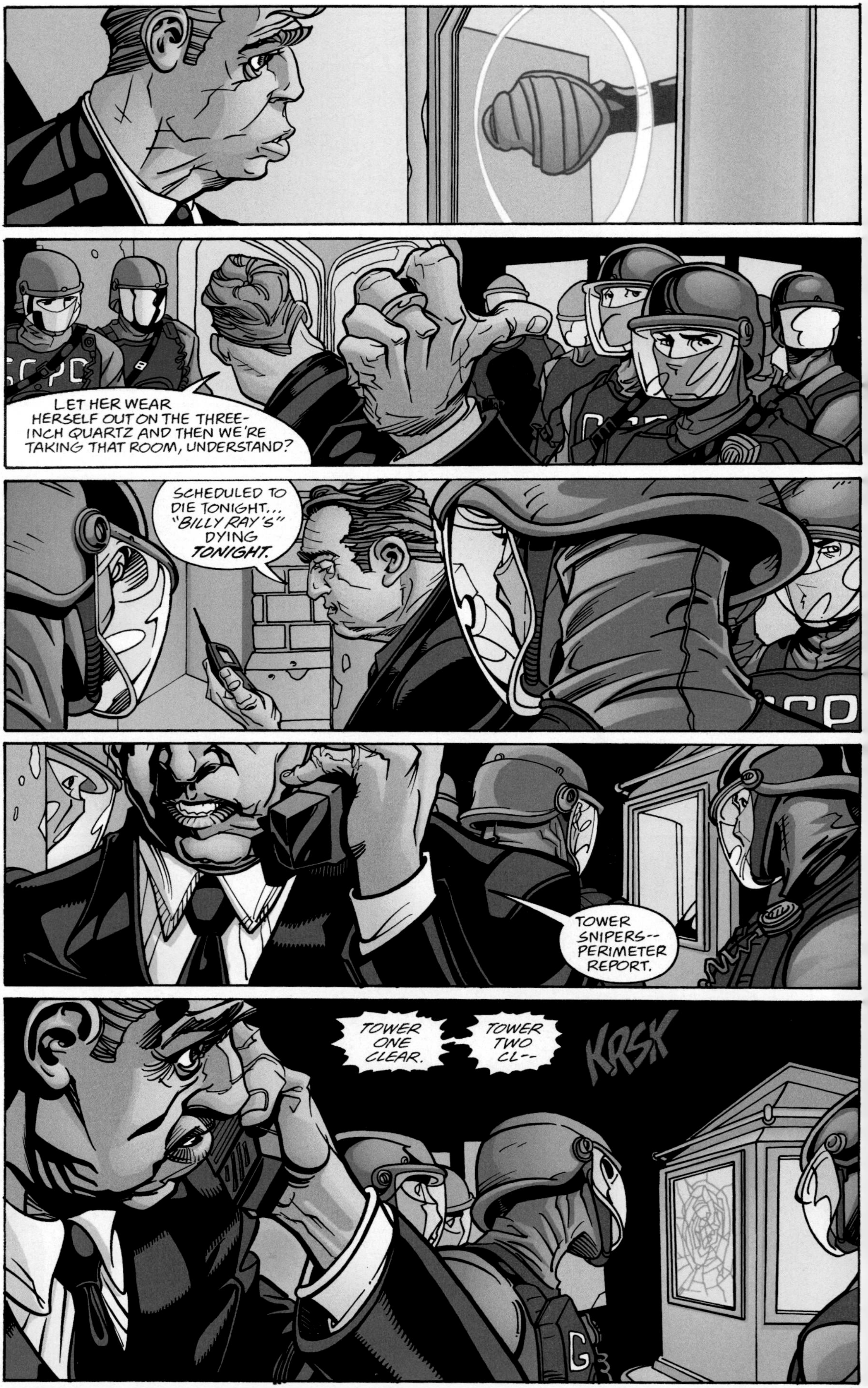
LET HER WEAR HERSELF OUT ON THE THREE-INCH QUARTZ AND THEN WE'RE TAKING THAT ROOM, UNDERSTAND?
SCHEDULED TO DIE TONIGHT... "BILLY RAY'S" DYING TONIGHT.
TOWER SNIPERS-- PERIMETER REPORT.
TOWER ONE CLEAR.
TOWER TWO CL--
KRSK

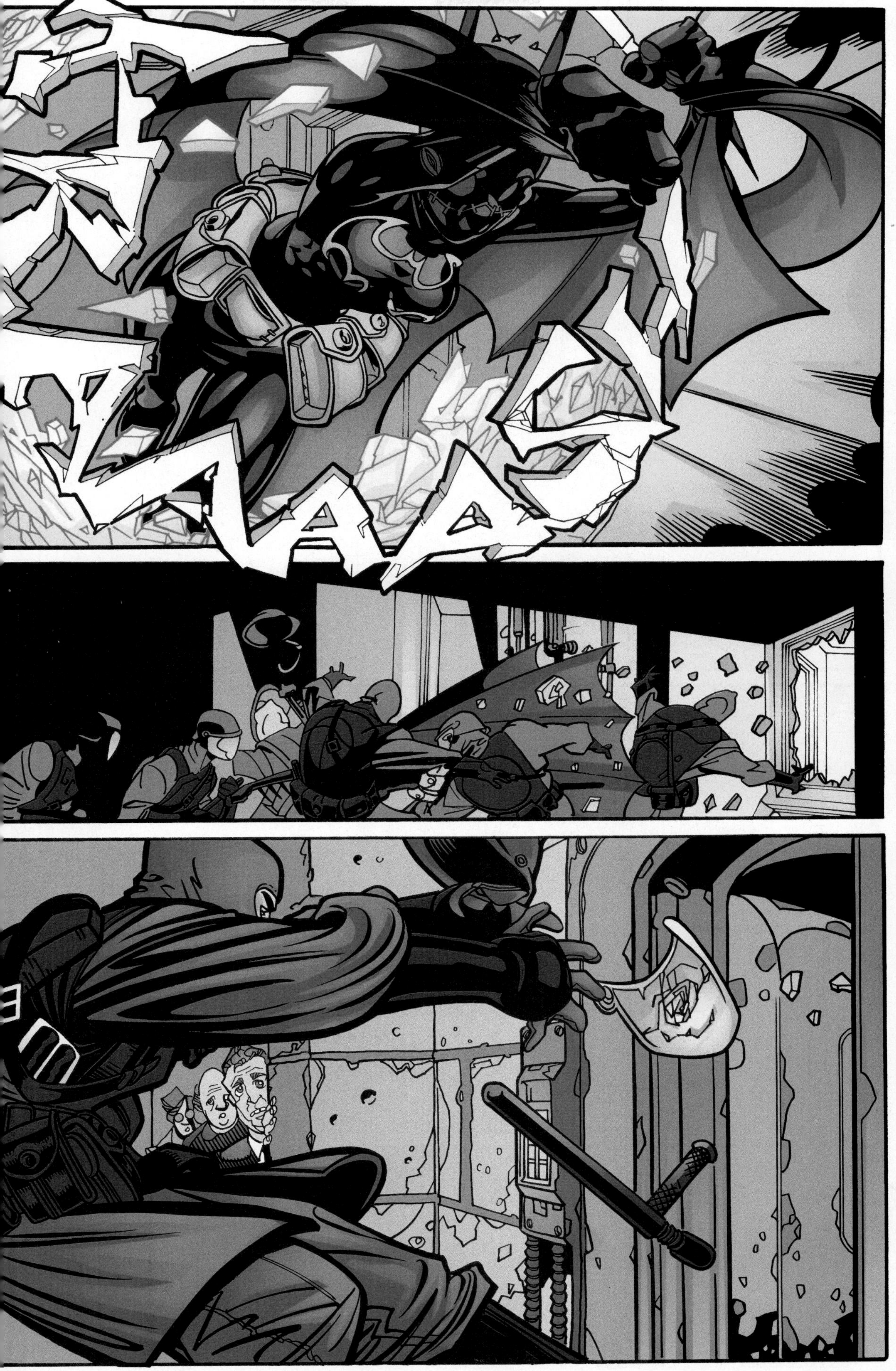

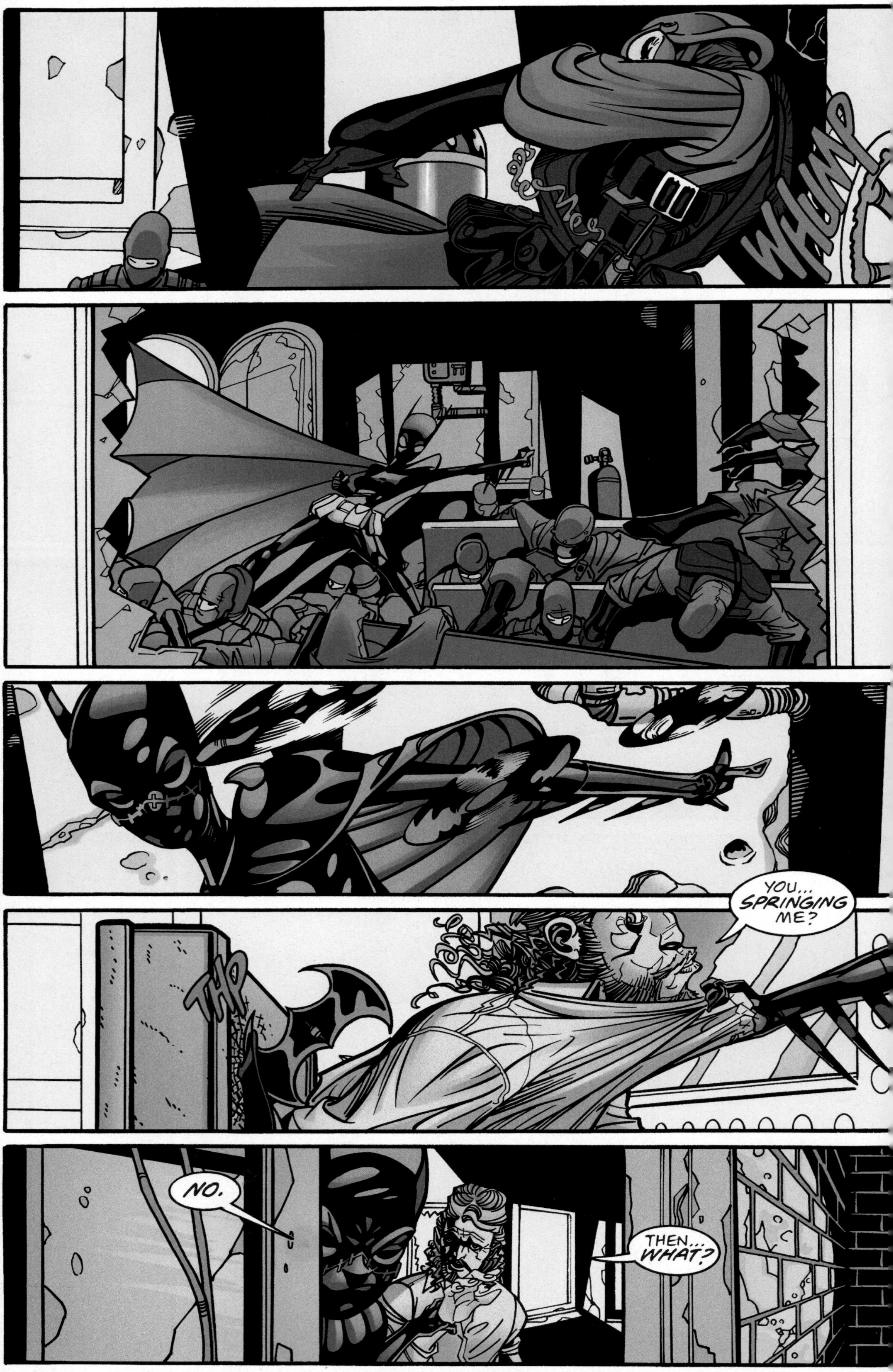
WHUMP
YOU... SPRINGING ME?
THP
NO.
THEN... WHAT?

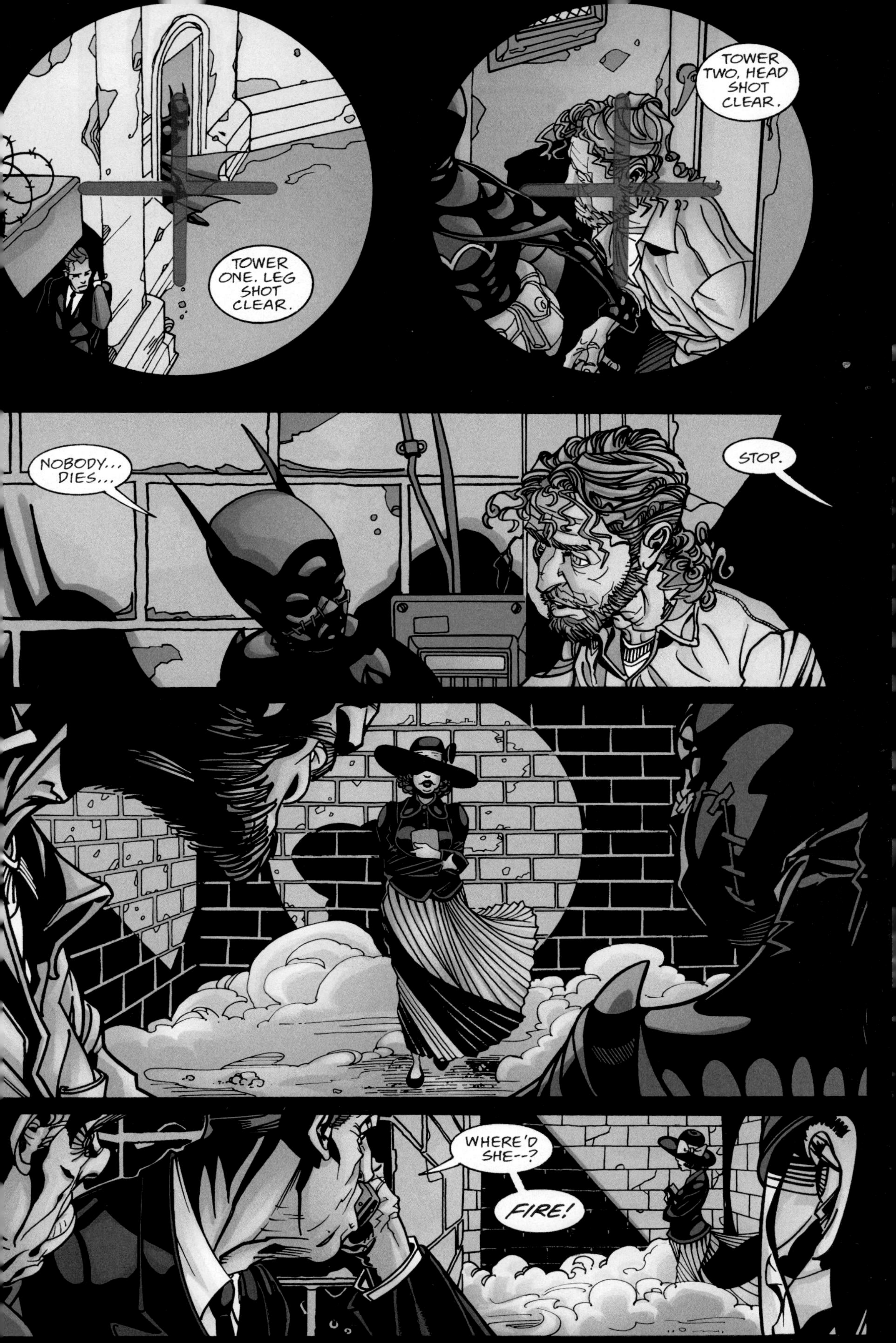
TOWER ONE. LEG SHOT CLEAR.
TOWER TWO, HEAD SHOT CLEAR.
NOBODY... DIES...
STOP.
WHERE'D SHE--?
FIRE!

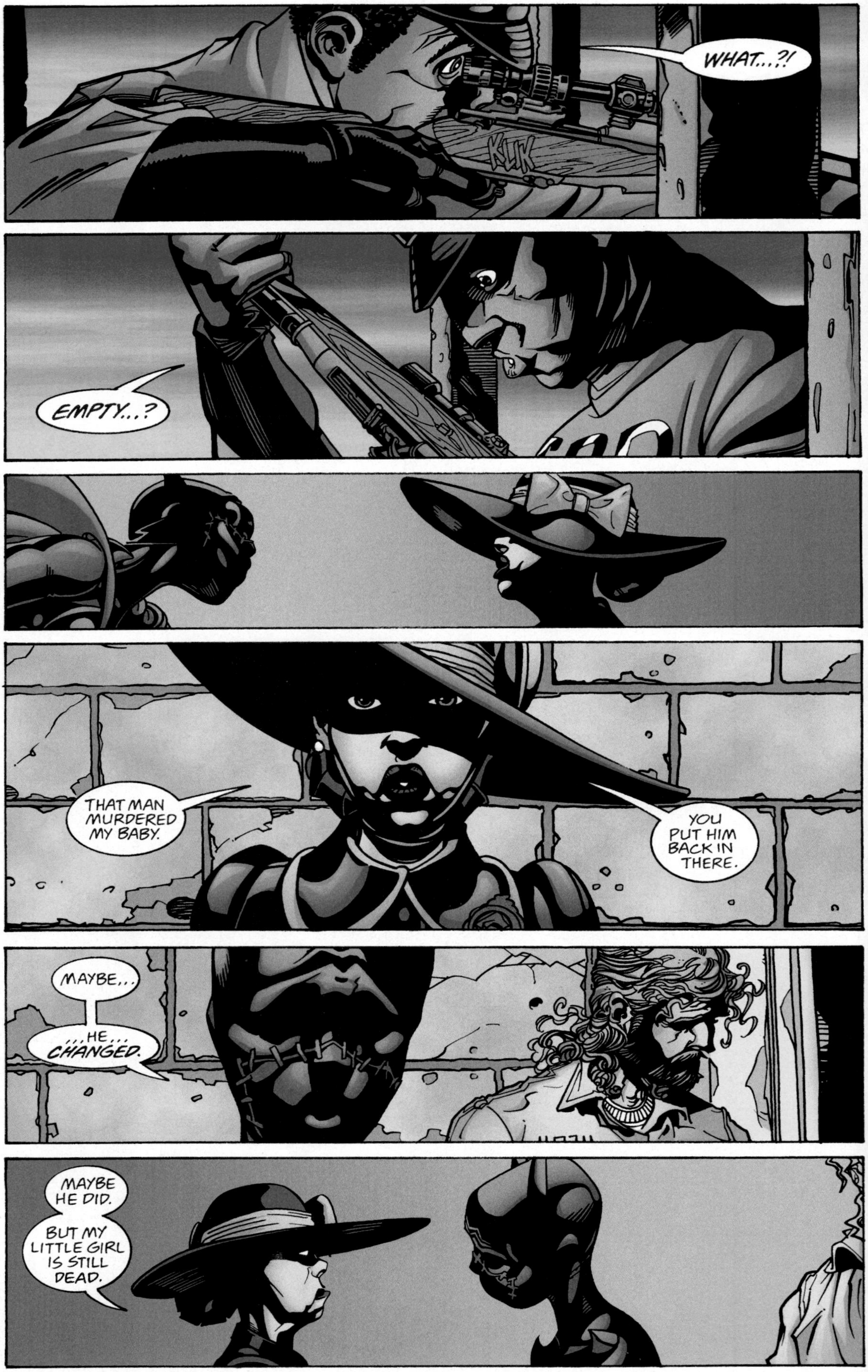
WHAT...?!
KLIK
EMPTY...?
THAT MAN MURDERED MY BABY.
YOU PUT HIM BACK IN THERE.
MAYBE...
...HE... CHANGED.
MAYBE HE DID.
BUT MY LITTLE GIRL IS STILL DEAD.

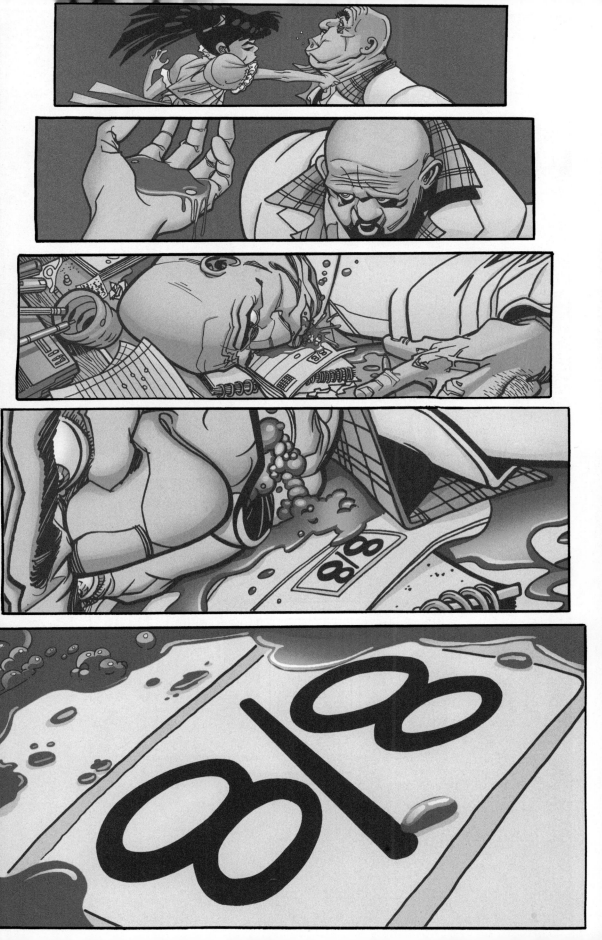

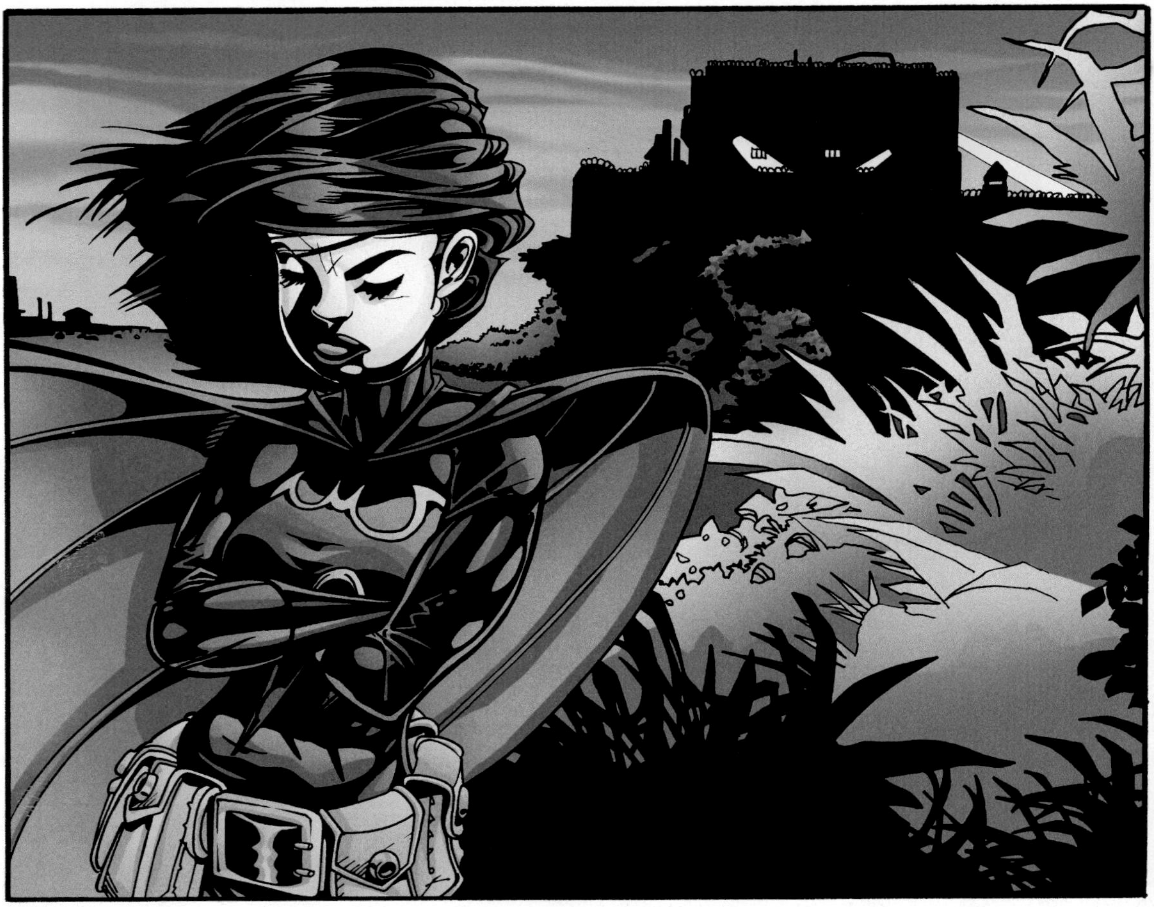

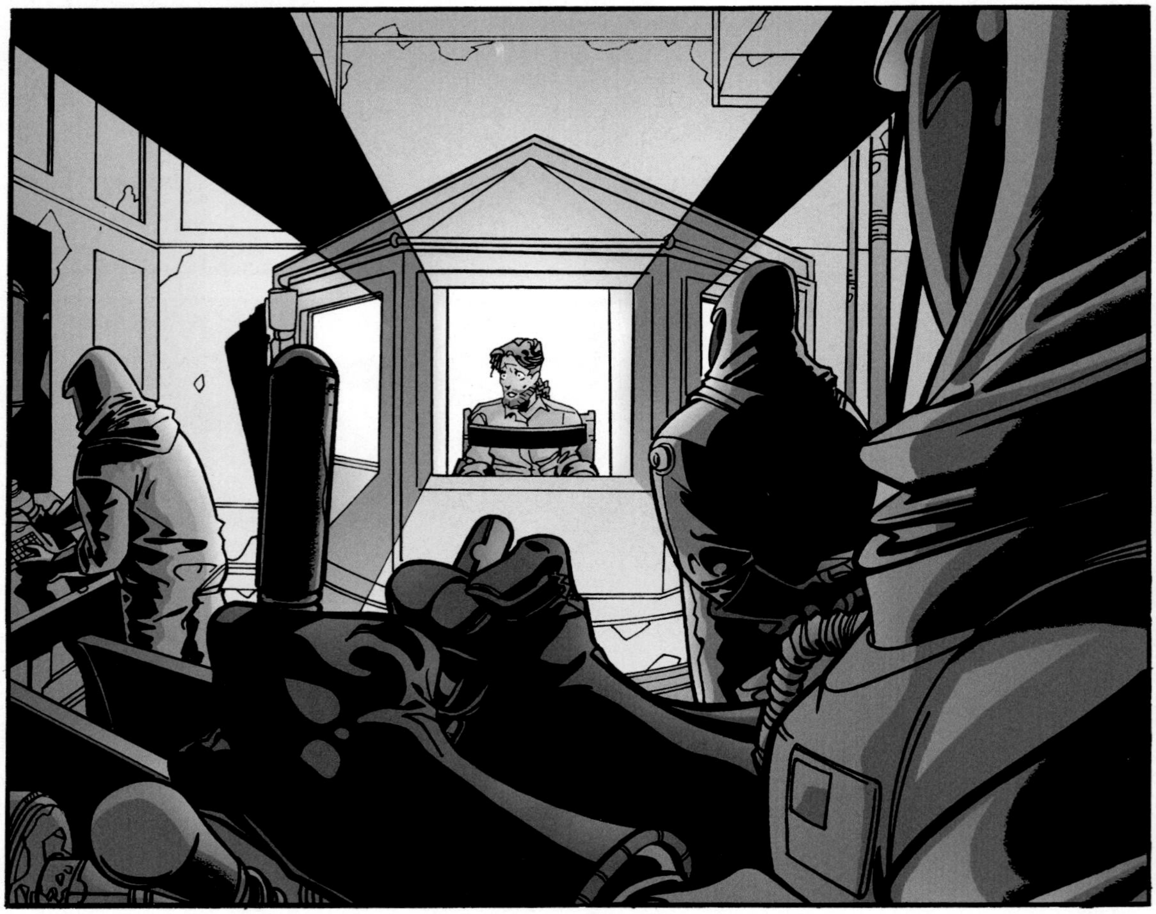

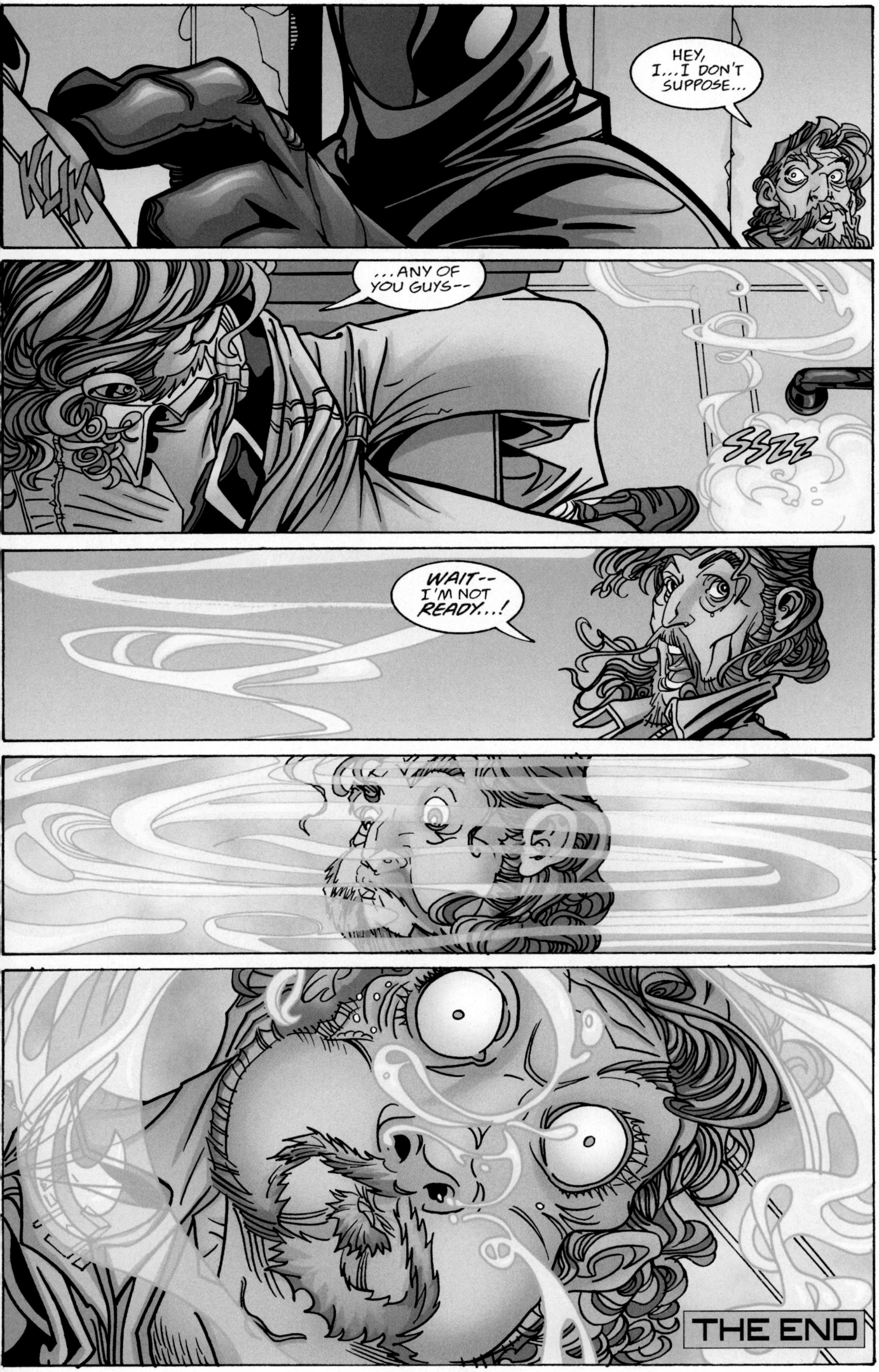
KLIK
HEY, I...I DON'T SUPPOSE...
...ANY OF YOU GUYS--
SSZZZ
WAIT-- I'M NOT READY...!
THE END

BATGIRL #20 cover by Damion Scott,
Robert Campanella & Patrick Martin

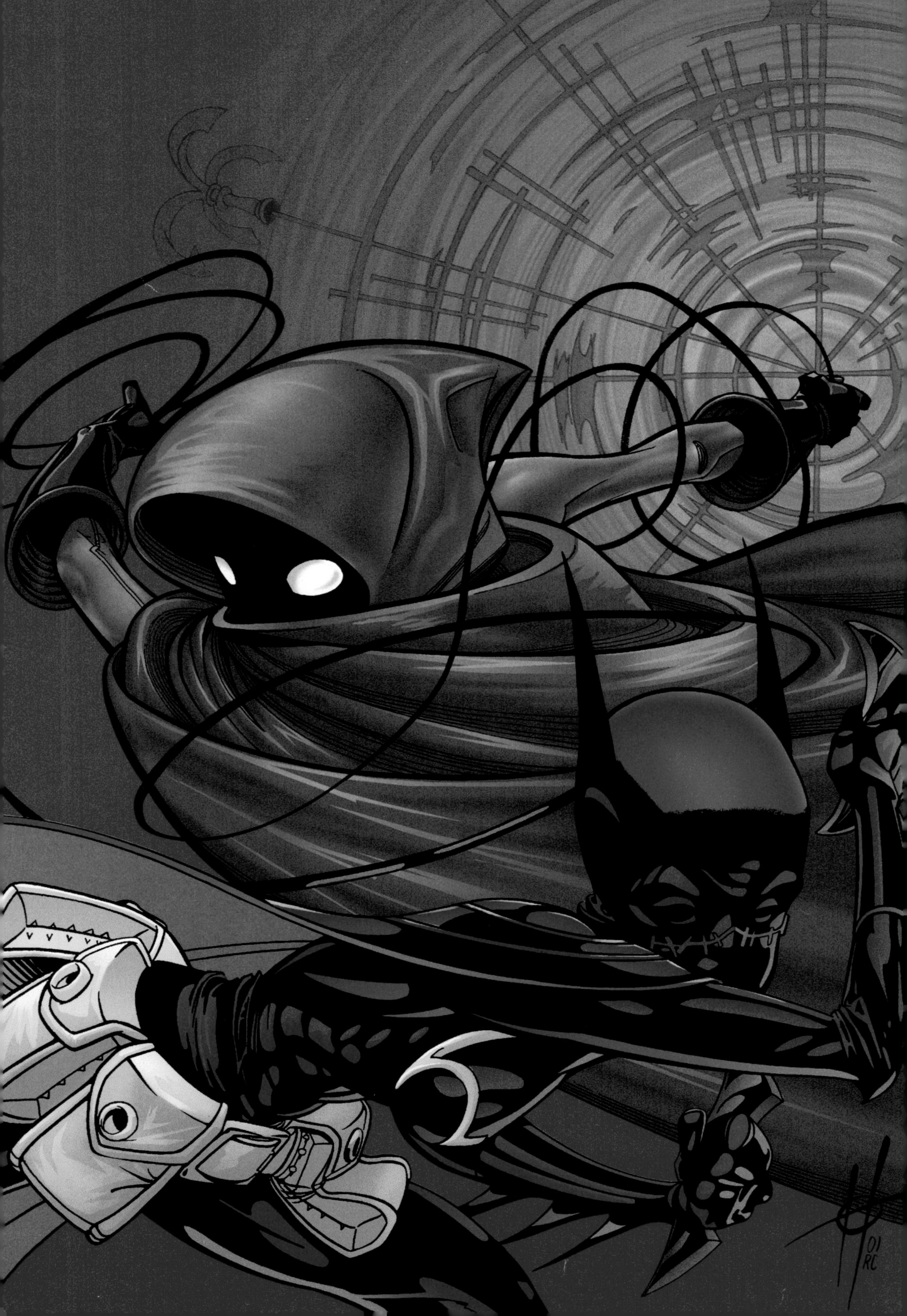

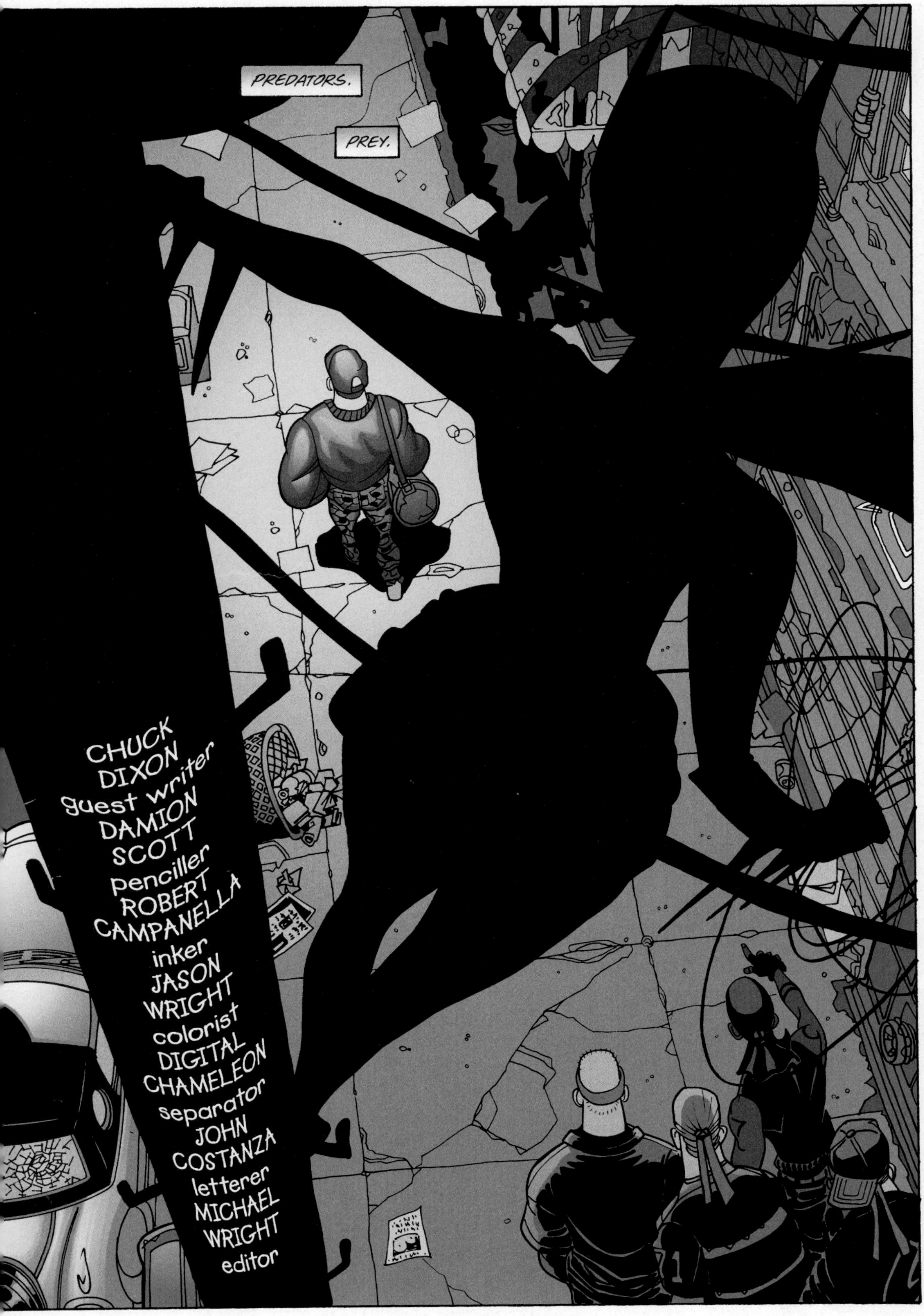
PREDATORS.
PREY.
CHUCK DIXON guest writer
DAMION SCOTT penciller
ROBERT CAMPANELLA inker
JASON WRIGHT colorist
DIGITAL CHAMELEON separator
JOHN COSTANZA letterer
MICHAEL WRIGHT editor

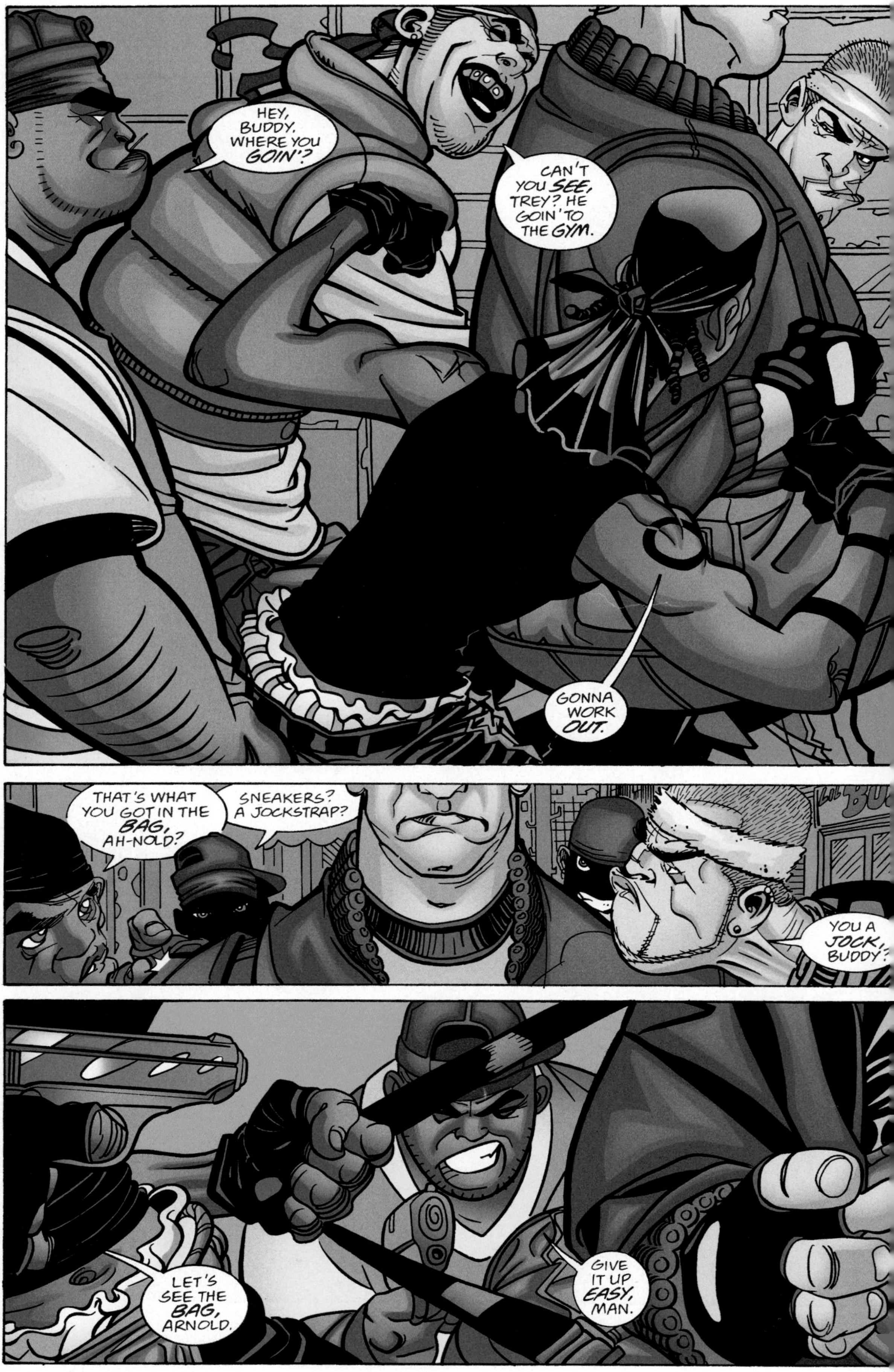
HEY, BUDDY. WHERE YOU GOIN'?
CAN'T YOU SEE, TREY? HE GOIN' TO THE GYM.
GONNA WORK OUT.
THAT'S WHAT YOU GOT IN THE BAG, AH-NOLD?
SNEAKERS? A JOCKSTRAP?
YOU A JOCK, BUDDY?
LET'S SEE THE BAG, ARNOLD.
GIVE IT UP EASY, MAN.

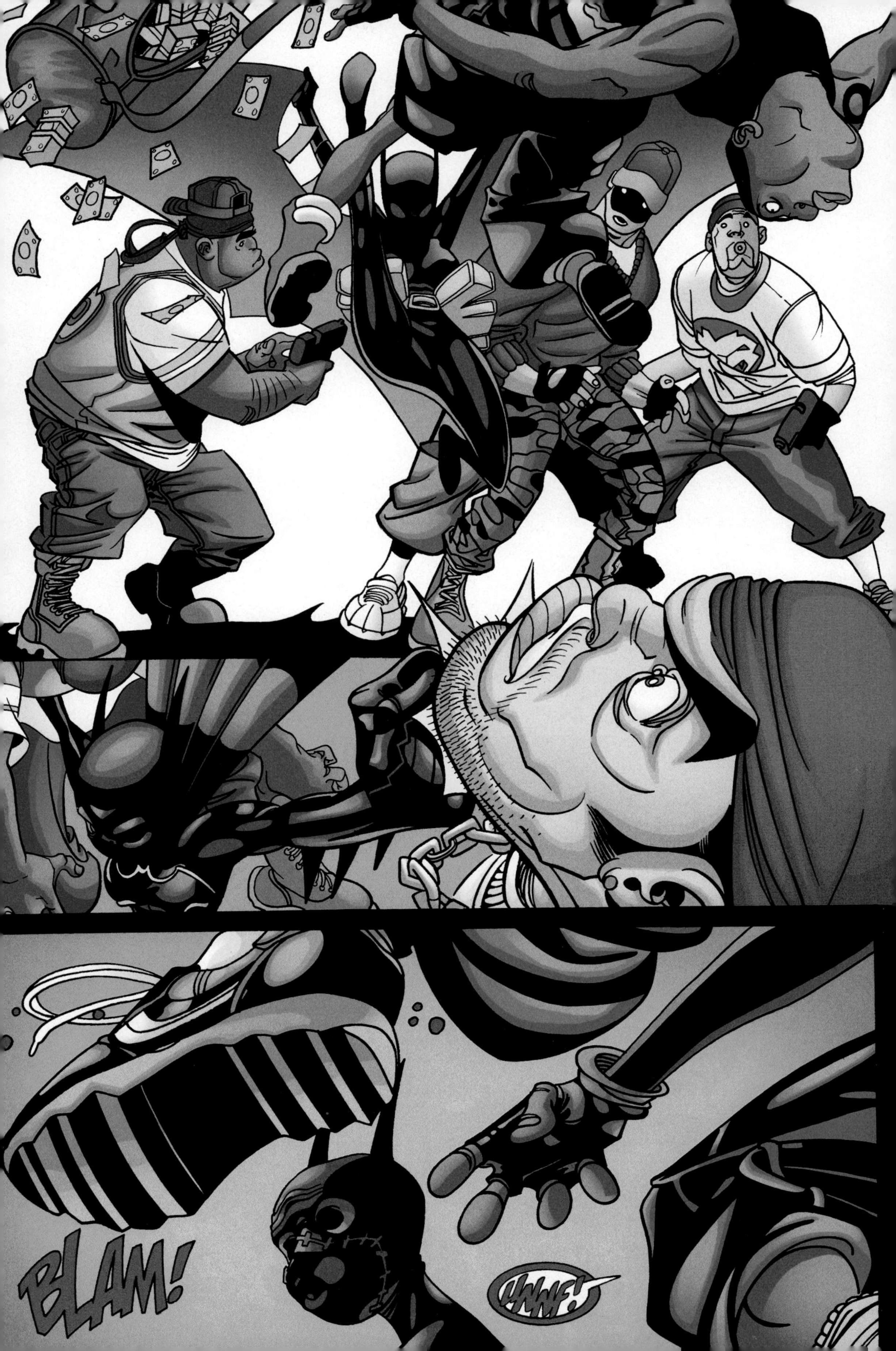
BLAM!
UNNF!

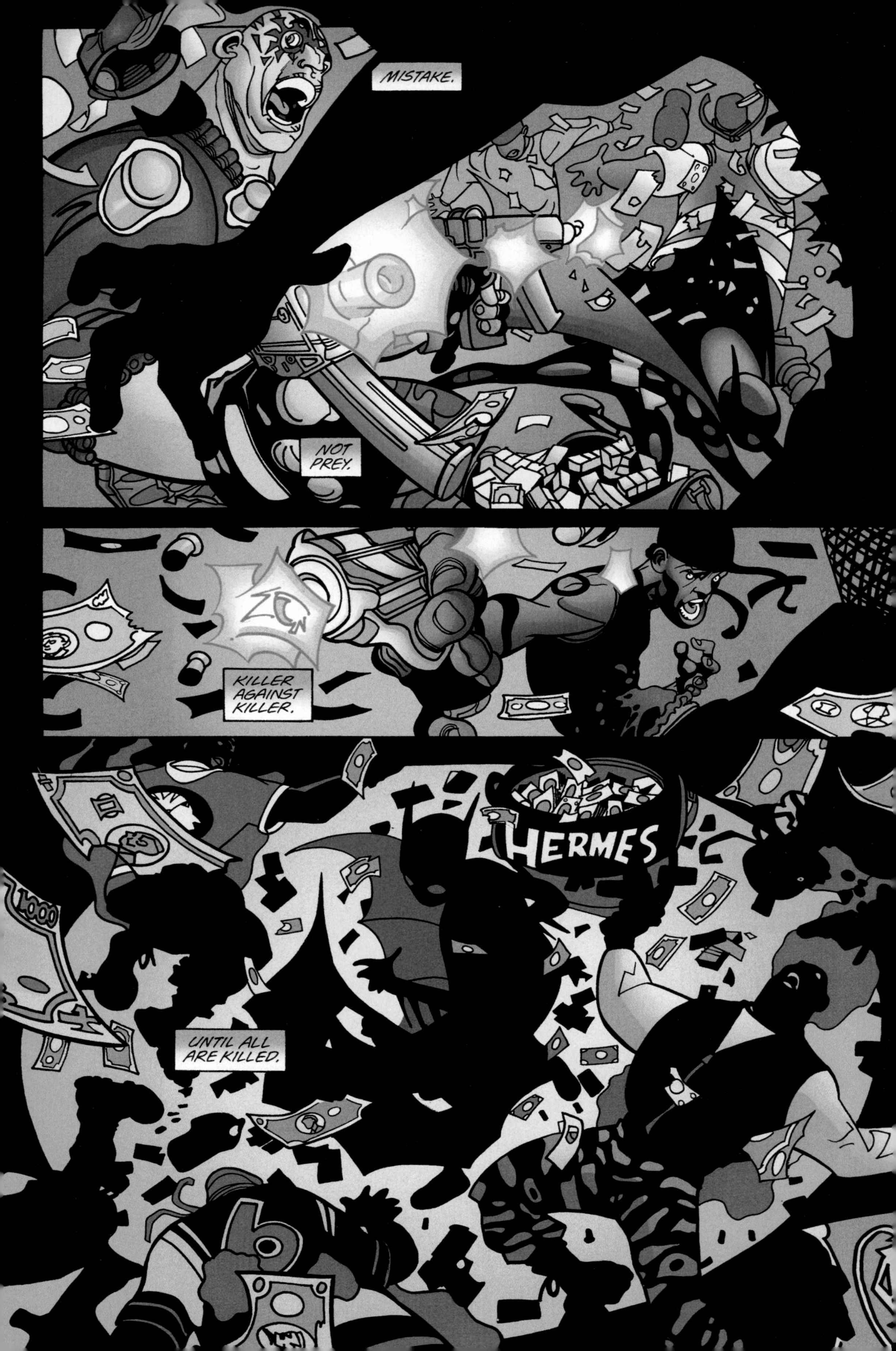
MISTAKE.
NOT PREY.
KILLER AGAINST KILLER.
HERMES
UNTIL ALL ARE KILLED.

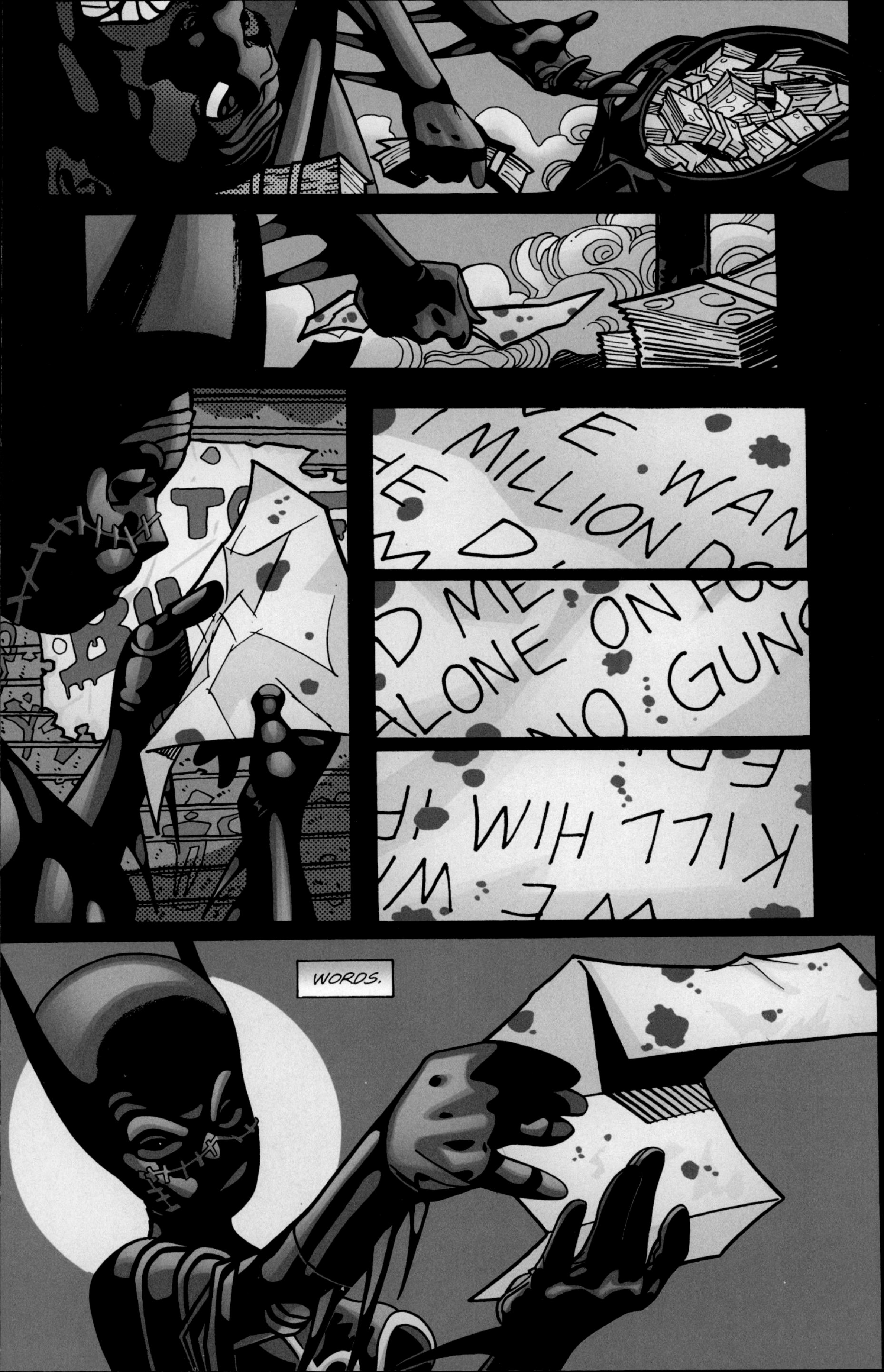
MILLION
ALONE ON
KILL HIM
WORDS.

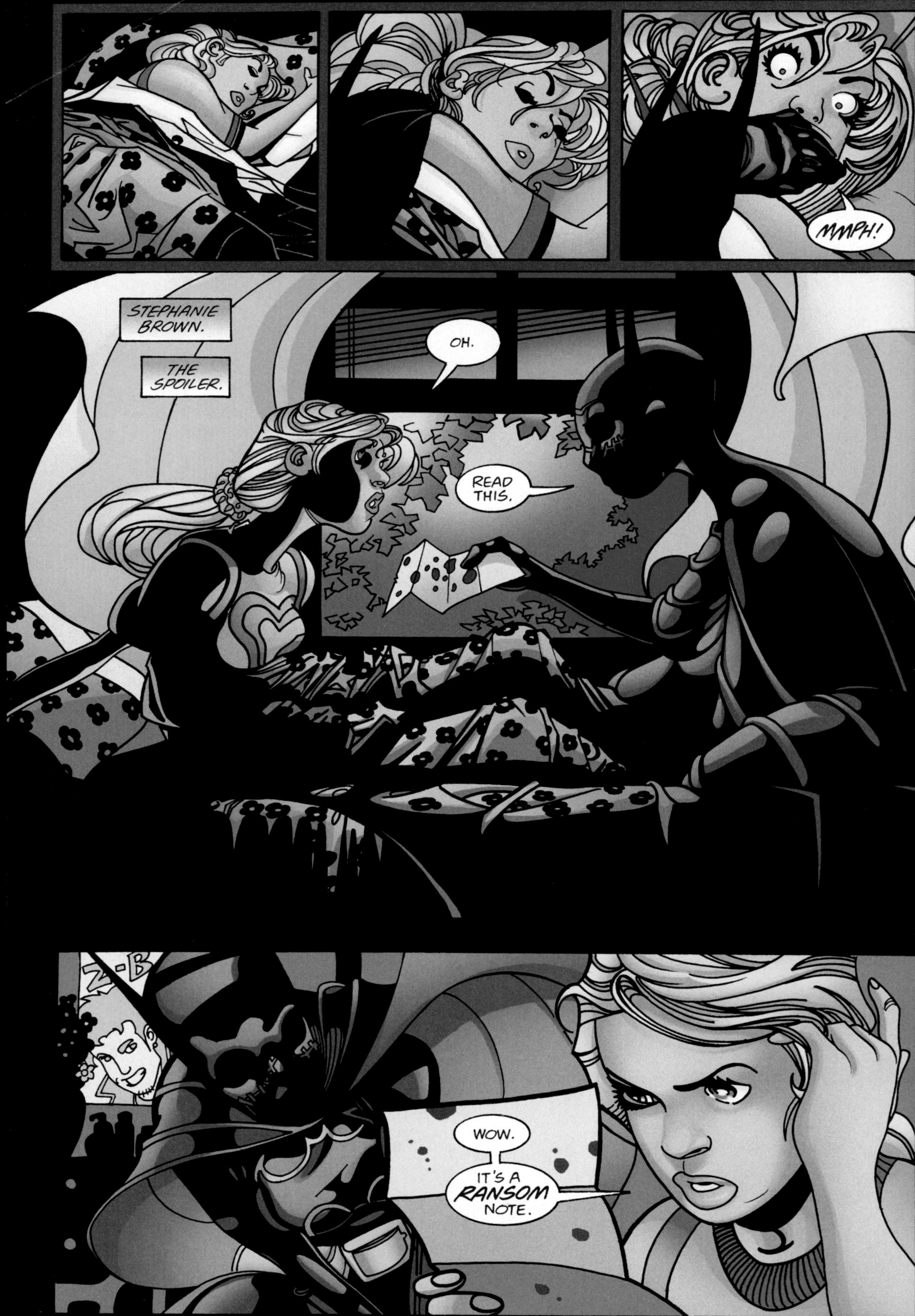
MMPH!
STEPHANIE BROWN.
THE SPOILER.
OH.
READ THIS.
WOW.
IT'S A RANSOM NOTE.

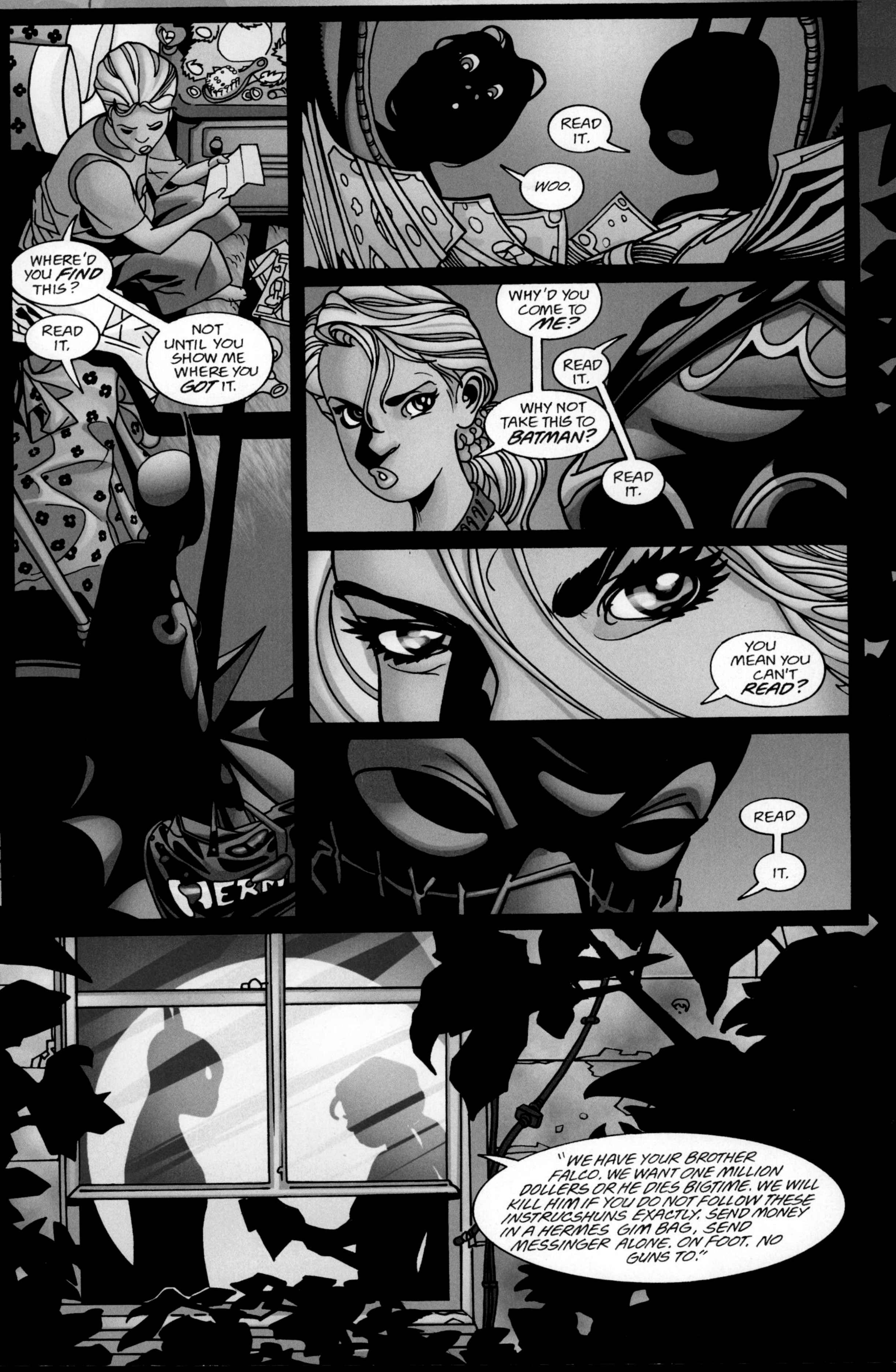

READ IT.
WOO.
WHERE'D YOU FIND THIS?
READ IT.
NOT UNTIL YOU SHOW ME WHERE YOU GOT IT.
WHY'D YOU COME TO ME?
READ IT.
WHY NOT TAKE THIS TO BATMAN?
READ IT.
YOU MEAN YOU CAN'T READ?
READ
IT.
"WE HAVE YOUR BROTHER FALCO. WE WANT ONE MILLION DOLLERS OR HE DIES BIGTIME. WE WILL KILL HIM IF YOU DO NOT FOLLOW THESE INSTRUCSHUNS EXACTLY. SEND MONEY IN A HERMES GIM BAG. SEND MESSINGER ALONE. ON FOOT. NO GUNS TO."

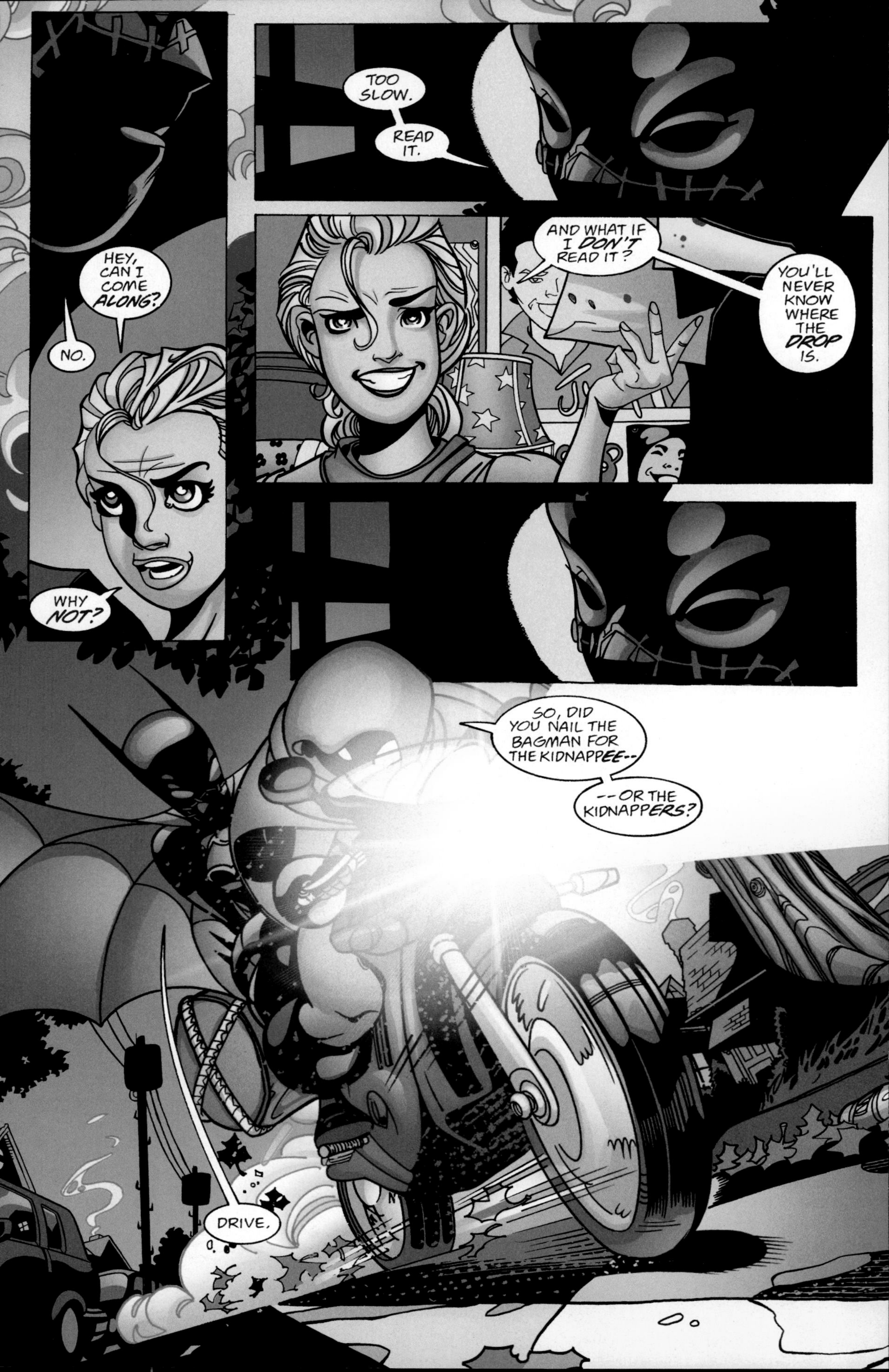
HEY, CAN I COME ALONG?
NO.
WHY NOT?
TOO SLOW.
READ IT.
AND WHAT IF I DON'T READ IT?
YOU'LL NEVER KNOW WHERE THE DROP IS.
SO, DID YOU NAIL THE BAGMAN FOR THE KIDNAPPEE--
--OR THE KIDNAPPERS?
DRIVE.

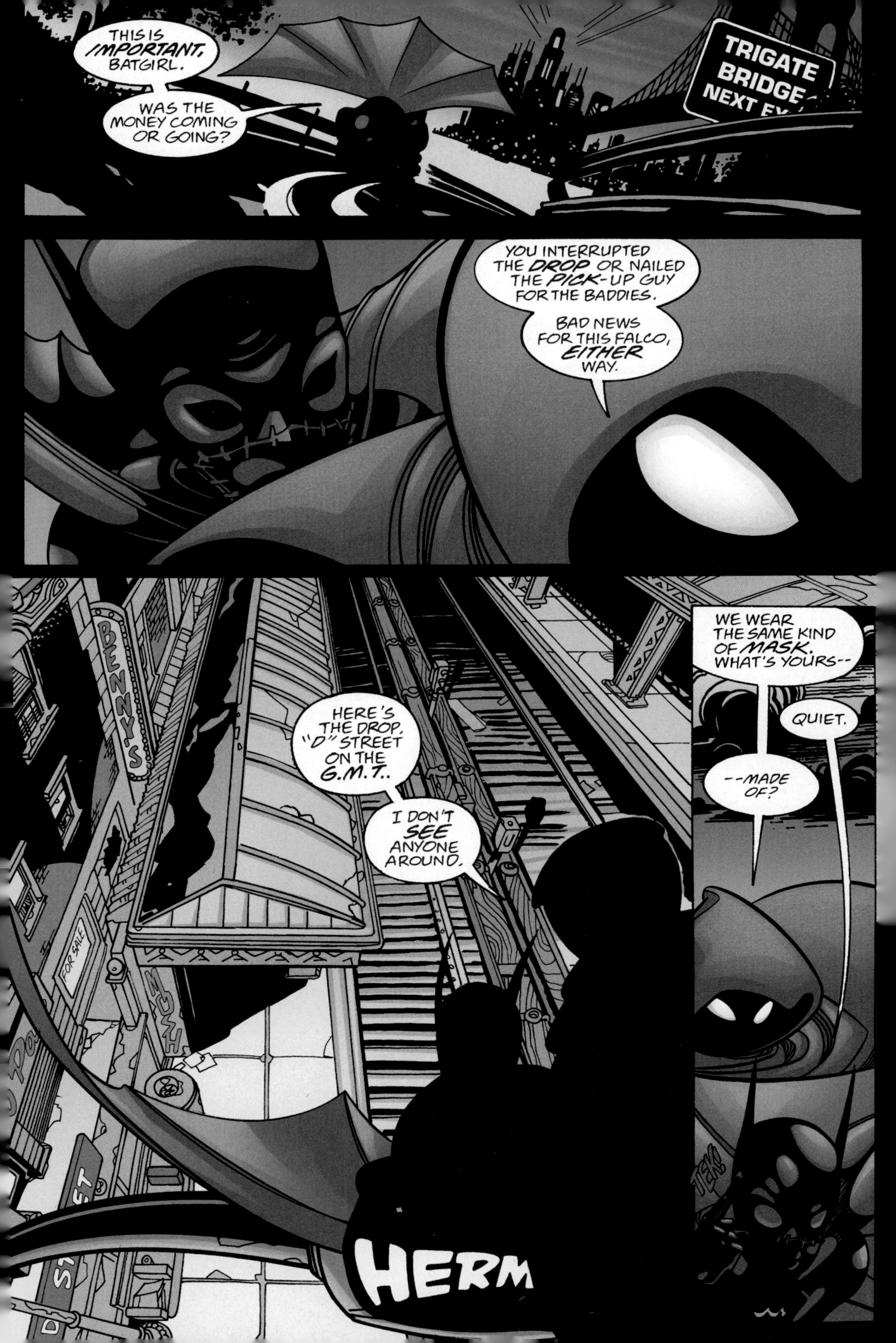
TRIGATE BRIDGE NEXT EX
THIS IS IMPORTANT, BATGIRL.
WAS THE MONEY COMING OR GOING?
YOU INTERRUPTED THE DROP OR NAILED THE PICK-UP GUY FOR THE BADDIES.
BAD NEWS FOR THIS FALCO, EITHER WAY.
BENNY'S
HERE'S THE DROP. "D" STREET ON THE G.M.T..
I DON'T SEE ANYONE AROUND.
FOR SALE
WE WEAR THE SAME KIND OF MASK. WHAT'S YOURS--
QUIET.
--MADE OF?
HERM

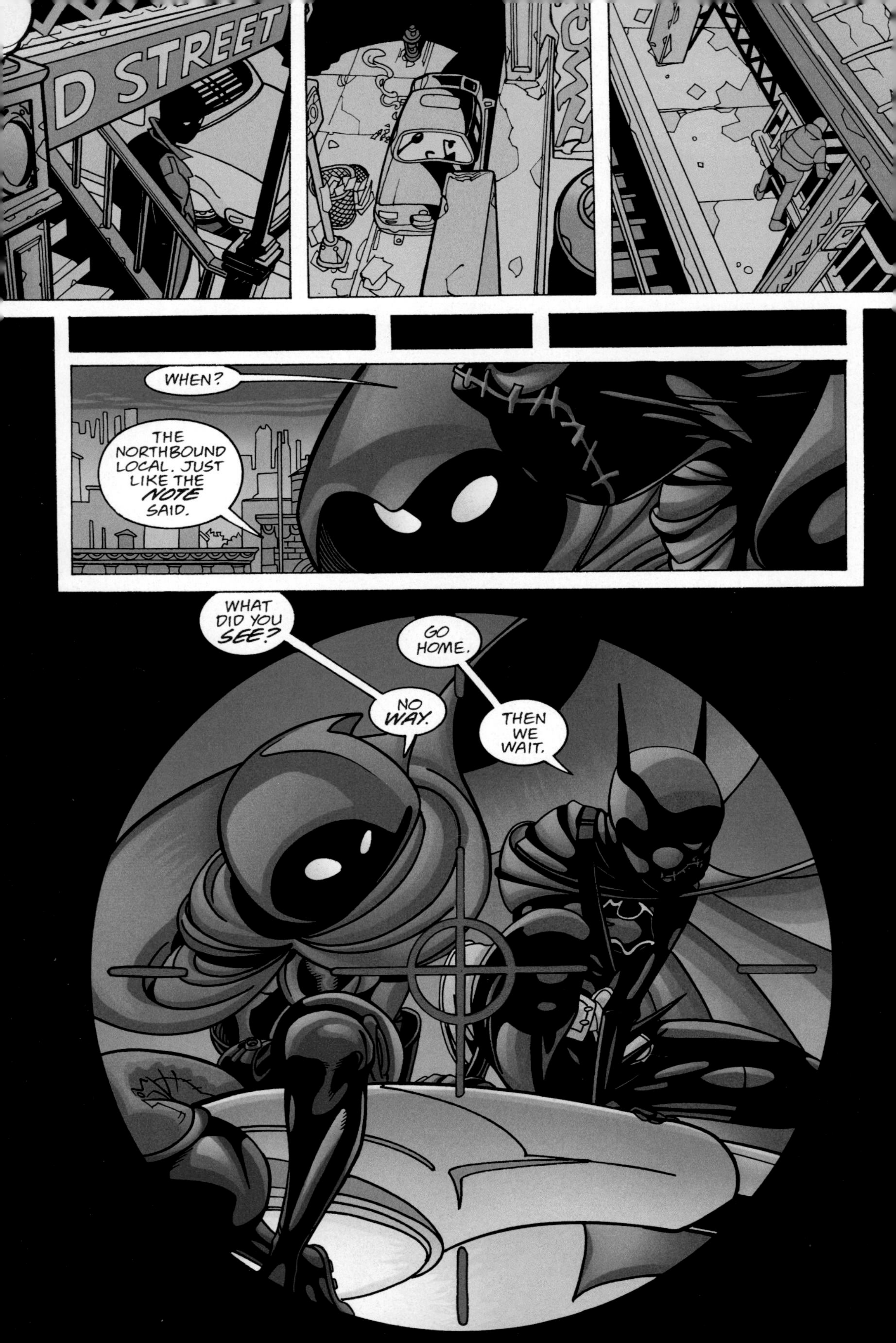
D STREET
WHEN?
THE NORTHBOUND LOCAL. JUST LIKE THE NOTE SAID.
WHAT DID YOU SEE?
NO WAY.
GO HOME.
THEN WE WAIT.

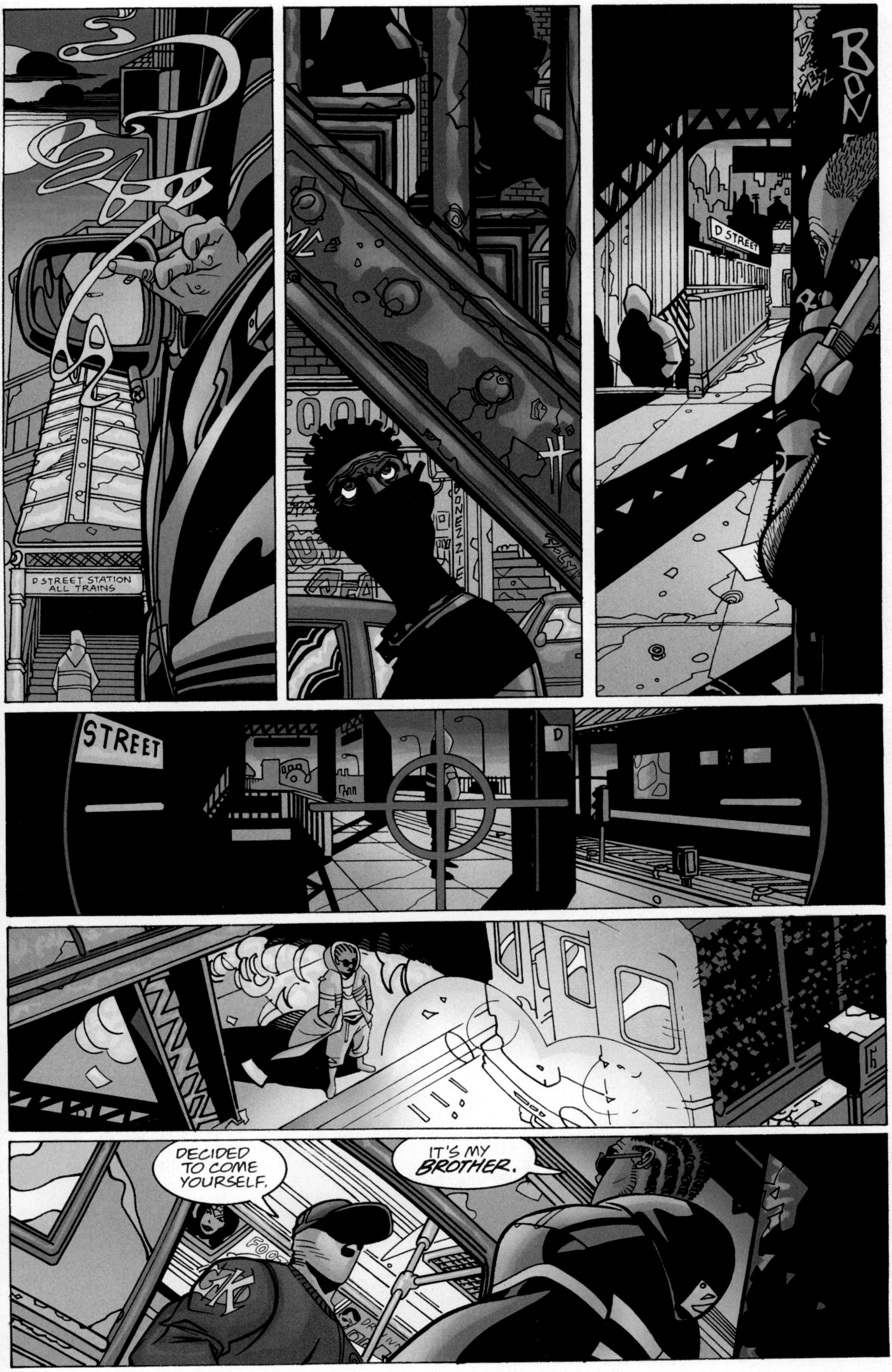
D STREET STATION
ALL TRAINS
D STREET
STREET
D
DECIDED TO COME YOURSELF.
IT'S MY BROTHER.

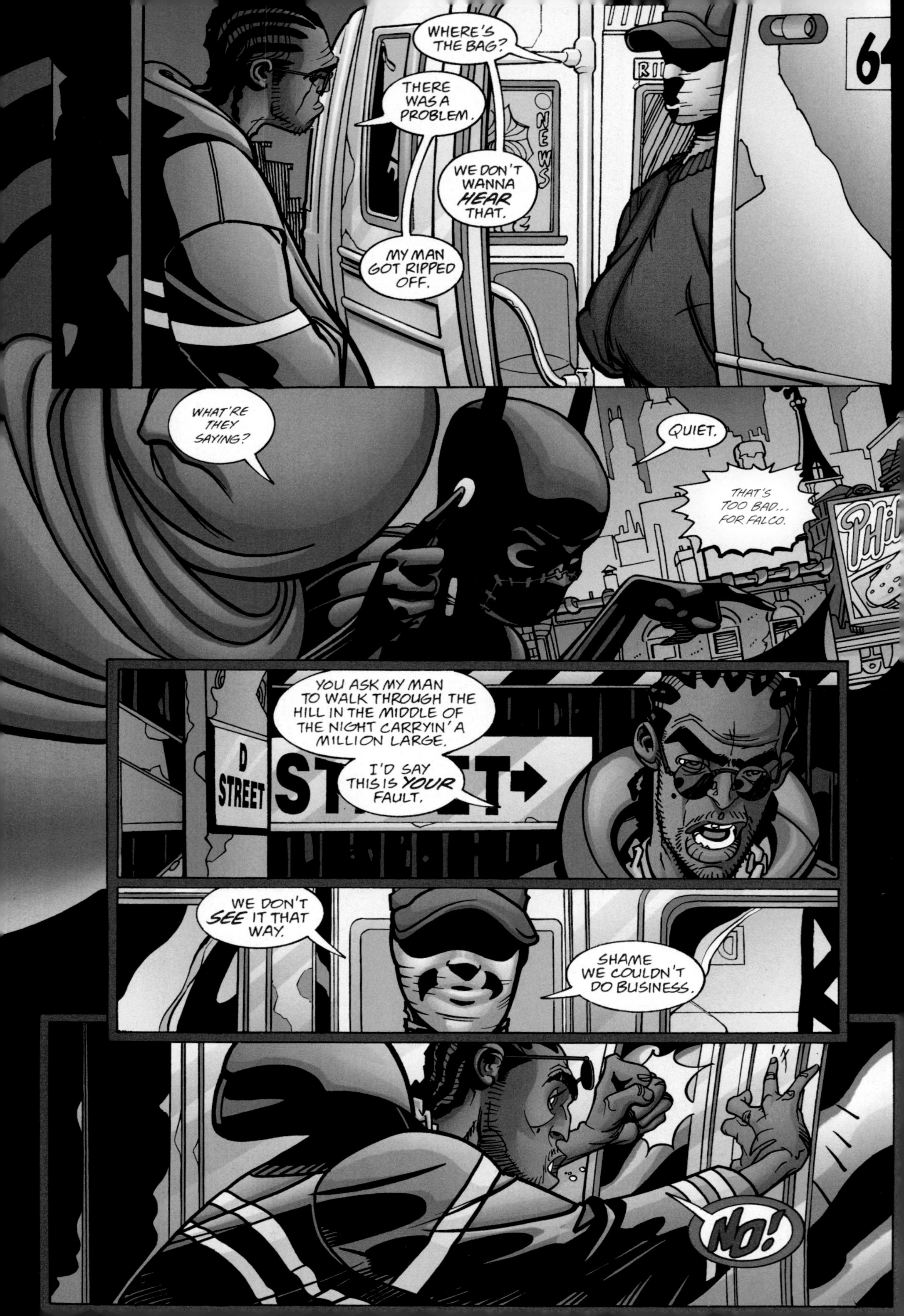
WHERE'S THE BAG?
THERE WAS A PROBLEM.
WE DON'T WANNA HEAR THAT.
MY MAN GOT RIPPED OFF.
WHAT'RE THEY SAYING?
QUIET.
THAT'S TOO BAD... FOR FALCO.
D STREET
YOU ASK MY MAN TO WALK THROUGH THE HILL IN THE MIDDLE OF THE NIGHT CARRYIN' A MILLION LARGE.
I'D SAY THIS IS YOUR FAULT.
WE DON'T SEE IT THAT WAY.
SHAME WE COULDN'T DO BUSINESS.
NO!

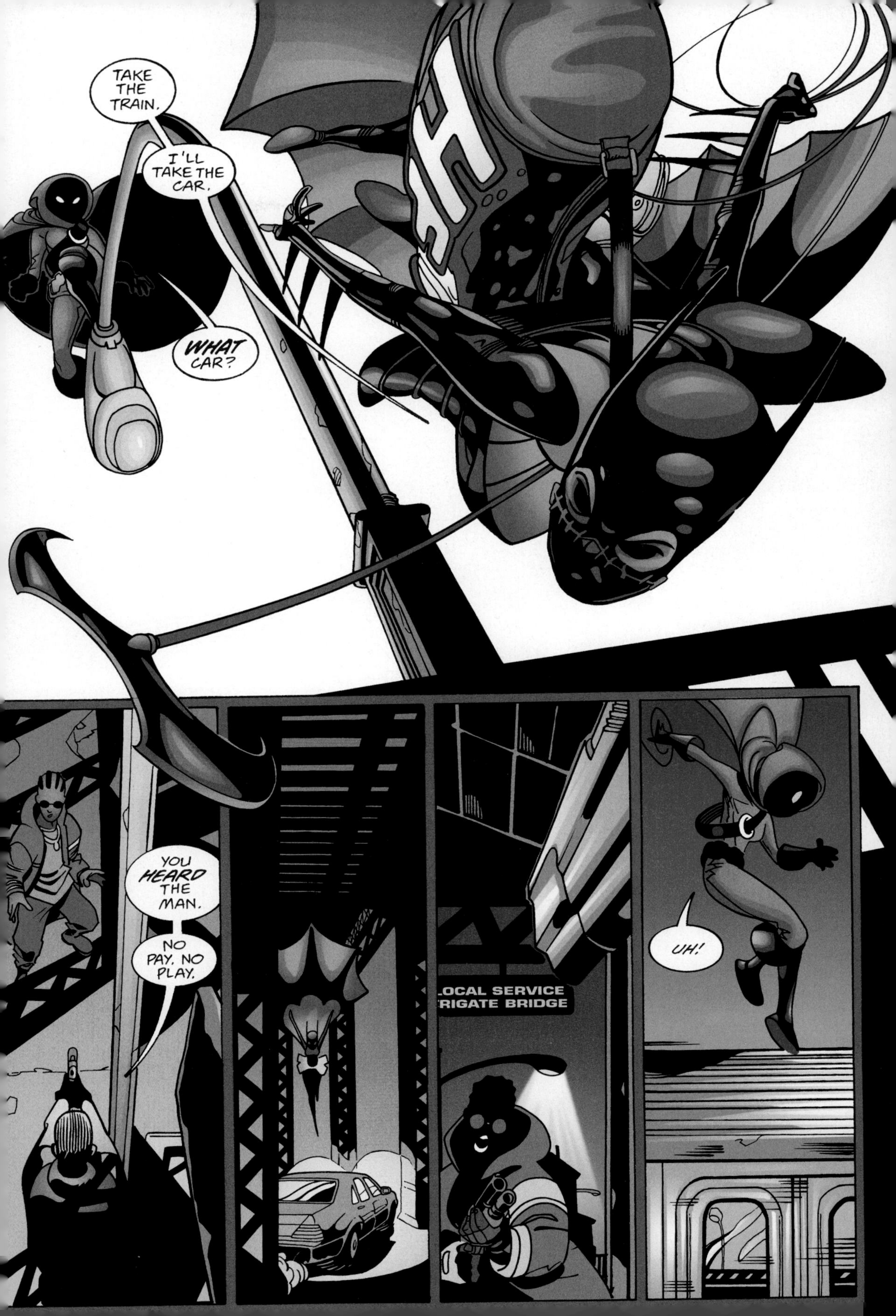

TAKE THE TRAIN.
I'LL TAKE THE CAR.
WHAT CAR?
YOU HEARD THE MAN.
NO PAY, NO PLAY.
LOCAL SERVICE
TRIGATE BRIDGE
UH!

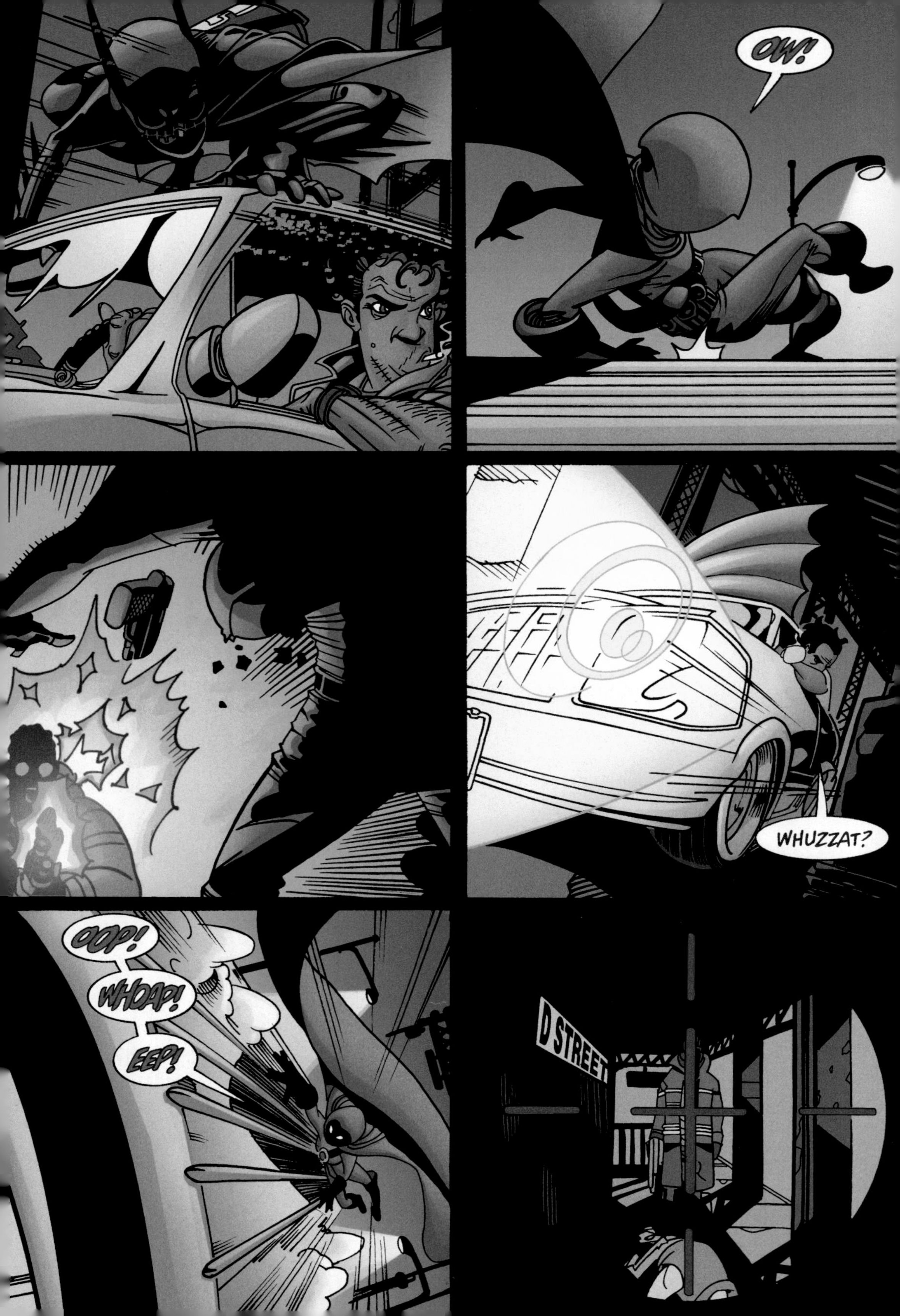
OW!
WHUZZAT?
OOP!
WHOAP!
EEP!
D STREET

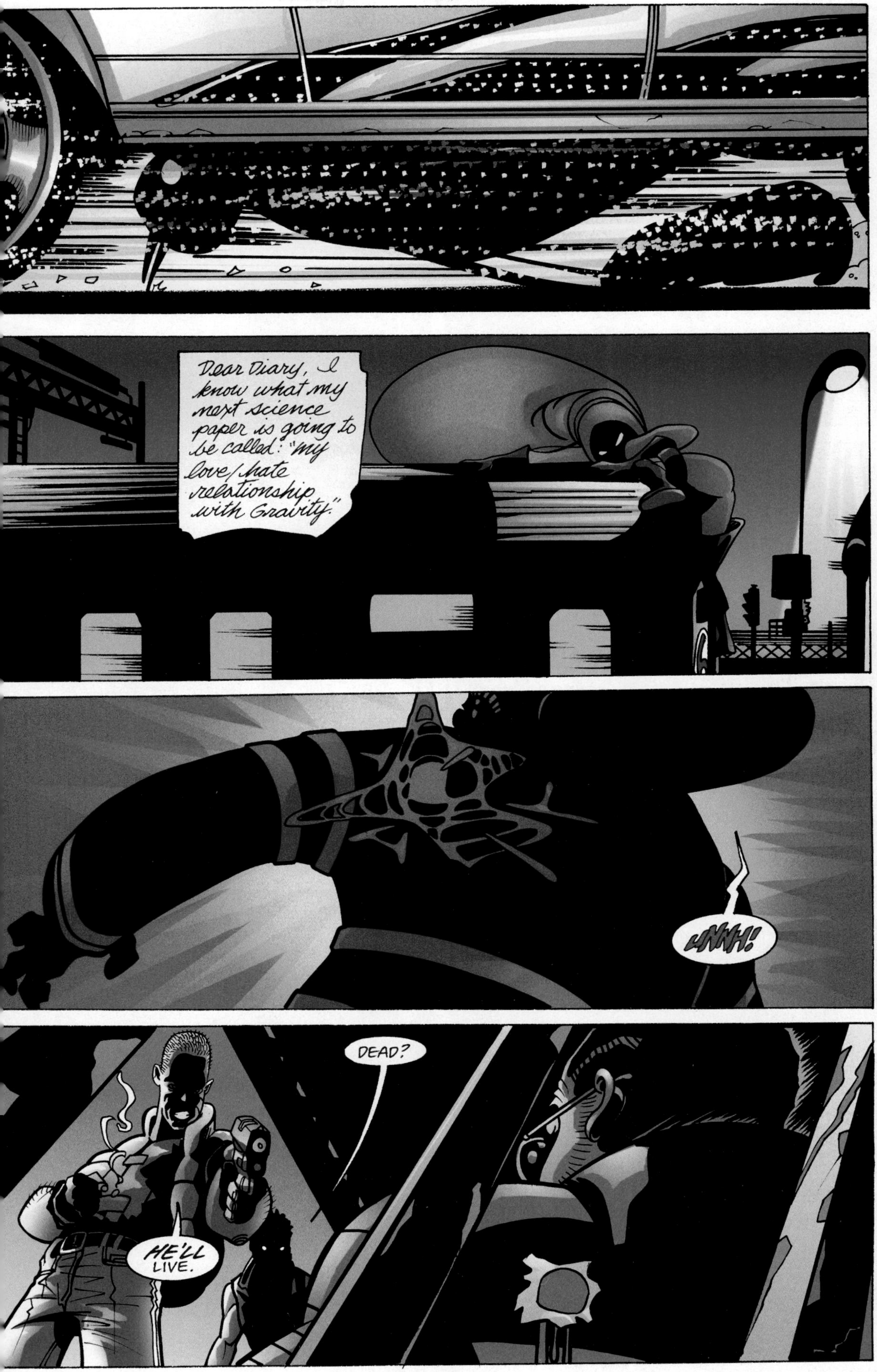
Dear Diary, I know what my next science paper is going to be called: "My love/hate relationship with Gravity."
UNNH!
DEAD?
HE'LL LIVE.

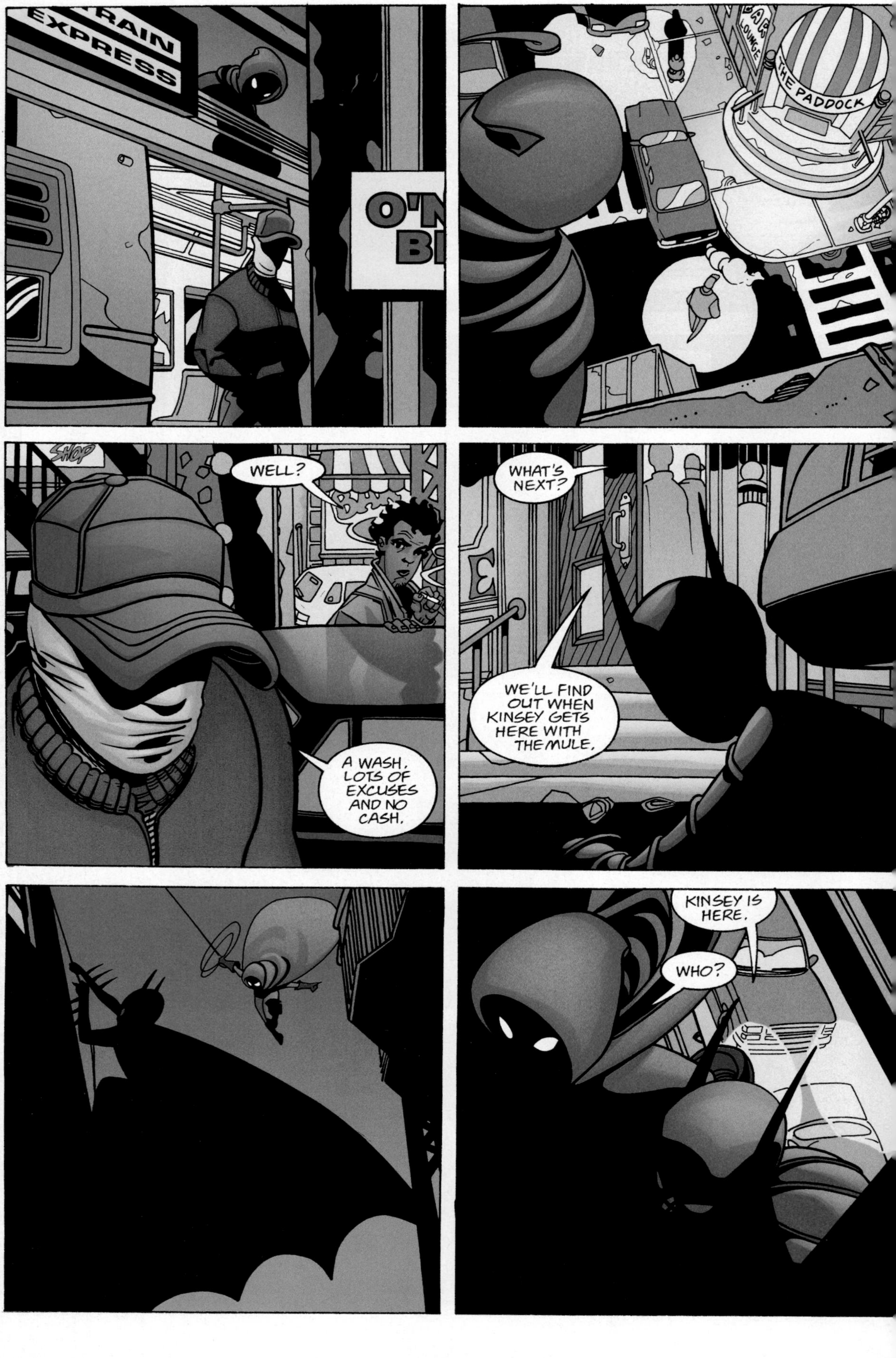

TRAIN
EXPRESS
THE PADDOCK
LOUNGE
SHOP
WELL?
A WASH, LOTS OF EXCUSES AND NO CASH.
WHAT'S NEXT?
WE'LL FIND OUT WHEN KINSEY GETS HERE WITH THE MULE.
KINSEY IS HERE.
WHO?

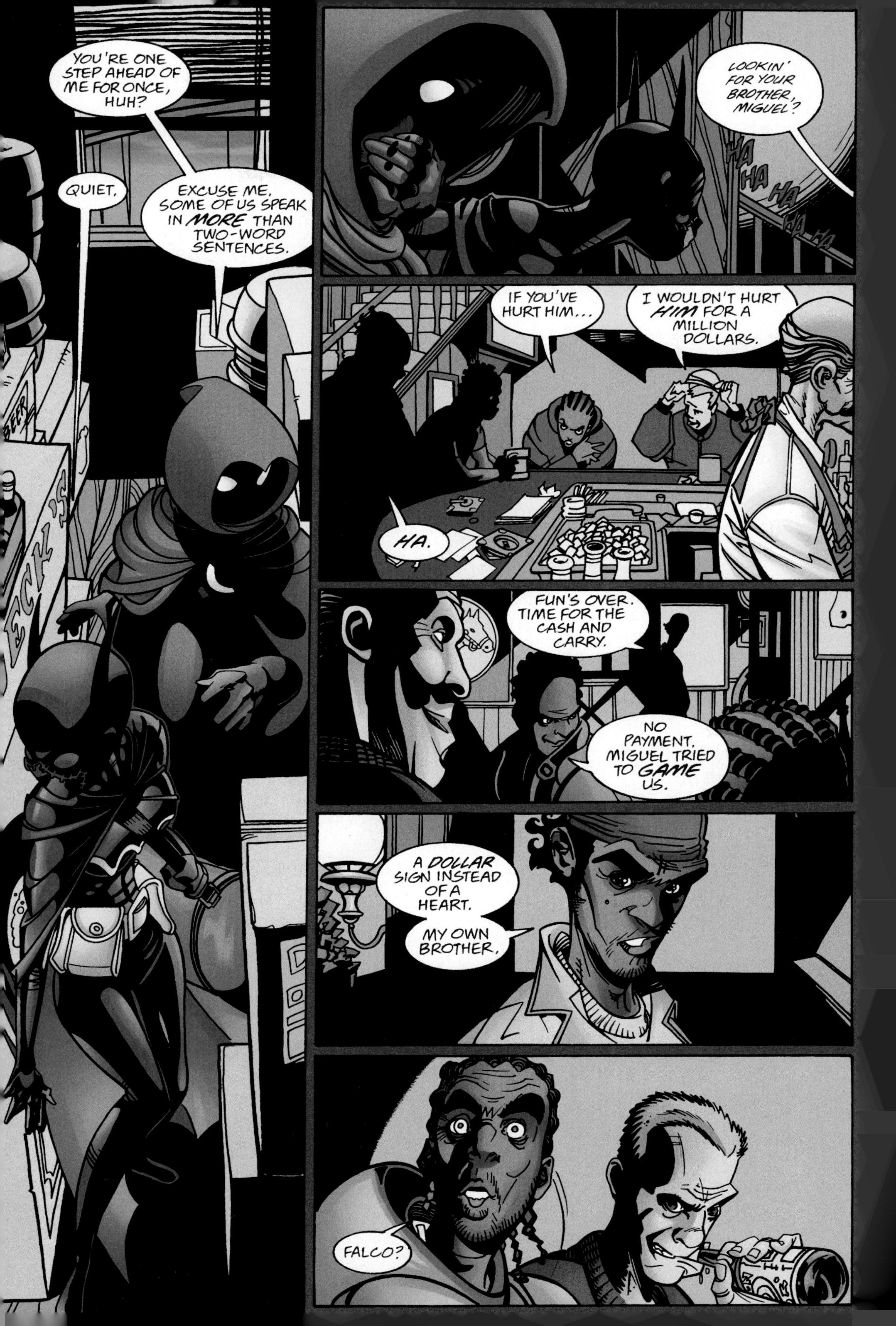
YOU'RE ONE STEP AHEAD OF ME FOR ONCE, HUH?
QUIET.
EXCUSE ME, SOME OF US SPEAK IN *MORE* THAN TWO-WORD SENTENCES.
LOOKIN' FOR YOUR BROTHER, MIGUEL?
HA HA HA HA HA HA
IF YOU'VE HURT HIM...
I WOULDN'T HURT *HIM* FOR A MILLION DOLLARS.
HA.
FUN'S OVER. TIME FOR THE CASH AND CARRY.
NO PAYMENT. MIGUEL TRIED TO *GAME* US.
A *DOLLAR* SIGN INSTEAD OF A HEART.
MY OWN BROTHER.
FALCO?

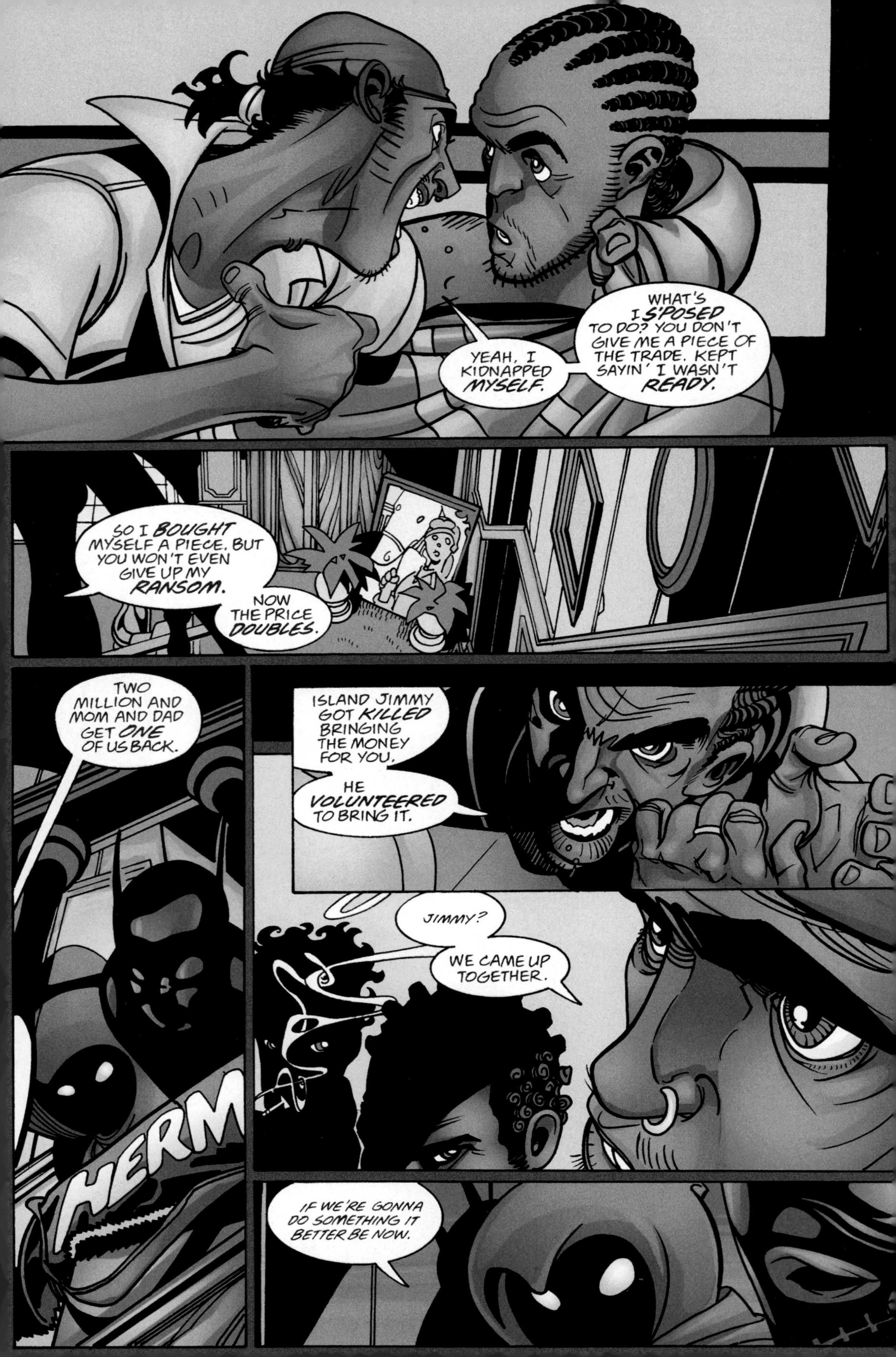
YEAH, I KIDNAPPED MYSELF.
WHAT'S I S'POSED TO DO? YOU DON'T GIVE ME A PIECE OF THE TRADE. KEPT SAYIN' I WASN'T READY.
SO I BOUGHT MYSELF A PIECE, BUT YOU WON'T EVEN GIVE UP MY RANSOM.
NOW THE PRICE DOUBLES.
TWO MILLION AND MOM AND DAD GET ONE OF US BACK.
ISLAND JIMMY GOT KILLED BRINGING THE MONEY FOR YOU.
HE VOLUNTEERED TO BRING IT.
JIMMY?
WE CAME UP TOGETHER.
HERM
IF WE'RE GONNA DO SOMETHING IT BETTER BE NOW.

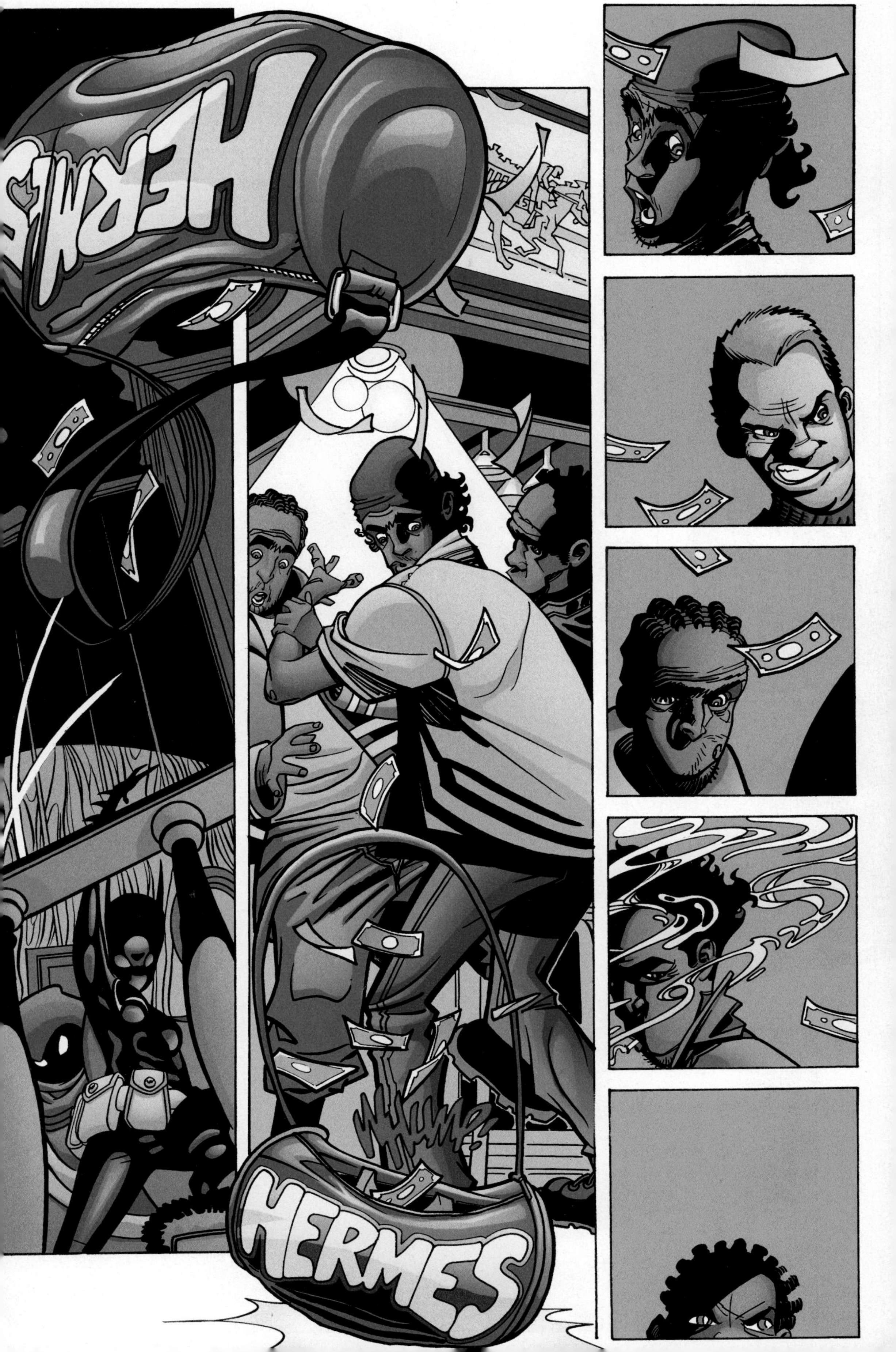

HERMES
WHUMP!
HERMES

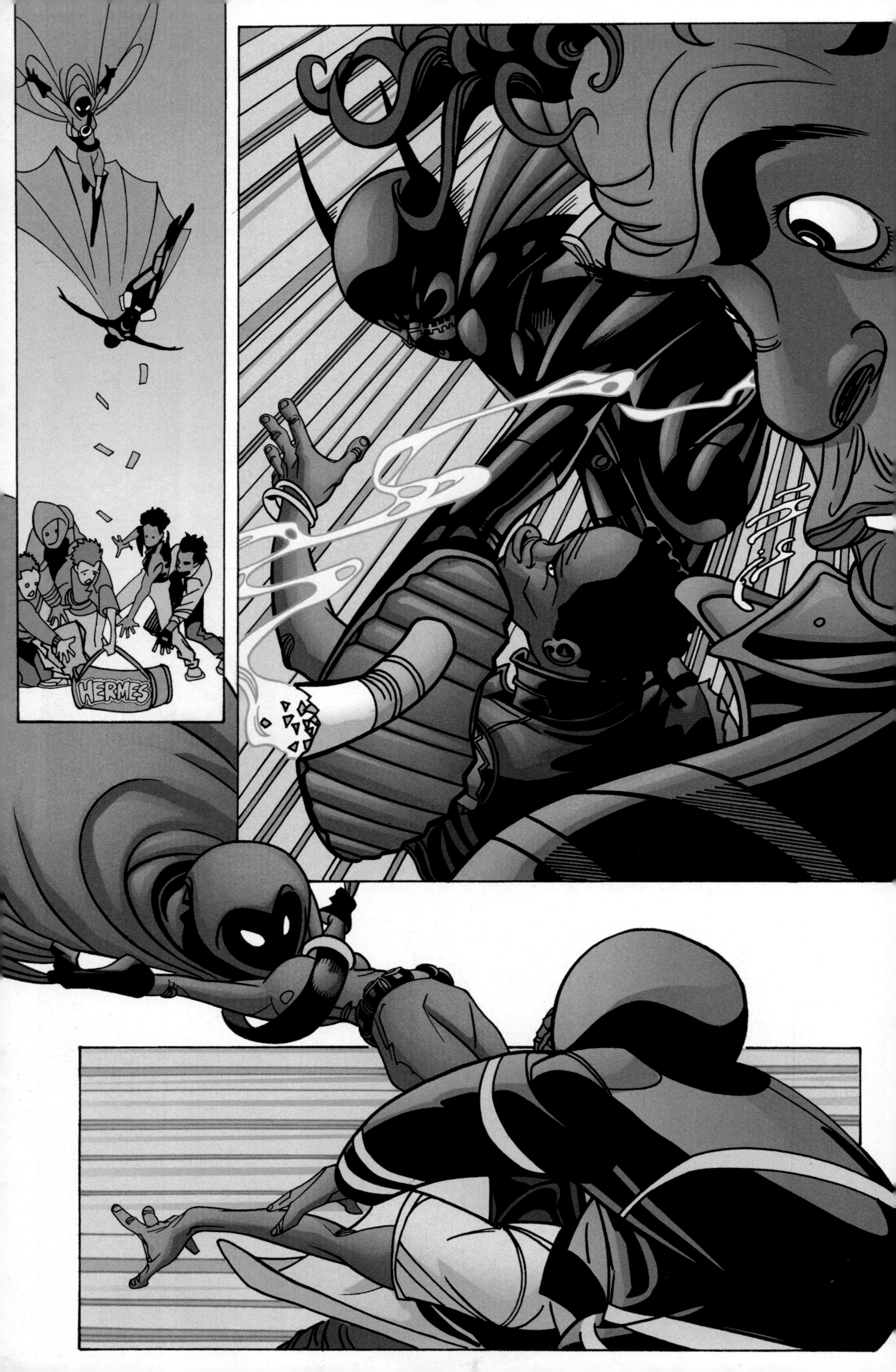
HERMES

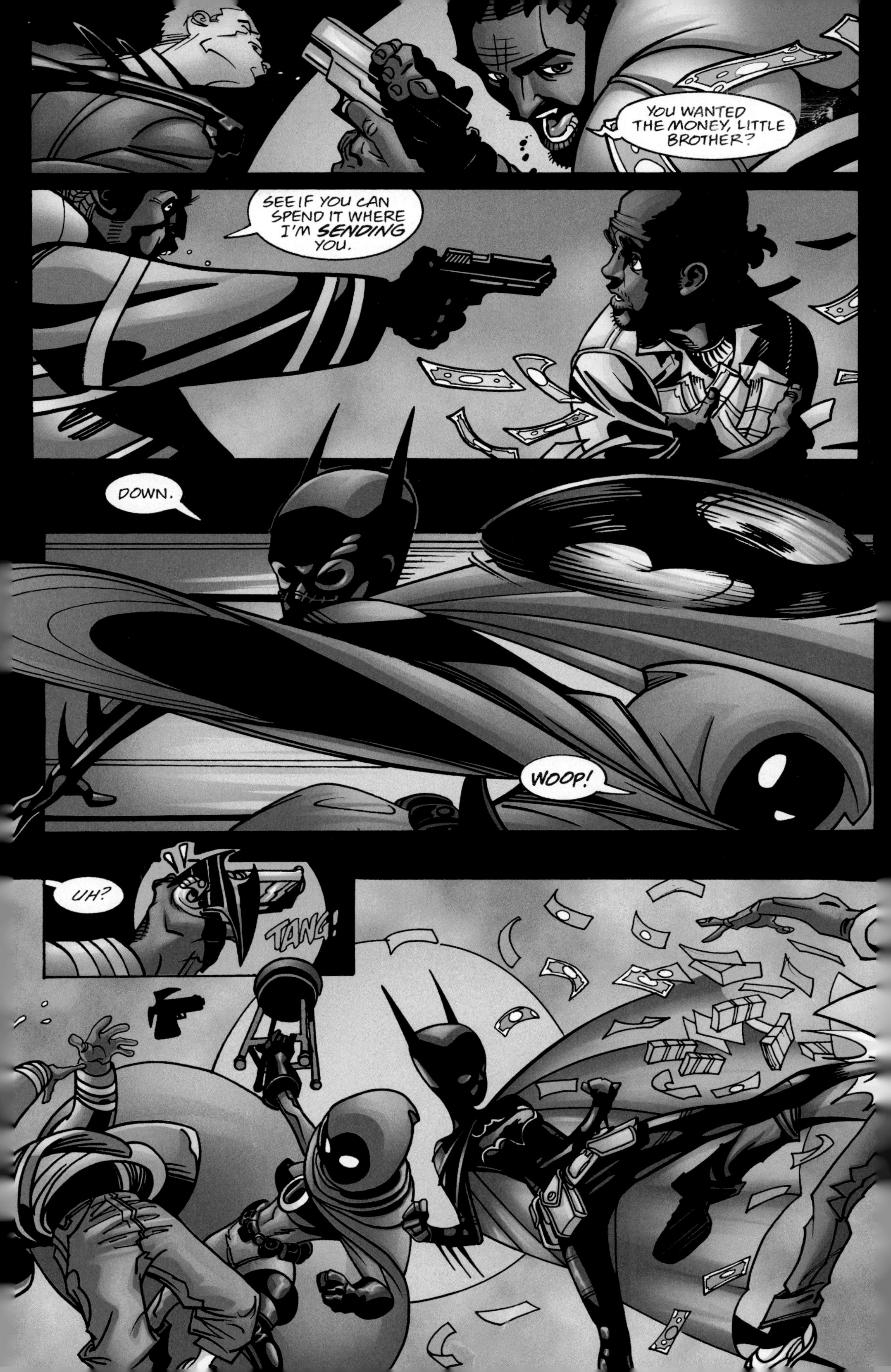
YOU WANTED THE MONEY, LITTLE BROTHER?
SEE IF YOU CAN SPEND IT WHERE I'M *SENDING* YOU.
DOWN.
WOOP!
UH?
TANG!

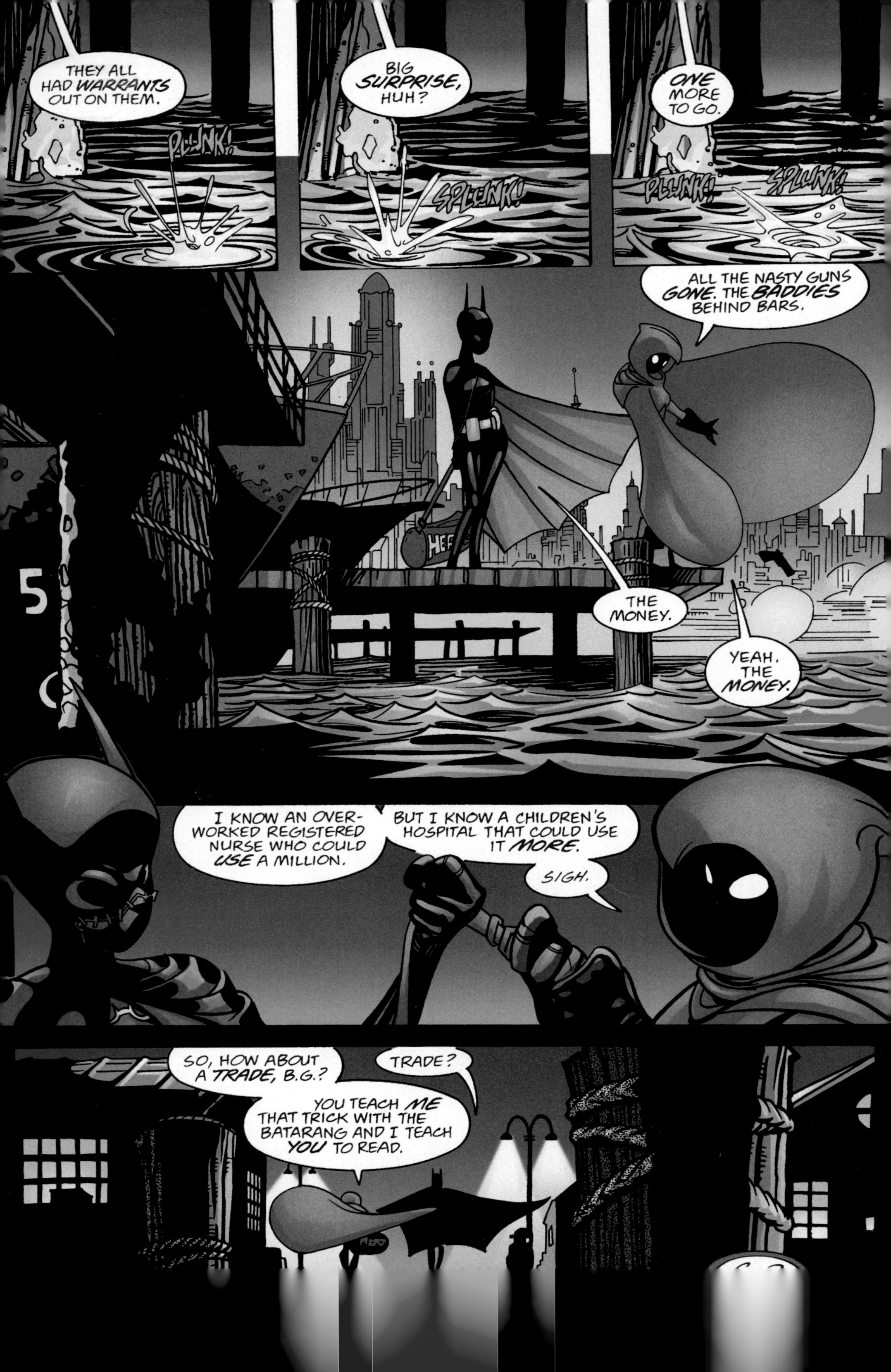

THEY ALL HAD WARRANTS OUT ON THEM.
PLUNK!
BIG SURPRISE, HUH?
SPLUNK!
ONE MORE TO GO.
PLUNK!
SPLUNK!
ALL THE NASTY GUNS GONE. THE BADDIES BEHIND BARS.
THE MONEY.
YEAH, THE MONEY.
5
I KNOW AN OVER-WORKED REGISTERED NURSE WHO COULD USE A MILLION.
BUT I KNOW A CHILDREN'S HOSPITAL THAT COULD USE IT MORE.
SIGH.
SO, HOW ABOUT A TRADE, B.G.?
TRADE?
YOU TEACH ME THAT TRICK WITH THE BATARANG AND I TEACH YOU TO READ.

BATGIRL #21 cover by Tim Sale

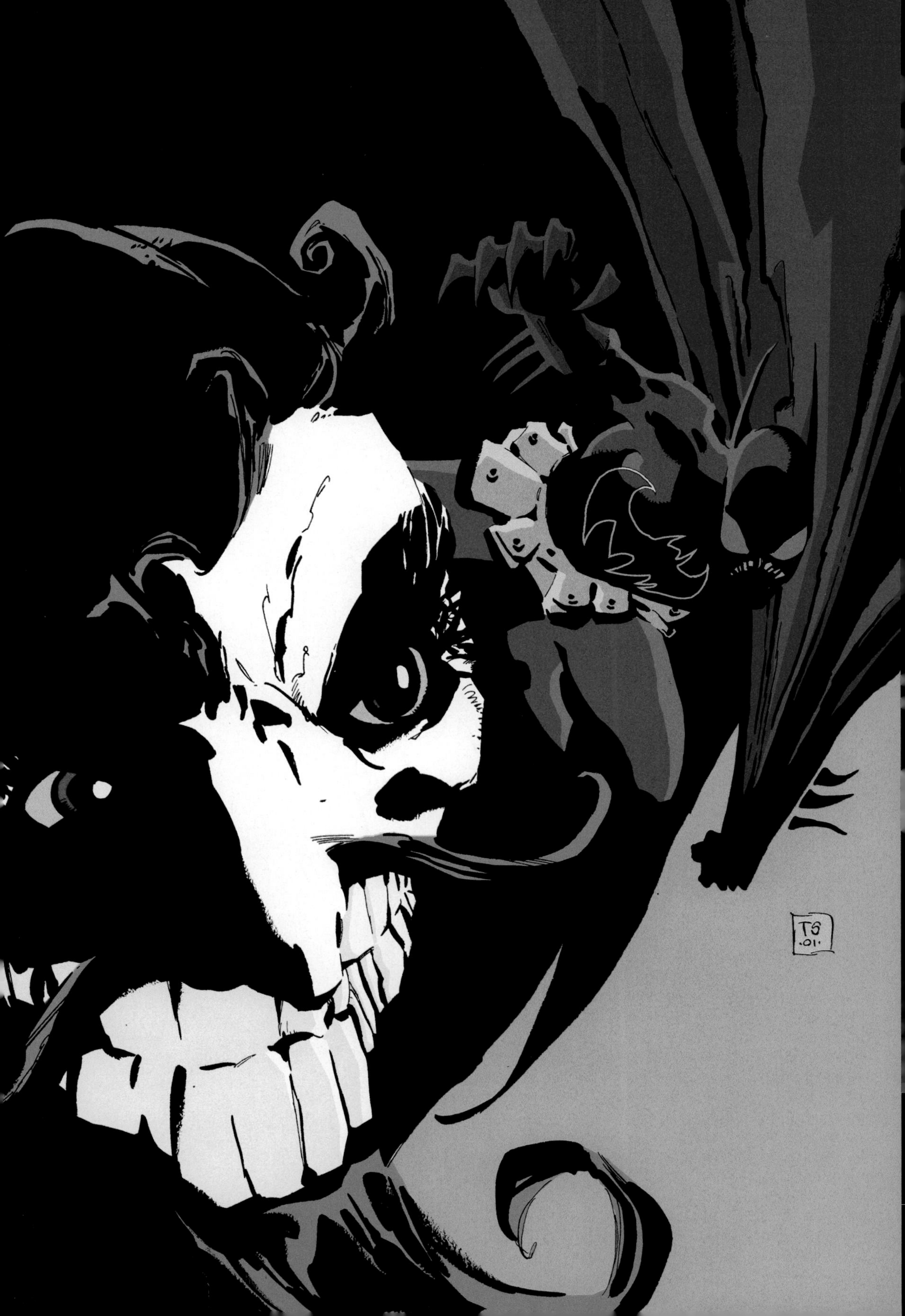
TS
·01·

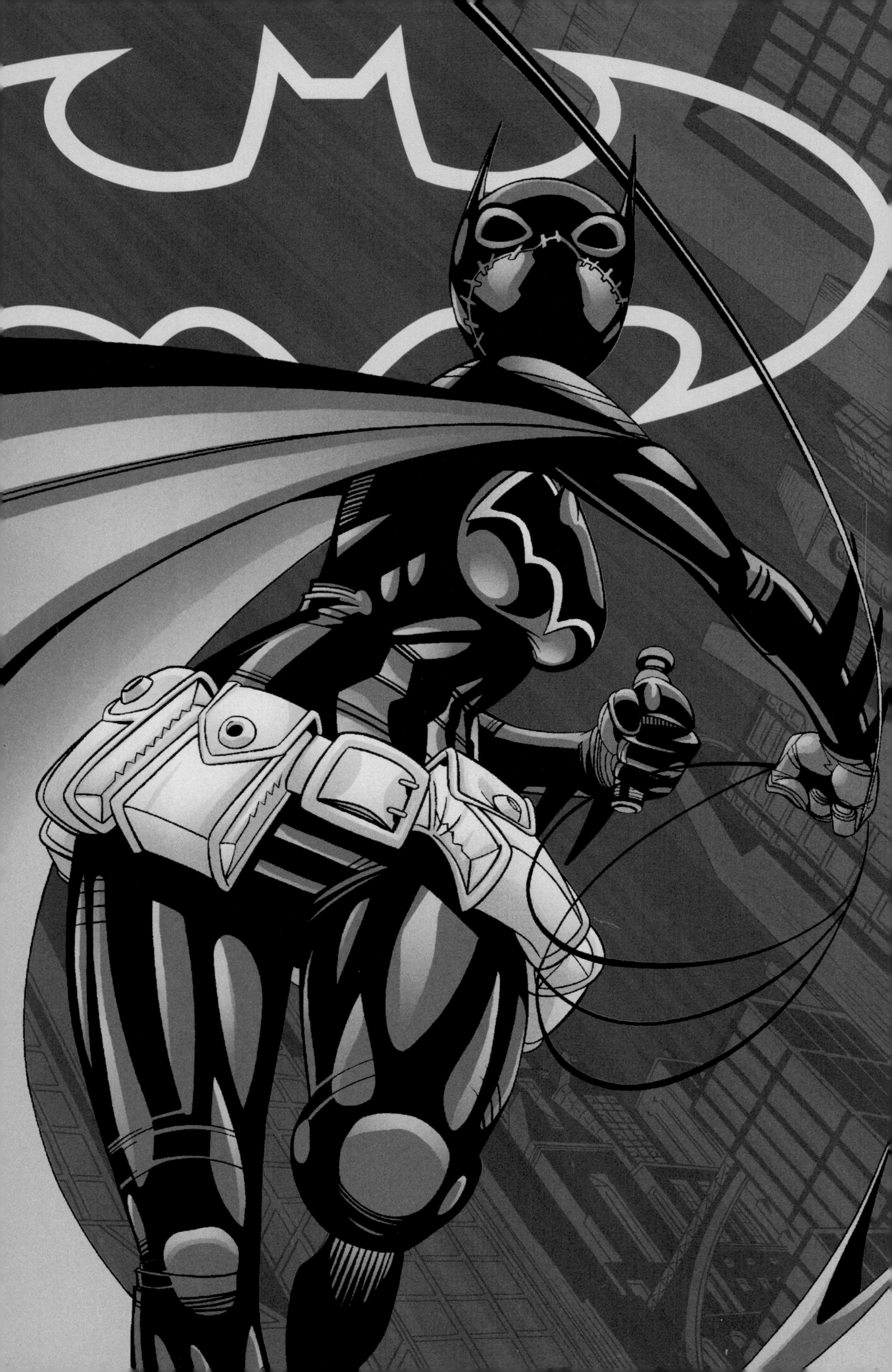

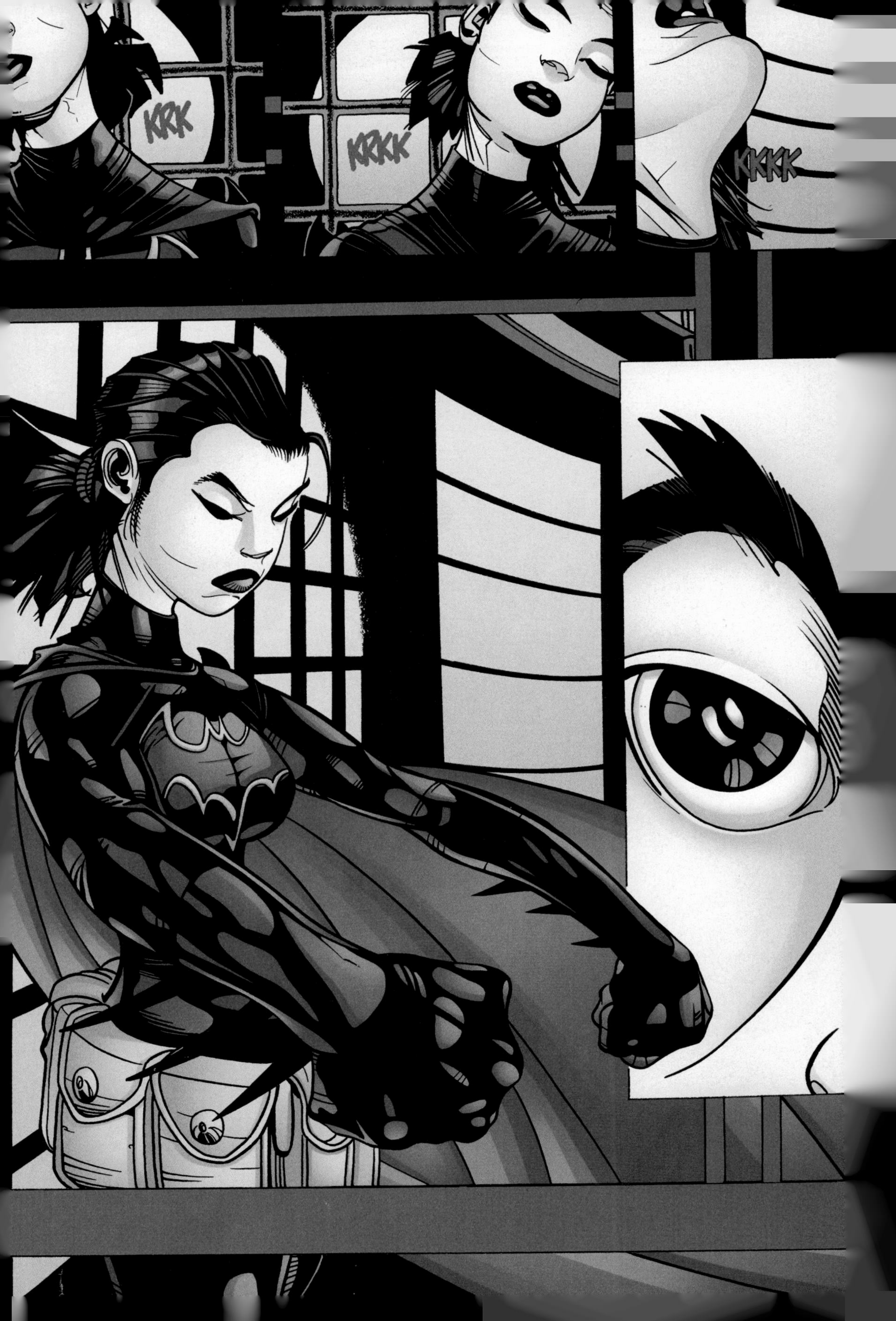
KRK
KRKK
KKKK

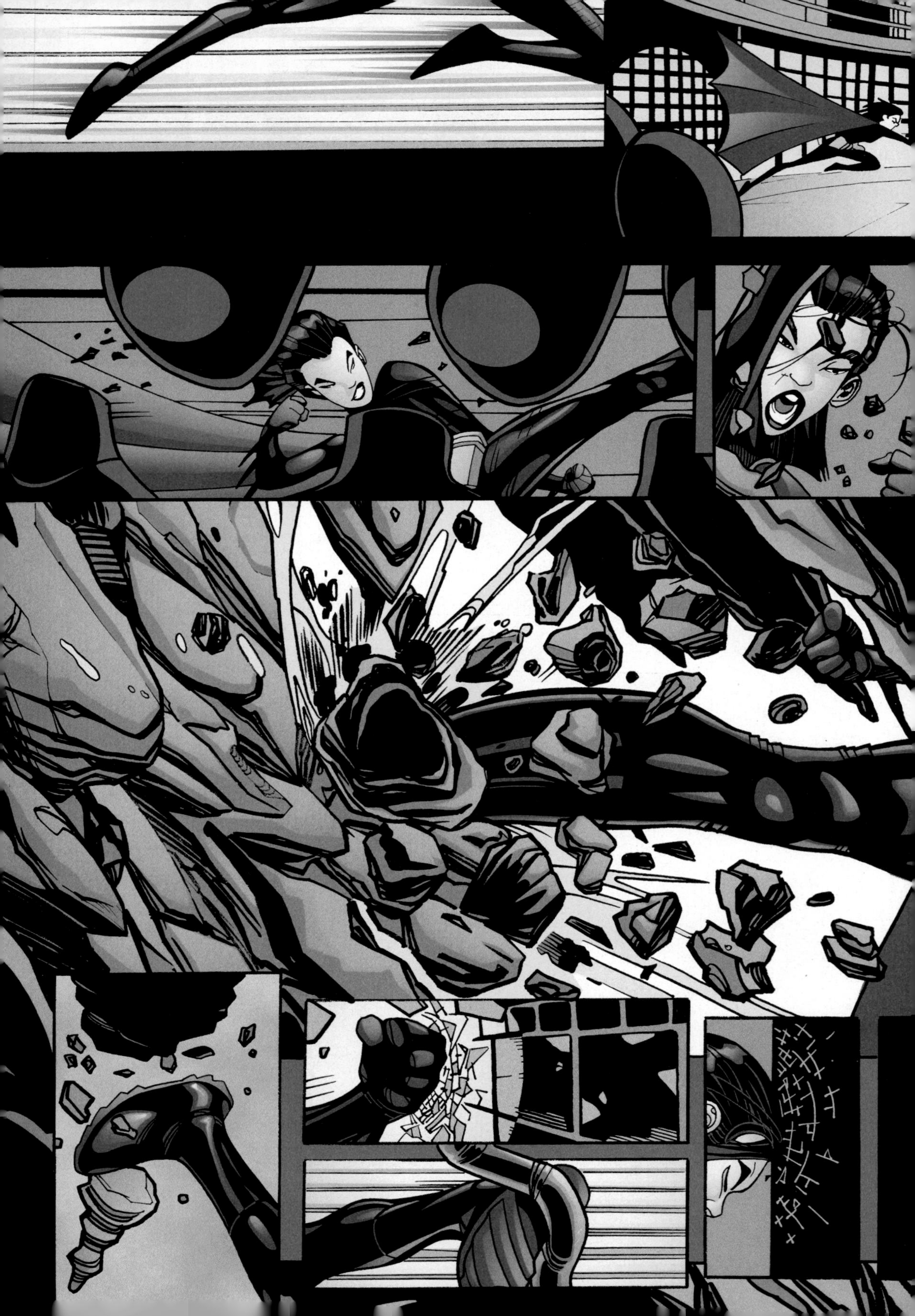

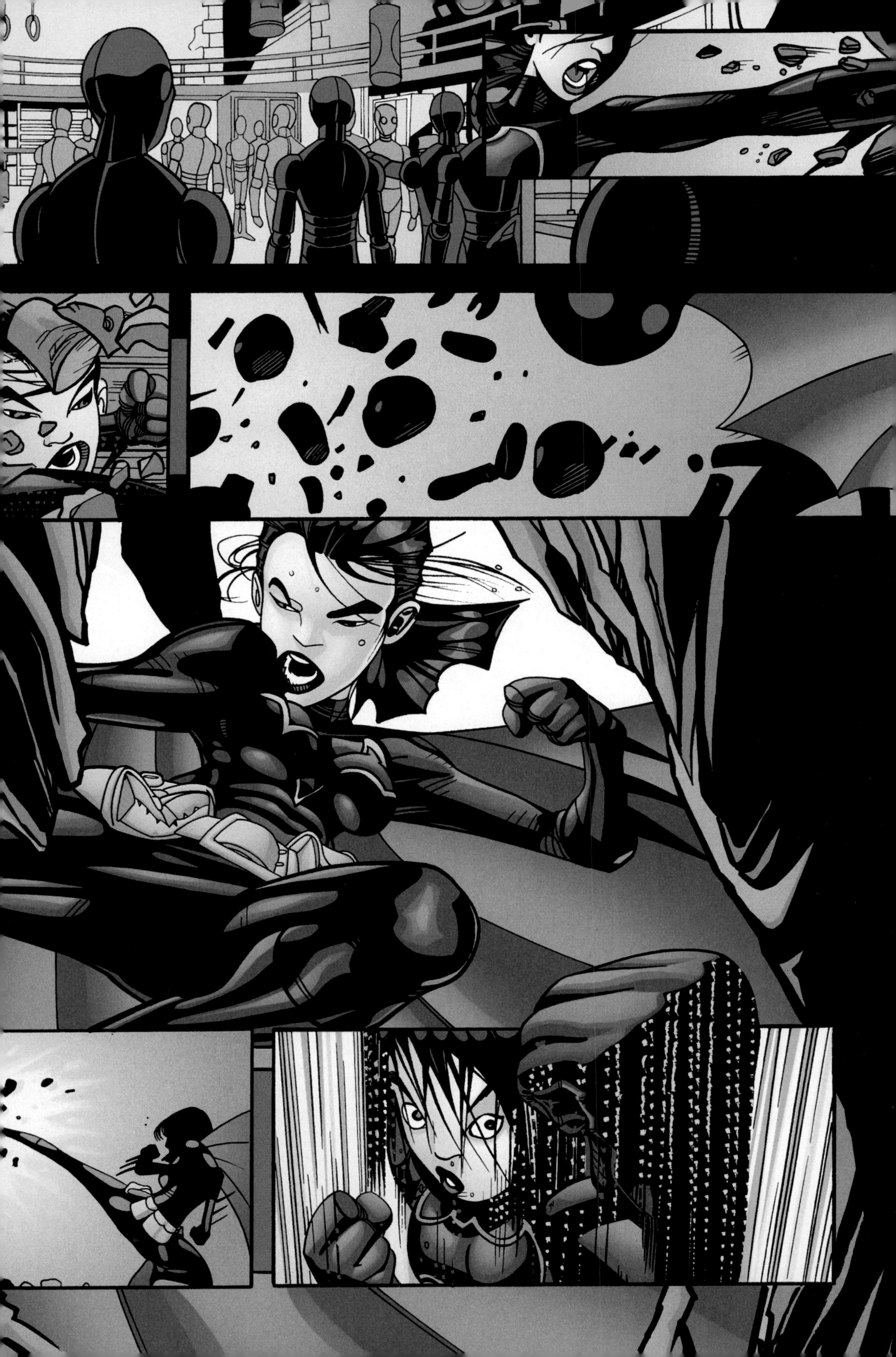

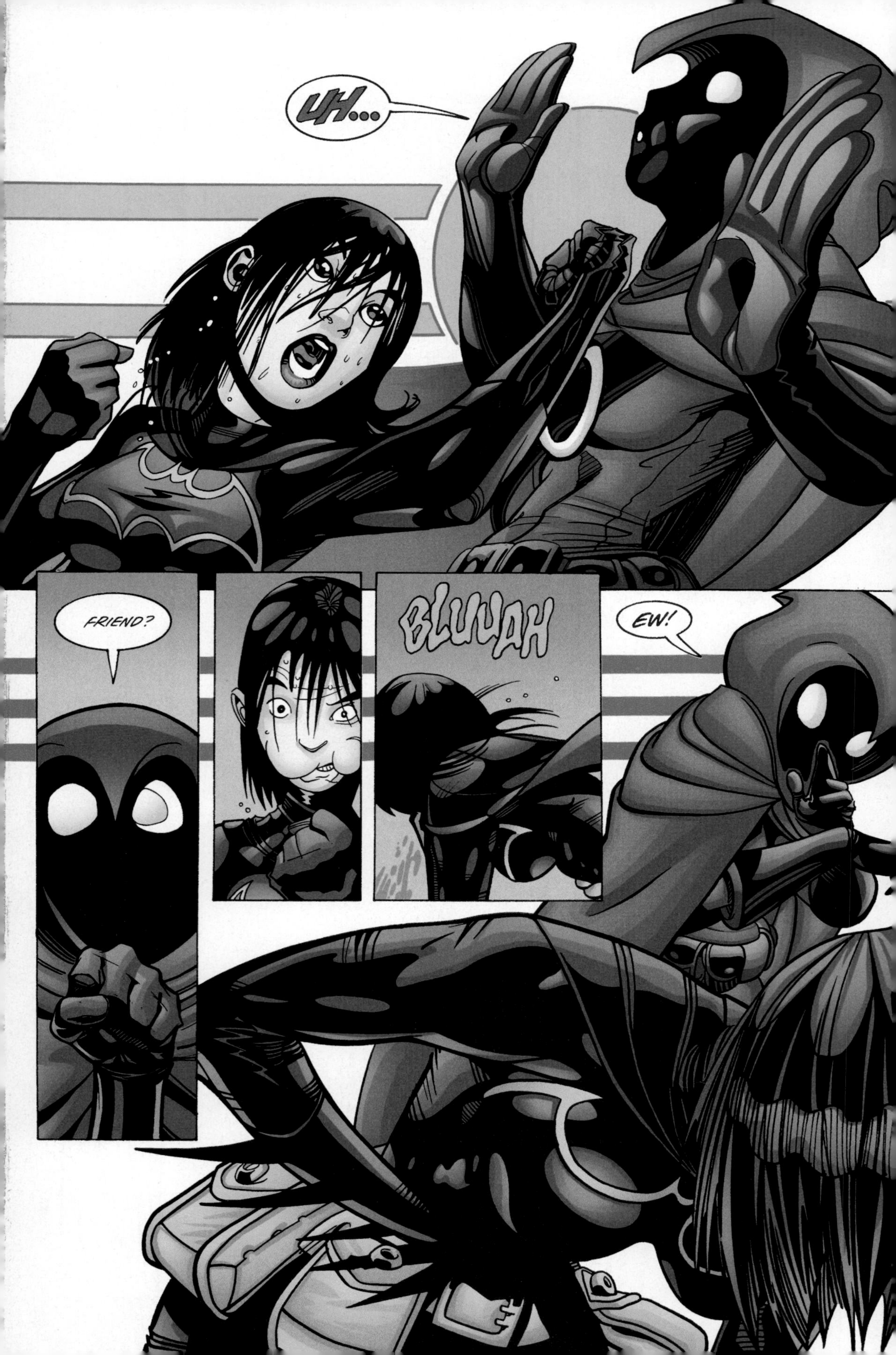
UH...
FRIEND?
BLUUAH
EW!

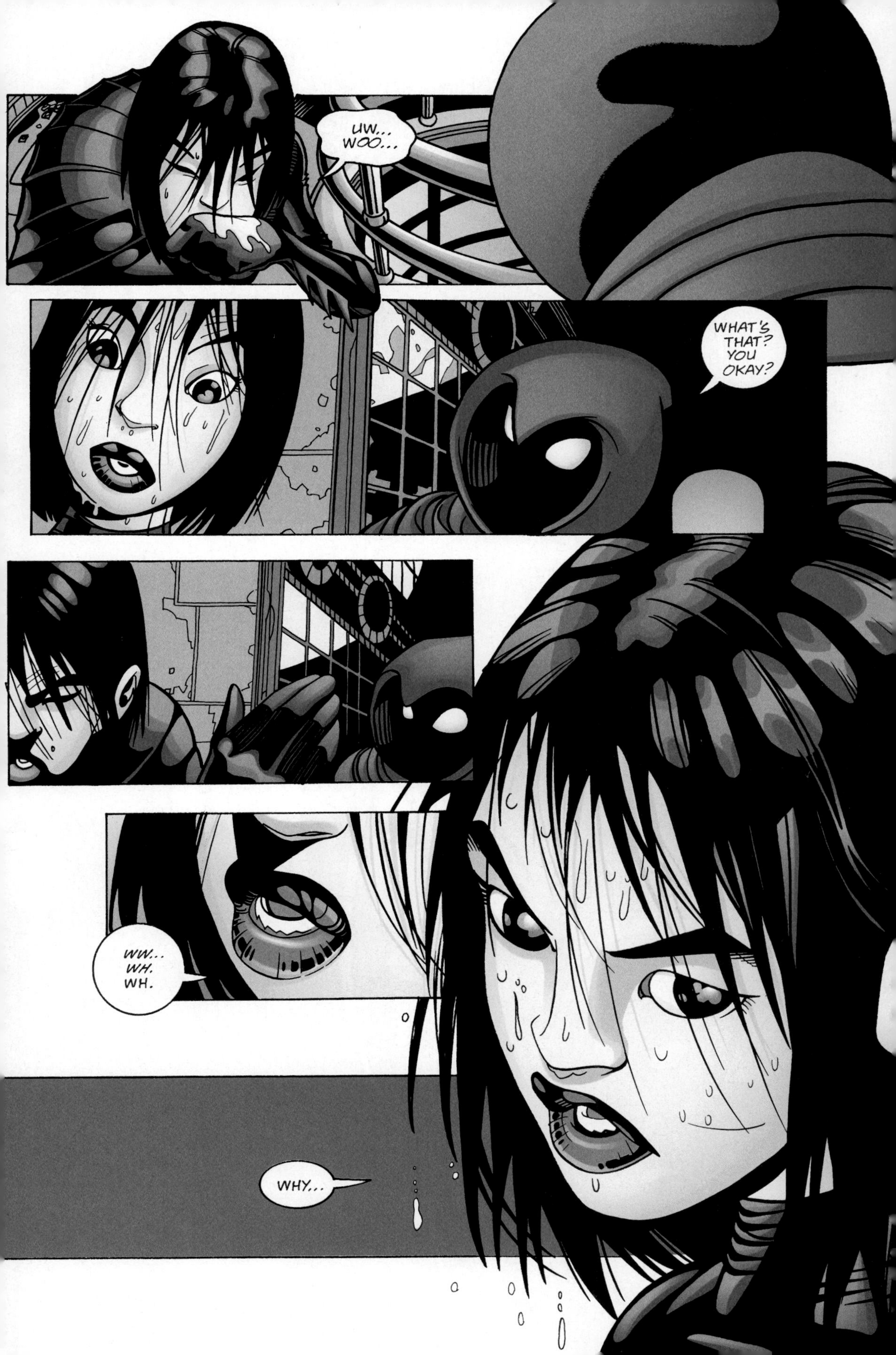
UW... WOO...
WHAT'S THAT? YOU OKAY?
WW... WH. WH.
WHY...

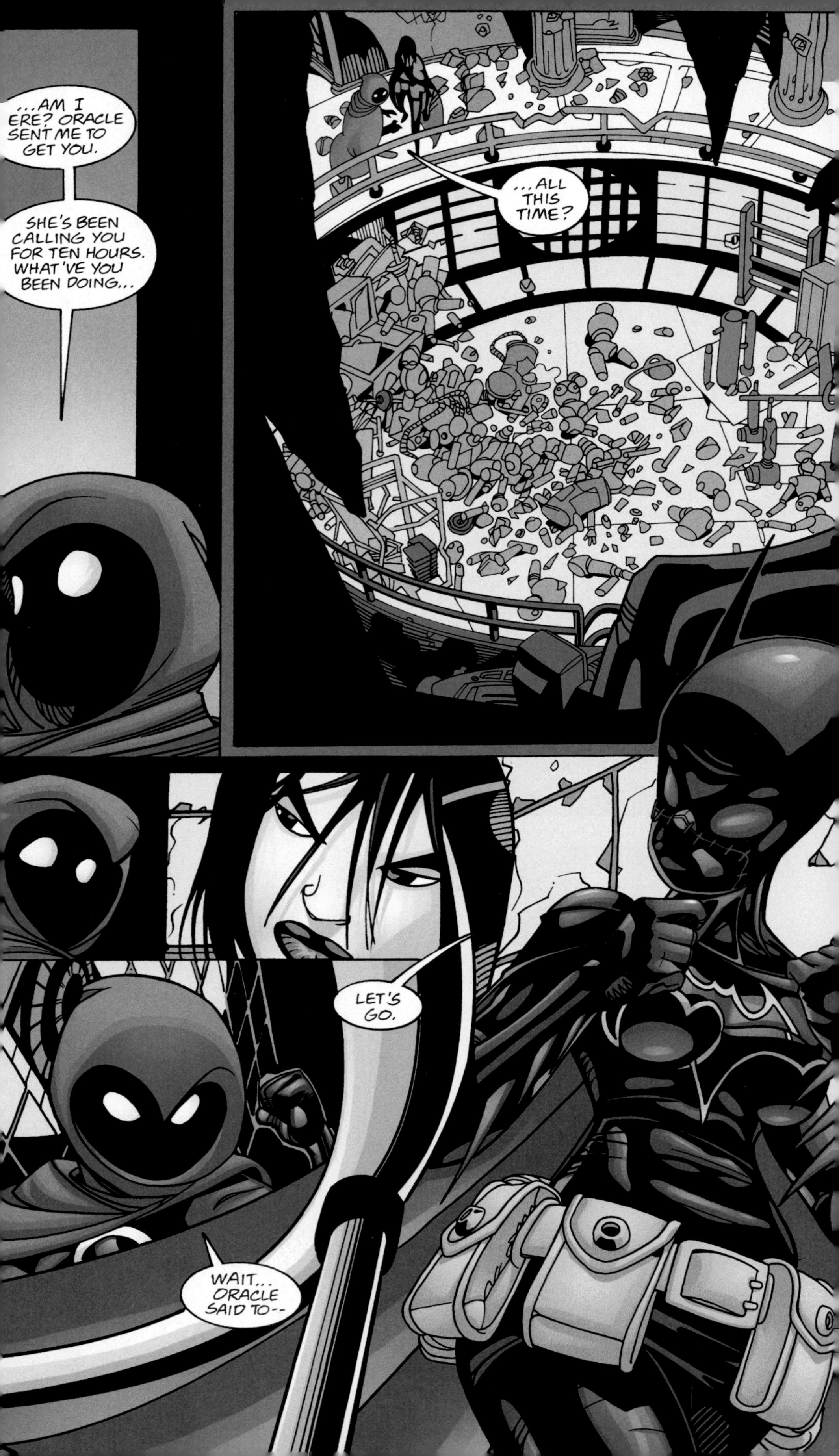
...AM I ERE? ORACLE SENT ME TO GET YOU.
SHE'S BEEN CALLING YOU FOR TEN HOURS. WHAT'VE YOU BEEN DOING...
...ALL THIS TIME?
LET'S GO.
WAIT... ORACLE SAID TO--

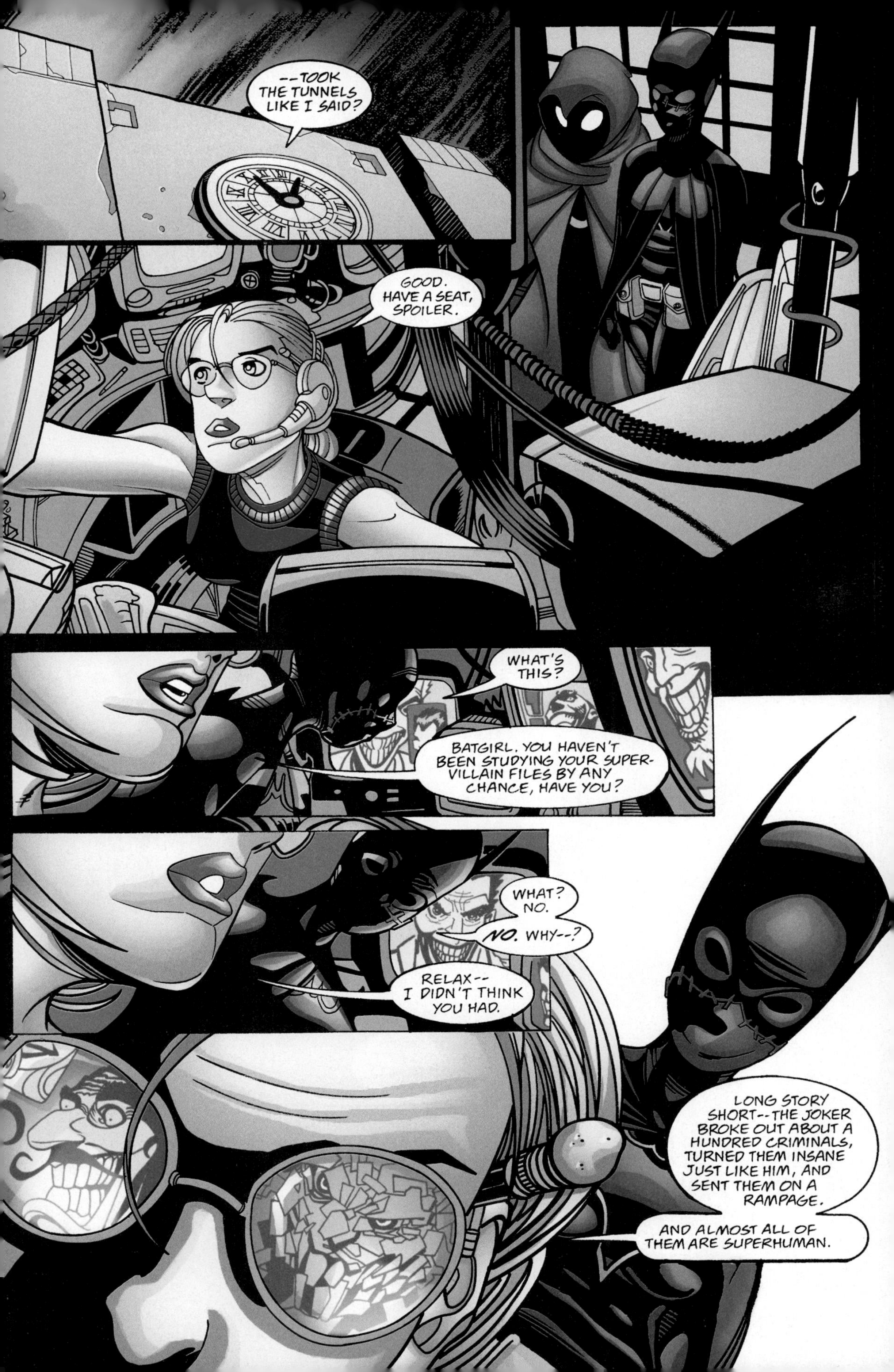
--TOOK THE TUNNELS LIKE I SAID?
GOOD. HAVE A SEAT, SPOILER.
WHAT'S THIS?
BATGIRL. YOU HAVEN'T BEEN STUDYING YOUR SUPER-VILLAIN FILES BY ANY CHANCE, HAVE YOU?
WHAT? NO.
NO. WHY--?
RELAX-- I DIDN'T THINK YOU HAD.
LONG STORY SHORT--THE JOKER BROKE OUT ABOUT A HUNDRED CRIMINALS, TURNED THEM INSANE JUST LIKE HIM, AND SENT THEM ON A RAMPAGE.
AND ALMOST ALL OF THEM ARE SUPERHUMAN.

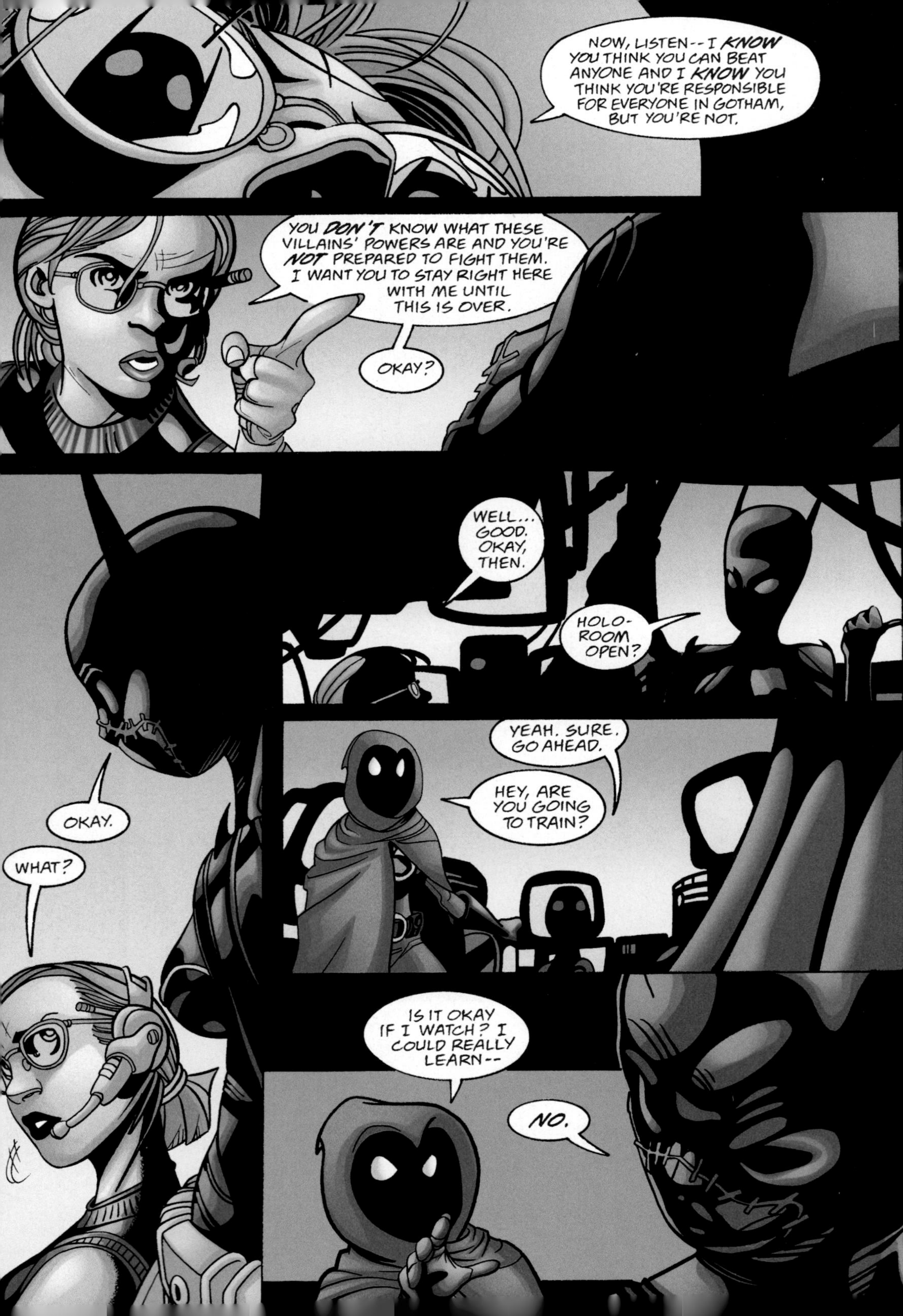

NOW, LISTEN-- I KNOW YOU THINK YOU CAN BEAT ANYONE AND I KNOW YOU THINK YOU'RE RESPONSIBLE FOR EVERYONE IN GOTHAM, BUT YOU'RE NOT.
YOU DON'T KNOW WHAT THESE VILLAINS' POWERS ARE AND YOU'RE NOT PREPARED TO FIGHT THEM. I WANT YOU TO STAY RIGHT HERE WITH ME UNTIL THIS IS OVER.
OKAY?
OKAY.
WHAT?
WELL... GOOD. OKAY, THEN.
HOLO-ROOM OPEN?
YEAH. SURE. GO AHEAD.
HEY, ARE YOU GOING TO TRAIN?
IS IT OKAY IF I WATCH? I COULD REALLY LEARN--
NO.

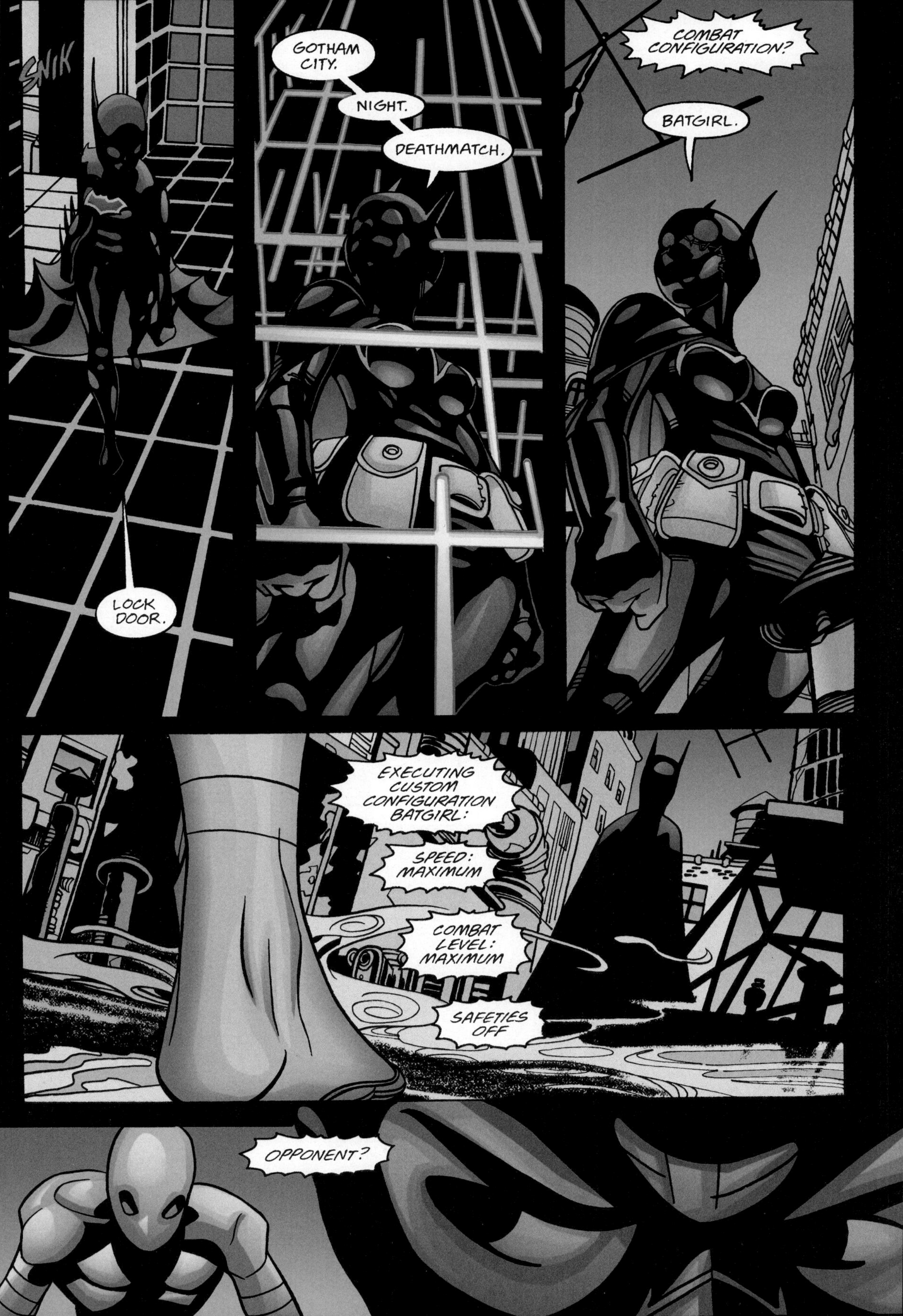
SNIK
LOCK DOOR.
GOTHAM CITY.
NIGHT.
DEATHMATCH.
COMBAT CONFIGURATION?
BATGIRL.
EXECUTING CUSTOM CONFIGURATION BATGIRL:
SPEED: MAXIMUM
COMBAT LEVEL: MAXIMUM
SAFETIES OFF
OPPONENT?

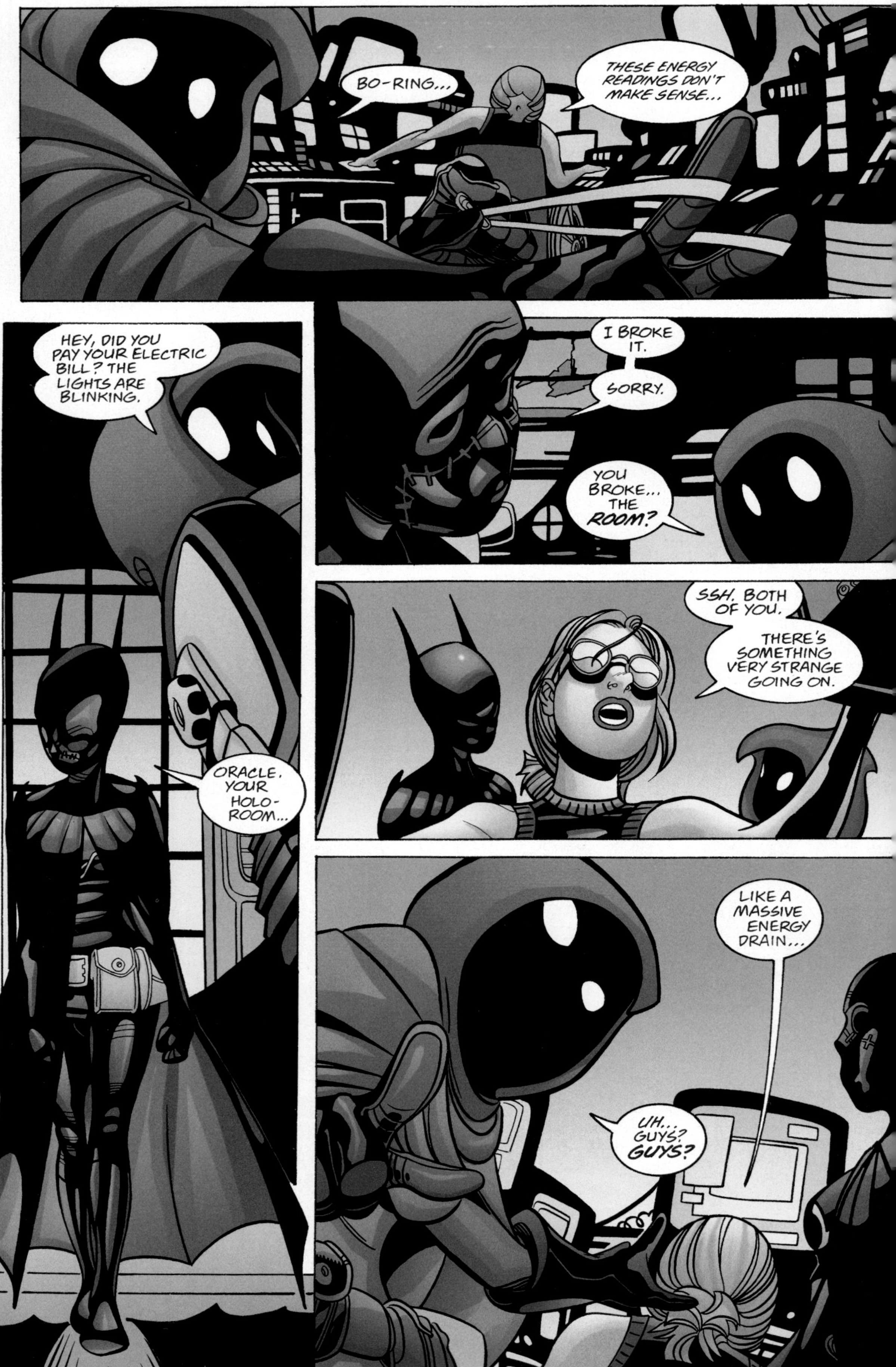
BO-RING...
THESE ENERGY READINGS DON'T MAKE SENSE...
HEY, DID YOU PAY YOUR ELECTRIC BILL? THE LIGHTS ARE BLINKING.
I BROKE IT.
SORRY.
YOU BROKE... THE ROOM?
ORACLE. YOUR HOLO-ROOM...
SSH. BOTH OF YOU.
THERE'S SOMETHING VERY STRANGE GOING ON.
LIKE A MASSIVE ENERGY DRAIN...
UH... GUYS? GUYS?

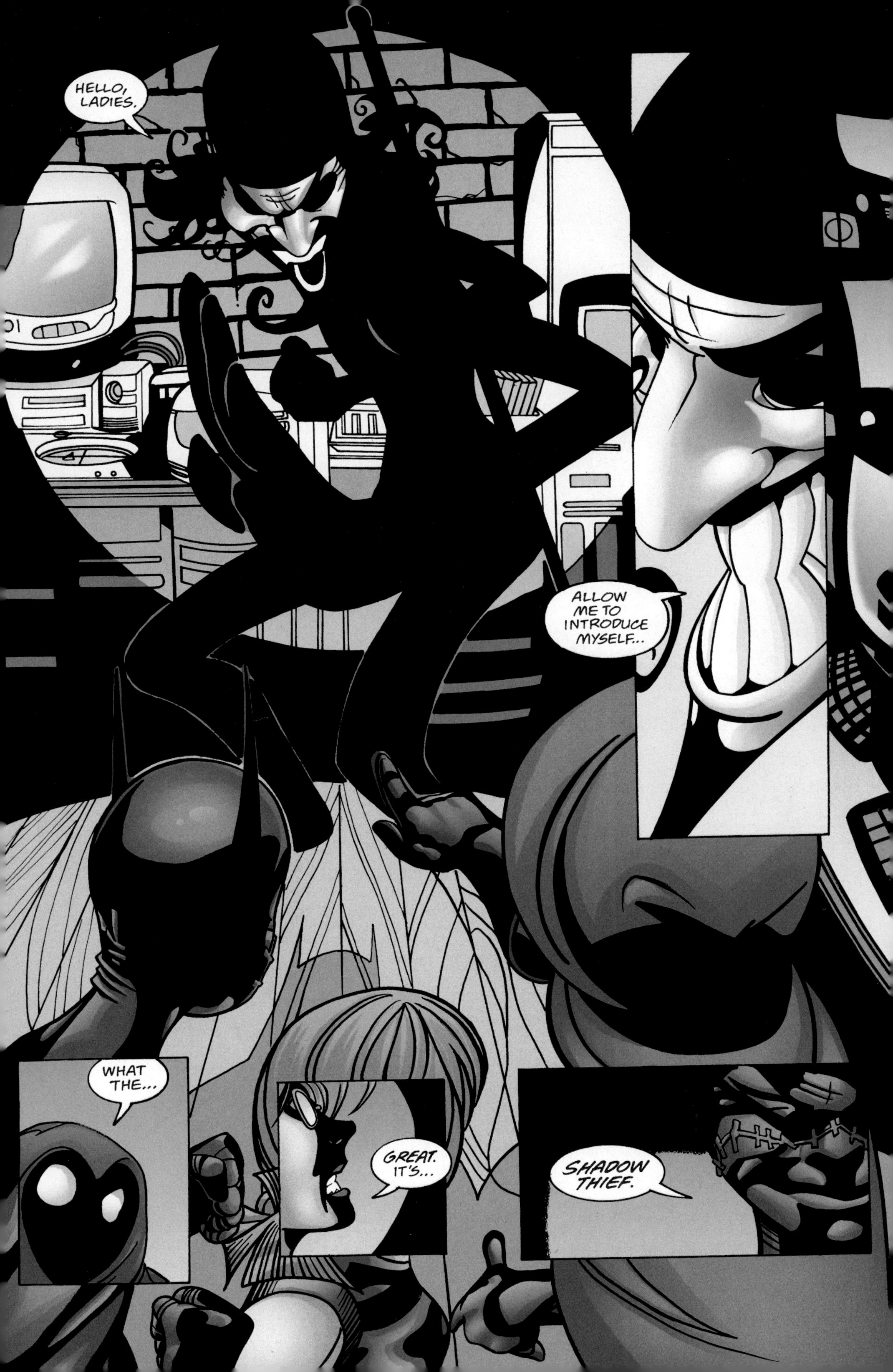
HELLO, LADIES.
ALLOW ME TO INTRODUCE MYSELF...
WHAT THE...
GREAT. IT'S...
SHADOW THIEF.

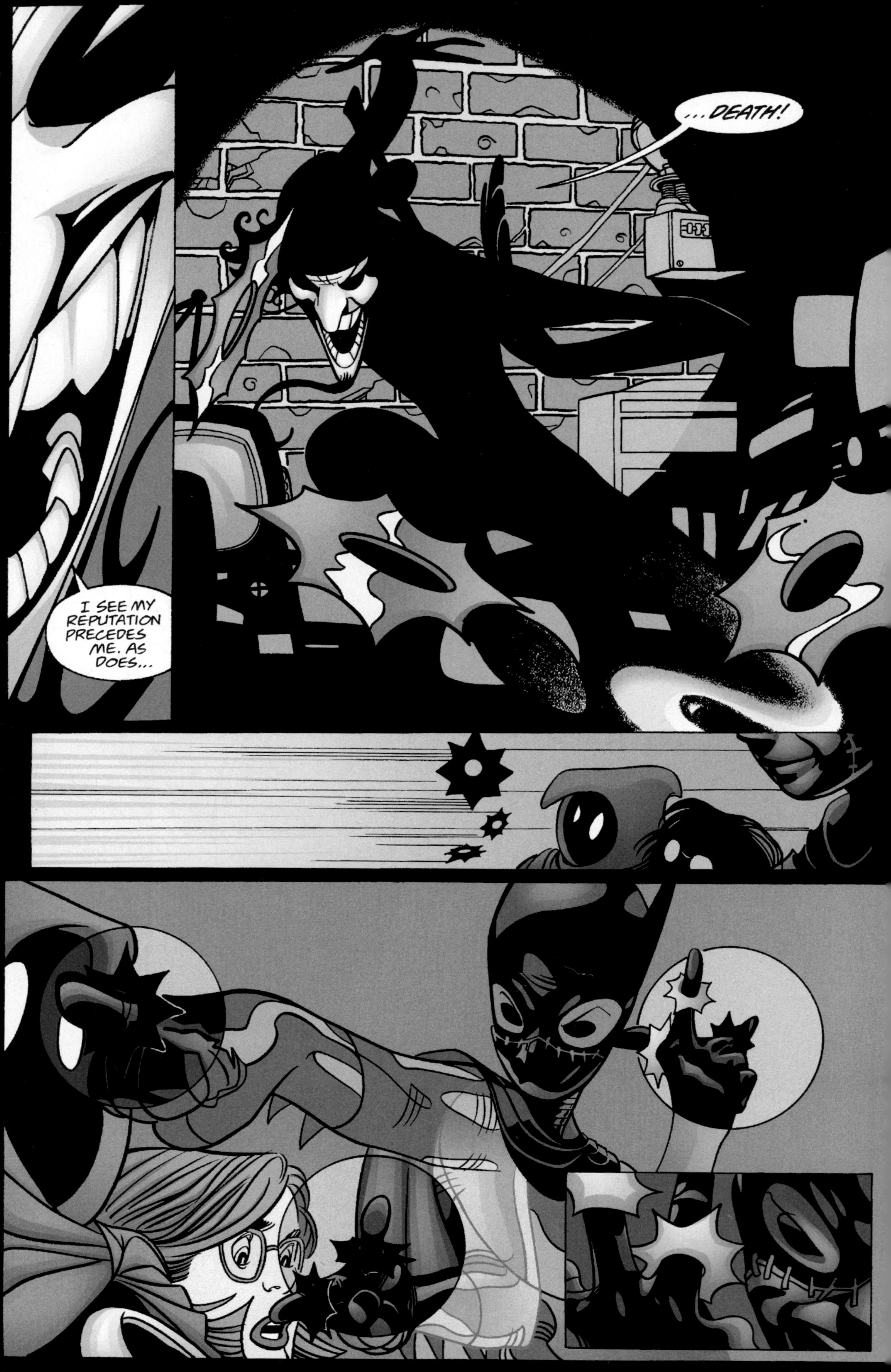
I SEE MY REPUTATION PRECEDES ME. AS DOES...
...DEATH!

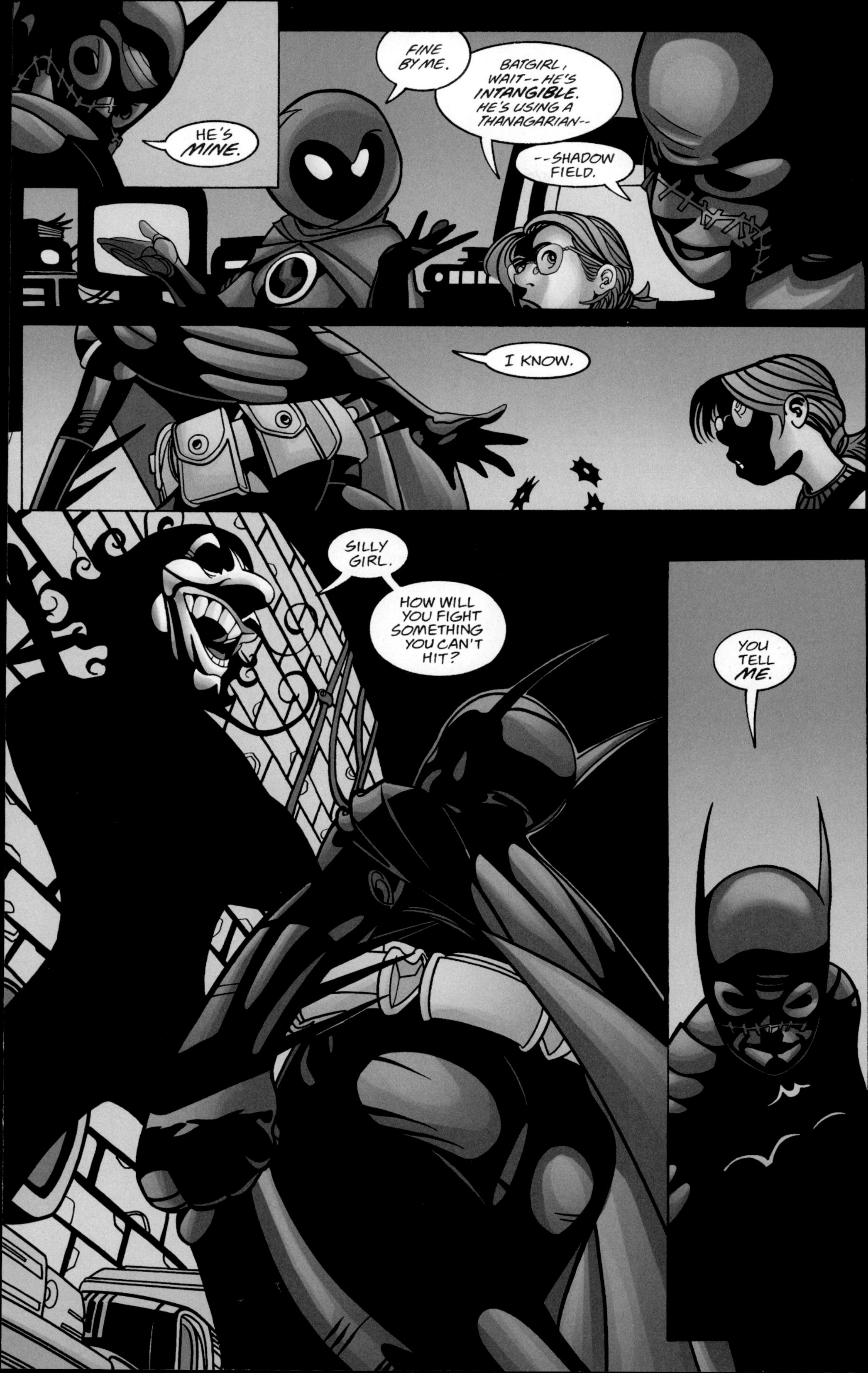
HE'S MINE.
FINE BY ME.
BATGIRL, WAIT-- HE'S INTANGIBLE. HE'S USING A THANAGARIAN--
--SHADOW FIELD.
I KNOW.
SILLY GIRL.
HOW WILL YOU FIGHT SOMETHING YOU CAN'T HIT?
YOU TELL ME.

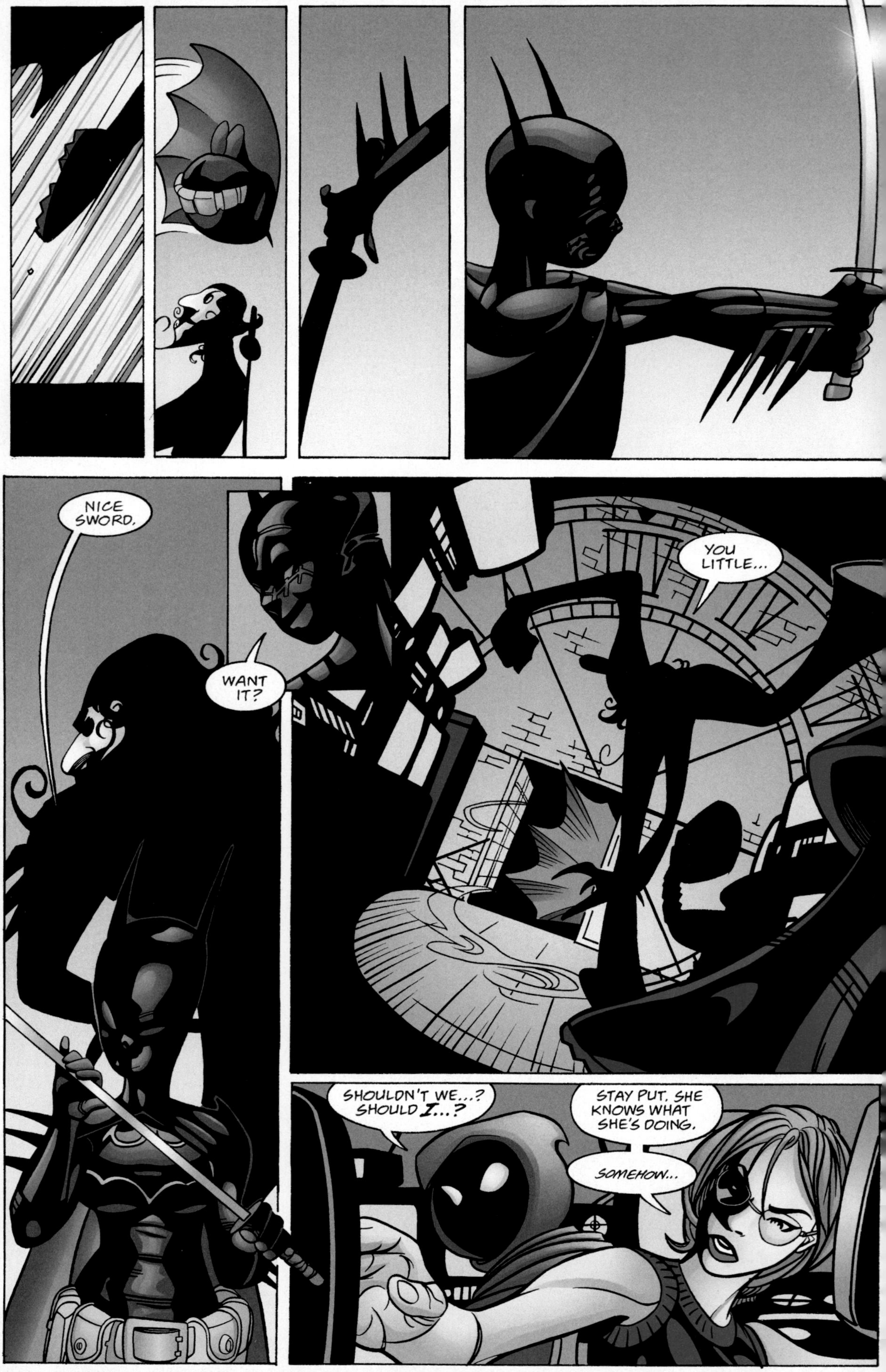
NICE SWORD.
WANT IT?
YOU LITTLE...
SHOULDN'T WE...? SHOULD *I*...?
STAY PUT, SHE KNOWS WHAT SHE'S DOING.
SOMEHOW...

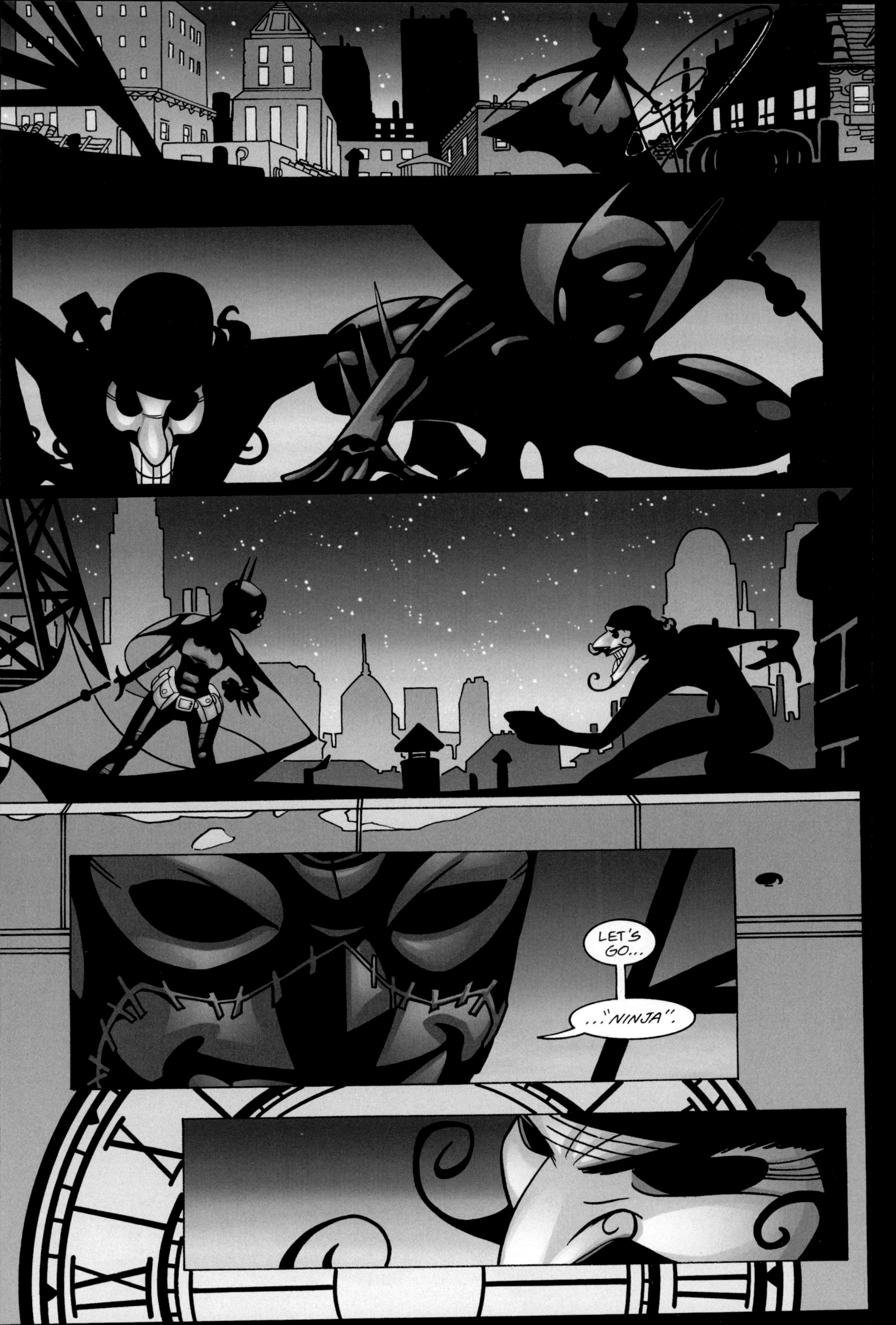
LET'S GO...
..."NINJA".

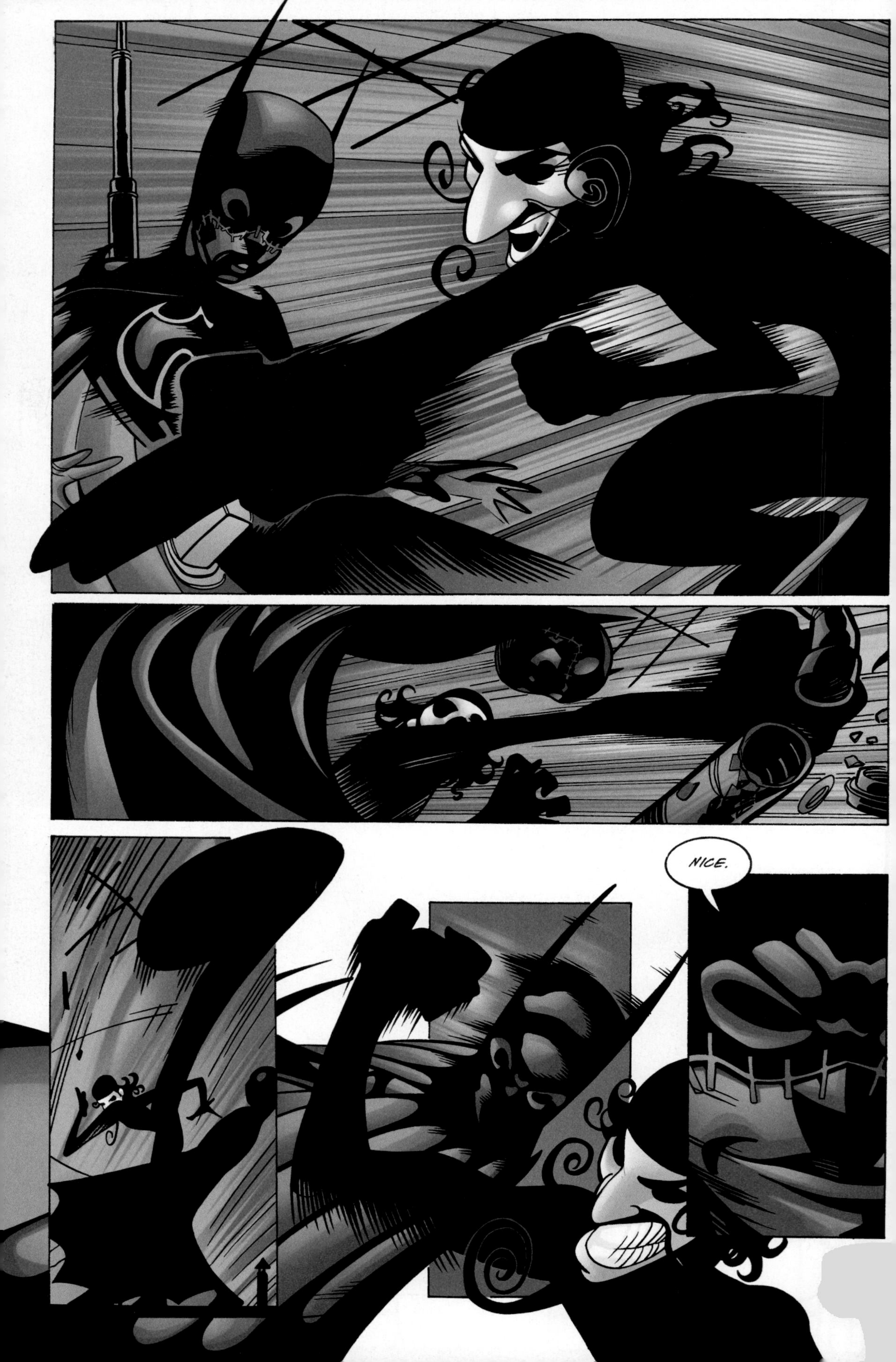
NICE.

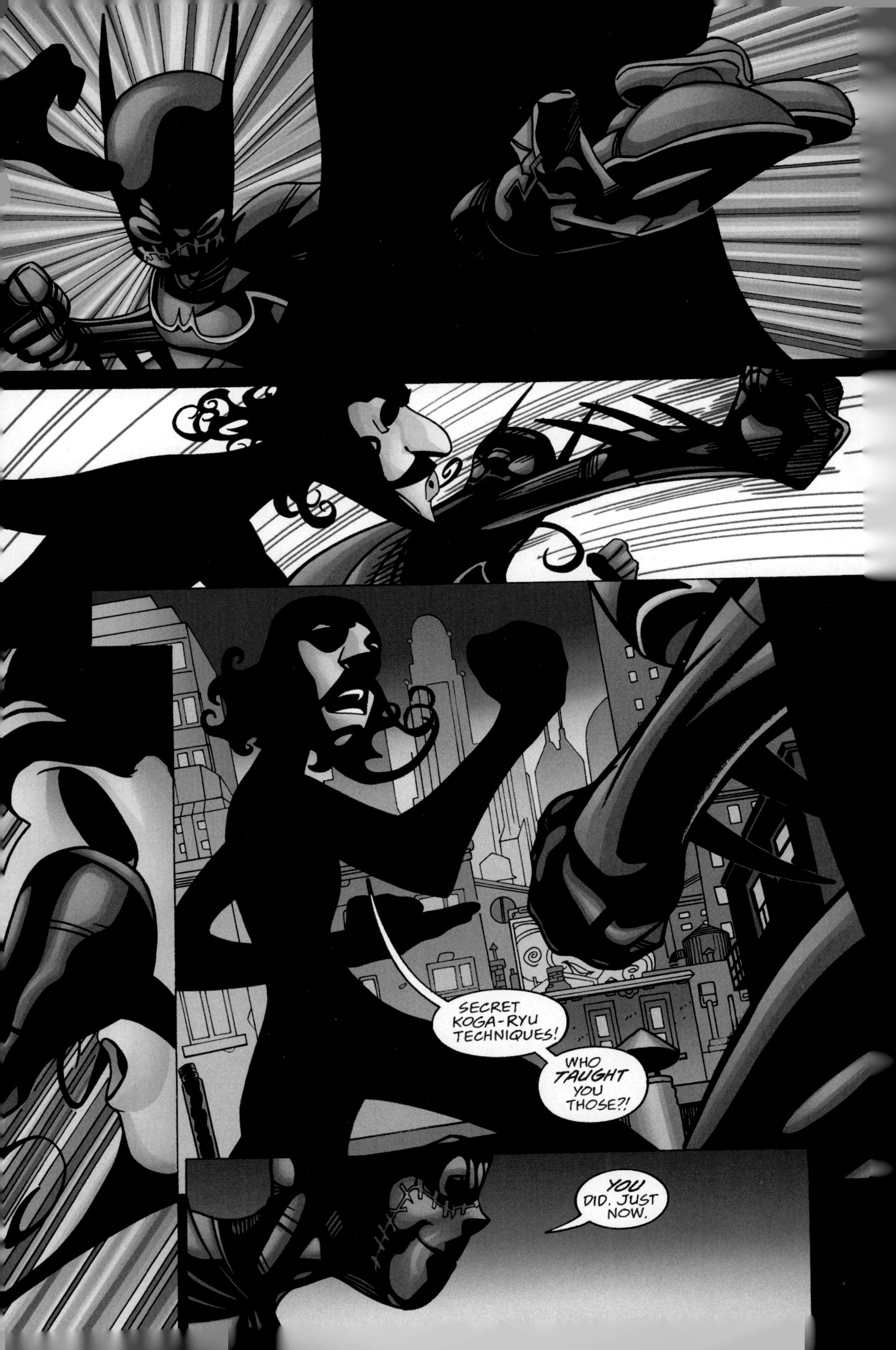
SECRET KOGA-RYU TECHNIQUES!
WHO TAUGHT YOU THOSE?!
YOU DID. JUST NOW.

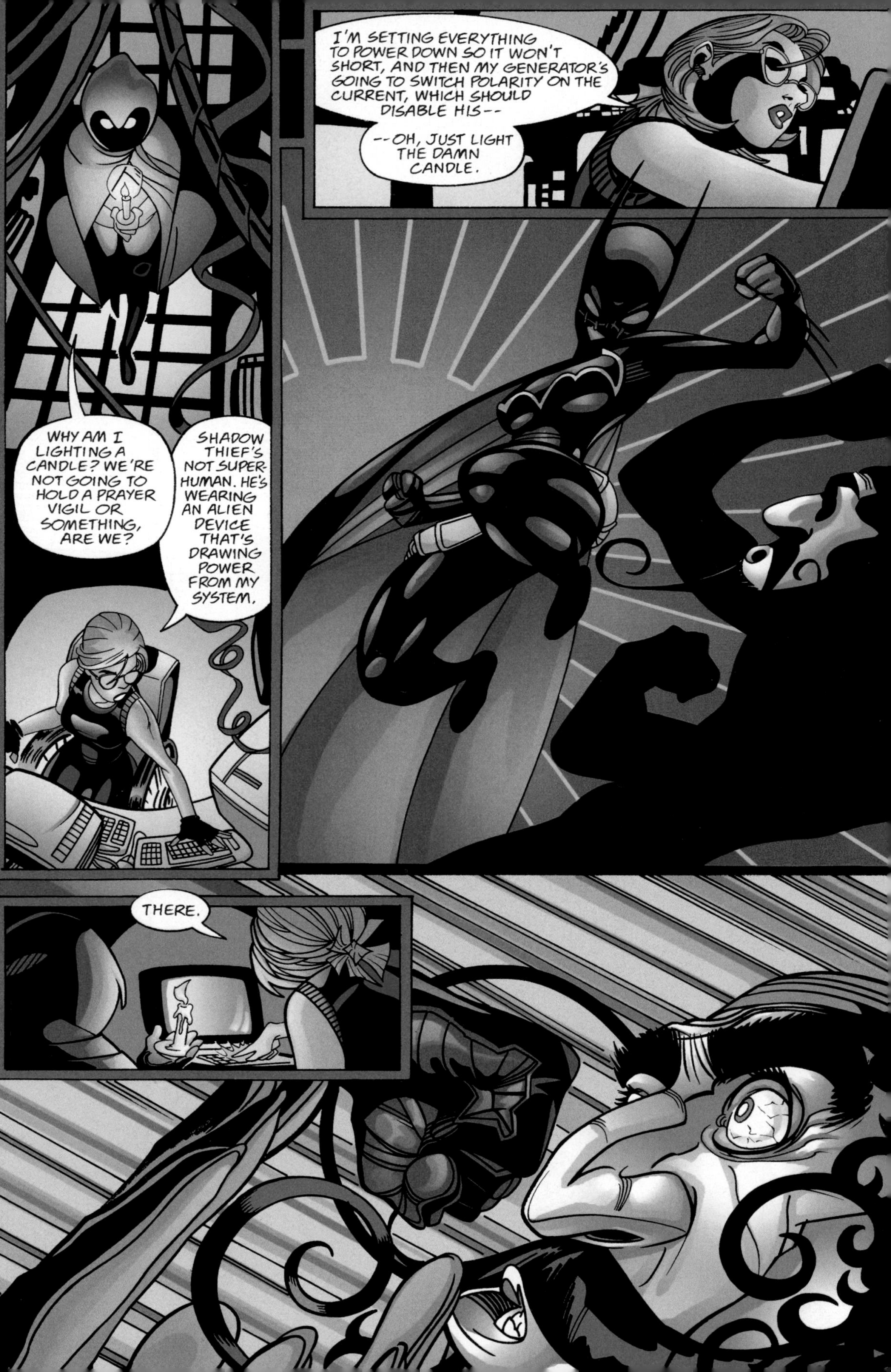
I'M SETTING EVERYTHING TO POWER DOWN SO IT WON'T SHORT, AND THEN MY GENERATOR'S GOING TO SWITCH POLARITY ON THE CURRENT, WHICH SHOULD DISABLE HIS--
--OH, JUST LIGHT THE DAMN CANDLE.
WHY AM I LIGHTING A CANDLE? WE'RE NOT GOING TO HOLD A PRAYER VIGIL OR SOMETHING, ARE WE?
SHADOW THIEF'S NOT SUPER-HUMAN. HE'S WEARING AN ALIEN DEVICE THAT'S DRAWING POWER FROM MY SYSTEM.
THERE.

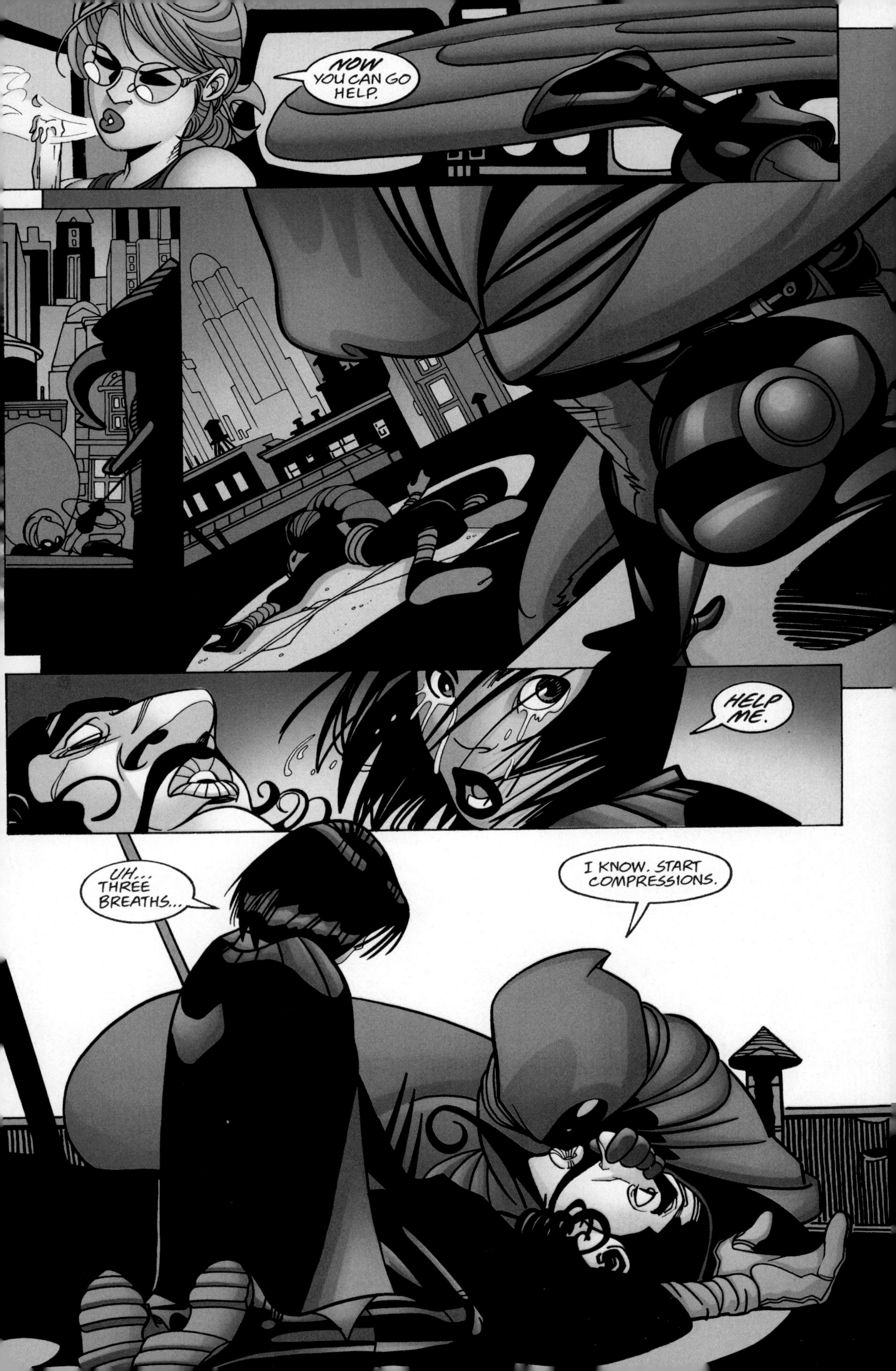
NOW YOU CAN GO HELP.
HELP ME.
UH... THREE BREATHS...
I KNOW. START COMPRESSIONS.

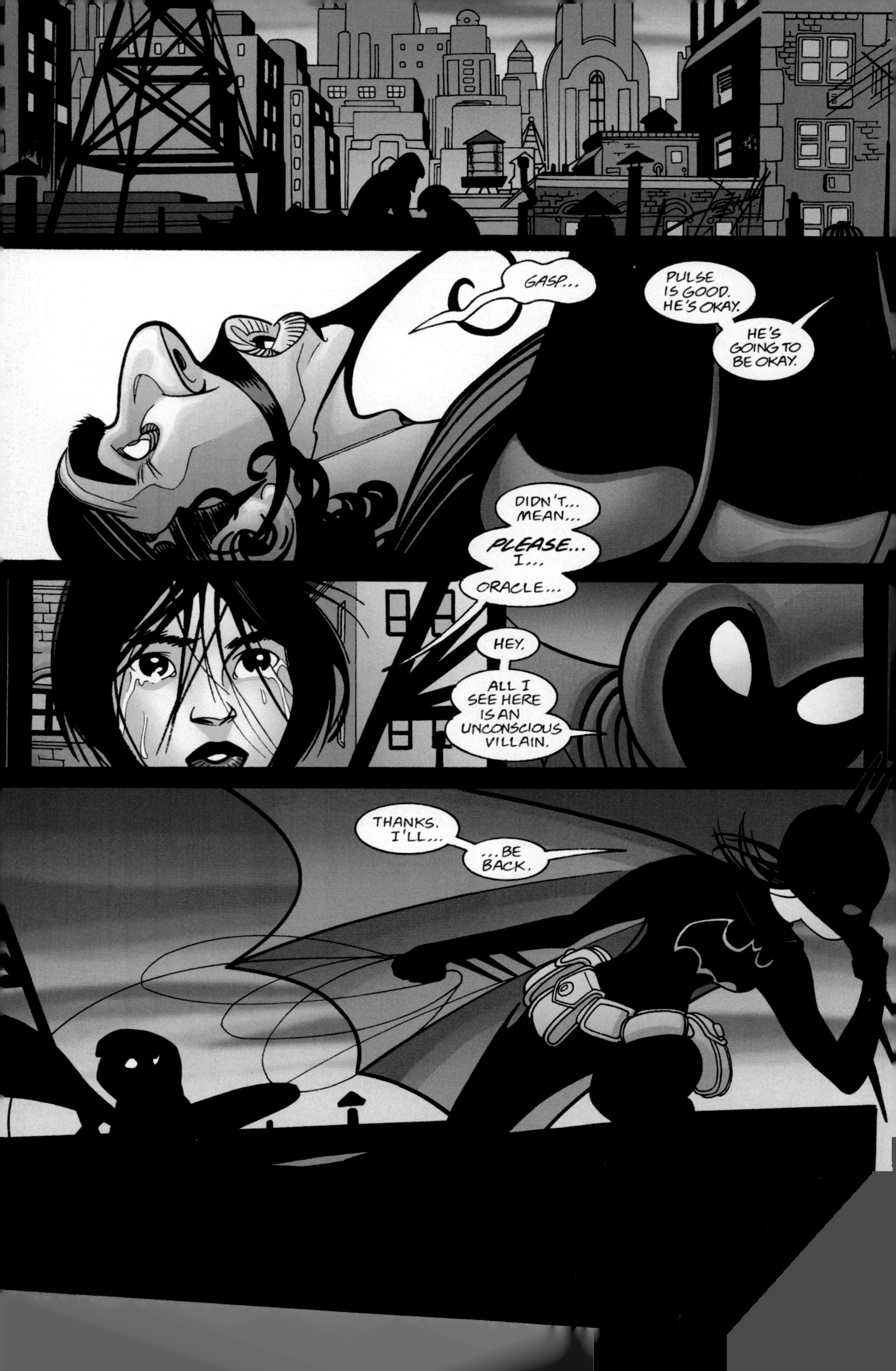
GASP...
PULSE IS GOOD. HE'S OKAY.
HE'S GOING TO BE OKAY.
DIDN'T... MEAN...
PLEASE... I...
ORACLE...
HEY.
ALL I SEE HERE IS AN UNCONSCIOUS VILLAIN.
THANKS. I'LL...
...BE BACK.

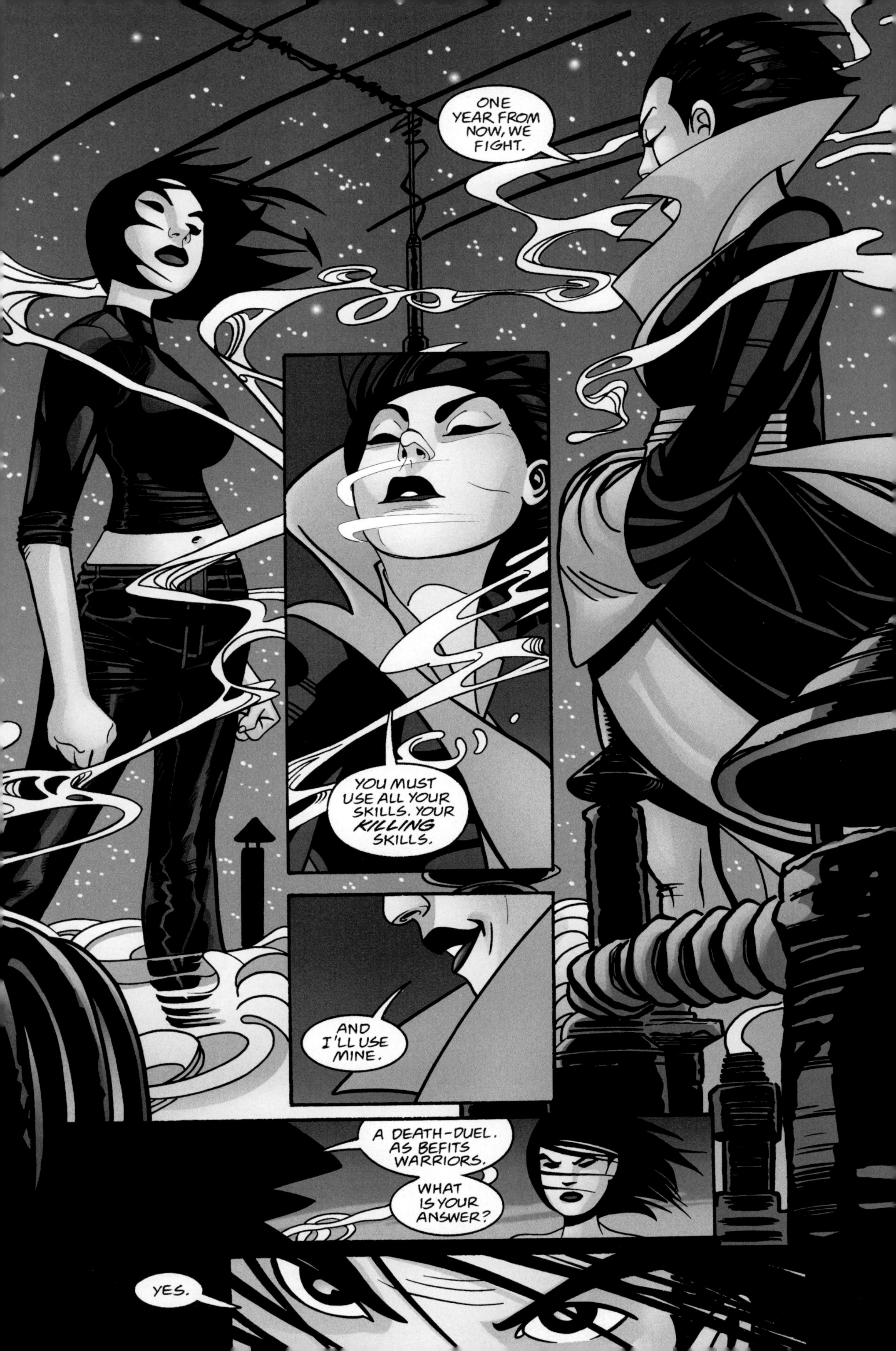
ONE YEAR FROM NOW, WE FIGHT.
YOU MUST USE ALL YOUR SKILLS. YOUR *KILLING* SKILLS.
AND I'LL USE MINE.
A DEATH-DUEL. AS BEFITS WARRIORS.
WHAT IS YOUR ANSWER?
YES.

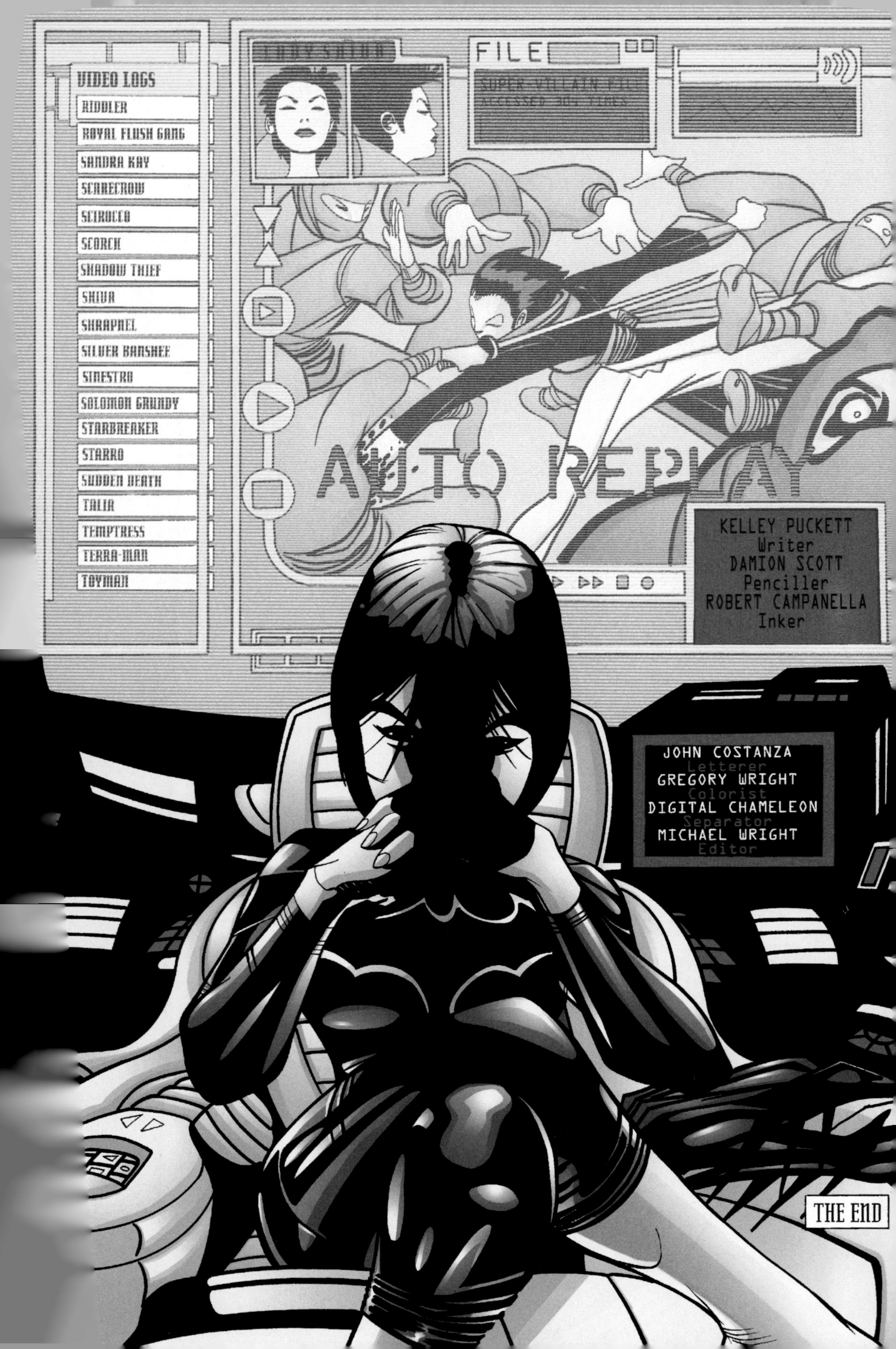
VIDEO LOGS
RIDDLER
ROYAL FLUSH GANG
SANDRA KAY
SCARECROW
SCIROCCO
SCORCH
SHADOW THIEF
SHIVA
SHRAPNEL
SILVER BANSHEE
SINESTRO
SOLOMON GRUNDY
STARBREAKER
STARRO
SUDDEN DEATH
TALIA
TEMPTRESS
TERRA-MAN
TOYMAN
FILE
AUTO REPLAY
KELLEY PUCKETT
Writer
DAMION SCOTT
Penciller
ROBERT CAMPANELLA
Inker
JOHN COSTANZA
Letterer
GREGORY WRIGHT
Colorist
DIGITAL CHAMELEON
Separator
MICHAEL WRIGHT
Editor
THE END

BATGIRL #22 cover by Damion Scott, Robert Campanella & Patrick Martin

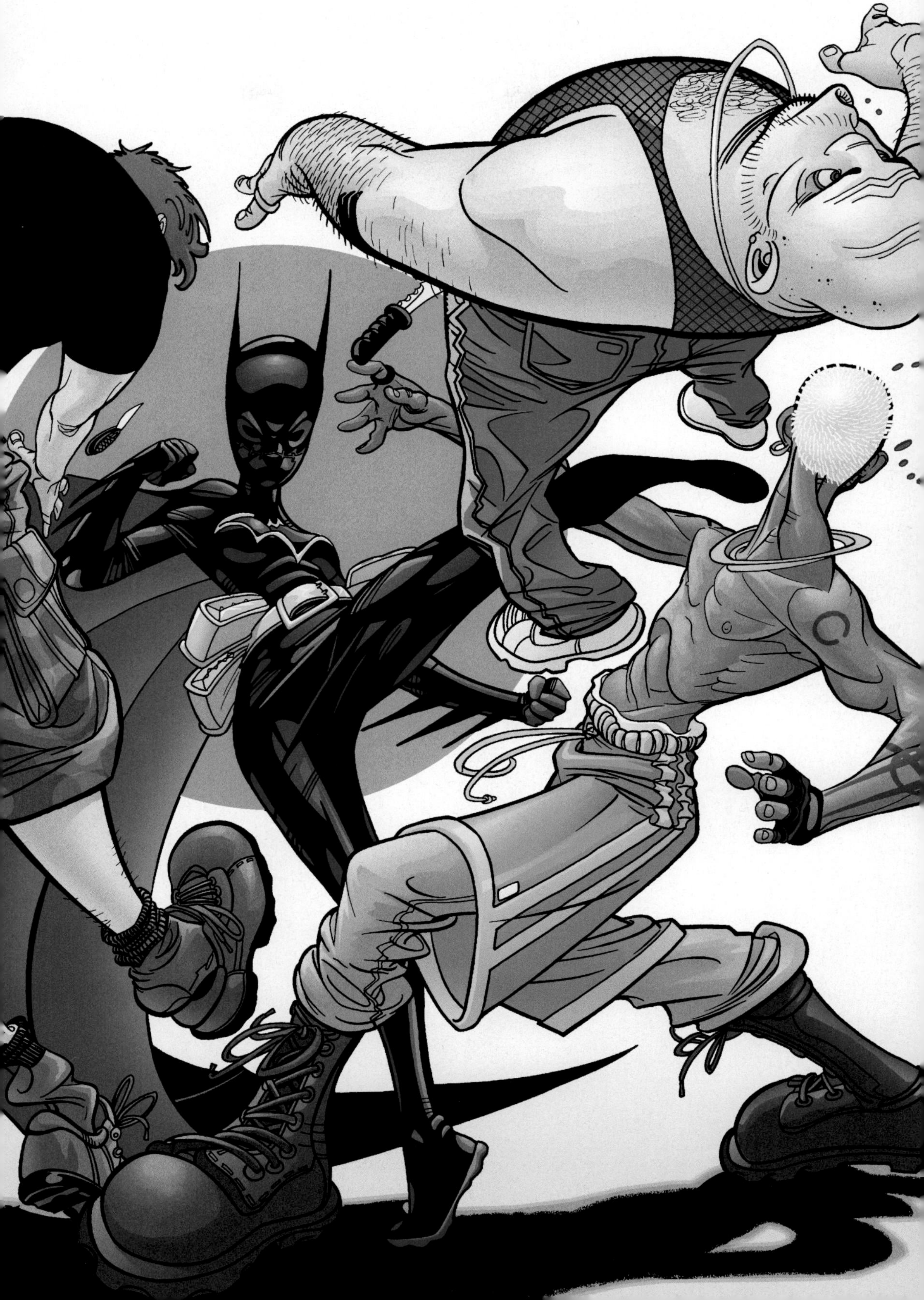

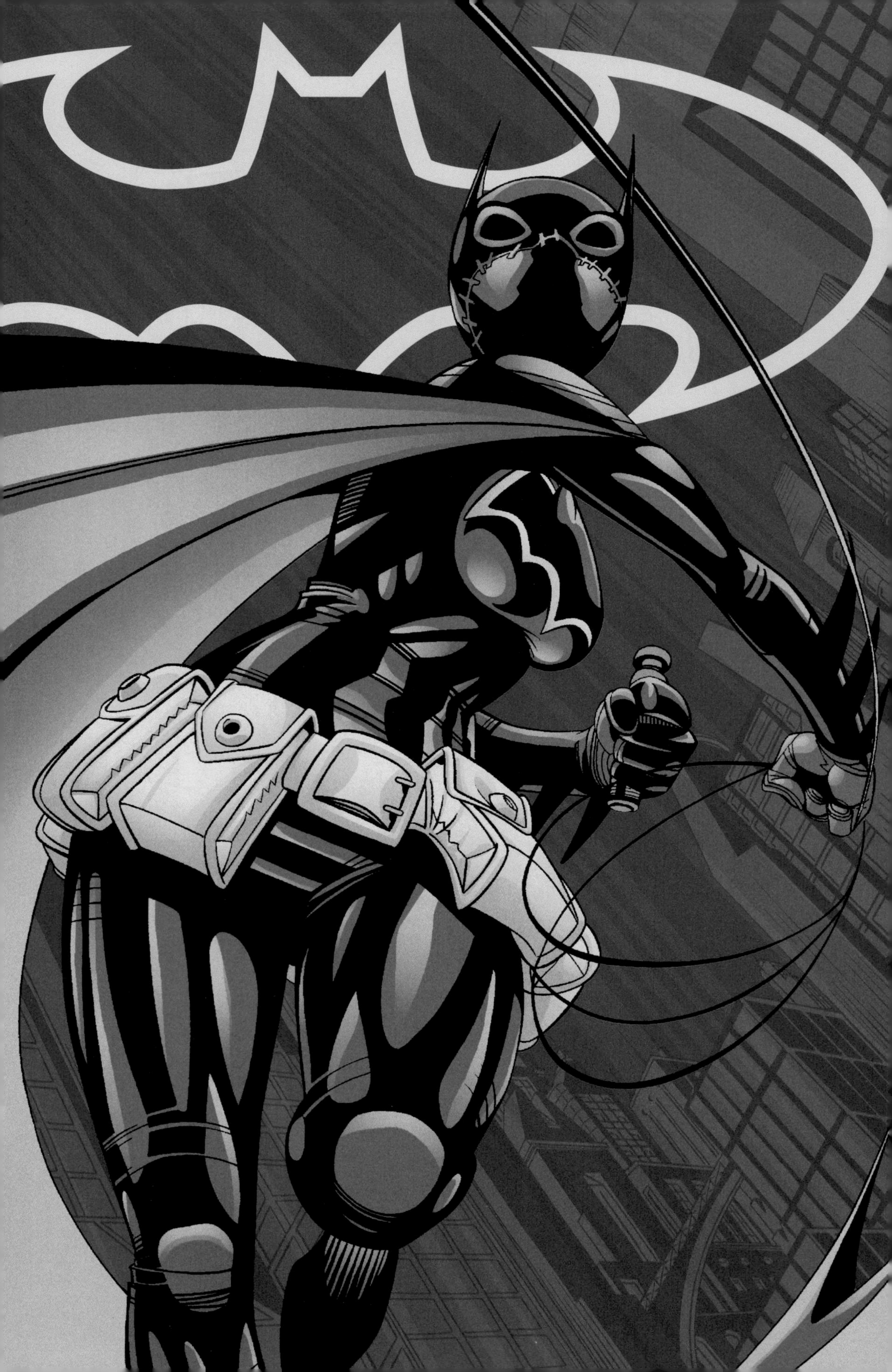

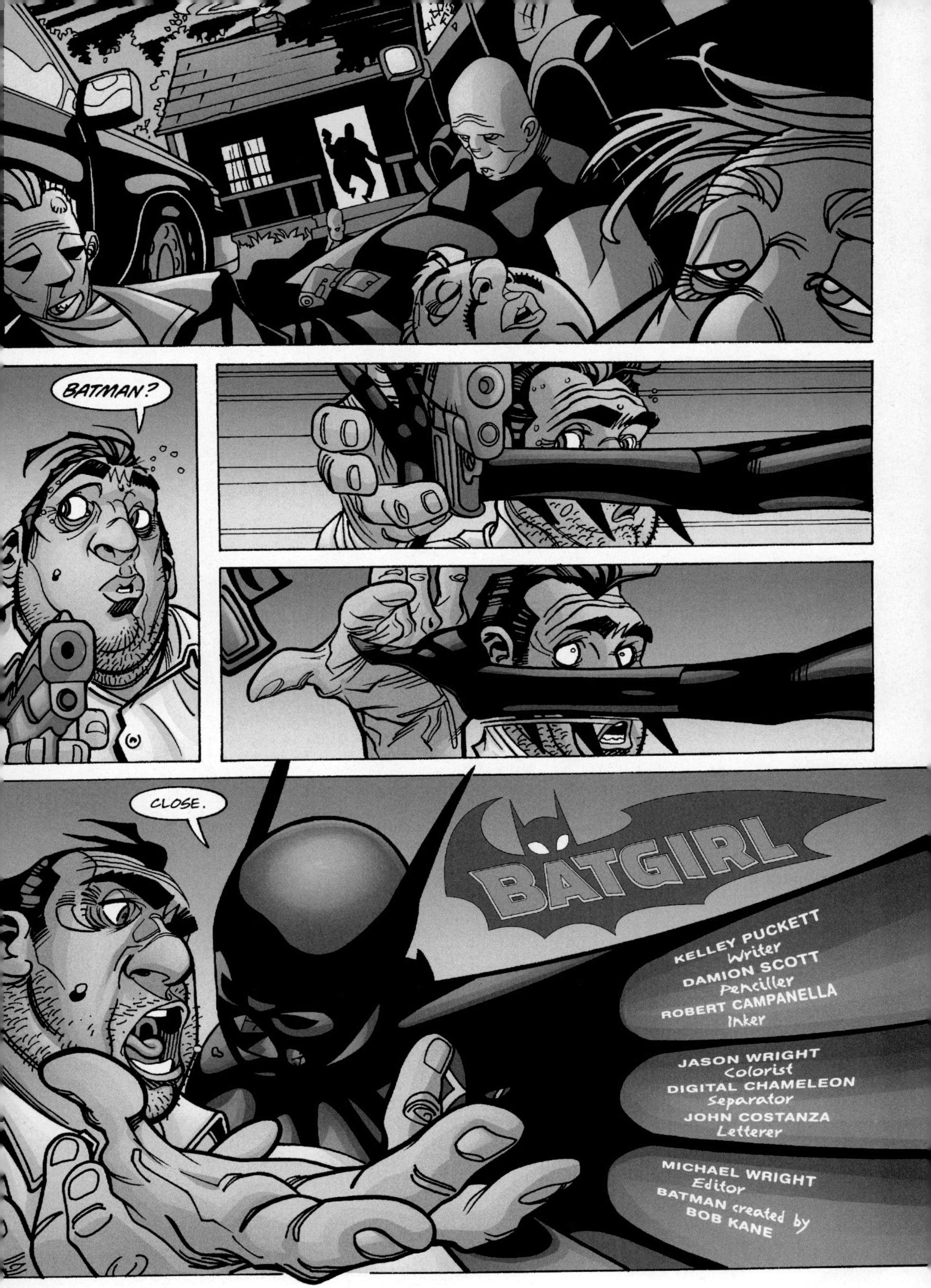
BATMAN?
CLOSE.
BATGIRL
KELLEY PUCKETT
Writer
DAMION SCOTT
Penciller
ROBERT CAMPANELLA
Inker
JASON WRIGHT
Colorist
DIGITAL CHAMELEON
Separator
JOHN COSTANZA
Letterer
MICHAEL WRIGHT
Editor
BATMAN created by
BOB KANE

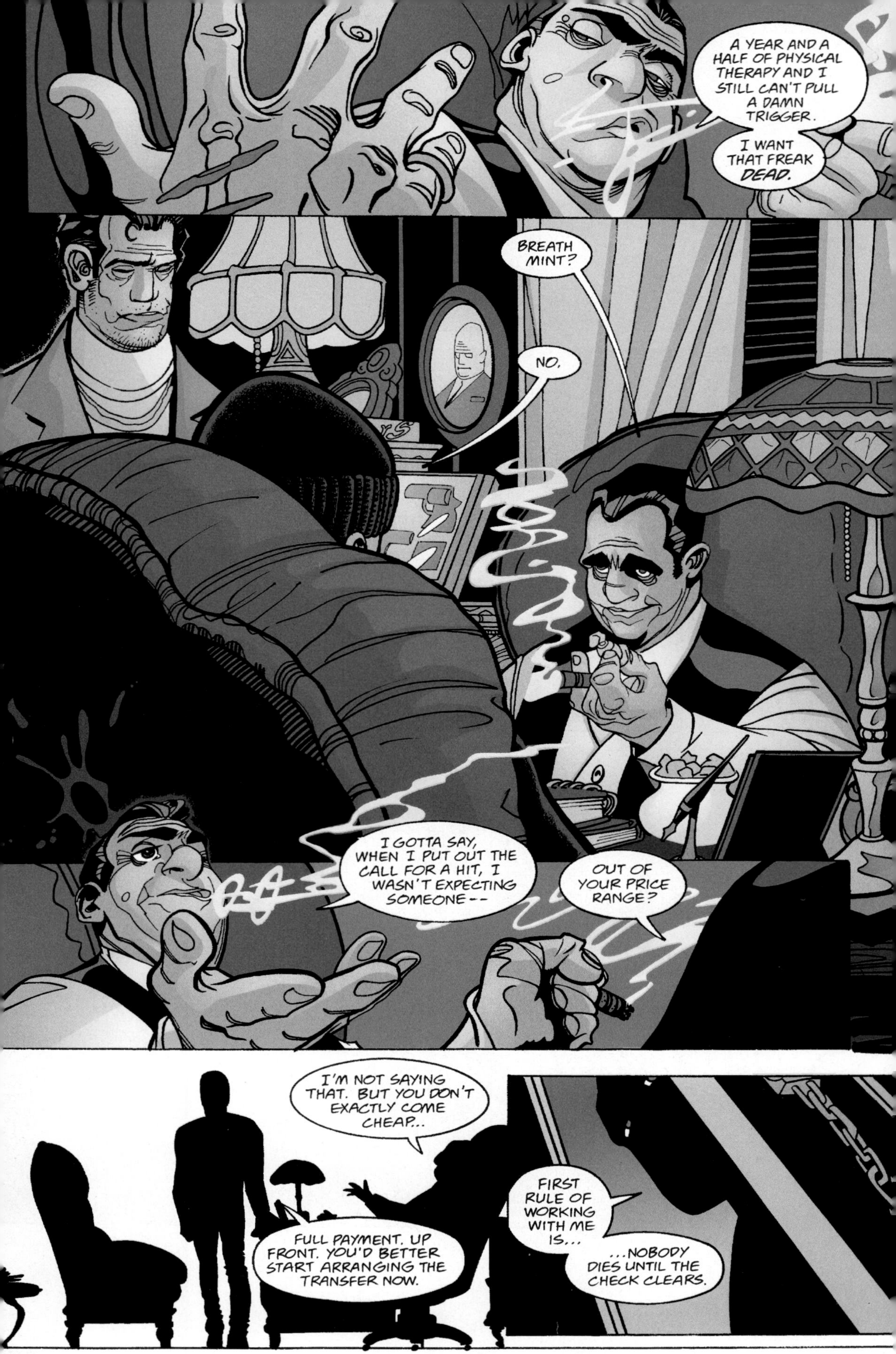
A YEAR AND A HALF OF PHYSICAL THERAPY AND I STILL CAN'T PULL A DAMN TRIGGER.
I WANT THAT FREAK DEAD.
BREATH MINT?
NO.
I GOTTA SAY, WHEN I PUT OUT THE CALL FOR A HIT, I WASN'T EXPECTING SOMEONE--
OUT OF YOUR PRICE RANGE?
I'M NOT SAYING THAT. BUT YOU DON'T EXACTLY COME CHEAP...
FULL PAYMENT. UP FRONT. YOU'D BETTER START ARRANGING THE TRANSFER NOW.
FIRST RULE OF WORKING WITH ME IS...
...NOBODY DIES UNTIL THE CHECK CLEARS.

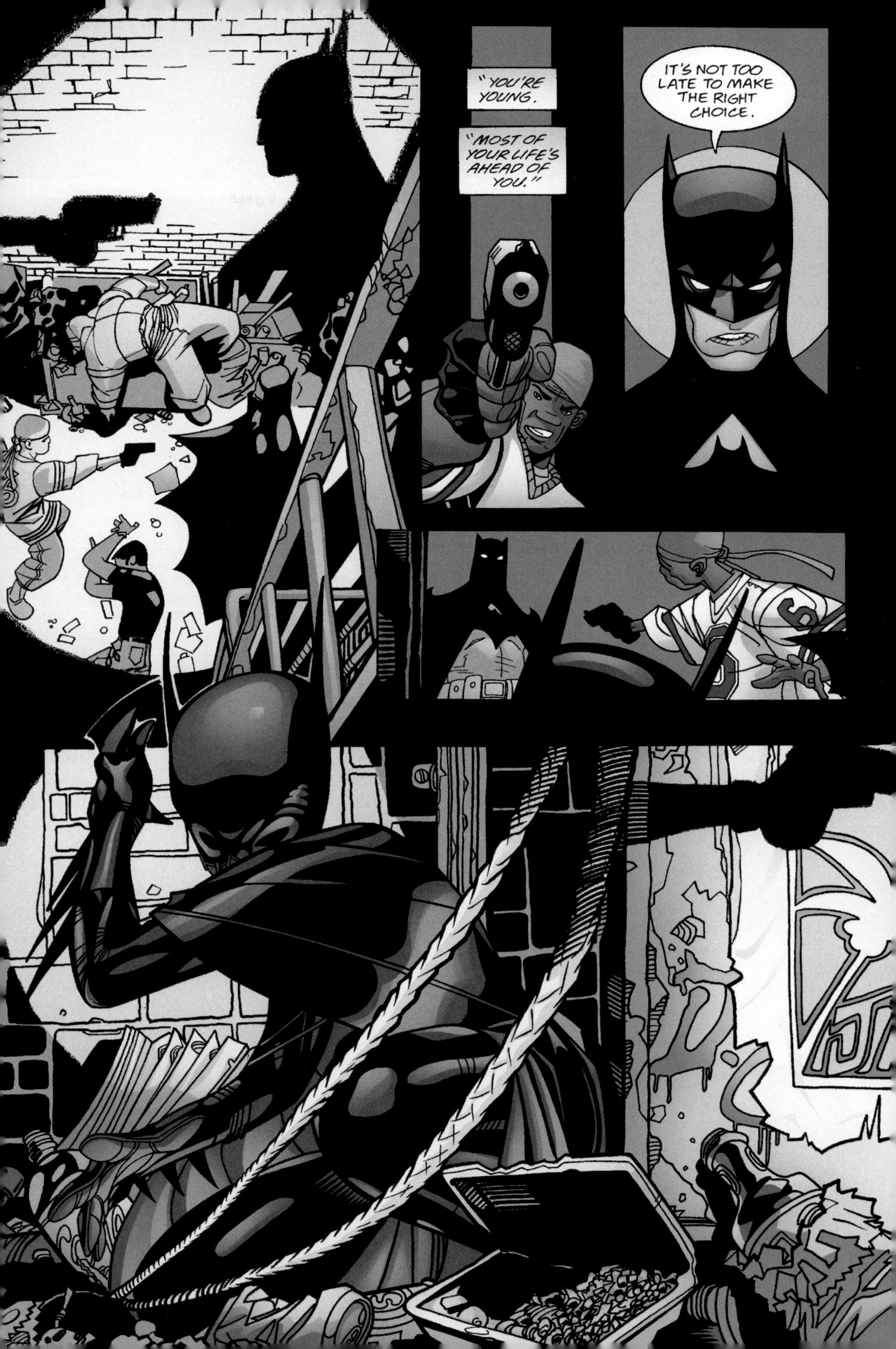
"YOU'RE YOUNG.
"MOST OF YOUR LIFE'S AHEAD OF YOU."
IT'S NOT TOO LATE TO MAKE THE RIGHT CHOICE.

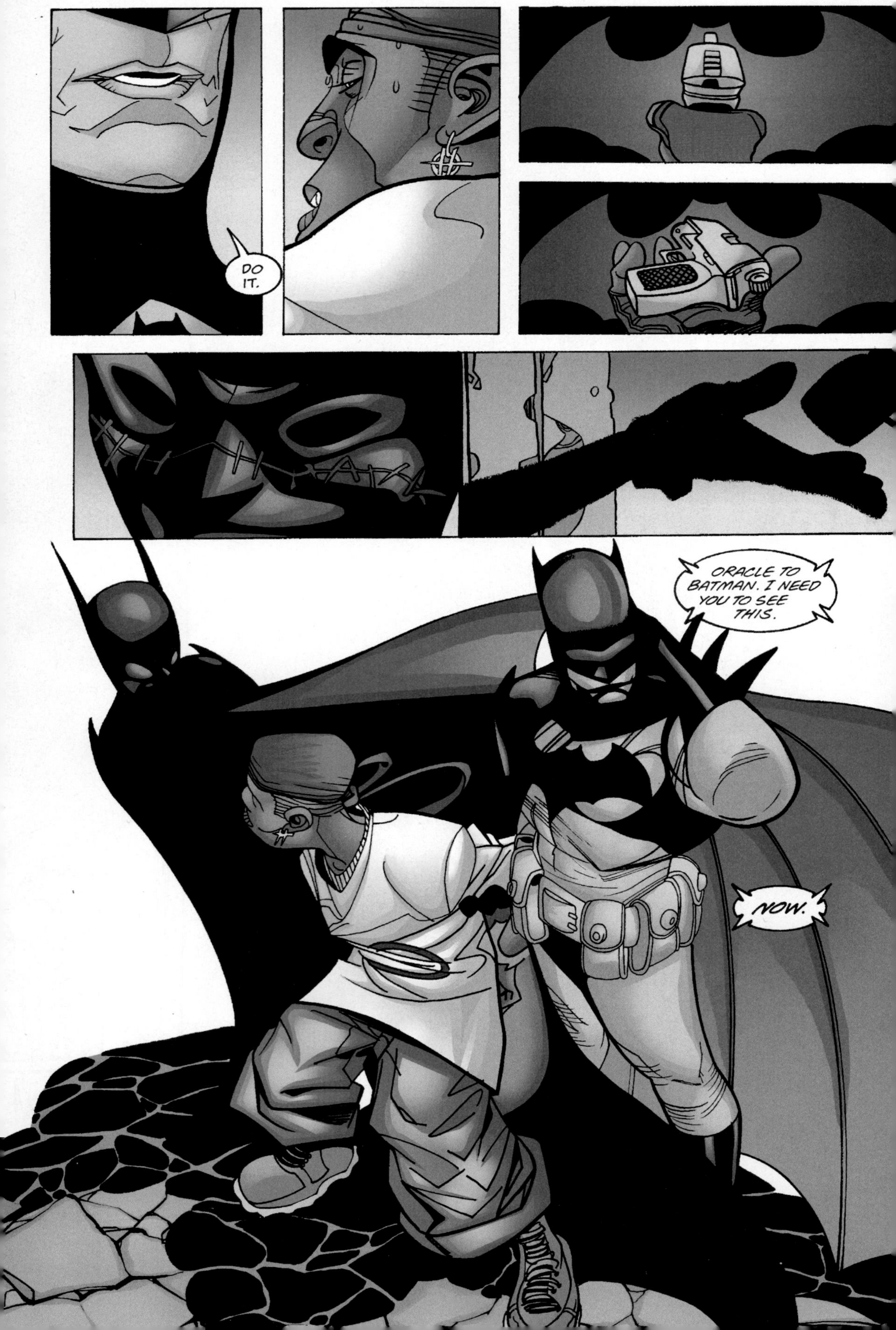
DO IT.
ORACLE TO BATMAN. I NEED YOU TO SEE THIS.
NOW.

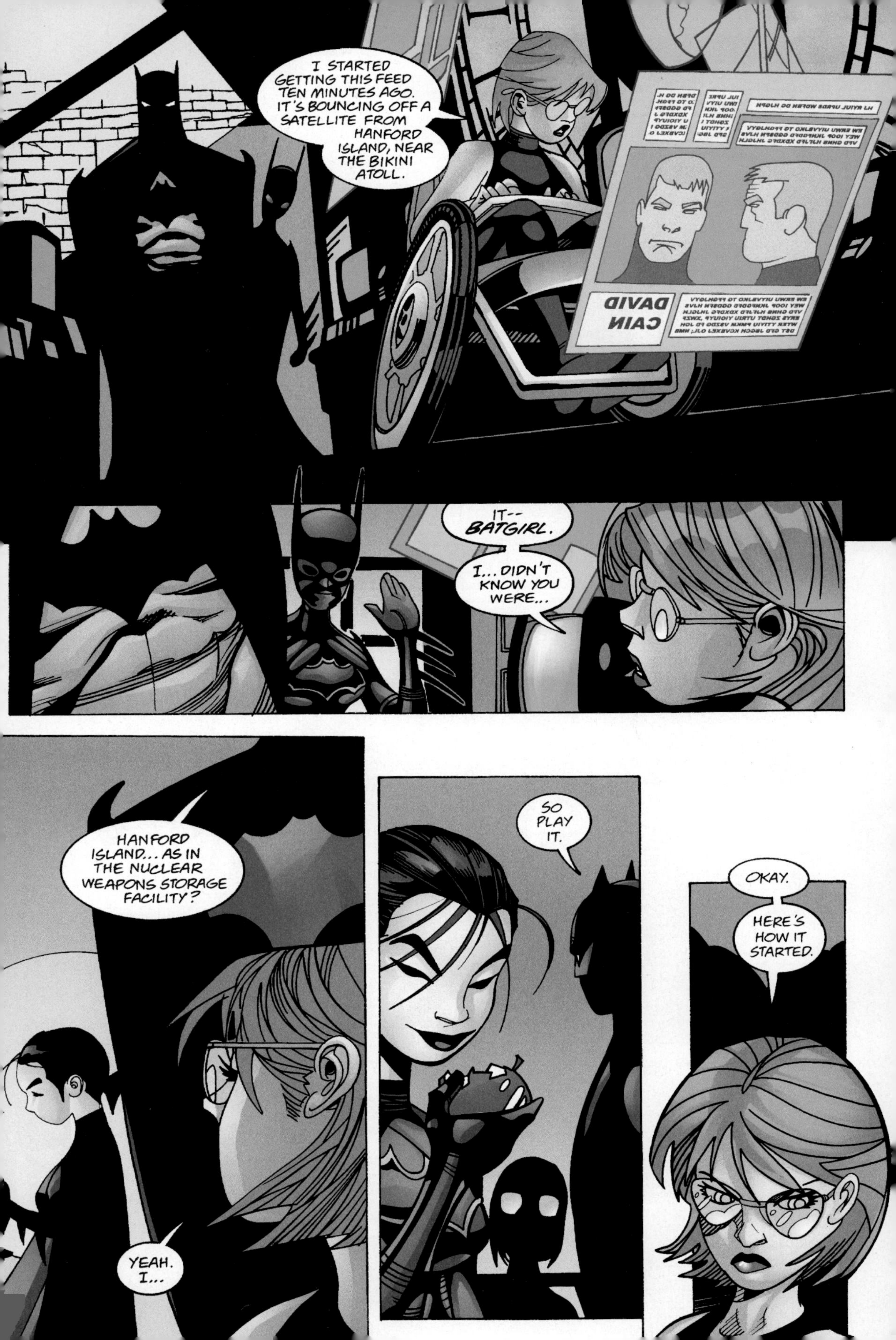
I STARTED GETTING THIS FEED TEN MINUTES AGO. IT'S BOUNCING OFF A SATELLITE FROM HANFORD ISLAND, NEAR THE BIKINI ATOLL.
DAVID CAIN
IT-- BATGIRL.
I... DIDN'T KNOW YOU WERE...
HANFORD ISLAND... AS IN THE NUCLEAR WEAPONS STORAGE FACILITY?
YEAH. I...
SO PLAY IT.
OKAY.
HERE'S HOW IT STARTED.

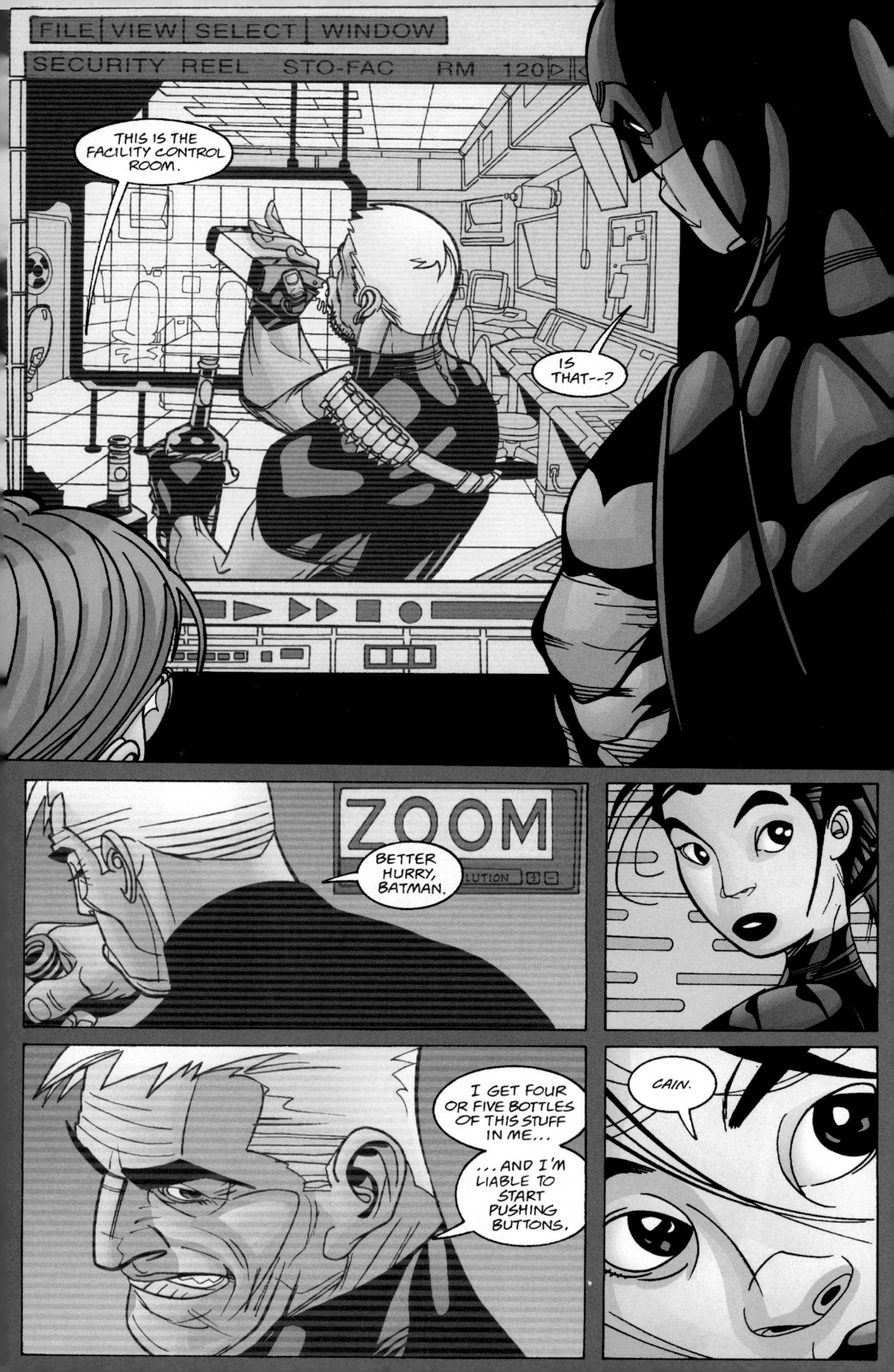
FILE VIEW SELECT WINDOW
SECURITY REEL STO-FAC RM 120
THIS IS THE FACILITY CONTROL ROOM.
IS THAT--?
ZOOM
BETTER HURRY, BATMAN.
I GET FOUR OR FIVE BOTTLES OF THIS STUFF IN ME...
...AND I'M LIABLE TO START PUSHING BUTTONS.
CAIN.

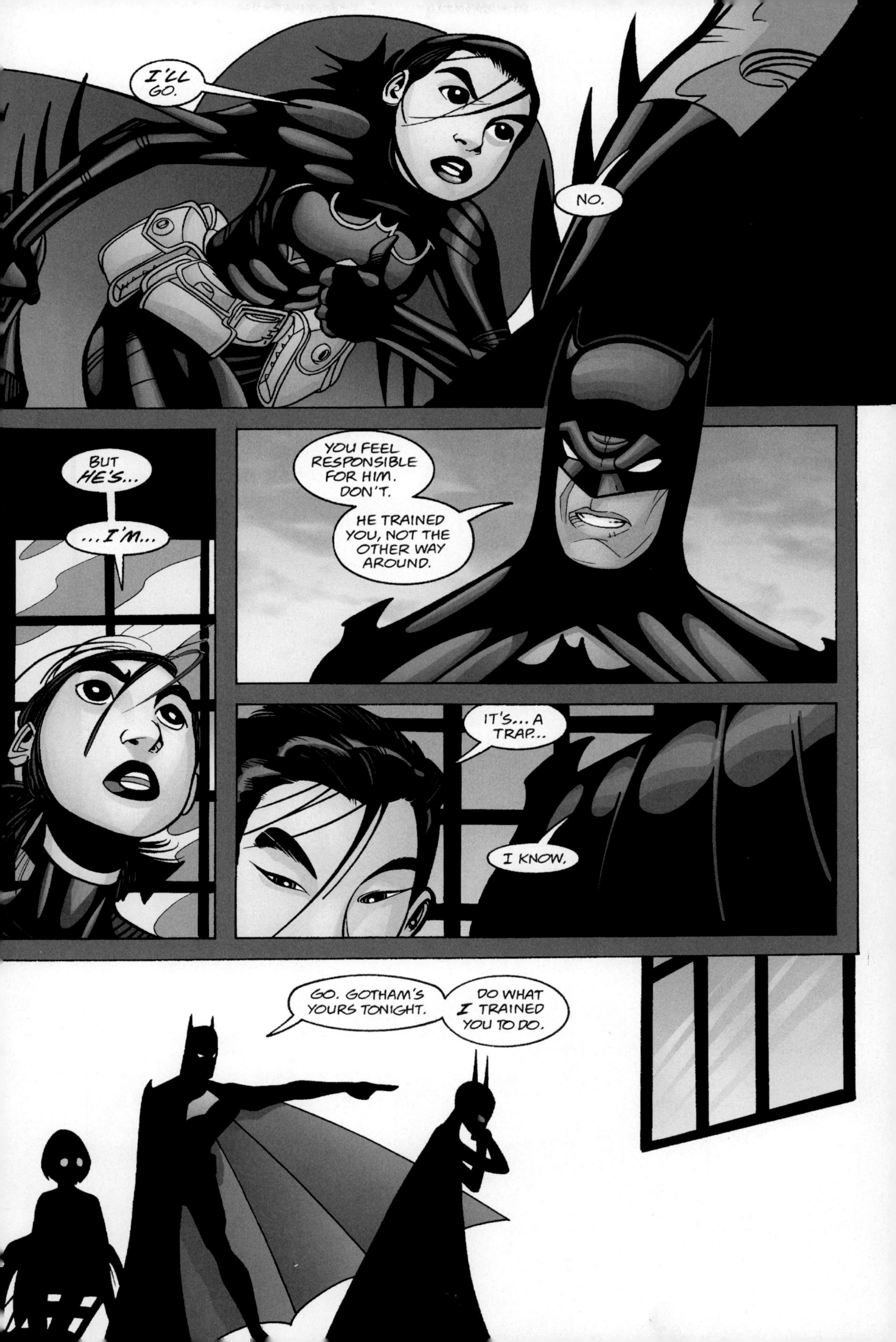
I'LL GO.
NO.
BUT HE'S...
...I'M...
YOU FEEL RESPONSIBLE FOR HIM. DON'T.
HE TRAINED YOU, NOT THE OTHER WAY AROUND.
IT'S... A TRAP...
I KNOW.
GO. GOTHAM'S YOURS TONIGHT.
DO WHAT I TRAINED YOU TO DO.

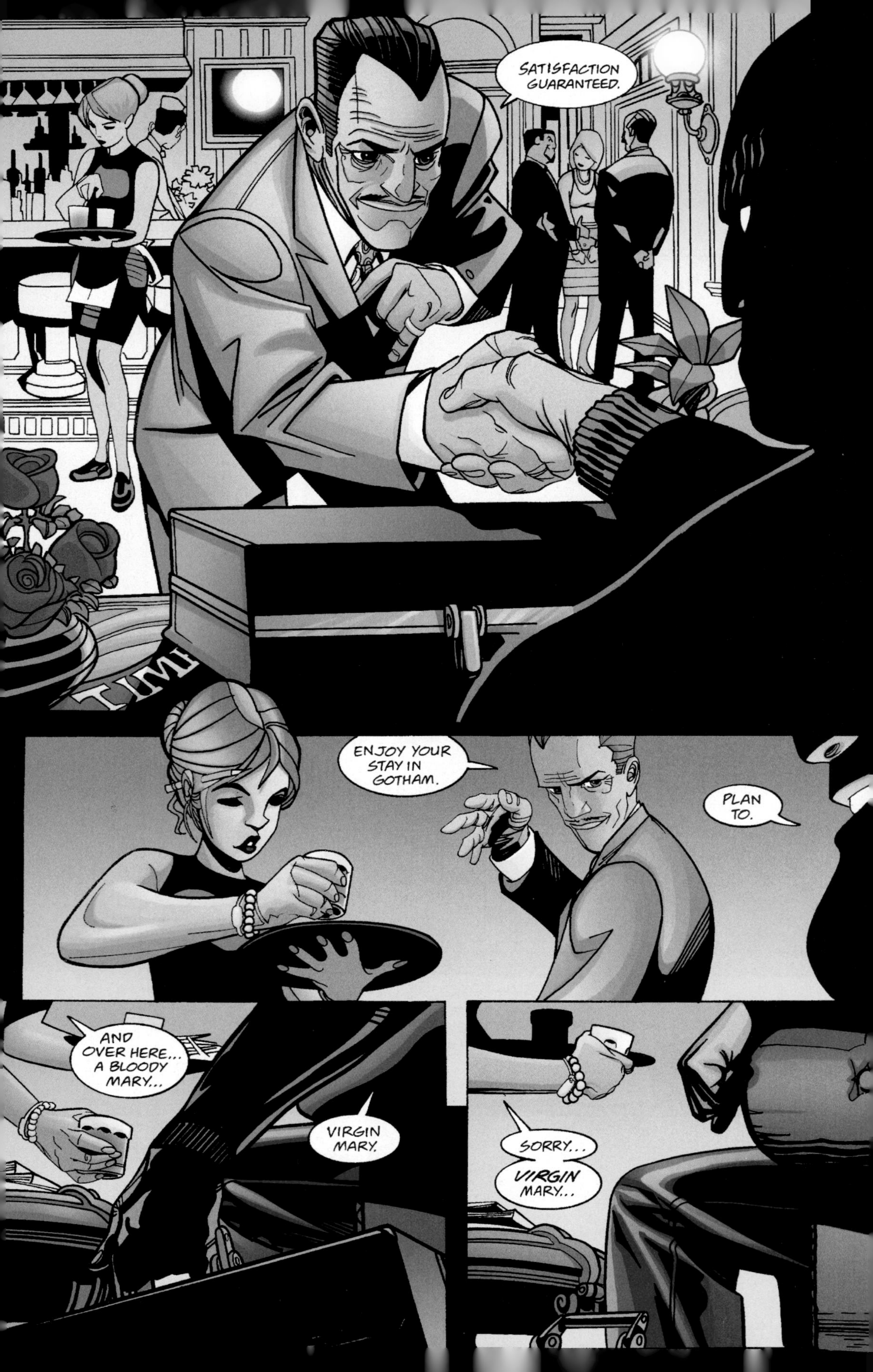
SATISFACTION GUARANTEED.
ENJOY YOUR STAY IN GOTHAM.
PLAN TO.
AND OVER HERE... A BLOODY MARY...
VIRGIN MARY.
SORRY...
VIRGIN MARY...

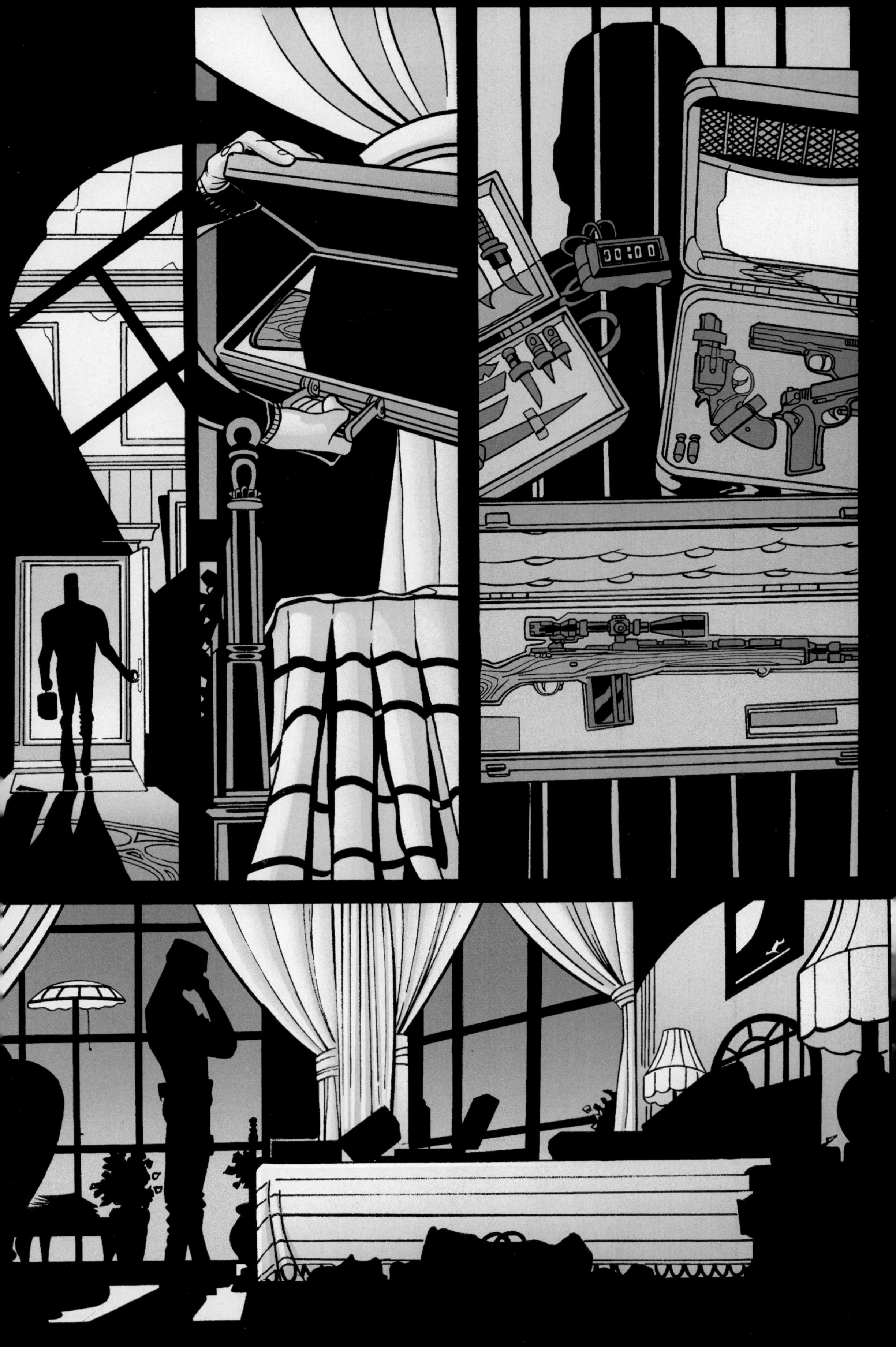
00:00

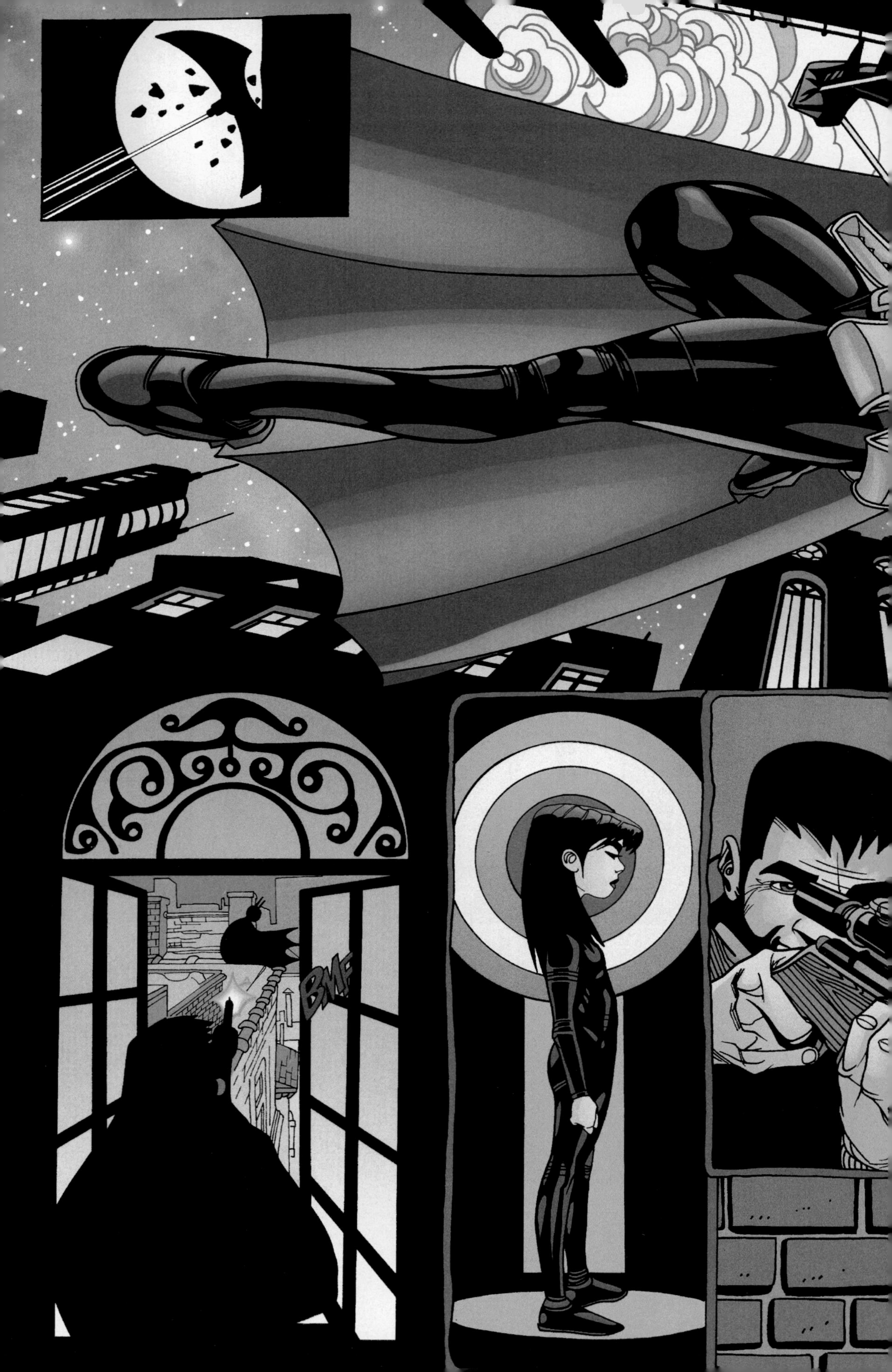
BMF

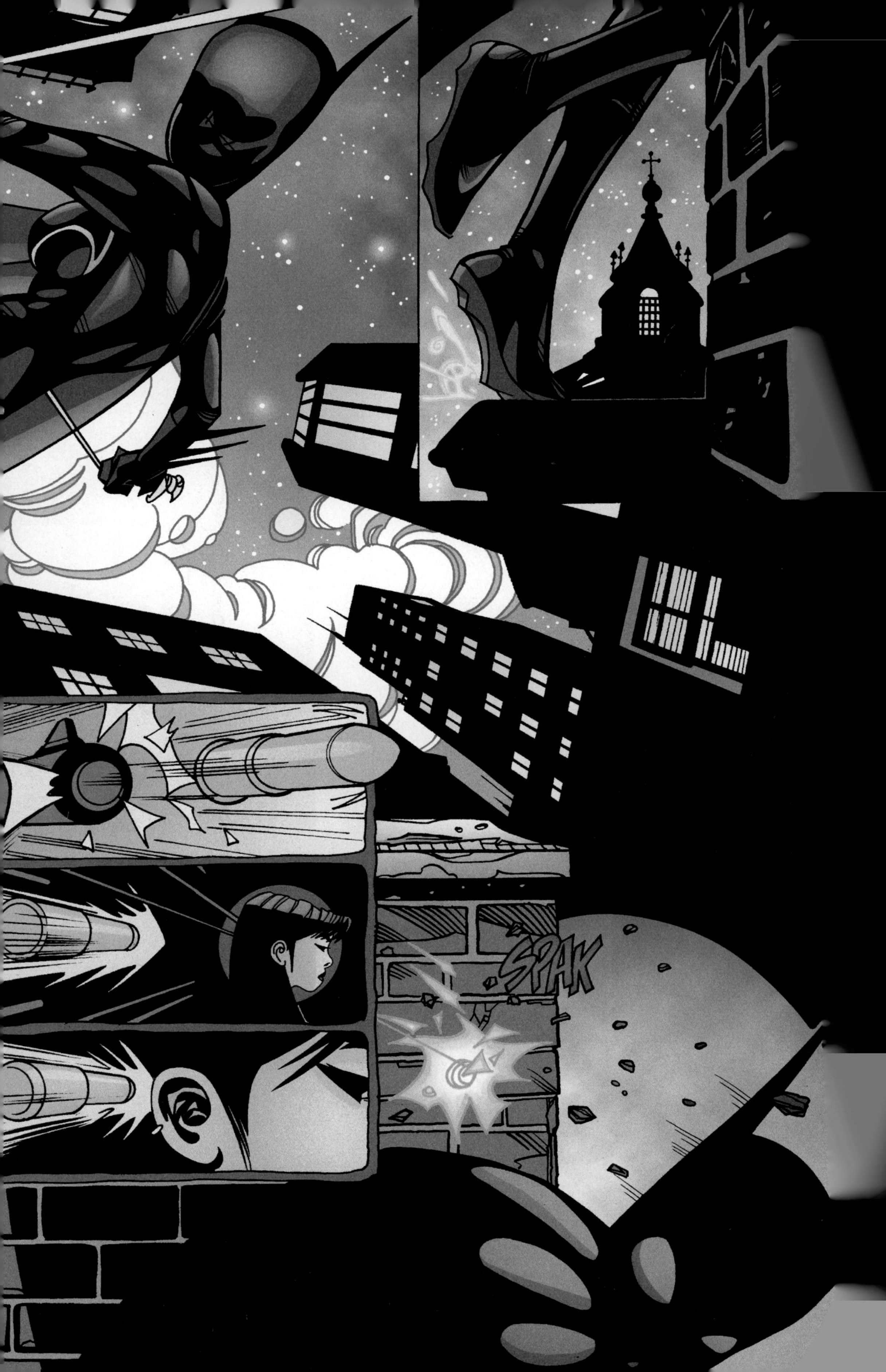
SPAK

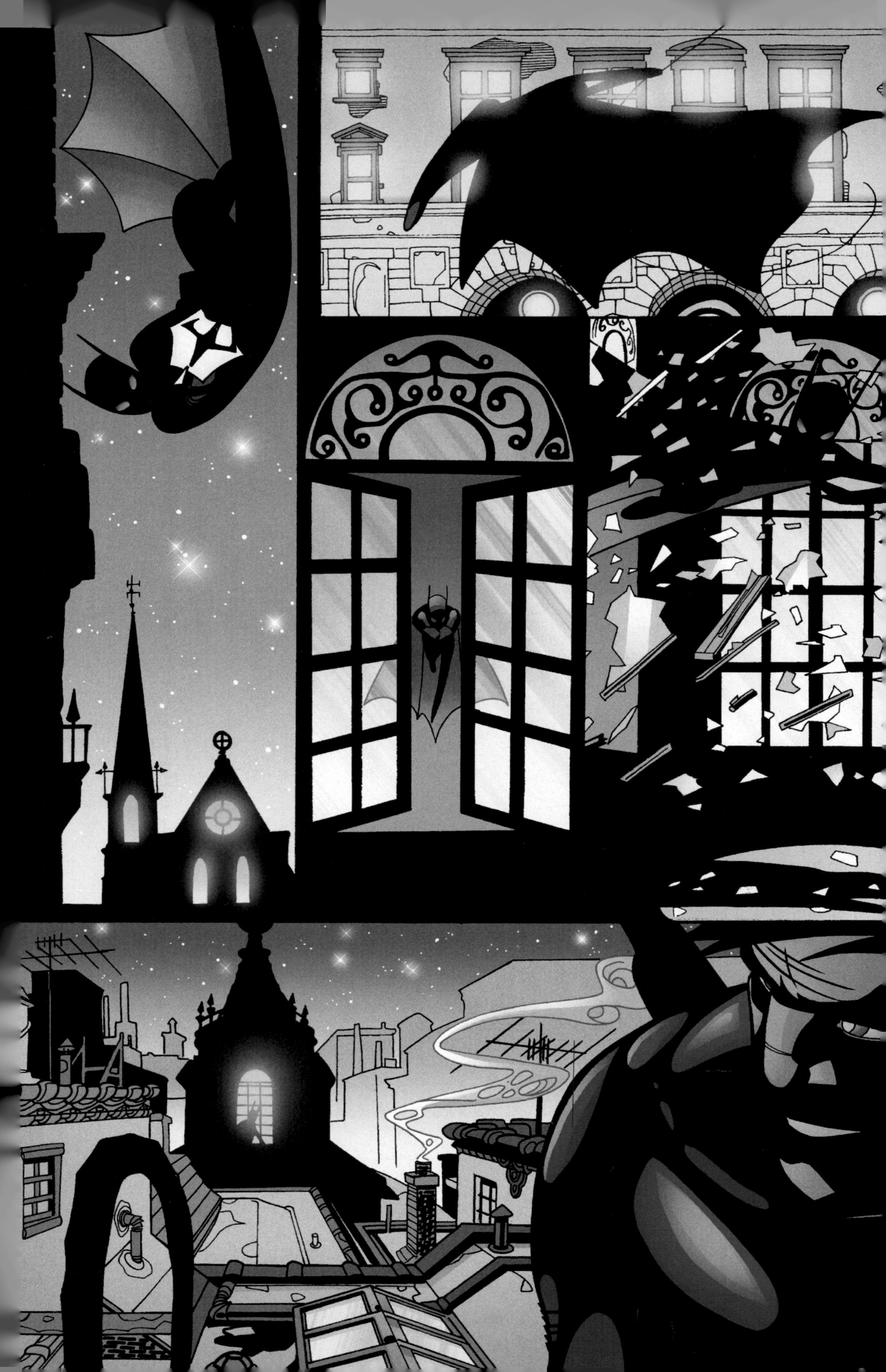

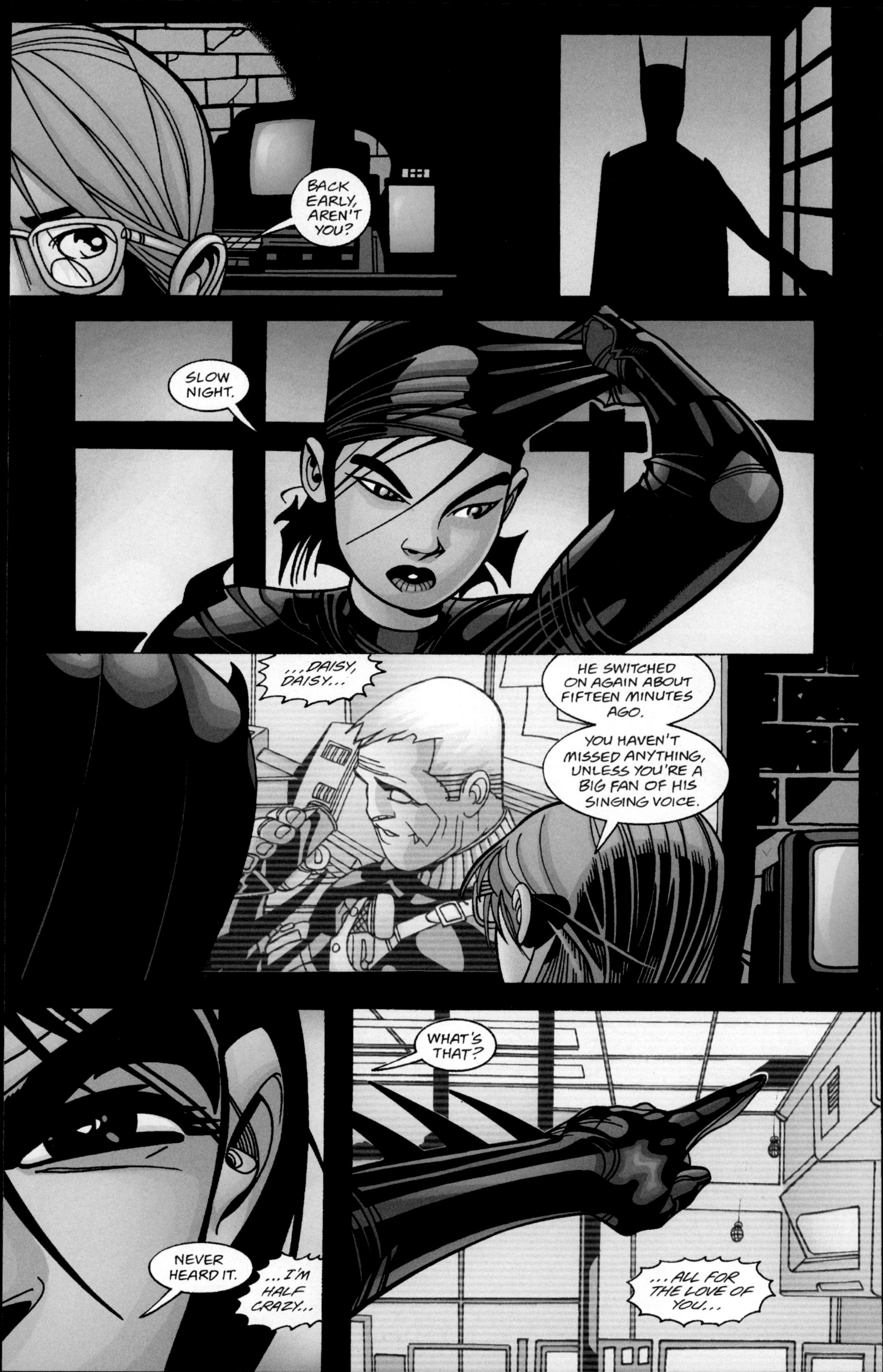
BACK EARLY, AREN'T YOU?
SLOW NIGHT.
...DAISY, DAISY...
HE SWITCHED ON AGAIN ABOUT FIFTEEN MINUTES AGO.
YOU HAVEN'T MISSED ANYTHING, UNLESS YOU'RE A BIG FAN OF HIS SINGING VOICE.
WHAT'S THAT?
NEVER HEARD IT.
...I'M HALF CRAZY...
...ALL FOR THE LOVE OF YOU...

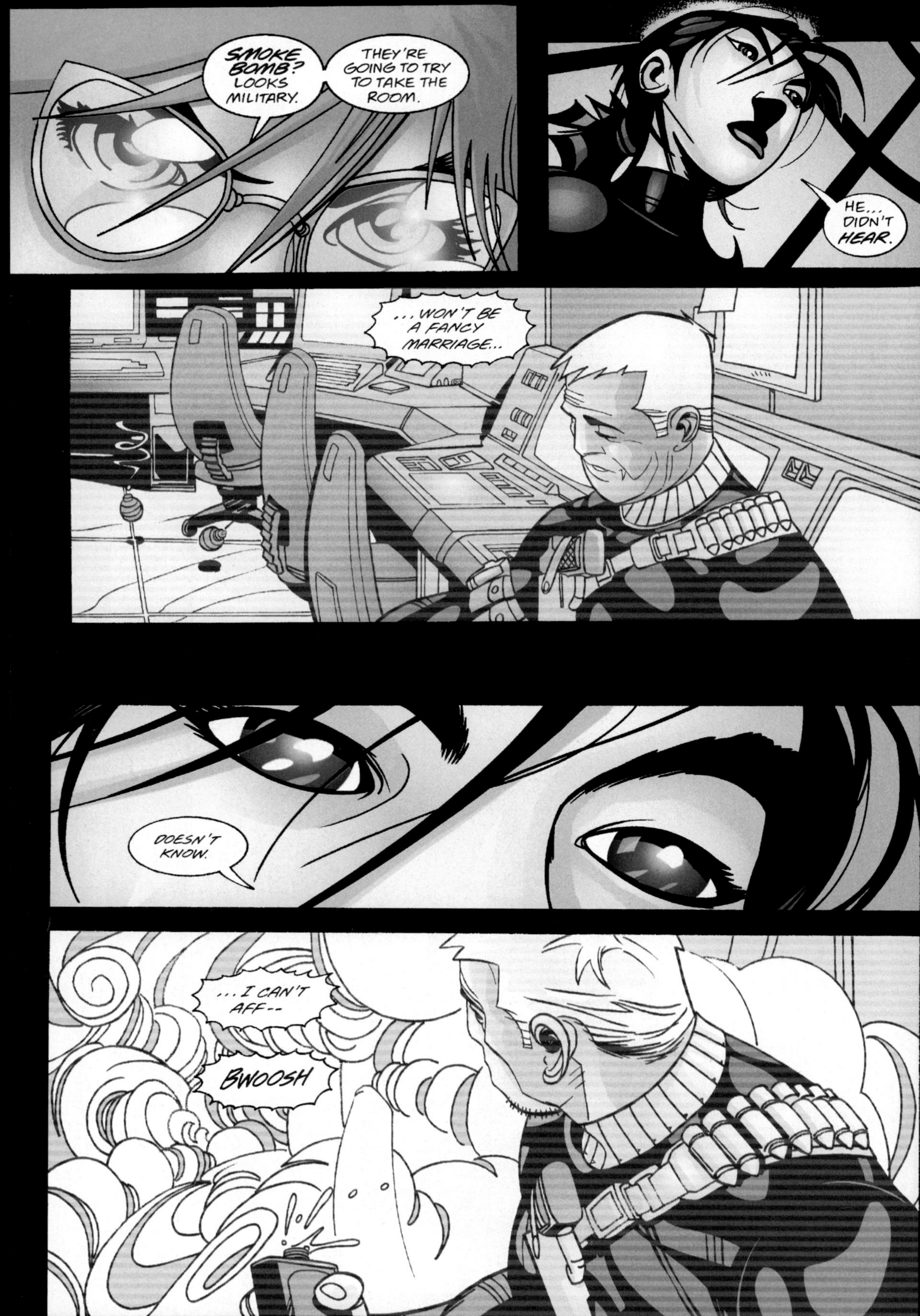
SMOKE BOMB? LOOKS MILITARY.
THEY'RE GOING TO TRY TO TAKE THE ROOM.
HE... DIDN'T HEAR.
...WON'T BE A FANCY MARRIAGE...
DOESN'T KNOW.
...I CAN'T AFF--
BWOOSH

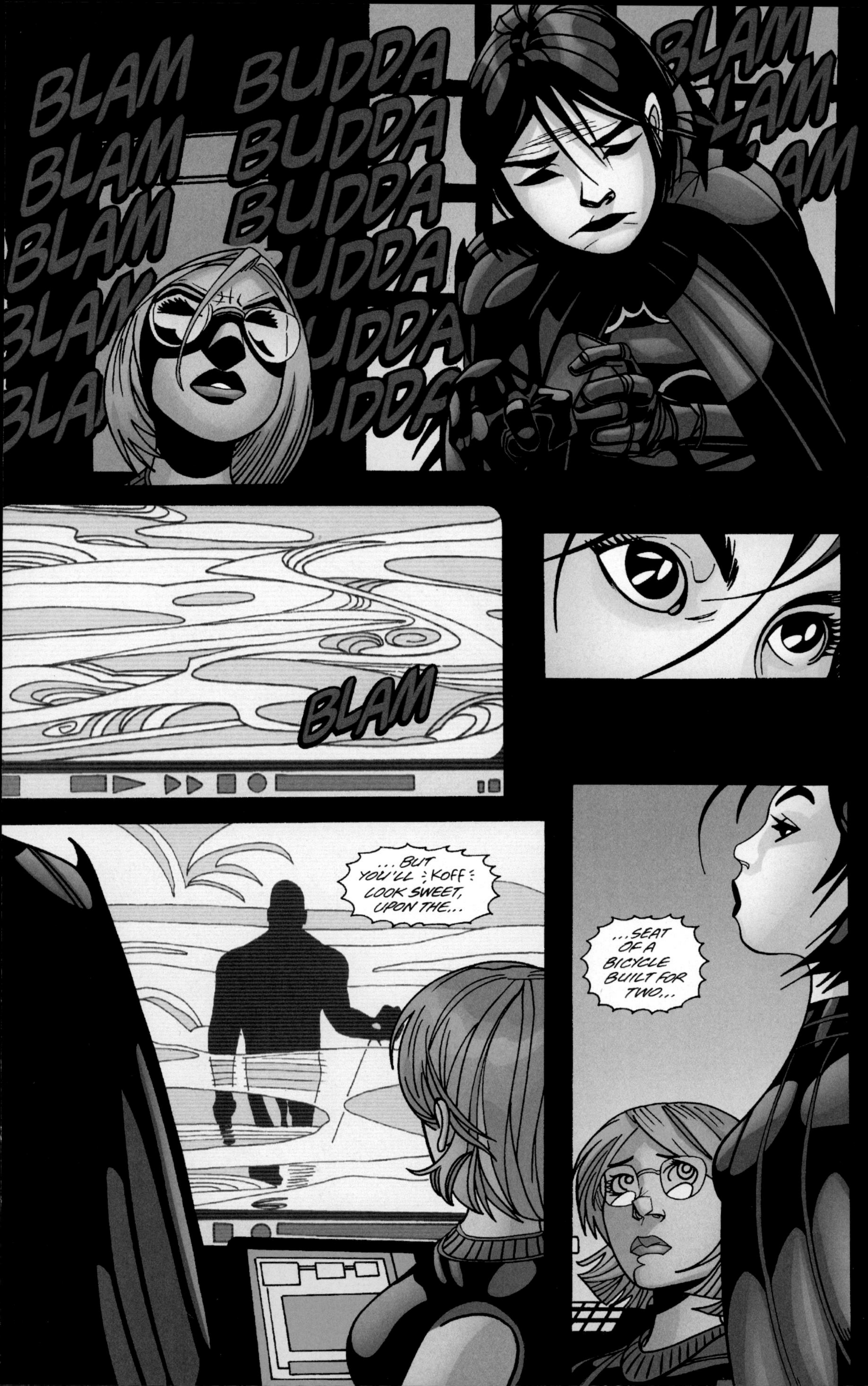
BLAM BLAM BLAM BLAM BLAM
BUDDA BUDDA BUDDA BUDDA BUDDA BUDDA
BLAM BLAM BLAM
BLAM
...BUT YOU'LL :KOFF: LOOK SWEET, UPON THE...
...SEAT OF A BICYCLE BUILT FOR TWO...

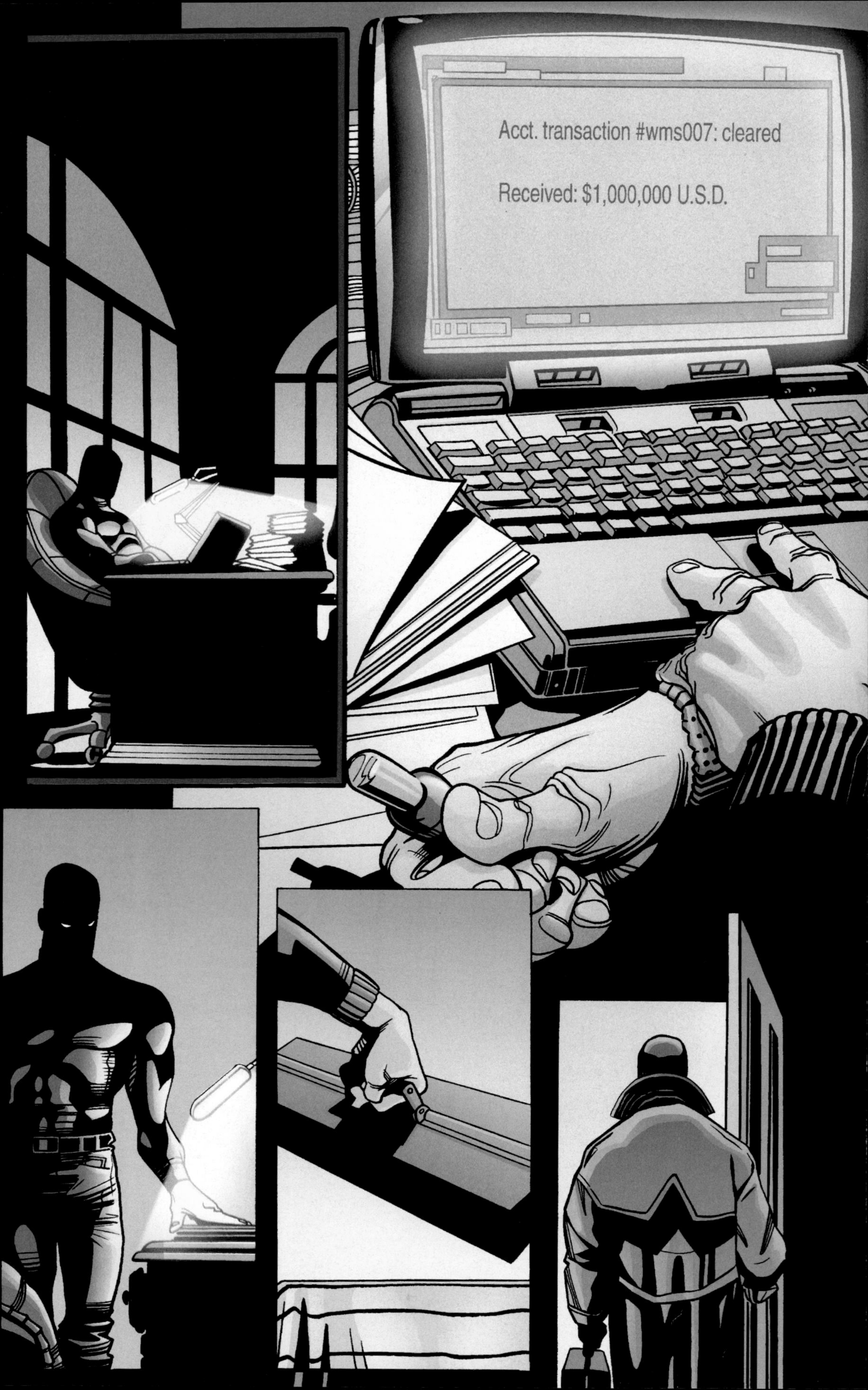
Acct. transaction #wms007: cleared
Received: $1,000,000 U.S.D.

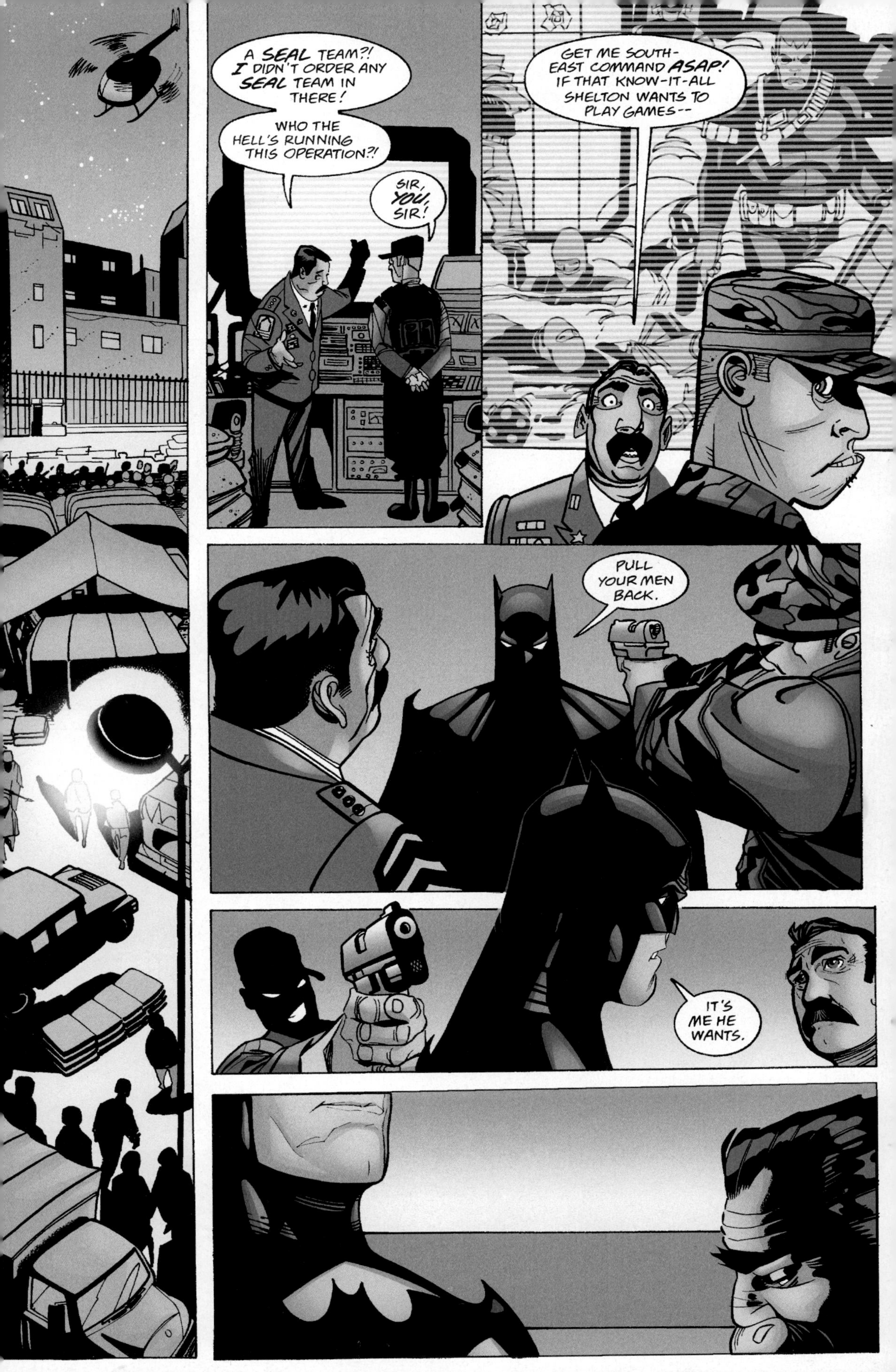
A SEAL TEAM?! I DIDN'T ORDER ANY SEAL TEAM IN THERE!
WHO THE HELL'S RUNNING THIS OPERATION?!
SIR, YOU, SIR!
GET ME SOUTH-EAST COMMAND ASAP! IF THAT KNOW-IT-ALL SHELTON WANTS TO PLAY GAMES--
PULL YOUR MEN BACK.
IT'S ME HE WANTS.

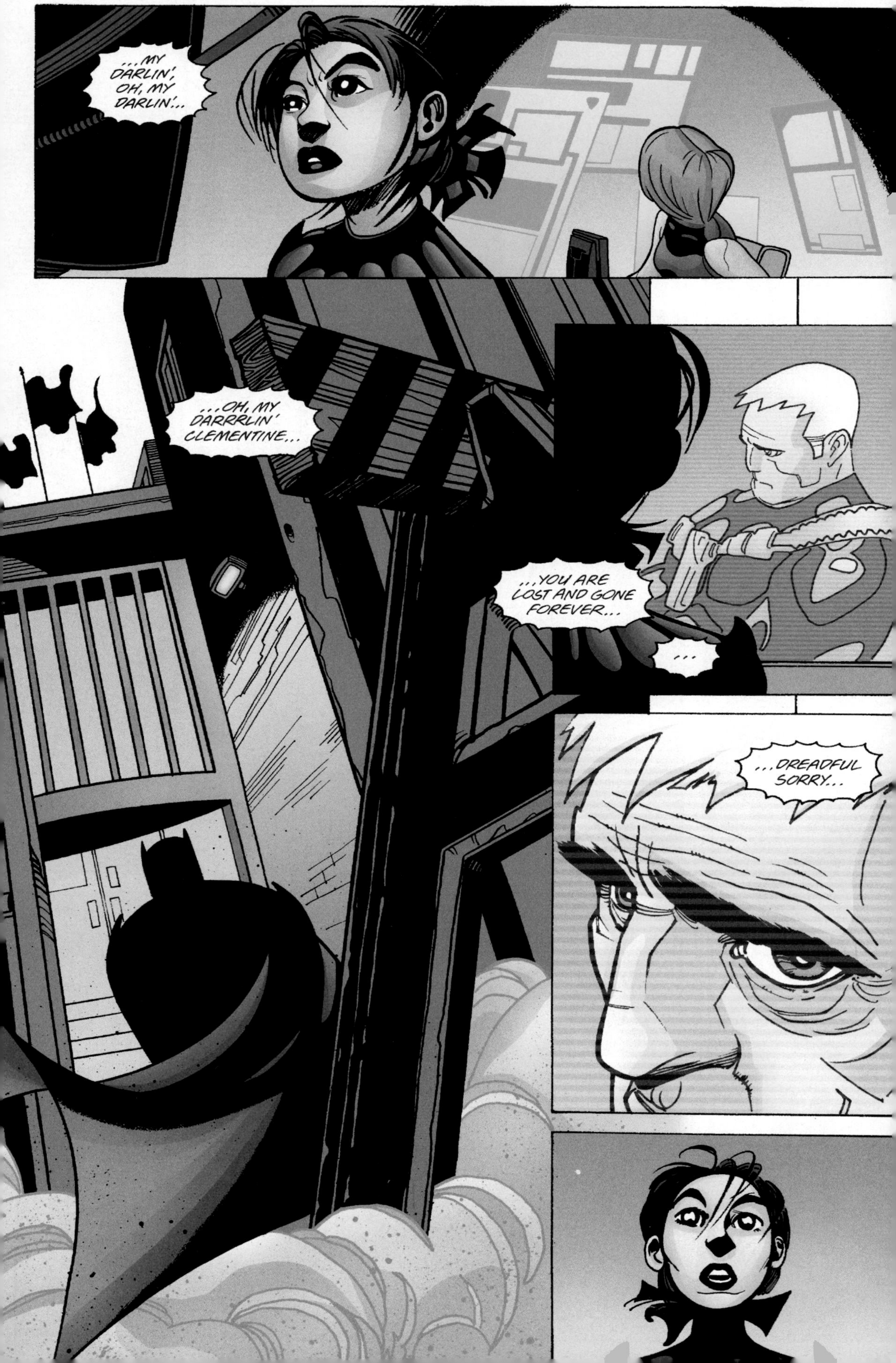
...MY DARLIN', OH, MY DARLIN'...
...OH, MY DARRRLIN' CLEMENTINE...
...YOU ARE LOST AND GONE FOREVER...
...
...DREADFUL SORRY...

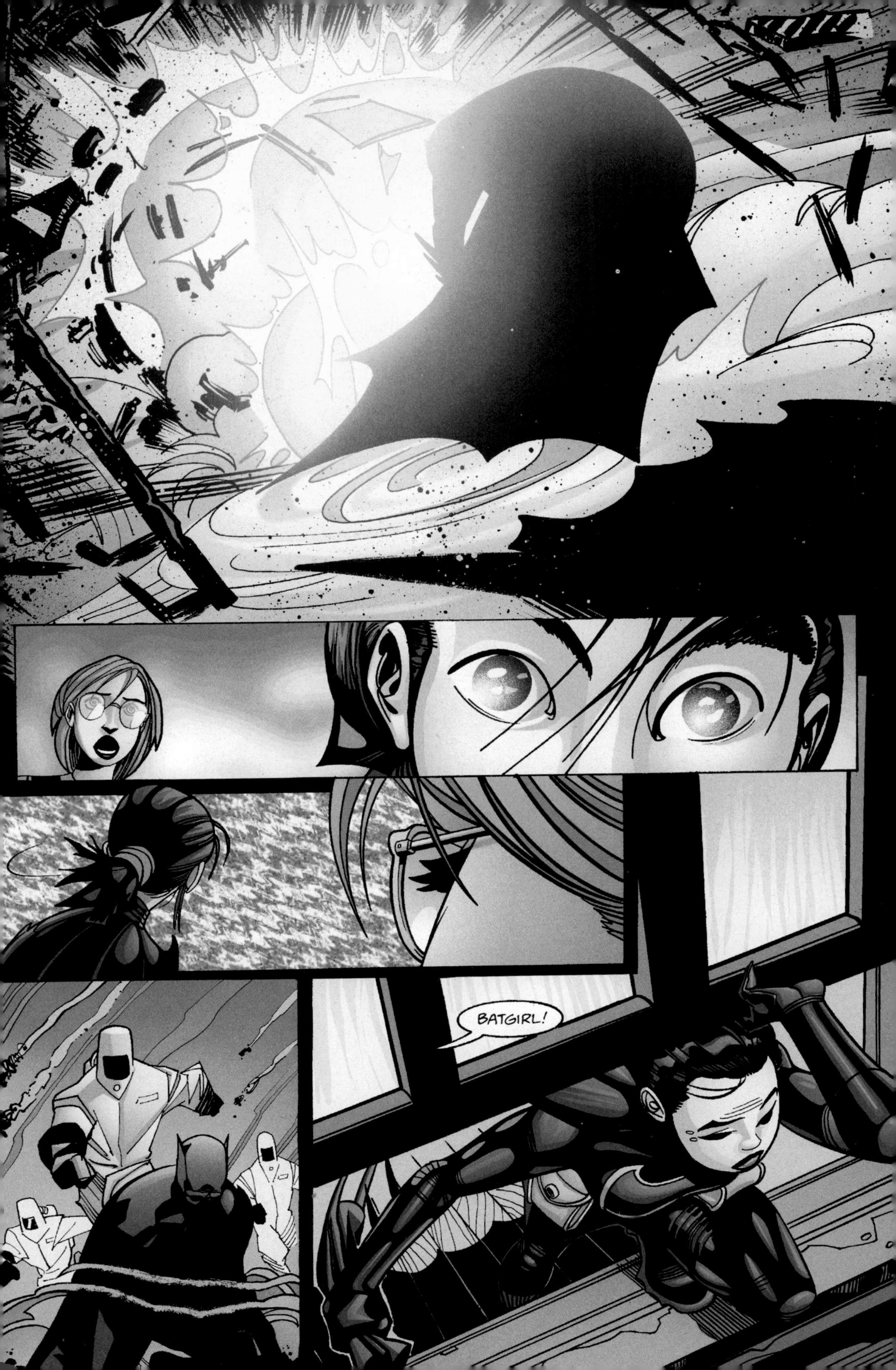
BATGIRL!

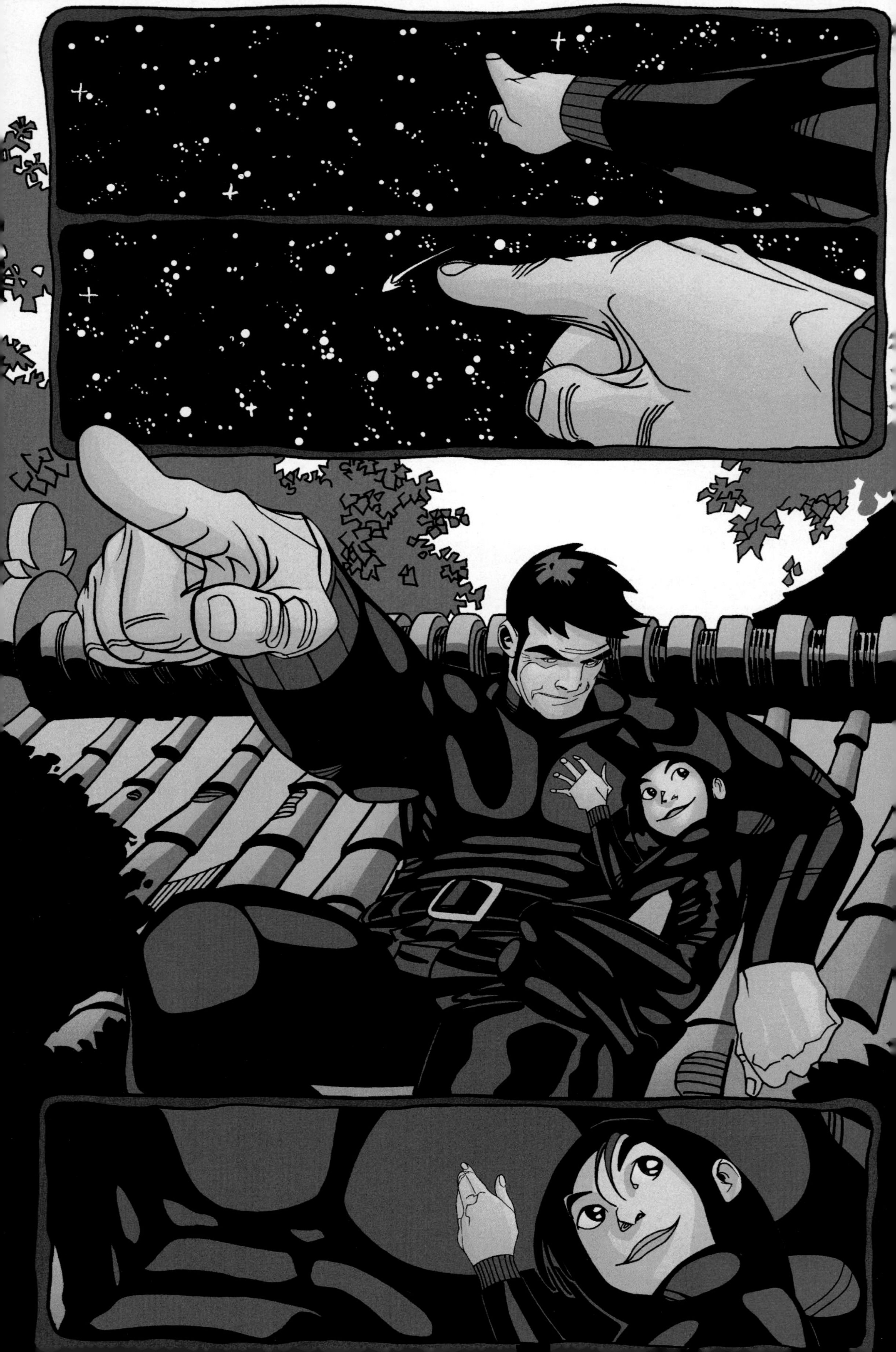

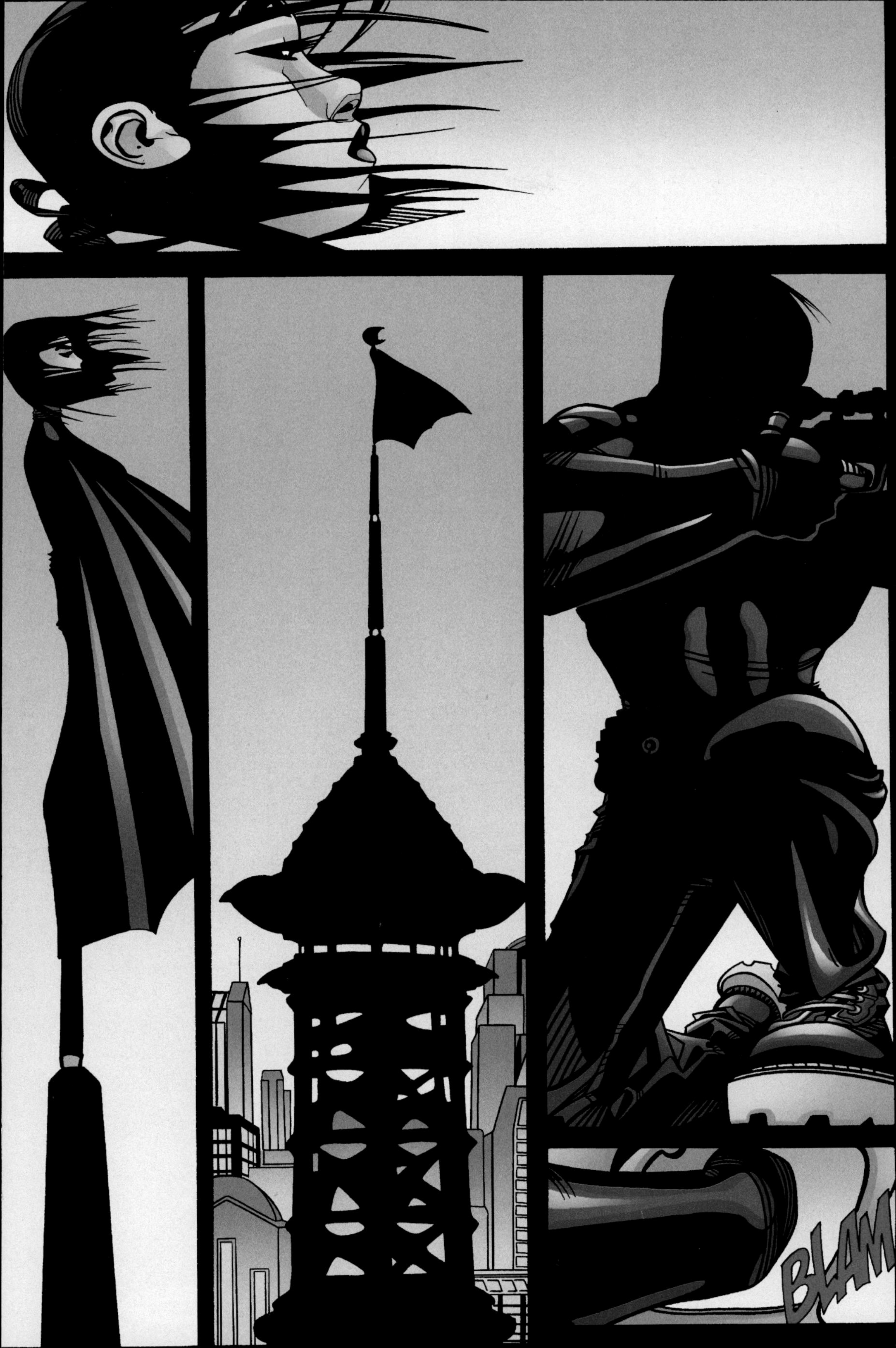
BLAM

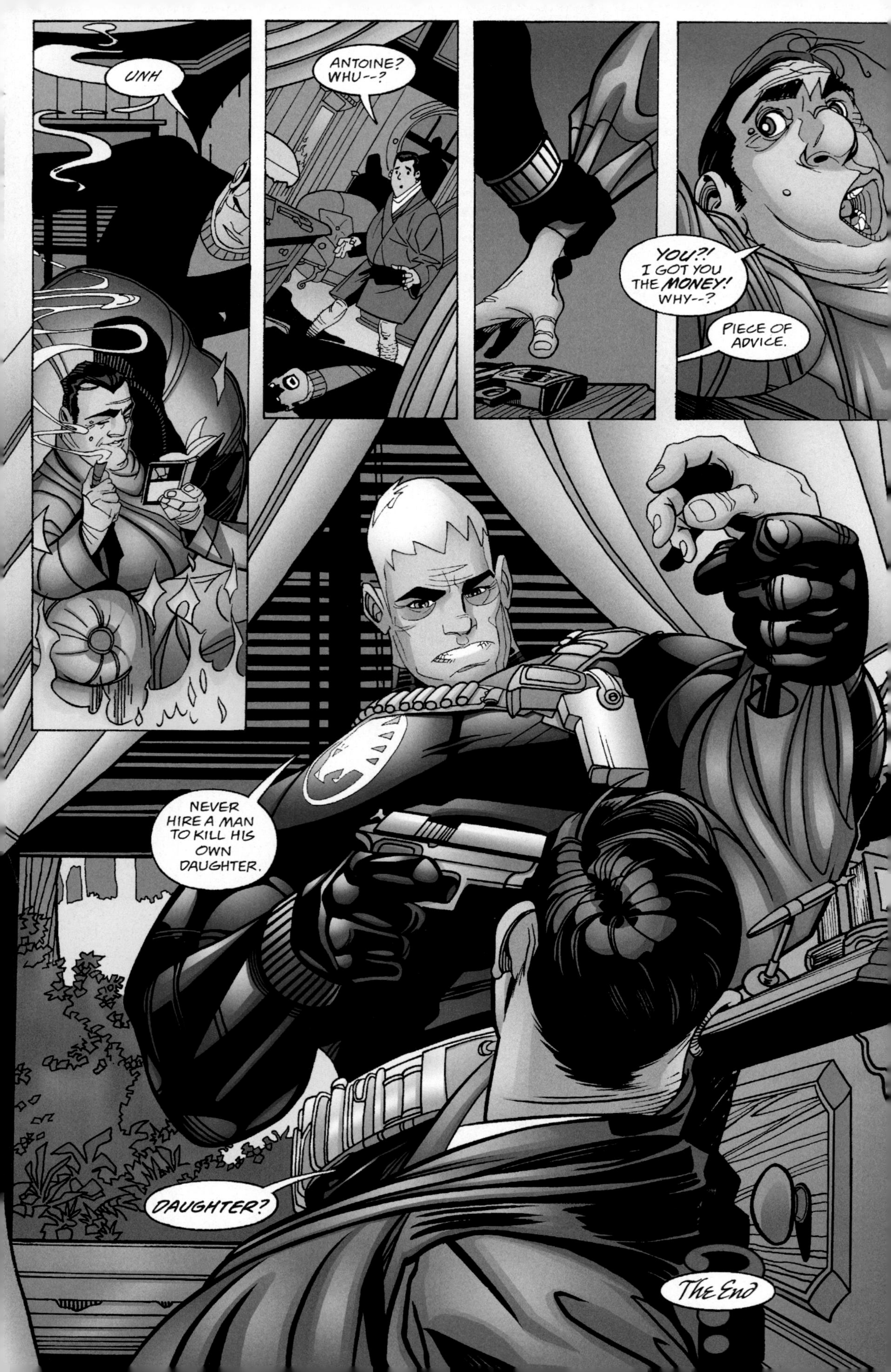

UNH
ANTOINE? WHU--?
YOU?! I GOT YOU THE MONEY! WHY--?
PIECE OF ADVICE.
NEVER HIRE A MAN TO KILL HIS OWN DAUGHTER.
DAUGHTER?
The End

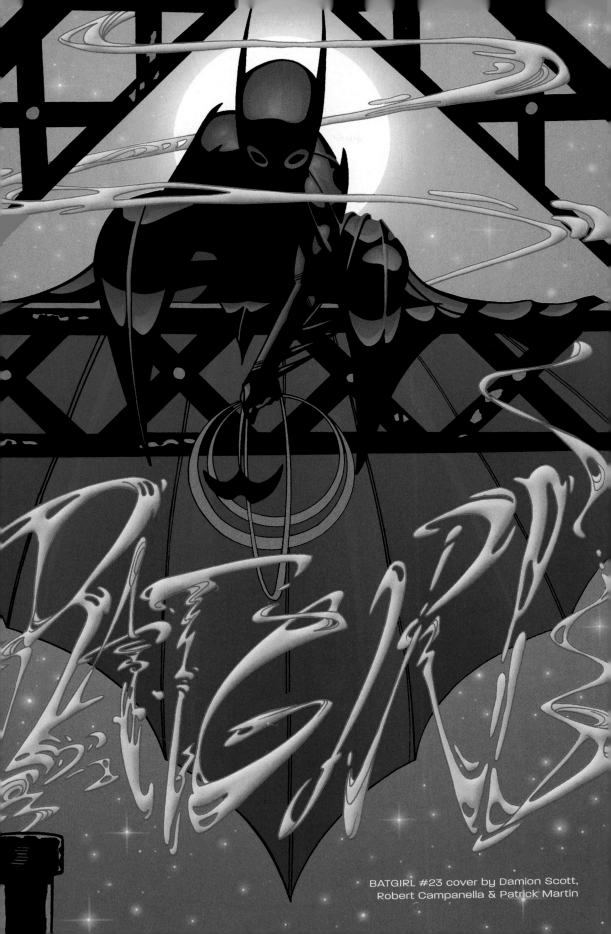

BATGIRL #23 cover by Damion Scott,
Robert Campanella & Patrick Martin

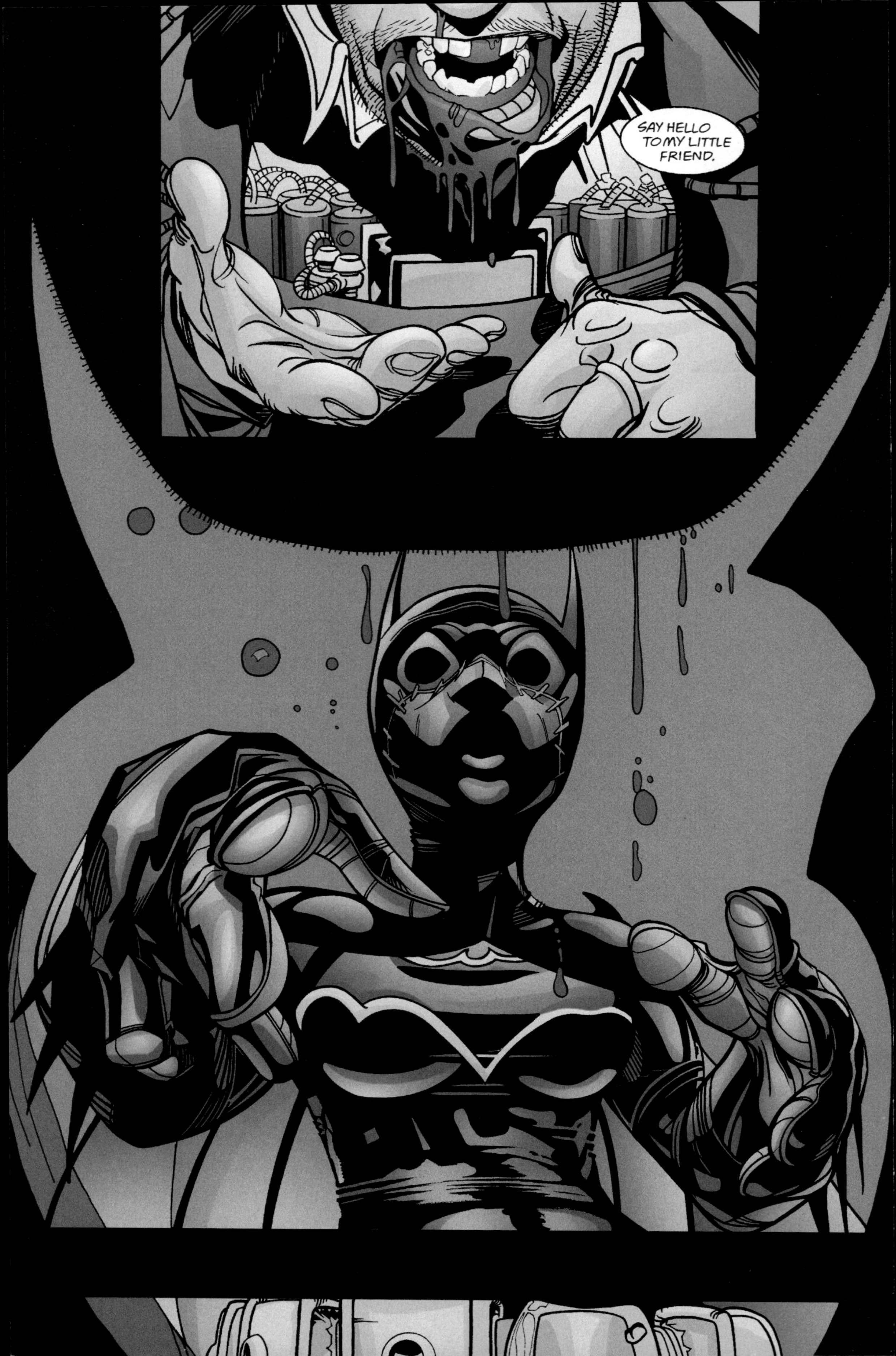
SAY HELLO
TO MY LITTLE
FRIEND.

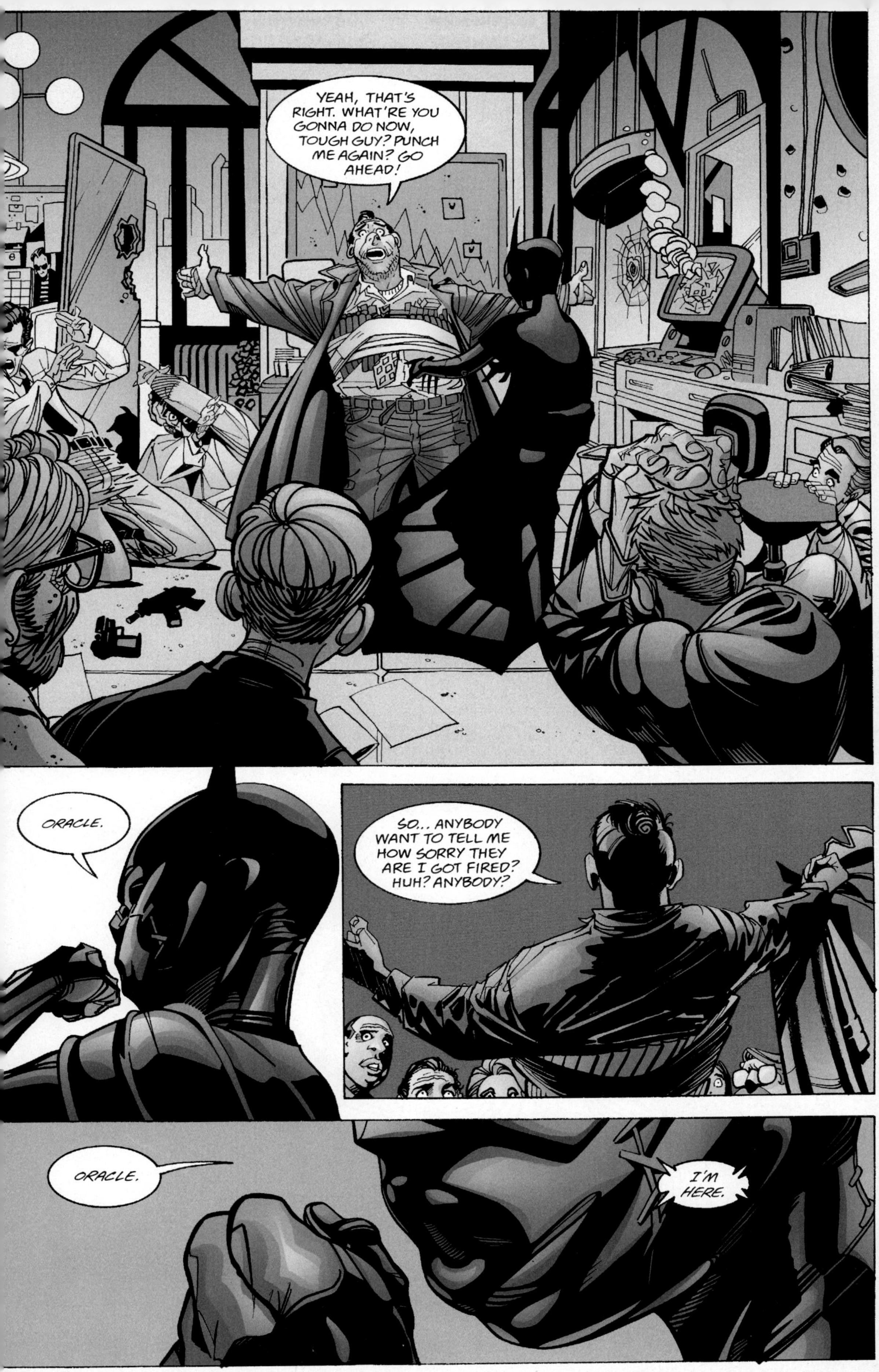
YEAH, THAT'S RIGHT. WHAT'RE YOU GONNA DO NOW, TOUGH GUY? PUNCH ME AGAIN? GO AHEAD!
ORACLE.
SO... ANYBODY WANT TO TELL ME HOW SORRY THEY ARE I GOT FIRED? HUH? ANYBODY?
ORACLE.
I'M HERE.

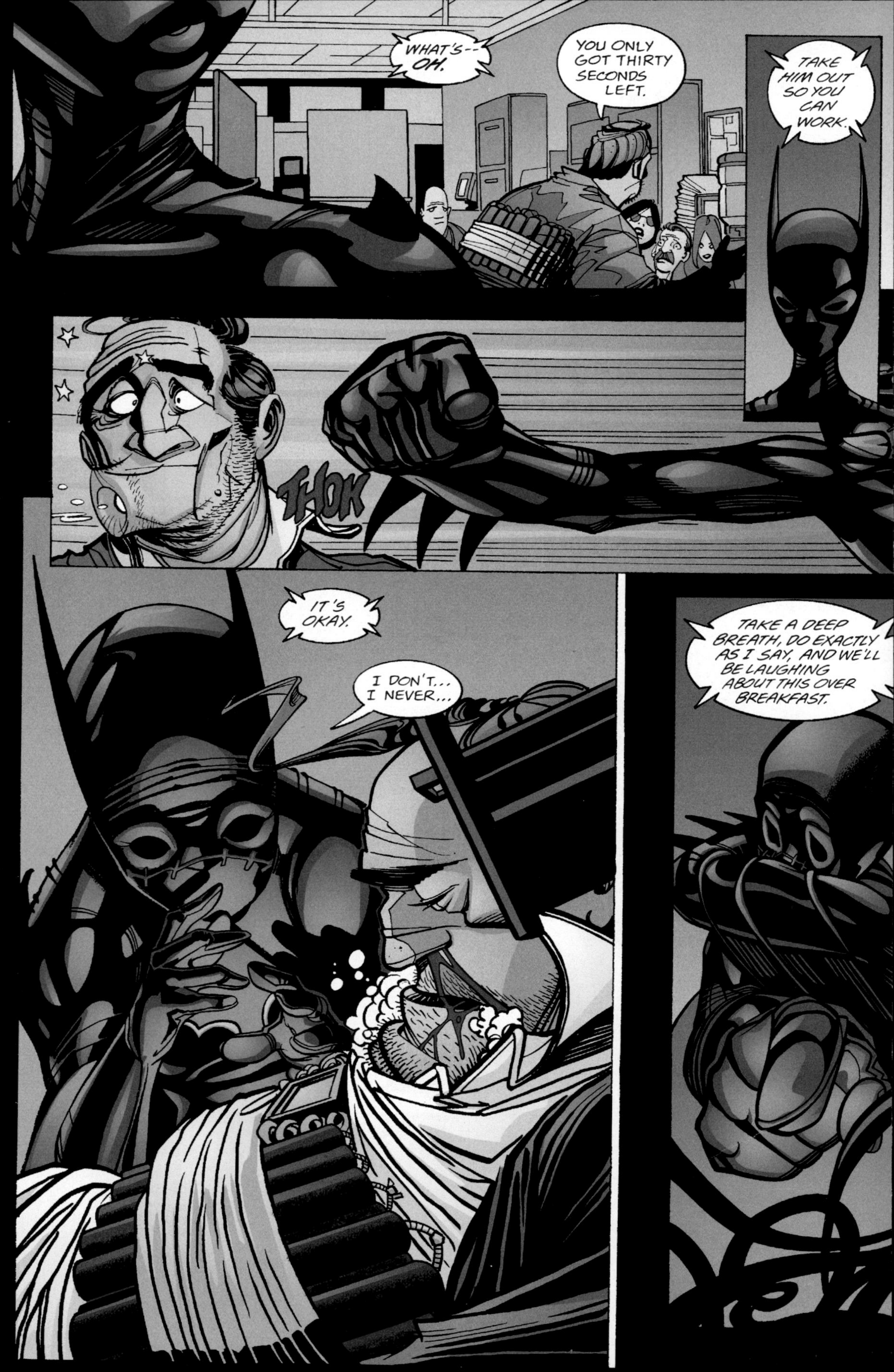
WHAT'S-- OH.
YOU ONLY GOT THIRTY SECONDS LEFT.
TAKE HIM OUT SO YOU CAN WORK.
THOK
IT'S OKAY.
I DON'T... I NEVER...
TAKE A DEEP BREATH, DO EXACTLY AS I SAY, AND WE'LL BE LAUGHING ABOUT THIS OVER BREAKFAST.

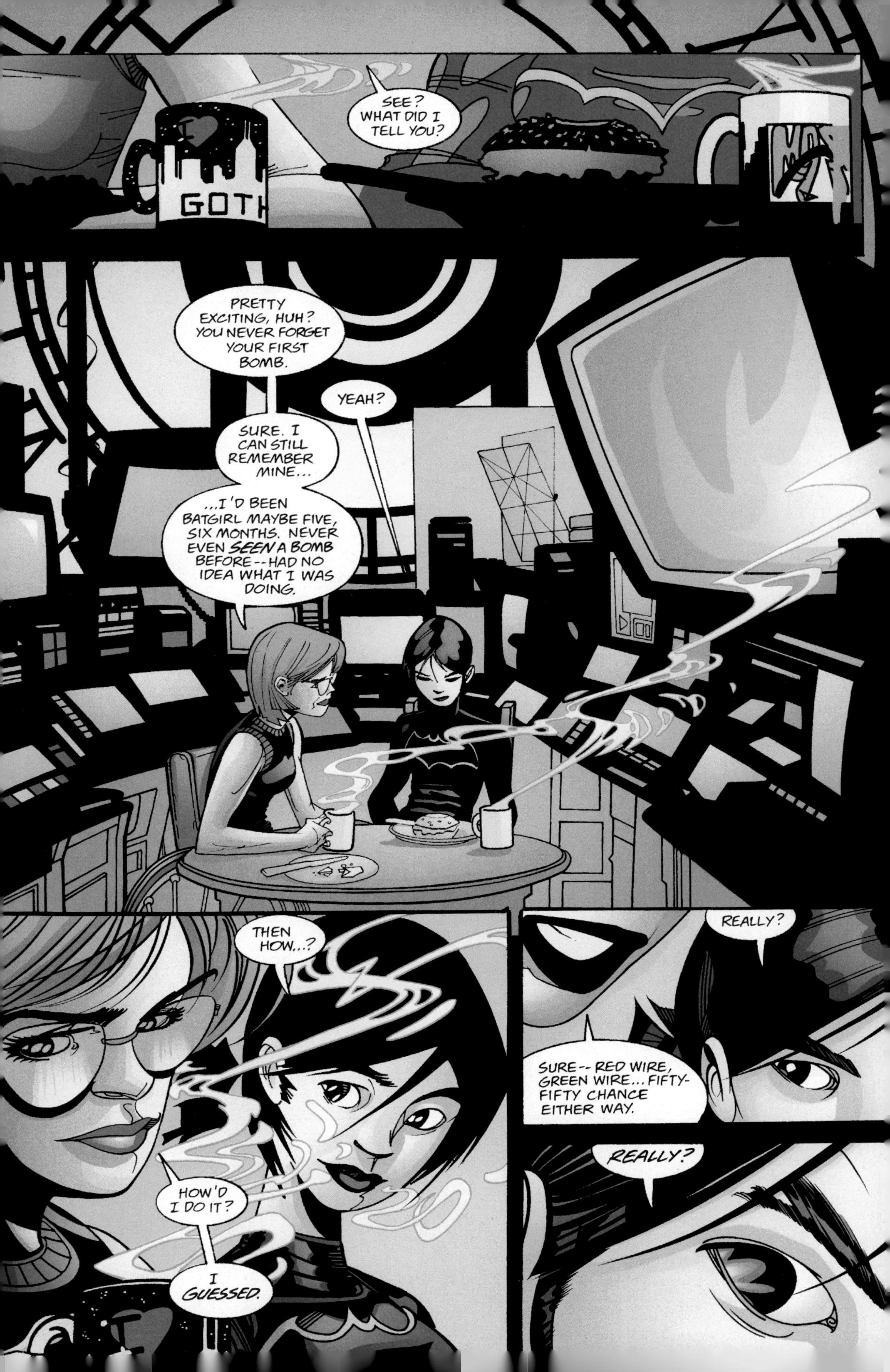
GOTH
SEE? WHAT DID I TELL YOU?
PRETTY EXCITING, HUH? YOU NEVER FORGET YOUR FIRST BOMB.
YEAH?
SURE. I CAN STILL REMEMBER MINE...
...I'D BEEN BATGIRL MAYBE FIVE, SIX MONTHS. NEVER EVEN SEEN A BOMB BEFORE--HAD NO IDEA WHAT I WAS DOING.
THEN HOW...?
HOW'D I DO IT?
I GUESSED.
REALLY?
SURE-- RED WIRE, GREEN WIRE... FIFTY-FIFTY CHANCE EITHER WAY.
REALLY?

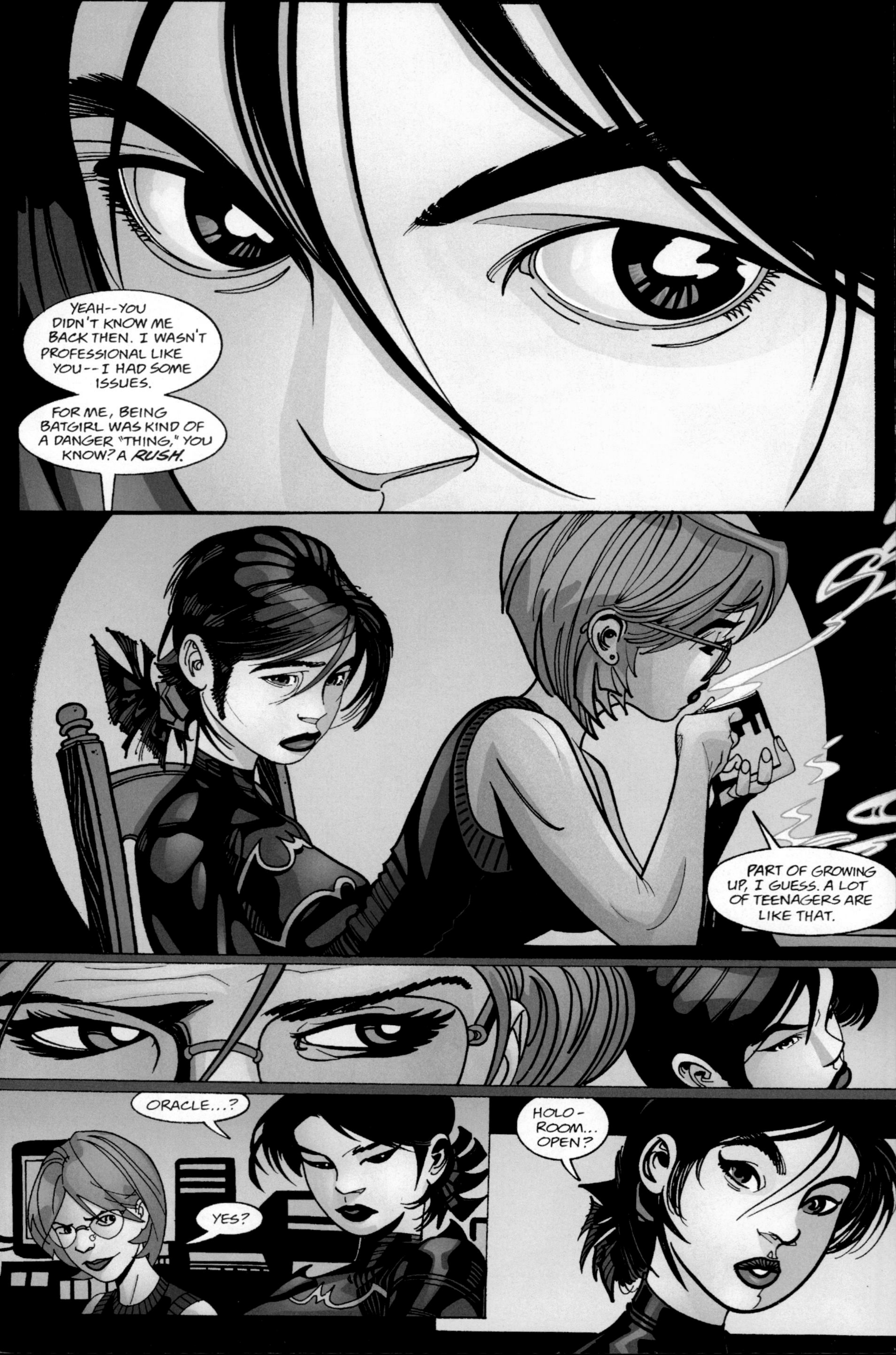
YEAH--YOU DIDN'T KNOW ME BACK THEN. I WASN'T PROFESSIONAL LIKE YOU--I HAD SOME ISSUES.
FOR ME, BEING BATGIRL WAS KIND OF A DANGER "THING," YOU KNOW? A RUSH.
PART OF GROWING UP, I GUESS. A LOT OF TEENAGERS ARE LIKE THAT.
ORACLE...?
YES?
HOLO-ROOM... OPEN?

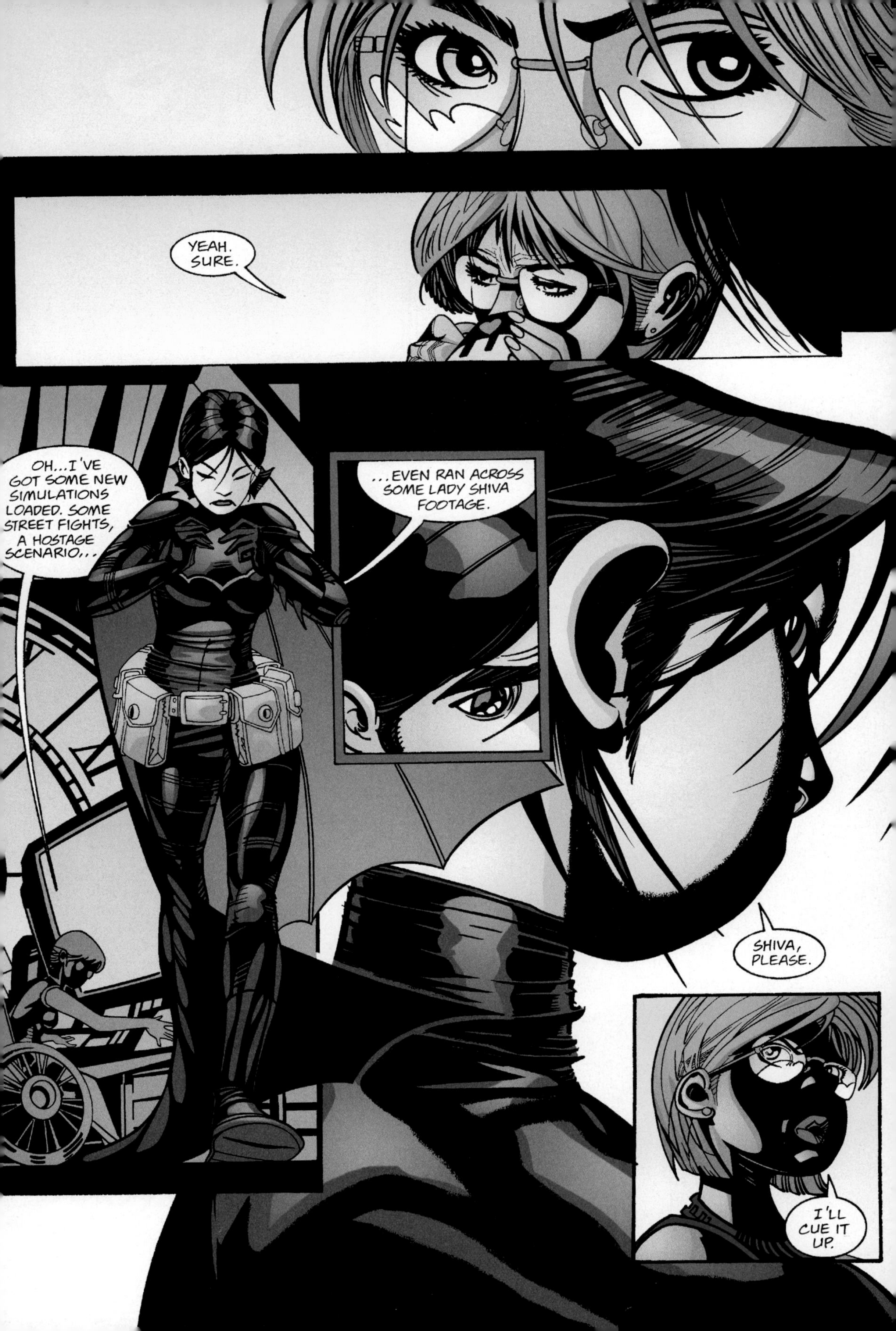
YEAH. SURE.
OH...I'VE GOT SOME NEW SIMULATIONS LOADED. SOME STREET FIGHTS, A HOSTAGE SCENARIO...
...EVEN RAN ACROSS SOME LADY SHIVA FOOTAGE.
SHIVA, PLEASE.
I'LL CUE IT UP.

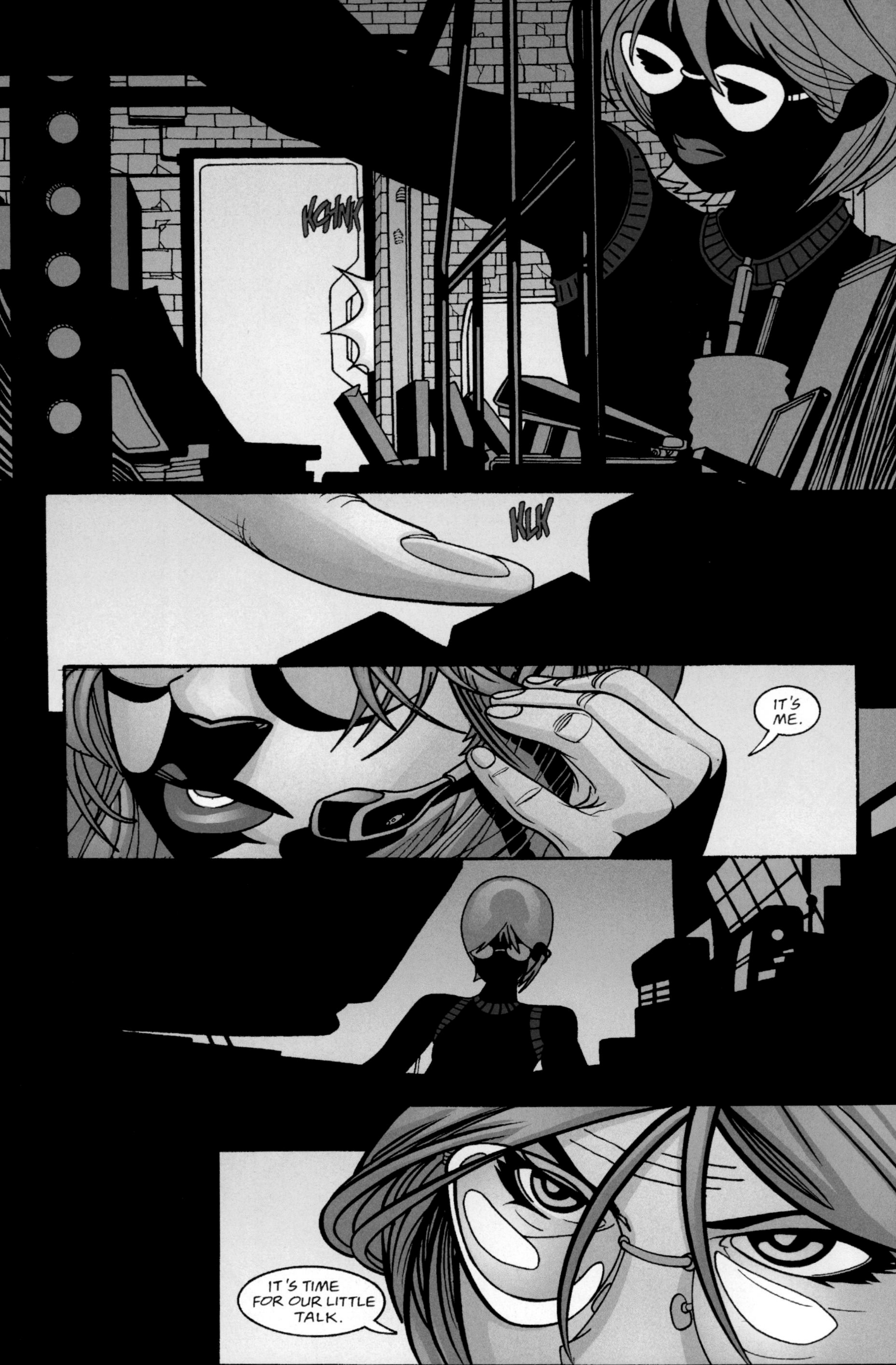
KCHINK
KLK
IT'S ME.
IT'S TIME FOR OUR LITTLE TALK.

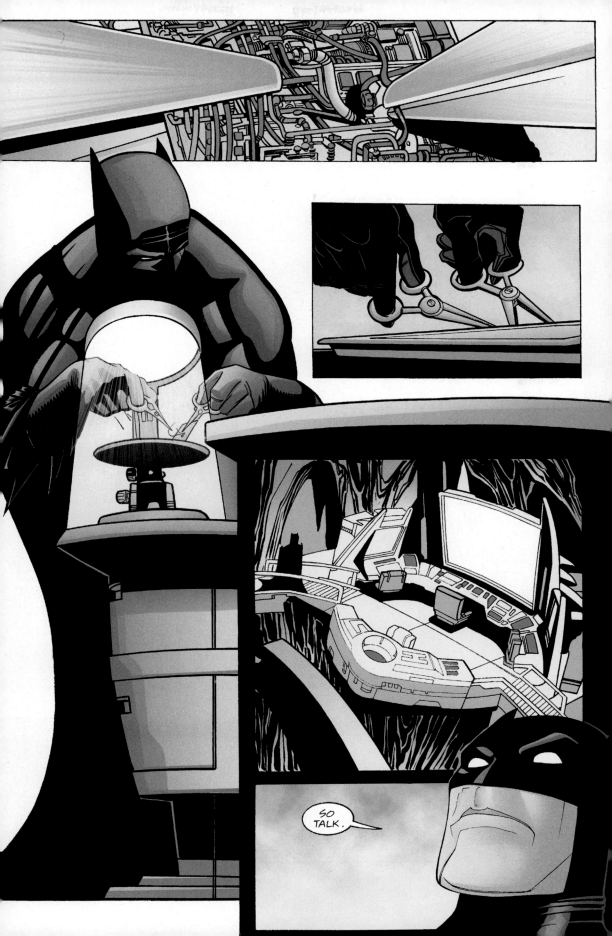

SO
TALK.

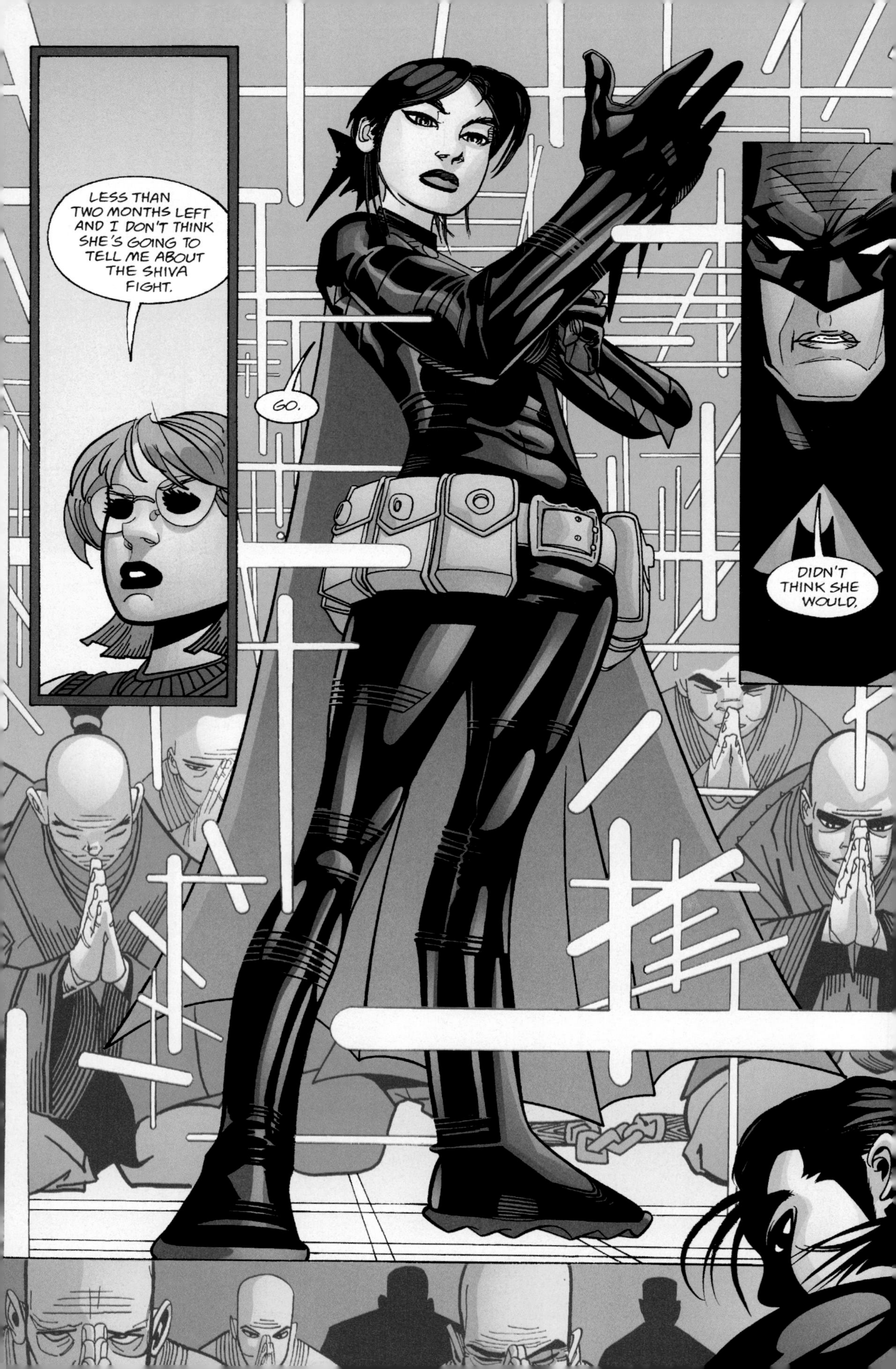
LESS THAN TWO MONTHS LEFT AND I DON'T THINK SHE'S GOING TO TELL ME ABOUT THE SHIVA FIGHT.
GO.
DIDN'T THINK SHE WOULD.

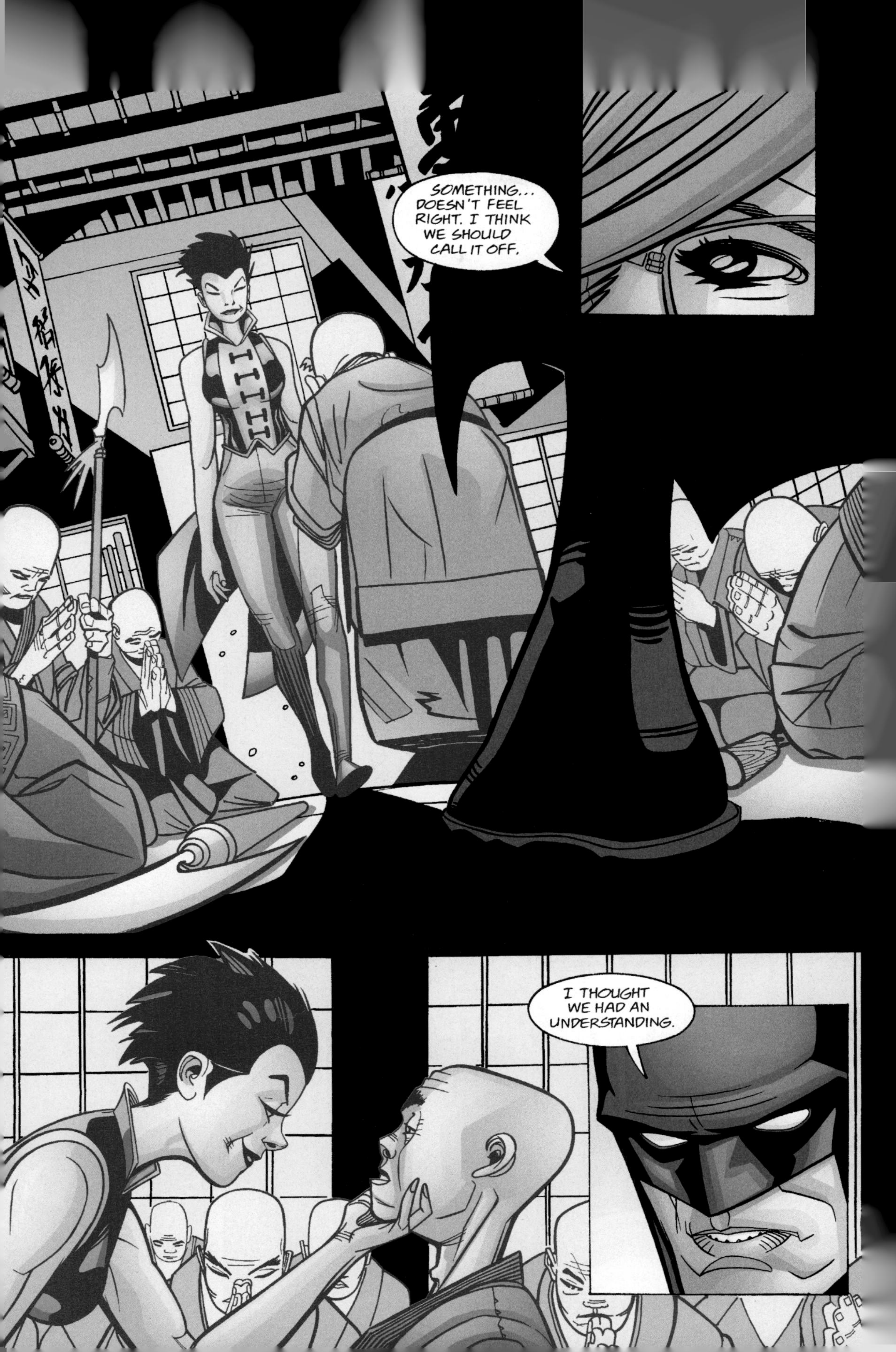
SOMETHING... DOESN'T FEEL RIGHT. I THINK WE SHOULD CALL IT OFF.
I THOUGHT WE HAD AN UNDERSTANDING.

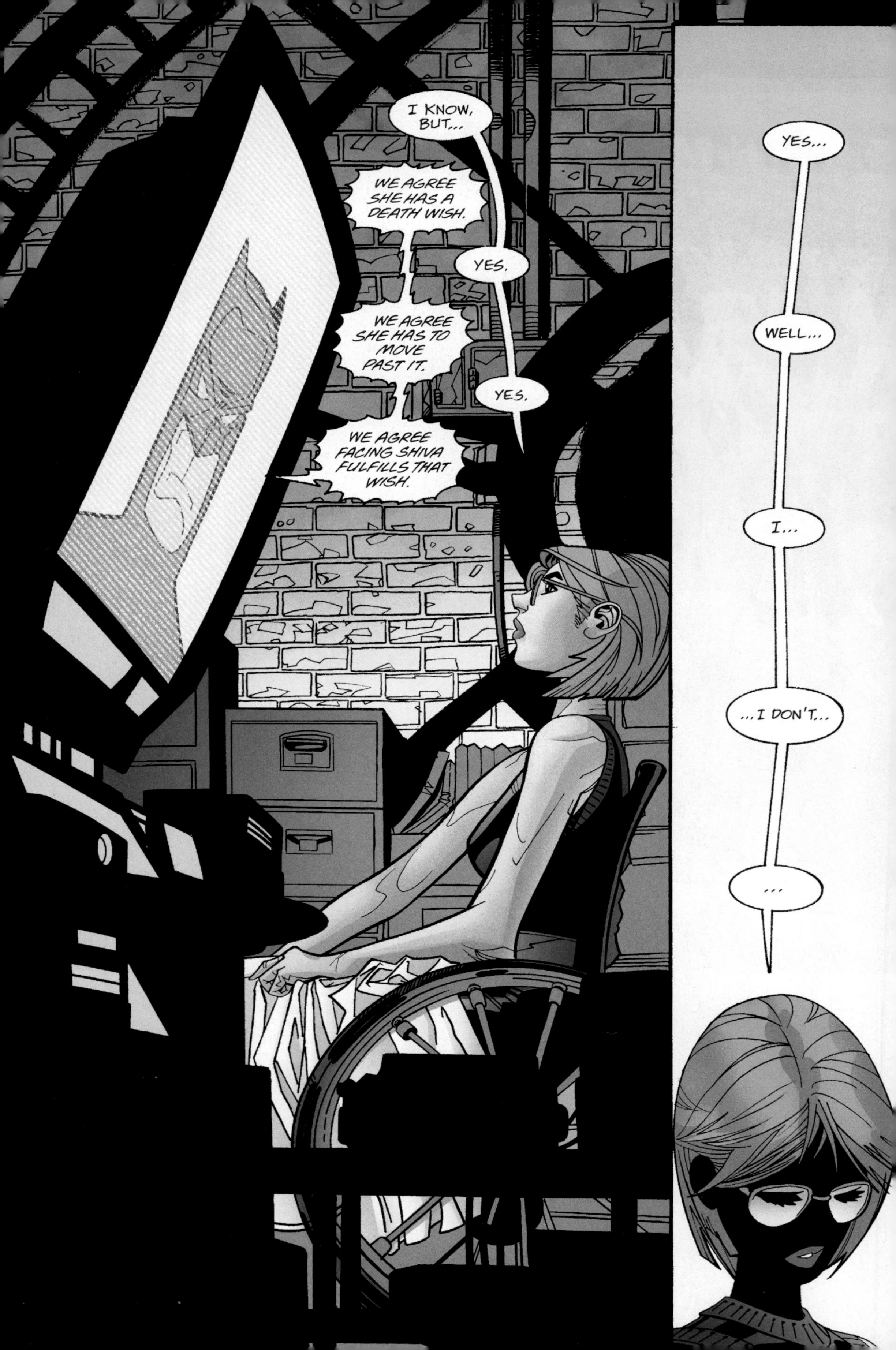
I KNOW, BUT...
WE AGREE SHE HAS A DEATH WISH.
YES.
WE AGREE SHE HAS TO MOVE PAST IT.
YES.
WE AGREE FACING SHIVA FULFILLS THAT WISH.
YES...
WELL...
I...
...I DON'T...
...

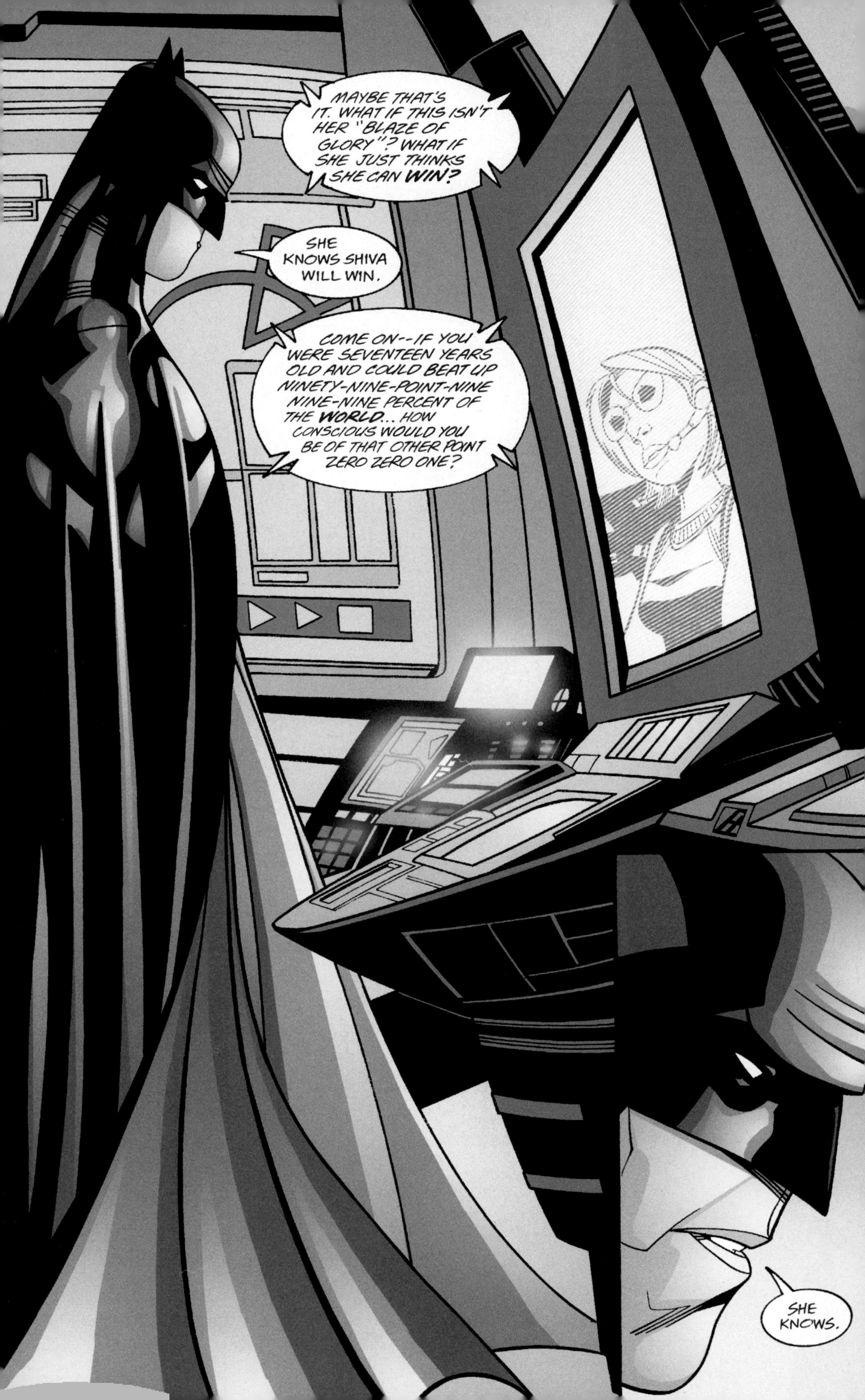
MAYBE THAT'S IT. WHAT IF THIS ISN'T HER "BLAZE OF GLORY"? WHAT IF SHE JUST THINKS SHE CAN WIN?
SHE KNOWS SHIVA WILL WIN.
COME ON--IF YOU WERE SEVENTEEN YEARS OLD AND COULD BEAT UP NINETY-NINE-POINT-NINE NINE-NINE PERCENT OF THE WORLD... HOW CONSCIOUS WOULD YOU BE OF THAT OTHER POINT ZERO ZERO ONE?
SHE KNOWS.

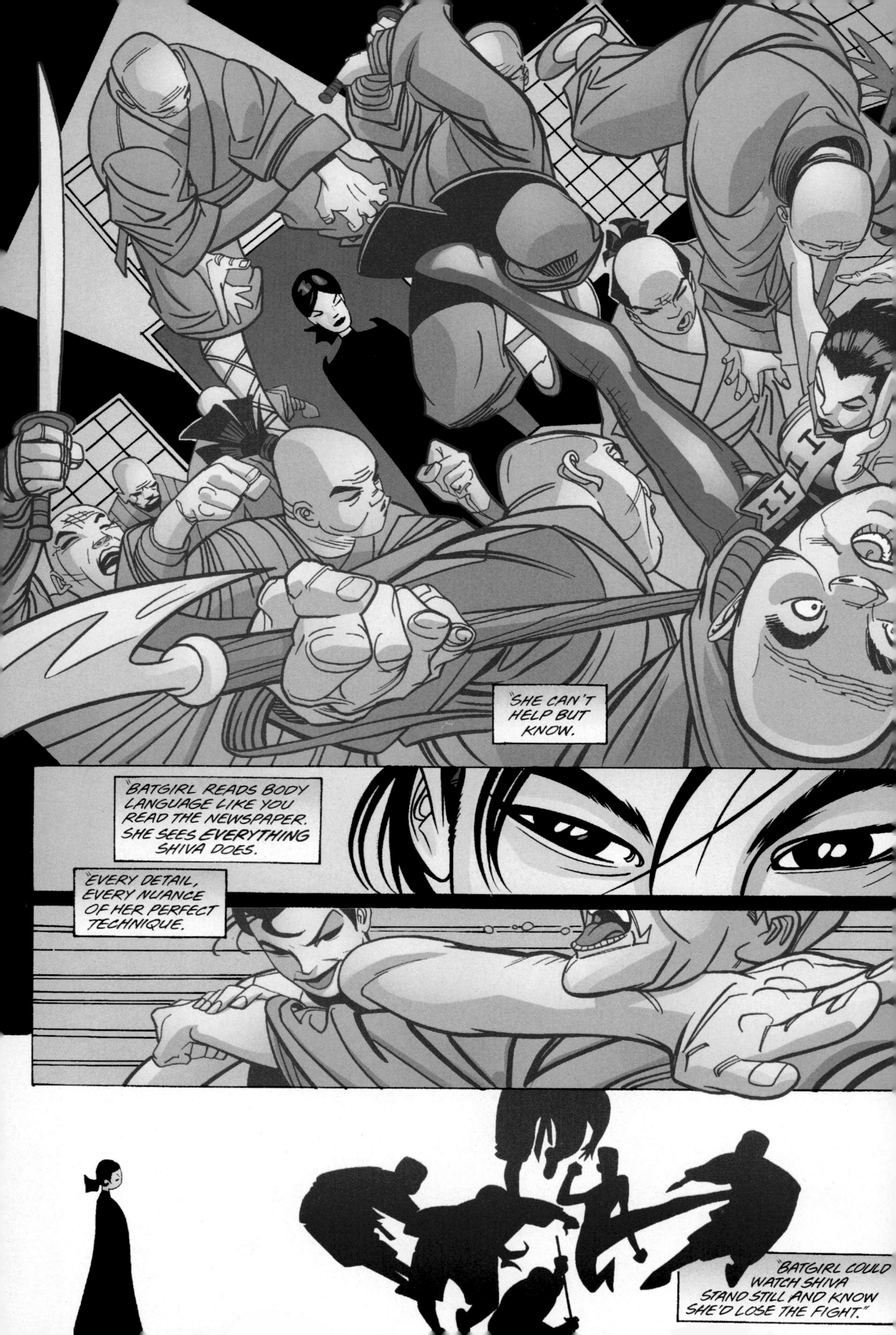
"SHE CAN'T HELP BUT KNOW.
"BATGIRL READS BODY LANGUAGE LIKE YOU READ THE NEWSPAPER. SHE SEES EVERYTHING SHIVA DOES.
"EVERY DETAIL, EVERY NUANCE OF HER PERFECT TECHNIQUE.
"BATGIRL COULD WATCH SHIVA STAND STILL AND KNOW SHE'D LOSE THE FIGHT."

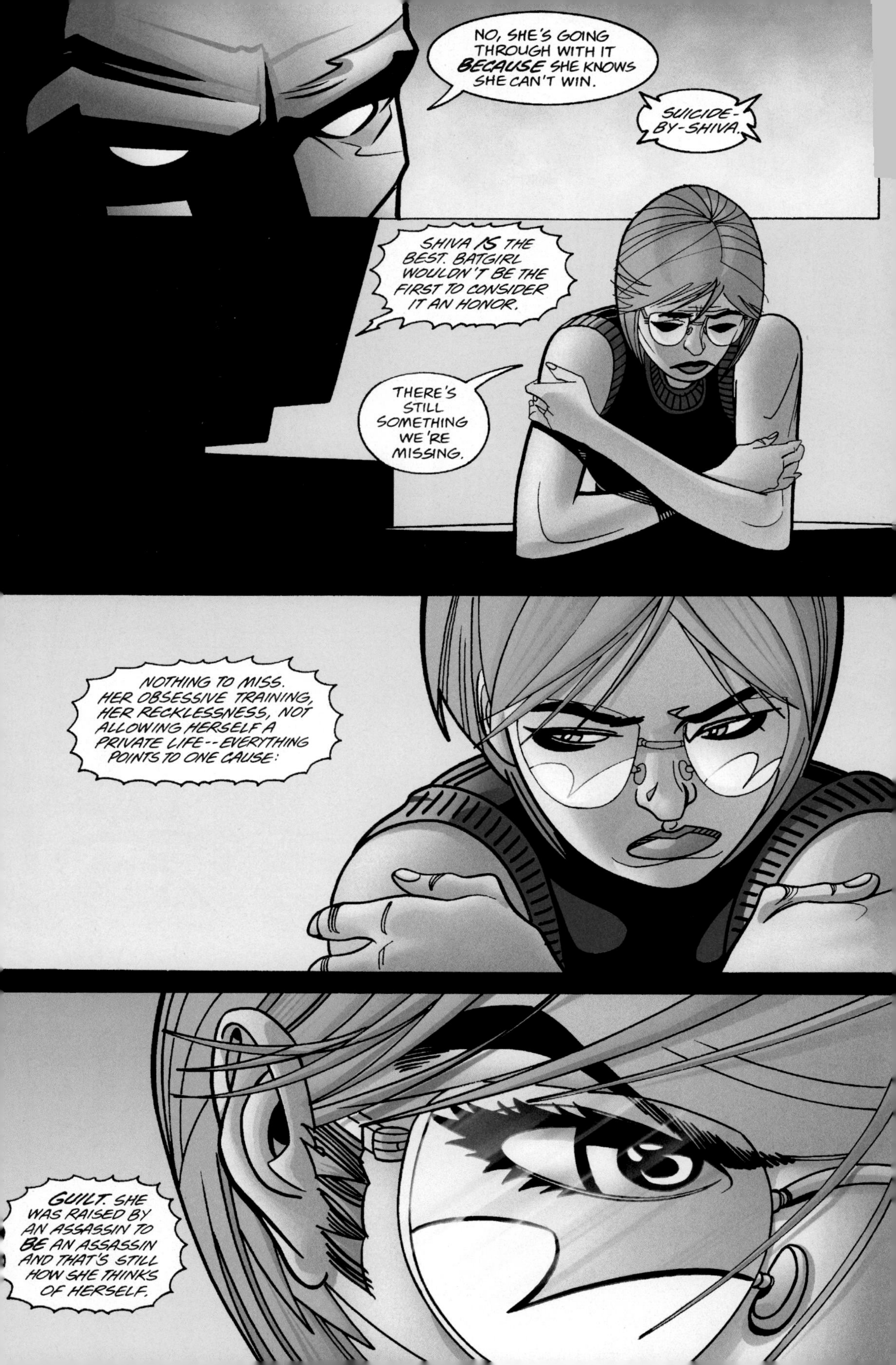
NO, SHE'S GOING THROUGH WITH IT BECAUSE SHE KNOWS SHE CAN'T WIN.
SUICIDE-BY-SHIVA.
SHIVA IS THE BEST. BATGIRL WOULDN'T BE THE FIRST TO CONSIDER IT AN HONOR.
THERE'S STILL SOMETHING WE'RE MISSING.
NOTHING TO MISS. HER OBSESSIVE TRAINING, HER RECKLESSNESS, NOT ALLOWING HERSELF A PRIVATE LIFE--EVERYTHING POINTS TO ONE CAUSE:
GUILT. SHE WAS RAISED BY AN ASSASSIN TO BE AN ASSASSIN AND THAT'S STILL HOW SHE THINKS OF HERSELF.

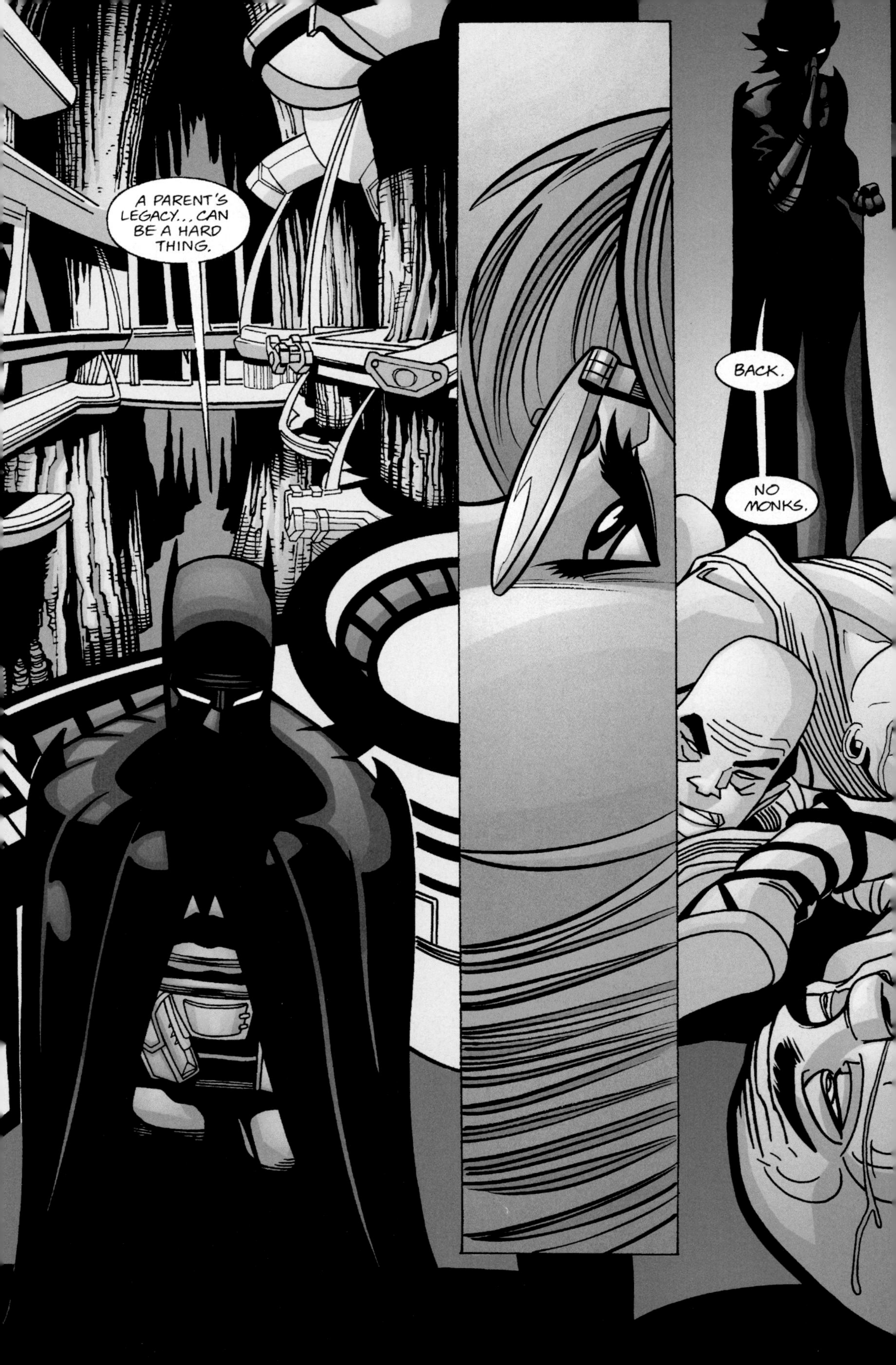
A PARENT'S LEGACY... CAN BE A HARD THING.
BACK.
NO MONKS.

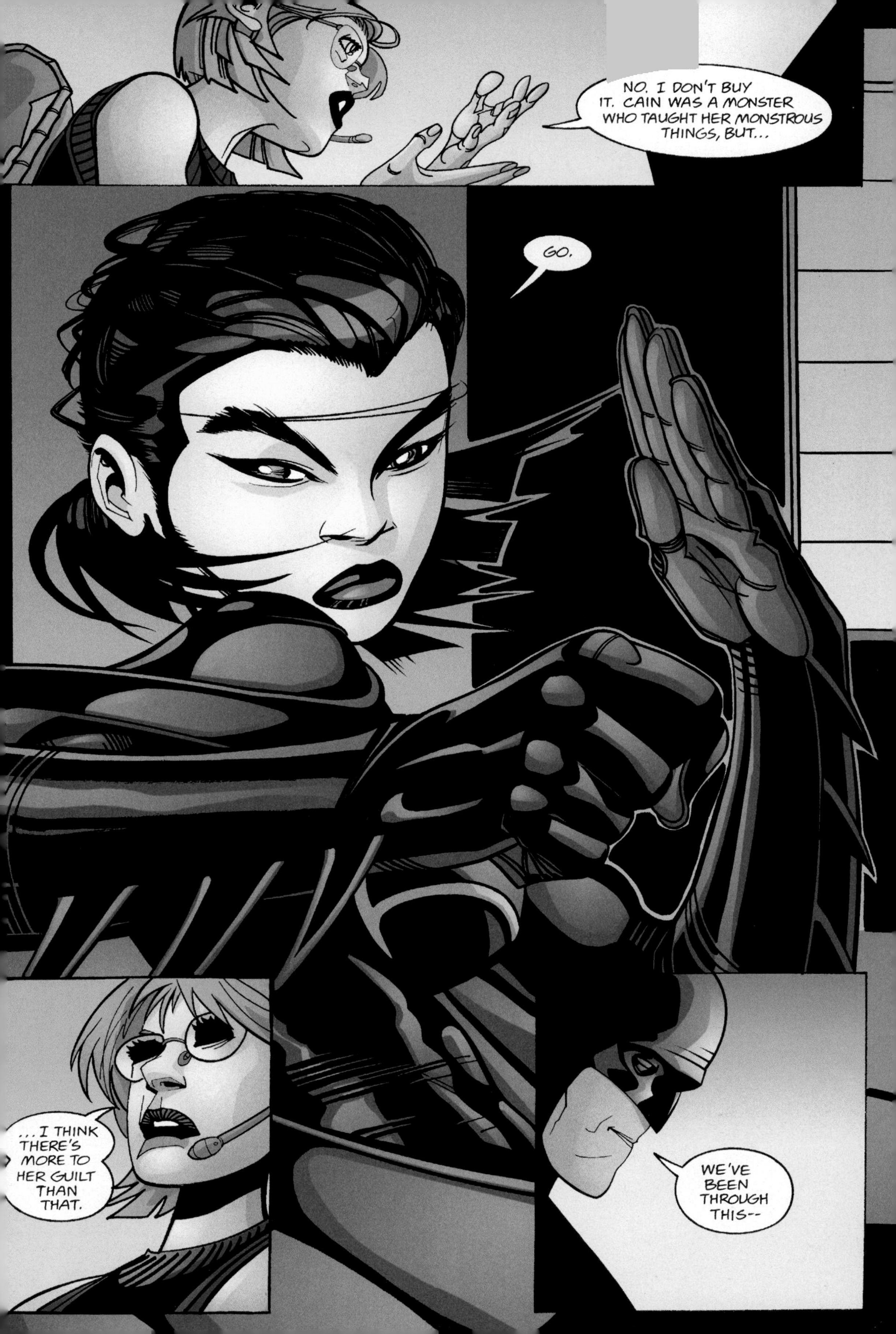
NO. I DON'T BUY IT. CAIN WAS A MONSTER WHO TAUGHT HER MONSTROUS THINGS, BUT...
GO.
...I THINK THERE'S MORE TO HER GUILT THAN THAT.
WE'VE BEEN THROUGH THIS--

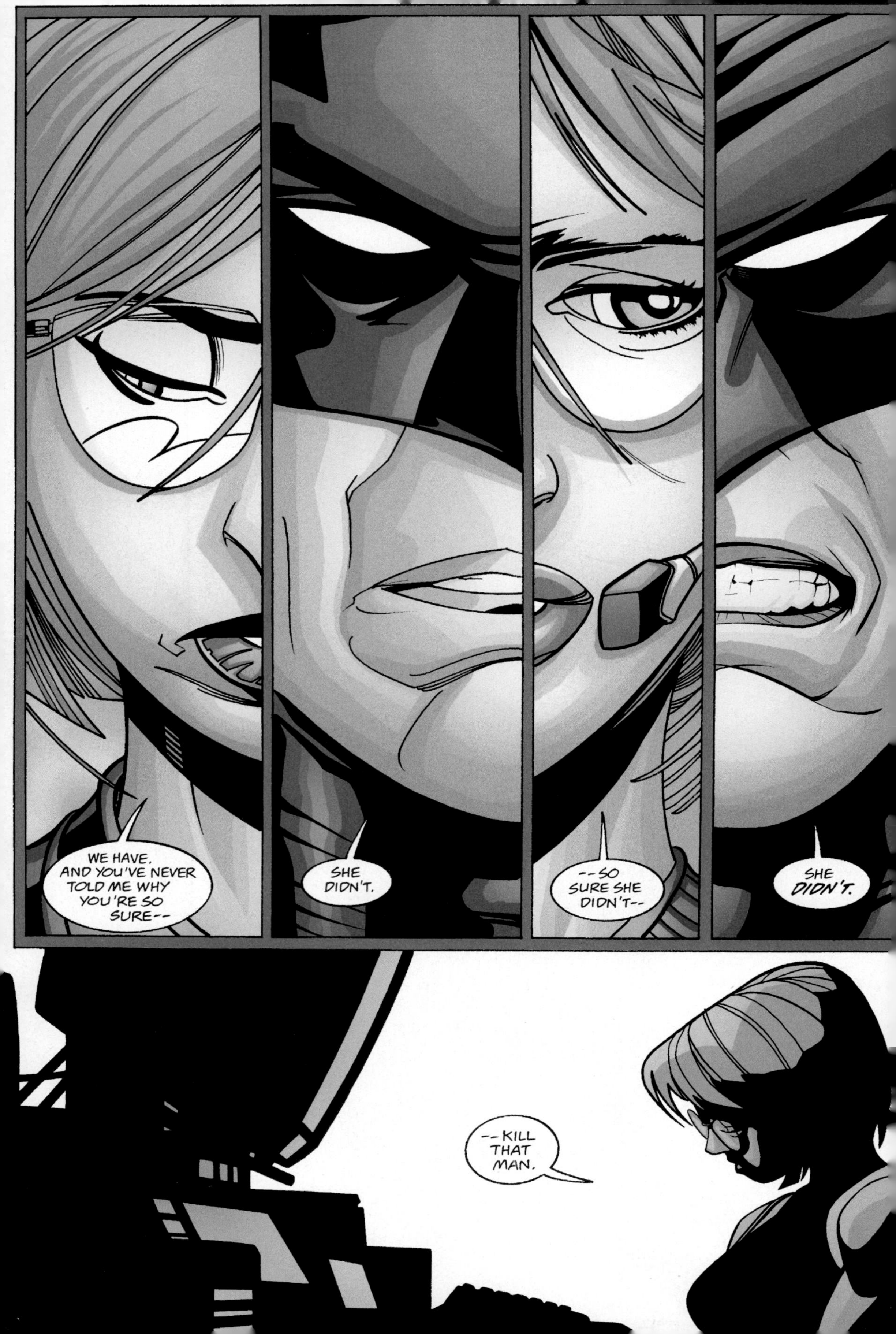
WE HAVE. AND YOU'VE NEVER TOLD ME WHY YOU'RE SO SURE--
SHE DIDN'T.
--SO SURE SHE DIDN'T--
SHE *DIDN'T.*
--KILL THAT MAN.

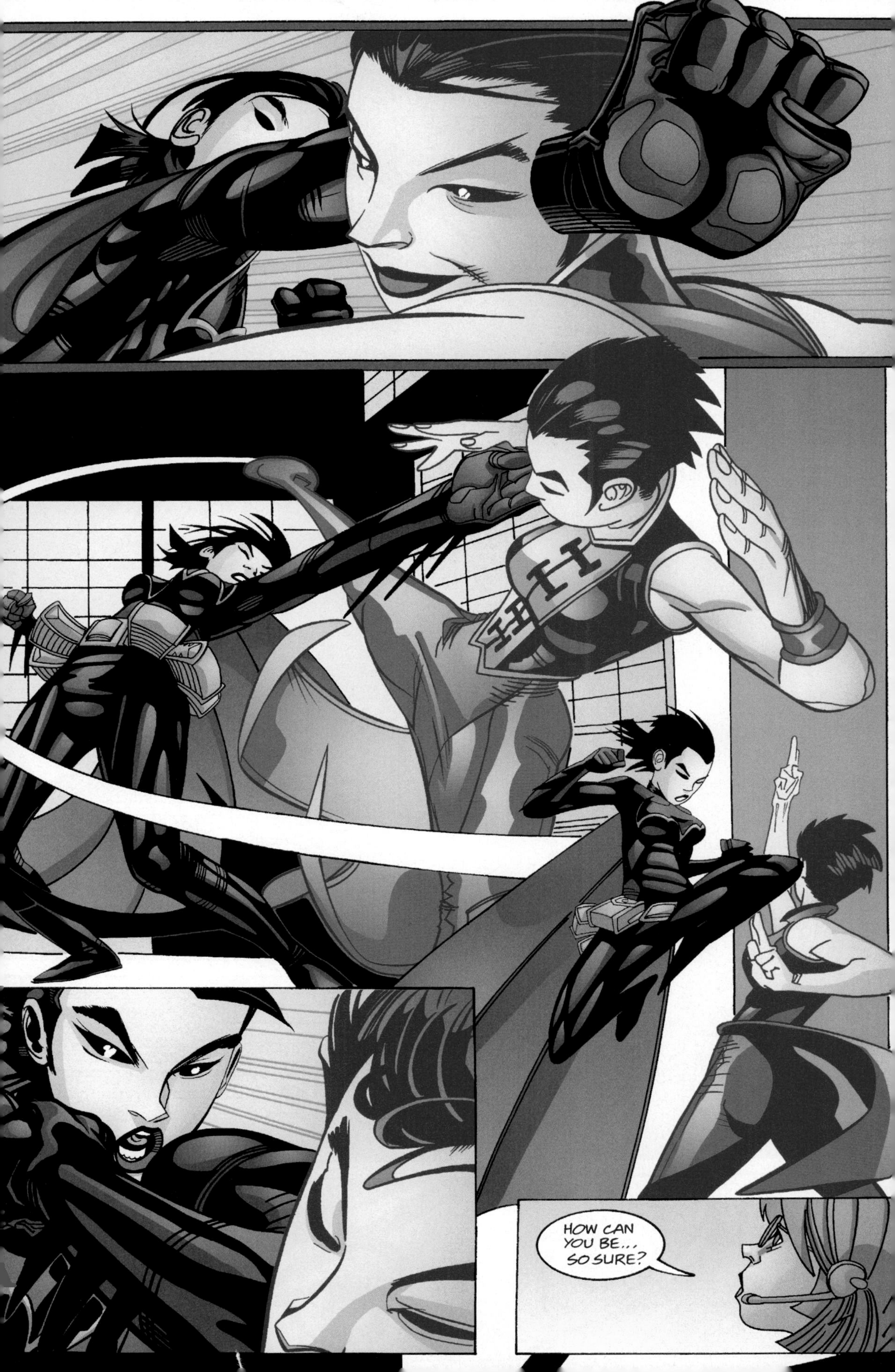
HOW CAN YOU BE... SO SURE?

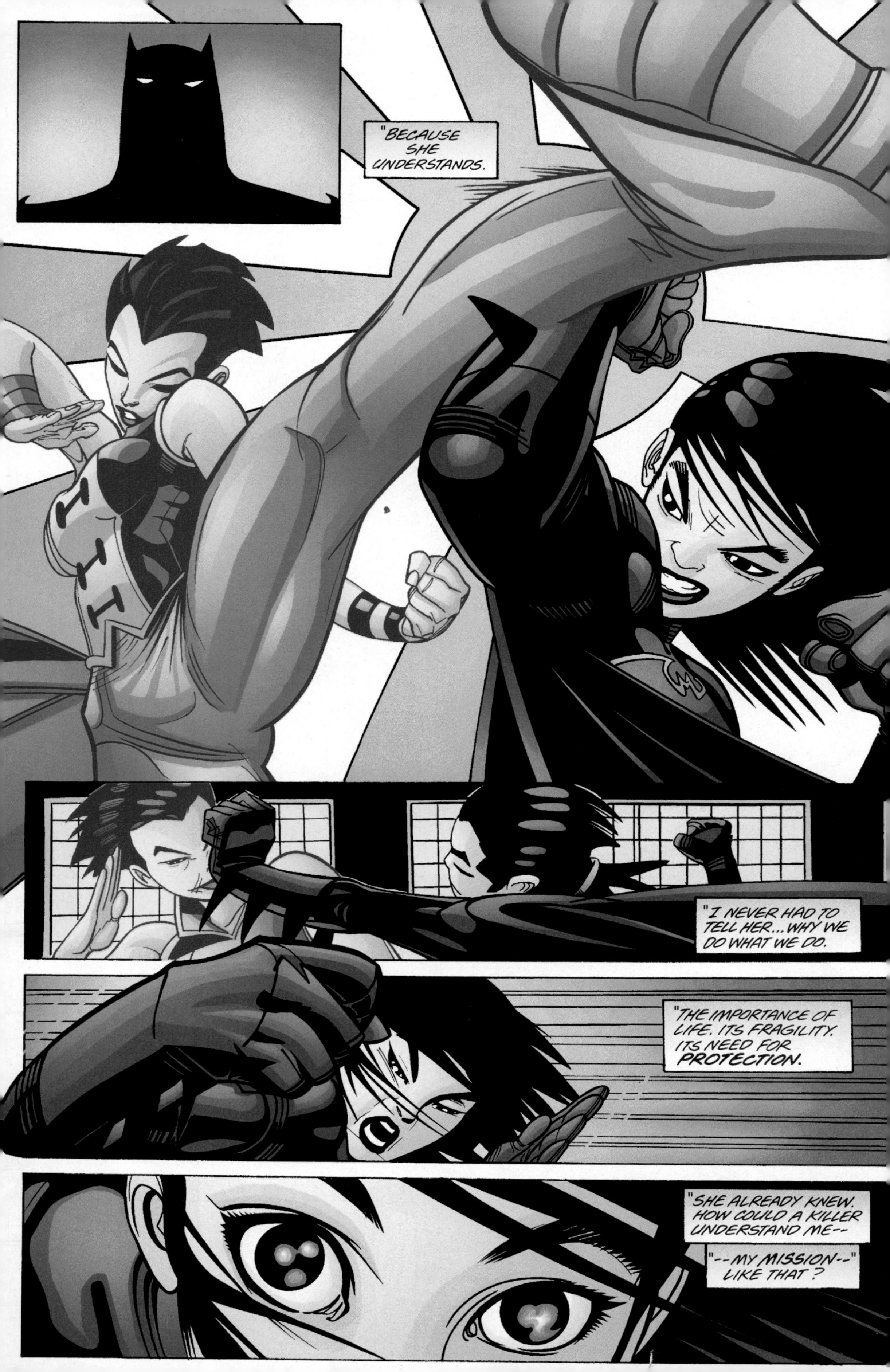
"BECAUSE SHE UNDERSTANDS.
"I NEVER HAD TO TELL HER... WHY WE DO WHAT WE DO.
"THE IMPORTANCE OF LIFE. ITS FRAGILITY. ITS NEED FOR PROTECTION.
"SHE ALREADY KNEW. HOW COULD A KILLER UNDERSTAND ME--
"--MY MISSION--" LIKE THAT?

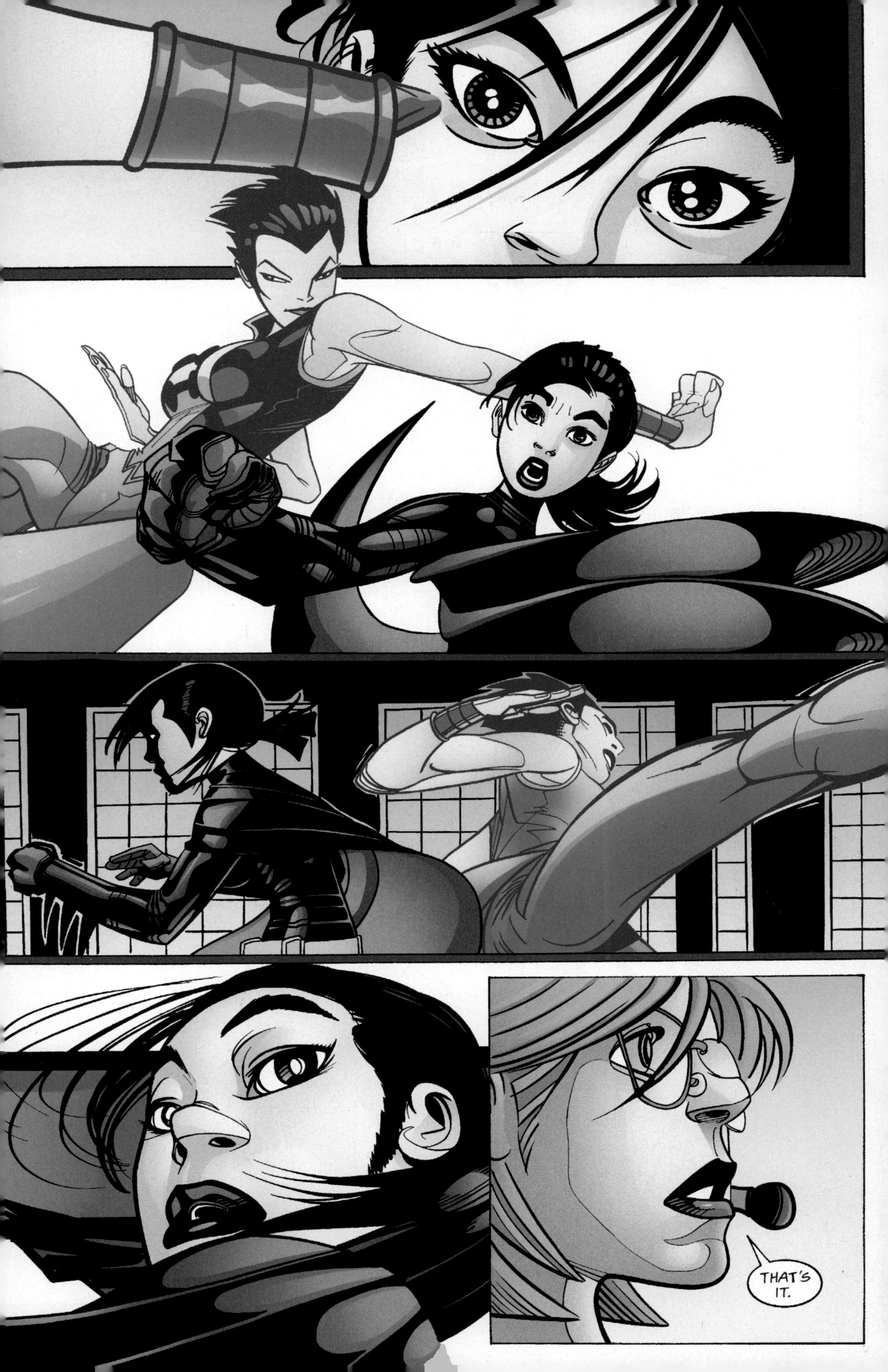
THAT'S IT.

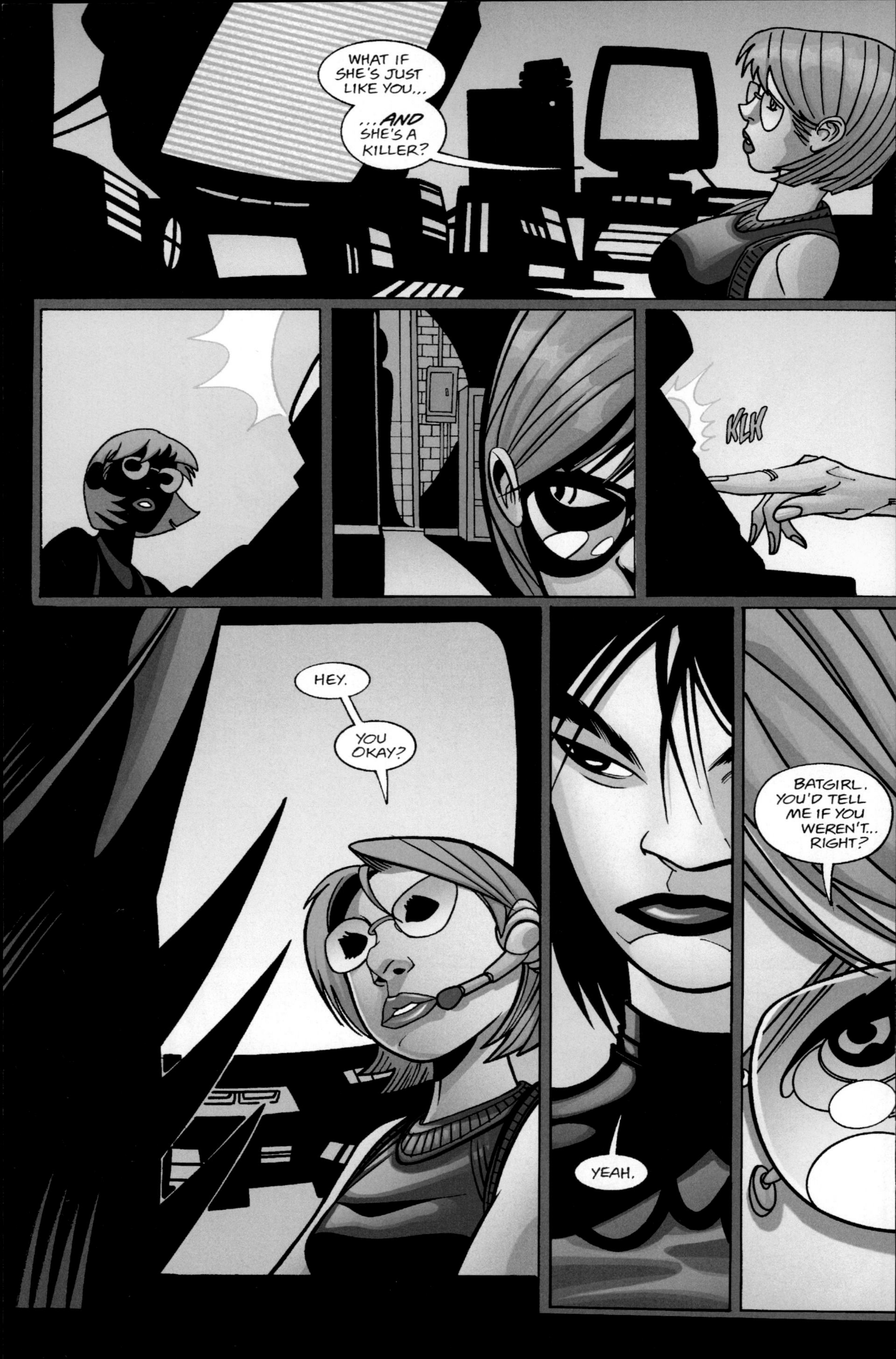

WHAT IF SHE'S JUST LIKE YOU...
...AND SHE'S A KILLER?
KLK
HEY.
YOU OKAY?
BATGIRL. YOU'D TELL ME IF YOU WEREN'T... RIGHT?
YEAH.

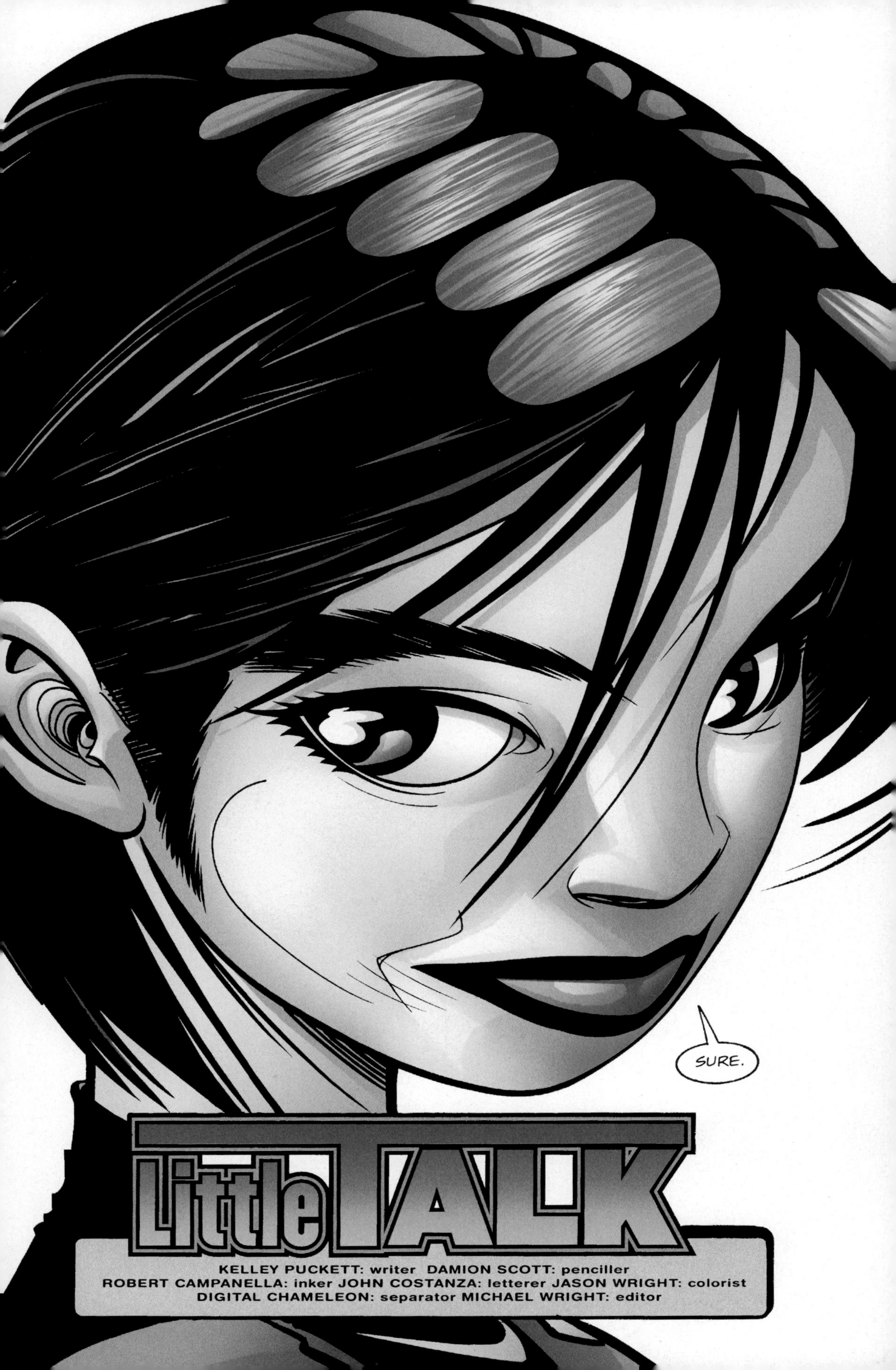
SURE.
Little TALK
KELLEY PUCKETT: writer DAMION SCOTT: penciller
ROBERT CAMPANELLA: inker JOHN COSTANZA: letterer JASON WRIGHT: colorist
DIGITAL CHAMELEON: separator MICHAEL WRIGHT: editor

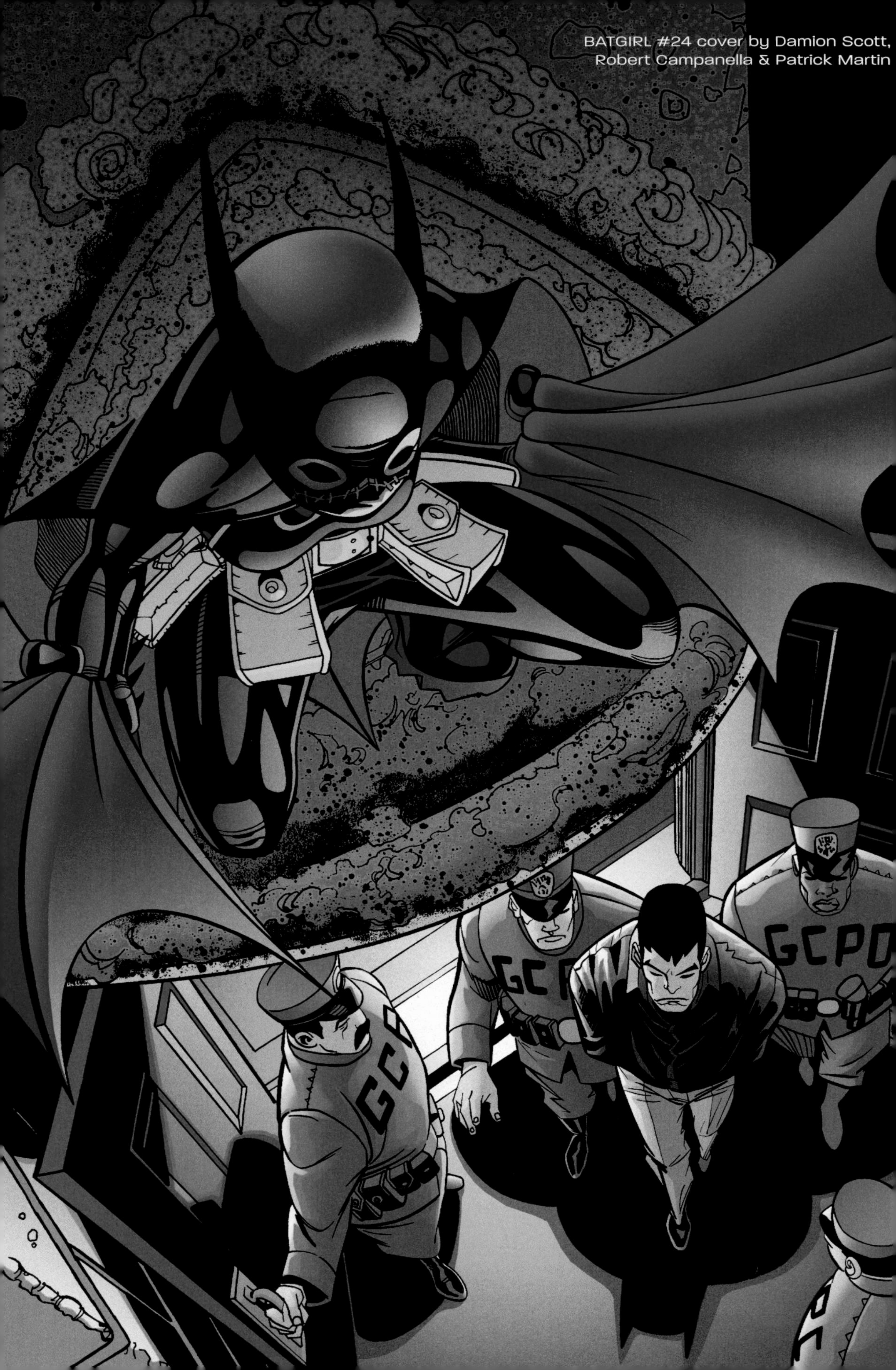
GCPD

BATGIRL #24 cover by Damion Scott,
Robert Campanella & Patrick Martin

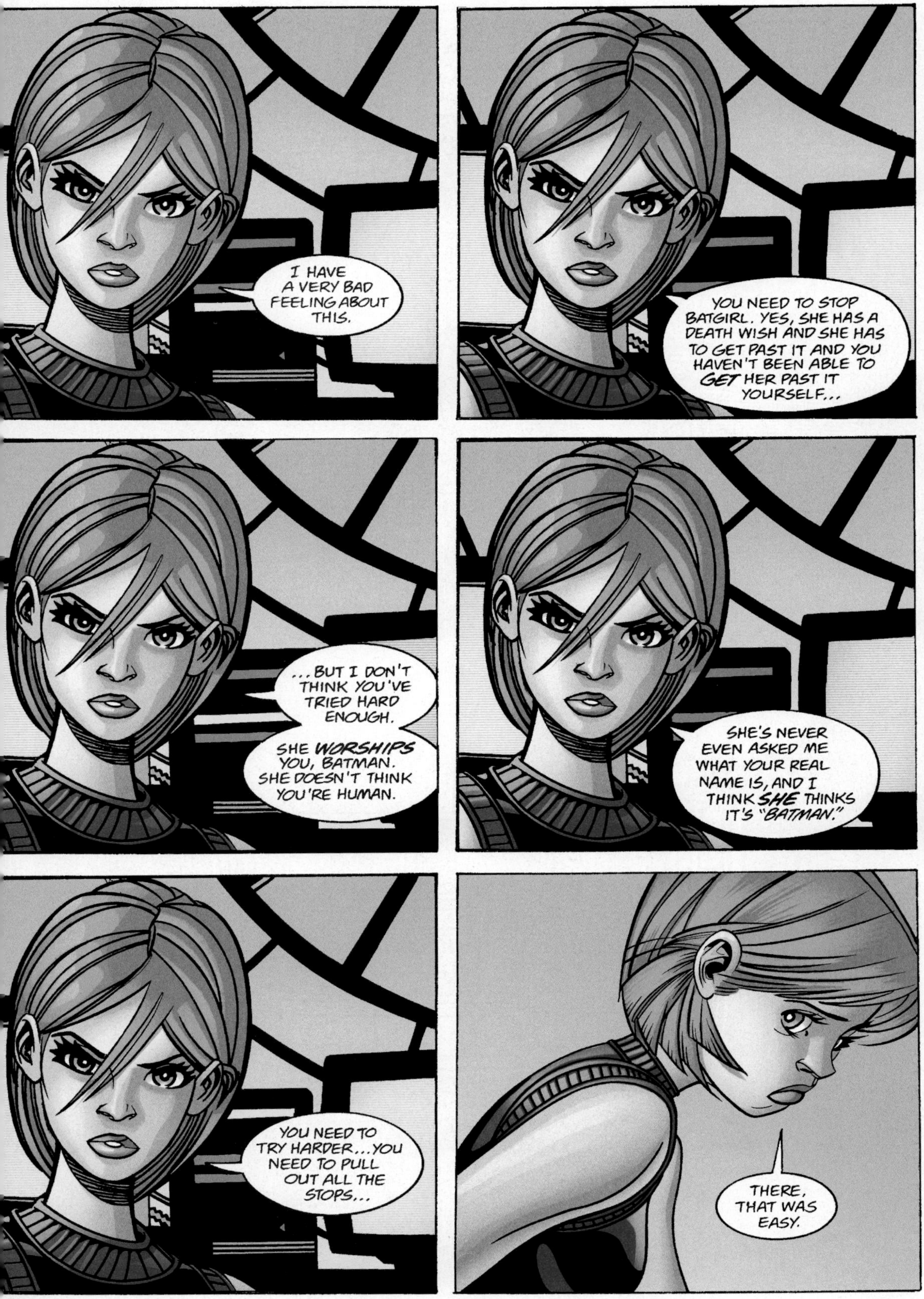
I HAVE A VERY BAD FEELING ABOUT THIS.
YOU NEED TO STOP BATGIRL. YES, SHE HAS A DEATH WISH AND SHE HAS TO GET PAST IT AND YOU HAVEN'T BEEN ABLE TO GET HER PAST IT YOURSELF...
...BUT I DON'T THINK YOU'VE TRIED HARD ENOUGH.
SHE WORSHIPS YOU, BATMAN. SHE DOESN'T THINK YOU'RE HUMAN.
SHE'S NEVER EVEN ASKED ME WHAT YOUR REAL NAME IS, AND I THINK SHE THINKS IT'S "BATMAN."
YOU NEED TO TRY HARDER...YOU NEED TO PULL OUT ALL THE STOPS...
THERE, THAT WAS EASY.

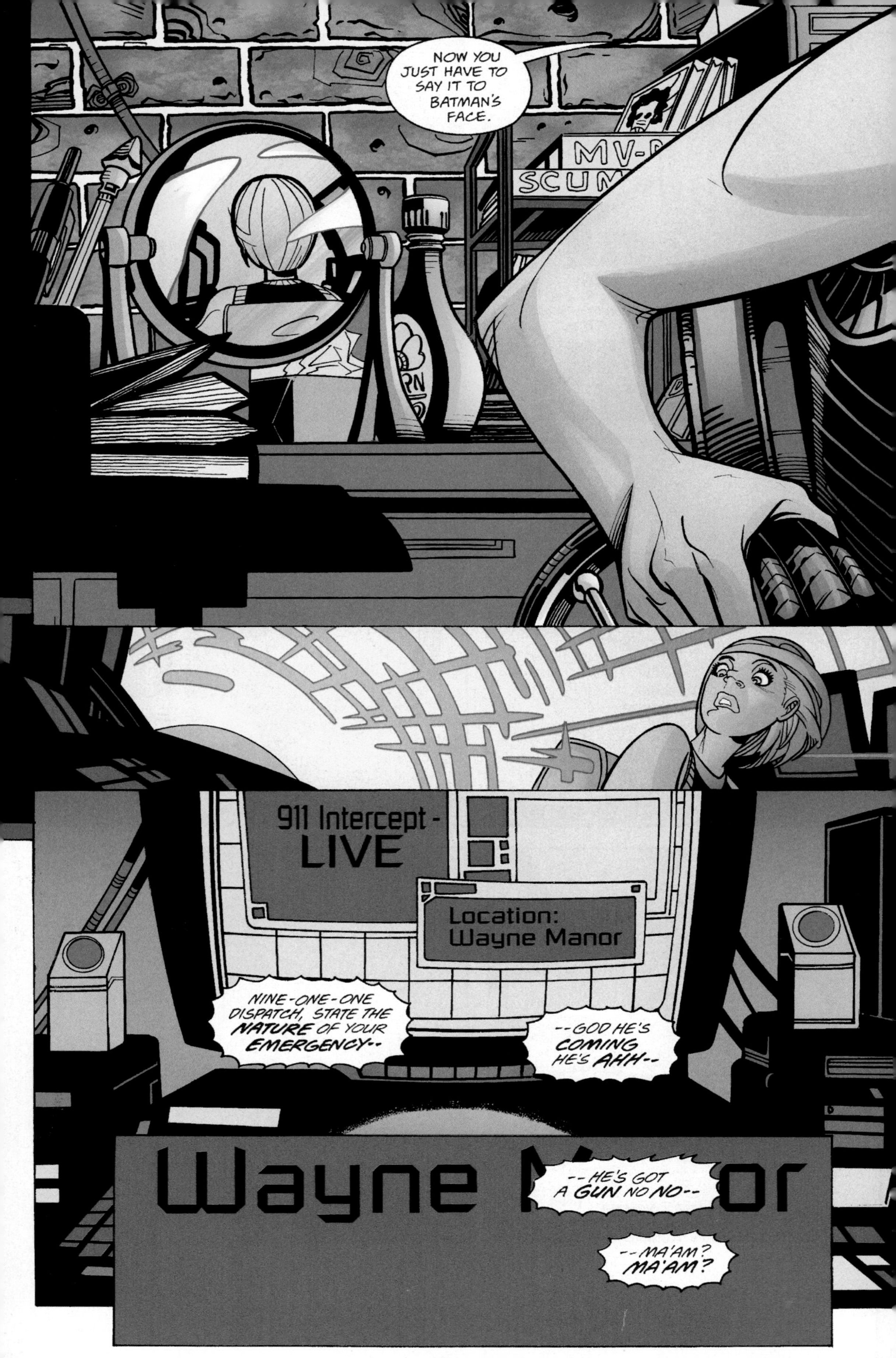
NOW YOU JUST HAVE TO SAY IT TO BATMAN'S FACE.
911 Intercept - LIVE
Location: Wayne Manor
NINE-ONE-ONE DISPATCH, STATE THE NATURE OF YOUR EMERGENCY--
--GOD HE'S COMING HE'S AHH--
--HE'S GOT A GUN NO NO--
--MA'AM? MA'AM?

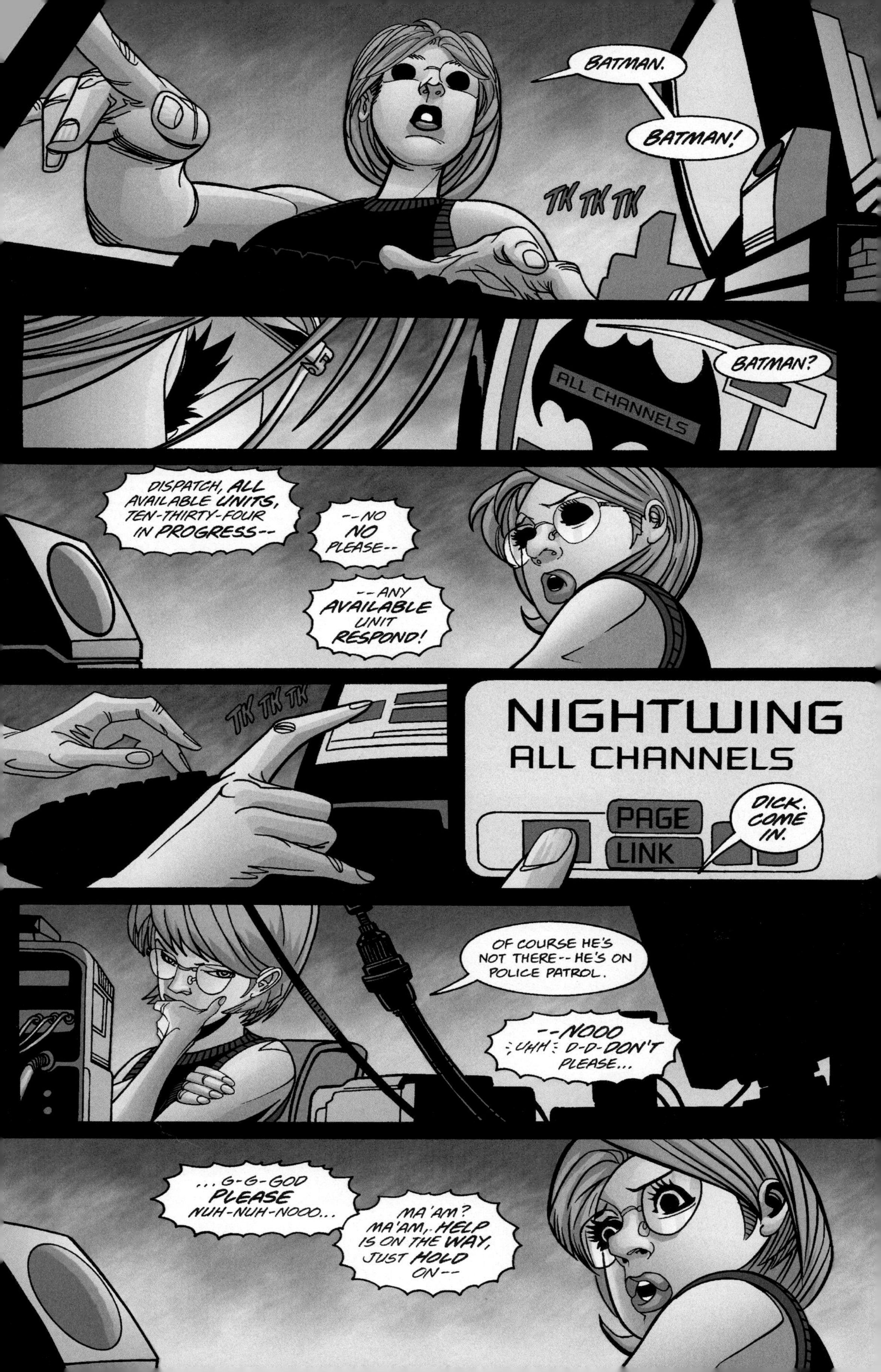

BATMAN.
BATMAN!
TK TK TK
BATMAN?
ALL CHANNELS
DISPATCH, ALL AVAILABLE UNITS, TEN-THIRTY-FOUR IN PROGRESS--
--NO NO PLEASE--
--ANY AVAILABLE UNIT RESPOND!
TK TK TK
NIGHTWING
ALL CHANNELS
PAGE
LINK
DICK. COME IN.
OF COURSE HE'S NOT THERE--HE'S ON POLICE PATROL.
--NOOO UHH D-D-DON'T PLEASE...
...G-G-GOD PLEASE NUH-NUH-NOOO...
MA'AM? MA'AM, HELP IS ON THE WAY, JUST HOLD ON--

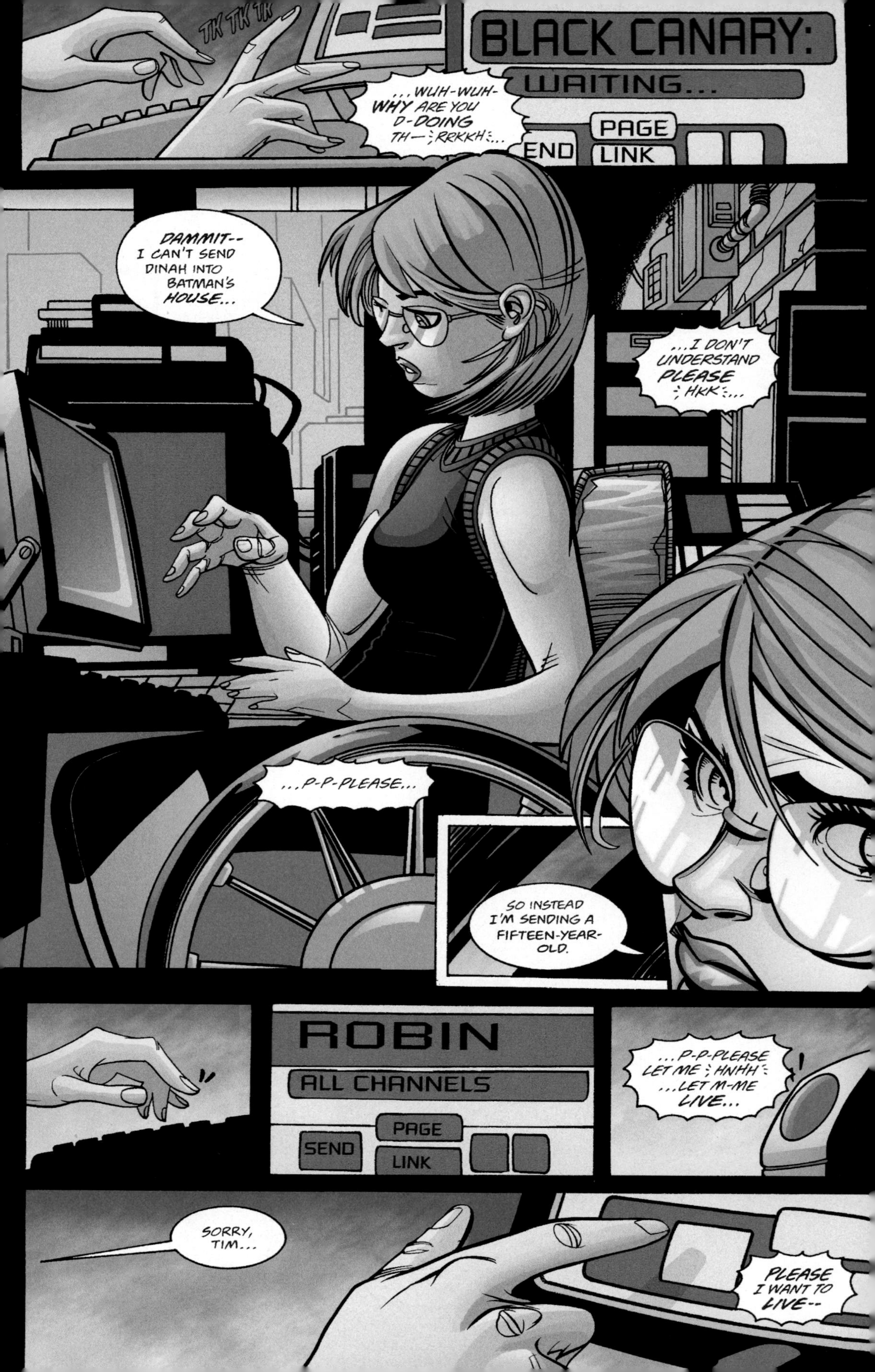
TK TK TK
BLACK CANARY:
WAITING...
...WUH-WUH-WHY ARE YOU D-DOING TH--RRKKH...
END
PAGE
LINK
DAMMIT-- I CAN'T SEND DINAH INTO BATMAN'S HOUSE...
...I DON'T UNDERSTAND PLEASE HKK...
...P-P-PLEASE...
SO INSTEAD I'M SENDING A FIFTEEN-YEAR-OLD.
ROBIN
ALL CHANNELS
SEND
PAGE
LINK
...P-P-PLEASE LET ME HNHH ...LET M-ME LIVE...
SORRY, TIM...
PLEASE I WANT TO LIVE--

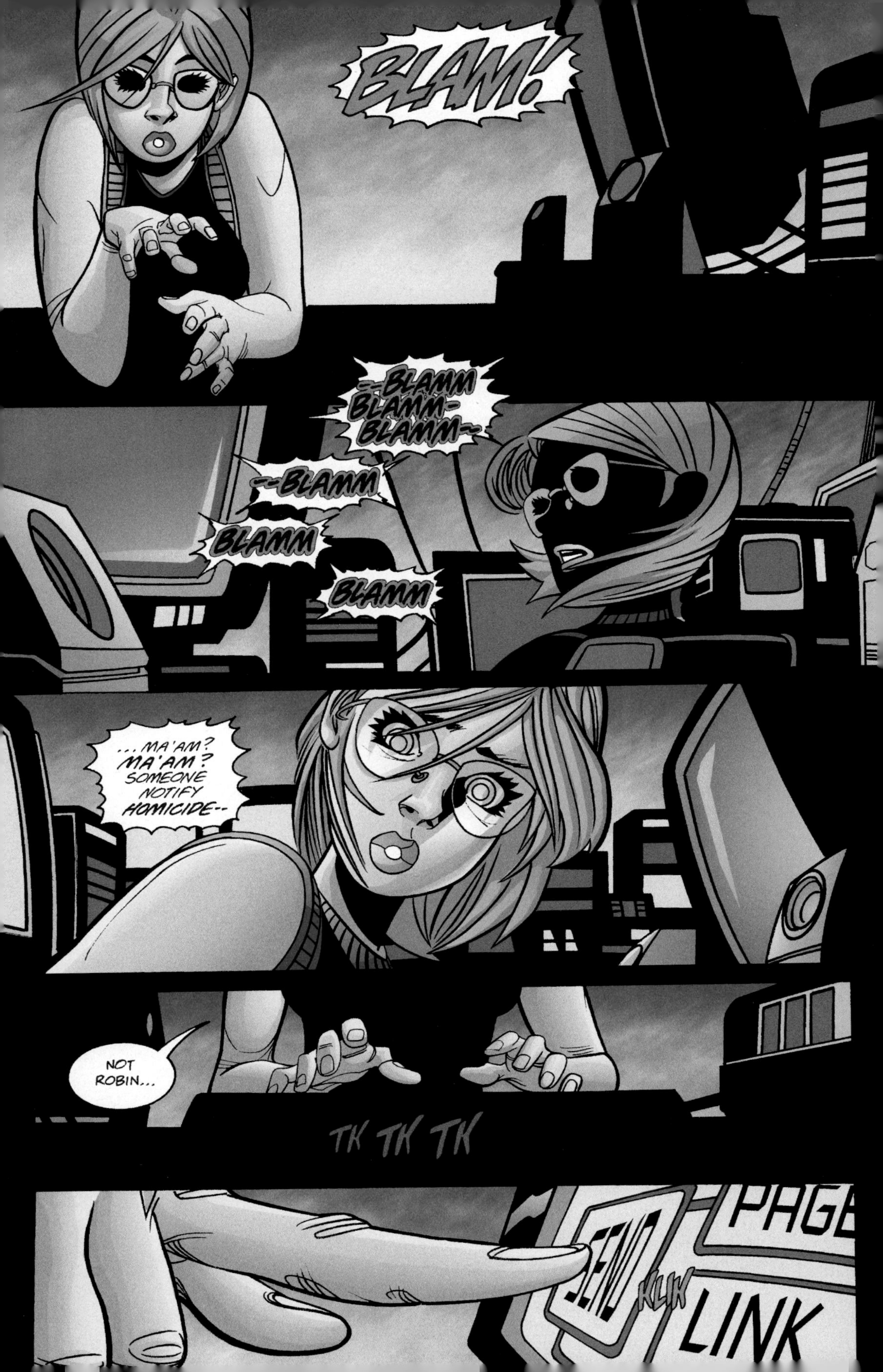
BLAM!
--BLAMM BLAMM-BLAMM--
--BLAMM
BLAMM
BLAMM
...MA'AM? MA'AM? SOMEONE NOTIFY HOMICIDE--
NOT ROBIN...
TK TK TK
PAGE
SEND
KLIK
LINK

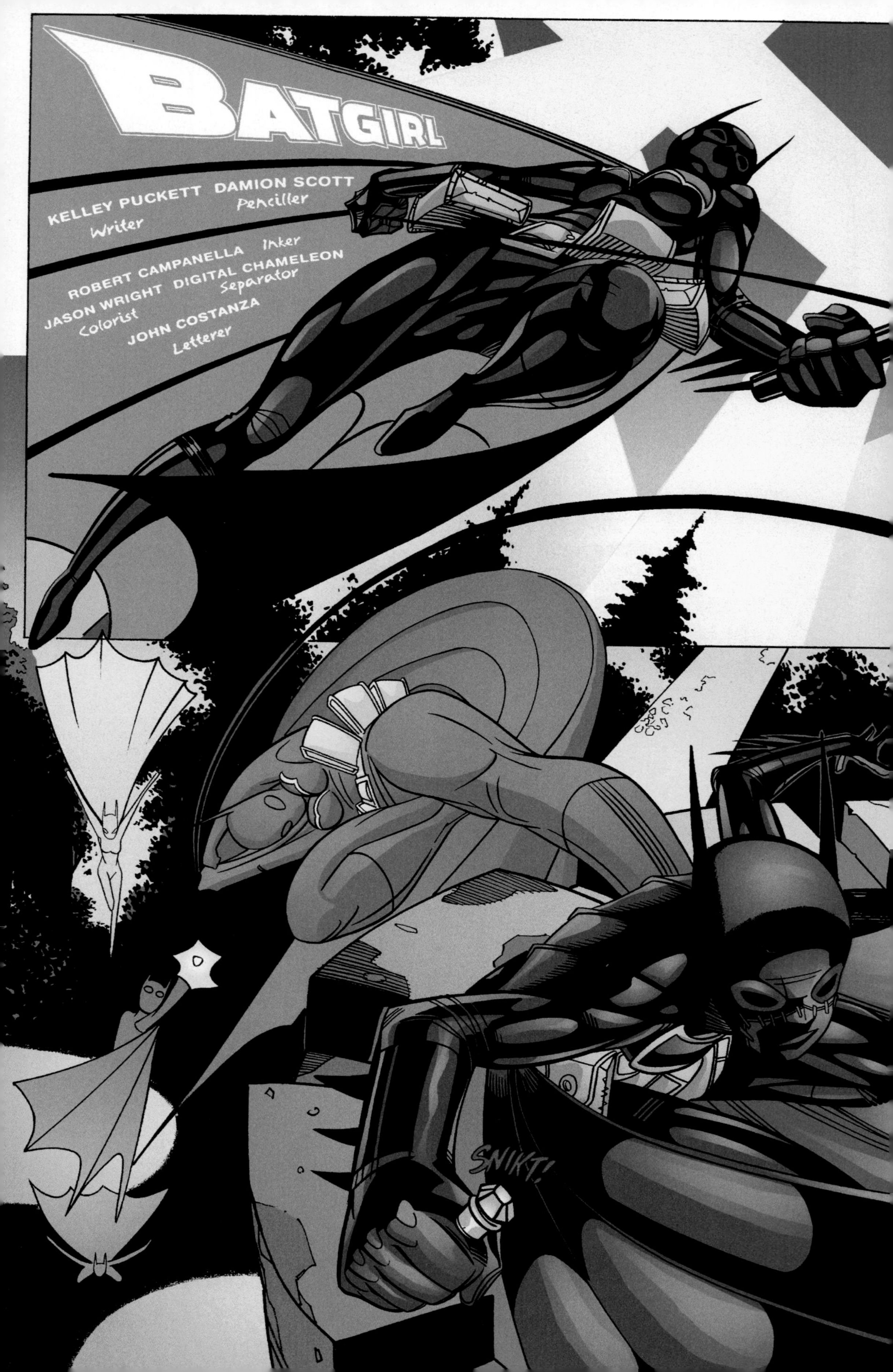
BATGIRL
KELLEY PUCKETT Writer
DAMION SCOTT Penciller
ROBERT CAMPANELLA Inker
JASON WRIGHT Colorist
DIGITAL CHAMELEON Separator
JOHN COSTANZA Letterer
SNIKT!

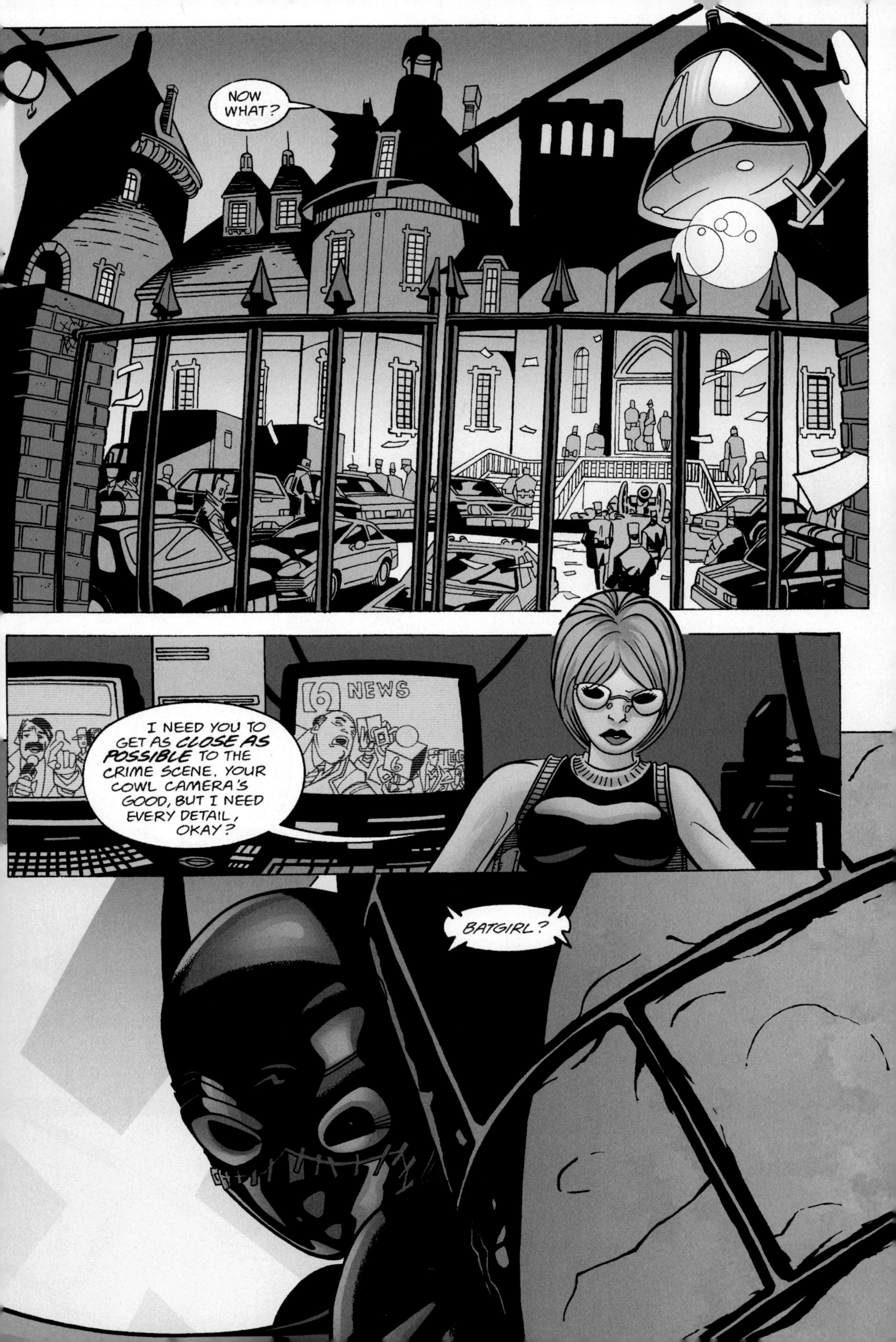
NOW WHAT?
I NEED YOU TO GET AS CLOSE AS POSSIBLE TO THE CRIME SCENE. YOUR COWL CAMERA'S GOOD, BUT I NEED EVERY DETAIL, OKAY?
BATGIRL?

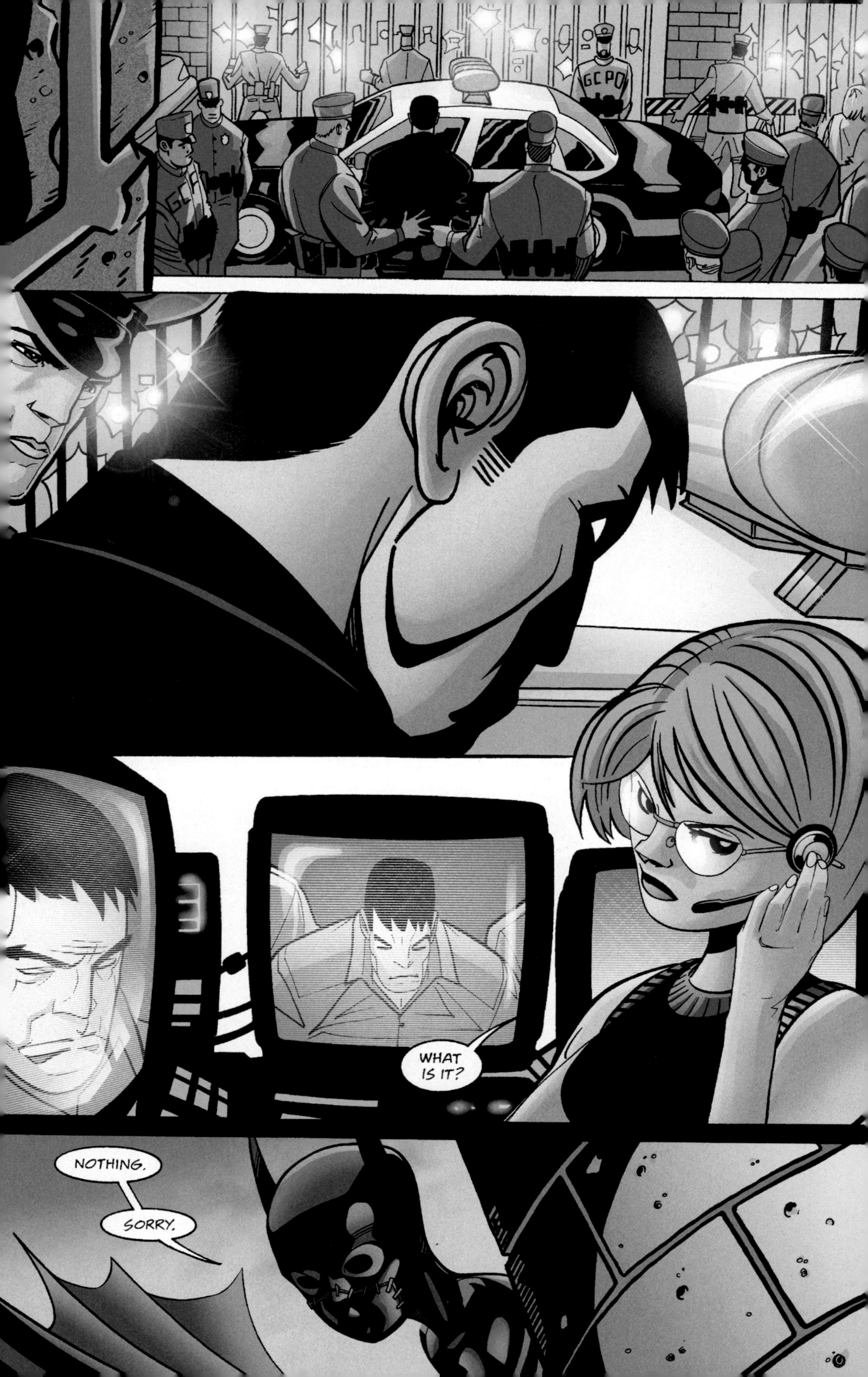
GCPD
WHAT IS IT?
NOTHING.
SORRY.

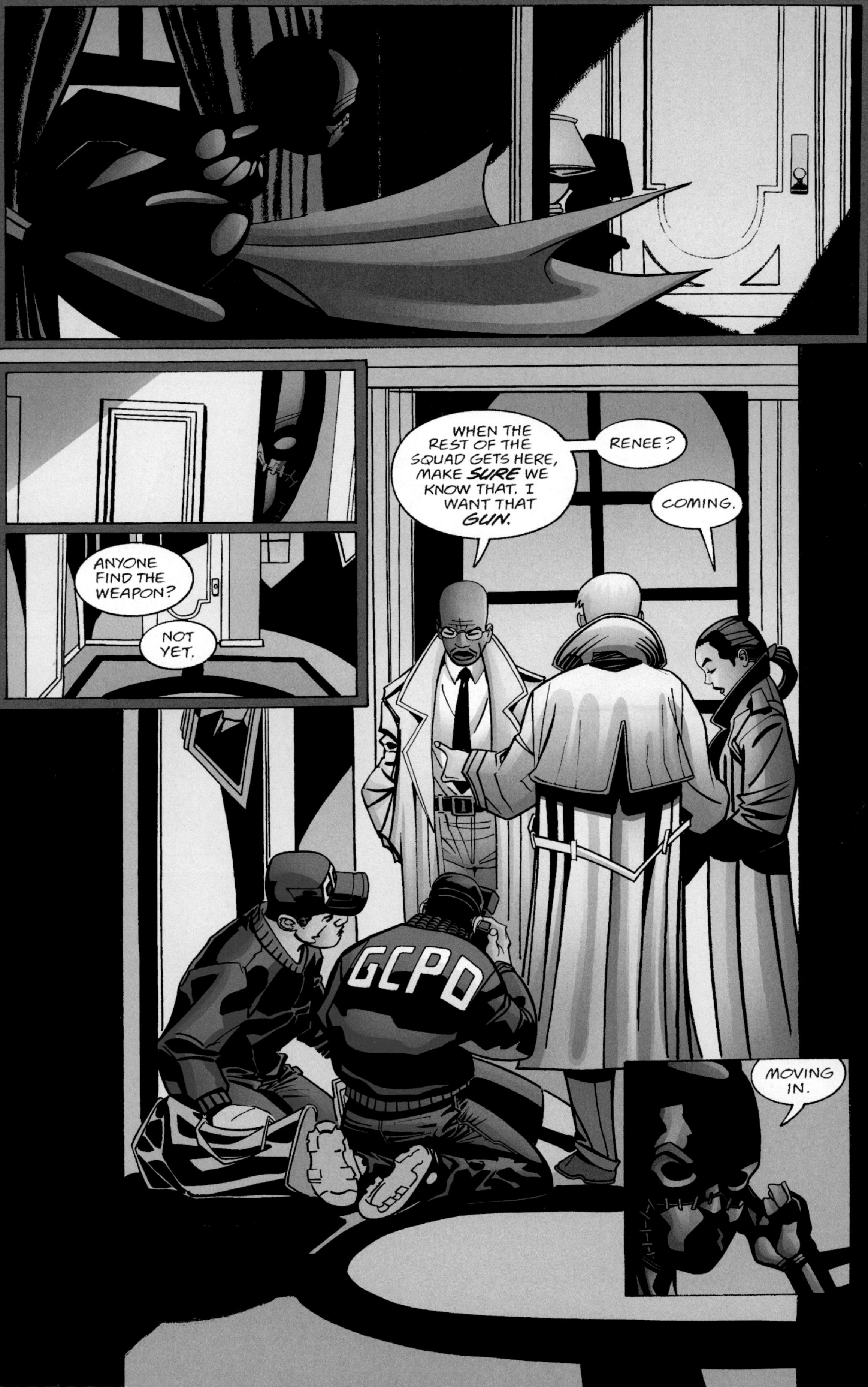
ANYONE FIND THE WEAPON?
NOT YET.
WHEN THE REST OF THE SQUAD GETS HERE, MAKE SURE WE KNOW THAT. I WANT THAT GUN.
RENEE?
COMING.
MOVING IN.

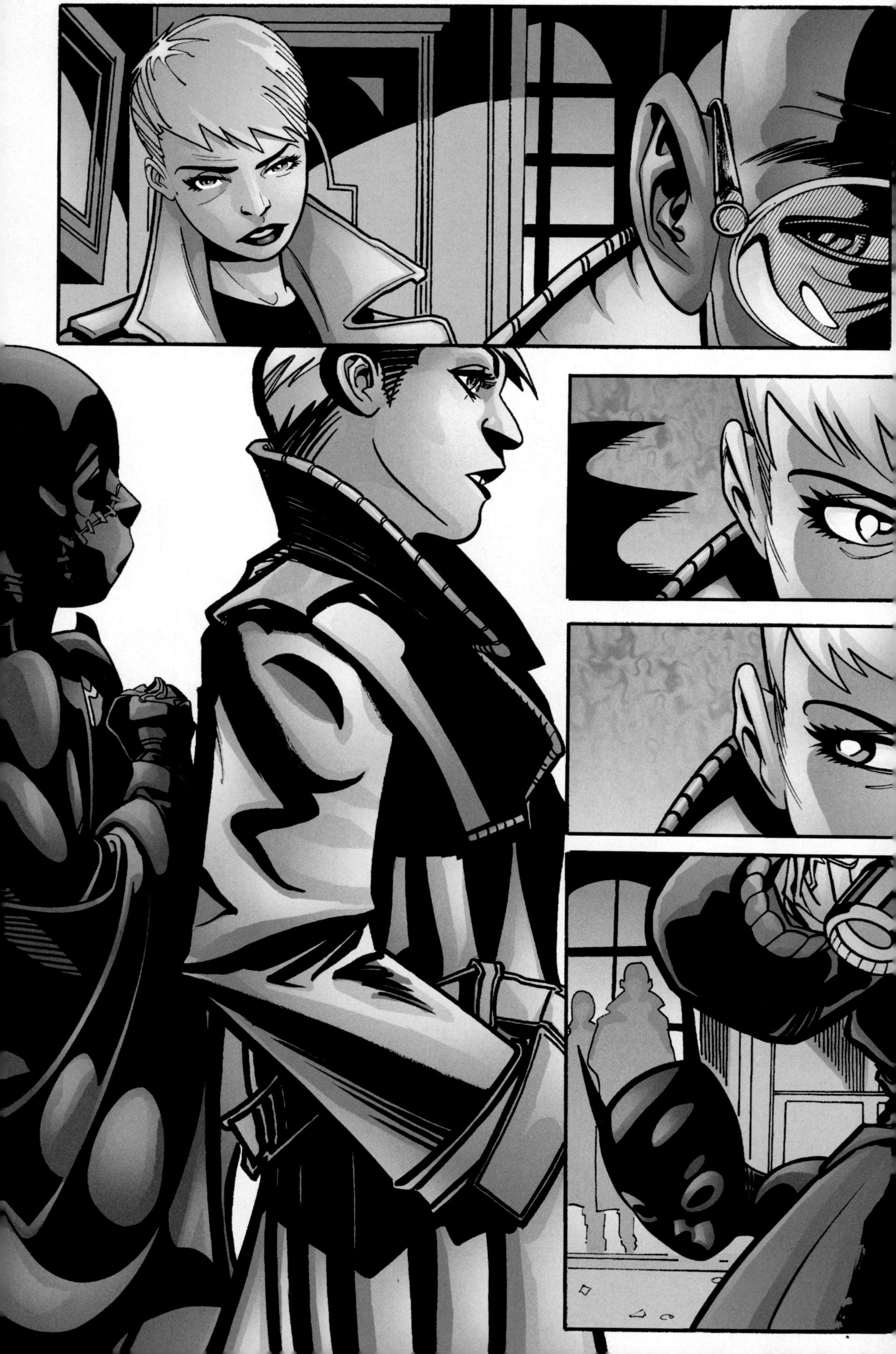

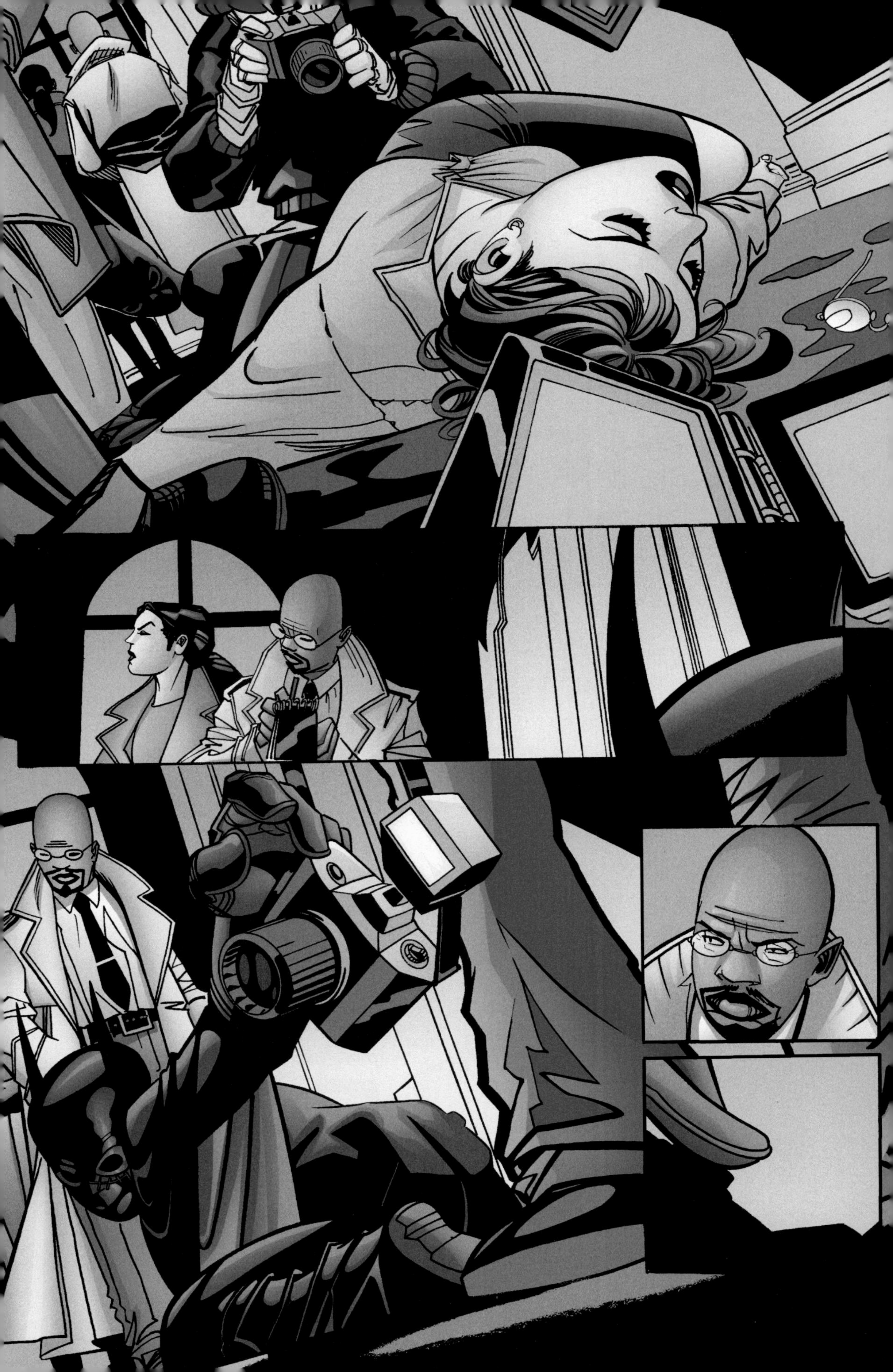

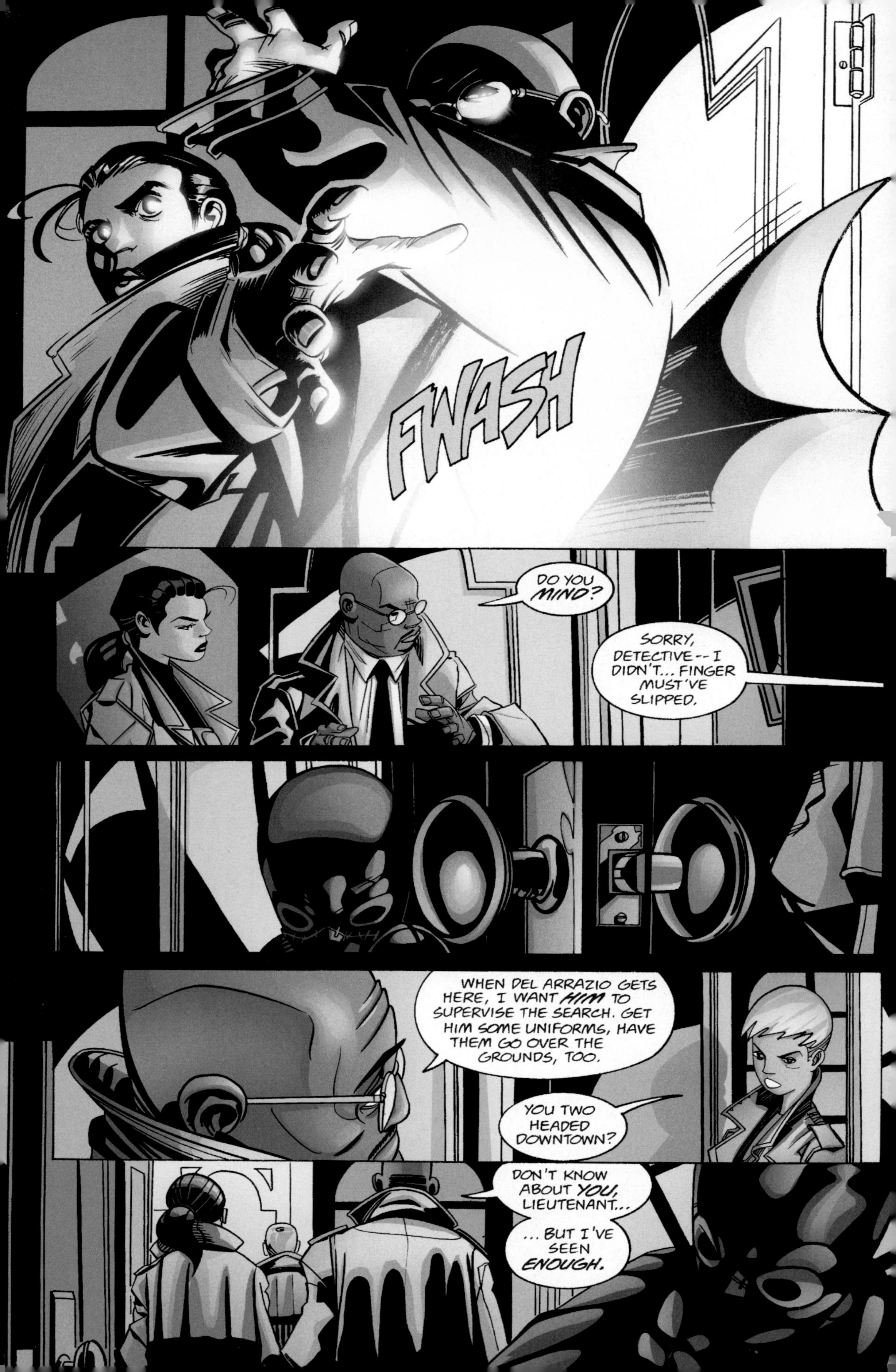
FWASH
DO YOU MIND?
SORRY, DETECTIVE-- I DIDN'T... FINGER MUST'VE SLIPPED.
WHEN DEL ARRAZIO GETS HERE, I WANT HIM TO SUPERVISE THE SEARCH. GET HIM SOME UNIFORMS, HAVE THEM GO OVER THE GROUNDS, TOO.
YOU TWO HEADED DOWNTOWN?
DON'T KNOW ABOUT YOU, LIEUTENANT...
...BUT I'VE SEEN ENOUGH.

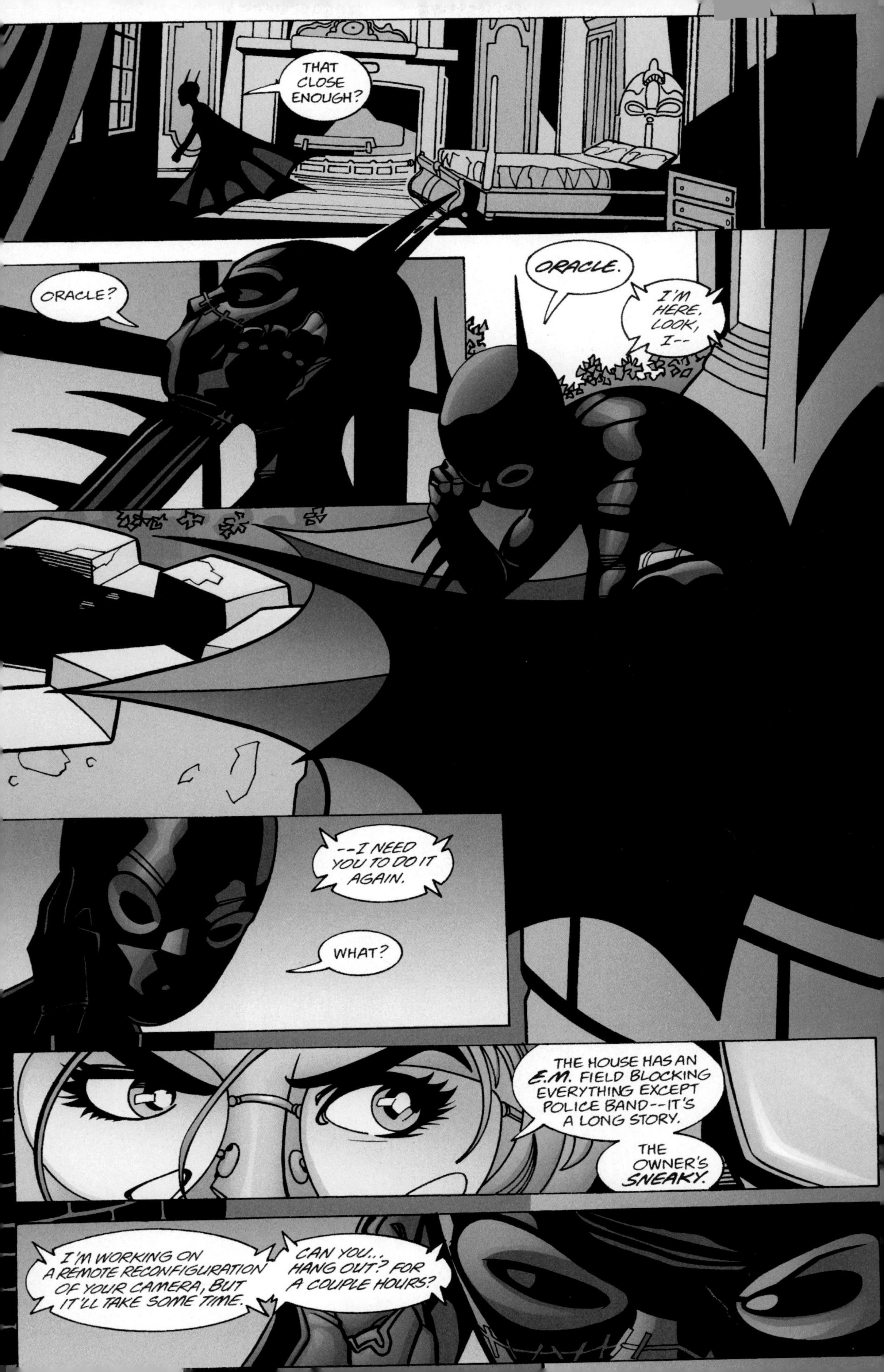
THAT CLOSE ENOUGH?
ORACLE?
ORACLE.
I'M HERE. LOOK, I--
--I NEED YOU TO DO IT AGAIN.
WHAT?
THE HOUSE HAS AN E.M. FIELD BLOCKING EVERYTHING EXCEPT POLICE BAND--IT'S A LONG STORY.
THE OWNER'S SNEAKY.
I'M WORKING ON A REMOTE RECONFIGURATION OF YOUR CAMERA, BUT IT'LL TAKE SOME TIME.
CAN YOU... HANG OUT? FOR A COUPLE HOURS?

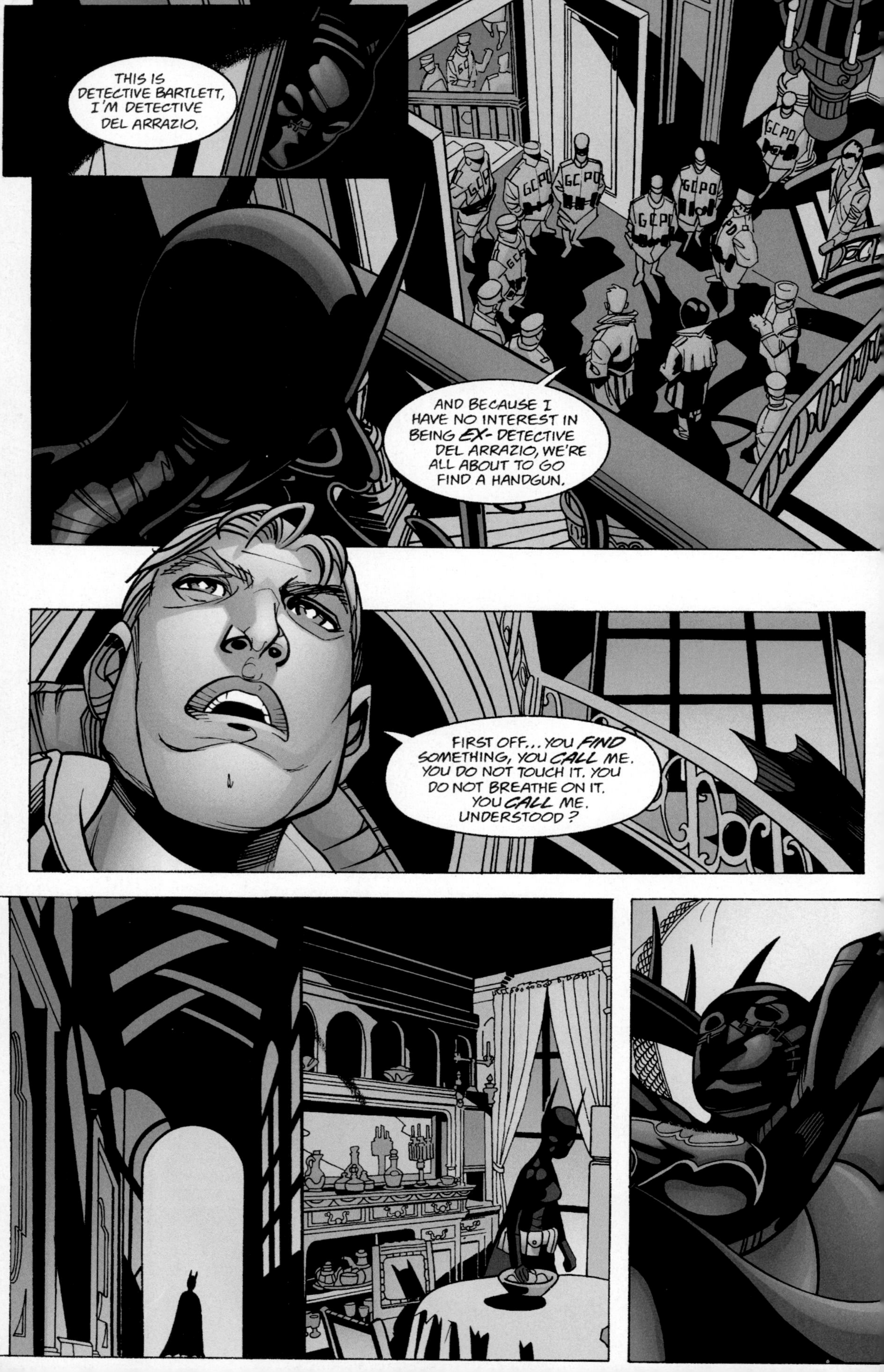
THIS IS DETECTIVE BARTLETT, I'M DETECTIVE DEL ARRAZIO.
AND BECAUSE I HAVE NO INTEREST IN BEING EX- DETECTIVE DEL ARRAZIO, WE'RE ALL ABOUT TO GO FIND A HANDGUN.
FIRST OFF... YOU FIND SOMETHING, YOU CALL ME. YOU DO NOT TOUCH IT. YOU DO NOT BREATHE ON IT. YOU CALL ME. UNDERSTOOD?

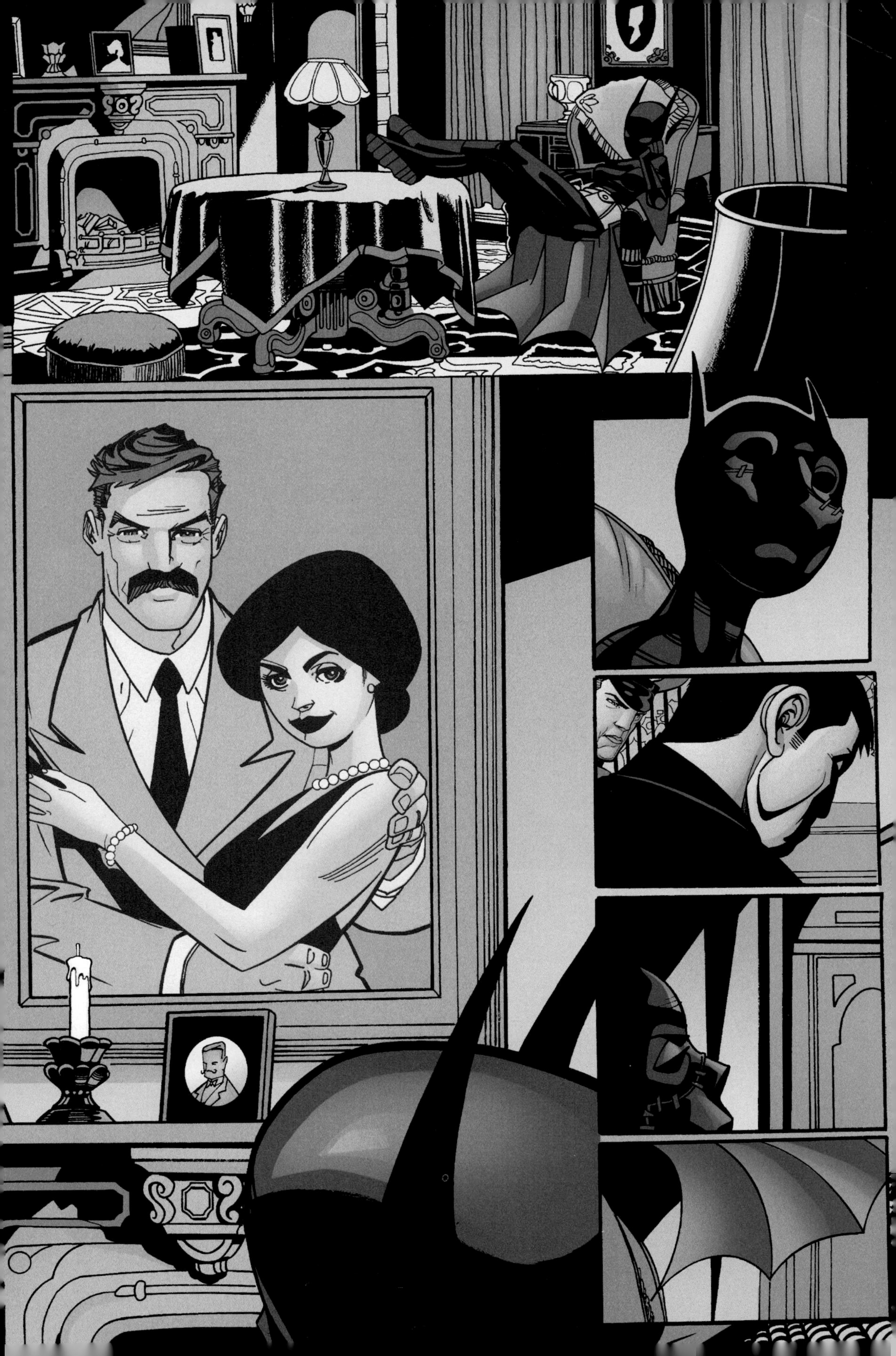

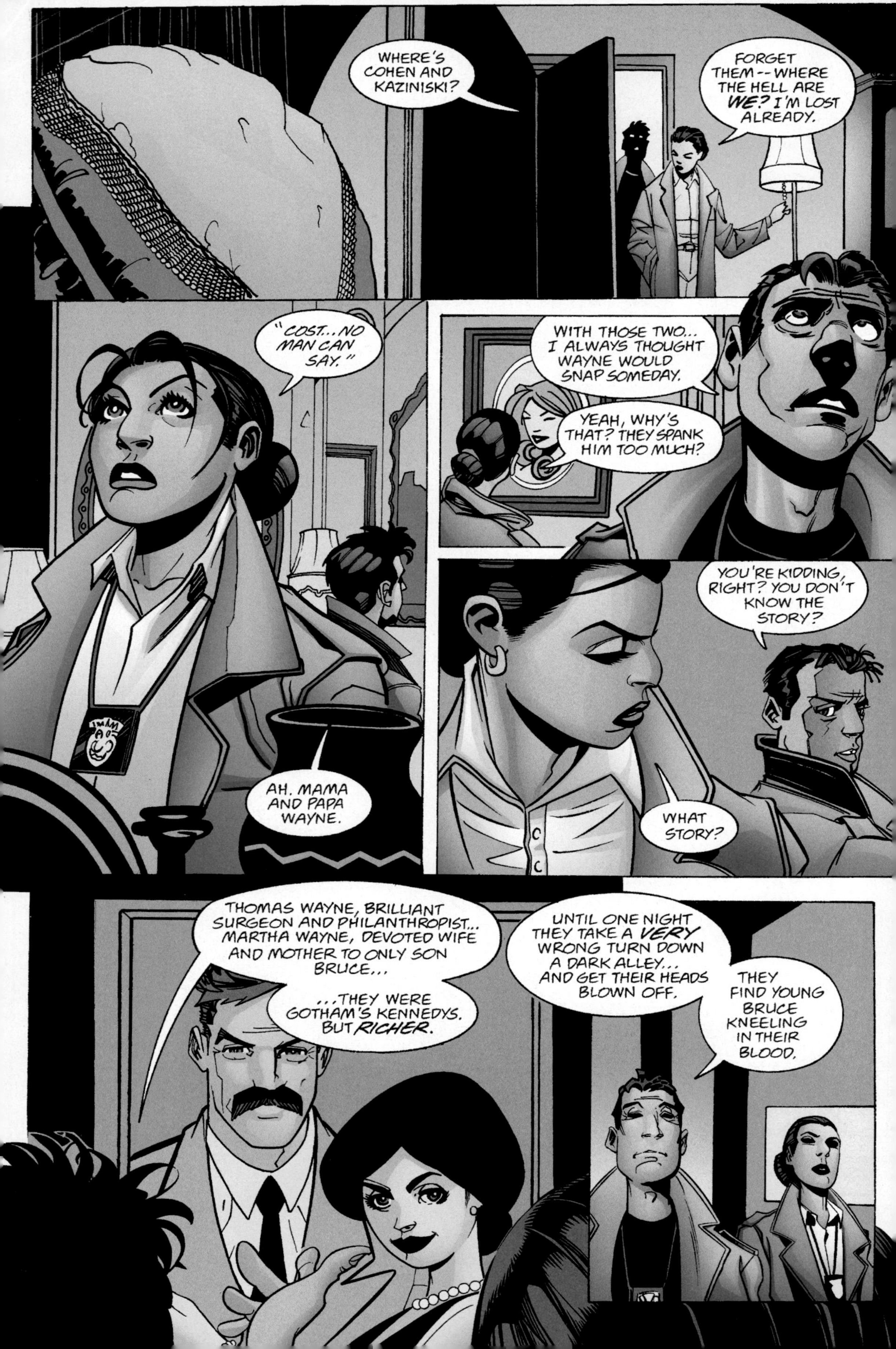
WHERE'S COHEN AND KAZINISKI?
FORGET THEM -- WHERE THE HELL ARE WE? I'M LOST ALREADY.
"COST... NO MAN CAN SAY."
AH. MAMA AND PAPA WAYNE.
WITH THOSE TWO... I ALWAYS THOUGHT WAYNE WOULD SNAP SOMEDAY.
YEAH, WHY'S THAT? THEY SPANK HIM TOO MUCH?
YOU'RE KIDDING, RIGHT? YOU DON'T KNOW THE STORY?
WHAT STORY?
THOMAS WAYNE, BRILLIANT SURGEON AND PHILANTHROPIST... MARTHA WAYNE, DEVOTED WIFE AND MOTHER TO ONLY SON BRUCE...
...THEY WERE GOTHAM'S KENNEDYS. BUT RICHER.
UNTIL ONE NIGHT THEY TAKE A VERY WRONG TURN DOWN A DARK ALLEY... AND GET THEIR HEADS BLOWN OFF.
THEY FIND YOUNG BRUCE KNEELING IN THEIR BLOOD.

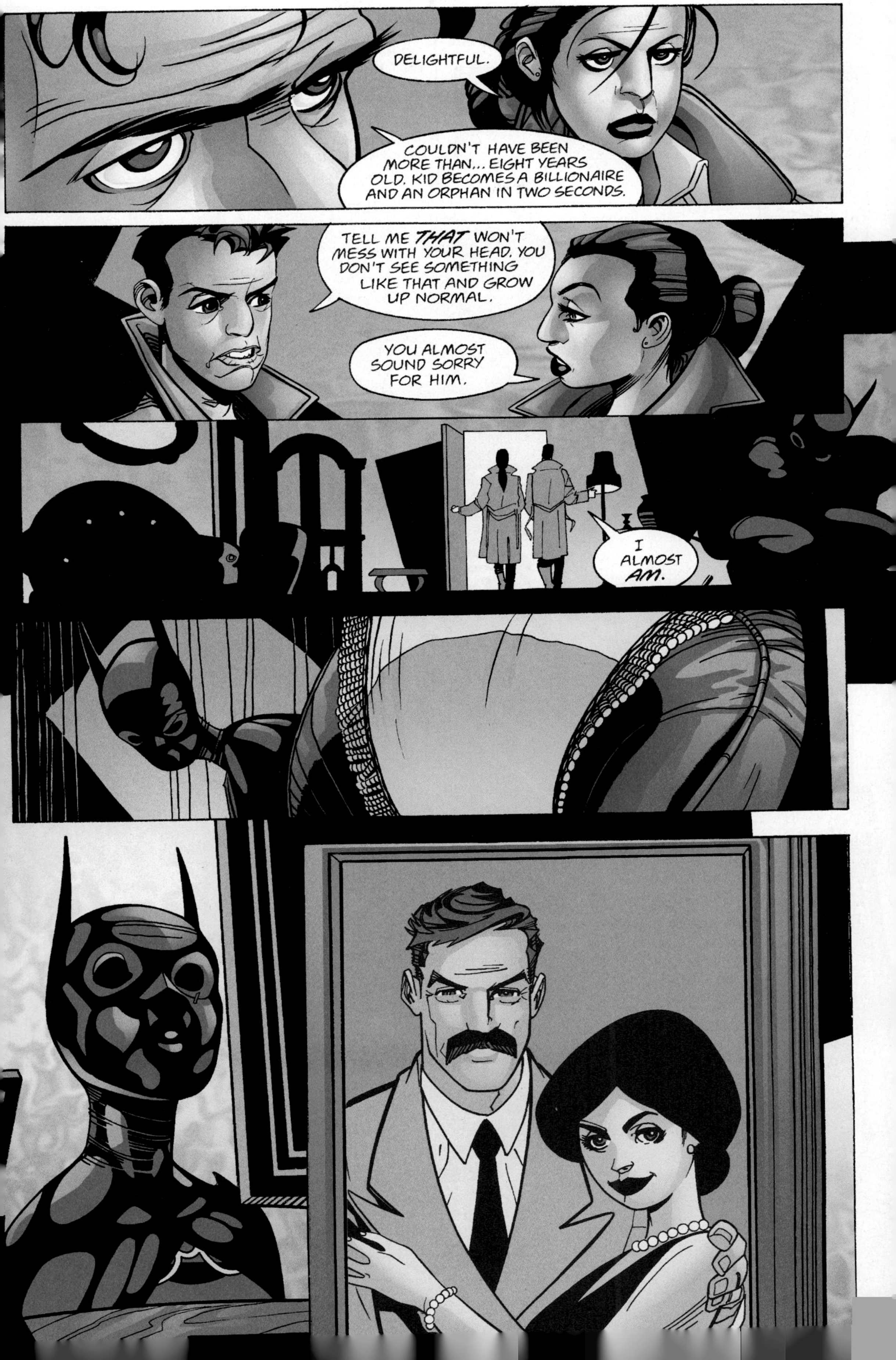
DELIGHTFUL.
COULDN'T HAVE BEEN MORE THAN... EIGHT YEARS OLD. KID BECOMES A BILLIONAIRE AND AN ORPHAN IN TWO SECONDS.
TELL ME THAT WON'T MESS WITH YOUR HEAD. YOU DON'T SEE SOMETHING LIKE THAT AND GROW UP NORMAL.
YOU ALMOST SOUND SORRY FOR HIM.
I ALMOST AM.

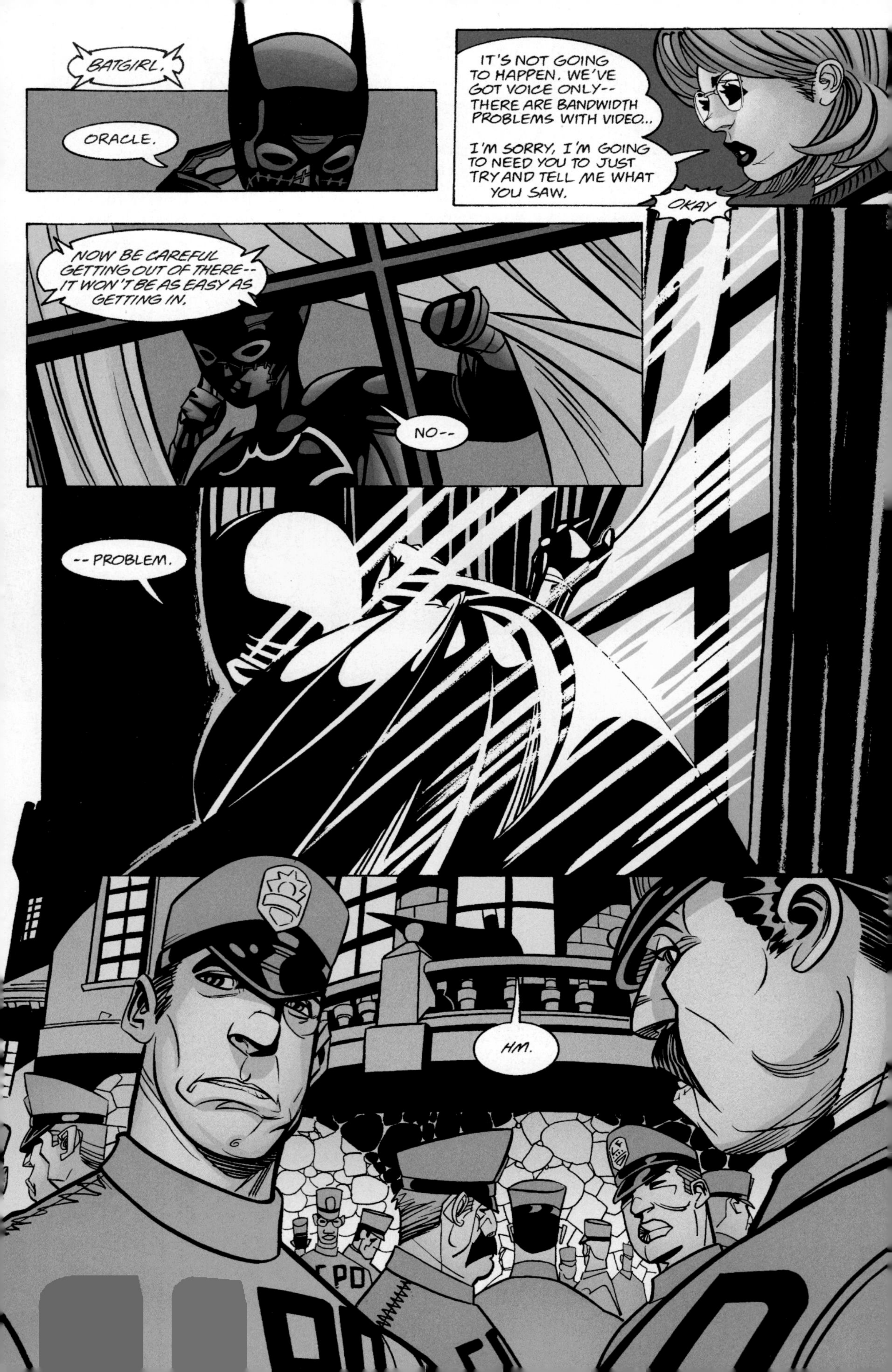
BATGIRL.
ORACLE.
IT'S NOT GOING TO HAPPEN. WE'VE GOT VOICE ONLY-- THERE ARE BANDWIDTH PROBLEMS WITH VIDEO...
I'M SORRY, I'M GOING TO NEED YOU TO JUST TRY AND TELL ME WHAT YOU SAW.
OKAY
NOW BE CAREFUL GETTING OUT OF THERE-- IT WON'T BE AS EASY AS GETTING IN.
NO--
--PROBLEM.
HM.
GPD

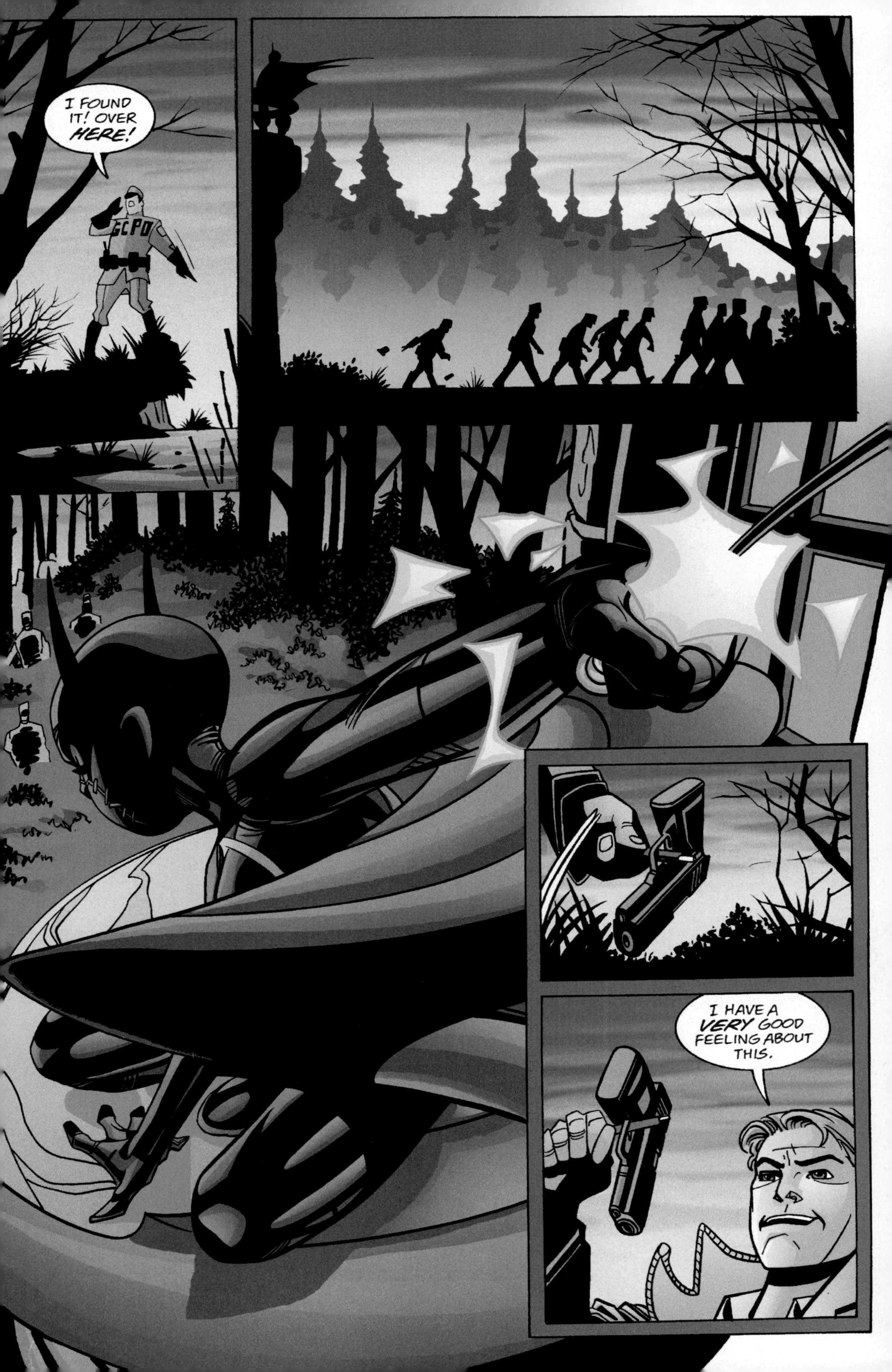
I FOUND IT! OVER HERE!
I HAVE A VERY GOOD FEELING ABOUT THIS.

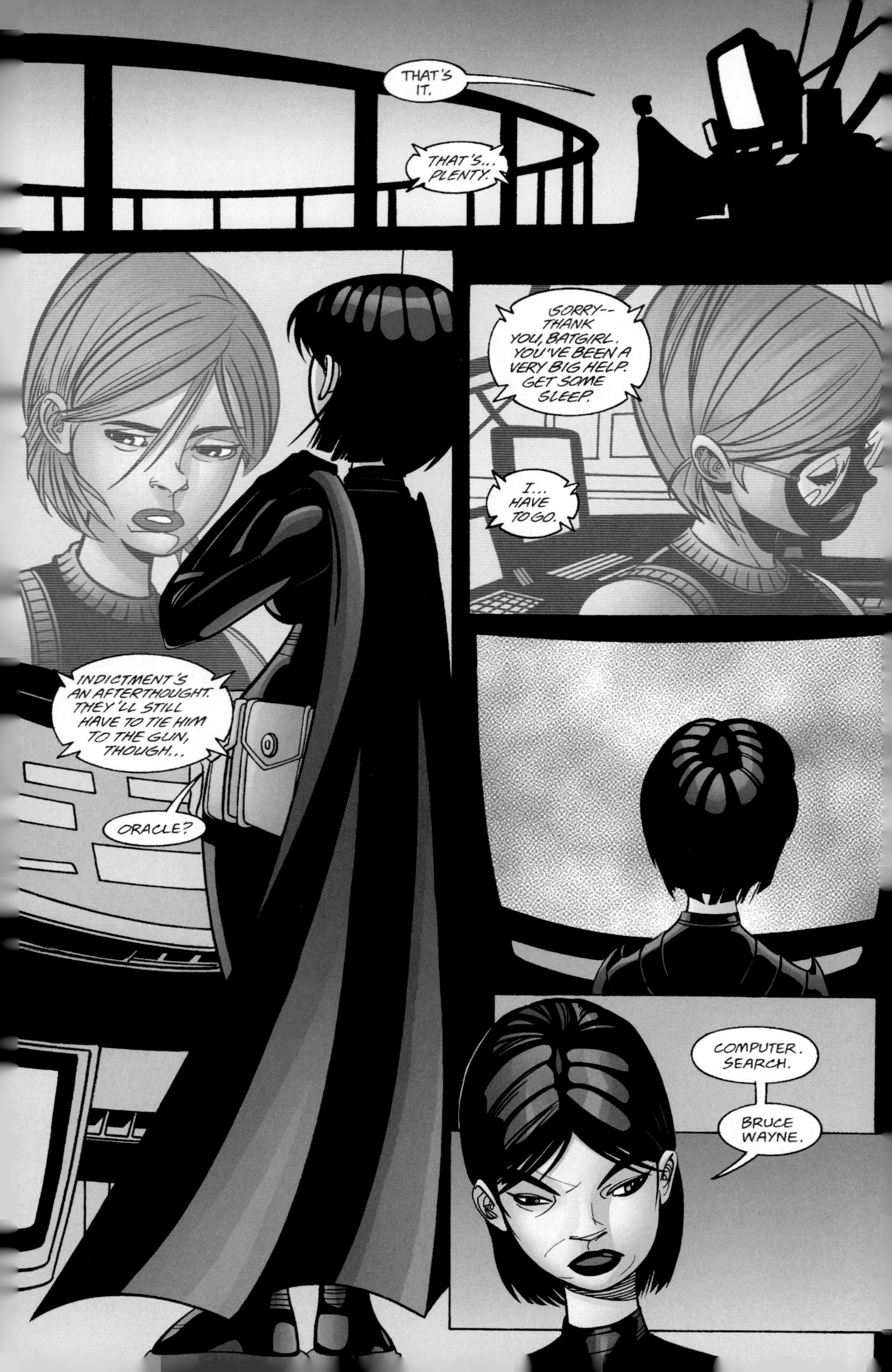
THAT'S IT.
THAT'S... PLENTY.
SORRY-- THANK YOU, BATGIRL. YOU'VE BEEN A VERY BIG HELP. GET SOME SLEEP.
I... HAVE TO GO.
INDICTMENT'S AN AFTERTHOUGHT. THEY'LL STILL HAVE TO TIE HIM TO THE GUN, THOUGH...
ORACLE?
COMPUTER. SEARCH.
BRUCE WAYNE.

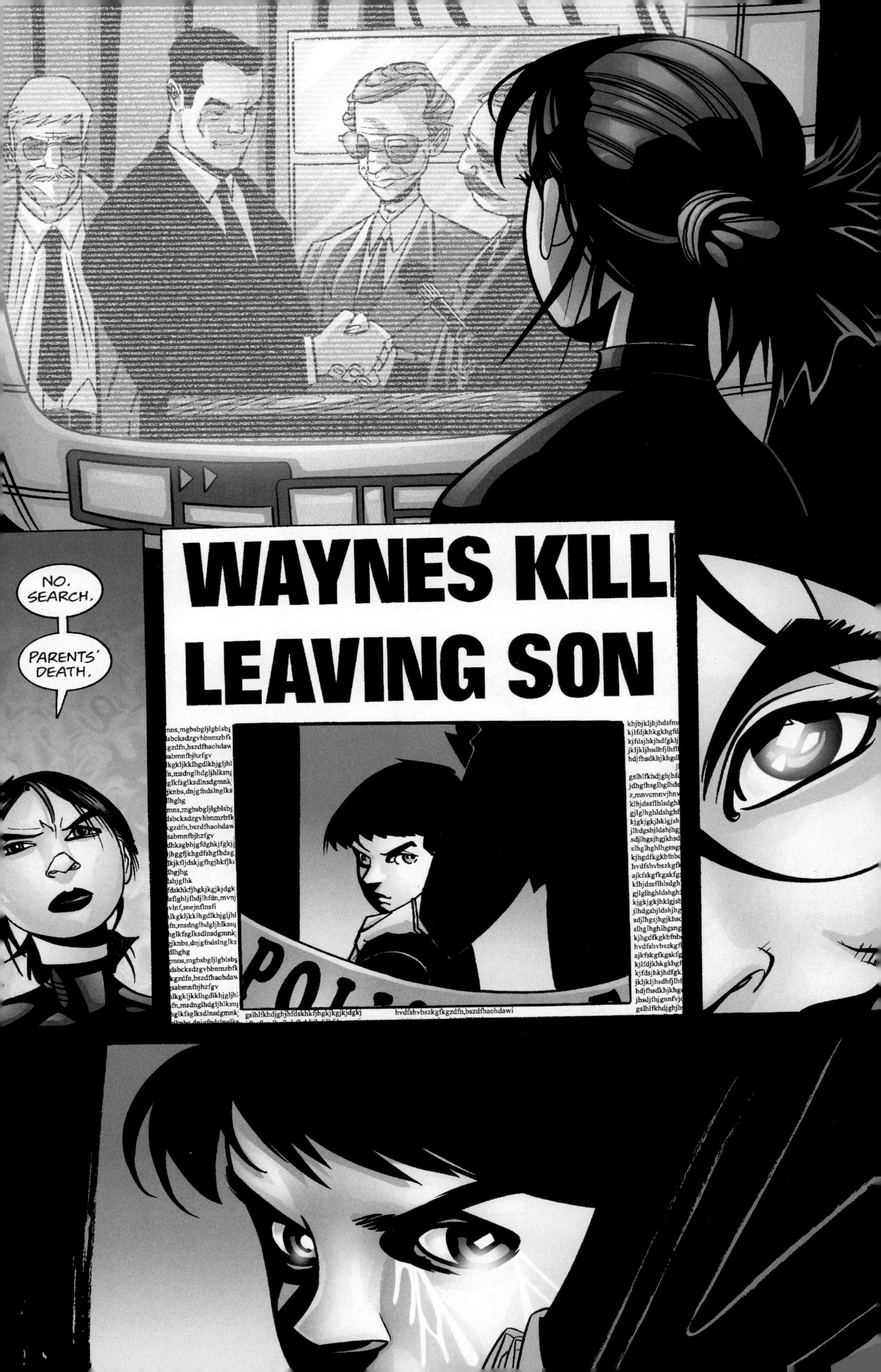
NO. SEARCH.
PARENTS' DEATH.
WAYNES KILL
LEAVING SON

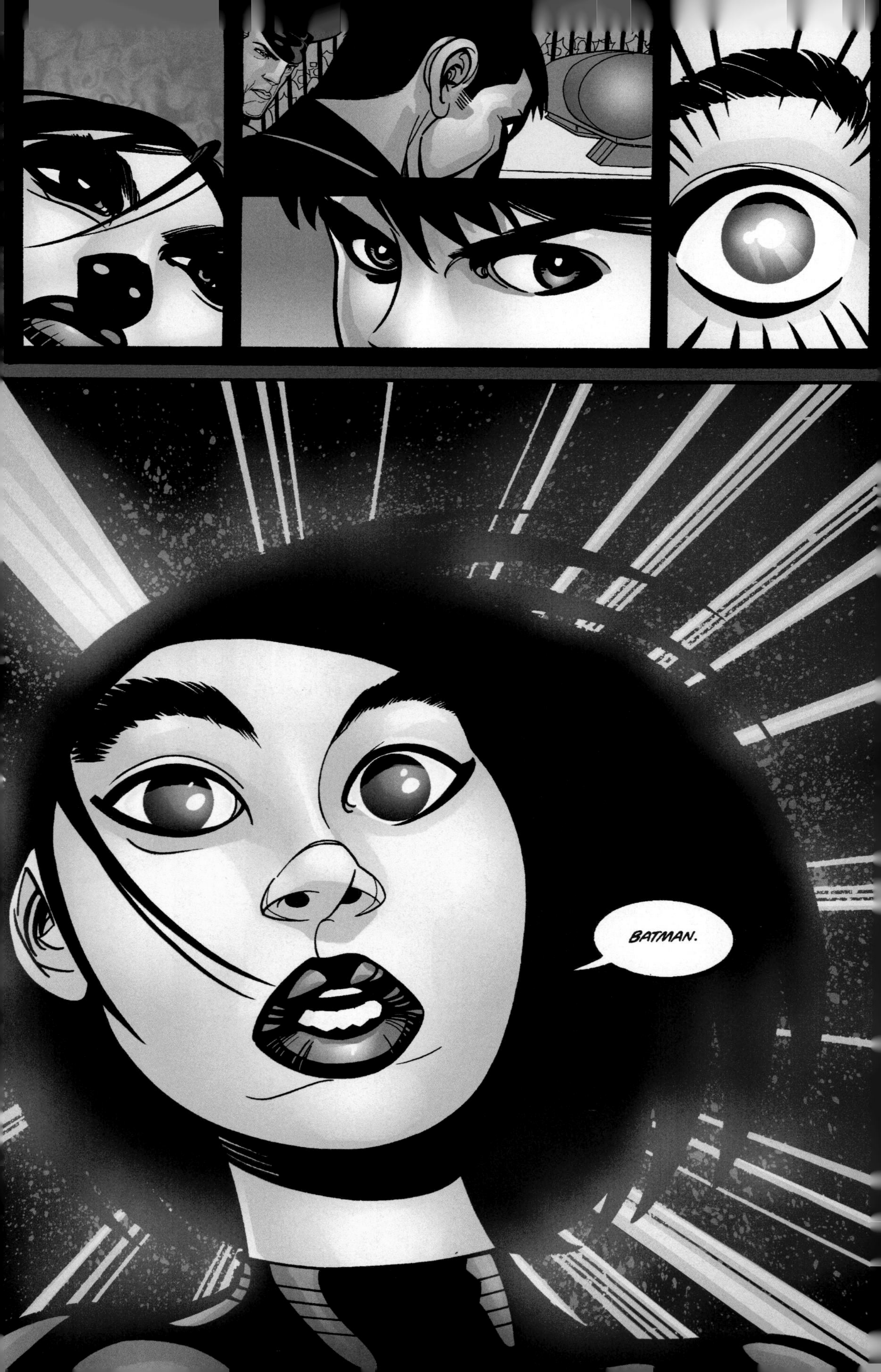
BATMAN.

BATGIRL #25 cover by Damion Scott,
Robert Campanella & Patrick Martin

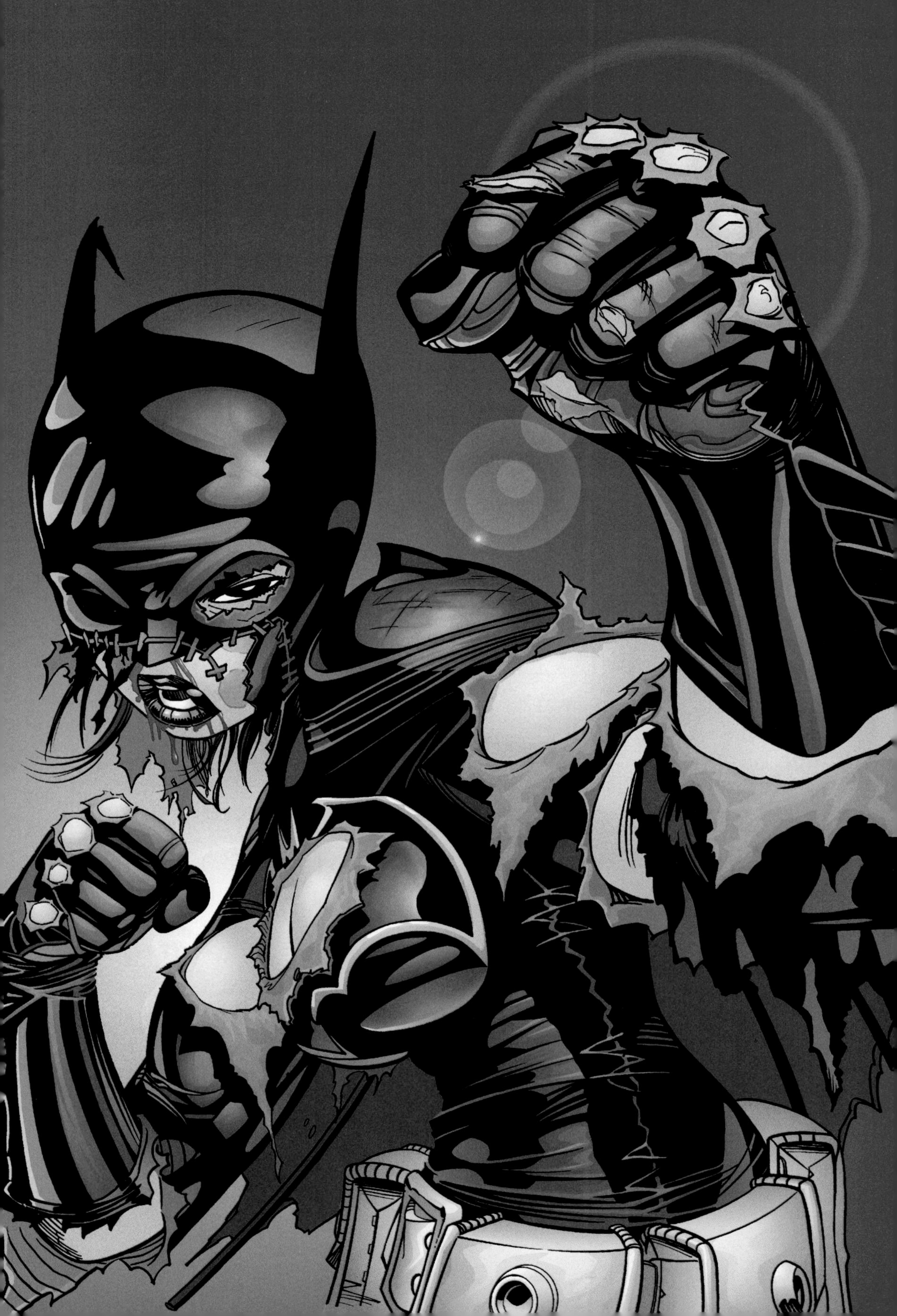

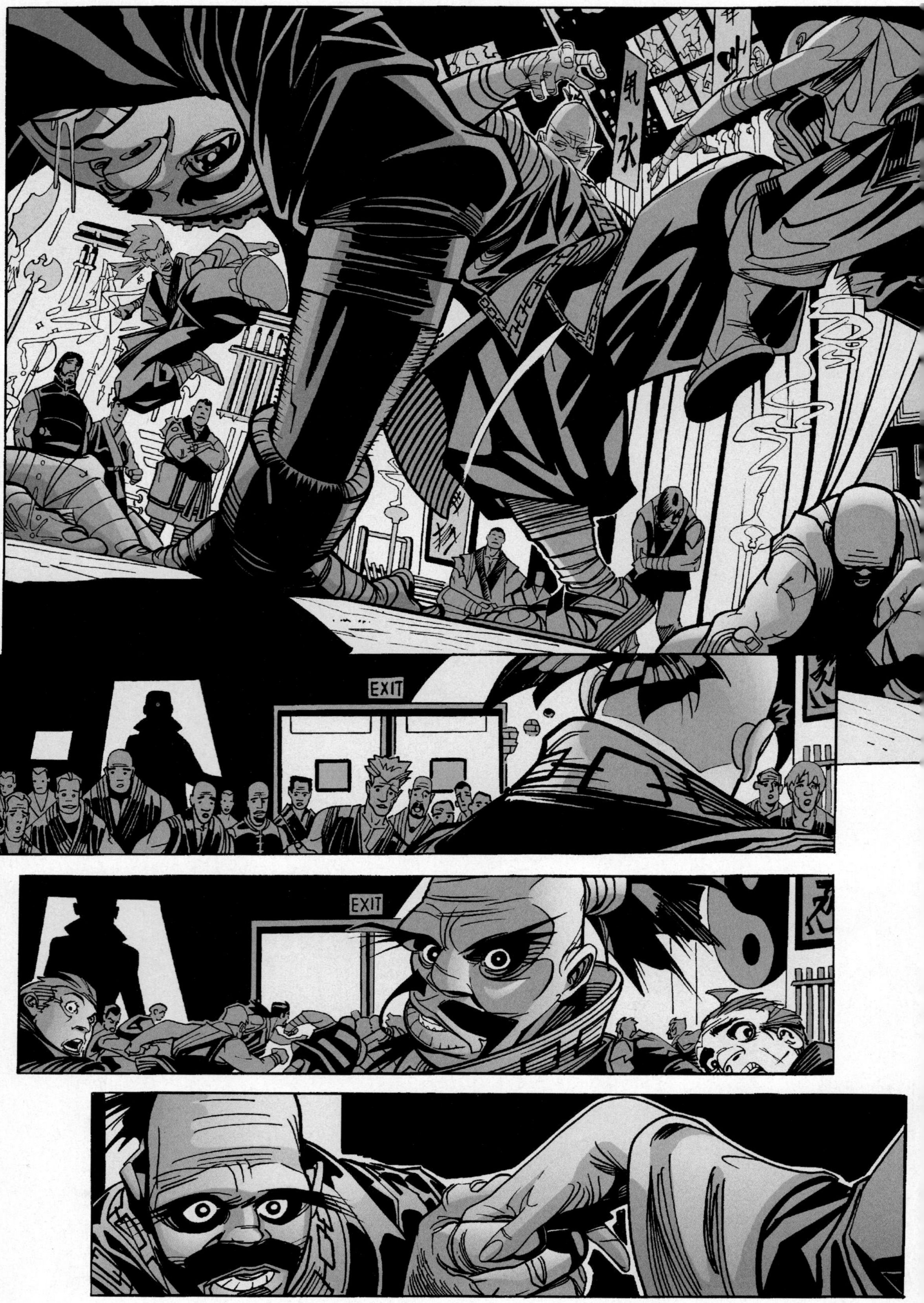
EXIT
EXIT

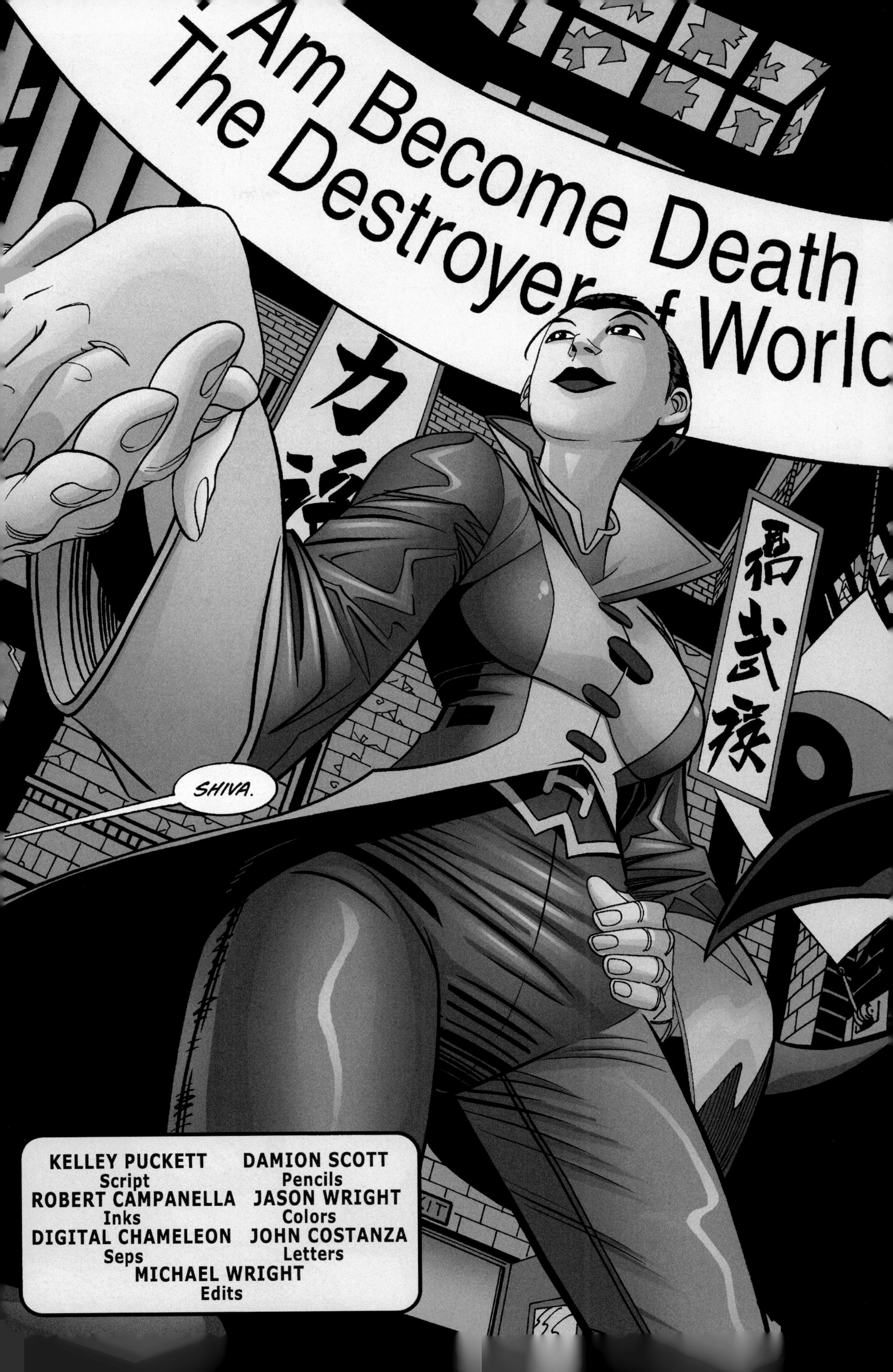
Am Become Death
The Destroyer f Worl
SHIVA.
KELLEY PUCKETT Script
DAMION SCOTT Pencils
ROBERT CAMPANELLA Inks
JASON WRIGHT Colors
DIGITAL CHAMELEON Seps
JOHN COSTANZA Letters
MICHAEL WRIGHT Edits

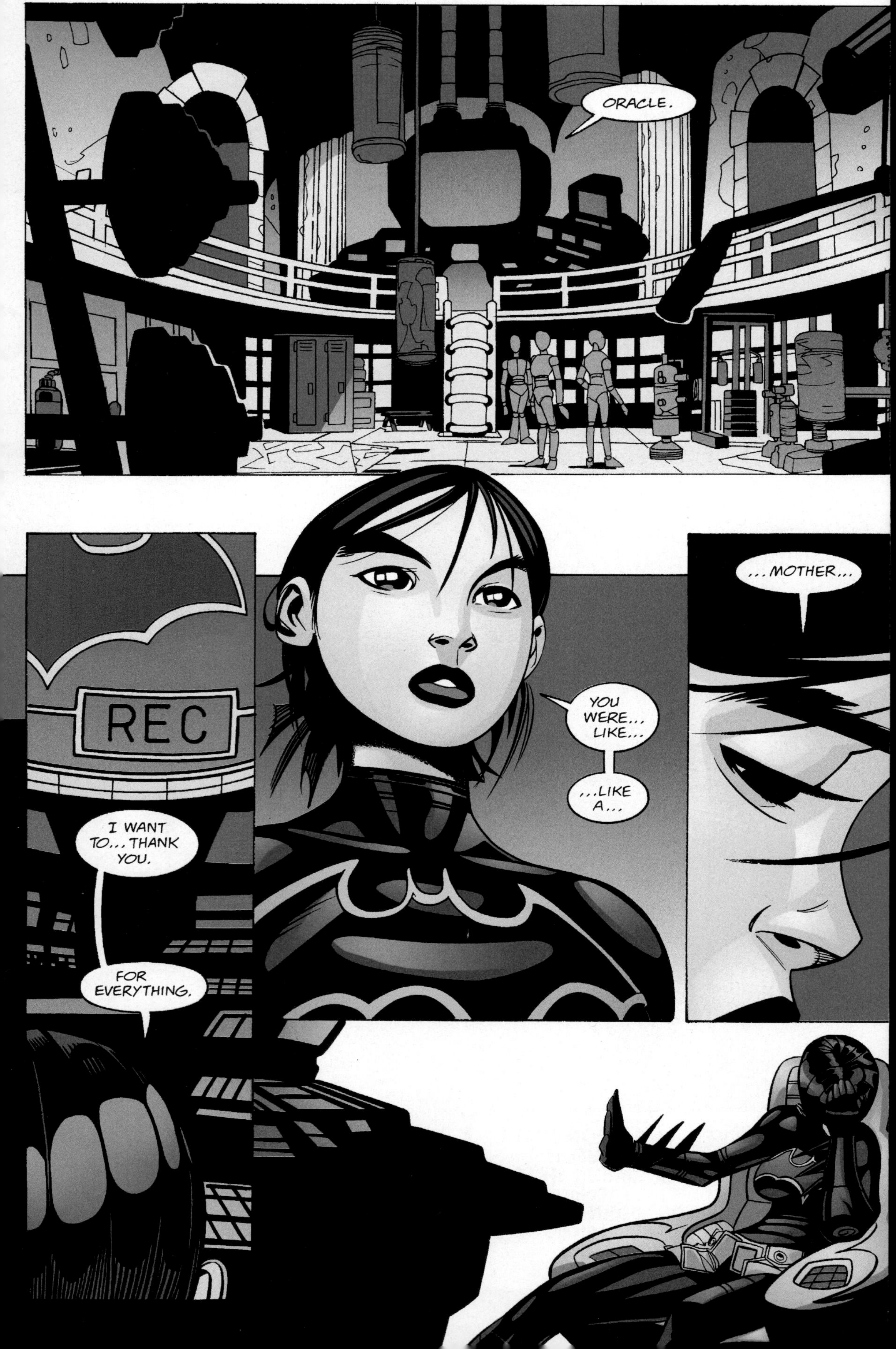
ORACLE.
YOU WERE... LIKE...
...LIKE A...
...MOTHER...
I WANT TO... THANK YOU.
FOR EVERYTHING.

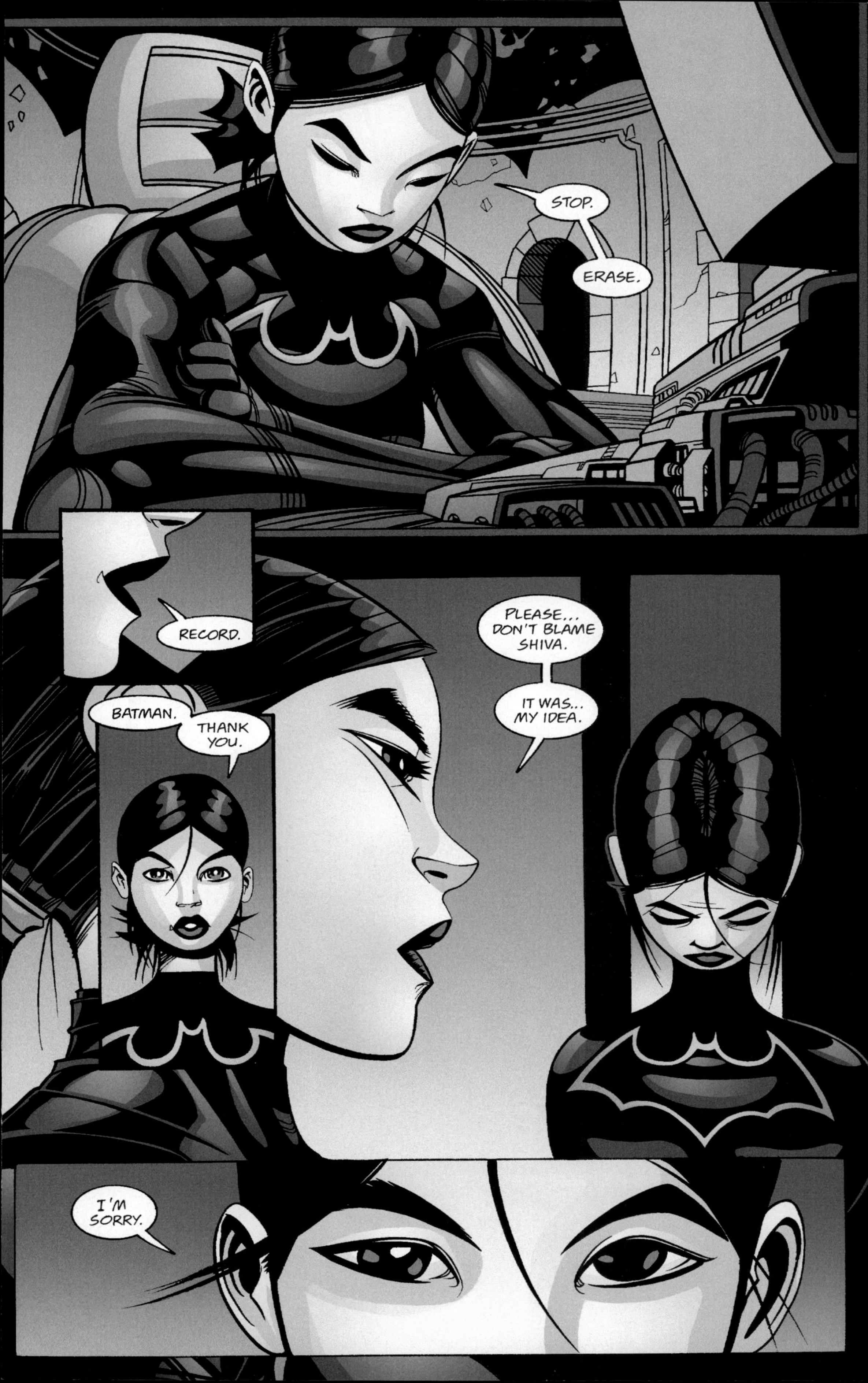
STOP.
ERASE.
RECORD.
BATMAN.
THANK YOU.
PLEASE... DON'T BLAME SHIVA.
IT WAS... MY IDEA.
I'M SORRY.

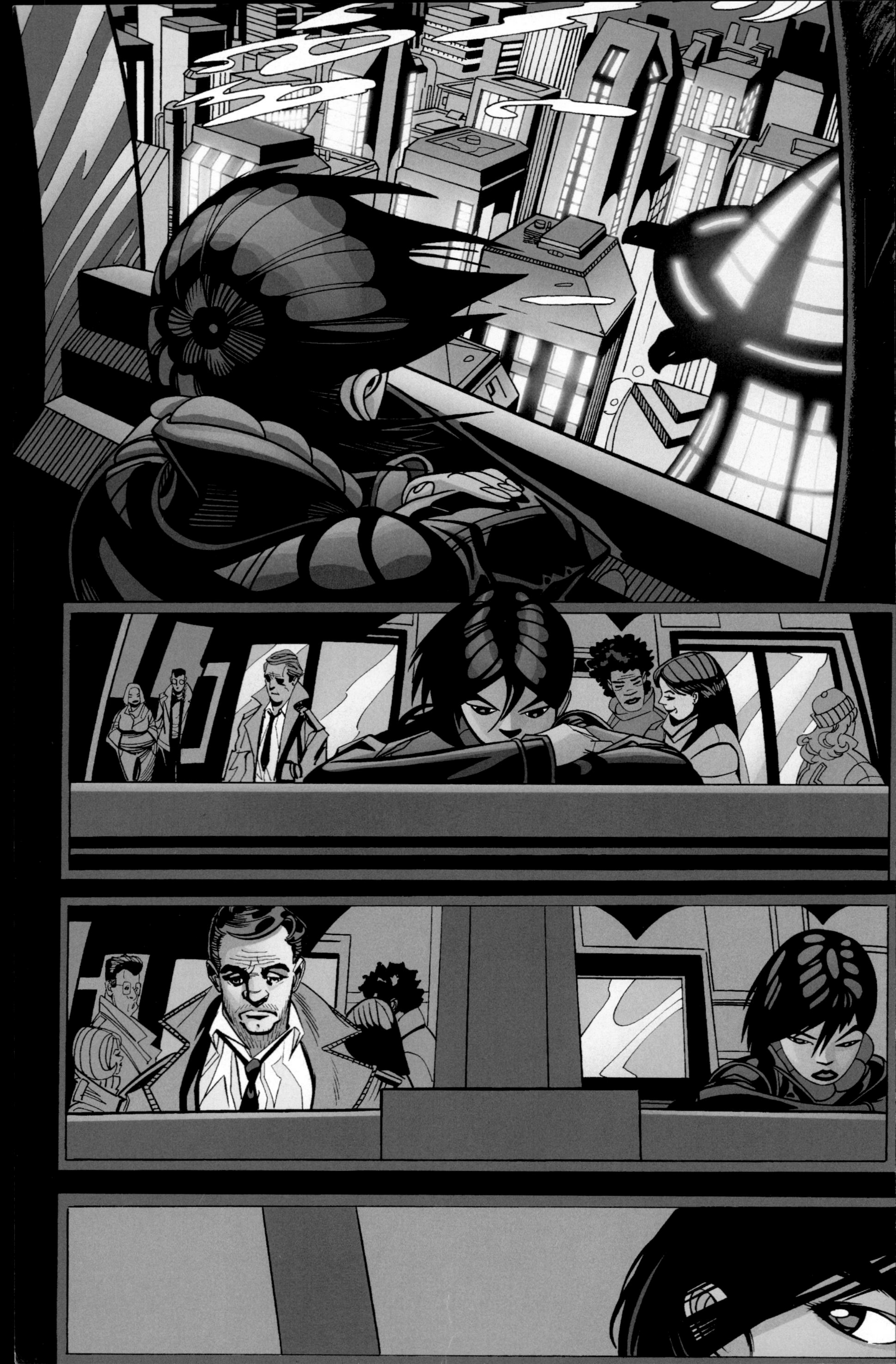

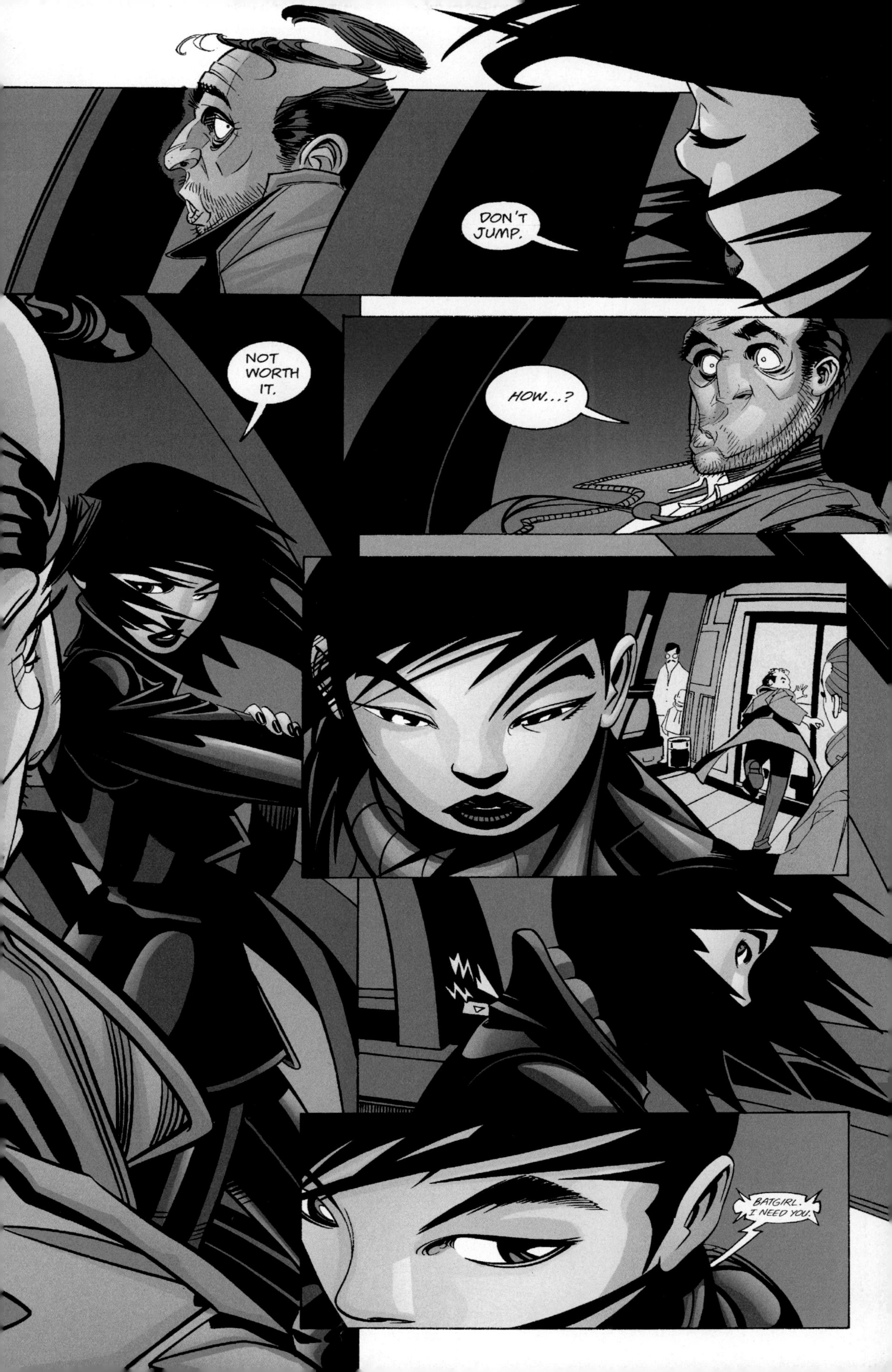
DON'T JUMP.
NOT WORTH IT.
HOW...?
BATGIRL. I NEED YOU.

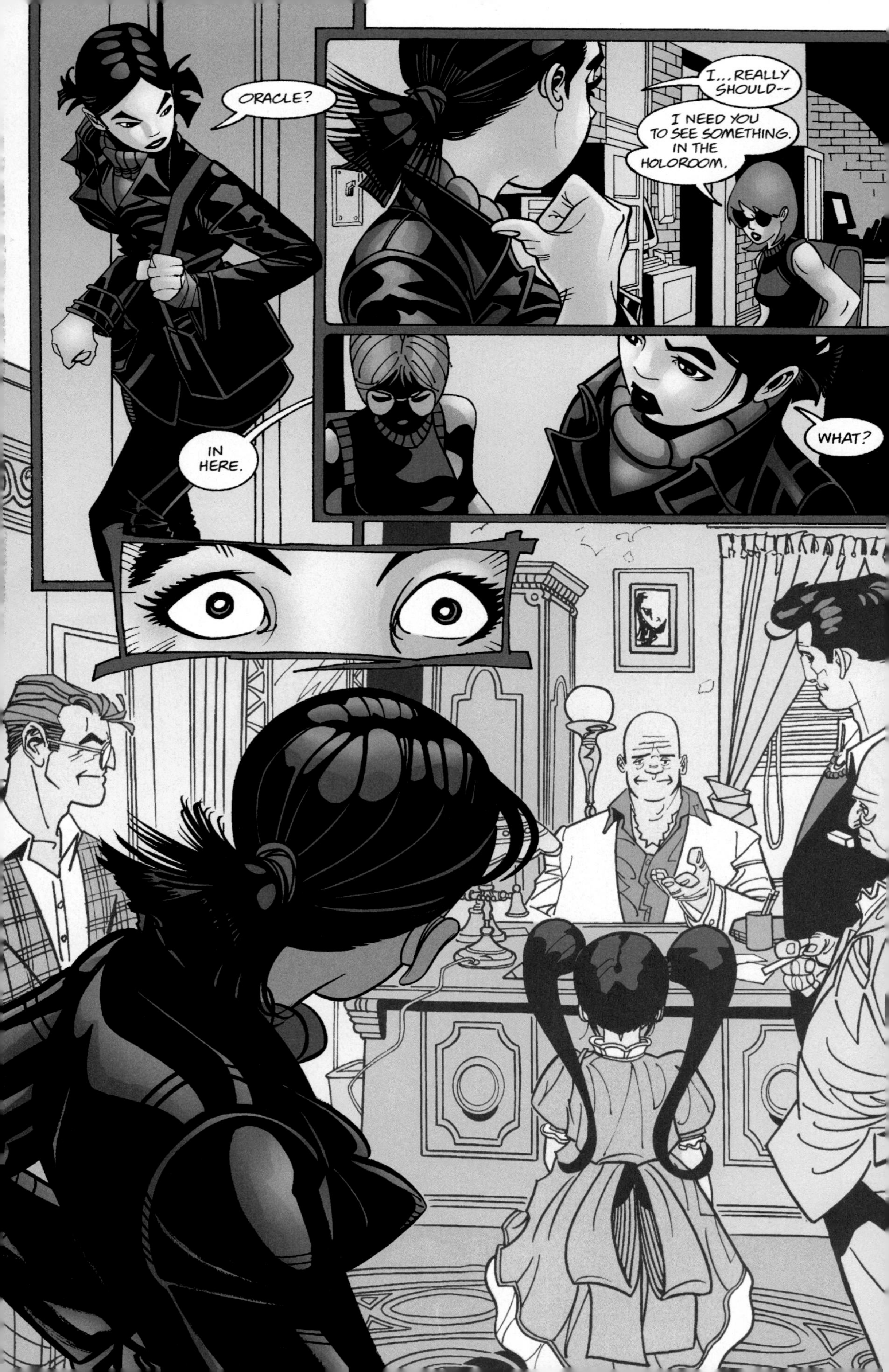
ORACLE?
I... REALLY SHOULD--
I NEED YOU TO SEE SOMETHING. IN THE HOLOROOM.
IN HERE.
WHAT?

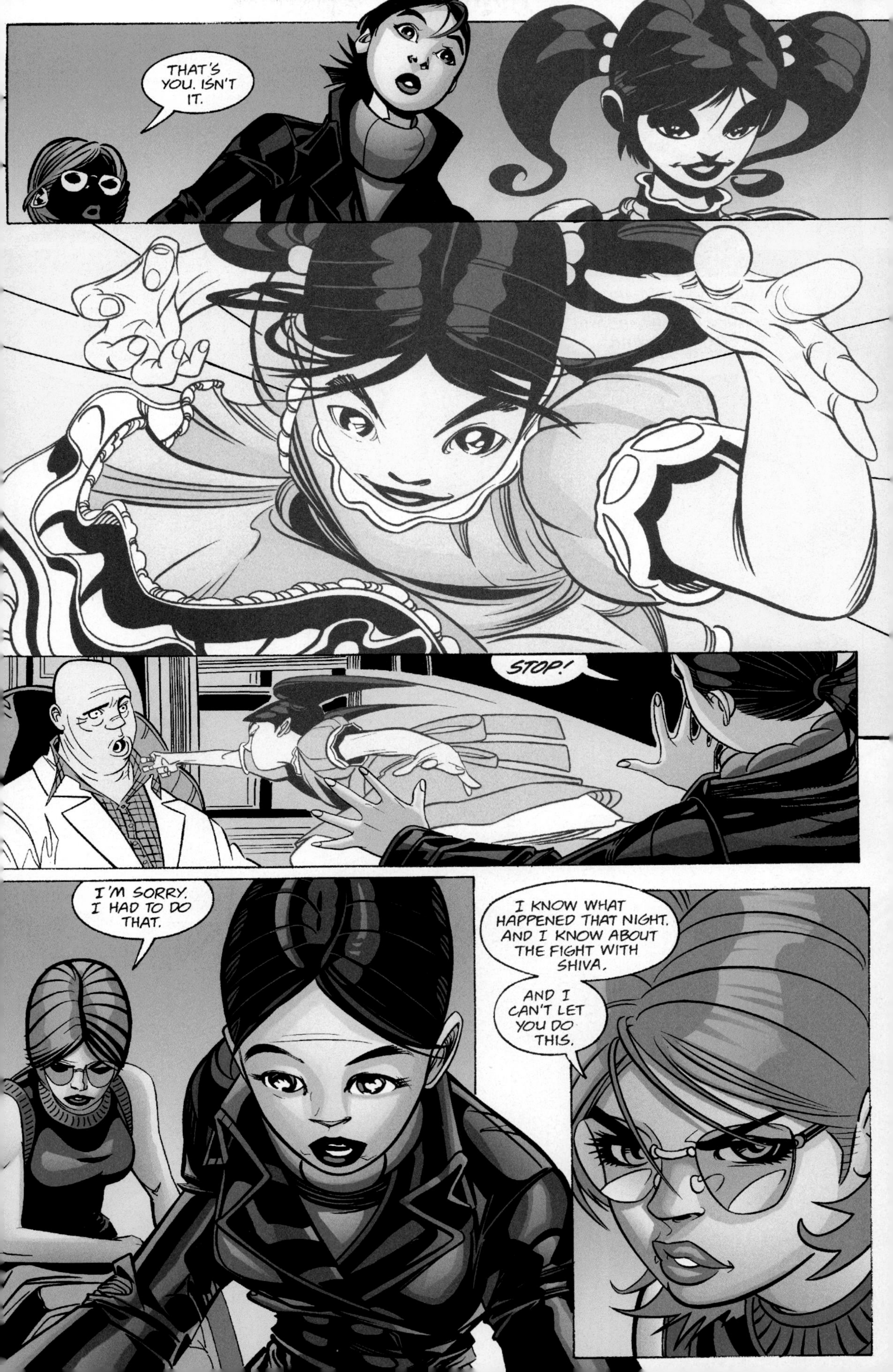
THAT'S YOU. ISN'T IT.
STOP!
I'M SORRY. I HAD TO DO THAT.
I KNOW WHAT HAPPENED THAT NIGHT. AND I KNOW ABOUT THE FIGHT WITH SHIVA.
AND I CAN'T LET YOU DO THIS.

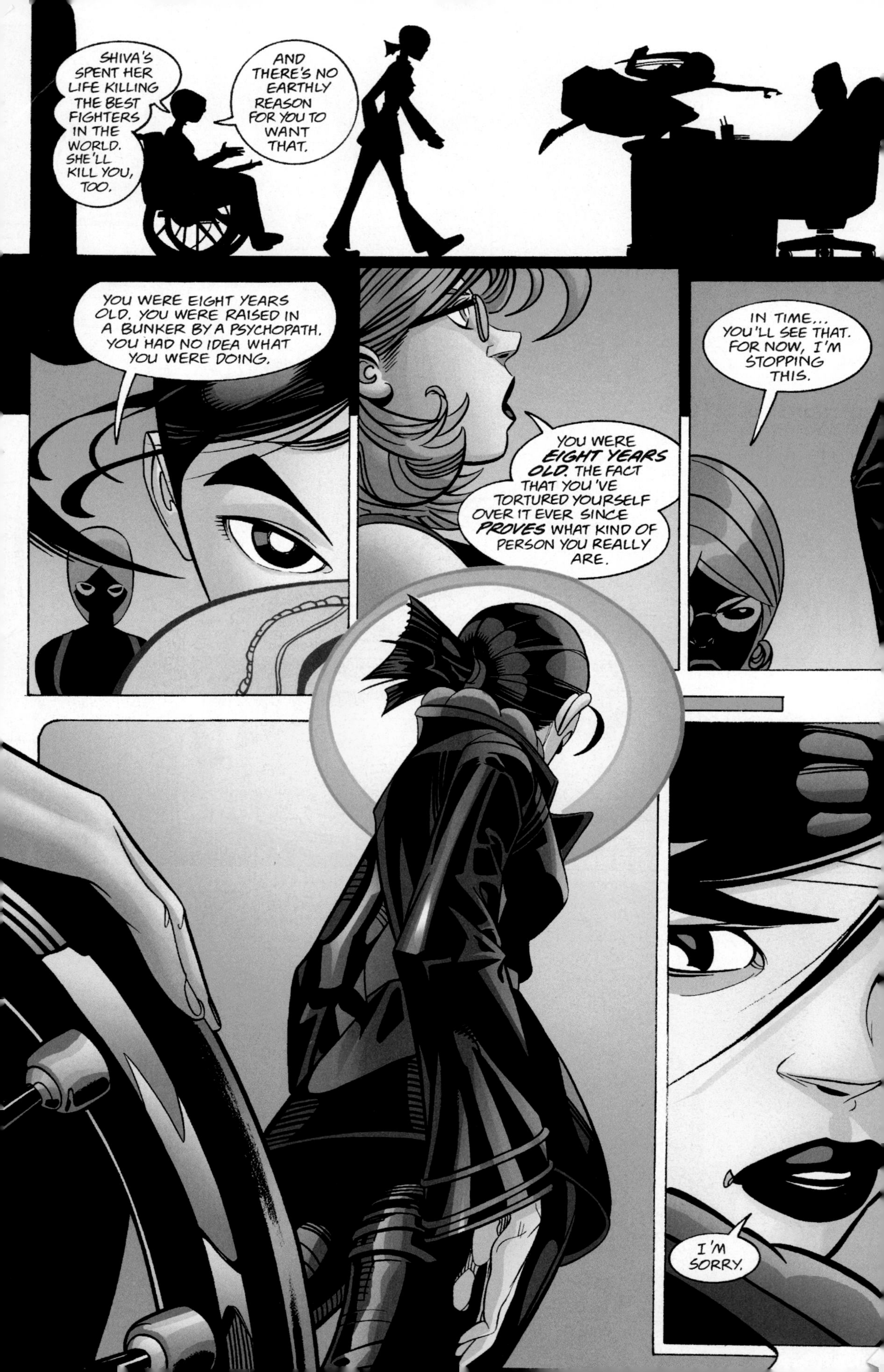
SHIVA'S SPENT HER LIFE KILLING THE BEST FIGHTERS IN THE WORLD. SHE'LL KILL YOU, TOO.
AND THERE'S NO EARTHLY REASON FOR YOU TO WANT THAT.
YOU WERE EIGHT YEARS OLD. YOU WERE RAISED IN A BUNKER BY A PSYCHOPATH. YOU HAD NO IDEA WHAT YOU WERE DOING.
YOU WERE EIGHT YEARS OLD. THE FACT THAT YOU'VE TORTURED YOURSELF OVER IT EVER SINCE PROVES WHAT KIND OF PERSON YOU REALLY ARE.
IN TIME... YOU'LL SEE THAT. FOR NOW, I'M STOPPING THIS.
I'M SORRY.

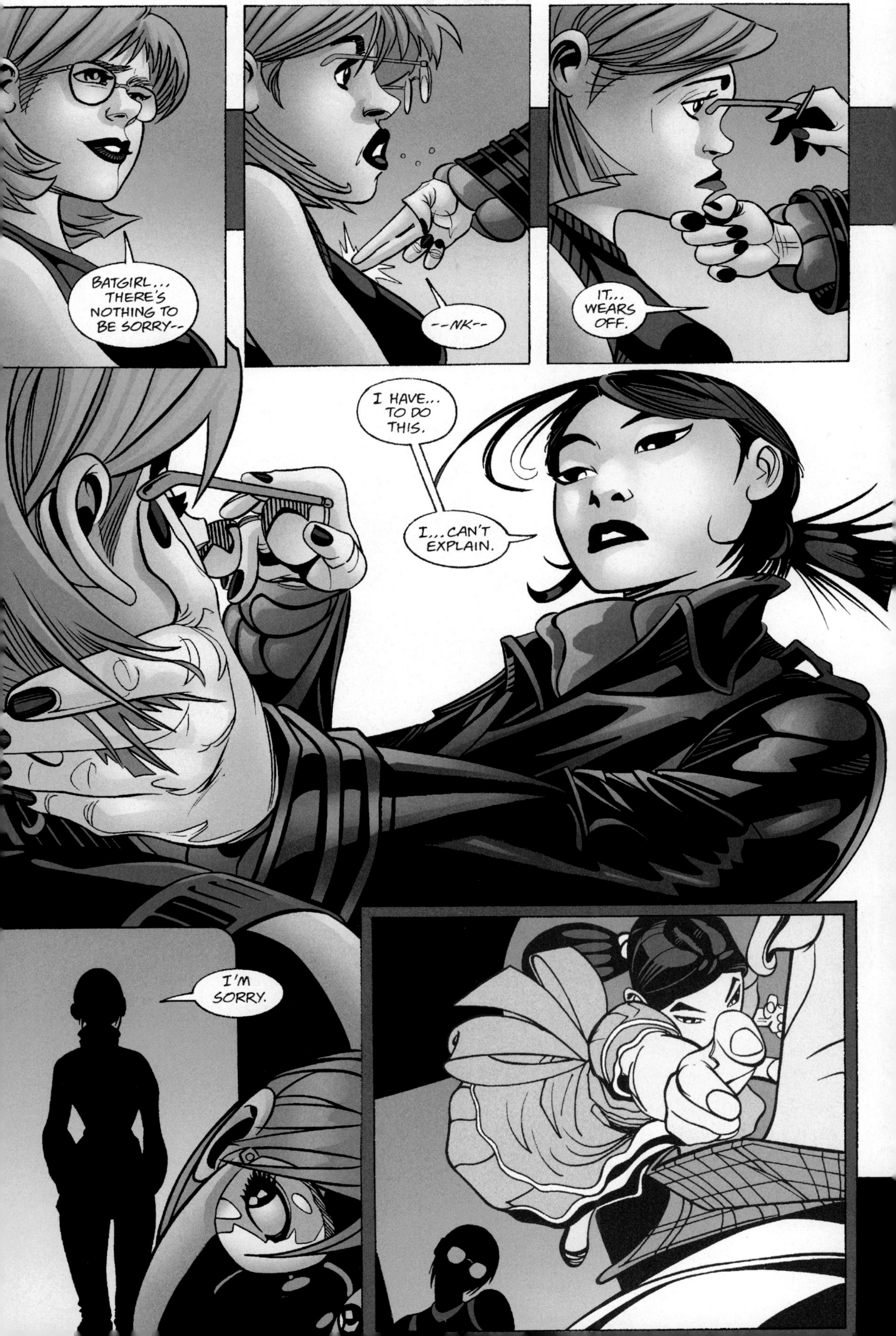
BATGIRL... THERE'S NOTHING TO BE SORRY--
--NK--
IT... WEARS OFF.
I HAVE... TO DO THIS.
I...CAN'T EXPLAIN.
I'M SORRY.

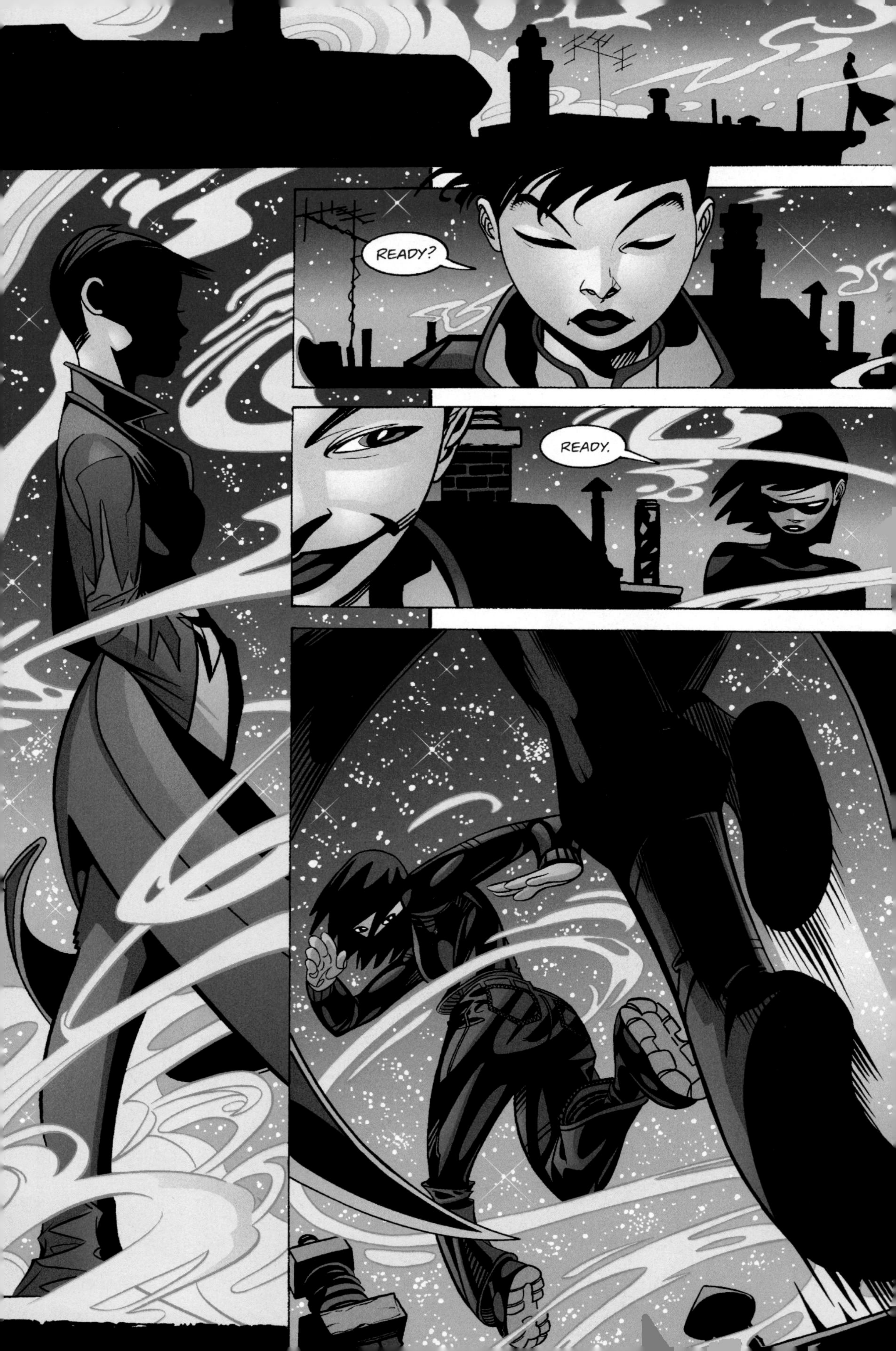
READY?
READY.

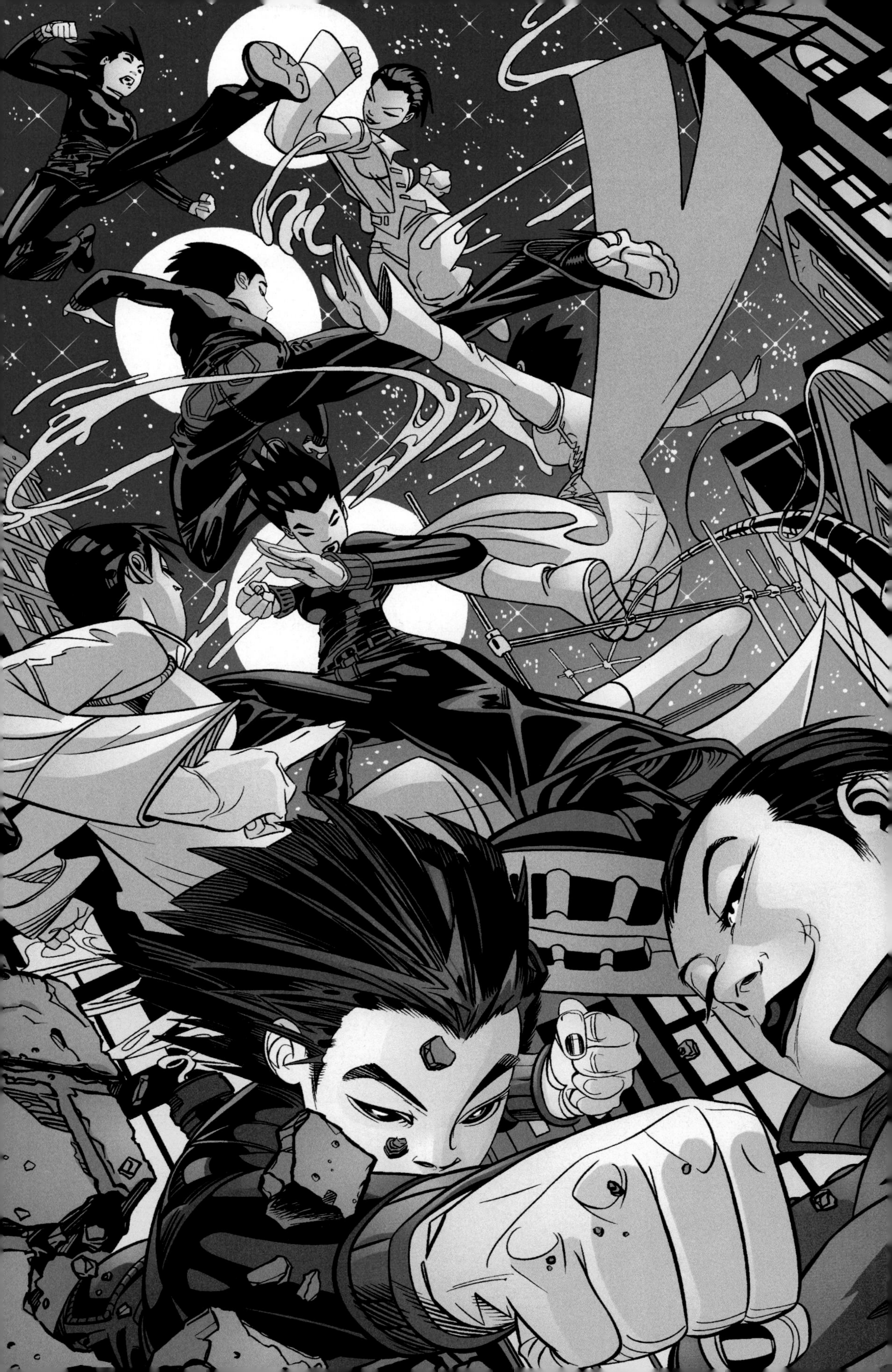

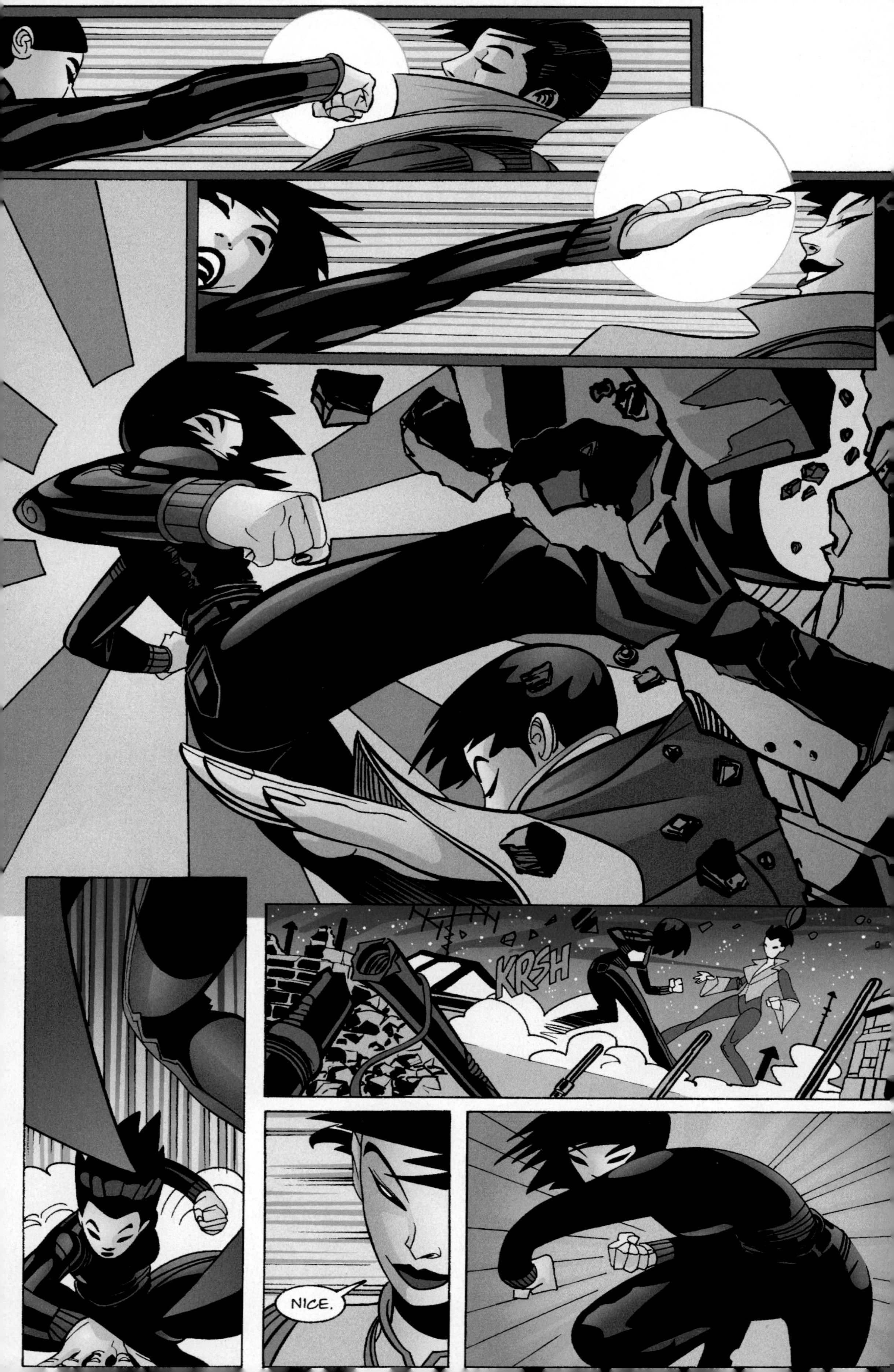
KRSH
NICE.

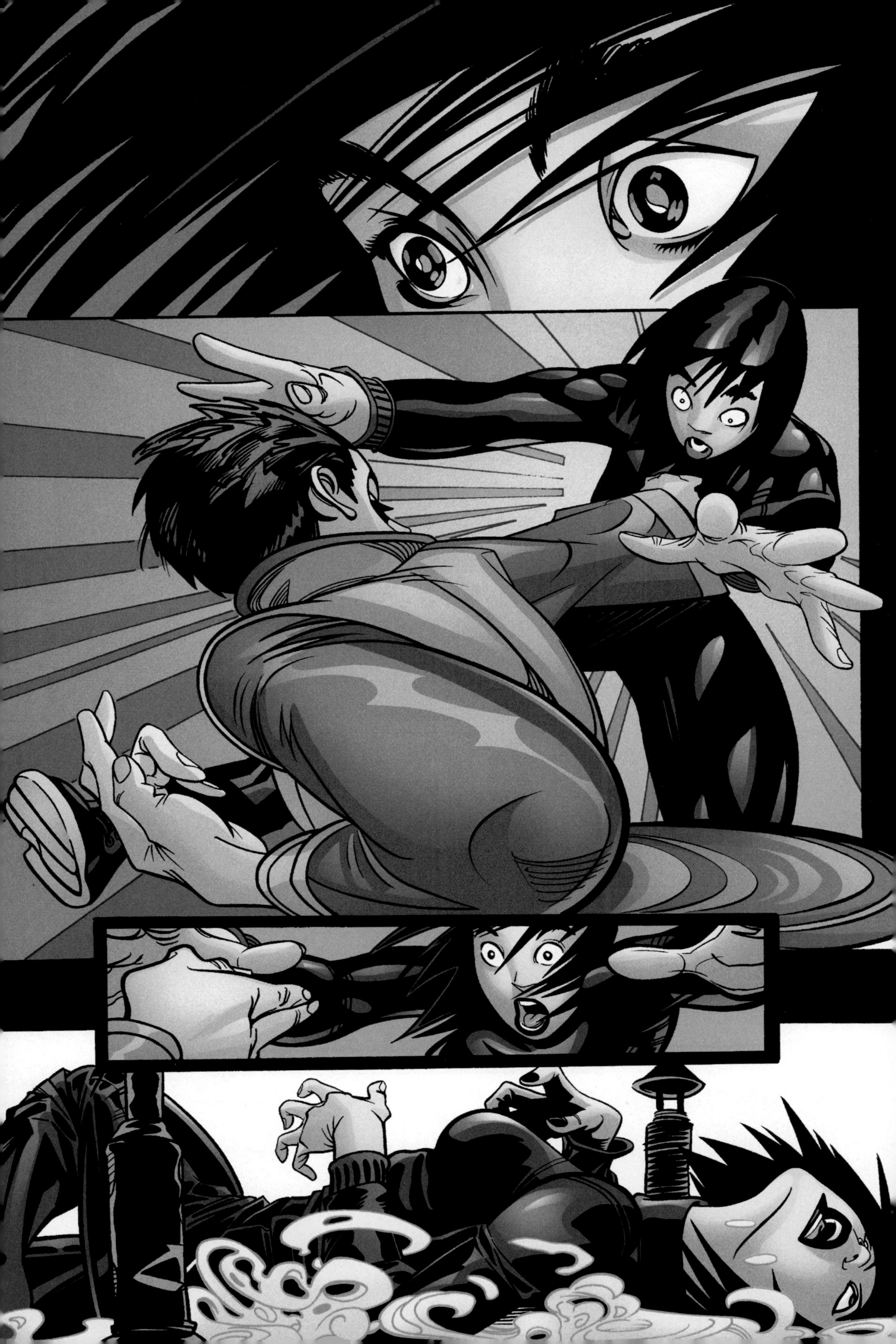

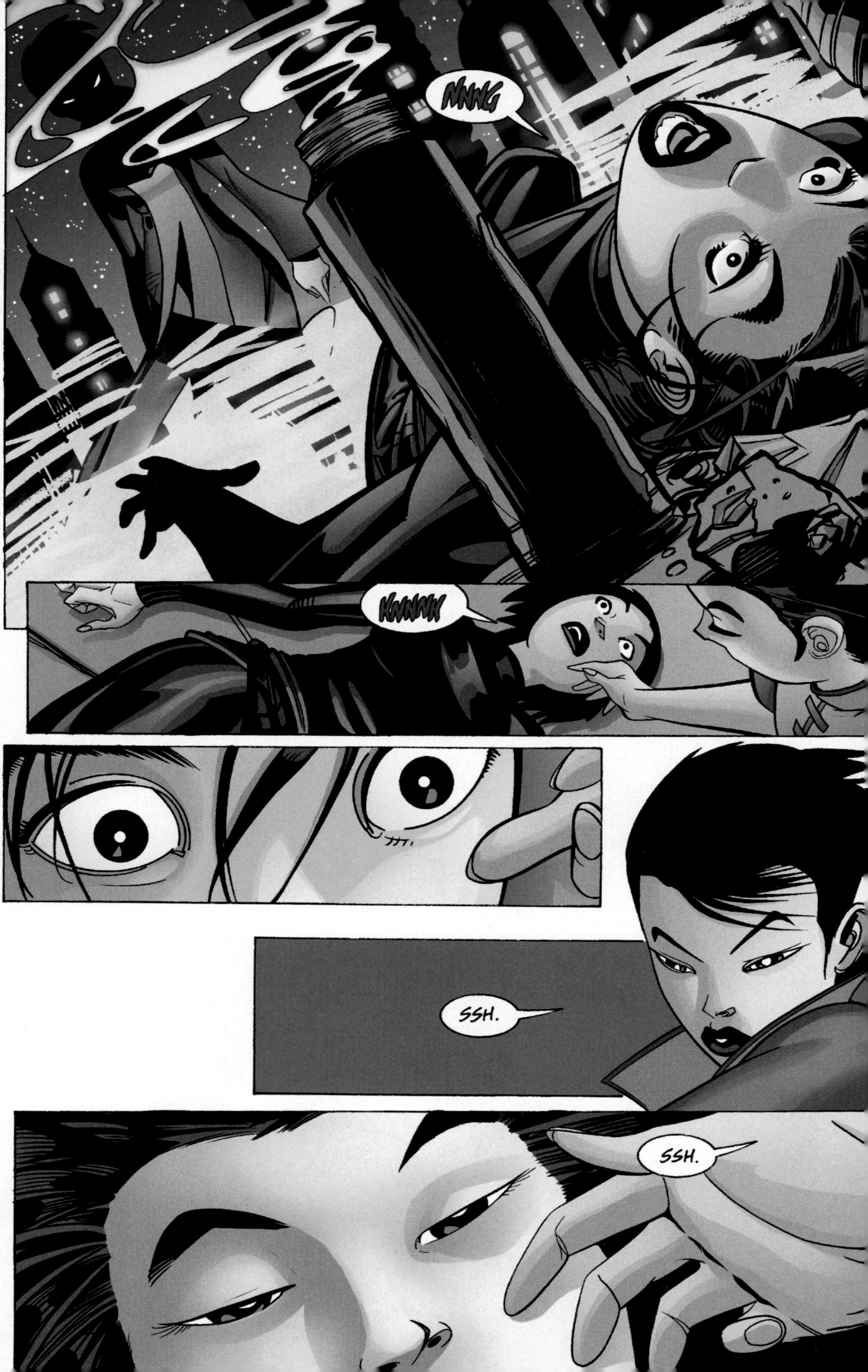
NNNG
KNNNK
SSH.
SSH.

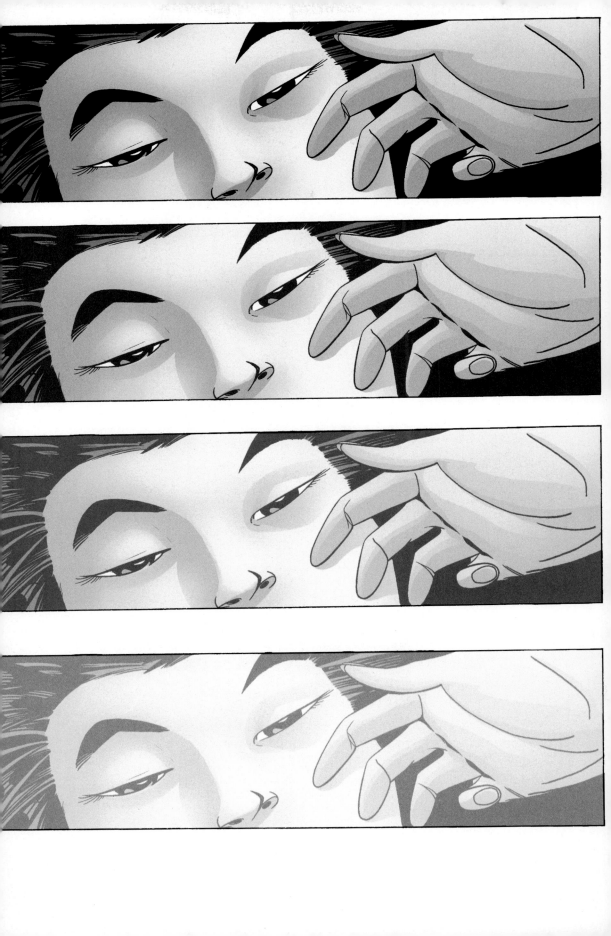

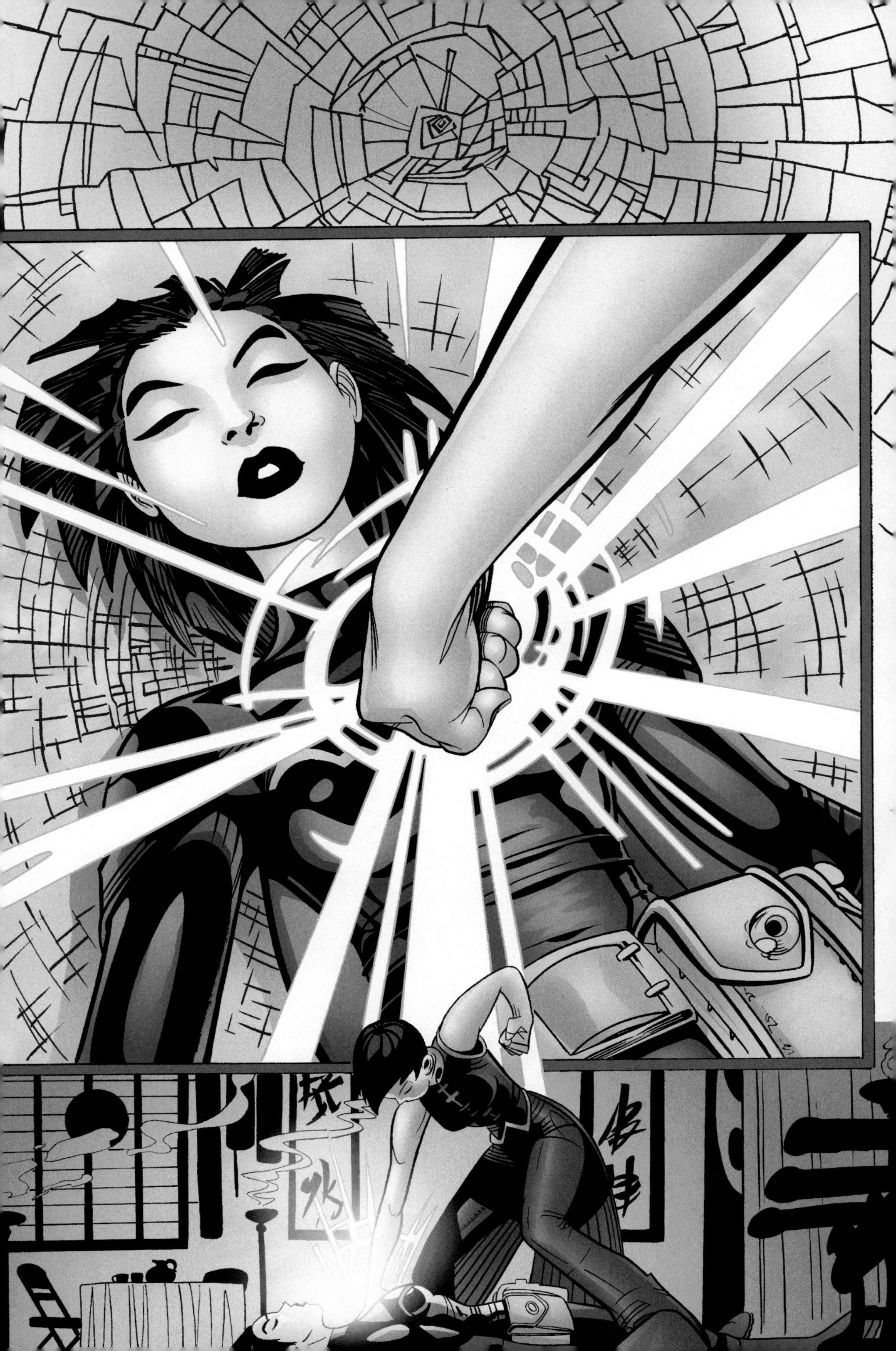

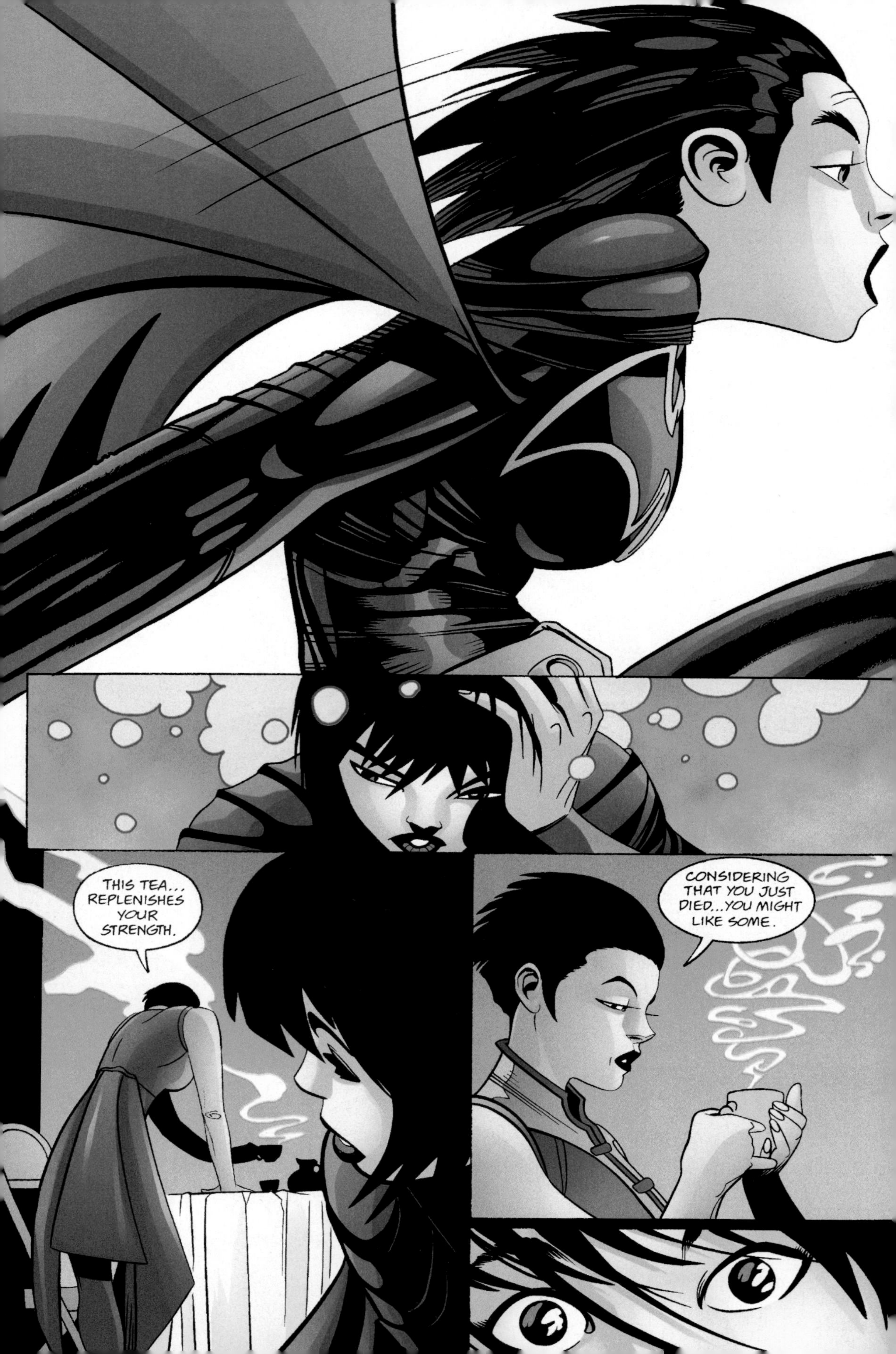
THIS TEA... REPLENISHES YOUR STRENGTH.
CONSIDERING THAT YOU JUST DIED...YOU MIGHT LIKE SOME.

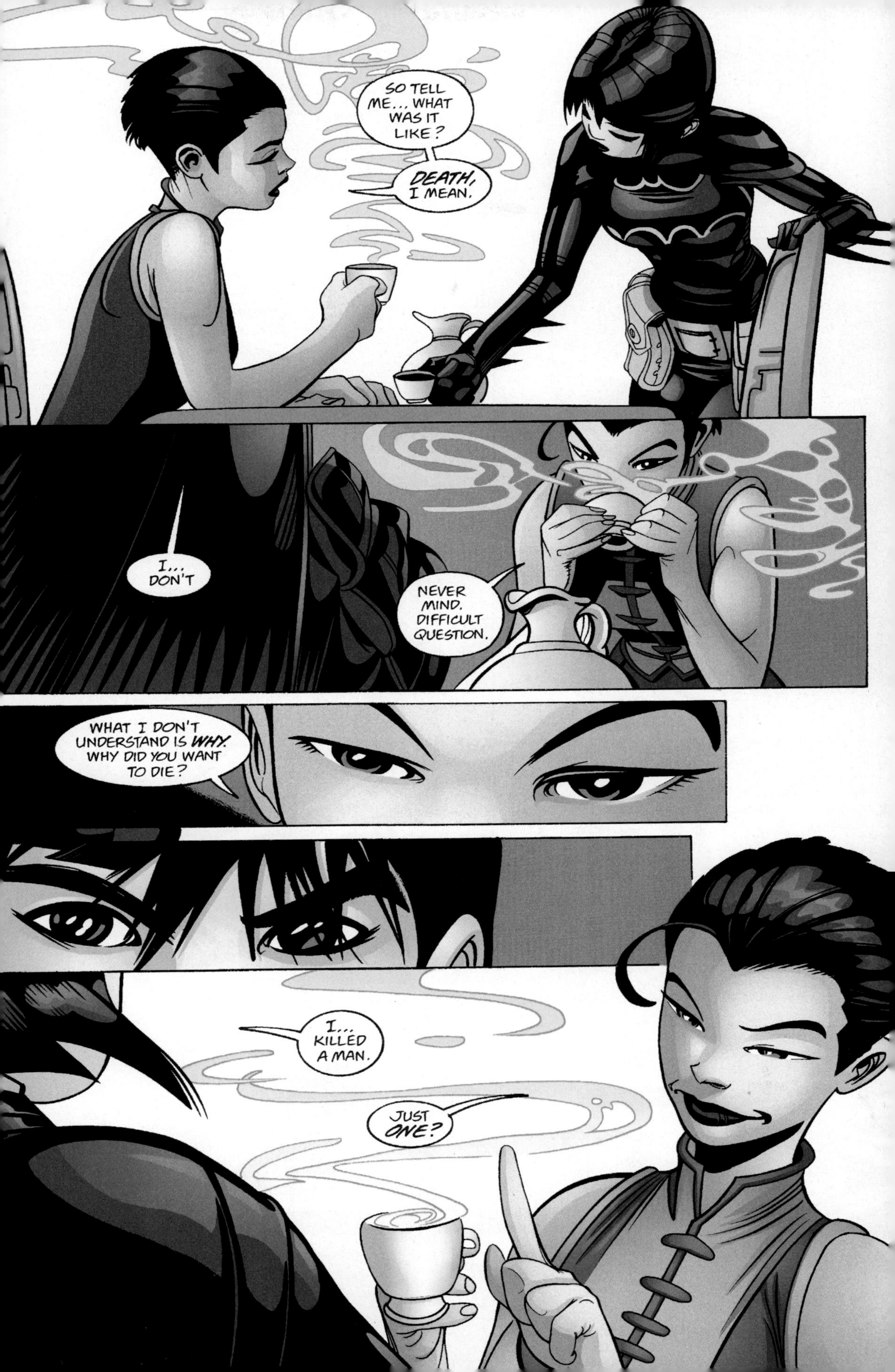
SO TELL ME... WHAT WAS IT LIKE?
DEATH, I MEAN.
I... DON'T
NEVER MIND. DIFFICULT QUESTION.
WHAT I DON'T UNDERSTAND IS WHY. WHY DID YOU WANT TO DIE?
I... KILLED A MAN.
JUST ONE?

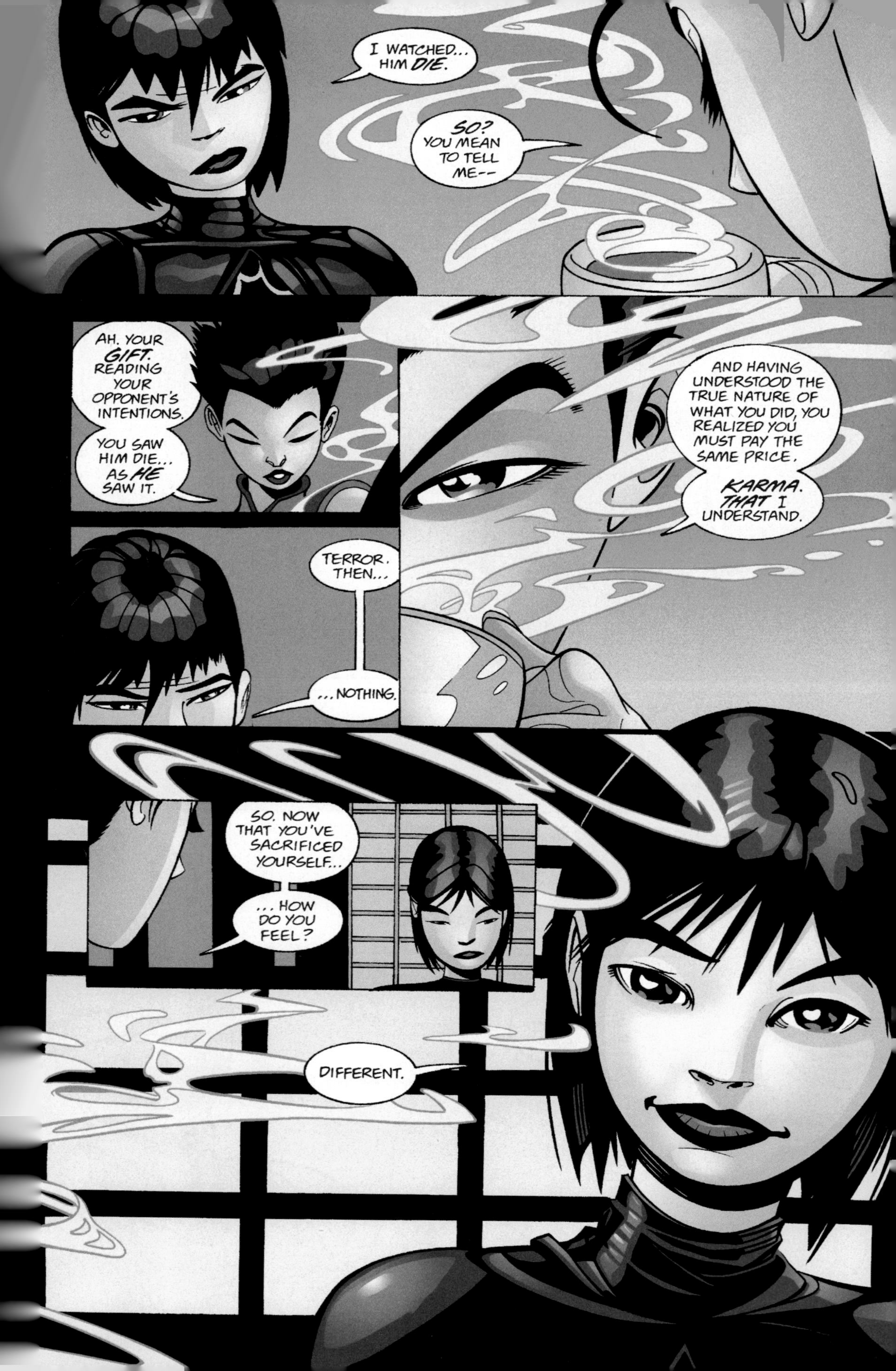
I WATCHED... HIM DIE.
SO? YOU MEAN TO TELL ME--
AH. YOUR GIFT. READING YOUR OPPONENT'S INTENTIONS.
YOU SAW HIM DIE... AS HE SAW IT.
AND HAVING UNDERSTOOD THE TRUE NATURE OF WHAT YOU DID, YOU REALIZED YOU MUST PAY THE SAME PRICE.
KARMA. THAT I UNDERSTAND.
TERROR. THEN...
...NOTHING.
SO. NOW THAT YOU'VE SACRIFICED YOURSELF...
...HOW DO YOU FEEL?
DIFFERENT.

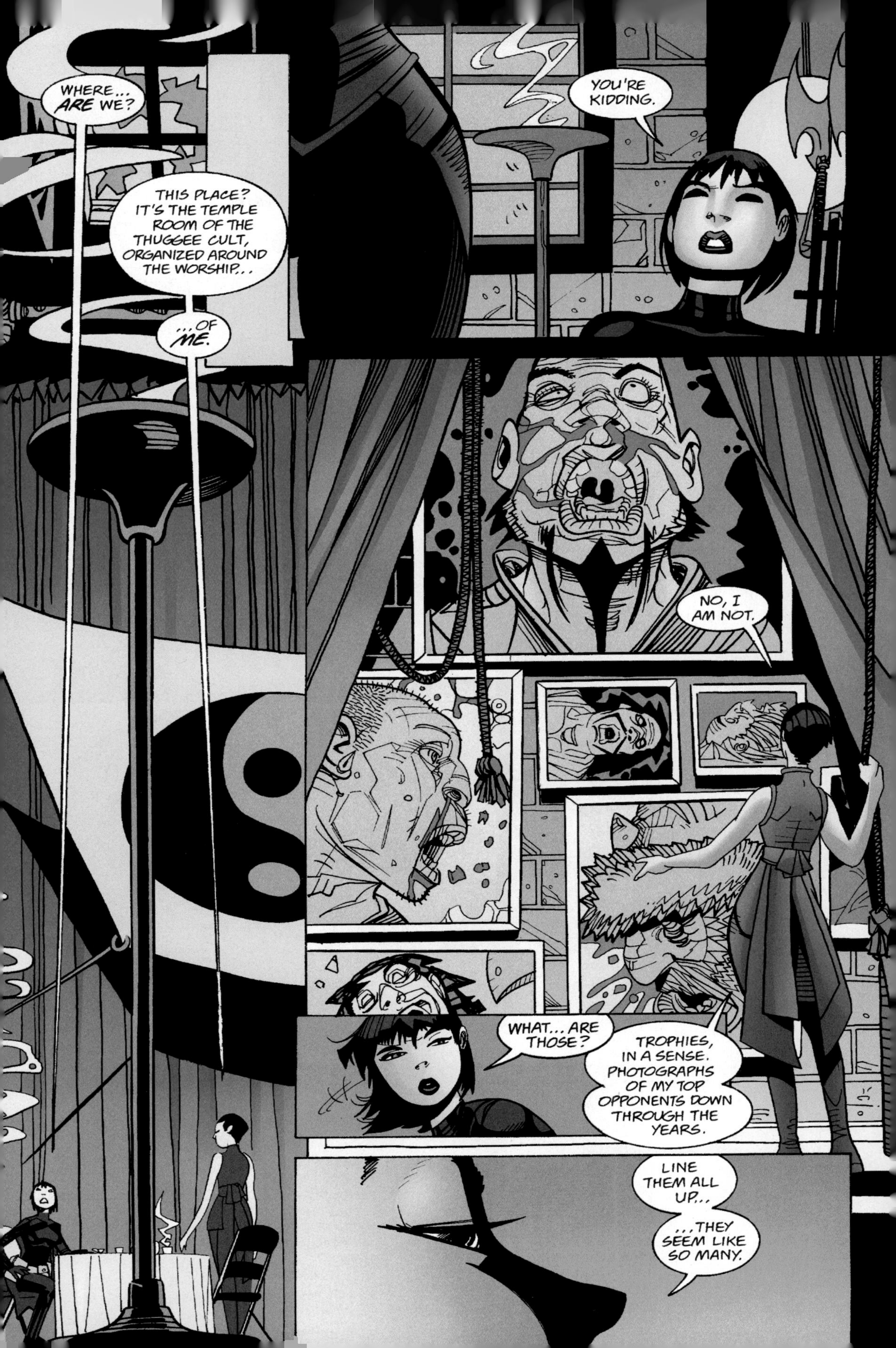
WHERE... ARE WE?
THIS PLACE? IT'S THE TEMPLE ROOM OF THE THUGGEE CULT, ORGANIZED AROUND THE WORSHIP...
...OF ME.
YOU'RE KIDDING.
NO, I AM NOT.
WHAT... ARE THOSE?
TROPHIES, IN A SENSE. PHOTOGRAPHS OF MY TOP OPPONENTS DOWN THROUGH THE YEARS.
LINE THEM ALL UP...
...THEY SEEM LIKE SO MANY.

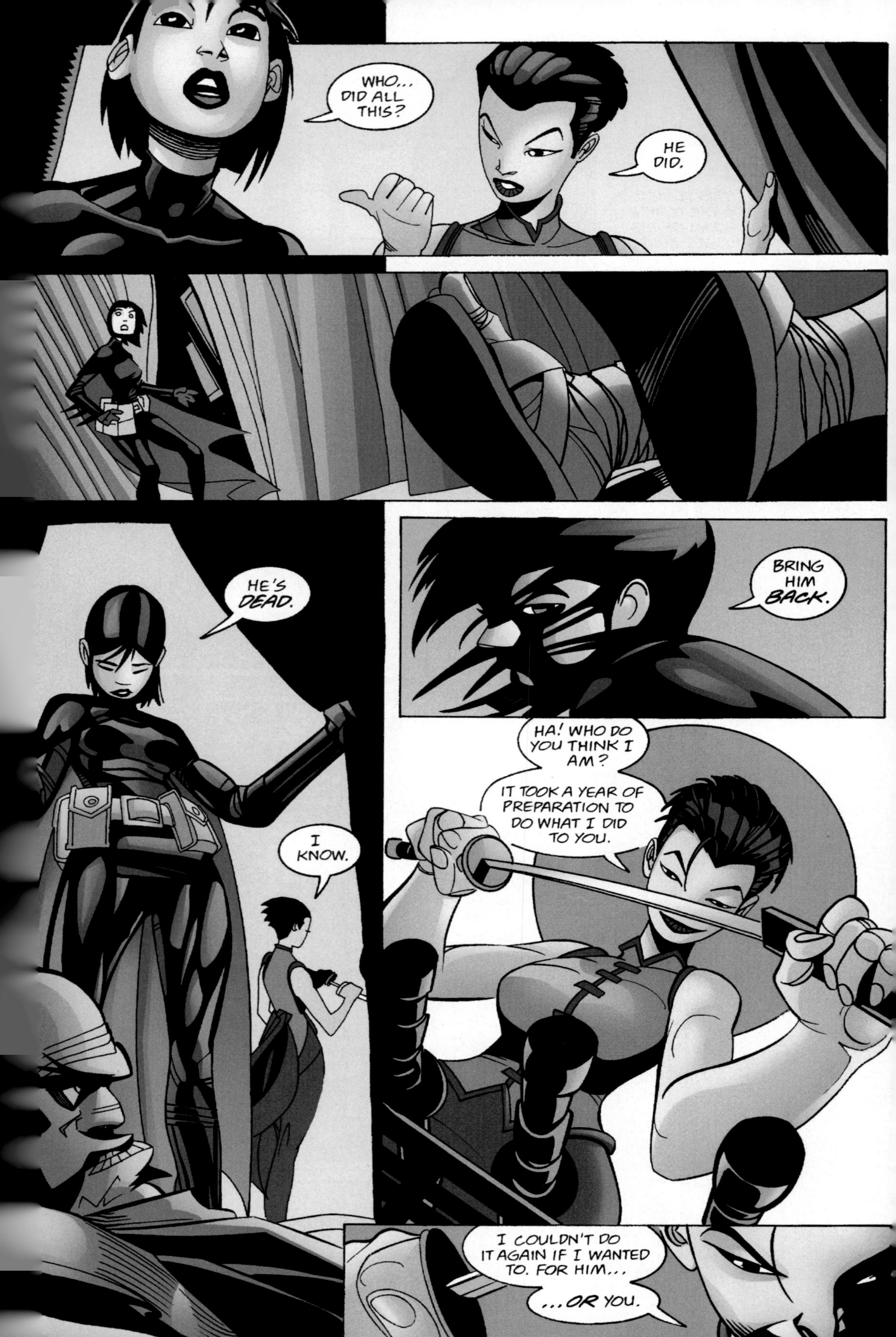
WHO... DID ALL THIS?
HE DID.
HE'S DEAD.
I KNOW.
BRING HIM BACK.
HA! WHO DO YOU THINK I AM?
IT TOOK A YEAR OF PREPARATION TO DO WHAT I DID TO YOU.
I COULDN'T DO IT AGAIN IF I WANTED TO. FOR HIM...
...OR YOU.

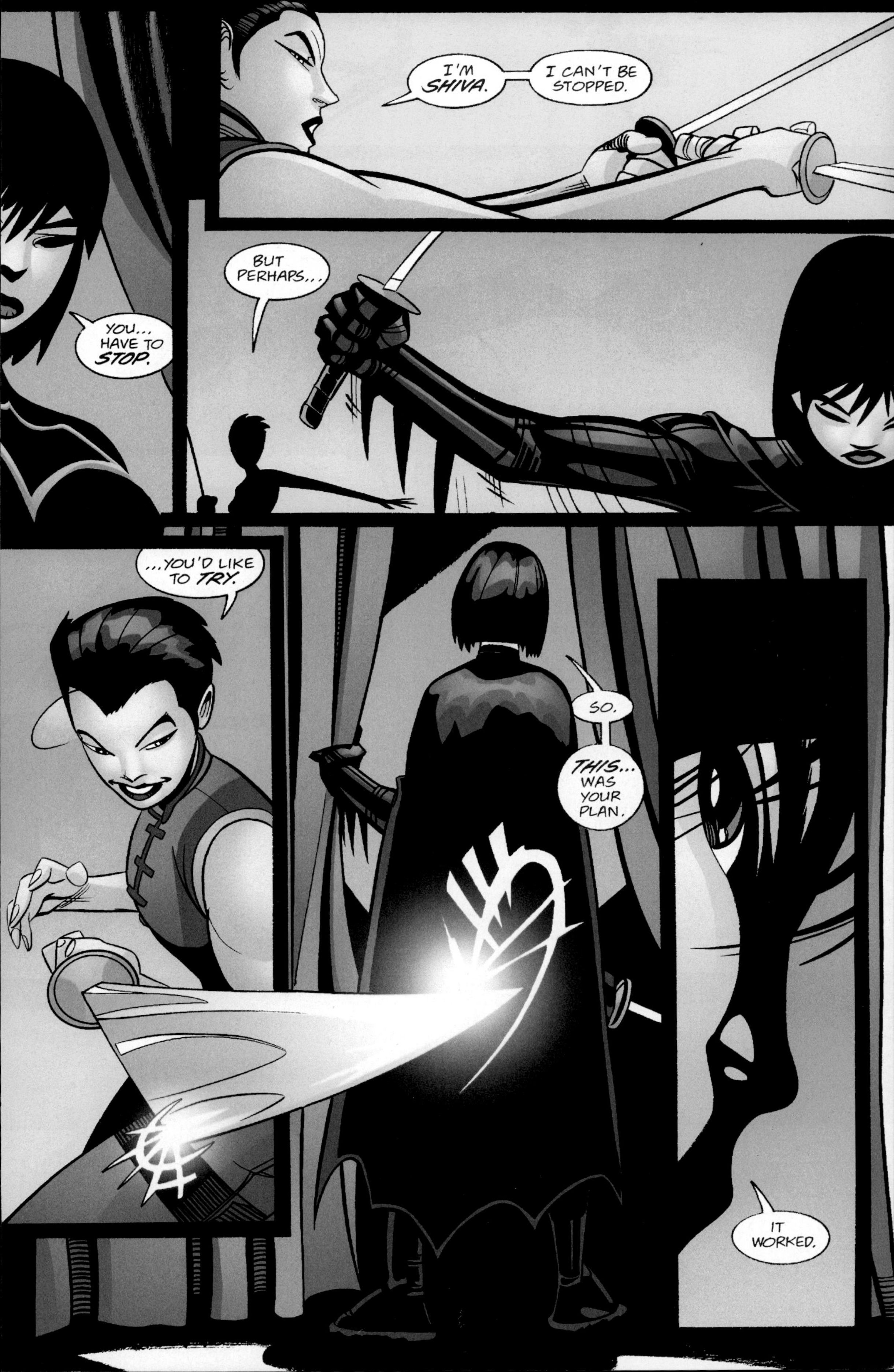
I'M SHIVA.
I CAN'T BE STOPPED.
YOU... HAVE TO STOP.
BUT PERHAPS...
...YOU'D LIKE TO TRY.
SO.
THIS... WAS YOUR PLAN.
IT WORKED.

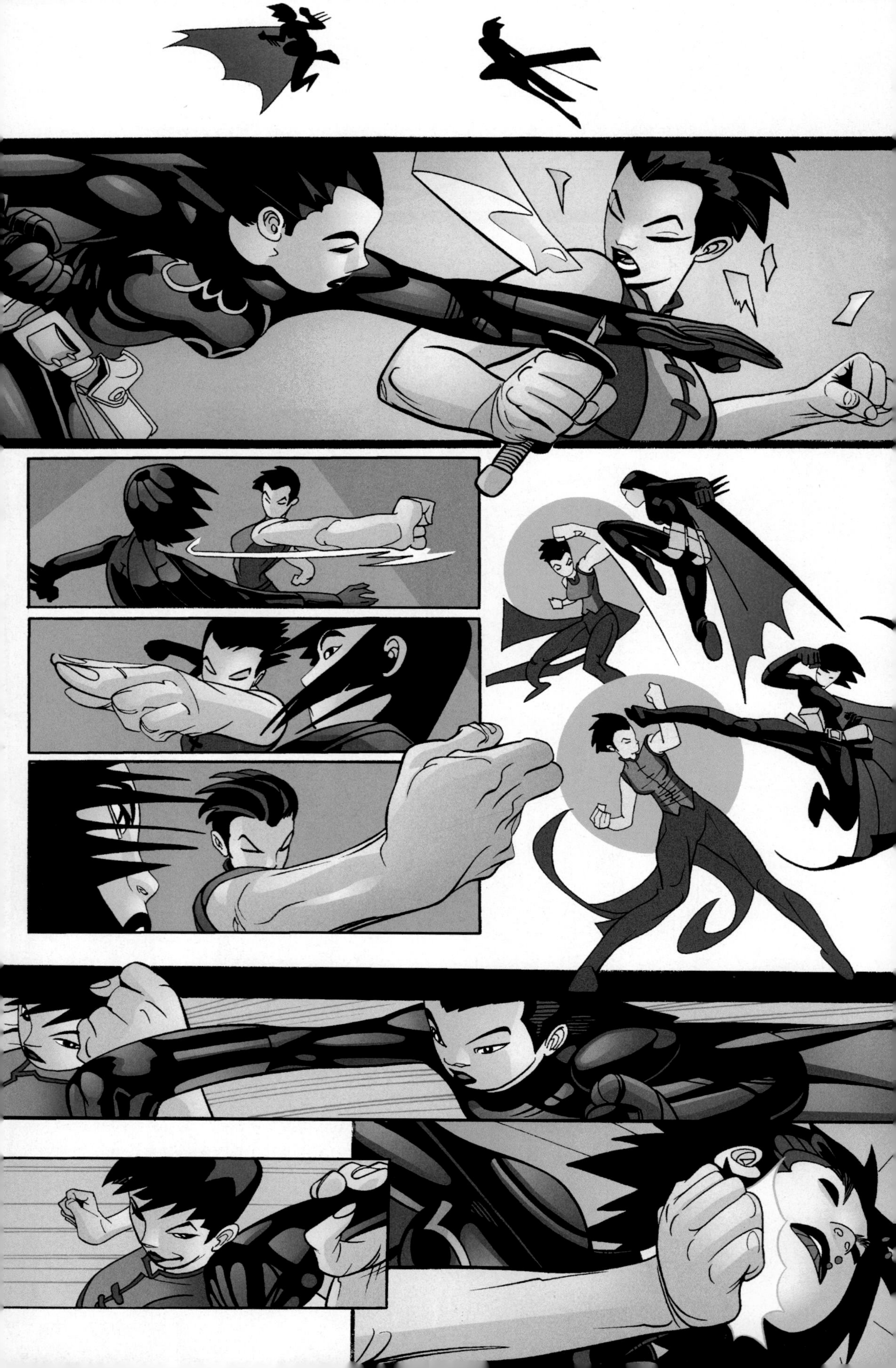

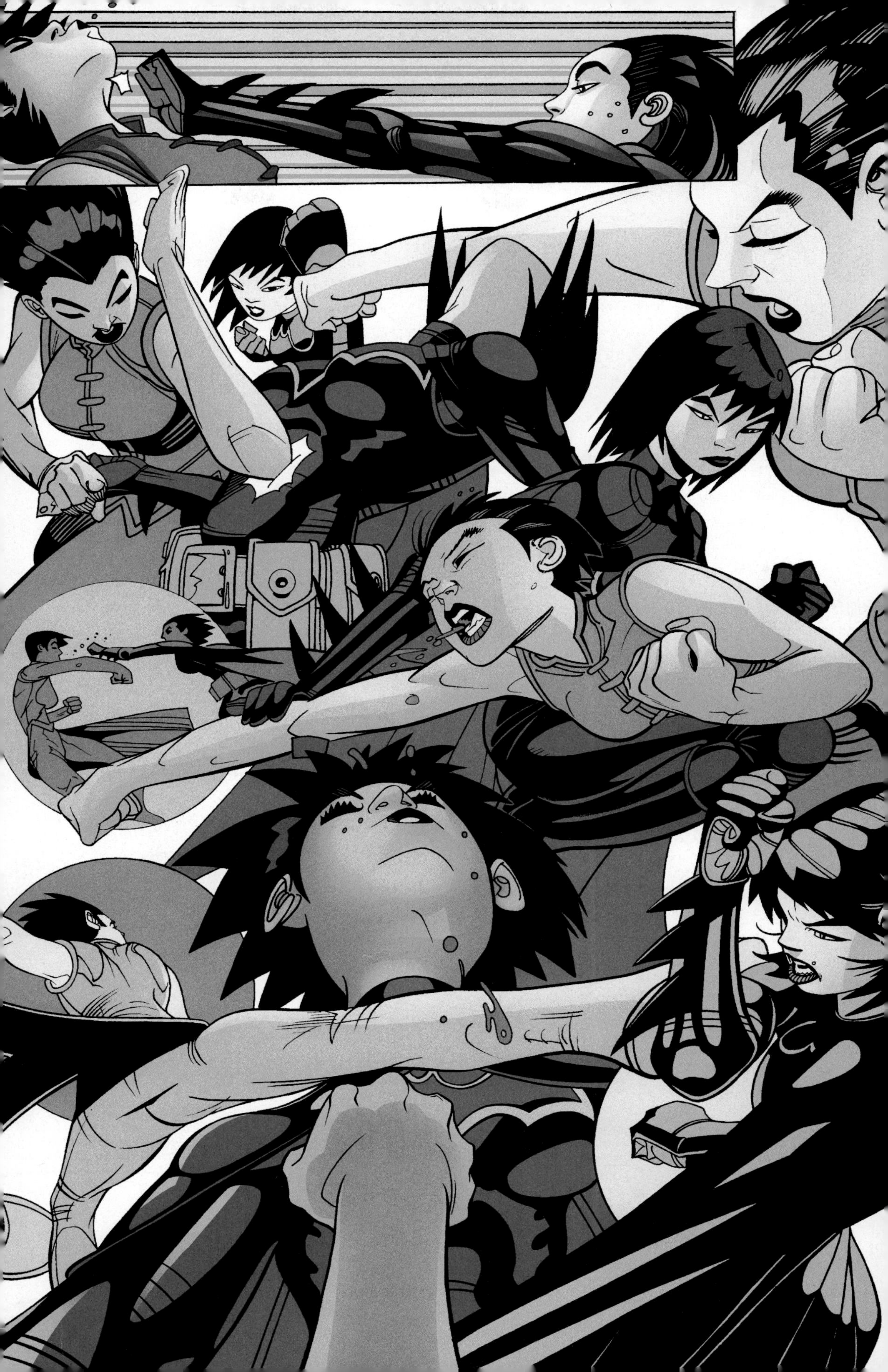

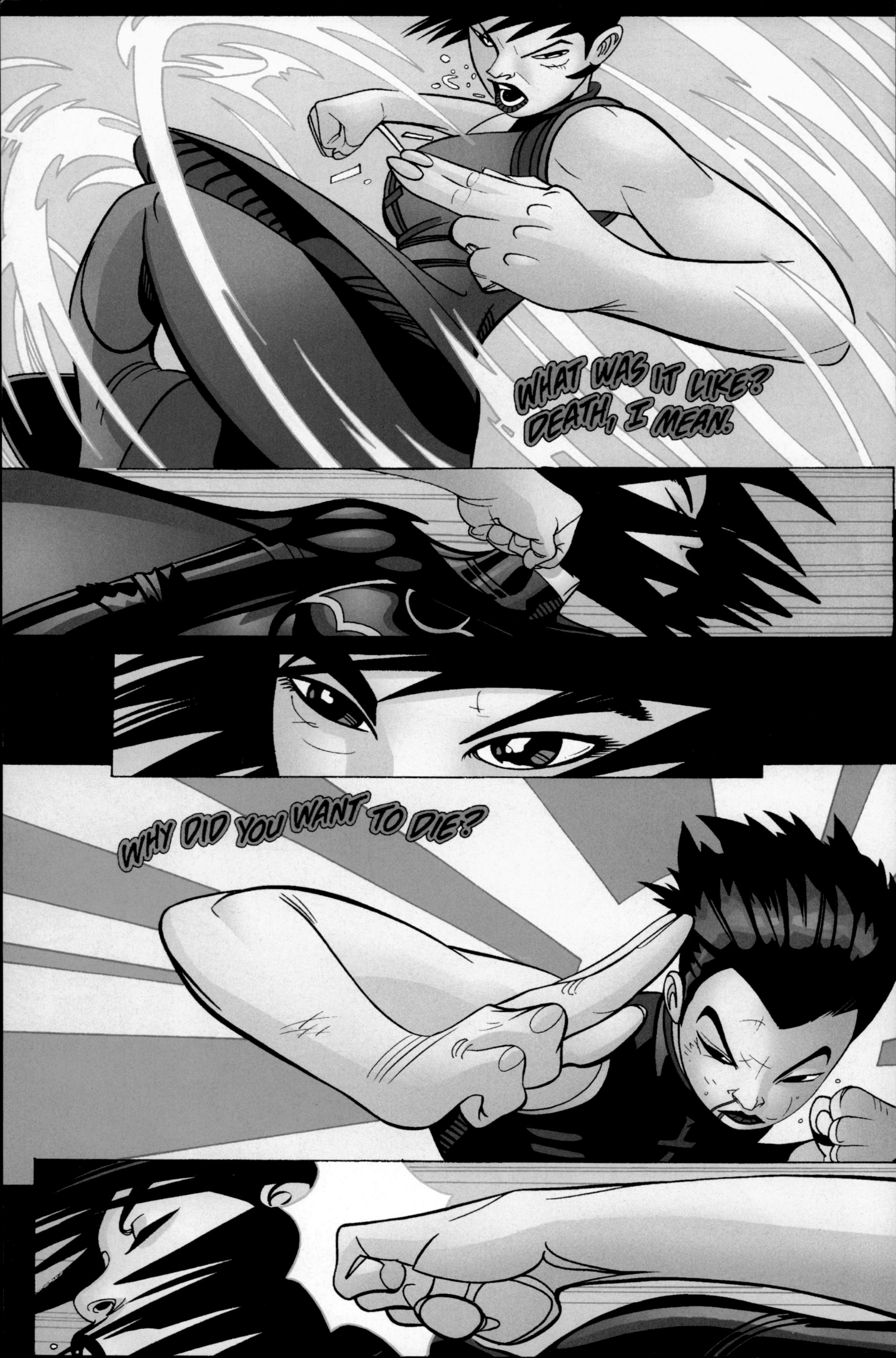
WHAT WAS IT LIKE? DEATH, I MEAN.
WHY DID YOU WANT TO DIE?

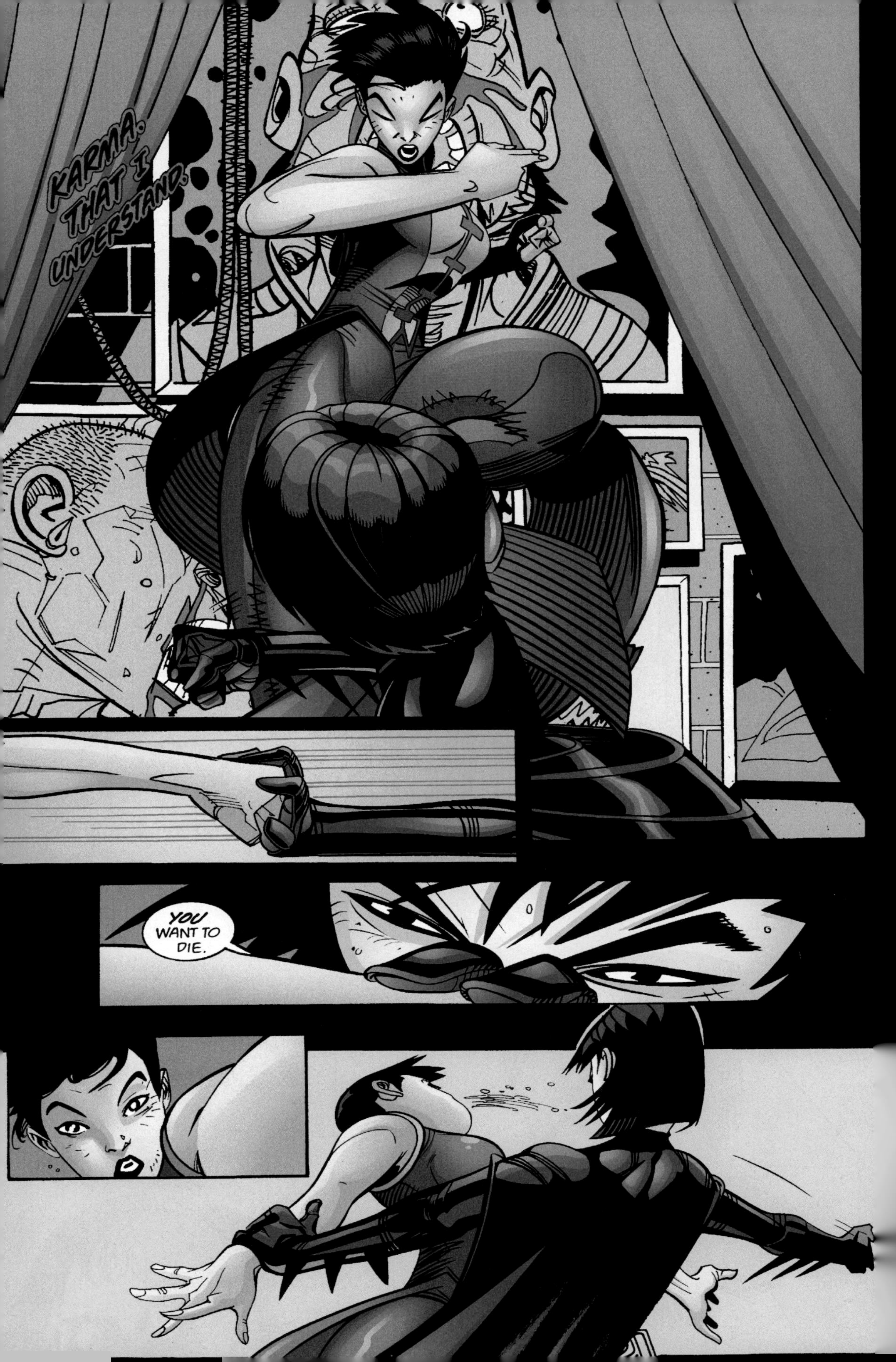
KARMA. THAT I UNDERSTAND.
YOU WANT TO DIE.

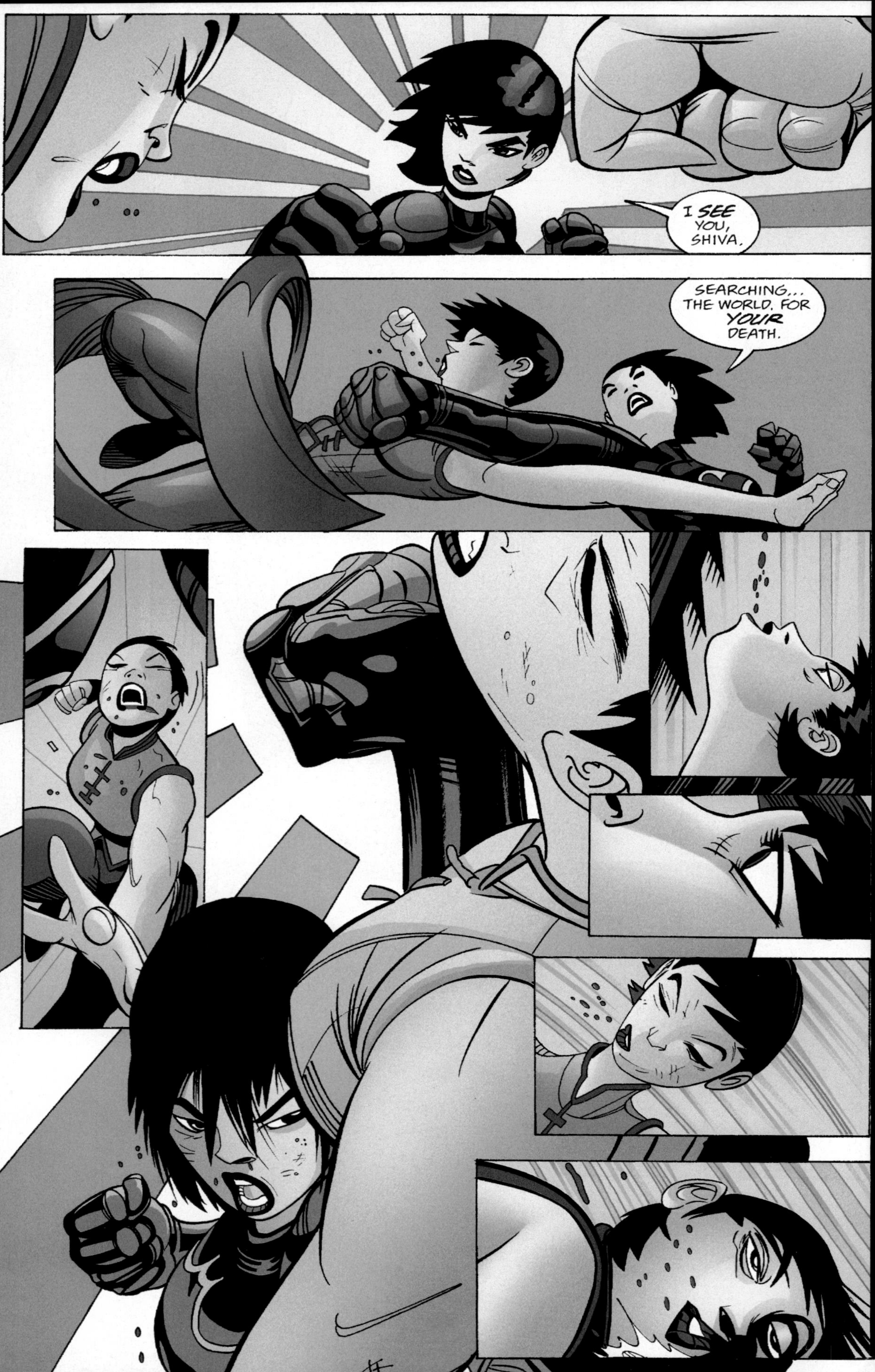
I SEE YOU, SHIVA.
SEARCHING... THE WORLD. FOR YOUR DEATH.

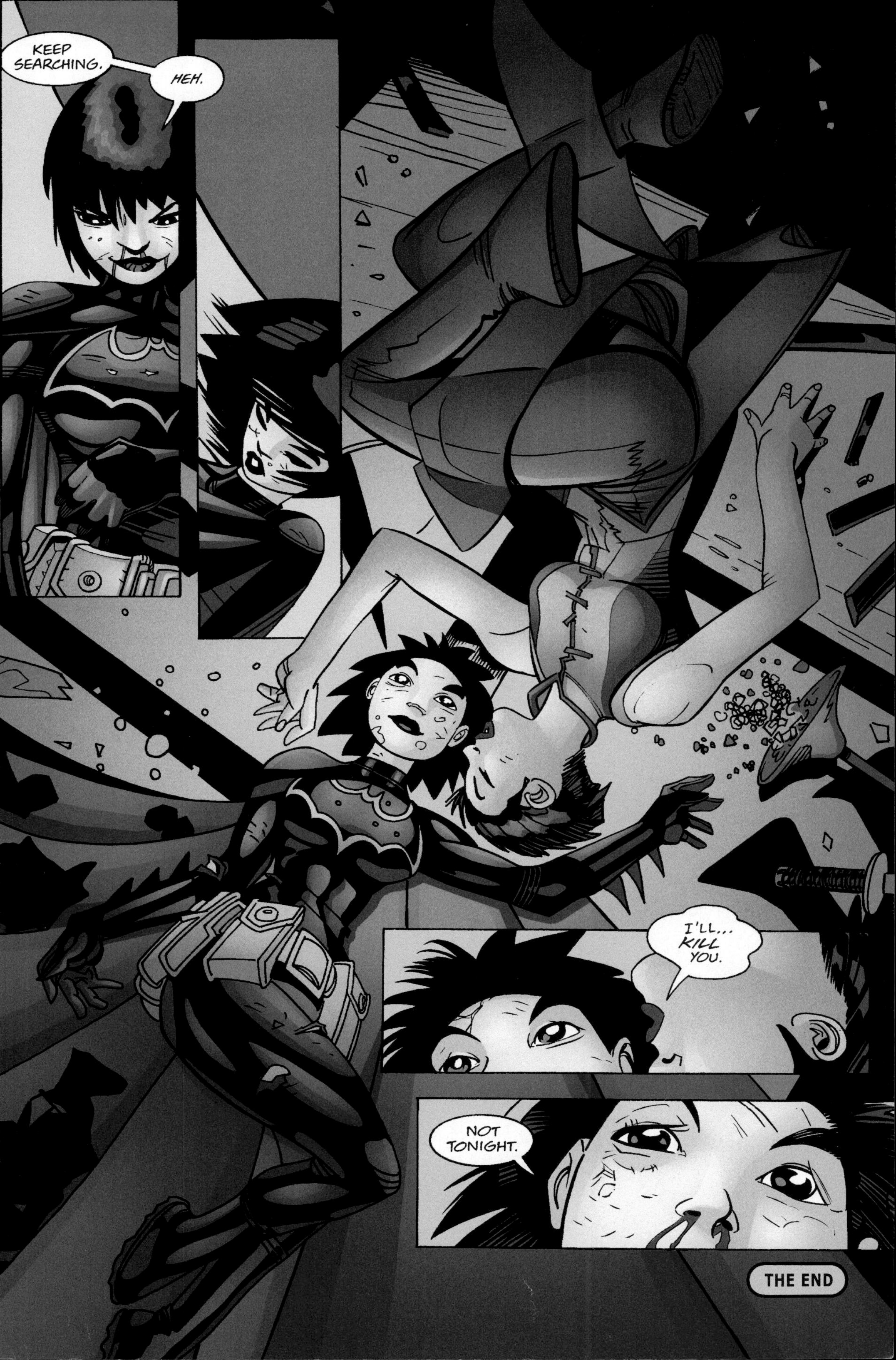
KEEP SEARCHING.
HEH.
I'LL... KILL YOU.
NOT TONIGHT.
THE END

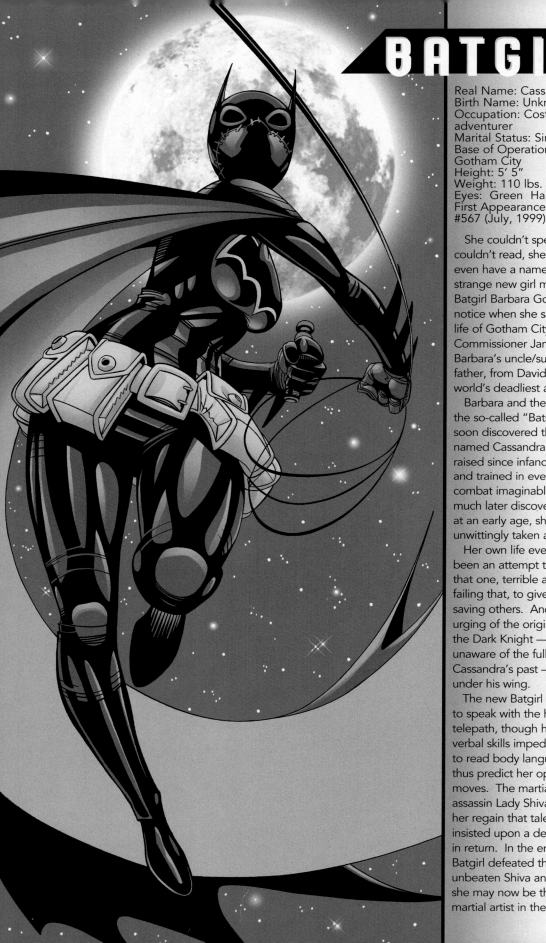

BATGIRL

Real Name: Cassandra Cain
Birth Name: Unknown
Occupation: Costumed
adventurer
Marital Status: Single
Base of Operations:
Gotham City
Height: 5' 5"
Weight: 110 lbs.
Eyes: Green Hair: Black
First Appearance: BATMAN
#567 (July, 1999)

She couldn't speak, she
couldn't read, she didn't
even have a name. But this
strange new girl made former
Batgirl Barbara Gordon take
notice when she saved the
life of Gotham City Police
Commissioner James Gordon,
Barbara's uncle/surrogate
father, from David Cain, the
world's deadliest assassin.

Barbara and the rest of
the so-called "Batsquad"
soon discovered that the girl
named Cassandra had been
raised since infancy by Cain,
and trained in every form of
combat imaginable. It was
much later discovered that,
at an early age, she had
unwittingly taken a man's life.

Her own life ever since has
been an attempt to atone for
that one, terrible action or,
failing that, to give her life
saving others. And so, at the
urging of the original Batgirl,
the Dark Knight — then
unaware of the full extent of
Cassandra's past — took her
under his wing.

The new Batgirl would learn
to speak with the help of a
telepath, though her new
verbal skills impeded her abili
to read body language and
thus predict her opponent's
moves. The martial artist and
assassin Lady Shiva helped
her regain that talent, but
insisted upon a deathmatch
in return. In the ensuing fight
Batgirl defeated the previousl
unbeaten Shiva and proved
she may now be the greatest
martial artist in the world.

LADY SHIVA

Real Name: Shiva Wu-San
Occupation: Martial artist
Marital Status: Single
Base of Operations: Unknown
Height: 5′ 8″
Weight: 135 lbs.
Eyes: Brown
Hair: Black
First Appearance: RICHARD DRAGON, KUNG-FU FIGHTER #5 (DECEMBER-JANUARY 1975/1976)

In the history of martial arts, one name stands above all the rest: Shiva.

Lady Shiva Wu-San has devoted her entire life to the quest for perfection in the martial arts, traveling to every corner of the globe in pursuit of a new technique, a better opponent, another form.

This single-minded passion has led her to become the premier martial artist in the world. Not even Batman has successfully defeated her in solo hand-to-hand combat. In fact, only one person has ever beaten Shiva — Batgirl.

At their first meeting, Shiva could see that, at last, she had found someone to potentially rival herself. But she sensed something was keeping Batgirl from achieving her full potential. Shiva therefore agreed to help unlock that potential, for a price: Batgirl must then meet her in a battle to the death one year later.

Batgirl agreed to the fight and arrived at the proper time, not expecting to survive the encounter. Instead, she realized that Shiva also had a subliminal deathwish; it was this insight, along with her unsurpassed skill and physical prowess, which allowed Batgirl to triumph.

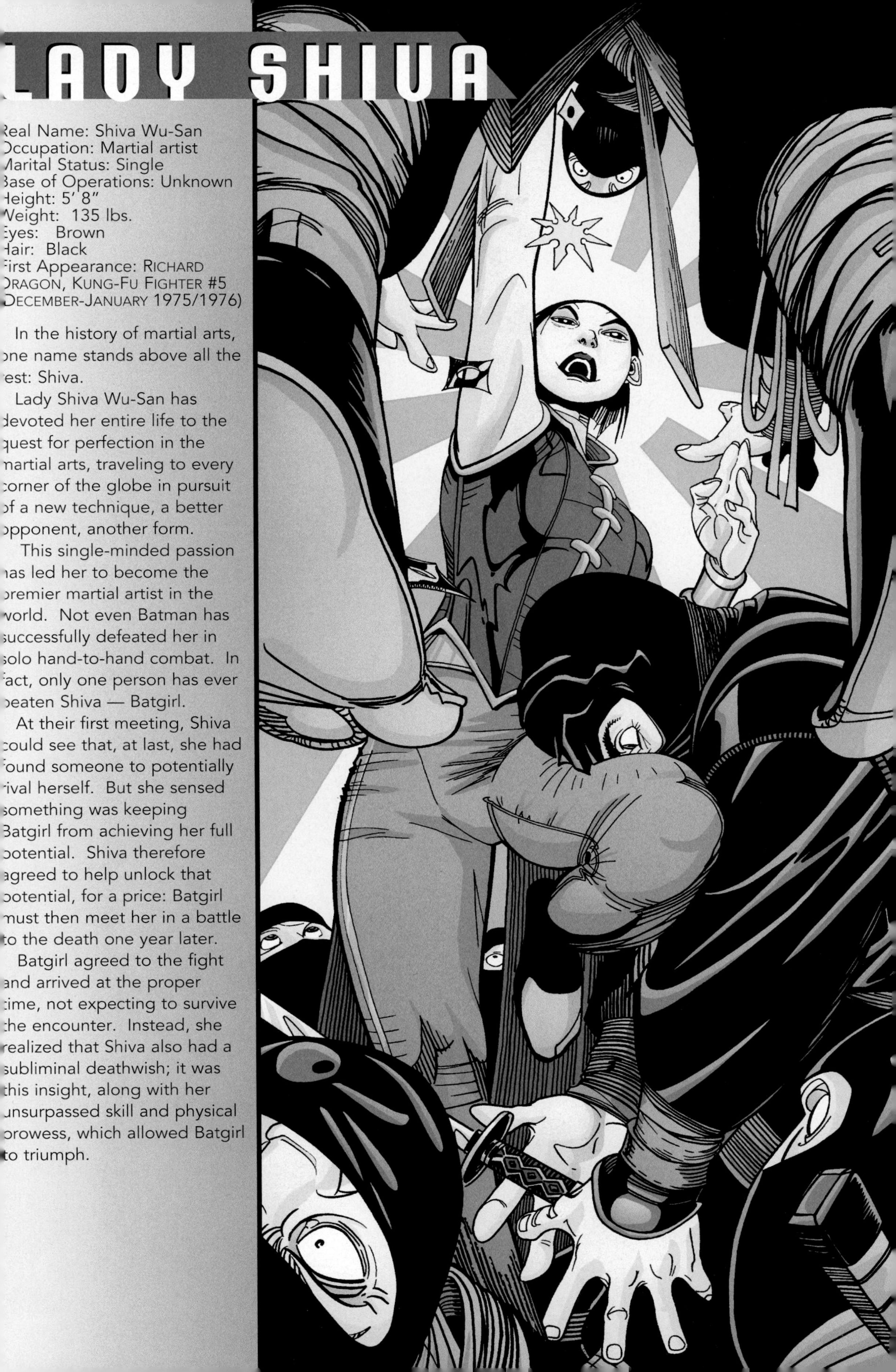

Real Name: Barbara Gordon
Occupation: Information specialist
Marital Status: Single
Height: 5′ 11″
Weight: 126 lbs.
Eyes: Green Hair: Red
First Appearance: SUICIDE SQUAD #23 (January, 1989)

There is little she doesn't already know. There is nothing she can't find out.

If knowledge is truly power, Oracle is one of the most powerful people on the planet.

Despite having her spine shattered by the Joker's bullet, Barbara Gordon refused to give up. Recognizing she could no longer be the kind of super-hero she had been, she instead devoted all her time to developing one of the world's most complex and powerful computer systems and set to work accumulating information, renaming herself "Oracle." Blessed with a photographic memory, Barbara reads dozens of the world's top newspapers and magazines daily. She's also constantly gathering information from other, less public sources, such as the CIA's mainframe, not to mention the data networks of the FBI, NSA and Interpol (all without their knowledge or consent).

Oracle has proven an absolutely invaluable resource to the Batman and his allies, as well as countless other super-heroes, very, very few of whom know anything about the person behind the name. Black Canary, in particular, has become a close partner over the years, the two of them forging a bond strengthened by their very different personalities. Her long-standing friendship with Dick Grayson, the original Robin — now known as Nightwing — has become much more intimate recently.

ORACLE

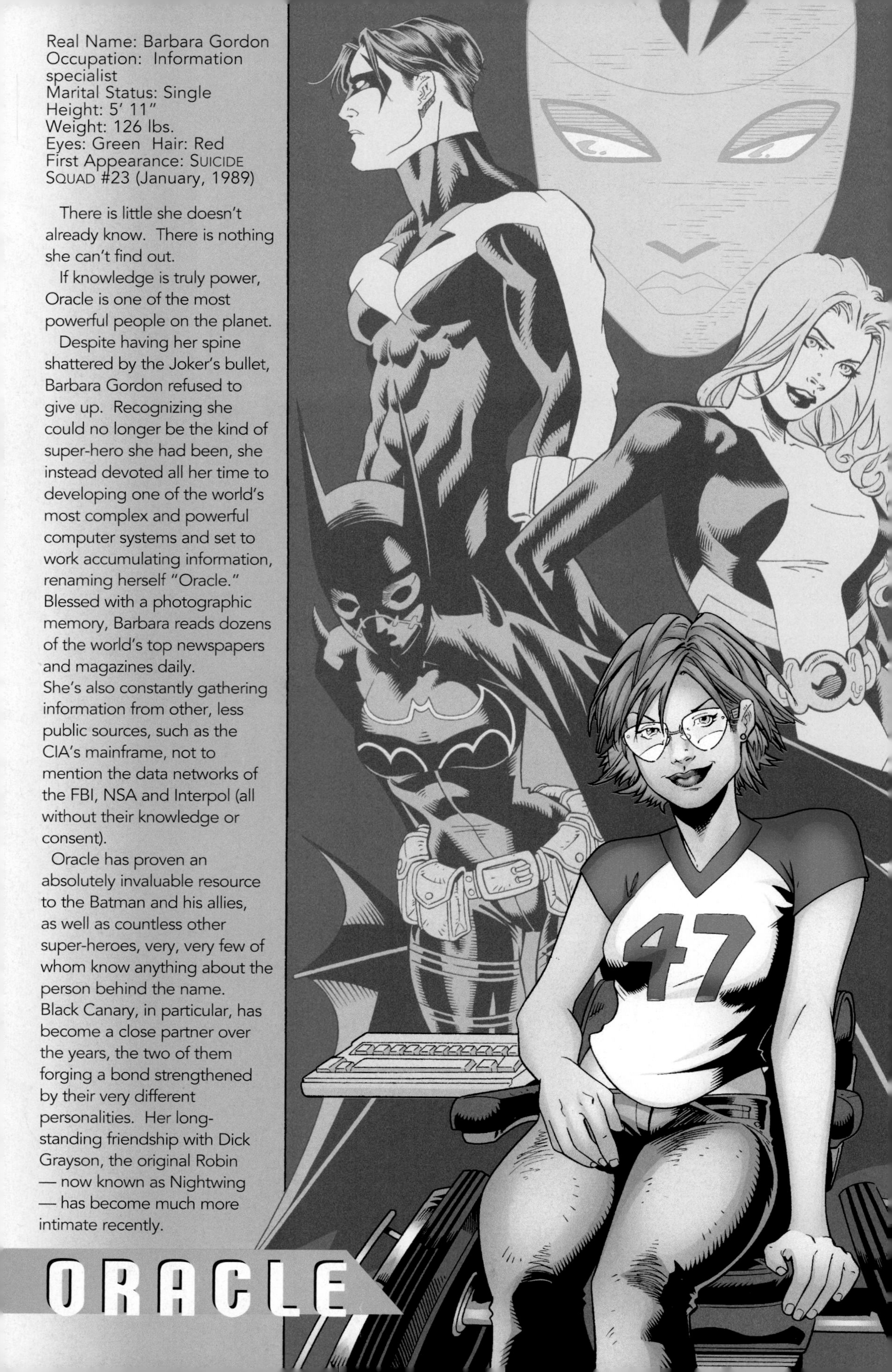
47

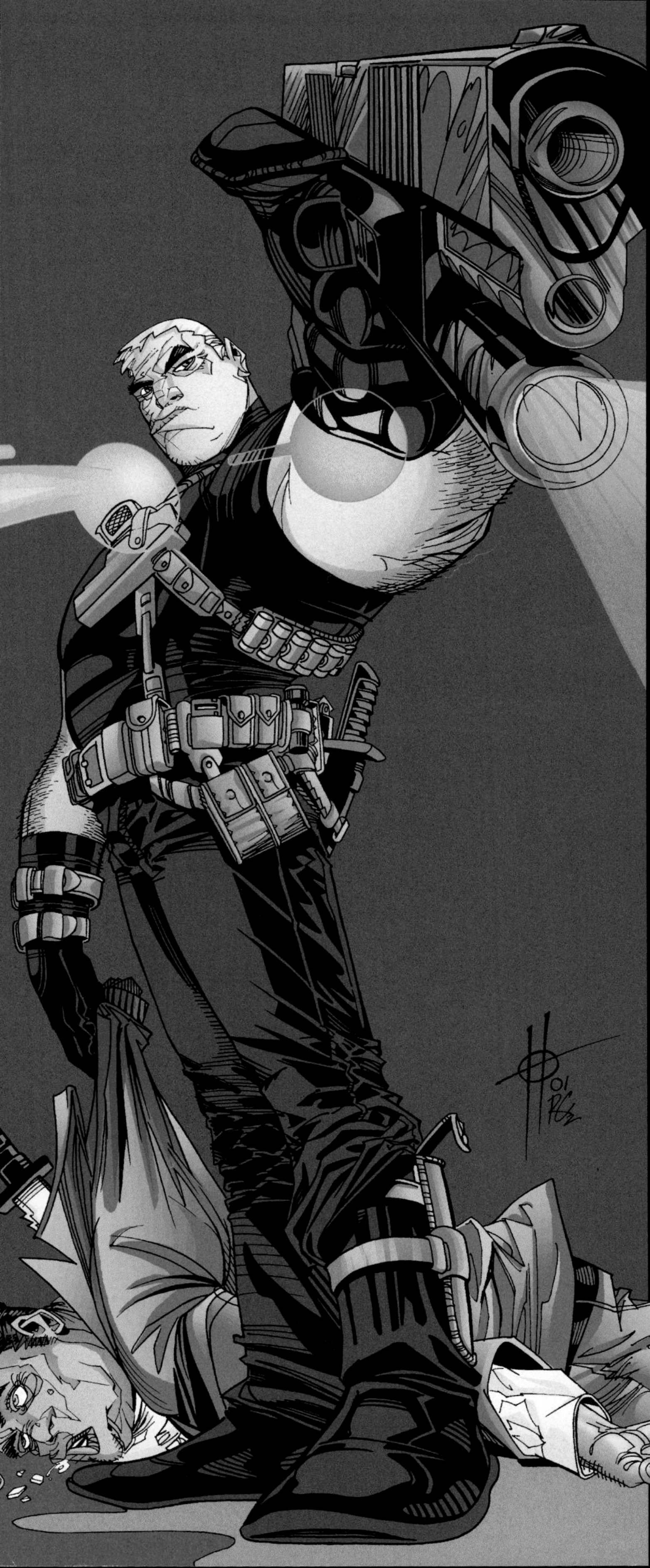

CAIN

Real Name: David Cain
Occupation: Assassin
Marital Status: Single
Base of Operations: Varying
Height: 6′ 2″ Weight: 245 lbs.
Eyes: Blue Hair: Gray
First Appearance: BATMAN #567 (July, 1999)

If you want to kill someone, hire a hit man. If you want to kill someone closely guarded, utterly secluded or completely untouchable, get Cain.

David Cain is one of the world's premier assassins, taking out some of the most famous and powerful people on the planet, no matter how seemingly impossible the task.

Exceptionally meticulous, Cain's success can be partially attributed to the way he always plans far ahead for any contingency: hence his decision to train someone to be his partner and eventual successor. Several attempts failed before he succeeded in acquiring a child who, at an extraordinarily early age, showed stunning physical prowess — the female who would one day become Batgirl.

Naming her Cassandra, Cain trained the young girl in every imaginable form of violence, from hand-to-hand combat to weapons and explosives. To further her skills, Cain never taught her how to speak; instead, physical movement became her language — she learned to read a person's body language as well and easily as other people can understand speech. This skill led Batgirl to be able to predict exactly what her opponents were going to do, sometimes before they knew it themselves.

Batgirl left Cain immediately after performing her first assassination, shattered by the experience of ending another person's life. Cain was surprisingly devastated by her disappearance and has never been the same since. He has never quite given up hope that someday she might return to his life.

BATGIRL

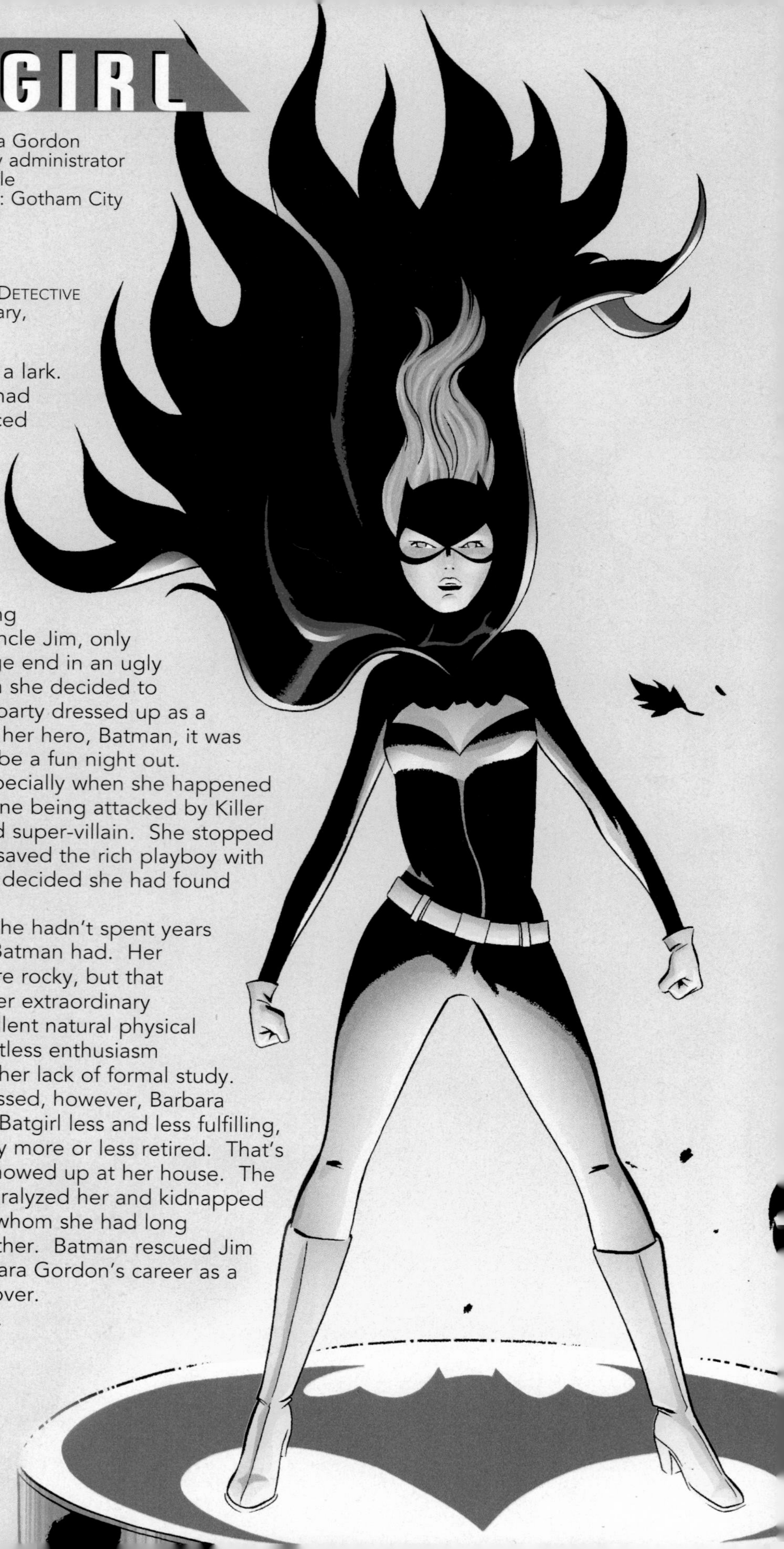

Real Name: Barbara Gordon
Occupation: Library administrator
Marital Status: Single
Base of Operations: Gotham City
Height: 5′ 11″
Weight: 126 lbs.
Eyes: Green
Hair: Red
First Appear-ance: DETECTIVE COMICS #359 (January, 1967)

It all started as a lark. Barbara Gordon had already experienced more than enough tragedy in her life — losing both her parents in a senseless car accident and being taken in by her Uncle Jim, only to see his marriage end in an ugly divorce. So when she decided to go to a costume party dressed up as a female version of her hero, Batman, it was just supposed to be a fun night out.

And it was. Especially when she happened to see Bruce Wayne being attacked by Killer Moth, a costumed super-villain. She stopped the bad guy and saved the rich playboy with little trouble, and decided she had found her calling.

Unfortunately, she hadn't spent years training the way Batman had. Her earliest forays were rocky, but that didn't stop her; her extraordinary intelligence, excellent natural physical abilities and relentless enthusiasm compensated for her lack of formal study.

As the years passed, however, Barbara found her role as Batgirl less and less fulfilling, and she eventually more or less retired. That's when the Joker showed up at her house. The Joker shot and paralyzed her and kidnapped her Uncle Jim — whom she had long considered her father. Batman rescued Jim Gordon, but Barbara Gordon's career as a crimefighter was over.
Or so it seemed…

"Simone and artist Ardian Syaf not only do justice to Babs' legacy, but build in a new complexity that is the starting point for a future full of new storytelling possibilities. A hell of a ride."—IGN

START AT THE BEGINNING!

BATGIRL
VOLUME 1: THE DARKEST REFLECTION

DC COMICS
"THIS IS A MUST-BUY SERIES."
— THE NEW YORK TIMES
THE NEW 52!
BATGIRL
VOLUME 1
THE DARKEST REFLECTION
GAIL SIMONE ARDIAN SYAF VICENTE CIFUENTES

BATGIRL VOL. 2: KNIGHTFALL DESCENDS

THE NEW 52!
BATGIRL
VOLUME 2
KNIGHTFALL DESCENDS
GAIL SIMONE ARDIAN SYAF ED BENES VICENTE CIFUENTES

BATGIRL VOL. 3: DEATH OF THE FAMILY

THE NEW 52!
BATGIRL
VOLUME 3
DEATH OF THE FAMILY
GAIL SIMONE DANIEL SAMPERE

BATWOMAN VOL. 1: HYDROLOGY

THE NEW 52!
BATWOMAN
VOLUME 1 HYDROLOGY
J.H. WILLIAMS III W. HADEN BLACKMAN

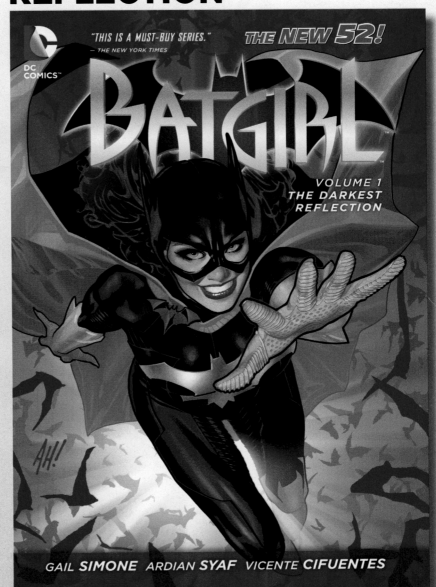

"Chaotic and unabashedly fun."—IGN

"I'm enjoying HARLEY QUINN a great deal;
it's silly, it's funny, it's irreverent."
—COMIC BOOK RESOURCES

HARLEY QUINN
VOLUME 1: HOT IN THE CITY

AMANDA **CONNER**   JIMMY **PALMIOTTI**   CHAD **HARDIN**
STEPHANE **ROUX**   ALEX **SINCLAIR**   PAUL **MOUNTS**